The INCLUSIVE CLASSROOM

Educating Exceptional Children

Tanya

Tanya

The INCLUSIVE CLASSROOM

Educating Exceptional Children

Jac Andrews and Judy Lupart
University of Calgary

Dan Bachor
University of Victoria

Carol Crealock
University of Western Ontario

Curt Dudley-Marling
York University

Anthony Marini
University of Calgary

David Piper
St. Mary's University

Nelson Canada

International Thomson Publishing
The trademark ITP is used under license

Canadian Cataloguing in Publication Data
Andrews, Jac, 1952-
The inclusive classroom: educating exceptional
children

Includes bibliographical references.
ISBN   0-17-603497-9

1. Gifted children - Education -Canada.
I. Lupart, Judy Lee. II. Title.

LC3995.3.A63 1993   371.95'0971   C93-093841-0

Acquisitions Editor: Charlotte Forbes
Editorial Manager: Nicole Gnutzman
Supervising Editor: Linda Collins
Developmental Editor: Heather Martin
Art Director: Bruce Bond
Design: Julia Hall
Cover Design: Julia Hall
Cover Art: Artwork by J.W. Stewart, copyright 1993, used by permission.

Printed and bound in Canada
3 4   BG

CONTENTS

◇ PREFACE AND CONCEPTUAL OVERVIEW

The Inclusive Classroom: Educating Exceptional Children is for those who are working (or preparing to work) with students in Canadian classrooms, including regular and special educators, counsellors, teachers' aides, psychologists, social workers, language specialists, physical and occupational therapists, other related professionals, and parents. As an introductory text, the book provides an overview of information related to teaching students in today's classrooms, with particular emphasis on the concept of inclusive education. *Inclusive education* refers to the merging of regular and special education into a unified educational system in order to meet the diverse needs of all students. From our perspective, the Canadian classroom is an *inclusive mosaic* because it mirrors the multidimensional fabric of our society.

The challenge of writing this textbook was to present ideas and practices that addressed the realities of Canada's present educational environment while at the same time guiding the reader toward a consideration of emerging themes and practices. For example, even though many educational institutions (e.g., public schools, colleges, and universities) provide separate special and regular education programs, we have stressed the need for a unified educational system. Additionally, while many educational programs are organized by categories of exceptional children (e.g., gifted education), we present information that is related to students' learning and behavioural characteristics rather than to those categories.

Lastly, many educators follow traditional behaviouristic theories of learning and instruction that emphasize the events and activities of the learning environment. We, however, emphasize a more transactional view of learning and instruction, namely, the view that the teaching-learning process centrally involves the teacher and the learner. The actions and processes undertaken by the teacher and learner interact in a dynamic fashion to influence the quantity and quality of learning; moreover, learning and instruction are made up of many components involving an interaction of cognitive, developmental, sociocultural, and environmental variables.

MAJOR THEMES

The major underlying themes of this textbook are:

- ◆ Students should be educated in their community school, and made to feel that they belong.
- ◆ Teachers should be sensitive to individual differences and accept student diversity.
- ◆ Teachers should work together within a unified system of education in order to meet the diverse needs of students.
- ◆ Contemporary educational practices should be dynamic, holistic, collaborative, adaptive, student-centred, and ecological.
- ◆ All teachers should be teachers of children with special needs.

- Learning is a cognitive, sociocultural, developmental, and behavioural process.
- The classroom should be thought of as a microcosm of Canadian society.
- Parents should be considered as partners in the educational process.
- Educational assessment involves problem-solving and decision-making.
- *Theories* of learning and teaching are related to the *practice* of learning and teaching.
- Students should have differentiated curriculum and individualized educational programs.
- Effective teaching involves effective classroom management.
- Learning strategies help students enhance and control their learning.
- Effective education requires attention to both the academic and social development of students.
- Diversity in the classroom is a tremendous resource for learners, and must be tapped by having classrooms where teachers and students share the centre stage.
- Equity is the way to excellence.

ORGANIZATION OF THE TEXT

The book comprises fifteen chapters that are divided into six parts. Part 1, "Transitions in Education," is the foundation of the text. Chapter 1 provides an in-depth discussion of the process of inclusive education. Chapter 2 traces the history of, and provides a rationale for, inclusive education. It also discusses the educational guidelines and policies that ensure a free and appropriate education for all students in Canada. Chapter 3 presents the theories that have come to dominate current educational thinking and practice, and that have the greatest relevance for understanding the teaching and learning process.

Part 2, "Students with Special Needs," addresses the diverse educational characteristics of students in inclusive classrooms. Chapter 4 provides extensive coverage of the definitions and issues related to exceptional learning and behaviour, as well as an in-depth discussion of the information-processing characteristics of students. Chapter 5 focuses on students in the mainstream who face linguistic and cultural challenges.

Part 3, "School and Home Partnership," considers the importance of professional and parent collaboration. Chapter 6 deals with the concept of the inclusive team, and examines some of the specific contributions that various educational professionals can offer as they work together to meet the diverse needs of students. In Chapter 7, we discuss how the school and home partnership can be initiated, maintained, and developed.

Part 4, "Preparation for Teaching and Learning," provides essential information on the process of teaching and learning. Chapter 8 focuses on the assessment practices of teachers in the classroom and offers some useful suggestions for determining the strengths and weaknesses of students, and for monitoring their learning progress. Chapter 9 examines classroom management in the context of teaching, and includes substantive discussion of three major components of effective classroom management—*proaction, support,* and *reaction* —that involve effective teaching practices. Chapter 10 details the academic skills and the difficulties students experience in the areas of word identification, oral language, reading, writing, spelling, and mathematics. This chapter also examines instructional methods teachers can use to promote their students' learning, as well as the relationship of these methods to current and dominant educational theories. Chapter 11 presents important considerations for program planning, and discusses ways to help teachers make instructional decisions.

Part 5, "Critical Instructional Considerations," focuses on three areas that teachers should promote with their students: *strategic learning and thinking, social ability,* and *living and learning in a community.* Chapter 12 discusses the use of learning strategies in the classroom setting. Chapter 13 presents assessment procedures for determining students' social ability, and provides some instructional methods and approaches for encouraging its development. Chapter 14 discusses the social principles of teaching and learning that can make education meaningful for everyone.

Part 6, "Emerging Issues and Future Directions," contains one last chapter that considers the salient issues within the present educational context, as well as emerging issues and themes. In addition, Chapter 15 considers some promising directions, at all levels of education, that may bring about the successful merging of regular and special education into a unified system of education.

FEATURES OF THE TEXT

Each of the six major parts of the book opens with a *part introduction* that provides a brief rationale and outline of the key concepts presented in the respective chapters. At the beginning of each chapter, we provide a list of *chapter objectives* that highlight the major goals of the chapter. In the *glossary-cum-index* at the end of the book, we offer definitions of all the key terms that appear in the chapters.

Throughout the text, we present *figures* and *tables* illustrating assessment and instructional methods, which readers can modify and use with their students. We also include *case studies* to highlight important topics, and to provide a practical demonstration of certain ideas. *Photos* of teachers and other related professionals, parents, and students appear throughout in order to show the relationship of the information presented in this book to practice.

At the beginning and end of each chapter major concepts and key points are overviewed in an *introduction* and *summary* (or *conclusion*). Each chapter opens with a *vignette* that highlights salient ideas and captures the reader's interest. End-of-chapter *questions* help direct readers to the main ideas of the chapter, and the list of *references* that concludes each chapter allows readers to enhance their awareness of the research and work being done in the educational field. Finally, a print *test bank* of approximately six hundred multiple-choice items covering the fifteen chapters accompanies the text.

ACKNOWLEDGEMENTS

In preparing and completing this textbook, we owe a large debt of gratitude to M.J. Samuelson, who helped us type, format, and edit the manuscripts, as well as transform our figures and tables from rough drafts into polished products. Thanks, as well, to Sandy Mann for all of her help with the case studies, and to Vianne Timmons and Val Blair for all of their efforts in developing the test bank.

For their assistance with the photos, we would like to thank Lorraine Templeton, Deborah Hamilton, and the administrators, teachers, students, and parents associated with the Calgary public school system.

We would also like to thank the contributing authors, Dan Bachor, Carol Crealock, Curt Dudley-Marling, Anthony Marini, and David Piper, for their diligence and commitment to this project.

The development of this book has been greatly enhanced by the efforts of many people at Nelson Canada. Particular appreciation is extended for our editor, Charlotte Forbes, who contributed creative ideas and suggestions, provided support, encouragement, and direction, and who displayed continual enthusiasm and commitment. We would also like to thank all the reviewers of our draft chapters for their guidance and insightful perspectives: Richard Freeze, University of Manitoba; Robert Gall, University of Lethbridge; Jack Goldberg, University of Alberta; James Hanrahan, McGill University; N.L. Hutchinson, Queen's University; Larry Morton, University of Windsor; Marion Porath, University of British Columbia; Glenn W. Sheppard, Memorial University; and Alexander M. Wilson, Mount Allison University.

Finally, for their help and encouragement, our gratitude to the members of our families, who make living and working worthwhile, and to whom we dedicate this book.

To
Deborah Hamilton
Jenna Hamilton-Andrews
Chad Hamilton-Andrews

and

Michael Lupart
Michael Lupart
Vanessa Lupart

TRANSITIONS IN EDUCATION

P A R T

1

*C*urrently, *the educational field in Canada is experiencing a paradigm shift. The* traditional paradigm *is* characterized *by a dual system of educational service delivery (regular and special education) for meeting the diverse learning needs of all students. This divisive model has resulted in student classification and categorization, segregated learning environments, fragmented programming and instruction, and "top-down" decision-making practices. The* new paradigm *is characterized by a unified system of educational service delivery (a merger of special and regular education) to address the unique learning needs of all students. This inclusive model has been adopted and implemented by an increasing number of schools, and has resulted in integrated learning environments, holistic programming and instruction, and collaborative-based decision-making practices.*

The shift from the traditional paradigm to the new paradigm has required changes in educational thought and practice. These changes are reflected in the widespread movement toward inclusive education; an upsurge in applied research and instructional practice associated with cognitive, developmental, and social-cultural theories of learning; growing support for collaborative exchanges across professional disciplines; and new legislative directions in all of Canada's provinces and territories.

The present era of Canadian education is challenging and exciting. Many educators are advocating a

A NOTE FROM THE AUTHORS

unified (inclusive) educational system that will foster lifelong learning, provide educational quality and equity, facilitate independent learning and thinking, promote a school-home partnership, encourage living and learning in a community, and develop academic and social competence. Moreover, educators are trying to achieve these goals by consulting and collaborating with one another, and by providing adaptive instruction for all students. This process requires positive attitudes, beliefs, and values regarding inclusive education as well as enabling conditions to initiate, maintain, and foster a united educational system.

This section of the book presents the conceptual, historical, and theoretical foundations for inclusive education, and provides an overview of current practices and trends in Canadian education. Chapter 1 defines the concept of inclusive education, describes the desired outcomes of a unified educational system, overviews the critical features of the inclusive education process, and presents some of the issues and conditions that affect the ability of educators to provide inclusive education. Chapter 2 comprehensively reviews the history of inclusive education, and provides a detailed summary of the legal and legislative directions of the Canadian provinces and territories relative to inclusive education. Finally, Chapter 3 presents an overview of the theoretical perspectives that have come to dominate current educational thinking and practice.

INCLUSIVE EDUCATION: THE MERGING OF SPECIAL AND REGULAR EDUCATION INTO A UNIFIED EDUCATION SYSTEM

CHAPTER OBJECTIVES

To stress the importance of inclusive education.

To provide information regarding the emergence of inclusive education.

To discuss the major goals of inclusive education.

To stress the importance of consultation, collabo-

ration and adaptive instruction to the merger of regular and special education.

To note the teacher characteristics and enabling conditions that affect the merger of regular and special education.

In December of 1982, James was born prematurely at six and one-half months, weighing 1.5 kg. His twin brother died at birth and James suffered from a lack of oxygen. The doctor reassured the parents by telling them that James's physical development would seem slow, but not to worry about it. It was only ten months later that a neurologist declared that James had cerebral palsy, and that it would probably affect his motor skills but not his intellectual development.

In his first year, James was very ill. He suffered through severe bronchitis, which was later followed by chicken pox and what seemed to be continual colds and ear infections. His second year was much healthier, and, according to his parents, he started growing "normally." James appeared to use a lot of energy learning basic skills; every single gesture required a considerable amount of concentration and determination. At two years and six months he began talking, and by four

years of age, with the help of a physiotherapist, he was toilet-trained and able to awkwardly walk, drink, and eat by himself. Although he had expressive and receptive language delays, James's speech was clear and fluent.

James's parents did not stop their careers because they had a child with special needs. His family was extremely positive toward him and was constantly supportive of all his efforts. According to James's Mom and Dad, their most important objective was to convince James that "the road might be difficult to follow at times, but he could make it." Like his brother and sister, James attended a day care before entering elementary school.

When James was four years old, his parents wanted to register him in the neighbourhood pre-kindergarten program. However, the principal did not want to impose this "extra load" on his teacher. He suggested that James register in a special school for mentally retarded children. Mother's reply was that she wanted James to attend his neighbourhood school and be able to socialize with students of his own age. Furthermore, she insisted that he did not demonstrate any signs of mental retardation and would, with support and guidance, be able to cope effectively with the daily classroom routines and the teacher's expectations. Although the principal was reluctant to admit James, the teacher willingly accepted James into her classroom, and the school was able to assign a part-time aide to help James while at school. By the end of the year, his teacher said that it was not as difficult as she had first thought. Moreover, she reported that all the other students had benefited immensely from James's presence and participation in the class. He had become academically and socially integrated and was liked by his classmates due to, among other things, his keen sense of humour.

James's Grade 2 experience was much more challenging because of his teacher's attitude. James's mother and father sensed that his teacher was annoyed by the inclusion of James in her classroom, particularly because of the lack of resources and assistance provided her. Unlike the previous years, James did not have an aide assigned to him, due to budget restrictions. Furthermore, James's teacher did not have previous experience with exceptional children and felt very pressured and uncomfortable with the "extra load." Unfortunately, this placement resulted in few curricular modifications for James and little individualized programming and instruction. During this year, James would often come home frustrated and sad. His parents were forewarned that this experience could be part of the risks they agreed to take when they involved James in the "real world," so, they tried to compensate for these frustrations by offering all the support and care they could give. They volunteered as much time as they could to the teacher and her classroom. Furthermore, they reinforced the view with James that his teacher was also having difficulty coping with the circumstances and struggling to do her best. Hence, it was the system and not him that she was sometimes reacting to.

The following year, the family moved to another city. In her first contact on the phone with the school's principal, James's mother mentioned that her son had some communication difficulties and was severely physically impaired. Without knowing the details, the answer from the principal was, "So what!" From that school year on, James's inclusion within school and classrooms was never a problem. Hand in hand, his new Grade 3 teacher (he was not able to walk on his own)

gave him a tour of the school during his first day, and introduced him to the school's resource personnel and to his classmates as a new member of the school. His teacher organized his working space with two tables on which were displayed his books and his special typewriter (within six months James was an expert typist and doing reports for others). James was expected to follow the same program as his peers (with some modifications), and he made it; he participated in the outdoor activities, played soccer as a goalie, competed in oral debates, and played at recess with his peers.

During Grade 3, James started stuttering. The teacher, his classmates, and his family were very patient, and tried to reduce his tension by providing positive reinforcement when he remained calm and spoke slowly. At home, the parents practiced "hugging therapy," which meant as soon as James started to panic when talking to others, they would hug him and calm him down. The technique proved to be successful, since James stopped stuttering by the end of the year.

During his first three years of school, James's motor skills were deficient. He was falling all the time and it was difficult for him to, for example, drink from a regular glass or write without his special typewriter. However, his academic and social achievements were spectacular, and he proved to be an outstanding student. He was described by his teachers as "survivor," which meant that he met his challenges with success. His self-motivation and his determination made him a winner.

His Grade 4 teacher noted that James was exceptional not only because of his physical handicap but also because of his remarkable intellectual and social capacities. She felt that James was "wasting" his time in Grade 4 and got him promoted to Grade 5.

From this time on, he has continued to shine both academically and socially. He has won four awards of excellence in different subjects, and writes articles for the school's journal. He has been nominated by his peers to be in charge of the peer support program of the school, and is a member of a downhill skiing club.

James's life today appears to be healthy and active. He goes to his neighbourhood school and enjoys his learning experiences. He plays with his friends at school, goes to day care, and is a member of the school choir and drama club. Along with spending a lot of time with his family on the weekends, he skis, goes to boy scout meetings, and always has time to play with his best friends at his home or theirs. And it seems that this is the way it should be.

◇ INTRODUCTION

One of the most significant improvements in education over the past couple of decades has been the increased partnership between special and regular education teachers (Will,1986), a partnership that has grown because of the educational challenges teachers are facing in today's schools. The most significant challenge is to meet the individual learning needs of *all* students. One response is to create a unified education system that considers student diversity as a reflection of our society. We refer to this unified concept as **inclusive education** and believe that it is currently the predominant educational trend.

In this chapter, we discuss the salient aspects of inclusive education (see Figure 1.1), which we view as a merger of special and regular education into a unified educational system. From our perspective, this merger requires special and regular educators to consult and collaborate with one another, and to provide adaptive instruction to all their students. The successful merging of special and regular education depends on the positive attitudes, beliefs, and values of educators, and on the presence of enabling conditions. We also believe that the major goals of the unified educational system are to foster lifelong learning, provide educational quality and equity, facilitate independent learning and thinking, promote a school-home partnership, encourage living and learning in a community, and develop the academic and social competence of all students.

We first present critical developments in the field of education over the last few decades that have led to inclusive education. Next, we outline the goals of inclusive education before discussing the critical procedures (consultation, collaboration, adaptive instruction) involved in the successful merging of special and regular education. The final section of this chapter provides an overview of the attitudes, beliefs, values, and enabling conditions that affect the ability of special and regular educators to establish a unified educational system.

◆ inclusive education: the merger of special and regular education into a unified educational system

✳ *Major components of sp. needs*

Figure 1.1

The Salient Aspects of Inclusive Education

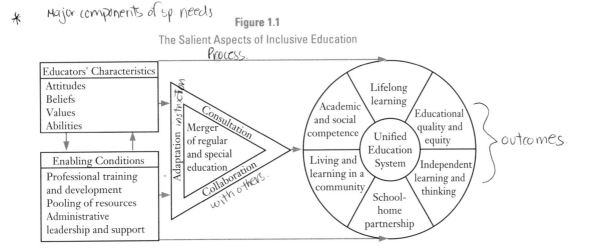

◆ THE FOUNDATION OF INCLUSIVE EDUCATION

In the 1960s and 1970s, there was a major push for special education as parents and teachers of children with varying abilities came to believe that traditional education was not meeting the needs of their children, and therefore not achieving their desired goals (e.g., academic and social competence, and equal access and opportunity to a robust educational experience). Hence, a variety of special education services emerged consisting of specially trained personnel, curriculum options, and special classes with smaller and more homogeneous enrolments. It was assumed that individual programming, instructional modifications, and teachers specially trained in areas of exceptionality would lead to more effective educational experiences for children with special needs.

In the 1980s, the optimism began to erode as the downside of the special education movement became evident. The fact that more children were being assessed also meant that more children were being labelled and segregated. There was increasing concern that the focus in special education on the remediation of deficits was having adverse effects. Many students in special classes were still having difficulty reaching their academic potential, still failing to make the "school to life" transition, and still having problems relating with their peers, generalizing and transferring information from one context to another, and developing a positive sense of self.

Another growing recognition in the 1980s was that special education could not deal with the dramatic increase of children in need of special services, particularly in light of the declining resources available to assist them. Coincidentally, a growing number of disadvantaged children were falling through the cracks because they did not fit the criteria of one of the categories of exceptionality, and yet demonstrated a need for special programming in order to reach their potential. These children included the poor, the chemically dependent, pregnant teenagers, students with low aspirations, homeless children, dropouts, and a rising number of children for whom English was a second language.

◆ PRESENT EDUCATIONAL TRENDS

Despite the faded optimism that characterized the 1980s, that decade saw developments from educational research and practice that were to provide the basis for a more effective and unified educational system for dealing with student diversity. *First*, over the last decade, advances in cognitive psychology have emerged, in both academic and applied settings, which indicate that our ability to develop students' higher cognitive processes may be improved (French, 1991; Kirby & Williams, 1991; Leong & Randhawa, 1989; Mulcahy, Short, & Andrews, 1991; and Segal, Chipman, & Glaser, 1985). In the educational field, there has been a significant increase in the desire of professionals in school districts, colleges, and universities to find ways of increasing their students' capacity to learn, think, and behave more effectively. Recent years have witnessed the emergence of various cognitive education programs aimed at enhancing students' learning and thinking with the hope that they might become more independent learners and more efficient problem-solvers (see Chapter 12).

Second, in the 1980s the importance of social ability and the need to incorporate social skills within the curriculum was recognized. A widespread belief emerged that education should attend to both the academic and social development of students (see Chapter 13). Moreover, people began to support the idea that a classroom should be a community where all children have the right to belong and to talk, work, and share together (see Chapter 14). *Thirdly*, the 1980s saw increasing disenchantment with traditional assessment approaches. There was a shift from standardized assessment to dynamic assessment, which has resulted in a greater focus on the *process* of learning—what the child is doing that facilitates learning, or not doing that impedes learning, and how nonintellectual factors such as motivation, affect, and personality intertwine (Lidz, 1990; Samuels, Lamb, & Oberholtzer, 1992). Along with increased emphasis on process assessment there has also been greater emphasis on practical classroom-based assessment, which has resulted in more useful information with respect to program planning and intervention (see Chapter 8).

Fourth was the movement in education toward **adaptive instruction**. Emerging from research were principles and practices related to effective program planning and instruction that assisted teachers in modifying classroom environments to correspond to student differences, and in teaching students how to cope more effectively with academic and social tasks (see Chapters 9, 10, and 11). The principles included such things as frequent monitoring of students' performance, modelling effective learning strategies, and promoting independent problem-solving and decision-making. The practices included the use of cooperative learning procedures, tutoring systems, reciprocal teaching methods, multisensory lesson designs, mastery learning models, and computer-assisted instruction programs.

Fifth was the movement away from child **labelling** and **categorization** toward identifying the conditions that result in variant performance levels (see Chapter 4).The idea that learning difficulties reside solely in the child was being replaced by the idea that the process of learning is complex, and that learning problems can result from an interaction of factors such as educational context, teaching methodology, and academic task.

A *sixth* important development in the 1980s was the realization in the educational community that the dramatic increase of immigrants to Canada was changing the ethnic and linguistic composition of the classroom (Bell, 1991). Indeed, we now recognize that the classroom is a microcosm of Canadian society consisting of children from different cultural backgrounds. The increase of children with second-culture and second-language experiences presents a challenge to the educational system (Kach & DeFaveri, 1987),

◆ adaptive instruction: modifying classroom environments and instruction to accommodate the unique learning needs of each student

◆ labelling: the classifying of exceptional students on the basis of their primary disabilities or disorders

◆ categorization: a system of classification whereby individuals become eligible to receive special education services based on assessment criteria and labelling practices

which requires that teachers become sensitive to the communication and cultural needs of their students, and try to promote their cultural identity (see Chapter 5).

Seventh was the recognition that the education of all students requires the coordinated and collaborative efforts of parents and teachers, who need to share the responsibility for all children's academic and social development (see Chapters 6 and 7). *Lastly,* our educational experiences in the 1980s reinforced the need to broaden the education curriculum, in order for teachers to meet the needs of all students, and to foster respect for individual differences and similarities among all students within the classroom (see Chapter 10).

◇ IMPLICATIONS OF THE EMERGING TRENDS

The trends from the last couple of decades have provided impetus for the merging of regular and special education into a unified educational system. The emerging belief of the 1990s is that all teachers are responsible for addressing all students' unique learning needs—a belief that is encapsulated in slogans such as, "*All teachers are teachers of children with special needs.*" The increasing numbers of children in need of individualized programming, the expanding knowledge and skill of teachers with respect to student diversity, effective assessment, and teaching methodologies, and the lower levels of funding for special services suggest that the slogan for the 21st century might be, "*It is normal to be different.*" The current emphasis on the integration of special-needs children into the mainstream suggests that, in the future, special education and regular education will be considered not separate disciplines but rather parts of a unified system that will be dynamic, holistic, collaborative, and focused on the individual needs of all children. Educational leaders, we believe, will increasingly advocate for a unified (inclusive) educational system, while school systems will undergo major transitions in order to: (1) foster lifelong learning, (2) provide educational equity and quality, (3) facilitate independent learning and thinking, (4) promote a school-home partnership, (5) encourage living and learning in a community, and (6) develop academic and social competence.

◇ THE GOALS OF INCLUSIVE EDUCATION

Goals which were in Fig. circle
(1) what are the goals
(2) what do they mean?

The six goals of inclusive education noted above collectively reflect the belief that educators should ensure that all children are provided opportunities to maximize their potential in the mainstream of regular education. Furthermore, they represent the desired outcomes of all educators' efforts within a unified educational system.

LIFELONG LEARNING

Although children share common characteristics, each is unique, with different interests and aspirations (Brown, 1988). To ensure that children gain personal satisfaction in their educational experiences, and are provided with the foundation for **lifelong learning,** requires an integrated and flexible educational process. It involves not only appropriate service delivery but also dedicated people who are involved in the child's day-to-day life, and who strive to make the child's experiences as full and enjoyable as possible. It requires teachers to be understanding, empathic, and knowledgeable about students' cognitive, developmental, and cultural needs, as well as to be energetic and creative with respect to program planning and instruction.

All children should be encouraged to view learning as a lifelong adventure. Teachers can foster this idea by projecting an excitement about learning, and by demonstrating its value beyond the classroom. Children need to be shown that learning can be fun and meaningful. They also need to discover ways to direct and control their learning by themselves. Lastly, the idea that learning is active, modifiable, ongoing, and usable should be reinforced and modelled by the teacher so that students can understand and appreciate how their lives are continually enriched through the process of learning. Pearpoint (1989) comments that lifelong learning is "something we all are engaged in every moment," and that "our future will be determined less by our technological expertise than by our excellence in developing our human resources" (p. 250).

EQUITY AND QUALITY

A major goal of inclusive education is to integrate all children and ensure that they have fair and equal access to normal school experiences. We believe that each child has the right to be a full member of his or her community school; that schools should provide an opportunity for children to learn among their friends; that schools should strive to be communities that value diversity (Forest & Lusthaus, 1989); and that educational options and choices that ensure quality educational service within a unified system should be available to children and their parents. This type of educational system regards all children as equally accepted members of heterogeneous classrooms.

Position statements from departments of education across all of the provinces and territories in Canada (Csapo & Goguen, 1989) reveal a clear and uniform message regarding integration: "the present and future trend is to increase and improve the integration of children with individual needs within the mainstream of the school environment." The rationale for integration is based on several assumptions: first, all children can become more **acculturated** by being with their peers, and thereby acquiring through observing and modelling age-appropriate behaviours and skills; second, all children can acquire academic and social competencies through interactions

◆ lifelong learning: effective education that goes beyond curriculum and grade levels to emphasize critical thinking and problem-solving

◆ acculturation: a process in which individuals merge their own cultural needs and identity with those of the dominant group

that occur naturally within the classroom (Hartup, 1983); and, third, all children can gain an appreciation of individual differences. However, these things are not likely to occur unless they are planned and promoted. Successful integration depends on the degree of communication and participation allowed within the environment, as well as on the flexibility and willingness of all members in the environment to support integration.

Ultimately, it is the quality of education that is of central importance to advocates of inclusive education. According to Marfo and Nesbit (1989), quality education

> does not have to do merely with the setting in which education is provided. Quality education results from realistic educational goal setting, appropriate educational content that is determined and guided by realistic goals, and instructional support systems that are selected on the basis of each child's strengths, needs, and limitations. An important guiding principle in dealing with any heterogeneous group is that no fixed or predetermined learning environments or instructional strategies are best or even appropriate for all children (p. 195).

From our perspective, we must strive for a unified system that promotes belonging, stresses individualization and options for all students, fosters cooperative professional relationships, and focuses on the child (Stainback & Stainback, 1984).

LEARNING AND THINKING

There is an urgent need for educators to focus their endeavours on the development of higher-level cognitive skills that enable students to become independent learners and creative problem-solvers. Because of our rapidly changing technological environment, these skills are more important today than ever (Mulcahy, Andrews, & Peat, 1989). Hence, the development of children's learning and thinking skills is a major goal of inclusive education.

Generally, research over the last decade shows that many children with learning difficulties tend to be passive rather than active learners: they believe neither that they have personal control over their learning, nor that their efforts influence their achievement; they tend to be dependent rather than independent learners; they tend to use deficient and/or inefficient strategies when doing academic tasks; and they do not typically monitor their performance. Specifically, many children with learning difficulties are unable to monitor their reading comprehension to ensure that they are obtaining meaning from text (Wong, 1985); unable to apply task-appropriate strategies (Torgesen, 1980); unable to plan organizational strategies for approaching a task (Wong, 1982); unable to engage in strategic behaviour in order to restore meaning when there has been a breakdown in understanding; and unable to change or modify their strategies to meet varying task demands (Palincsar & Brown, 1987).

Advances in cognitive psychology over the past decade have resulted in the development of cognitive education programs that focus on learning and thinking skills (see Mulcahy, Short, & Andrews, 1991). These programs range from developing intellectual competence (e.g., Feuerstein, Rand, Hoffman, & Miller, 1980; Sternberg, 1985), operational reasoning (e.g., Lipman, Sharp, & Oscanyan, 1980; Nickerson & Adams, 1983), and problem-solving ability (e.g., de Bono, 1980; Meichenbaum, 1980), to providing more procedural techniques and skills for mastering academic and social tasks (e.g., Dansereau, 1984; Deshler & Schumaker, 1986; Weinstein & Underwood, 1985).

Many teachers have adopted these programs to help them develop their students' learning and thinking skills. Research clearly points to the effectiveness of cognitive interventions with differing populations (see Deshler, Warner, Schumaker, & Alley, 1983; Hallahan et al., 1983, in the area of learning disabilities; Scott, 1988, in the area of gifted education; Dansereau, 1985; Weinstein, 1982, with college students; Brown & Campione, 1977; Mulcahy, 1980, with children who have cognitive deficiencies), and within a wide assortment of subject areas (see Jones, Palincsar, Ogle, & Carr, 1987; Wittrock, 1986). Research at the University of Alberta over the past few years has also supported the utility of cognitive intervention (Andrews, 1984; Lupart & Mulcahy, 1983). For example, a longitudinal research project at the University of Alberta from 1984 to 1988 demonstrated that students can benefit in both the academic and social domains from teachers trained in cognitive strategy instruction (Mulcahy, Andrews, & Peat, 1989). Summarizing the findings of various intervention studies, Jones (1986) concludes that

> [c]ognitive instruction has the potential to alter substantially the capability of the learner, especially the low achieving learner, in much the same way that microchips radically altered the capability of the computer—Explicit learning strategy training facilitates learning for low achieving students, and there is strong data to suggest that cognitive instruction decreases the differences between younger and older students (pp. 8-9).

SCHOOL-HOME PARTNERSHIP

Families are one of the most important foundations for children's learning and development. Families typically provide children with attention, guidance, and stability. They "provide security and protection from vulnerability; they pick up the pieces when things go wrong; and they have the potential to ensure that their members' most fundamental needs of love and caring are met. Indeed, families are the anchors that many of us need to survive in the world" (Strully & Strully, 1989, p. 214). Families also facilitate their child's membership in communities and schools. Along with serving some very important functions related to their children's social and academic development, families are the most knowledgeable about their children's unique strengths, weaknesses, and interests.

Schools are also important foundations for children's learning and development. They provide a place where knowledge can be developed, skills can be acquired, and friendships can emerge. They also facilitate children's membership within communities, and promote the development and maintenance of social values and norms. Moreover, like families, schools are very knowledgeable about students' individual learning characteristics and behavioural tendencies.

As major stakeholders in children's learning and development, families and schools can offer each other valuable information and support. The organization and management of their partnership in children's education, however, needs to be carefully planned. Parents as partners is discussed in depth in Chapter 7. For now, it is sufficient to say that parents can be involved in their children's education in several ways, for example, as a resource for assessing and evaluating their child's educational and social needs, and as a source of input for program planning and instruction. The coordinated effort of parents and teachers can lead to substantial contributions to children's educational service and social-emotional development. Hence, parents as partners is a major goal of inclusive education.

LIVING AND LEARNING IN A COMMUNITY

An important outcome of inclusive education would be that all children benefit from the various relationships and associations available within the community. As noted by Judith Snow (1989),

> All individuals, regardless of their differences, must be regarded as an unusual gift, not a burden, to the broader social structure. People must see that differences do not have to be fixed or cured. Instead, each individual's gifts must be discovered, accepted and shaped. Every person must be welcomed, celebrated, listened to, challenged, and supported in every environment to develop all of his or her potential talents. The individual's contributions must be facilitated and used for the betterment of the wider group (p. 223).

The concept of living and learning in a community is further discussed in Chapters 5 and 14. For now, it is important to note that the aim of inclusive education is to foster and maintain learning environments in which children can talk, work, and share together. These environments are seen as places where differences are accepted and respected, and where interactions among the students are encouraged and strengthened. A further goal is to reinforce the community spirit in the classroom and help class members become more cooperative and understanding of each other's individual characteristics.

ACADEMIC AND SOCIAL COMPETENCE

A priority of inclusive education is to be more responsive to the differential abilities of children in both the academic and social domains. There is no blueprint to guide teachers with respect to this priority. However, a successful plan may involve the creation of a nonthreatening and nurturing school environment in which teachers can share ideas and concerns among themselves (Correa, 1990). Other strategies for success may involve the development and use of *cooperative learning models, proactive and supportive management, cognitive strategy instruction*, and *social skills programs* (see Chapters 9 and 13 for further discussion).

Now that we understand some of the goals of inclusive education, let us focus our attention on how these goals can be achieved. From our perspective, the process involves the merger of regular and special education.

◆ THE MERGER OF REGULAR AND SPECIAL EDUCATION

The idea to merge regular and special education into a unified educational system structured to meet the unique needs of all students evolved from the mainstreaming movement. **Mainstreaming** was the predominant educational trend of the 1980s. Its focus is on serving the needs of exceptional students in the least restrictive environment. Although the ideological arguments in support of mainstreaming are compelling, many educators, administrators, teachers, parents, and researchers have given evidence and testimony to its associated imperfections and limitations. This has led to a change of thinking regarding how educational systems can respond to the diverse needs of all students in an effective and equitable manner (Flynn & Kowalczyk-McPhee, 1989).

In this section, we review current issues regarding mainstreaming, and point out how some of its drawbacks have led us to support inclusive education.

◆ mainstreaming: the accommodation of students with special needs in a regular education setting

CURRENT ISSUES

Since the early 1970s, the mainstreaming movement has mushroomed in Canadian schools. Propelled by the widespread criticism of segregated schooling, the civil rights movement, and the discriminatory effects of categorization and labelling, educators and parents have optimistically awaited the results of studies evaluating the effectiveness of mainstreaming programs. Unfortunately, these results have not been clear-cut, and conflicting evidence has had to be reassessed (Asher & Taylor, 1981; Gottlieb, 1981; Johnson, Johnson, & Maruyama, 1983; MacMillan, Jones, & Meyers, 1976; O'Neil, 1984).

Stainback, Stainback, Courtnage, and Jaben (1985) suggest that the concept of mainstreaming, in which regular classroom teachers are expected to adapt instruction to meet a wide range of students' needs, is difficult to implement given the structure of today's schools. They note that the traditional graded structure of schools has become one of the foremost barriers to the individualization of educational programming. Stainback et al. (1985) refer to this situation as forcing the child to "fit" an imperfect system, which attempts to "fix" what is wrong with the child. Stainback et al. propose that schools need to modify existing structures to be consistent with the following assumptions about children:

1. Students vary from one another in regard to the age at which they are ready to learn specified objectives.
2. Students vary from one another in regard to the rate at which they learn given objectives.
3. Students vary within themselves in regard to how fast they progress through the objectives in different curricular areas (p. 147).

Key modifications would include a move toward nongraded groupings, providing for flexible pacing, evaluation, and programming based on standards that are geared toward the performance of the individual student, and a large-scale de-emphasis of categorical programs and labelling.

While certain advocacy groups are committed to the full-scale implementation of mainstreaming in schools, there are a number of crucial functional barriers to this end, among them the following:

- The recognition that services for exceptional students often involve other governmental departments such as family and social services, health, and the solicitor general. Each has different funding structures and priorities, and there is typically no coordinating mechanism for interjurisdictional planning and policy development.
- Most provinces have developed policies that require all children to attend school. Children who were previously institutionalized, or provided for in specialized schools, are now being served in the public schools. The diverse needs that these children present have been described as "specific, and often specialized, health care services such as catheterization, suctioning and gastrotomy feeding to more socially related needs related to drug and alcohol abuse, family breakup and behavioral and emotional disorders" (Alberta Education Response Centre, 1990, p. 25). Such services are well beyond the traditional roles of education.
- Both rural and smaller districts may have particular difficulty in providing the necessary range of noninstructional services.
- Larger urban centres are increasingly burdened as students from smaller jurisdictions move into the cities where specialized services are more readily available.

The policies and decisions that these problems give rise to will ultimately impact on all governmental, educational, and community levels. Our focus is on the improved organization and service delivery in the schools through a merger of regular and special education. We believe that the expertise and teaching innovations that have been developed within both disciplines can be united. As Stainback and Stainback (1984) state:

> Dichotomizing students into two basic types (special and regular), maintaining a dual system of education, separate professional organizations, separate personnel preparation programs, and separate funding patterns does very little to foster the values inherent in the mainstreaming and integration movement of the past decade. . . . The issue is not whether there are differences among students. There are obviously differences, even extreme differences. . . . However, this should not be used as a justification to label, segregate, or maintain a dual system of education. With careful planning, it should be possible to meet the unique needs of all students within one unified system of education—a system that does not deny differences, but rather a system that recognizes and accommodates for differences (p. 109).

An example of this type of system is the Ontario Waterloo Region Roman Catholic Separate School Board, which is being restructured in order to achieve one unified system in which all children will have access and equal opportunity for success in education. According to Flynn and Kowalcyzk-McPhee (1989), this school board became committed to the idea that their schools should provide an integrated instructional program that could meet the needs of all students through a variety of options, and in a flexible, differentiated, and equitable manner. The direction and impetus for this contemporary educational trend stems from a major movement within the education field called the *regular education initiative*.

◆ THE REGULAR EDUCATION INITIATIVE

One of the key thrusts of the **regular education initiative (REI)** is the merging of special and regular education expertise in an attempt to eliminate some of the documented problems associated with segregated special education—and, at the same time, preserve the rich knowledge base that has been developed in the special education field—through the cooperative professional development of both special and regular education teachers (Stainback & Stainback, 1984, 1985; Stainback, Stainback, & Forest, 1989).

Gersten and Woodward (1990) provide an extensive review of problems associated with traditional **special education pull-out programs,** which have been described as a "dumping ground" for any student experiencing difficulties with the regular classroom curriculum. They point to factors such as the marked increase in students classified as learning disabled in the past two decades; the lack of distinction between students classified as learning disabled and remedial students; the confusion and apparent variety in school policy and definition of learning disabilities; and the fact that once students are placed in special education, they typically remain there for an extended

◆ regular education initiative (REI): movement to transfer responsibility for exceptional students from special education teachers to regular education teachers

◆ special education pull-out program: special segregated instruction for students who are experiencing difficulties with the regular classroom curriculum

period. Such factors have led some educators to conclude that regular teachers are abdicating their responsibilities toward exceptional students.

Taking the opposite perspective, Miller (1990) describes this trend as a "disenfranchisement" of regular teachers who, feeling overwhelmed by all of the legislative, procedural, legal, and technical issues associated with special education, have simply "deferred to the perceived expertise and knowledge of the special education staff" (p. 17). It is noteworthy that similar sentiments were voiced in a major Canadian document, namely, the CELDIC Report, *One Million Children* (Roberts & Lazure, 1970): "teachers (and others) were made to feel that only specialists could help the handicapped child. In this process, the front line person is made to feel inadequate, and the child is segregated as being different, because of the special treatment provided" (p. 6).

Related to this trend is the ever-increasing research showing that the presumed benefits of special education pull-out classes (i.e., smaller classes, individualized instruction, and special programs) have created even more difficulties—especially for students with minor learning problems—in effecting full-time reintegration into the regular program. Problems have included disruption and time lost moving to and from the resource room; failure to connect resource assistance with regular class instruction; the use of different curriculum materials in resource and regular classrooms; and the fact that students miss part of what regular students experience during resource room time (Allington & McGill-Franzen,1989).

The REI attempts to eliminate many of these problems through the provision of effective instruction within the mainstream of regular education. Proponents of this initiative emphasize the use of effective instructional and learning strategies in order to realize exceptional students' learning potential. Fulfilling this initiative will require the merging of what special education teachers and regular education teachers now do separately into one service delivery format. The process is not a simple one, although the recent literature in this area is optimistic about what can be achieved in such a merger (Stainback & Stainback, 1984, 1985; Stainback et. al., 1989).

Despite its initial appeal, the REI movement has been criticized on several fronts. First, the feasibility of providing specialized instruction within the mainstream of regular education has been questioned (Kauffman, Gerber, & Semmel, 1988). Is it realistic to expect regular classroom teachers to serve the needs of all students within the regular classroom? Critics such as Mesinger (1985) suggest that the expectation is unrealistic, or premature at best, stating that "not enough academically proficient persons are entering teacher training" (p. 511). Others have argued that there is insufficient research evidence of school programs based upon REI principles to warrant the full-scale elimination of current special education services (McKinney & Hocutt, 1988).

A second point of contention is the core assumption that regular teachers are going to be willing participants in the REI process (Davis, 1989). The concerns and fears that regular teachers have expressed regarding the advent of regular class placement of special needs students are well documented (Childs, 1981; Corman & Gottlieb, 1979; Horne, 1983; Hudson, Graham, & Warner, 1979). Many teachers are uneasy about the prospects of teaching children with special needs, partly out of the misconceptions about exceptionality and partly out of concern that there will be insufficient support mechanisms provided. As Keogh (1988) notes, "It is strange logic that calls for the regular system to take over responsibility for pupils it has already demonstrated it has failed" (p. 20).

The REI is not a plan for action. Rather, it is a collection of views from a variety of authors (e.g., Gartner & Lipsky, 1989; Lilly, 1986; Reynolds, Wang, & Walberg, 1987; Stainback & Stainback, 1984; Wang, Reynolds, & Walberg, 1986) that has generated a lot of attention regarding our current system of education. We agree with Jenkins, Pious, and Jewell (1990) that

> the REI offers a provocative way to focus our thinking about better ways to organize and provide services even though it is not a carefully detailed plan that specifies the bricks and mortar, the building schedule, the use of resources, and the personnel needed to build a structure. Based on this view, it is also clear that the REI could eventually be expressed in many ways, incorporating combinations and permutations of the best that the field has to offer in effective services. But we are a long way from even laying the foundation for this effort (p. 481).

The major tenet of the REI is that classroom teachers should have the overall responsibility for educating children with learning problems. The inference from the REI literature is that regular classroom teachers should have the ultimate responsibility for educating all students assigned to them; making and monitoring major instructional decisions for all of the students in their class; providing instruction that follows a normal developmental curriculum; managing instruction for diverse populations; and finding, using, and coordinating assistance for students who require more intense services than those provided to their peers (Jenkins et al., 1990).

What we draw from reading the REI literature is that all children have the right to be educated in their community schools, and that classroom teachers have the ultimate authority and responsibility for educating them. This does *not* mean that all children will receive all instructional services in the regular classroom. Rather, it means that if a **transdisciplinary team** (see Chapters 6 and 7) determines that students require instruction beyond the normal developmental curriculum, need services beyond the ability of the classroom teachers (e.g., mobility training or speech reading), or require the provision of specialized services, then the team (which includes the classroom teacher) ensures that students receive this help in their community school. Moreover, the classroom teacher is in charge of orchestrating all the required elements of his or her program plan (Jenkins et al., 1990).

◆ transdisciplinary team: members of a group who share information and skills across a variety of topic areas and professional domains

From our perspective, inclusive education depends on the extent to which classroom teachers can accept the responsibilities outlined above; school administrations can provide the support and resources necessary for accommodating their students in their schools; teachers can adapt their instruction to deal with student diversity; and regular and special education teachers can collaborate and communicate with each other, and it is this last necessity to which we turn now.

◇ COLLABORATION AND CONSULTATION IN THE SCHOOLS

Process part of model.

◆ collaborative consultation: mutual exchange of information between professionals of all disciplines in order to address legal and instructional decisions concerning the needs of exceptional children

Idol and West and their colleagues (Idol, Paolucci-Whitcomb, & Nevin, 1986; West & Cannon, 1988; West & Idol, 1990) have developed consultation models based on the concept of **collaborative consultation,** which they define as an interactive process that allows individuals with diverse expertise to work together in efforts to assist students with special needs. Consultation models are designed to prevent and remediate learning and behaviour problems, and to coordinate instructional programs (West, Idol, & Cannon, 1989). According to their consultative model, regular and special education teachers, as well as other team members, should negotiate their responsibilities and expectations, define the nature and parameters of the immediate problem, generate and select intervention recommendations, implement plans for action, evaluate the intervention, and redesign the intervention if needed (West & Idol, 1990).

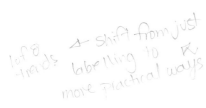 *a shift from just labelling to more practical ways*

The consultation and collaboration movement has shifted educators' orientation from a "reactive posture to a more proactive and preventative one" (Johnson, Pugach, & Devlin, 1990, p. 10). As Johnson et al. note (1990), a true partnership requires special and regular education teachers to recognize the limits of their own training, and administrators to encourage collegiality and teacher empowerment. Teachers must also keep the child as the focal point, and share each other's expertise to solve problems. Johnson et al. (1990) recommend the following steps for producing a collaborative environment:

◆ Sanction collaborative efforts at the administrative level to give teachers the encouragement, freedom, and support they need to engage in mutual problem-solving.

◆ Allow sufficient time for teachers to interact by having others, such as parent volunteers and teacher aides, assist with clerical work and other noninstructional tasks.

◆ Provide opportunities for special and regular education teachers to co-teach in order to foster a greater mutual understanding of each other's unique expertise.

◆ Reserve in-service meetings for collaborative problem-solving among teachers and other professionals who could work in teams in order to capitalize on each other's expertise and to develop problem-solving strategies.

Despite their appeal, collaborative consultation models have produced mixed opinions. Some critics report that communication problems arise

because of personal and professional defensiveness (Hansen & Hansen, 1978), while others believe that the process takes too much time (Miller & Sabatino, 1978). From our perspective, these issues can be resolved with careful planning and open dialogue. In summarizing research supporting consultant models, Nevin and Thousand (1987) concludes, "Teachers in schools with a consulting teacher assumed more direct roles and engaged in more direct activities with handicapped learners' referral, assessment, curriculum development, implementation of teaching/learning activities, and evaluation when compared to their counterparts" (p. 277). (For further discussion of consultation and collaboration, see Chapter 6.)

◆ ADAPTIVE INSTRUCTION   → Part of process of inclusive ed. Model.

Inclusive education requires teachers to be responsive and adaptive to the unique learning needs of all students. Regular and special education teachers need to be innovative, collaborative, and accommodative in their efforts to deal with student diversity. There is no one way to support the needs of a diverse school population. Indeed, adaptive instruction assumes that each teacher will identify and provide a wide range of instructional supports that are needed by individual students to effectively master the learning and behavioural objectives (Wang, 1989).

According to a number of authors (Glaser, 1977; Reynolds & Birch, 1988; Walberg & Wang, 1987; Wang, 1980, 1989), adaptive instruction requires teachers to assess the characteristics and capabilities of each student (see Chapter 8); collaborate and consult with others to plan developmentally appropriate instruction (see Parts 3 and 4); make environmental and individual accommodations to facilitate student learning; manage and instruct students in ways that permit mastery of content at a pace suited to individual abilities, needs, and interests (see Chapters 9 and 10); foster students' independent and strategic learning and thinking (see Chapter 12); promote the social ability and social integration of all students (see Chapter 13); and provide opportunities for students to better understand, appreciate, and respect their peers as well as to experience partnership and leadership (see Chapters 5 and 14).

Wang (1989) states that "one of the basic premises of effective adaptive instruction programs is that a variety of educational objectives, instructional materials, and learning tasks is needed; furthermore, success in achieving instructional objectives requires a wide selection of teaching and learning strategies" (p. 184). The successful implementation and practice of procedures associated with adaptive instruction depends on the beliefs, values, and attitudes of the teachers regarding student diversity, and on the enabling conditions of the educational environment.

◆ TEACHERS' BELIEFS, VALUES, AND ATTITUDES

in lecture.

Many teacher characteristics affect the process of inclusive education, for example, the type and level of educational training and the number of years of teaching experience (Berryman & Berryman, 1981; Ogletree & Atkinson, 1982; Winzer, 1984; Winzer & Rose, 1986). Arguably, the more training and experience teachers have in special-needs education and programming, the greater their chances for successfully implementing educational programs and practices based on inclusive education. Additionally, if classroom teachers are sincerely willing to take on the responsibility of teaching children with diverse learning and behavioural needs, the chances for effective inclusive education are greatly increased. Inclusive education also depends on certain necessary values. Teachers need to value: learning as a lifelong process in which they share responsibility with parents for maximizing the quality of children's lives; the need to enrich children's competencies in both the academic and social domains; their colleagues and the benefits of collaboration; and, perhaps most importantly, the goals of inclusive education.

It has been suggested that the most critical element of inclusive education is the attitude of classroom teachers toward children with special needs (Hannah, 1988). Teachers' attitudes affect not only what happens in classroom settings (McClaskey & Quay, 1987) but also the instructional option that is chosen for students (Budgell, 1986; Safran, Safran, & Barcikowski, 1985). Unfortunately, many teachers are opposed to having children with diverse needs in their classrooms (Childs, 1981; Hudson et al., 1979; Jamieson, 1984; Jones, Gottlieb, Guskin, & Yoshida, 1978). This finding suggests that teachers must be given opportunities to confront their biases so that constructive and workable solutions can be developed (Desharnais, 1980).

Attitudes vary according to types of disabilities (Schloss & Miller, 1982), the types of perceptions people have about disabilities (Bartel & Guskin, 1976), and the labels assigned to children with disabilities (Algozzine, Mercer, & Countermine, 1977). Teachers' attitudes influence the nature of the interaction between students and teachers, as well as the students' achievement (Brophy & Good, 1974). Schulz, Carpenter, and Turnbull (1991) point out that

> teachers constantly communicate important attitudinal messages to students about individual differences. It becomes obvious to all students whether teachers favor high-achieving students; feel respect, pity, or disgust for students who have special problems; believe that every person has inherent value; or are prejudiced against those who are different. Teachers are much more transparent than they care to believe (p. 413).

Teachers' attitudes about children with diverse needs can be changed through accurate information and positive encounters (Johnson & Johnson, 1984; Stainback et al., 1985). As Schulz et al. (1991) comment, "Sometimes teachers only get to know handicapped children and youth as students. They know a student's level of performance, particular disability, curriculum needs, and learning styles; but that is not enough. It is also important to know the student as an individual, and, furthermore, to find joy and naturalness in the relationship" (p. 416). But some teachers doubt their ability to make a difference in children's learning (O'Reilly & Duquette, 1988), while others are anxious about dealing with diverse populations of students (Nader, 1984). We next examine enabling conditions that might provide teachers opportunities to develop positive attitudes about children with diverse needs, to integrate students into their classrooms, and to consult and collaborate with others regarding teaching approaches, thereby achieving the goals of inclusive education.

◆ ENABLING CONDITIONS FOR INCLUSIVE EDUCATION

· Know what enabling conditions are – terms or general

The merger of regular and special education will not happen quickly or easily. As discussed above, the process requires regular and special educators to consult and collaborate with one another, and to plan and provide adaptive instruction for all children. Moreover, it depends on teachers' positive attitudes and the resources available for them to successfully develop and maintain a unified system of education. From our perspective, the most important enabling conditions are: *professional training and development*, *pooling of resources*, and *administrative leadership and support*.

PROFESSIONAL TRAINING AND DEVELOPMENT

Many teachers lack information about students considered to be exceptional or special, and believe, therefore, that they are underprepared to teach them (Post & Roy, 1985). Pre-service and in-service teacher training that includes direct contact with children who have diverse needs might foster positive attitudes and give teachers greater confidence about their ability to teach these children. For example, Glass and Meckler (1972) provided a summer workshop for elementary teachers to assist them in their instruction of mildly handicapped children. By the end of the workshop, teachers were more positive about integration, and viewed themselves as better able to accommodate their programming and teaching for these children. Ministries of education should encourage education departments in universities and colleges to pool their resources in order to give all educators a strong base in the teaching/ learning process. Moreover, colleges and universities should prepare teachers-in-training to deal with diversity in the classroom (Stainback & Stainback, 1984).

Teacher federations agree that present training methods fail to provide successful integrated learning experiences (Csapo, 1981). Teachers need information that will broaden their understanding and appreciation of children with special needs—information, for example, on how to identify learning problems, and on how to adapt the environment and their instruction to accommodate those problems. Their courses should include such things as dynamic assessment, individual educational planning, adaptive instruction, differentiated learning, multicultural education, and holistic curriculum development. Additionally, teacher training should include practical training in, and experience with, consultative and collaborative practices in schools. Thousand and Villa (1989) point out that for "school personnel to be most effective in their collaborations with one another and their instruction of students, they need to share common concepts, vocabulary, and training in instructional strategies that are founded in sound research and theory" (p. 95).

POOLING OF RESOURCES

Inclusive education will need the resources and the personnel to address the unique needs of all students. A high quality of service requires well-trained teachers, support personnel (e.g., teachers' aides), transportation services, school building modifications, material resources (e.g., assessment instruments, program materials, and instructional aides). Inclusive education will impose additional financial demands on school boards during a time when, in many provinces, the share for educational spending that is borne by the provincial governments is steadily shrinking (Csapo, 1981). Money allocation and cost-effectiveness with respect to inclusive education must be addressed. According to Stainback and Stainback (1989), "What is needed is an integration of the resources and personnel from special education into regular education—to broaden the capabilities of regular education to meet the unique educational needs of all students" (p. 255).

Considerable money and time is currently spent in assessing and classifying students in order to make special education placement decisions. In an inclusive educational system, however, everyone would qualify for assistance, and resources could be redirected to instructional assessment and program planning. As Stainback and Stainback (1984) envision it, "If . . . a given number of students required instruction in an alternative communication system, self-care skills, or advanced physics, the cost estimates to operate such services could constitute the justification for monetary appropriations, rather than categories of labelled children" (p. 108).

no.

ADMINISTRATIVE LEADERSHIP AND SUPPORT

Inclusive education depends on administrative leaders to promote the merger of special and regular education; support integrated learning; develop supportive networks with the community; foster respect for individual differences; promote consultative, cooperative, and adaptive educational practices; promote the goals of inclusive education; and empower teachers. On this last point, we believe that it is critical that administration help teachers help themselves cope with the frustrations and stresses involved in inclusive education. As Vivian Correa (1990) notes, "When teachers are empowered they have input in restructuring school policies and procedures that better reflect their perspective. Teachers who are entrusted with responsibility for school-based changes and school-based management arrive at solutions to problems that more accurately meet the needs of students, parents, and communities" (p. 8). Her suggestions as to how schools can create programs that reflect teacher leadership include teachers:

- deciding the nature of staff development programs to advance their knowledge of new and effective educational practices
- developing their skills in working together through formal instruction in such things as collaboration, parent communication, and problem solving
- developing functional, meaningful, and flexible curricula for their students
- scheduling time to collaborate with others in providing effective instruction.

The process of inclusive education requires the full support and guidance of administrators and supervisors at the school district level. As Karagianis and Nesbit (1980), note, "It is necessary that administrators and supervisors be well-versed concerning education of the exceptional child. They must be ready (*and willing*) to provide direction and to evaluate the proposals of teachers and principals who share in the process" (p. 5). We believe that the initiation, development, maintenance, evaluation, and improvement of inclusive education practices should be a school-based responsibility. From this perspective, we recommend to schools the following general steps:

1. Have teachers collectively discuss such things as their philosophy of education, and their attitudes, beliefs, and values regarding integrated teaching and learning, and then decide what educational goals they want to achieve in their school.
2. Have teachers record the information arising from their discussions, and note what they might require to reach their goals. These enabling conditions might include support personnel, programs and materials, reduction of class sizes, in-service training, and so forth.
3. Draw up a list of responsibilities for all school personnel, including teachers, principals, assistant principals, program coordinators, support staff , psychologists, reading specialists, speech and language specialists, occupational and physical therapists, medical personnel, social workers, counsellors, mental health practitioners, and parents.
4. Develop suggestions for the implementation, maintenance, evaluation, and continuation of service delivery needs, along with a school budget for the overall plan.
5. Set up an internal committee to review the final report, and to make recommendations. Have the proposal reviewed by all personnel in the school, and from the feedback make modifications where agreed upon.
6. Submit the report for school district review and feedback.
7. After district approval, implement the plan and thereafter evaluate and modify where necessary. Provide staff development through in-services and workshops on a continual basis.

◆ CONCLUSION

The process of inclusive education requires considerable preparation and commitment. Not only does the process need to be decided upon and acted upon, but it also needs to be continually monitored and evaluated. The process cannot be considered as a one-shot approach, but rather as a multifaceted endeavour taking place over an extended period of time. The goals of inclusive education will not be accomplished quickly, and the process itself will take time to evolve and grow. Commitment on the part of all those involved in the educational process is a prerequisite for the emergence of a unified system of education that can meet the unique needs of all students.

QUESTIONS
◆◆◆◆◆◆◆◆◆◆◆◆◆◆

1. What is inclusive education and what are its goals?

2. What are some of the educational developments that have led to the concept of inclusive education?

3. What are some of the problems associated with the regular education initiative?

4. What are some things that regular and special educators will have to do once they are joined within a unified educational system?

5. What are some enabling conditions that can allow teachers to be more responsive to children with diverse needs?

REFERENCES

Alberta Education Response Centre. (1990). *Special education review: A discussion paper*. Edmonton: Alberta Education.

Algozzine, G., Mercer, C. D., & Countermine, T. (1977). The effects of labels and behavior in teacher expectations. *Exceptional Children*, 131-132.

Allington, R., & McGill-Franzen, A. (1989). School response to reading failure: Instruction for chapter 1 and special education students in grades two, four, and eight. *Elementary School Journal*, 79, 529-542.

Andrews, J. (1984). *An exploration of study strategies used by spelling disabled children: A qualitative comparison of three teaching approaches*. M.A. thesis, University of Alberta, Edmonton, Alberta, Canada.

Asher, S. R., & Taylor, A. R. (1981). Social outcomes of mainstreaming: Sociometric assessment and beyond. *Exceptional Education Quarterly*, 1(4), 13-30.

Bartel, N. R., & Guskin, S. (1976). A handicap as a social phenomenon. In W. M. Cruikshank (Ed.), *The psychology of exceptional children and youth* (pp. 74-114). New Jersey: Prentice-Hall.

Bell, K. J. (1991). Language learning in Canadian classrooms: Our heritage of multiculturalism. In R. Short, L. Stewin, & S. McCann (Eds.), *Educational psychology: Canadian perspectives* (pp. 320-333). Toronto: Copp Clark Pitman.

Berryman, J., & Berryman, C. (1981). *Use of the attitudes towards mainstreaming scale with rural Georgia teachers*. (ERIC Document Reproduction Service No. ED 201-240.)

Brophy, J., & Good, T. (1974). *Teacher-student relationships: Causes and consequences*. New York: Holt, Rinehart & Winston.

Brown, A. L., & Campione, J. C. (1977). Training strategic study time apportionment in educable retarded children. *Intelligence*, 1, 94-107.

Brown, R. I. (1988). *Quality of life for handicapped people*. New York: Croom Helm.

Budgell, P. (1986). Drifting toward segregation. *British Journal of Special Education*, 13, 94-95.

Childs, R. E. (1981). Perception of mainstreaming by regular classroom teachers who teach mainstreamed educable mentally retarded students in the public schools. *Education and Training of the Mentally Retarded*, 16(3), 225-227.

Corman, L., & Gottlieb, J. (1979). Mainstreaming mentally retarded children: A review of research. In N. R. Ellis (Ed.), *International review of research in mental retardation, Volume 9* (pp. 251-275). New York: Academic Press.

Correa, V. I. (1990). Advocacy for teachers. *Teaching Exceptional Children, Winter*, 7-9.

Csapo, M. (1981). Teachers' federations in the mainstream. *B. C. Journal of Special Education*, 5(3), 197-218.

Csapo, M., & Goguen, L. (1989). *Special education across Canada: Issues and concerns for the 90s*. Vancouver: Centre for Human Development and Research.

Dansereau, D. F. (1984). *Cooperative learning strategies*. Paper presented at the Conference on Study and Learning Strategies, Texas A & M University.

Dansereau, D. F. (1985). Learning strategy research. In J. Segal, S. Chipman, & R. Glaser (Eds.), *Thinking and learning skills, Volume 1: Relating instruction to research*. Hillsdale, NJ: Lawrence Erlbaum.

Davis, W. E. (1989). The regular education initiative debate: Its promises and problems. *Exceptional Children*, 55, 440-446.

de Bono, E. (1980). *Teaching thinking*. New York: Penguin.

Desharnais, W. (1980). Address to coordinators, supervisors, directors of special education. *B. C. Journal of Special Education*, 4, 3-12.

Deshler, D., Warner, M., Schumaker, J. B., & Alley, G. R. (1983). Learning strategies intervention model: Key components and current status. In J. D. McKinney & L. Feagons (Eds.), *Current topics in learning disabilities: Volume 1*. Norwood, NJ: Ablex.

Deshler, D., & Schumaker, J. (1986). Learning strategies: An instructional alternative for low achieving adolescents. *Exceptional Children*, 52(6), 583-590.

Feuerstein, R., Rand, Y., Hoffman, M. B., & Miller, R. (1980). *Instrumental enrichment: An intervention program for cognitive modifiability*. Baltimore, MD: University Park Press.

Flynn, G., & Kowalczyk-McPhee, B. (1989). A school system in transition. In S. Stainback, W. Stainback, & M. Forest (Eds.), *Educating all students in the mainstream of regular education*. Toronto: Paul H. Brookes.

Forest, M., & Lusthaus, E. (1989). Promoting educational equality for all students. In S. Stainback, W. Stainback, & M. Forest (Eds.), *Educating all students in the mainstream of regular education* (pp. 43-57). Toronto: Paul H. Brookes.

French, F. (1991). Cognitive instructional practices in today's schools: Promise or fallacy? In R. Short, L. Stewin, & S. McCann (Eds.), *Educational psychology: Canadian perspectives* (pp. 77-100). Toronto: Copp Clark Pitman.

Gartner, A., & Lipsky, D. K. (1989). *The yoke of special education: How to break it*. Rochester, NY: National Centre on Education and the Economy.

Gersten, R., & Woodward, J. (1990). Rethinking the regular education initiative: Focus on the classroom teacher. *Remedial and Special Education*, 11(3), 7-16.

Glass, R. M., & Meckler, R. S. (1972). Preparing elementary teachers to instruct mildly handicapped children in regular classrooms: A summer workshop. *Exceptional Children*, 39, 152-156.

Glaser, R. (1977). *Adaptive education: Individual diversity and learning*. New York: Holt, Rinehart & Winston.

Gottlieb, J. (1981). Mainstreaming: Fulfilling the promise? *American Journal of Mental Deficiency*, 86, 115-126.

Hallahan, D. P., Hall, R. J., Ianna, S. O., Kneedler, R. D., Lloyd, J. W., Loper, A. B., & Reeve, R. E. (1983). Summary of research findings at the University of Virginia learning disabilities research institute. *Exceptional Education Quarterly*, 4(1), 95-111.

Hannah, M. E. (1988). Teacher attitudes toward children with disabilities: An ecological analysis. In H. E. Yuker (Ed.), *Attitudes toward persons with disabilities* (pp. 154-170). New York: Springer-Verlag.

Hansen, P., & Hansen, S. (1978). *Mainstreaming: International perspectives*. Paper presented at the world congress on future special education, Sterling, Scotland.

Hartup, W. W. (1983). Peer relations. In P. H. Mussen (Ed.), *Handbook of child development, Volume 4.: Socialization, personality and social development* (pp. 103-196). New York: John Wiley.

Horne, M. D. (1983). Elementary classroom teacher attitudes toward mainstreaming. *The Exceptional Child*, 30, 93-98.

Hudson, F., Graham, S., & Warner, M. (1979). Mainstreaming: An experimentation of the attitudes and needs of regular classroom teachers. *Learning Disabilities Quarterly*, 2, 58-62.

Idol, L., Paolucci-Whitcomb, P., & Nevin, A. (1986). *Collaborative consultation*. Austin, TX: Pro-Ed.

Jamieson, J. D. (1984). Attitudes of educators toward the handicapped. In R. J. Jones (Ed.), *Attitudes and attitude change in special education: Theory and practice* (pp. 206-222). Reston, VA: Council for Exceptional Children.

Jenkins, J. R., Pious, C. G., & Jewell, M. (1990). Special education and the regular education initiative: Basic assumptions. *Exceptional Children, 56*, 479-491.

Johnson, D., & Johnson, R. (1984). Classroom learning structure and attitudes towards handicapped students in mainstream settings: A theoretical model and research evidence. In R. Jones (Ed.), *Attitudes and attitude change in special education* (pp. 118-142). Reston, VA: Council for Exceptional Children.

Johnson, D. W., Johnson, R. T., & Maruyama, G. (1983). Interdependence and interpersonal attraction among heterogeneous and homogeneous individuals: A theoretical formulation and a meta-analysis of the research. *Review of Educational Research, 53*(1), 5-54.

Johnson, L., Pugach, M., & Devlin, S. (1990). Professional collaboration. *Teaching Exceptional Children, Winter*, 9-11.

Jones, B. F. (1986). Quality and equality through cognitive instruction. *Educational Leadership, April*, 6-11.

Jones, A. L., Gottlieb, J., Guskin, S., & Yoshida, R. K. (1978). Evaluating mainstreaming programs: Models, caveats, considerations and guidelines. *Exceptional Children, 44*, 588-601.

Jones, B. F., Palincsar, A., Ogle, D., & Carr, E. (1987). *Strategic teaching and learning: Cognitive instruction in the content areas.* Produced by the Association for Supervision and Curriculum Development, Alexandria, VA.

Kach, N., & DeFaveri, I. (1987). What every teacher should know about multiculturalism. In L. Stewin & S. McCann (Eds.), *Contemporary educational issues: The Canadian mosaic* (pp. 228-238). Toronto: Copp Clark Pitman.

Karagianis, L. D., & Nesbit, W. C. (1980). Special education: A changing perspective for educational administrators. *The Canadian Administrator, 9*,(4), 1-6.

Kauffman, J. M. (1989). The regular education initiative as Reagan-Bush education policy: A trickle-down theory of education of the hard-to-teach. *Journal of Special Education, 23*(3), 256-278.

Kauffman, J. M., Gerber, M. M., & Semmel, M. I. (1988). Arguable assumptions underlying the regular education initiative. *Journal of Learning Disabilities, 21*, 6-11.

Keogh, B. K. (1988). Improving services for problem learners: Rethinking and restructuring. *Journal of Learning Disabilities, 21*, 19-22.

Keogh, B. K. (1990). Narrowing the gap between policy and practice. *Exceptional Children, 57*, 186-190.

Kirby, J. R., & Williams, N. H. (1991). *Learning problems: A cognitive approach*. Toronto: Kagan & Woo.

Leong, C. K., & Randhawa, B. S. (1989). *Understanding literacy and cognition: Theory, research, and application*. New York: Plenum.

Lidz, C. S. (1990). Some thinking about dynamic assessment. *Teaching, Thinking and Problem Solving, 12*(2), 10-12.

Lilly, M. S. (1986). The relationship between general and special education: A new face on an old issue. *Counterpoint, 6*(1), 10.

Lipman, M., Sharp, A., & Oscanyan, F. (1980). *Philosophy in the classroom* (2nd ed.). Philadelphia: Temple University Press.

Lupart, J., & Mulcahy, R. (1983). *Text driven versus conceptually driven processing in good and poor readers: A developmental perspective*. Canadian Psychological Association Annual Meeting, Winnipeg, Canada.

MacMillan, D., Jones, R., & Meyers, C. (1976). Mainstreaming the mildly retarded: Some questions, cautions, and guidelines. *Mental Retardation, 14*, 3-10.

Marfo, K., & Nesbit, W. C. (1989). Egalitarian versus pedagogical concerns in education: The case of integration in special education. In M. Csapo & L. Goguen (Eds.), *Special education across Canada* (pp. 179-198). Vancouver: Centre for Human Development and Research.

McClaskey, M., & Quay, L. (1987). Effects of coaching on handicapped children's social behavior and teachers' attitudes in mainstreamed classes. *The Elementary School Journal, 87*, 424-435.

McKinney, J. D., & Hocutt, A. M. (1988). Policy issues in the evaluation of the regular education initiative. *Learning Disabilities Focus, 4*(1), 15-23.

Meichenbaum, D. (1980). Cognitive behavior modification with exceptional children: A promise yet unfulfilled. *Exceptional Education Quarterly, 1*, 83-88.

Mesinger, J. F. (1985). Commentary on "Rationale for the merger of special and regular education" or, Is it now time for the lamb to lie down with the lion? *Exceptional Children, 51(6)*, 510-512.

Miller, L. (1990). The regular education initiative and school reform: Lessons from the mainstream. *Remedial and Special Education, 11*(3), 17-22.

Miller, T. L., & Sabatino, D. (1978). An evaluation of the teacher consultant model as an approach to mainstreaming. *Exceptional Children, 45*, 86-91.

Mulcahy, R. F. (1980). Memory: Some selective aspects. In R. F. Jarmen (Ed.), *Issues in developmental disabilities*. University Microfilms International.

Mulcahy, R. F., Andrews, J., & Peat, D. (1989). Cognitive education: A longitudinal examination. In C. K. Leong & B. S. Randhawa (Eds.), *Literacy and cognition: Theory, research and instructional implications* (pp. 287-314). New York: Plenum.

Mulcahy, R. F., Short, R., & Andrews, J. (1991). *Enhancing learning and thinking*. New York: Praeger.

Nader, A. (1984). Teacher attitude toward the elementary exceptional child. *International Journal of Rehabilitation Research, 7*, 37-46.

Nevin, A., & Thousand, J. (1987). Avoiding or limiting special education referrals: Changes and challenges. In M. C. Wang, M. C. Reynolds, & H. J. Walberg (Eds.), *Handbook of special education: Research and practice, Volume 1: Learner characteristics and adaptive education* (pp. 273-286). New York: Pergamon.

Nickerson, R. S., & Adams, M. J. (1983). Introduction. In *Project intelligence: The development of procedures to enhance thinking skills: Teacher's manual*. Cambridge, MA: Harvard University and Bolt, Beranek and Newman.

Ogletree, E., & Atkinson, L. (1982). *Mainstreaming teachers favor mainstreaming*. (ERIC Document Reproduction Service No. ED 233 027.)

O'Neil, G .P. (1984). Some reflections on the integration of moderately mentally handicapped students (TMR) in Ontario schools. *Canadian Journal of Exceptional Children, 1*(1), 19-22.

O'Reilly, R., & Duquette, C. (1988). Experienced teachers look at mainstreaming. *Education Canada, Fall*, 9-13.

Palincsar, A. S., & Brown, A. L. (1987). Enhanced instructional time through attention to metacognition. *Journal of Learning Disabilities, 20*, 66-75.

Pearpoint, J. (1989). Reflections on a quality education for all students. In S. Stainback, W. Stainback, & M. Forest (Eds.), *Educating all students in the mainstream of regular education* (pp. 249-254). Toronto: Paul H. Brookes.

Post, L., & Roy, W. (1985). Mainstreaming in secondary schools: How successful are plans to implement the concept? *NASSP Bulletin, 69,* 71-79.

Reynolds, M. C., & Birch, J. W. (1988). *Adaptive mainstreaming: A primer for teachers and principals* (3rd ed.). New York: Longman.

Reynolds, M. C., Wang, M. C., & Walberg, H. J. (1987). The necessary restructuring of special and regular education. *Exceptional Children, 53*(5), 391-398.

Roberts, C.A., & Lazure, M.D. (Eds.). (1970). *One million children: A national study of Canadian children with emotional and learning disorders.* Toronto: Crainford.

Safran, S., Safran, J., & Barcikowski, (1985). Classroom context and teachers' perceptions of problem behaviors. *Journal of Educational Psychology, 77,* 20-28.

Samuels, M., Lamb, C., & Oberholtzer, L. (1992). Dynamic assessment of adults with learning difficulties. In H. C. Haywood & D. T. Zurich (Eds.), *Interactive assessment.* New York: Springer-Verlag.

Schloss, P., & Miller, S. R. (1982). Effects of the label "institutionalized" vs. "regular class student" on teacher expectations. *Exceptional Children, 46*(4), 363-364.

Schultz, J. B., Carpenter, C. D., & Turnbull, A. P. (1991). *Mainstreaming exceptional students: A guide for classroom teachers* (3rd ed.). Toronto: Allyn & Bacon.

Scott, M. E. (1988). Learning strategies can help. *Teaching Exceptional Children, Spring,* 30-33.

Segal, S., Chipman, S., & Glaser, R. (1985). *Thinking and learning skills, Volume 1: Relating instruction to research.* Hillsdale, NJ: Lawrence Erlbaum.

Snow, J. A. (1989). Systems of support: A new vision. In S. Stainback, W. Stainback, & M. Forest (Eds.), *Educating all students in the mainstream of regular education* (pp. 221-231). Toronto: Paul H. Brookes.

Stainback, W., & Stainback, S. (1984). A rationale for the merger of special and regular education. *Exceptional Children, 51,* 102-111.

Stainback, S., & Stainback, W. (1985). The merger of special and regular education: Can it be done? *Exceptional Children, 51,* 517-521.

Stainback, W., & Stainback, S. (1989). Common concerns regarding merger. In S. Stainback, W. Stainback, & M. Forest (Eds.), *Educating all students in the mainstream of regular education* (pp. 255-274). Toronto: Paul H. Brookes.

Stainback, W., Stainback, S., Courtnage, L., & Jaben, T. (1985). Facilitating mainstreaming by modifying the mainstream. *Exceptional Children, 52,* 144-152.

Stainback, S., Stainback, W., Forest, M. (1989). *Educating all students in the mainstream of regular education.* Toronto: Paul H. Brookes.

Sternberg, R. J. (1985). Instrumental and componential approaches to the nature and training of intelligence. In S. Chipman, J. Segal, & N. R. Glaser (Eds.), *Thinking and learning skills, Volume 2: Current research and open questions* (pp. 216-243). Hillsdale, NJ: Lawrence Erlbaum.

Strully, J. L., & Strully, C. F. (1989). Family support to promote integration. In S. Stainback, W. Stainback, & M. Forest (Eds.), *Educating all students in the mainstream of regular education* (pp. 213-219). Toronto: Paul H. Brookes.

Thousand, J. S., & Villa, R. A. (1989). Enhancing success in heterogeneous schools. In S. Stainback, W. Stainback, & M. Forest, (Eds.), *Educating all students in the mainstream of regular education* (pp. 89-103). Toronto: Paul H. Brookes.

Torgesen, J. K. (1980). Conceptual and educational implications of the use of efficient task strategies by learning disabled children. *Journal of Learning Disabilities, 51,* 33-37.

Walberg, H. J., & Wang, M. C. (1987). Effective educational practices and provisions for individual differences. In M. C. Wang, M. C. Reynolds, & H. J. Walberg (Eds.), *Handbook of special education: Research and practice, Volume 1: Learner characteristics and adaptive education* (pp. 113-128). Oxford, England: Pergamon.

Wang, M. C. (1980). Adaptive instruction: Building on diversity. *Theory into Practice, 19*(2), 122-127.

Wang, M. C. (1989). Accommodating student diversity through adaptive instruction. In S. Stainback, W. Stainback, & M. Forest, (Eds.), *Educating all students in the mainstream of regular education* (pp. 183-197). Toronto: Paul H. Brookes.

Wang, M. C., Reynolds, M. C., & Walberg, H. J. (1986). Rethinking special education. *Educational Leadership, 44*(1), 26-31.

Weinstein, C. E. (1982). A meta-curriculum for remediating learning strategies deficits in academically underprepared students. In L. Noel & R. Levitz (Eds.), *How to succeed with academically underprepared students.* Iowa City: American College, Testing Service Centre for Advancing Educational Practice.

Weinstein, C. E., & Underwood, V. L. (1985). Learning strategies: The how of learning. In J. W. Segal, S. F. Chipman, & R. Glaser (Eds.), *Thinking and learning skills, Volume 1: Relating instruction to research* (pp. 241-258). Hillsdale, NJ: Lawrence Erlbaum.

West, J. F., & Cannon, G. S. (1988). Essential collaborative consultation competencies for regular and special educators. *Journal of Learning Disabilities, 21,* 56-63.

West, J. F., & Idol, L. (1990). Collaborative consultation in the education of mildly handicapped and at-risk students. *Remedial and Special Education, 11*(1), 22-31.

West, J. F., Idol, L., & Cannon, G. (1989). *Collaborative consultation in the schools: An in-service and pre-service curriculum for teachers, support staff, and administrators.* Austin, TX: Pro Ed.

Will, M. (1986). *Educating students with learning problems—A shared responsibility.* Washington, DC: U. S. Department of Education, Office of Special Education and Rehabilitation Services.

Winzer, M. (1984). Attitudes of educators and non-educators toward mainstreaming. *Exceptional Children, 59,* 23-26.

Winzer, M., & Rose, C. (1986). Mainstreaming exceptional students: Use of the attitude survey with teachers in British Columbia. *Journal of Special Education, 10*(4), 309-319.

Wittrock, M. C. (1986). *Handbook of research on teaching* (3rd ed.). London: Macmillan.

Wong, B. Y. L. (1982). Strategic behaviors in selecting retrieval cues in gifted, normal achieving and learning disabled children. *Journal of Learning Disabilities, 15,* 33-40.

Wong, B. Y. L. (1985). Metacognition and learning disabilities. In D. L. Forest-Pressley, G. E. Mackinnon, & T. G. Waller (Eds.), *Metacognition, cognition and human performance.* Toronto: Academic Press.

HISTORICAL AND LEGISLATIVE FOUNDATIONS FOR INCLUSIVE EDUCATION

CHAPTER 2

CHAPTER OBJECTIVES

To provide an overview of the historical origins of present programs for children with exceptional learning needs.

To review the unique educational provisions for special needs children at each historical phase.

To identify the influences of historical progression regarding appropriate education for all students.

To examine the effect of litigation and legislation on development of programs for students with special needs.

To provide an overview of current educational provisions for children with exceptional needs within each of the Canadian provinces and territories.

Back to the Books:

Two-Year Fight With System Wins Boy New School Experience

Robbie Marshall wheeled into his local high school this morning to take a place among teenagers in Sherwood Park.

The persistent 16-year-old fought and won a two-year battle with Sherwood Park's Catholic school board to gain admittance to Archbishop Jordan High School.

"He's really looking forward to it," said Robbie's father, Robert. "He's been anticipating this day all summer."

Robbie, who has spina bifida, has spent most of his school life in classes for the handicapped. Now in a Grade 10 class with other teenagers, his new world of academics and teenage anxieties is a far cry from the class for the trainable mentally handicapped he left in June.

"It's not only a new school, it's a whole new system," Robert Marshall says. "This is a kid who's been totally segregated his whole school life."

His parents and teachers hope the experience won't overpower Robbie's desire to succeed.

"We just hope this works out well," says Archbishop principal Aurell Royer. "All the teachers are very positive about it. We're going to give it our best shot."

Marshall has long believed his son's learning was hindered by time missed for twenty major operations and by years of exposure to diluted programming. In the past, Robbie's class activities included trips to the mall to learn to shop and make change, something the teenager does easily on his own.

The Marshalls' problems started nearly two years ago when Robbie announced he'd quit school rather than spend more years in special classes, where students concentrate on life skills rather than curriculum courses.

When Sherwood Park's Catholic school board refused Robbie admittance to a regular Grade 10 class, the family spent more than $5,000 to fight a series of appeals that ended at the doorstep of Education Minister Jim Dinning.

An Alberta Education review committee ruled in April Robbie should be given the chance to integrate. Dinning's final approval, however, didn't come until mid-June.

After a two-year fight to place him—Robbie should not be in a mentally handicapped class—the Marshalls have no expectations beyond raising a well-adjusted school boy.

"We just want him to be in a normal class with normal kids," Marshall says. "Everything else is a bonus."

On Tuesday, the teachers who will work with Robbie gave the new student a tour of the school. To accommodate Robbie the school had to find a special desk and make alterations in the washroom.

Source: *The Edmonton Journal*, September 4, 1991.

◇ INTRODUCTION

Today's schools differ from those of the past in their recognition of the diverse learning needs of students. Within any typical Canadian classroom, this diversity is evidenced in a multitude of ways. Some students contribute significantly to classroom discussions, and yet have extreme difficulty expressing their ideas in written form. Some students mingle easily with their classmates, whereas others are most often seen by themselves, or possibly with a single best friend. Other students show exceptional achievement in a subject area such as mathematics, and yet find it difficult to read texts that are written for children in earlier grades. When new concepts are introduced, some students readily assimilate the material, and oftentimes expand on an idea through a synthesis with their background experience. In contrast, some students require lengthy discussion and practice before they are able to understand newly introduced material. Even within a particular subject area, it is not uncommon to find that a student can handle particular aspects such as computation in mathematics, and yet be completely lost when it comes to problem-solving.

While most teachers would agree that meeting the individual learning needs of all students is a desirable and logical philosophy for educators, its actual implementation and practice has become increasingly problematic. One of the primary reasons for this is the growing presence of special-needs students in the regular classroom. Students who were traditionally served in a variety of special segregated education settings such as the resource room, special class, or even special schools are returning to the regular classroom. Students who were previously taught by specially trained teachers, with specialized teaching materials, are moving into the **mainstream**. The reasons for this movement are multifaceted and complex, stemming from historical, economic, social, political, pedagogical, technological, and theoretical fac-

 mainstream: general or dominant educational system consisting of physical, intellectual, social, and emotional components

tors that will be detailed throughout the book. Whatever the source or the reasons, the trends are clear: general classroom teachers are increasingly expected to deal with students with a variety of special needs and conditions.

The authors' purpose in this book is to provide prospective teachers with a framework for understanding individual student learning needs and the special learning needs of exceptional children. In recognition of the diversity of learning needs that every classroom teacher must address, we introduce a variety of skills and strategies that will be most helpful in the general classroom. It is our firm belief that most students are best served in the general classroom, and that through the practice of good teaching, guided by relevant theory and research, the learning potential of all students can be effectively developed. A full description of inclusive education and the mainstreaming process has been provided in the previous chapter. Before moving to classroom applications, we will consider the various historical, legislative, and theoretical factors that have culminated in the present concept of serving the needs of regular and exceptional students in the mainstream.

◇ PROGRESSIVE INCLUSION

The Canadian movement toward individualized education and the **least restrictive environment** for all students has followed a pattern of *progressive inclusion* that was similarly evident in the United States (Reynolds & Birch, 1988; Reynolds, 1989), and, to a lesser extent, Europe (Hardman, Drew, Egan, & Wolf, 1990; Hallahan and Kauffman, 1991; Ramasut, 1989). As

least restrictive environment: the environment that provides maximum educational benefit to exceptional students, together with minimum disruption to the educational progress of their nonexceptional peers

Reynolds (1989) describes it, there are at least four significant strands that characterize the gradual shift that has taken place in Western schools in the development of services for children with exceptional learning needs (see Table 2.1).

Table 2.1
The Progressive Inclusion Change Process
◆ From distal to proximal arrangements ◆ From separation to integration ◆ From selection/rejection decisions to placement decisions ◆ From "two-box" arrangements to a continuum

The first element is *the move from distal to proximal placements*. Initially, care for children with disabilities was provided in residential institutions, which served a large geographic area and which resulted in the removal of many children from their homes and communities. For example, it was common practice for Alberta students with visual disabilities to be sent to institutions in Ontario as late as the 1970s (Conn-Blowers & McLeod, 1989). Today we see a shift from **distal placements** to **proximal placements**, which involve providing educational service in settings within the home community and, most preferably, within inclusive classes in neighbourhood schools.

The second strand to characterize progressive inclusion is *the move from separation to integration*. Over the years there has been a notable conceptual and attitudinal shift, from an initial emphasis on physically separate provisions for children with highly visible disabilities (involving a preoccupation with labelling and the transfer of students from regular classes into special day schools or classes), to the current practice of part-time pull-out or resource-room classes and/or full integration into regular classes. For example, Gittins (1980) reports that during the 1960-61 school term, there were 249 teachers to serve 3,592 students enrolled in special classes throughout British Columbia. In just nine years, these figures multiplied to 849 teachers serving 10,247 students with exceptional learning needs in special classes. Educational alternatives were not available for students who did not fit the existing criteria of any given category of student with exceptional needs. In contrast, a report by Nessner (1990) reveals that in 1986, 51 percent of Canadian children (aged 5-14) with disabilities were attending regular schools, 30 percent were attending special classes in regular schools, and 6 percent were attending special schools. These figures reveal a trend toward greater inclusion of students with exceptional learning needs in regular schools.

The third trend is described as *the move from selection/rejection decisions to placement decisions*. From the early 1900s to the hiatus during the 1970s, schools used tests to justify the removal of exceptional students from the mainstream. This practice was bolstered by the well-established and unchallenged assumption that these students needed specially trained teachers,

◆ **distal placement**: placing exceptional students in the location farthest from the mainstream

◆ **proximal placement**: placing exceptional students in the location closest to the mainstream

italics

special teaching methods, and special materials. Services for children with exceptional learning needs became contingent on their meeting the categorical criteria set by the school system. If the child fit all the criteria, a special class placement was provided; if not, the regular classroom remained the only option, even though the student might be experiencing significant difficulties there. Eventually, systematic research investigations and a critical review of the results (Madden & Slavin, 1983; Ruhl, 1983; Wang, Reynolds, & Walberg, 1987), coupled with some notably eloquent treatises that raised important questions about the efficacy of special education practice in general (Dunn, 1968; Gartner & Lipsky, 1987), led to a major conceptual shift in which students' individual learning needs were given priority over labelling and removal concerns. There was increasing emphasis on creating more diverse placement options in the schools, such as part-time instructional support and resource-room programs, in order to serve the instructional needs of any child who was experiencing difficulty in the regular classroom.

The final thrust in North American schools is *the move from separate special education and regular education systems to a continuum of services*, in which the overriding goal is to deliver services in the least restrictive environment, i.e., in the most normal educational setting possible that would provide the maximum opportunity for the development of individual learning abilities. The transition to unified and philosophically integrated systems of education for all students has been substantially advanced by U.S. education initiatives such as "the regular education initiative" (Jenkins, Pious, & Jewell, 1990; Slavin, 1990); "the restructuring of schools" (Reynolds, Wang & Walberg, 1987); and "the merger of regular and special education" (Stainback, Stainback, & Bunch, 1989a; Stainback & Stainback, 1984).

◆ HISTORICAL FOUNDATIONS OF INCLUSION IN CANADA

The theme of progressive inclusion outlined above has been generally applied to both U.S. and Canadian contexts. Nevertheless, as Chambers (1980) points out, Canadian educational history is unique in two respects. First, unlike the United States, Canada has never had a federal mandate for education. Rather, it is the responsibility of each province and territory to determine policy in educational matters. As Chambers (1980) notes, "Throughout Canada, there is no one, no minister, no agency responsible for the education of Canadian children" (p. 2). The second factor unique to Canadian educational history is the extensive involvement of the church, which contributed substantially, particularly in the early years, to the expansion and development of educational services. Such efforts were counterproductive in the sense that they relieved provincial governments of not only considerable expense, but, in some instances, responsibility as well. As Chambers (1980) points out, "Free public education was not originally a goal of our country" (p. 2).

Correspondingly, these early circumstances were in the long run a deterrent to the development of a quality education system. Indeed, Winzer (1990) asserts that "[a]dvances in Canadian education and social welfare took place only after the wealth of the provinces increased sufficiently to allow people to feel they could afford to turn from their colonial preoccupation with survival and material development" (p. 62). In Canada, the historical progression of appropriate education for all students begins with the total exclusion of handicapped individuals prior to the mid-1800s. The transition to contemporary inclusive schools and classrooms is traced in the following section. Table 2.2 summarizes the major periods of progressive inclusion in Canadian education.

Table 2.2
History of Progressive Inclusion in Canadian Education

Time Period	Key Descriptor	Predominant Educational Trend
Early History	Exclusion	Elitist orientation, education reserved for privileged classes. Handicapped individuals were scorned and excluded from general society.
1800s	Institutionalization	Separate residential schools and institutions provided care primarily for visible handicapped students.
1900-1950	Segregation	Public education system develops. Special schools and classes are formed. Residential schools increased and became larger.
1950s and 1960s	Categorization	Increased numbers and categories of special classes, particularly for high incidence exceptional learners. Testing, labelling emphasis. Low incidence students remain in residential schools.
1970s	Integration	Philosophical shift to promote education for handicapped students in the least restrictive environment. Placement alternatives are developed. Moderate and severe handicapped students are served within the public school.
1980s	Mainstreaming	Emphasis on serving the needs of high incidence exceptional students in the regular classroom. Physical, social, instructional needs are met in the least restrictive environment.
1990s	Inclusion	Merging of special education and regular education into a unified education system. Student-centred, individual learning needs are the focus.

KEY DATES, PEOPLE, AND EVENTS

Early History: Exclusion

The first educational institute in Canada, College of Quebec, was established by the Jesuits in 1640. Initial instruction was largely spiritual, and gradually other subjects such as reading, writing, Latin, and grammar were introduced (Abbott, 1990). Blankenship & Lilly (1981) note that for the greater part of the history of civilization, education was an elitist institution—with the primary recipients coming from the wealthy and upper classes—that excluded the majority of school-age children. Any provisions that were available for the less fortunate in society were due to the humanistic and charitable concerns of an individual or group, often associated with the church.

The haphazard nature of educational provisions in these times is captured in Brehaut's (1984) summary description by a St. Catharine's teacher in 1795: "By observation and enquiry, I am inclined to think that education of youth is too much neglected in this Province. In some parts they have masters, in others none; and indeed those who have masters had almost as well be without them" (p. 7). The fate of children with disabilities was, at this point, not an educational matter, but rather an issue of basic care that was adopted by religious groups and physicians, predominantly within specifically designated residential schools or institutions.

The 1800s: Institutionalization

Just prior to the turn of the 20th century, provisions for exceptional children in Canada were limited and, for the most part, entirely separate from the mainstream education system. Children with hearing, vision, or **orthopedic handicaps** were the first to receive care, often on the recommendation of a physician. Chambers (1980) comments that "the medical profession became the chief agency of referral and the medical model became predominant for the whole area of what we now refer to as exceptionality" (p. 3). Several provinces including Nova Scotia, New Brunswick, Ontario, Quebec, Manitoba, and British Columbia established special residential schools during the 1800s, primarily to serve children with serious sensory defects. The efforts of religious bodies and key educational reform leaders such as Ronald McDonald in Quebec, and John Barrett McGann in Ontario were particularly instrumental in advancing the concept of educating children with disabilities.

Certain concepts that have guided special education during the current century were, in fact, developed as early as the 1700s and incorporated into some of the teaching practices initiated in North American institutions during the 1800s. Much of this early work was carried out by scholars interested in children with sensory impairments in special institutions such as the Winnipeg School for the Deaf and the Frederick Fraser School for the Blind in Halifax. Hallahan and Kauffman (1991) list ideas, already well established in

orthopedic handicap: physical handicap resulting from a deformity of bones, joints, ligaments, muscles, or tendons

European society during the 1800s, that were similarly reflected in the instruction provided by early North American pioneers in special education:

◆ Individualized instruction.

◆ Ordering the sequence of instructional tasks from less to more complex.

◆ Providing maximal learning through the stimulation of all sensory abilities.

◆ The structuring of the environment to invite intellectual discovery.

◆ Using immediate feedback to reinforce correct performance.

◆ An emphasis upon those skills which enabled one to function in society.

◆ The full actualization of potential as a key educational goal (p. 19).

From these early schools came specialized approaches that are commonly used in today's classrooms, such as the use of sign language for students with hearing impairments, and the development of a braille alphabet to assist students with visual impairments. Such advances notwithstanding, only a limited proportion of the special populations that are recognized today were served in the 1800s, and of those only a small percentage enjoyed the benefits of educational provisions incorporating such concepts.

In contrast to the innovative developments for children with vision and hearing impairments, the circumstances for other children with exceptional needs were grim. The initial impetus for **institutionalization** grew out of a social welfare concern for children who were often neglected or abandoned. As their numbers grew, more and bigger institutions were established to provide basic care for these children. Residential facilities, including institutions, asylums, and orphanages, were established, principally in Quebec and Ontario, to provide care for children who were (to use the terms of that time) deaf, blind, mentally retarded, crippled, delinquent, and vagrant. Winzer (1990) notes that the lack of clear differentiation of categories of exceptionality resulted in the inappropriate institutionalization of children, who were mentally handicapped, insane, vagrant, and delinquent, together in single facilities. These public institutions, or human warehouses, became a dumping ground for young children rejected by their families.

By the latter part of the 19th century, reformers were able to influence public attitudes to the degree that more appropriate provisions, particularly for poor, vagrant, and delinquent children, were provided in institutions such as reformatories and trade schools. The growing emphasis on educational or training aspects, as opposed to mere **custodial provision**, stemmed from the assumption that such training would equip residents for economic self-sufficiency and in the meantime teach them skills that would contribute to the maintenance of the institutions. Of the Ontario School for the Deaf in Belleville, MacIntyre (1984) writes: "Over time, the school developed a series of vocational programs emphasizing practical skills, beginning with those needed around the farm and house and advancing to such trades as wood working and shoe repairing. Printing trades were also taught, partially under

◆ institutionalization: the practice of placing children with exceptional needs—both physical and mental—in residential settings and care facilities that are entirely separate from the mainstream education system

◆ custodial provision: depersonalized care facility for exceptional children that provides minimal basic physical care

the assumption that deaf individuals would be particularly suited to working in the noisy environs of print shops" (p. 104).

Gradually, a free public education system began to emerge across the country. Innovative and progressive work that was being carried out, particularly with the highly visible handicapped students, as well as the growing trend toward the training and education of institutionalized children, became the foundation for development in the first half of the next century.

1900-1950: Segregation

The continued efforts of Canadian educational reformers such as Egerton Ryerson and John Barrett McGann, combined with an influx of immigrants at the turn of the century, led to a large-scale movement toward publicly supported schooling. By 1918, only Quebec and Newfoundland lacked compulsory education attendance laws (Stainback, Stainback, & Forest, 1989). This opened the doors for many middle- and lower-class students, but not, as yet, for children with disabilities or handicaps.

Despite the careful groundwork that had been laid by enlightened educators, other developments of this time created major barriers against moving students with sensory impairments or intellectual disabilities into the regular education system. Most notably, early 20th-century IQ-testing advancements, used to promote the **eugenics movement**, spawned an especially critical period of public scorn toward individuals who were diagnosed as mentally retarded, with widespread calls for their mandatory sterilization and segregation. So powerful were the effects of the eugenics movement that the massive custodial-based institutionalization of mentally retarded individuals was publicly condoned, creating some spillover of negativism toward other exceptional groups. Thus, in the first years of this century, the fate of children with disabilities was dictated by medical and religious disciplines, as well as by public attitudes. With provincial governments continuing to shirk responsibility even for regular educational development, provisions for students with disabilities were left largely to families, to the benefaction of the churches, or to provincial social-welfare systems.

Fortunately, there were enough strong-willed and progressive reformers to gradually turn the tide. Initial efforts focused on children with physical problems and illnesses, and began with the establishment of facilities such as the Montreal Children's Memorial Hospital and the Toronto Hospital for Sick Children, in the first decade of the century (Winzer, 1990). As new developments in the educational and health systems evolved, so too did programs and forms of service delivery. In less than two decades, special education classes were being incorporated into the general education system.

For example, MacIntyre (1984) describes the exceptional efforts of Dr. Helen MacMurchy, a predominant reformer of Ontario school systems, to open up special classes for mentally retarded children. She mounted a campaign based upon reports and petitions, which led to the creation of the

◆ eugenics movement: early 20th-century movement that advocated legislation to prevent procreation by mentally retarded individuals

1914 Auxiliary Classes Act, and "established entry requirements (including the necessity for a full examination), provided for residential schools, and defined the general structure and size of special classes" (p. 107). These early efforts set in place a solid framework for special classes that would be used until the end of the Second World War. This trend gradually extended to the regular school system, where a variety of day classes began to develop in Ontario and throughout the rest of Canada.

Despite the contributions of Dr. MacMurchy and others to the integration of exceptional needs students into the public school system, there remained considerable pressure to keep special-needs students out of regular classes, and thus special classes became a recognizable feature of many urban schools by the mid-1920s (Chaves, 1977). Gearheart, Weishahn, and Gearheart (1988) note that the widespread use of special classes in public schools resulted in the practice of increasing referrals to special classes on the part of regular educators, with special education only too willing to accept the challenge that diversity and increased numbers of students provided. It was generally accepted that handicapped children were much better served in these special classes due to the reduced teacher-pupil ratio, the use of special teaching methods, resources, equipment, and programs suited to the particular exceptional group, and the provision of specially trained teachers. Moreover, the public system continued to insist that it was unequipped to deal with extremely deviant children, and emphasized the cost-saving benefits of pooling **low-incidence** students into one special class, or school, covering a wider geographical area. This period saw a continued growth, throughout Canada, of asylums and residential institutions for children who were severely mentally and physically disabled.

◆incidence: the number of specifically defined exceptional individuals in the population at a given time

Despite the fact that an increasing number of special-needs students were being served by the public school system, special-class provisions perpetuated the isolation and segregation of students with disabilities. Despite the numerous rationalizations of educators favouring special-class placement for children with exceptionalities, Gearheart et al. (1988) point out that "special classes were sometimes dumping grounds, other times a vehicle for segregation, and in some geographic areas a way to do something for culturally different or bilingual children without actually starting a bilingual program" (p. 10). Similar criticisms were beginning to surface concerning the educational provisions for students who were intellectually disabled. The seeds of dissatisfaction were in place, and this tendency began to dominate educational thought by mid-century.

not detail

1950s and 1960s: Categorization

The push to improve educational provisions for handicapped students, and to bring service into the mainstream of regular education, largely resulted from the proliferation of parent and professional associations. During this period, parents and professionals began to lobby governments, and to organize their efforts and concerns through the establishment of local, provincial, and national groups. High-profile groups that remain strong today, such as the Canadian Association for the Mentally Retarded (currently the Canadian Association for Community Living) and the Canadian Association for Children and Adults with Learning Disabilities, were established during the 1950s and 1960s. The Canadian branch of the Council for Exceptional Children was established in 1958, providing teachers, parents, and related professionals an opportunity for voicing issues and sharing educational concerns. Without a federal governmental body having jurisdiction over educational matters, connections with well-established national organizations offered a means for country-wide discussion and support.

In many provinces, it was common practice for parent interest groups, most notably advocates for students with intellectual limitations, to establish special education schools or classes. These early facilities were operated separately from the regular education system, with parents, volunteers, and occasionally trained teachers carrying the major responsibility for funding and the development and delivery of instructional programs. Such efforts to provide more personalized attention and educationally relevant experiences for children, whose only available option was placement in impersonalized, residential institutions, were an important step to the eventual inclusion of special classes in regular schools during the late 1960s and early 1970s (Conn-Blowers & McLeod, 1989).

Modest change was beginning to take shape in the public schools. Motivated by the growing discontent concerning the "dumping ground" characterization of special education classes, school boards began to review their assessment and placement policies. They attempted to clarify operational definitions of students by category of exceptionality, along with the assessment criteria and documentation necessary for placement determinations. This resulted in increased demands for testing and for greater differentiation in the categories of students served. For example, Church (1980) provides statistics for the Alberta Department of Education that show an increase from three categories in 1950 to nine recognized categories of service provision in 1970. Generally, provinces and territories began to assume funding responsibility for educational provisions for exceptional-needs students. The move toward testing for labelling purposes (as opposed to assessment to determine individual learning needs) established a particularly strong precedent for special education practice in general, and remains entrenched in many school districts today, despite opposing trends.

1970s: Integration

The 1970s was an eventful decade for the progressive inclusion movement throughout Canada. There was significant philosophical and attitudinal shift away from the emphasis on special classes toward a concern that "the educational system should educate handicapped children in the least restrictive

◆ integration: full participation of exceptional students in regular education class

environment and should guarantee every child adequate social adjustment and maximum school achievement" (Robichaud & Enns, 1980, p. 202). The movement toward **integration** was the result of a growing backlash against segregated special classes. Educators had begun to note that handicapped students were rarely returned to the regular classroom once they were placed in special classes, and labelling practices that had been the cornerstone of special education placement and delivery systems were now seen as discriminatory, and as giving rise to inappropriate stereotypes.

Prompted by a seminal article by Dunn (1968), who called into question the widespread practice of special-class segregation of mildly handicapped students, a plethora of efficacy studies were conducted during this decade. There was wide-scale assessment of the academic progress and social adjustment of students placed in special classes, in comparison with students with exceptional learning needs who remained in regular classes. Little difference between the two groups with respect to school achievement levels was found (Budoff & Gottlieb, 1976; Bradfield, Brown, Kaplan, Rickert, & Stannard, 1973), and students with disabilities, regardless of placement, were seen to have lower social status than students without disabilities (Corman & Gottlieb, 1978).

The mounting concern over the viability of special classes was part of a larger, more pervasive shift in public attitudes toward disabled individuals. This change was spearheaded by parent and professional advocacy groups, and by a variety of legal and legislative actions in the U.S. that had significant impact on education provisions for children with exceptional learning needs. The central themes of the shift were **normalization** and **deinstitutionalization**, and its most notable educational outcomes were: (1) the creation of educational placement alternatives, such as resource rooms and part-time special classes (Deno, 1973); and (2) an increased enrolment of students with moderate and severe disabilities in public schools (Csapo & Goguen, 1980).

◆ normalization: the belief that all exceptional children are entitled to an education and living environment as close to the cultural norm as possible

◆ deinstitutionalization: the movement to remove disabled individuals from residential institutional care and place them in home community settings that support and foster their independence and quality of life

The publication of the CELDIC Report, *One Million Children* (Roberts & Lazure, 1970) was to be a primary force in the future of special education. The report was the result of work done by the Commission on Emotional and Learning Disorders in Children, which was formed in 1966 in response to increasing demands by parents, teachers, and other concerned citizens that the educational and emotional needs of children be properly addressed in the schools. The main educational concepts to emerge from this document were: (1) every child has the right to the education required to realize his or her full potential; (2) the financing of education for *all* students is the responsibility of the educational authorities; and (3) students with exceptional learning needs should remain integrated with other students as long as possible. The report further recommended that categorical approaches to special education be eliminated in favour of instruction that is based on individual learning characteristics.

The impact of the CELDIC Report was bolstered by the work of Wolfensberger at the Toronto-based National Institute of Mental Retardation (Wolfensberger, Nirge, Olshansky, Perske, & Roos, 1972). Wolfensberger espoused the philosophical view that *all* persons with disabilities should have access to educational and living environments as close to normal as possible. Normalization advocates stressed that persons with disabilities have the same needs, desires, and hopes as those without, and should therefore be kept in the mainstream, rather than set apart through the creation of artificial, isolating conditions. Stainback et al. (1989) note that "[t]his principle and the subsequent modifications that focused more on social image enhancement or social valorization (Wolfensberger, 1984) have played a profound role in reducing segregationist practices" (p. 10).

Other developments in this period included revisions in teacher-training programs to ensure that prospective teachers better understood the learning needs of exceptional students, and the greater involvement of universities in training professionals to carry out research and evaluation of special education programs. These recommendations were advanced by the Hardy, McLeod, Minto, Perkins, and Quance (1971) report, *Standards for Education of Exceptional Children in Canada*, and, accordingly, several Canadian universities implemented courses and specialization programs in special education and exceptionality during this decade.

The 1970s were also notable for a renewed interest in provincial and territorial legislation, especially as it related to the legal implications of providing education for students with exceptional needs. During this period, several provinces introduced new school acts and amendments in response to the growing demand for appropriate education for students with special needs (see the following section for further discussion). In addition, individual cases that challenged educational practice also began to reach the courts.

For example, in the late 1970s the much-publicized case of Shelley Carrière, a 10-year-old child with cerebral palsy, came before the Alberta courts. Shelley was initially labelled as **mentally handicapped**, and the County of Lamont assumed all costs for her attendance at Glenrose School Hospital in Edmonton. In 1977, Glenrose dismissed Shelley, recommending that, since the county lacked the facilities to accommodate a child in a wheelchair, she attend a private Edmonton school serving children with multiple disabilities. Shelley's parents took legal action against the existing legislation, which allowed for certain instances of student exclusion from school. In 1978, the Supreme Court of Alberta ruled that the County of Lamont had the responsibility to educate Shelley, and that she had the right to obtain an appropriate education within the home community school in Chipman.

The *Carrière* case is one of the few parent-initiated actions in Canada to use the legal system to bring about change in the educational system for students with exceptional needs. As will become apparent in the section on the legislative foundations of special education, the use of legal powers to settle such disputes has been far less widespread in Canada than it has been in the United States. Nevertheless, bold initiatives such as the U.S. federal

◆ mentally handicapped: a level of intellectual functioning and adaptive skills low enough to prevent a child from obtaining benefits from ordinary school education

◆ Public Law 94-142: U.S. legislation that mandates free and appropriate public education for every child between the ages of 3 and 21

legislation of **Public Law 94-142** have played a significant role in promoting legislation-based educational change in Canadian provinces and territories.

1980s: Mainstreaming

The 1980s were progressive in two major respects: (1) a Canadian literature base on special education began with the publication of two key works—the Csapo and Goguen (1980) publication *Special Education across Canada: Issues and Concerns for the 80's*, and the Kysela (1980) monograph *The Exceptional Child in Canadian Education*; and (2) the general move toward integration of exceptional students began to focus on the concept of *mainstreaming*, a term Robichaud and Enns (1980) define as the "trend toward integrating the mildly handicapped as much as possible into the regular classroom" (p. 202). Hallahan and Kauffman (1991) suggest that since the 1980s special educators have shifted from an efficacy perspective on mainstreaming to an emphasis on its ethical aspects.

This decade saw growing pressure on school boards and provincial and territorial governments to give serious attention to the inevitability of mainstreaming special-needs students into the regular classroom. It was also a decade of considerable confusion because, despite widespread support for mainstreaming, there were limited means and precedents to suggest the most effective method for its implementation. Concerned groups tended to operate in isolation, with schools and boards, governmental departments, parent groups, and universities addressing the problem each from their separate and unique perspective.

One essential distinction between the 1980s and the 1990s is that the majority of school boards and provincial and territorial governments of the former decade continued to perpetuate categorical services for students with exceptional learning needs, thus maintaining a dual system of regular and special education (Stainback et al., 1989a). At the same time, schools were being increasingly pressured by their communities, and by society in general, to succeed in the mainstreaming process. Regular teachers were growing concerned about the central role they were expected to take in the mainstreaming process (Lupart, 1987; Winzer, 1985). Here was yet another duty or responsibility tacked onto an already excessive teaching load. In the majority of situations, this concern was justified. School districts had begun to serve more students with exceptional needs in the regular classroom, but they were not supplying teachers with the knowledge and experience needed to deal appropriately with the unique educational challenges that each exceptional child presented (Larrivee, 1981).

These problems notwithstanding, a report compiled by the Council of Ministers of Education (1989) indicates that, based on the results of a cross-Canada survey, the "provinces and territories have now developed very specific directives, guidelines and handbooks that make provision for the broad spectrum of education needs" (p. 14). All provincial and territorial educational ministries and departments have developed systems, based on a philosophy of integration, that offer a continuum of service. Nevertheless, there persists a preoccupation with the issues associated with categorical views of exceptionality, and with the continuance of a dual system of service delivery in the schools. According to current educational leaders in the field, these matters constitute the primary barriers to the mainstreaming process, and will be of primary concern in the current decade (Reynolds, Wang, & Walberg, 1987; Stainback et al., 1989a; Stainback & Stainback, 1984).

1990s: Inclusion

As schools continue to grapple with various means of implementing mainstreaming philosophies and programs, new ideas have emerged in the recent literature, including such concepts as the regular education initiative (Jenkins et al., 1990; Slavin, 1990; McKinney & Hocutt, 1988); the restructuring of schools (Reynolds et al., 1987; Villa, Thousand, Stainback, & Stainback, 1992); the merger of regular and special education (Stainback et al., 1989a; Stainback & Stainback, 1984; Mesinger, 1985); and professional school-based teaming through a process of collaborative consultation (Idol, 1993; Idol, Paolucci-Whitcomb, & Nevin, 1986; Nevin, Thousand, Paolucci-Whitcomb, & Villa, 1990; Freeze, Bravi, & Rampaul, 1989; Porter, 1991; Porter & Collicott, 1992). While these ideas are examined elsewhere in the text, it is important to recognize what they represent in terms of the overall historical-conceptual framework outlined in this chapter.

In essence, the new thinking is based on the belief that the full realization of normalization principles in our present educational system is dependent upon a complete **paradigm shift** and restructuring of the schools. In other words, there must be a dismantling of the dual system of special education and regular education (Stainback et al., 1989a; Lipsky & Gartner, 1989). The "adding on" or "moving in" approach to mainstreaming that has been adopted by the majority of school systems in Canada simply will not work. The two traditional educational systems need to be joined together into one unified system of service delivery (see Figure 2.1). It must be further recognized that new ways of viewing the general education system, in addition to the traditional special education system, are integral to the success of a unified system.

Inclusive education refers to a unified education system that sees student diversity as a source of enrichment and challenge. The resources of schools must be realigned so as to provide maximum support for teachers in their daily efforts to help all students develop to the fullest extent possible. The knowledge base that special education has developed separately over the past decades must be incorporated into general education practice through a combination of effective teaching practices, collaborative consultation, and organizational restructuring. Artificial designations such as categories, IQs, grade levels, and so forth must be replaced with the student-centred focus of

◆ paradigm shift: process by which the fundamental principles, foundations, and philosophy of the educational system are changed to accommodate current research, values, and legal/pedagogical isues

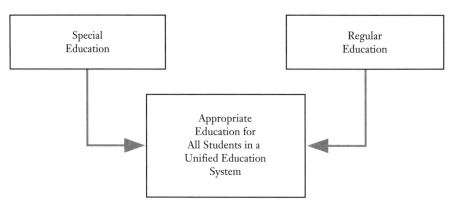

Figure 2.1
Restructuring Regular and Special Education

determining individual learning strengths and needs, and with the differentiation of instruction and resources to ensure that the learning potential of all students is tapped. The philosophical basis for inclusive education, then, is a belief that all students should be included within the regular classroom, and that any removal of a student to other educational settings must be justified on the basis of individual learning needs, not categorical membership.

Table 2.3 outlines many of the concepts that represent schools in transition from the "old paradigm" to the "new paradigm" inclusive education approach. The focus of educational services for all children moves away from a structured school-centred basis (i.e., special provisions for a limited number of identified students with exceptional learning needs) to one that is student-centred. Rather than having educational support divided into regular and special education systems, a holistic school-based approach is assumed to address the needs of all students within the school. This emphasis replaces a static one-way model of identification, testing, labelling, placement, and programming (which constrains the work of educational professionals through ever-increasing complex policies and regulations) with a more dynamic, interactive system of operation.

Assessment is no longer the responsibility of one or two isolated experts, who confirm or establish a diagnosis or label for the child having difficulty in the regular classroom. Instead, the regular classroom teacher is seen to be the primary professional in collaboration with families to help the child achieve his or her full learning potential. Consequently, the teacher assumes a central role in both assessment and instructional differentiation in the inclusive classroom, by focusing on the learner in the classroom context. Instead of using single tests, indexes, or scores to label students, teachers work in collaboration with other support professionals to determine the instructional needs of students, and address those needs through the provision of mediated instruction, which accommodates a variety of learning styles, and which offers sufficient differentiation of approaches, strategies, and materials. The

Table 2.3 Schools in Transition: Old Paradigm vs. New Paradigm Schools in Transition	
Old Paradigm	**New Paradigm**
◆ static	◆ dynamic
◆ fragmented	◆ holistic
◆ isolated expert	◆ collaborative
◆ single tests index or score	◆ multiple measures developmental
◆ school-centred, justifying who's "in" or "out"	◆ student-centred
◆ labelling	◆ instructional needs
◆ standardized/comparative	◆ focused on learner in context/mediated
◆ artificial	◆ ecological

artificial world of the special classroom, where students are classified as being either "in" or "out," is replaced with an inclusive classroom that celebrates and respects student diversity. The ecology of the classroom is the primary responsibility of the inclusive teacher, who is challenged to create a community of learners for all students in the inclusive classroom. (These concepts will be discussed in detail in the chapters that follow.)

We next review the legislative foundations that govern Canadian schools. In contrast to the U.S. system, which has been significantly affected by federal legislation, Canadian schools operate on the basis of provincial and territorial school acts. Given this fact, it is not surprising that there is considerable variation in the way that schools across the country are meeting the needs of students with exceptionalities. The following section focuses on legal and legislative trends in the provinces and territories, and provides a brief overview of current progress in the transition toward inclusive education.

◆ THE LEGAL CONTEXT OF SPECIAL EDUCATION

LITIGATION AND LEGISLATION

The values and beliefs of a society are reflected in the policies and guidelines under which its schools operate. As noted in the previous section, over the past fifty years, educational reform in Canada for students with special needs has resulted from two factors: (1) the efforts of parent pressure groups, professional reformers, and professional organizations; and (2) successful court challenges and litigation. These have been the primary catalysts for the acceptance of students with special needs in schools and in the community at large, and for the formulation of legislation and educational guidelines and policies that ensure a free and appropriate education for all students in Canada. As a prerequisite to understanding the legislation and accompanying guidelines and policies, we begin with a discussion of two often confused terms—litigation and legislation.

Concerns about special education and the legal rights of parents and their special needs children are centred on two primary issues: the right to have provision of special education program placement, and the right to refuse the recommendation of the school for special education program placement. The processes of litigation and legislation are conceptually joined by these two issues. *Litigation* refers to a process that occurs through a court system, and typically involves an individual or a small group of people filing a suit. Zuker (1988) defines litigation as "[a] case, controversy, or lawsuit between two or more parties for the purpose of enforcing an alleged right or recovering money damages for a breach of duty" (p. 247). For example, a parent may file a suit against a school board for not providing an appropriate education in the school jurisdiction in which the child and parents live. A somewhat different litigation process is referred to as a *class action suit*, which, if successful, affects all defined persons in a given school jurisdiction. If a parent of a learning-disabled child sues a school system, on behalf of all children in the school jurisdiction who are learning disabled, for lack of special classes and wins the decision of the court, then all learning-disabled students in that jurisdiction will benefit.

Important to understanding the connection between litigation and legislation processes is the notion that once a number of successful litigations have taken place, the need for legislation to correct a social inequity is recognized. For example, a province may have had various suits filed in several school jurisdictions concerning the lack of special programs, appropriate placements, or appropriate programs for students who are intellectually disabled, learning disabled, or visually impaired. Such multiple litigations will typically lead to a change in existing laws, or to new legislation to resolve specific inadequacies. Moreover, the lawmakers are influenced by prevailing public attitudes, which have over the past fifty years favoured the rights and educational needs of children who are exceptional, as well as by the legal and legislative developments occurring in other provinces and countries.

Mandell and Fiscus (1981) define *legislation* as "laws or bills which are enacted by a majority vote of lawmakers" (p. 26). The levels of jurisdiction that constitute the legal foundations of education in Canada are federal, provincial, and local (Zuker, 1988). Laws from all three levels influence the system and delivery of education in our schools. Federal authority is derived from the constitutional provisions laid out in the 1867 British North America (BNA) Act, which, patriated in the Constitution Act of 1982 (Constitution Act, 1982), maintains specific rights and privileges concerning denominational, separate, or alternative schools, as well as minority language educational rights.

Although the federal government maintains some control over educational matters through federal departments, the primary responsibility for education lies with the provincial level of jurisdiction. The enactment of Section 15(2) of the Canadian Charter of Rights and Freedoms in 1985 may, however, create the means for increased legislative power to challenge the lack of educational rights for the handicapped. Section 15(2) states that all individuals are "equal before and under the law," and have the "right to the equal protection and equal benefit of the law without discrimination and, in particular, without discrimination based on … mental and physical disability." Poirier, Goguen, and Leslie (1988) surmise that on the basis of recent actions taken by Canadian appeal courts, in which section 15(2) was cited, it is doubtful that future educational decisions will differ markedly from traditional practice. Nevertheless, it is important to recognize that the legislative machinery is in place at the federal level to effectively influence educational policy and practice, especially in provinces lagging behind in service provision for handicapped students (Poirier & Goguen, 1986).

Provincial authority relies on the statutes enacted by the legislatures that provide the legal framework within which the educational system is governed. Supplementary to these statutes, the associated school acts provide a variety of rules and regulations set out by various departments of education. Zuker (1988) notes that "[p]rovinces have education departments responsible for education while adhering to the schools act, regulations, policies, and collective agreements. Although these departments maintain control over teacher certification, curriculum, budget allocation, and textbooks, many responsibilities have been decentralized" (p. 5). For example, school administration and supervision is normally carried out at the local school-board level, although most provinces have provincially funded schools for students who are hearing impaired, and, in a few provinces, for students who are blind, learning disabled, aphasic, or behaviourally disordered. Therefore, although the basic framework for provinces is the same, it is not surprising that there is considerable variation among provinces concerning direction and service provision for special education.

Local school boards act as agents of the province, each within a particular geographically defined area. The operational powers and duties are set out in the school act and, at the local level, authority depends on policies established through resolutions of the local school boards. Funding is provided through a combination of local property taxes and provincial grants. Each province and territory has its own unique funding formula for the distribution and allocation of school grants, and special education programs and services have always been highly dependent on such funding. For example, Kelly (1985) notes that a survey of 1983 special education funding costs across Canada reveals that, on average, the provincial/territorial governments pay 78.3 percent of the total amount of special education costs. The recent emphasis on the provision of a free and appropriate education for all students, and on the mainstreaming movement, has necessitated a restructuring of funding provisions in many provinces (Kelly, 1985; Alberta Department of Education, 1989; Lawton & Wignall 1989). Provincial/territorial discretionary power over educational matters ensures basic operational consistency across school jurisdictions, but, at the same time, is flexible enough to accommodate specific local student characteristics and interests.

Before moving to a detailed discussion of current Canadian legislation, it is instructive to consider the forces that promote change in the educational system. Change does not happen quickly in educational institutions, and characteristically follows major trends in the larger society. Recent changes in the legal system—changes that uphold the rights of all children to receive a free and **appropriate education** in Canada—have resulted from the collective influence of parent and advocacy groups, private litigation actions in the courts, and the passage, in the United States, of Public Law 94-142 (1975), the Education for all Handicapped Children Act.

PUBLIC LAW 94-142 *yes*

Public Law 94-142 made it mandatory for all handicapped children in the United States to receive a free and appropriate education, and with its passage in 1975 made special education a national concern. The legislation outlines regulations and required actions on the part of *all* teachers and school systems. In other words, discrepancies and service gaps that could be identified in certain school systems throughout the U.S. were targeted for change. Public Law 94-142 clearly represented a move away from a special class or segregated system of educational service to the more current principles of least restrictive environment and normalization—ideas that lie at the heart of mainstreaming philosophy. Embodied within this legislation are key concepts that have been variously considered and incorporated into provincial legislation across Canada, and that can be seen as the benchmarks for special education reform in Canada over the past decade and a half. These key concepts are briefly outlined below.

- *Zero reject.* **Zero reject** refers to the concept that all children, regardless of the type or level of their handicap, must be provided with an appropriate and free education. The problem of functional barriers (e.g., lack of transportation), support services (e.g., speech therapy and medical aid), and in-service education for teachers is addressed in the legislation.
- *Nondiscriminatory evaluation.* **Nondiscriminatory evaluation** is specifically geared toward the classification of students and the development of appropriate educational programs for them. Evaluation must be carried out before educational placement decisions have been made, as well as every three years after the initial classification of "handicapped." Unbiased assessment is required to ensure that racial or cultural factors do not discriminate against students.
- *Individualized education.* An individualized education program, or IEP, must be developed for every student identified as handicapped who receives special education, and must include information concerning the student's level of educational performance; instructional goals and objectives; times, duration, and extent of special service and regular education;

appropriate education: educational practice that recognizes the abilities, needs, and rights of all children to reach their full academic potential in the least restrictive environment

zero reject: component of U.S. Public Law 94-142, which states that all children—regardless of type or level of handicap—must be provided with a free and appropriate education

nondiscriminatory evaluation: unbiased procedures used to classify students and develop programs for them as well as procedures for regular evaluation. Parents must be notified and encouraged to appear at the IEP development meeting, which is attended by the student's teacher, the student (when appropriate), a school system representative, and an evaluation team member or other qualified individual.

- *Least restrictive environment.* This provision captures the philosophy that students with handicaps should have as much access as possible to meaningful interaction with peers who are nonhandicapped. It is recognized that a continuum of placement possibilities (i.e., regular class, resource room, special classroom) must be considered before choosing the environment that meets the social and instructional needs of the student.

- *Due process.* This provision is to ensure that professionals and parents have adequate procedures in place to effect fair practice in the identification, referral, evaluation, and placement of a handicapped student. If conflicts arise in any of the above areas, then either the parent or the educator can request a due-process hearing. Decisions reached at such hearings, which are carried out at the local school system level, can be appealed to the state education agency, and beyond that to the appropriate state or federal court.

- *Parental participation.* Parents are encouraged to participate in all aspects of educational policy development including the determination of program priorities, budgets, and special education planning and advising. Also ensured in the provision is the parents' right to review, and to have explained, all educational records concerning their child, and the right to control the release of this information to outside agencies and personnel.

The concepts that are encompassed in Public Law 94-142 have had a major impact on educational thought and practice in Canada. Some Canadian provinces have followed a similar path of introducing comprehensive legislation to effect change. Other provinces and territories have instead provided general direction in their school acts, leaving greater autonomy and flexibility for local school jurisdictions to develop their own policies and procedures to accommodate students with exceptional learning needs. The specific direction of each province and territory will be reviewed in a subsequent section of this chapter.

MANDATORY VERSUS DISCRETIONARY POWER

In considering province-by-province provisions and service for students with exceptional needs, it is important to distinguish between two terms used in legislation. **Mandatory legislation** refers to any statute passed by the legislature that legally requires boards to provide education for all children regardless of their exceptionality. Provinces with mandatory legislation include Manitoba, New Brunswick, Newfoundland, Nova Scotia, Ontario, Alberta, Quebec, and Saskatchewan (Goguen, 1989). **Permissive legislation**, which applies to the educational legislation of the Northwest

- mandatory legislation: statute(s) or specific legal guidelines passed by the legislature requiring school boards to provide free and appropriate education for all students, regardless of their exceptionality

- permissive legislation: legislation that permits but does not legally require school boards to provide educational services for students with special needs

Territories, the Yukon, Prince Edward Island, and British Columbia, permits but does not legally require school boards to provide educational services for students with special needs.

Poirier et al. (1988) highlight the distinction between mandatory and permissive legislation by noting that "[e]ven in times when money is scarce and budgetary restrictions and cuts are envisaged, school boards in provinces with mandatory legislation may not abandon their duties under these statutes, unless the legislation is modified. Provinces with permissive legislation may exclude services to exceptional students without violating provincial law" (p. 18). However, as Poirier et al. (1988) suggest, the collective force of the Canadian Charter of Rights and Freedoms, human rights legislation, and administrative law "may have a great impact on the right of handicapped students to an education and on their rights to conditions without which the right to an education remains a theoretical right" (p. 31).

A notable example is provided by MacKay (1989), who describes the precedent-setting *Elwood* case which used the Charter of Rights and Freedoms to win a decision regarding the "rights of the mentally disabled to be integrated into the mainstream of Canadian schooling" (p. 150). The matter is not a trivial one, for as Winzer (1990) points out, if school boards are not taking the initiative to bring into effect policies and procedures that serve the needs of all students, or if there is wide discrepancy across a given province regarding the quality and type of provisions administered, there is a greater likelihood of pressure to adopt legislative policies to *ensure* that adequate provisions are made available for exceptional students.

Three factors raised by Poirier et al. (1988) in their analysis of Canadian education rights of children with exceptional needs further underline the significance of the powers and limitations of legal aspects of educational provisions. These factors are *appropriate education*, *right to resources*, and *parental involvement and procedural issues.*

Appropriate Education

The fact that the law protects the rights of children with exceptional needs to an education does not automatically mean that the education provided is most appropriate to the individual's abilities and needs, or that is necessarily provided in the least restrictive environment. Only three provinces—Quebec, Ontario, and Saskatchewan—have provincial education laws to ensure that the education provided will be appropriate to the needs and abilities of the child with exceptional needs (Poirier et al., 1988). Of course, it should not be assumed that provinces or territories lacking this sort of legislation are not meeting individual learning needs through other means. Many school districts of such provinces and territories have adopted innovative and advanced policies. The basic problem is with the discontinuity of policy, which becomes particularly evident in situations when a parent of an exceptional child enjoys a high level of service in one district, but finds the service considerably reduced in another district or province (Poirier et al., 1988).

Right to Resources *yes*

For many children with exceptional needs, appropriate education is hindered by an inadequate provision of resources, including access to school buildings, transportation, adequately trained personnel, and financing needs. Again, there is considerable variation from province to province in this area. For example, in the area of teacher certification, Ontario and Manitoba lie at one extreme, with the greatest amount of regulation. In these two provinces, specialized certification and/or course work is required for general special education, education of students who are deaf, blind, or intellectually disabled, as well as for individuals serving as special education coordinators. At the other extreme, Alberta, British Columbia, and Prince Edward Island have no special certification provisions beyond standard teacher certification.

Similar interprovincial discrepancies are noted by Godsell (1989) and Kelly (1985), who provide summary accounts of the various special education funding formulas used in Canada, and who describe how funding mechanisms can be differentially applied according to students, resources, and costs. The issue of special education funding is an important one in that certain funding formulas are dependent on the identification of students with exceptional learning needs before funding is released for individualized programming; this ties provinces or territories that adopt such formulas directly to a categorical approach. Other provinces, such as Alberta and Manitoba, have introduced block-funding procedures based on total student enrolments within a district; this allows the allocation of funding to be administered more flexibly, according to school division characteristics and needs. The block form of funding allocation is more compatible with inclusive education initiatives, but its effectiveness rests on the existence of a trained professional group able to translate special education dollars into inclusive and successful programs in schools.

Parental Involvement and Procedural Issues

The U.S. Education for All Handicapped Children Act (EAHCA) uses the term **due process** (discussed in the previous section) to describe the components deemed necessary to ensure that the educational needs of exceptional students are met. The term refers specifically to policies or procedures for screening, referral, assessment, and placement. As Poirier et al. (1988) note, "Whereas the child-finding procedures are compulsory in the United States, in Canada the general rule, except for Ontario, is that screening is done by teachers as a part of their job" (p. 76). This means that most provinces and territories are not legally compelled to carry out formal procedures to identify, assess, and place students with exceptional learning needs.

◆ **due process:** provision of U.S. Public Law 94-142 to ensure professionals and parents adequate and fair practice in the screening, identification, and placement of exceptional students

yes

The involvement of parents in due process and placement decisions is provided in the Education Acts of Saskatchewan and Ontario, but great disparities on this point are evident across Canada. Poirier et al. (1988) suggest that "[s]chool legislation … be changed to take into account the involvement of parents, the right to be heard, their right to see their child's record, and to make representation before their child is placed in a particular school setting" (p. 83).

It is difficult to determine what impact provincial and territorial legislation and the Charter of Rights and Freedoms will have on promoting inclusive education. Hill (1988) notes a recent increase in mainstreaming practices in both the regular school system and regular education classrooms, which suggests that moves are being made in the direction of inclusive education. The next section provides an overview of current provincial and territorial educational legislation, with summary information given in Table 2.4.[1]

◆ PROVINCIAL AND TERRITORIAL LEGISLATION

YUKON

uniqueness

The Yukon has recently introduced progressive legislation concerning mainstreaming provisions and rights for exceptional children. Sections in the Education Act (Yukon Territory, 1990) that cover children with exceptional needs are based on the principle of the least restrictive and most enabling environment. The philosophical foundation of the legislation is that all children will typically be best served in the regular classroom environment. Students with exceptional needs will initially be accommodated within this context, with any additional support and assistance deemed necessary to be provided. If the regular classroom is found not to be the most enabling for the student, then a continuum of educational alternatives is potentially available.

The legislation supports a noncategorical approach, in which (1) programs are determined on the basis of needs as opposed to labels; and (2) all children with exceptional needs are required to have an **individual educational plan (IEP)**, which must be signed by the parent before implementation. Recognized exceptional needs are those associated with intellectual, physical, emotional, or communicative characteristics, and thus the needs of gifted students are included in the legislation. Parents dissatisfied with any aspect of the education delivery system can appeal through an Educational Appeal Tribunal, which is appointed by the Minister of Education. The decisions of the tribunal are final and carry considerable weight in that they are registered with the Supreme Court of Canada.

Because of its recency, it is difficult to predict to what extent implementation of this legislation will be limited by financial constraints. The Yukon

◆ **individual education plan (IEP):** written plan developed by an educational team and consisting of short- and long-term goals that reflect and accommodate the assessed needs and abilities of a student with exceptional needs

---

1. Our word of appreciation to the individuals who gave their time and expertise in a validity check of the subsequent information, and who are acknowledged at the end of the chapter.

has the additional challenge of serving a small student population over a very large geographical area, making the provision of services for students with special needs even more difficult in comparison with other provinces. Nevertheless, it is important to recognize that the Yukon Education Act appears to address many of the shortcomings of a categorical approach to special education, and it is highly compatible with inclusive education initiatives.

NORTHWEST TERRITORIES

One of the most significant changes in recent educational practice in the Northwest Territories has been the inclusion of students with special needs into regular classrooms in schools within their home communities. In 1982, the Special Committee on Education produced a report, entitled *Learning, Tradition and Change*, which included a number of recommendations for special education and which ultimately spearheaded the formal move toward integration. In response to these recommendations, the NWT Department of Education developed *A Departmental Directive and Guidelines on Special Needs Education* (1986), which was based on a philosophy of mainstreaming. The central thrust of the document was the provision of community-based education for all students with special needs through individualized programming. Effective implementation of the philosophy was achieved through the establishment and funding support of an extensive network of support personnel (e.g., special needs consultants, special needs teachers, and special needs assistants).

In recent years, departmental funding mechanisms, initially based on incidence levels and programming for students with "special needs," have in many NWT regions/boards been revised and extended beyond the practices outlined in *A Departmental Directive*. More recent documents produced by the NWT Department of Education, such as *Education in the NWT* (1989) and *Our Students, Our Future: An Educational Framework* (1991), emphasize not only that all children have a right to an appropriate education, but that *all* children are unique in terms of needs, interests, strengths, feelings, and abilities. The Education Act (Northwest Territories, 1976) is currently under revision, while *A Departmental Directive and Guidelines on Special Needs Education (1986)* is similarly being updated and rewritten in the form of a territorial-wide policy on integration.

As the Northwest Territories has undergone this marked process of change and development, a number of key supports to the successful implementation of the mainstreaming philosophy and integration policy have emerged. These include: adequate funding to support implementation; public awareness initiatives to enhance understanding; on-going staff development and training; and the provision of specialized support services. The Department of Education is committed to the process of implementing integration of all students, and will continue to support boards of education as they strive to serve all students.

Table 2.4
Canadian Legislative Provisions for Exceptional Students

Province Or Territory	Most Recent Legislation	Supporting Documents	Key Word Descriptors
Alberta	School Act (amended Sept. 1, 1990)	Program Adequacy in Special Education (1987) Special Education Policy Handbook (1989) Special Education Manual (1987)	permissive inclusive zero-reject
British Columbia	School Act–Bill 87 (1989) School Regulation & Minister of Educ. Orders # 149/89 # 150/89	Guidelines for Programs and Services in Special Education (in preparation)	permissive, inclusive, noncategorical, local autonomy, learner focused
Manitoba	The Public Schools Act (1987)	Special Education in Manitoba: Policy and Procedural Guidelines for the Education of Students with Special Needs in the Public School System (1989)	mandatory integration
New Brunswick	New Brunswick Schools Act (1992)	Working Guidelines on Integration (1988) Integration Means All Our Children Belong (1987) Report of the Integration Review Committee (1989) Final Report on the Review of School Integration Special Committee on Social Policy and Development (1990) O.E.C.D./C.R.R.I. Report: Active Life for Disabled Youth—Integration in the Schools of New Brunswick, Perner (1991)	mandatory inclusion in regular classes
Newfoundland	The Schools Act (as amended) 1987; under revision	Special Education Policy Manual (1987) (revised 1992)	zero reject, team decision-making, comprehensive programming, teaching strategies

Northwest Territories	Education Act (1976; under revision)	Learning, Tradition & Change (March, 1982) A Departmental Directive & Guidelines on Special Needs Education (1986) Education in the NWT (1989) Our Students, Our Future: An Educational Framework (1990)	inclusion mainstreaming individualized programming
Nova Scotia	Education Act (consolidated in 1990)	Learning Disabled Students in the Nova Scotia Public School System (1990) Integration Implementation: The N.S. Teachers' Union Perspective (1990) Public School Programs (1991-93)	zero-rejection integration
Ontario	The Ontario Education Amendment Act (1980)	The Special Ontario Regulation 554/81 Education Information Handbook, Ontario Ministry of Education (1984)	mandatory; integration, legal rights, categorical, parent litigation
Prince Edward Island	PEI School Act (consolidated in 1988)	Special Education Policy	mandatory, noncategorical, zero-reject
Quebec	Education Act (1988)	Ministère de l'Éducation (1990) General education in the youth sector: Preschool, elementary school, and secondary school: 1991-92 directives	zero-reject, individualized and appropriate education, parent participation, shared decision-making
Saskatchewan	The Education Act (1978)	Special Education Policy Manual (1989)	mandatory, appropriate education, integration
Yukon	Education Act (1990, proclaimed August 13)	Special Education Handbook (in preparation) Special Education Policy (under revision)	mandatory, noncategorical, least restrictive/most enabling environment, neighbourhood school

hot detal

BRITISH COLUMBIA

Current thinking and practice relating to the education of children with exceptional needs in British Columbia has been significantly influenced by a comprehensive, province-wide study of education completed in 1988. The Royal Commission on Education Report, *A Legacy for Learners* (1988), contains eighty-three recommendations that address all aspects of education (e.g., curriculum, teacher supply and qualifications, system governance, and education finance) relevant to the development of a population that is "well prepared to meet the rapidly changing challenges of everyday life in the 21st century" (p. 1). Indicating a philosophical shift toward inclusive education, the Commission emphasizes in its recommendations a continuation of policies and programs, and the extension of educational and social services, where necessary, to support students with exceptional needs and their parents, as well as to assist teachers in the delivery of appropriate learning experiences within "normalized" classroom settings. Moreover, it recommends that the rights of students with exceptional needs and their parents be covered in the School Act and a procedure for disputes resolution provided.

The Commission's theme of "student-focused" education was incorporated in related documents from the office of the Minister of Education. For example, *Inter-Ministerial Protocols for the Provision of Support Services to Schools* (British Columbia, 1990) provides a detailed overview of a formalized plan of collaboration involving the Ministries of Education, Social Services and Housing, Health, and the Solicitor General in the provision of necessary support services to children in schools (e.g., nursing care, mental-health services, and occupational therapy). The plan is to be implemented over a ten-year period. A few of the protocols have been implemented, bringing about increased funding for speech/language pathology, occupational and physical therapy, and mental-health services, along with the operationalization of in-school supports for special needs students.

Bill 67 of the School Act (British Columbia, 1989) defines an educational program as an organized set of learning activities that are "designed to enable learners to develop their individual potential and to acquire the knowledge, skills and attitudes needed to contribute to a healthy society and a prosperous and sustainable economy" (pp. 6-7). The access statement (Section 2) and the definition of "educational program" (Section 1) articulate each child's entitlement to a program designed to meet his or her needs. Other features that pertain to meeting the needs of exceptional students are Appeals (Section 11), Parents' Entitlements and Responsibilities (Section 7), Student Records (Section 9), Special Purpose Grants (Section 131), and Support Services (Section 106).

The School Act (British Columbia, 1989) states that: "Unless the educational needs of a handicapped student indicate that the student's educational program should be provided otherwise, a board shall provide that student with an educational program in classrooms where the student is integrated with other students who do not have handicaps" (p. 33). Although the B.C.

legislation does not order full integration in all circumstances, the onus is clearly on school boards to defend decisions against placement in integrated learning environments. This legislation marks an important shift from ministry control to greatly increased school board autonomy and authority in the general governance of educational matters. As Roch (1991) notes, "the Ministry no longer has the authority to issue policies or dictate procedures for the delivery of special education services to schools, beyond what is stated in the *Act and Orders*" (p. 2).

The most recent Ministry of Education document, entitled *Year 2000: A Framework for Learning* (British Columbia, 1990), provides a review of previously developed documents, as well as an organizing framework for all program development, student assessment and evaluation, and reporting activities in British Columbia. Central principles are summarized below:
Learning and the Learner

1. Learning requires the active participation of the learner.
2. People learn in a variety of ways and at different rates.
3. Learning is both an individual and a social process.

Curriculum and Assessment

1. Curriculum and assessment should be learner focused.
2. Assessment and reporting should help students make informed choices (pp. 7-11).

As outlined in the numerous British Columbia documents, the foundations have now been set in place for the creation of a single unified system of education. The ensuing decade will be critical in determining the ultimate success of those foundations.

ALBERTA

The Alberta School Act (Alberta, 1988) recognizes that certain behavioural, communicational, intellectual, learning or physical characteristics—alone or in combination—may necessitate the provision of special education. Conn-Blowers and McLeod (1989), in specific reference to Section 29 of the Act, note that "[w]hen a student is determined by a school board to be in need of a special education program, the student is entitled to access to such a program" (p. 26). Prior to special education program placement, parents (and, if appropriate, students) shall be consulted. Jeffaries (1991) emphasizes that even though it is not explicitly stated, the provisions cover all areas of exceptionality, including students who are gifted. For parents who oppose the education provided to their child with exceptional needs, the School Act (Sections 104 and 105) contains appeal procedures involving a system of review by the Minister, as well as a Special Needs Tribunal (Section 30). The Special Needs Tribunal may be requested to examine decisions concerning the board's inability to provide an education that is appropriate to the student's needs. When a decision is made that favours the board's claim, a special-needs plan is developed or approved by the Special Needs Tribunal, and, after determining how appropriate provision of services will be carried out, the costs are apportioned between the school board and the government.

McLeod (1983) notes that during the 1980s Alberta moved toward increased decentralization and local decision-making concerning service delivery. The provincial education department continues to provide support, however, in the form of a revised block-funding system to enable boards to furnish programs for exceptional students (Conn-Blowers & McLeod, 1989), a *Special Education Policy Handbook* (Alberta Department of Education, 1989), and a series of handbooks on students with learning disabilities, students who are gifted and talented, and students with behaviour disorders. The handbooks are intended for use as resource manuals to assist regular classroom teachers in working with special-needs students. Other sources of professional support can be found in the journals produced by two Alberta Teachers' Association specialty councils—the Special Education Council's *Teaching Atypical Students in Alberta*, and the Gifted and Talented Education Council's *Alberta Gifted and Talented Education*. The Alberta Department of Education is currently preparing a document to support school districts in developing policies for the integration of special-needs students.

SASKATCHEWAN

The most recent legislation concerning elementary and secondary education in Saskatchewan is found in the Education Act (Saskatchewan Department of Education, 1978), with specific provisions for students with exceptional needs outlined in Sections 178, 184, and 185. Vickers (1981) notes that Saskatchewan legislation has been progressive in comparison with other provinces because of its mandatory provision that "every person between the ages of 6 and 21 years has the right to attend school . . . and to receive instruction appropriate to his age and level of educational achievement" (p. 94).

As outlined in Section 184, a "pupil with a disability" includes any student who is deemed unable to participate at an optimal level in the benefits of the ordinary school program by reason of personal limitations attributable to physical, mental, behavioural, or communicative disorders. School boards are required to provide educational services on behalf of students who are handicapped, and parents must be consulted before any assessment procedures and/or placement decisions are made (Section 178). A unique provision of "enabling legislation" is found under Section 185, which specifies that gifted students may be provided with special programs when the ordinary program of instruction is deemed to be insufficient.

A recent *Special Education Policy Manual* (Saskatchewan Department of Education, 1989), prepared by the Special Education Branch of Saskatchewan Education, gives a detailed overview of the philosophy, guiding principles, policies, programs, and funding provisions for students with exceptional needs in Saskatchewan. School divisions can use this document as a guide to the preparation of their annual special education master plan, as an inventory of special education provisions, and as a detailed plan of how the school board is serving students with exceptional needs, how the services and programs are being evaluated, and what the emerging needs of the division are.

Another feature distinguishing Saskatchewan from other provinces and territories is the organizational structure of the Department of Education. Special Education is one of six branches under the umbrella of Curriculum and Instruction, establishing a clear priority of appropriate instruction for exceptional learners. Accordingly, the *Special Education Policy Manual* details progressive concepts such as "modified curriculum and instruction"; "process and product modification"; and "transdisciplinary applications to instruction." Reports and articles on mainstreaming and inclusive education regularly appear in the *Saskatchewan Bulletin*, the publication of the Saskatchewan Teachers' Federation. Additional information is available to educators through the Special Education Information Network of Saskatchewan (SEINeS), an electronic information system that is provided free of charge by the Special Education Branch of the Saskatchewan Department of Education.

MANITOBA

Section 41(4) of the Manitoba Public Schools Act (1987) specifies that: "Every school board shall provide or make provision for education in Grades 1 to 12 inclusive for all resident persons who have the right to attend school." Provision of educational programs for students with exceptional learning needs is mandatory. Moreover, the most recent policy manual, *Special Education in Manitoba* (Manitoba Department of Education and Training, 1989), outlines specific directives for the placement and programming of students with special needs. All boards must provide a systematic assessment of student learning needs, and placement decisions are based on the philosophy of the most enabling environment. A team approach to decision-making, with representation by the parents (and the student, if possible) is used. For children with severe disabilities requiring the support of health services, mental health, or community service professionals, education personnel are designated to coordinate all support in the educational planning process. Educational planning is carried out and monitored regularly by the educational team, and special programming is outlined in a goal-directed individual education program (IEP). Finally, emphasis is given to early identification and program implementation.

The philosophical orientation of the province is evident in the comments of Len Derkach, former Minister of Education and Training: "The integration of the majority of students with special learning needs into the regular school system is not only desirable, but possible, with specialized supports. A range of alternatives are needed so that reasonable choices can be made available for all students" (Manitoba Department of Education and Training, 1989).

An innovative special education planning process, referred to as the Annual Division Action Plan (ADAP), has been implemented throughout Manitoba, with the intent of ensuring that all school boards develop a planning and evaluation process, and put a delivery system in place. The ADAP must include: (1) planning process; (2) philosophy and policies; (3) needs survey; (4) comprehensive service delivery system; (5) other division resources; (6) professional development activities; and (7) review of the ADAP (Manitoba Department of Education and Training, 1989, p. 15).

Professional support for educators involved in inclusive education is provided in the *Manitoba Association of Resource Teachers* (MART) *Journal*, and the *Manitoba Journal of Counselling*, which highlights special inclusive education projects such as the development of a mini-course for junior high schools (Sherman, 1988).

ONTARIO

The most recent education legislation in Ontario, popularly referred to as Bill 82, was enacted in December, 1980, under the Education Amendment Act (Ontario, 1980), and received full implementation in September, 1985. Various regulations under the Act were drafted in 1981, with Ontario Regulation 554 having the greatest relevance for students with exceptional needs and their parents. This legislation, which has been widely proclaimed as the most comprehensive legislation in Canada, is reminiscent of the U.S. Education for All Handicapped Children Act. Unlike the U.S. act, however, Bill 82 is clearly categorical and restorative in its orientation (Wilson, 1989). The restorative approach is synonymous with the traditional special educational "medical model" and can be contrasted with the preventative approach, which is holistic and child-centred (Wilson, 1984).

Wilson (1989) asserts that the current legislation in Ontario places "pressure upon school systems to interpret the law in a categorical manner" (p. 90), and, consequently, that boards have "geared their delivery systems to handle exceptional pupils in placements that depend heavily on categorical assignment" (p. 90). The problem that arises is that educators and school districts favouring a preventative approach, which is more compatible with mainstreaming and integration practice, have difficulty putting their beliefs into practice because they are accountable to the terms of the current legislation. Vickers (1981) is highly critical of the new legislation, commenting that "[a]t a time when most people have agreed that labels are for jars and not for people, the Ontario legislators have maintained outmoded notions of "trainable retarded children" (p. 95).

While the current legislation *does* foster the delineation of two systems within the public school system—regular education and special education—

it is very comprehensive and attempts to address several areas of educational rights for exceptional children and their parents. Some of the key principles (Wilson, 1983; *Special Education Information Handbook*, 1984) that the Education Amendment Act includes are:

- *Universal access.* All students have the right to receive appropriate special education services and programs.
- *Free education.* Special education programs and services must be provided at no extra cost to the child or family.
- *Appeal procedures.* Parents can appeal on the basis of disagreement with the identification of the pupil as exceptional, the decision of the board to not consider a pupil as exceptional, and, finally, the placement of a pupil as an exceptional student.
- *Early, ongoing identification.* Learning abilities and needs of exceptional pupils are to be identified early on, and procedures for regular review and assessment are required.
- *Appropriate programs.* All exceptional pupils must have a program plan that outlines the specific objectives and services required.
- *Defined exceptionalities.* Provision of special education services and programs is based upon the five groupings of behaviour, communication, intellectual, physical, and multiple exceptionality.

A study of the impact and implementation of the Ontario Education Amendment Act has been conducted by Silverman, Wilson, and Seller (1987). Among the implementation dimensions they examined were identification, program, review and evaluation, communication with staff, and communication with parents. Their research showed general progress, although low ratings were found in the "dimensions related to the provision of programs, their planning and monitoring and the evaluation of their effect" (p. 19). Dimensions examined for the evaluation of impact included goal specificity, goal relatedness, teacher effort, effort relatedness, use of resources, parental contact, and individual pupil plans. Again, Silverman, Wilson, and Seller (1987) discerned progress, but noted that "if teachers' instructional skills as they relate to the establishment of instructional objectives, program design and implementation, and ongoing evaluation are to be enhanced, it may require a concerted effort in providing in-service programs for teachers and principals, and acceptance of the consulting role to be played by resource personnel" (p. 23).

A number of initiatives currently being implemented will likely have significant impact on Bill 82. First, a consultation paper entitled *Integration of Exceptional Pupils—An Invitation to Respond* has been widely circulated, and response will guide future legislation as it pertains to the education of students with exceptional learning needs. Introduced in 1991, Bill 114 dealt with two aspects of existing legislation: the Identification, Placement and Review Committees (IPRCs), and the role of the Special Education Advisory Committees (SEACs). Legislative changes relating to these two areas, and to more general issues stemming from mainstreaming concerns, will be within the purview of the above-mentioned consultation paper. A further proposal, Bill 37—An Act to Amend the Education Act and Certain Other Acts With Respect to Special Education—is presently before the legislature. This bill, which is directed toward changes in the education of pupils with developmental handicaps, removes the previous "hard to serve" designation of existing legislation.

The Ontario example is one approach to the difficult and complex problem of ensuring that all students have a right to appropriate educational services, programs, and opportunities. Evaluation of this detailed legislative approach to the problem has only just begun, and so the extent of its success (or failure) remains to be seen.

QUEBEC

The 1980s saw significant reform in Quebec's school system (Champoux-Lesage, 1989). General changes included a revamping of the program of studies and a revision of the basic school organization. The overriding goal for all changes during this period was to promote individualized instruction for all students within the regular school system. Major changes in special education were initiated in the mid-1970s with the formation of a provincial task force mandated to review the education of children with learning and emotional problems (Comité provincial de l'enfance inadaptée [COPEX]). The government response to the COPEX (1976) report was the adoption of two key policy papers concerning special education (Ministère de l'Éducation du Québec [MEQ], 1979a; 1979b). Three guiding principles were highlighted in these two documents: (1) universal access to the public school system; (2) access to high-quality education and; (3) education in as normal an environment as possible. The policy recognizes the following categorical distinctions: learning problems, mental deficiency, sensory impairments, physical handicaps, socio-emotional problems, and multiple deviations (Smith, 1992); intellectually gifted students are not, therefore, recognized in these policy papers.

The principle of universal access outlines the right of exceptional students to attend school in their home jurisdictions, with provision for preschool and extension beyond normal school-leaving age. Quality education specifically refers to educational provisions adapted to the special needs of the individual student that are intended to maximize personal development. The third major theme of integration is based on an adaptation of the **cascade model**, and emphasizes a school environment that provides the most "normal" setting possible for children with special needs. According to Champoux-Lesage (1989), "[t]he integration of students with learning difficulties and disabled students into the regular classes is without question the part of the policy that has most affected the education of Quebec youth in the past decade. Within the school system, the ministerial policy is referred to as the Integration Policy" (p. 98).

cascade model: a system of service delivery for special-needs students that emphasizes more diverse regular classroom placements and fewer specialized segregated placements

The *Schools of Quebec* (MEQ, 1979a; 1979b) elaborates on the above themes, notably with respect to: the rights of exceptional students to a continuum of educational alternatives for a free and appropriate education; extended schooling; decentralization of special education services; accessible facilities; preventative measures such as early identification and compensatory education; assessment based on revised definition of disability category; development of individualized education plans; integration; and parental consultation and participation. The Quebec Education Act (Quebec, 1988) provides for a number of these, especially universal access with extended schooling for the handicapped (Section 1); individualized education plans (Section 47); adaptation of regular education services (Section 234); mandatory board policy governing pupil evaluation, integration, special classes, and program evaluation (Section 235); and, finally, a board-level advisory committee for parents of students with special needs (Sections 185-187).

Smith (1992) takes issue with many of the provisions contained in the Act, including the broadening of grounds for pupil expulsion; the board's right to provide service via an agreement with an outside body, without parental consent; the potential threat to student rights embodied in the new nomenclature of the handicapped; and ministerial discretion regarding confidentiality of student files. Moreover, Smith (1992) comments that "the lack of legislative provisions governing availability of services, accessibility of school facilities and parental rights concerning the assessment and placement of their children have not been addressed" (p. 47). In fact, a critical analysis undertaken by Smith in 1989 revealed substantial discrepancies between the stated goals of Quebec government policy and the legislative actions taken.

Champoux-Lesage (1989) forecasts that the 1990s will bring further affirmation in Quebec of the individualized approach to the education of all children. Specific goals that might be targeted include the continued socialization of students with learning difficulties and disabilities; a refinement of the role of parents as partners in the decision-making processes of schools; more progressive funding procedures; and a greater focus on evaluation systems for effective monitoring of changes in student populations and funding allocations. It will be interesting to see if such changes are produced out of legislative actions or through a systematic restructuring of schools in general.

NEW BRUNSWICK

Prior to 1986, New Brunswick students with special needs were covered under the Auxiliary Classes Act (New Brunswick, 1973) and legislation associated with the services and programs administered through the Atlantic Provinces Special Education Authority (APSEA). As such, there was only minimal provision for students with exceptional needs in the Schools Act. On the recommendation of the Correia and Goguen (1983) report, the province decided to repeal the Auxiliary Classes Act and enact legislation that would reflect current social, educational, and legislative trends. In 1986, new legislation was proclaimed in what was commonly referred to as Bill 85—An Act to Amend the Schools Act (New Brunswick, 1986).

Bill 85, now incorporated in the New Brunswick Schools Act (New Brunswick, 1992), makes it mandatory for school boards to provide educational programs and services for all children. The Bill emphasizes individual programming, and uses the term "special education program" to refer specifically to "one which provides for services based on an individual pupil's specific needs rather than on any category of handicap" (New Brunswick Department of Education, *Working Guidelines on Integration*, 1988, p. 3). The goal of educational integration encompassed in the new legislation is based on the following fundamental assumptions outlined by Roberts (1987):

1. The responsibility for ... educating all children must be shared by the Department of Education, the school district and the school.
2. The ultimate goals for learning and development are the same for all children.
3. Programs and services must be planned according to the individual needs of the student.
4. Individual characteristics and differences are to be expected in any instructional group of students.
5. The notion of homogeneity of pupil learning characteristics is not supported.
6. Educational integration is seen to be consistent with the ideology of multiculturalism and individual differences. (pp. 17-18)

While reaction to the 1986 integration legislation has been generally positive (Leavitt, 1989; Perner & Roberts, 1989), criticisms have been voiced. Cashion, Latchford, and Mureika (1989) are particularly critical of the widespread regular-class placement of exceptional students, which they say is detrimental to students' potential and actual learning needs. Other concerns raised include unrealistic parental expectations, unprepared teachers, limited resources and support personnel, and understaffed classes. Perner (1991) acknowledges the challenges brought about by the innovative legislation. She nevertheless points out that the 1990 series of public hearings in New Brunswick overwhelmingly—and positively—confirmed the direction that has been set.

NOVA SCOTIA

Nova Scotia is a member of the Atlantic Provinces Special Education Authority (APSEA), which operates in conjunction with New Brunswick, Newfoundland, and Prince Edward Island, and has a mandate to provide programs and services to children who are visually and hearing impaired, from birth to age 21. In 1980, this mandate was extended to include severely learning-disabled students, but a subsequent APSEA review report (Kendall, 1987), recommended that provisions for the learning disabled be re-examined. The Standing Committee on Human Resources (1990) was directed to study the issues concerning learning-disabled students, and in their report, *Learning Disabled Students in the Nova Scotia Public School System*, offered several recommendations concerning the need for student assessment, public awareness, teacher training, curriculum changes, financing, adult education, and policy development. APSEA maintains the funding responsibility for students with severe learning disabilities who require special placement.

A categorical approach to service is inherent within the funding system outlined in the *Report of the Commission on Public Education Finance* (Walker, 1981) in that: "Children whose disabilities resulted from mental retardation, social or emotional disorders, learning disabilities, sensory impairments, physical handicaps, serious health-related disabilities, speech and communication disorders, or children suffering with severe multiple handicaps were to be educationally supported by the funding allocated for special education" (Beuree, 1989, p. 118). One of the interesting trends of the 1980s, reported by Beuree (1989), is the decrease in students with mental handicaps, and a significant increase in pupils with behavioural/emotional/social problems, speech/language disabilities, and learning disabilities. At the school-board level, directives to improve appeal policies at the school and district level were sent out, and a provincial appeal procedure was established in 1988.

Significant progress toward the implementation of integration in Nova Scotia is attributable to the efforts of the Nova Scotia Teachers' Union (1990). A task force was established in 1989, with the mandate to "survey the membership to determine the status of integration implementation in the province" (p. 1). All NSTU members were invited to make their views known to the Committee, which received the involvement or input of some 4,500 teachers. The recommendations of the Task Force reflect a commitment to work toward integration, while cautioning that the process must be done gradually, and with careful planning, supports, and adequate funding. The Task Force's requirements for successful integration included legislative commitment, coordination of all major stakeholders, professional development alternatives, and a delivery system that is "non-categorical, classroom based, consultative and student centred" (Nova Scotia Teachers' Union, 1990, p. 24).

In 1991, the Minister of Education stated that "the issue is no longer whether most students with exceptional needs should or should not be integrated, but what support is needed to be successful" (Publication and Reference Release, Nova Scotia Department of Education, November 26, 1991, p. 1). More recently, the Minister of Education's office has stated that students who are gifted are to be recognized under the rubric of exceptionality, and are to be provided for through special education funding (Policy and Information Release, Nova Scotia Department of Education, August 25, 1992). It will be interesting to observe the fate of progressive trends in Nova Scotia schools over the next few years, and particularly those for funding support.

PRINCE EDWARD ISLAND

The policy for exceptional students in Prince Edward Island is quite straightforward, in that "[w]ith only a few exceptions all children attend public school" (MacLellan, 1990). Education provisions for all students are outlined in the PEI School Act (PEI, 1988), which reflects the philosophy that all students should be able to attend school with their peers. PEI is also a member of APSEA, the joint special education authority of the Atlantic Provinces, which serves primarily individuals with visual and hearing impairments. APSEA recommends that educational needs should be provided whenever possible, in the local district, or, if small numbers dictate, through interdistrict, provincial, or interprovincial services (MacLellan, 1989). Recent years have seen a notable trend toward greater decentralization and the use of itinerant teachers in order that students may remain in their home communities.

MacLellan (1985) raised a number of concerns about mainstreaming, focusing particularly on the need for staff development and in-service, and the need to align educational resources so as to satisfy individual student needs while remaining sensitive to parental wishes. Indeed, over the past decade, there has been an increase in the number of students who receive special education services, as well as significant increases in the number of specialized teachers (MacLellan, 1989). It is of interest to note that PEI has gone full circle: from exceptional children being assigned to regular classrooms; to a period starting in the 1960s in which small classes with specially trained teachers were provided; to an open-ended resource-room concept in which both nonexceptional and exceptional students are served (MacLellan, 1990). Specific actions to promote the mainstreaming of students with exceptional needs in the 1990s include training all elementary teachers to remediate language/learning disability students, and providing province-wide work experience programs for low academic-ability students at the high-school level (MacLellan, 1989).

NEWFOUNDLAND

The Schools Act (Newfoundland, 1987) was enacted in 1970, amended in 1987, and is currently being reviewed by the House of Assembly. It is anticipated that new legislation will follow the direction set forth by the Royal Commission on Newfoundland Education. This appointed group has been involved in a comprehensive review of all aspects of education in Newfoundland, and has recently suggested over two hundred recommendations concerning the Act.

The most recent summary of guidelines for educational provisions for exceptional students in the province of Newfoundland and Labrador is outlined in the 1987 and revised *Special Education Policy Manual* (Government of Newfoundland and Labrador, 1992). Its three major undercurrents are:

(1) individualized programming; (2) team work and decision-making; and (3) the involvement of parents (Melvin, 1990). This comprehensive document provides a clear delineation of Department of Education and school district responsibilities for the provision of special education services, as well as a detailed description of the screening, identification, referral, assessment, and program implementation aspects of service delivery. The policy reflects a noncategorical approach in that it focuses on individual learning strengths and needs as a method of determining appropriate educational learning needs. In support of an integration philosophy, Newfoundland emphasizes an adapted cascade model of service delivery, and, as outlined in Section 2A.4, "Each school district is encouraged to provide a wide range of services to meet the needs of students with exceptionalities within its jurisdiction" (Government of Newfoundland and Labrador, 1992).

What dictates the eventual placement of the child is a team-based assessment of the "most enhancing environment" for a given student. Policy concerning the concept of school-based teams is stipulated in Section 2.D.2., as follows: "Each school district must establish, at the school level, program planning teams responsible for programming, and monitoring" (Government of Newfoundland and Labrador, 1992). Teams would normally comprise the school principal (or vice-principal), the teachers involved, and the parents, and, depending on the individual requirements of the child, the special education coordinator, school counsellor, educational psychologist, speech-language pathologist, and representatives of other outside agencies.

Newfoundland is clearly aligned to an inclusive mosaic approach to serving the needs of all special students, in that it has developed policy on all aspects that are integral to effective program delivery. One of the key features that sets it apart from other provinces is its recognition that funding, training, and qualifications of personnel must be commensurate with service delivery. In Newfoundland, it is acknowledged that without sufficient professional preparation of its primary-service providers (i.e., teachers and special education specialists), the move toward an effective program of service delivery for exceptional students is severely hampered.

CONCLUSION

The brief overview provided in this section of the chapter reveals a wide diversity across the provinces and territories in terms of legislated educational provisions for exceptional children, as well as in the degree of readiness each shows for inclusive education. Just over ten years ago, Vickers (1981) charged that "the [Canadian] legislation is inadequate to achieve what is required. Essentially, the legislation is overly concerned with bureaucratic issues and questions of structure and power. Issues of entitlement and quality are wholly ignored" (p. 97).

Although there have been positive developments over the past decade, it is very clear that more work needs to be done. For example, MacKay (1989) notes that, in the 1990s, school boards will need to consider revising or rewriting their placement and program practices to ensure that they withstand the scrutiny of the law. Similarly, Goguen (1989) predicts that the 1990s should bring further clarification of the concept of "appropriate education," and the greater involvement of parents in educational decision-making. Most likely, we can expect to see more provinces adopt legislation, similar to that in Ontario, the Yukon, and Alberta, in which special education tribunals or review procedures provide a mechanism for conflict resolution between parents and school boards on matters concerning special education and mainstreaming, thus alleviating the need for cumbersome and costly litigation procedures.

◆ SUMMARY

This chapter began with a historical overview of the major events and circumstances that are relevant to the concept of progressive inclusion. Children with exceptionalities were initially neglected or excluded from society in general; however, since the establishment of a general public education system at the turn of the century, there has been progress toward including all students in the general education system. Within the schools, students were typically served in separate classes, and as the special education delivery system grew, so too did the number of special classes and special education categories.

Following a general trend of normalization throughout Canadian communities, and the considerable efforts of parent groups, schools began to create learning placement alternatives that provided a least restrictive environment for students who were identified as being disabled or handicapped. Integration programs were implemented, giving students who had been previously excluded from regular education new opportunities for interaction with their nonhandicapped peers. The philosophical, organizational, and practical problems resulting from a dual system of education for regular and special education led to the current move toward inclusive education.

What sets the inclusive education movement apart from previous movements involving students with exceptional needs is the fact that it is based on the concept of a restructuring and unification of the educational system for all students. Many successful inclusive education schools have abandoned the traditional special education approach to service delivery for students with exceptional learning needs by giving the regular classroom teacher primary responsibility. Moreover, many Canadian schools are incorporating new approaches, such as school-based teaming and collaborative consultation, to smooth this important but difficult transition.

The final section of this chapter examined the law and legislation as it pertains to the education of exceptional students. The fact that education matters are primarily a provincial concern has led to a great diversity of provisions. Some provinces have adopted very detailed and specific legislative solutions, whereas others have put more emphasis on changing resource allocation and philosophy. An overview of current provincial/territorial legislation reveals, however, a generalized trend toward the provision of individually appropriate instruction-based programs for all students within the regular school system.

We are rapidly moving toward a new century, and how we meet the challenge of inclusive education for all Canadian students will depend largely on the preparation, attitudes, and competence of our prospective teachers. Beyond the historical traditions and legislative directions that each province and territory establishes, future teachers will also need to base their pedagogic beliefs and practice on solid theoretical ground. We examine this domain in the next chapter.

QUESTIONS
◆◆◆◆◆◆◆◆◆◆◆◆◆

1. How do permissive legislation and mandated legislation differ? Construct a supportive argument for each.

2. Research on the effects of labelling and classification has been contradictory. Describe the positive and negative ramifications of this categorization practice.

3. Distinguish between "mainstreaming" and "integration" as models of educational service delivery.

4. How can preparation and competence of teachers affect service delivery to students in inclusive education?

5. On the basis of an analysis of each province's and territory's legal provisions for special education, identify the three provinces/territories most ready to implement inclusion. Justify your response.

ACKNOWLEDGEMENTS

Special mention is given to the following individuals for their review and comments on the first draft of the sections concerning the provinces and territories:

Janet Webster, Director, Special Programs, Education, Yukon.

Romeo Beatch, Coordinator, Special Needs, Northwest Territories Education.

Helen Balanoff, Director, Student Support, Northwest Territories Education.

Claudia Roch, Assistant Director, Educational Programs Department, Special Education Branch, Ministry of Education, British Columbia.

Frederica Bowden, Coordinator, Special Education, Ministry of Education, Educational Programs Department, Special Education Programs Branch, British Columbia.

David Jeffaries, Coordinating Director, Appeals and Student Attendance Secretariat, Alberta Education, Alberta.

Harvey Finnestad, Director, Alberta Education Response Centre, Alberta Education, Alberta.

Margaret Lipp, Director of Special Education, Saskatchewan Education, Saskatchewan.

Bert Cenerini, Director, Child Care & Development, Education and Training, Winnipeg, Manitoba.

Anne Jordan Wilson, Professor, Ontario Institute for Studies in Education, Toronto, Ontario.

William Smith, Director, The Learning Centre of Quebec, Montreal, Quebec.

Darlene Perner, Student Services Consultant, Student Services Branch, Department of Education, Fredericton, New Brunswick.

Sonia Mascuich, Assistant Professor, Mount St. Vincent University, Halifax, Nova Scotia.

Elinor MacLellan, Special Education Consultant, Department of Education, Charlottetown, Prince Edward Island.

Edith Furey, Division of Student Support Services, Department of Education, St John's, Newfoundland.

Edie Melvin, Consultant, Division of Student Support Services, Department of Education, St. John's, Newfoundland.

REFERENCES

Abbott, E. (Ed.). (1990). *Chronicle of Canada*, Montreal: Chronicle Publications.

Alberta. (1988). *School Act*. Edmonton, AB: Queen's Printer.

Alberta Department of Education. **(**1989). *Special education policy handbook*. Edmonton, AB: Crown in Right of Alberta.

Beuree, G. (1989). Special education in Nova Scotia: Nova Scotia revisited. In M. Csapo & L. Goguen (Eds.), *Special education across Canada* (pp. 117-125).Vancouver: Centre for Human Development and Research.

Blankenship, C., & Lilly, S. (1981). *Mainstreaming students with learning and behavioral problems*. New York: Holt, Rinehart & Winston.

Bradfield, H. R., Brown, J., Kaplan, P., Rickert, E., & Stannard, R. **(**1973). The special child in the regular classroom. *Exceptional Children, 39*, 384-390.

Brehaut, W. (1984). Trends in the history of Ontario education. In H. Oliver, M. Holmes, & I. Winchester (Eds.), *The house that Ryerson built: Essays in education to mark Ontario's bicentennial* (pp. 7-17). Toronto: OISE Press.

British Columbia. (1989). School Act. Victoria, BC: Queen's Printer.

British Columbia. (1990). *Inter-ministerial protocols for the provision of support services to schools*. Victoria, BC: Queen's Printer.

British Columbia. (1990). *Year 2000: A framework for learning*. Victoria, BC: Queen's Printer.

Budoff, M., & Gottlieb, J. (1976). Special class students mainstreamed: A study of an aptitude (learning potential) x treatment interaction. *American Journal of Mental Deficiency, 81*(1), 1-11.

Cashion, M., Latchford, S. & Mureika, J. (1989). Letter to the Minister of Education on integration policy. *Pathways, 13*(1), 7.

Chambers, J. (1980). A retrospective view of special education. In G. Kysela (Ed.), *The exceptional child in Canadian society*. Canadian Society for Studies in Education, Alberta Social Services and Community Health.

Champoux-Lesage, P. (1989). Special education in Quebec: Summary of present situation and future prospects. In M. Csapo & L. Goguen (Eds.), *Special education across Canada* (pp. 93-102). Vancouver: Centre for Human Development and Research.

Chaves, I. M. (1977). Historical overview of special education in the United States. In P. Bates, T. L. West, & R. B. Schmerl (Eds.), *Mainstreaming: Problems, potentials, and perspectives* (pp. 25-41). Minneapolis: National Support Systems Project.

Church, E. J. M. (1980). Special education in Alberta: Past accomplishments, present issues and future prospects. In M. Csapo & L. Goguen (Eds.), *Special education across Canada: Issues and concerns for the '80s* (pp. 23-38). Vancouver: Centre for Human Development and Research.

Comité provincial de l'enfance inadaptée. (1976). *L'éducation de l'enfance en difficulté d'adaptation et d'apprentissage au Québec*. Quebec: Ministère de l'Éducation.

Conn-Blowers, E. A., & McLeod, H. J. (1989). Special education in Alberta. In M. Csapo & L. Goguen (Eds.), *Special education across Canada* (pp. 19-27). Vancouver: Centre for Human Development and Research.

Constitution Act. (1982). Pt. 1: Charter of Rights and Freedoms [enacted by the Canada Act, 1982 (U.K.) c.11, Sched. B.].

Corman, L., and Gottlieb, J. (1978). Mainstreaming mentally retarded children: A review of research. In N. R. Ellis (Ed.), *International review of research in mental retardation, Volume 9* (pp. 251-275). New York: Academic Press.

Correia, C., & Goguen, L. (1983). *Final report of a study concerning the Auxiliary Classes Act of New Brunswick*. Fredericton, NB: Department of Education.

Council of Ministers of Education, Canada. (1989). *Special education information sharing project: Summary of responses*. Volume 2, No. 7.

Csapo, M., & Goguen, L. (Eds.). (1980). *Special education across Canada*. Vancouver: Centre for Human Development and Research.

Deno, E. (Ed.). (1973). *Instructional alternatives for exceptional children*. Reston, VA: Council for Exceptional Children.

Dunn, L. (1968). Special education for the mildly retarded: Is much of it justifiable? *Exceptional Children, 35*, 5-22.

Freeze, D. R., Bravi, G., & Rampaul, W. E. (1989). Special education in Manitoba: A consultative-collaborative services delivery model. In M. Csapo & L. Goguen (Eds.), *Special education across Canada* (pp. 47-80). Vancouver: Centre for Human Development and Research.

Gartner, A., & Lipsky, D. K. (1987). Beyond special education: Toward a quality system for all students. *Harvard Educational Review, 57*(4), 367-395.

Gearheart, B. R., Weishahn, M. W., & Gearheart, C. J. (1988). *The exceptional student in the regular classroom* (4th ed.). Columbus: Merrill.

Gittins, J. A. (1980). Special education in British Columbia. In M. Csapo & L. Goguen (Eds.), *Special education across Canada: Issues and concerns for the '80s* (pp. 3-14). Vancouver: Centre for Human Development and Research.

Godsell, E. J. (1989). Special education in Newfoundland: Costs, benefits, and funding formulas. In S. B. Lawton, & R. Wignall (Eds.), *Scrimping or squandering?: Financing Canadian schools*. Toronto: OISE Press.

Goguen, L. (1989). Evolving educational rights. In M. Csapo & L. Goguen (Eds.). *Special education across Canada* (pp. 159-166). Vancouver: Centre for Human Development and Research.

Government of Newfoundland and Labrador. (1992). *Special education policy manual*. Department of Education, Division of Special Education Services.

Hallahan, D. P., & Kauffman, J. M. (1991). *Exceptional children: Introduction to special education* (5th ed.). Englewood Cliffs, NJ: Prentice-Hall.

Hardman, M. L., Drew, C. J., Egan, M. W., & Wolf, B. (1990). *Human exceptionality: Society, school, and family* (3rd ed.). Boston: Allyn & Bacon.

Hardy, M. I., McLeod, J., Minto, H., Perkins, S. A., & Quance, W. R. (1971). *Standards for education of exceptional children in Canada: The SEECC report*. Toronto: Leonard Crainford.

Hill, J. L. (1988). Integration in Canada: Implications for the certification of regular education teachers (RETS). *Canadian Journal of Special Education, 4*(2), 123-131.

Idol, L. (1993). *Special educators's consultation handbook* (2nd ed.). Austin, TX: Pro-ed.

Idol, L., Paolucci-Whitcomb, P., & Nevin, A. (1986). Collaborative consultation. Rockville, MD: Aspen Systems.

Jenkins, J. R., Pious, C. G., & Jewell, M. (1990). Special education and the regular education initiative: Basic assumptions. *Exceptional Children, 56*(6). 479-491.

Jeffaries, D. (1991). Personal Communication, February 22.

Kelly, B. (1985). The funding and costs of special education: A report prepared for the Council of Ministers of Education, Canada. Halifax, NS: Department of Education.

Kendall, D. (1987). *A study to recommend future directions in regional service delivery*. Unpublished manuscript submitted to the Board of Directors, Atlantic Provinces Special Education Authority. Halifax, NS.

Kysela, G. (1980). *The exceptional child in Canadian education* (Seventh Yearbook), Canadian Society for the Study of Education.

Larrivée, B. (1981). Effect of in-service training on teacher's attitudes toward mainstreaming. *Exceptional Children, 48,* 34-39.

Lawton, S. B., & Wignall, R. (Eds.). (1989). *Scrimping or squandering?: Financing Canadian schools.* Toronto: OISE Press.

Leavitt, M. (1989). *Teaching all the children: Stories from the classroom.* Fredericton, NB: Department of Education.

Lipsky, D. K., & Gartner, A. (Eds.). (1989). *Beyond separate education: Quality education for all.* Baltimore, MD: Paul H. Brookes.

Lupart, J. L. (1987). Mainstreaming: What do the teachers think? *Calgary Regional Special Education Council Newsletter, 1*(1), 10-11.

MacIntyre, R. (1984). Special education. In H. Oliver, M. Holmes, & I. Winchester (Eds.), *The house that Ryerson built: Essays in education to mark Ontario's bicentennial* (pp. 103-113). Toronto: OISE Press.

MacKay, A. W. (1989). The Elwood case: Vindicating the educational rights of the disabled. In M. Csapo & L. Goguen (Eds.), *Special education across Canada* (pp. 149-157). Vancouver: Centre for Human Development and Research.

MacLellan, E. (1985). Some concerns about mainstreaming. *Canadian Journal of Special Education, 1*(1), 91-93.

MacLellan, E. (1989). Special education in Prince Edward Island. In M. Csapo & L. Goguen (Eds.), *Special education across Canada* (pp. 127-131). Vancouver: Centre for Human Development and Research.

MacLellan, E. (1990). Personal written communication. July 31.

Madden, N. A., & Slavin, R. E. (1983). Mainstreaming students with mild handicaps: Academic and social outcomes. *Review of Educational Research, 53* (4), 519-569.

Mandell, C.J., & Fiscus, E. (1981). *Understanding exceptional people.* New York: West.

Manitoba (1987). *The Public Schools Act.* Winnipeg, MB: Queen's Printer.

Manitoba Department of Education and Training. (1989). *Special education in Manitoba: Policy and procedural guidelines for the education of students with special needs in the public school system.* Winnipeg, Manitoba: Queen's Printer.

McKinney, J. D., & Hocutt, A. M. (1988). Policy issues in the evaluation of the regular education initiative. *Learning Disabilities Focus, 4*(1), 15-23.

McLeod, H.J. (1983). Special education in the 1980's: A decade of crisis and opportunity. *B.C. Journal of Special Education, 7*(3), 221-227.

Melvin, E. (1990). Written communication. July 20.

Mesinger, J. F. (1985). Commentary on "Rationale for the merger of special and special education" or, Is it now time for the lamb to lie down with the lion? *Exceptional Children, 51*(6), 510-512.

Ministère de l'Éducation du Québec. (1979a). *The schools of Quebec: Policy statement and plan of action.* Quebec: Author.

Ministère de l'Éducation du Québec. (1979b). *The schools of Quebec: Policy statement and plan of action: Children with difficulties in learning and adaption.* Quebec: Author.

Nessner, K. (1990). Children with disabilities. *Canadian Social Trends, 19,* 18-20.

Nevin, A., Thousand, J., Paolucci-Whitcomb, P., & Villa, R. (1990). Collaborative consultation: Empowering public school personnel to provide heterogeneous schooling for all—or, Who rang that bell? *Journal of Educational and Psychological Consultation 1*(1), 41-67.

New Brunswick (1973). Schools Act, chapter 5, Auxiliary Classes Act. Fredericton, NB: Queen's Printer.

New Brunswick. (1986). *Bill 85:* An Act to Amend the Schools Act. Fredericton, NB: Queen's Printer.

New Brunswick. (1992). Schools act. Fredericton, NB: Queens Printer.

New Brunswick Department of Education. (1988). *Working guidelines on integration.* Fredericton: Student Services Branch.

Newfoundland. (1987). *The schools act (Teachers' staffing) regulations.* St. John's, Newfoundland: Author.

Northwest Territories. (1976). Education Act. Yellowknife: Queen's Printer.

Northwest Territories Department of Education. (1982). *Learning tradition and change in the Northwest Territories.* Yellowknife: Special Committee on Education.

Northwest Territories Department of Education. (1986). *A departmental directive and guidelines for special needs education.* Yellowknife: Special Committee on Education.

Northwest Territories Department of Education. (1989). *Education in the Northwest Territories.* Yellowknife: Special Committee on Education.

Northwest Territories Department of Education. (1991). *Our students, our future: An educational framework.* Yellowknife: Special Committee on Education.

Nova Scotia Department of Education. (1991). *Publication and Reference Release.* (November 26).

Nova Scotia Department of Education. (1992). *Policy and Information Release.* (August 25).

Nova Scotia Teachers' Union. (1990). *Integration implementation: The Nova Scotia Teachers Union perspective.* Nova Scotia: Nova Scotia Teachers Union.

Ontario. (1980). Education Amendment Act, Bill 82. Toronto: Queen's Printer.

Perner, D. (1991). Personal communication. February 21.

Perner, D., & Roberts, D. (1989). Special education in New Brunswick: Approaching special regular education. In M. Csapo & L. Goguen (Eds.). *Special education across Canada* (pp. 103-115). Vancouver: Centre for Human Development and Research.

Poirier, D., & Goguen, L. (1986). The Canadian Charter of Rights and the right to education for exceptional children. *Canadian Journal of Education, 11,* 231-244.

Poirier, D., Goguen, L., & Leslie, P. (1988). *Exceptional rights of exceptional children in Canada: A national study of multi-level commitments.* Toronto: Carswell.

Porter, G. L. (1991). The methods and resource teacher: A collaborative consultant model. In G. L. Porter & D. Richler (Eds.), *Changing Canadian schools* (pp. 107-154). North York, ON: The Roeher Institute.

Porter, G. L., & Collicott, J. (1992). New Brunswick School Districts 28 and 29: Mandates and strategies that promote inclusive schooling. In R. Villa, J. Thousand, W. Stainback & S. Stainback (Eds.), *Restructuring for caring and effective education: An administrative guide to creating heterogeneous schools* (pp. 187-200). Baltimore, MD: Paul H. Brookes.

Prince Edward Island. (1988). School Act. Charlottetown, P.E.I.: Queen's Printer.

Public Law 94-142. (1975). Federal Register, Department of Health, Education, and Welfare. Vol. 42, No. 163, 121a.13.

Quebec. Education Act, S.Q. (1988) c. 84. Consolidated as Education Act, R.S.Q., c. 1-13.3.

Ramasut, A. (Ed.). (1989). *Whole school approaches to special needs*. London: Falmer.

Reynolds, M. C. (1989). An historical perspective: The delivery of special education to mildly disabled and at-risk students. *Remedial and Special Education, 10*(6), 7-11.

Reynolds, M. C., & Birch, J. W. (1988). *Adaptive mainstreaming: A primer for teachers and principals* (3rd ed.). New York: Longman.

Reynolds, M. C, Wang, M. C., & Walberg, H. J. (1987). The necessary restructuring of special and regular education. *Exceptional Children, 53*(5), 391-398.

Roberts, D. (1987). New Brunswick special education: A new beginning. *Education New Brunswick—Journal Edition*, 14-18.

Roberts, C. A., & Lazure, M. D. (Eds.). (1970). *One million children: A national study of Canadian children with emotional and learning disorders*. Toronto: Leonard Crainford.

Robichaud, O., & Enns, R. (1980). The integration issue. In M. Csapo & L. Goguen (Eds.), *Special education across Canada: Issues and concerns for the '80s* (pp. 201-214). Vancouver: Centre for Human Development and Research.

Roch (1991). Letter to author, May 2, 1991.

Royal Commission on Education. (1988). *A legacy for learners: Summary of findings*. British Columbia.

Ruhl, K. (1983). Mainstreaming. In R. E. Schmid and L. M. Nagata (Eds.), *Contemporary issues in special education* (2nd ed.) (pp. 2-25). New York: McGraw-Hill.

Saskatchewan. (1978). *The education act*. Regina, SK: Queen's Printer.

Saskatchewan Department of Education. (1989). *Special education policy manual*.

Sherman, S. (1988). Understanding and accepting exceptional students. *Manitoba Journal of Counselling, 14*(4), 5-8.

Silverman, H., Wilson, A. K., & Seller, W. (1987). *The Education Amendment Act, 1980 (Bill 82). Implementation study: Board policies and school level practices*. Toronto: Queen's Printer for Ontario.

Slavin, R. E. (1990). General education under the regular education initiative: How must it change? *Remedial and Special Education, 11* (3), 40-50.

Smith, W. J. (1989). *The education of exceptional children in Quebec: A study of government policy goals and legislative action*. Montreal: Service des relations professionnelles Talleyrand.

Smith, W. J. (1992). Special education policy in Quebec: Evolution or status quo? *Education Canada, 32*(1), 40-48.

Special Education Information Handbook. (1984). Toronto, ON: Ministry of Education.

Standing Committee on Human Resources. (1990). *Learning disabled students in the Nova Scotia public school system*. First Session of the Fifty-Fifth General Assembly, Halifax, NS.

Stainback, S., Stainback, W. (1984). A rationale for the merger of special and regular education. *Exceptional Children, 51*, 102-111.

Stainback, S., Stainback, W., & Bunch, G. (1989a). A rationale for the merger of regular and special education. In S. Stainback, W. Stainback, & M. Forest, (Eds.), *Educating all students in the mainstream of regular education* (pp. 15-26). Baltimore, MD: Paul H. Brookes.

Stainback, W., Stainback, S., & Bunch, G. (1989b). Introduction and historical background. In S. Stainback, W. Stainback & M. Forest (Eds.), *Educating all students in the mainstream of regular education* (pp. 3-26). Baltimore, MD: Paul H. Brookes.

Stainback, S., Stainback, W., & Forest, M. (Eds.). (1989). *Educating all students in the mainstream of regular education*. Baltimore, MD: Paul H. Brookes.

Vickers, D. H. (1981). Special students, special laws and special programs. *B.C. Journal of Special Education, 5*(2), 92-102.

Villa, R. A., Thousand, J. S., Stainback, W., & Stainback, S. (Eds.). (1992). *Restructuring for caring and effective education: An administrative guide to creating heterogeneous schools*. Baltimore, MD: Paul H. Brookes.

Walker, G. (1981). *Report of the Commission on Public Education Finance*. Halifax: Ministry of Education.

Wang, M. C., Reynolds, M. C., & Walberg, H. J. (Eds.). (1987). *Handbook of special education: Research and Practice, Volume 1: Learner Characteristics and adaptive education*. Oxford: Pergamon.

Wilson, A. K. (1983). *A consumer's guide to Bill 82: Special education in Ontario*. Occasional Papers/22. Toronto: OISE Press.

Wilson, A. K. (1984). *Opening the door: The key to resource models*. Toronto: Ontario Public School Teachers' Federation.

Wilson, A. K. (1989). Ontario's "Bill 82" in retrospect. In M. Csapo & L. Goguen (Eds.), *Special education across Canada* (pp. 81-92). Vancouver: Centre for Human Development and Research.

Winzer, M. (1985). Teacher attitudes toward mainstreaming: An appraisal of the research. *B.C. Journal of Special Education, 9*(2), 149-161.

Winzer, M. (1990). *Children with exceptionalities: A Canadian perspective* (2nd ed.). Scarborough, ON: Prentice-Hall.

Wolfensberger, W., Nirge, B., Olshansky, S., Perske, R, & Roos, P. (1972). *The principle of normalization in human services*. Toronto, ON: National Institute on Mental Retardation.

Wolfensberger, W. (1984). Social role valorization: A proposed new term for the principle of normalization. *Mental Retardation, 21*(6), 234-239.

Yukon Territory. (1990). *Statutes of the Yukon 1990 Education Act*. Government of the Yukon: Queen's Printer.

Zuker, M. A. (1988). *The legal context of education*. Toronto: OISE Press.

THEORETICAL FOUNDATIONS OF INCLUSIVE EDUCATION

CHAPTER OBJECTIVES

To determine how educational psychology theory has shaped special education knowledge.

To understand cognitive development in terms of information-processing theory, developmental theory, and sociocultural theory.

To differentiate between the definition of exceptionality and normalcy from each theoretical perspective.

To comprehend the educational implications of information-processing theory, developmental theory, and sociocultural theory.

To discuss the significance of each theory's contribution to the evolution of educational programming.

Jim and Sally live on an acreage outside a small town in a rural district in Manitoba. Jim is the vice-principal of the local high school, and his subject specialization is industrial arts. In fact, Jim is what most people would call a tinkerer, and during his spare time he is often found downstairs in the workshop working on some new fix-it project. Sally is a homemaker kept very busy caring for their active, four-year-old son Matthew. Matthew has a most inquisitive nature and loves nothing better than to be with his father down in the workshop. Acting as Daddy's assistant, Matthew beams with pride when a project is successfully completed and presented to his mother.

This particular day was Sunday, and Jim and Sally were enjoying a few extra hours of sleeping in. Sud-

denly, they were awakened by a loud clamour and cat squeal. Both leaped out of bed and dashed out into the kitchen, silently hoping that what awaited them out there wasn't as bad as it sounded. At the doorway, they stood still as they surveyed the room. There, by the counter, was Matthew, looking somewhat scared and a bit bewildered, holding a can of machine oil. Hovering guardedly in a far corner was Toby, the pet cat. His lovely rust-coloured fur was matted, sticking out in sharp spikes in all directions, and small drops of oil were beginning to drip to the floor. Jim and Sally's heads turned back to Matthew as they puzzled about the scene before them. Sally spoke first. "Matthew, what on earth has been going on here?" Matthew responded, "Well, the cat was squeaking, so I oiled him."

◆ INTRODUCTION

In the opening vignette, Matthew's linking his understanding of himself as his father's helper in the workshop inappropriately to the presumed condition of a cat might demonstrate an advanced ability to problem-solve, but it is clear to any adult that his solution was faulty. Information adults take for granted is not necessarily part of a child's reality. Children are not simply miniature models of adults, who perceive and understand the world in the same way. Most adults have an intuitive sense that children think differently from adults, but would be hard pressed to explain exactly how and why this is so.

The prospective inclusive education teacher who might have Matthew in the classroom must address certain questions. How can Matthew's unique learning needs and strengths be understood? How should the learning environment be structured to provide the necessary support and differentiation to foster the development of Matthew's problem-solving abilities and self-directed learning? How will his needs change from one grade level to the next? If Matthew is gifted, how will his learning needs be different from those of other students in the class? Whereas most teacher preparation programs concentrate on subject area specialization and instructional methods related to the discipline, the inclusive education teacher who adopts a student-centred approach will need to gain an understanding of the typical and exceptional developmental patterns of children. The theoretical foundations of these patterns are found in the field of educational psychology. This chapter will provide an overview of current theory and implications for inclusive education practice.

◆ INTERFACE OF THEORY AND PRACTICE

WHAT IS A THEORY?

A theory can be simply defined as a system of ideas that explains some area of interest. Theories can be broad in scope (e.g., a theory of evolution), or they can be based on principles of a specific subject (e.g., a theory of equations in mathematics). Theories can be speculative and loosely defined, as when one refers to a personal pet theory about male and female relationships, or they can be scientifically built on formally tested results. In the discipline of education, scientific observation is used to organize, summarize, and simplify knowledge useful to teaching practice. Hence, a theory of reading comprehension should include not only tested observations that can assist teachers in planning instruction in reading comprehension, but also broader explanations of the important relationships among the observations.

In education, these relationships are often organized according to a set of principles or a model. For example, educators rely on psychological principles to understand human development and behaviour. Principles are used

*read &
understand*

to make predictions about what is important, and probable, with respect to various aspects of children's learning, development, and growth. Similarly, a model, such as a model of reading comprehension, provides a blueprint or pictorial representation of the factors or elements believed to be most important to the understanding of reading comprehension.

In such disciplines as physics and mathematics, theories can be generated from absolute laws (often expressed in the form of equations) that are both predictive and infallible. In contrast, knowledge of the discipline in education must be applied to human behaviour. Consequently, the principles and models that guide teaching practice are not totally infallible, and are often revised, adapted, and even replaced when new observations or research cannot be adequately explained by the theory (or theories, if competing theories exist). Research provides the objective examination of a problem, or set of relationships, according to systematic procedures that are developed within a given discipline or area of interest. The research domains that contribute to educational practice stem from a variety of disciplines such as philosophy, sociology, psychology, education, science, and linguistics; however, the area of particular relevance for inclusive education is educational psychology.

The field of educational psychology is uniquely centred on the study of the teaching and learning process. The field, which brings together the disciplines of education and psychology, was beginning to form as a distinct discipline in North America at the turn of the century. From the start, two traditional perspectives have predominated in education—one based on Dewey's pragmatism, or functionalist view of education theory, and the other based on Thorndike's positivism, or scientific view of education theory (Hilgard, 1987). Functionalism attempted to apply psychology to real-life problems, with major emphasis on the development of theories of learning. Dewey's progressive education movement "was based on a philosophy of experiment, use, and innovation" (Walberg & Hartel, 1992, p. 9). Education was to be fashioned on the basis of children's needs and the ability to adapt in a changing world. Educational theorists and researchers who adopted this tradition were primarily concerned with the study of curricular innovations and approaches to be implemented in various schools, and with the devising of appropriate appraisal methods and evaluation techniques.

In contrast, Thorndike took the view that instructional practice and selection of instructional materials must be informed by psychological principles and experimental investigation. Although their research was primarily focused on the study of memory, attention, and habit in relation to learning, Thorndike and his colleagues also studied, over a period of forty years, animal intelligence and learning, laws of learning, statistical methods in education and psychology, achievement tests, group intelligence tests, individual differences, the preparation of instructional materials, and children's vocabulary (Charles, 1987).

As attitudes, concepts, and ideas about student exceptionality and the role of the school changed over the course of the century (see Chapter 2), so

◆ **behaviourist theory:** theory of educational psychology that focuses on observable behaviours, factors that relate to changes in behaviour, and the acquisition of new skills or knowledge that can be measured

too did educational psychology theory. **Behaviourist theory,** which has its roots in Thorndike positivism, significantly shaped much of the early thinking concerning differences in human abilities and behaviour, and was the impetus for a plethora of research studies examining student performance in virtually all areas of exceptionality. This knowledge base strongly influenced instructional procedures, and continues to have relevance for contemporary classrooms (we return to behaviourist theory later in this chapter).

Current thinking in educational psychology is dominated by cognitive theory, which has emerged over the past forty years. In general terms, cognitive theory pertains to the processes and mechanisms underlying human learning and development (Sternberg, 1984), and to the factors and influences that foster it (Slavin, 1988; Moll, 1990). Cognitive theory covers a broad spectrum of sub-areas in educational psychology, including information processing, memory, attention, cognitive strategies, learning, cognitive development, intelligence, creativity, exceptionality, the sociohistorical basis of cognition, instructional design, cognitive process-based instruction, as well as cognition and metacognition. The contribution of three cognitive theories that have relevance for teachers in an inclusive classroom will be examined in greater detail later in the chapter.

HOW DO THEORIES INFLUENCE PRACTICE?

◆ **educational psychology:** scientific study of factors important in creating educational environments that promote and nurture a child's intellectual and personal growth

Educational psychology is the scientific study of factors that help create educational environments designed to nurture intellectual and personal growth in children. The learner, the teacher, and the interactions between them are the basic areas of focus. Teachers are responsible for imparting the skills, knowledge, attitudes, and values that enable children to function effectively and independently in society. Their professional role is to translate experience, research, and theory into effective teaching practice in the classroom, and to be aware of the diversity of learning abilities and levels of cognitive development in their students. How can theory prepare the prospective teacher for the multifaceted role that inclusive education entails?

One way to understand the process is to consider a library subject catalogue in relation to the expanding knowledge base of educational psychology. At the beginning of the century, the indexes under this topic would have been limited to a few broad subheadings such as learning, intelligence, individual differences, and classroom instruction and management. As new theories became available, the knowledge base expanded to include applications to new subject areas, instruction procedures, classroom management and discipline approaches, and testing/assessment strategies. While this expansion of information sources has led to substantial improvements in instruction and in student learning, it has created a dilemma for those who are associated with the education field, namely, how can the individual teacher assimilate all there is to know?

Without an organizing framework, a whole library of research findings and educational principles is of limited value. When an individual visits the library to obtain information about a particular subject or topic, material can be quickly found by referring to the indexes organized on the basis of author, title, or subject. If the subject is unfamiliar, it is likely that the individual will initially choose materials that provide a broad overview of the topic. If, for example, the individual was interested in learning how to play chess, the reading materials on this subject would become more sophisticated as the person gained more experience in actually playing chess.

For the prospective teacher of students in an inclusive classroom, a somewhat similar process is experienced. A choice is made to enter the teaching profession, and having already experienced several years of being a student, and having observed a variety of teachers, the individual will likely already have a speculative or implicit theory about what teaching and learning are all about. Teacher preparation programs provide the initial phase of what becomes, for effective teachers, a lifelong learning process. The knowledge base of the discipline is presented over a variety of courses and practicum experiences, as students are introduced to relevant theory and research, and to the process of critically reviewing the available literature. By the time they successfully complete the teaching degree requirements, students will have acquired an extensive theory and knowledge base, along with basic professional competencies, to begin their teaching careers.

Some teachers erroneously believe that the learning process ends with the completion of formal studies. But effective teachers, like the novice chess player in the earlier example, reflect daily on classroom activity, and approach teaching as a constant problem-solving experience. Every interaction with students and colleagues offers an opportunity to reflect on the guiding theories that are germane to the discipline, and to confirm and rediscover those ideas that have the greatest applicability and utility for achieving student success. With increasing experience a teacher may find that some theories are of limited practical application, and yet provide a larger picture or framework to sort out the multitude of factors and circumstances that contribute to student success. Certain theories may provide explicit direction in planning instructional events or groupings, while others may offer direction in serving students with exceptional learning needs. Still others may be rejected entirely.

HOW DOES EDUCATIONAL PSYCHOLOGY THEORY APPLY TO INCLUSIVE EDUCATION?

There is no simple, straightforward answer to this question. No single textbook, research study, or theory covers all that one needs to know. Moreover, knowledge can be interpreted in a variety of ways, depending on one's perspective or experiences. In the past, teacher preparation programs were, for the most part, designed separately for regular and special education teachers.

However, it has become increasingly evident that, if the needs of a diverse student population within the inclusive classroom are to be met, the theory and knowledge base that was formerly imparted only to special education teachers must be made accessible to all teachers. Accordingly, teachers will need to know more about the typical and atypical cognitive growth and development patterns of children, and about ways to assess student talents, needs, and progress. Moreover, they will need to become familiar with the theories and research that have shaped special education knowledge: assessment procedures and strategies, the diversity of student learning and development, differentiated teaching approaches, instructional and behavioural management strategies, and curriculum adaptations for students unable to learn successfully in traditional regular classrooms.

Readers of this text are among the first generation of teachers who will be exposed to the developing concepts, principles, and theories of inclusive education as part of their initial teacher preparation. The majority of their teacher colleagues will have experienced traditional programs, and may, consequently, be reluctant to adopt inclusive education philosophy and practice. On the other hand, effective teachers who use a reflective, lifelong learning approach to their teaching will be interested in discovering new forms of knowledge that will enable them to better serve the needs of all students. In addition, effective teachers will be interested in sharing insights, gained over years of teaching practice, that can assist the novice inclusive education teacher in the effective application of his/her knowledge base.

◇ BEHAVIOURIST THEORY   *Know what its about*

The work of early behaviourist pioneers such as John B. Watson, Edwin Guthrie, and Edward L. Thorndike led the discipline of educational psychology away from the interest in internal mental processes toward the scientific, experimental analysis of observable behaviours. The goal for behavioural theorists was to systematically examine behaviour of all living beings in order to establish basic laws of learning. All forms of learning were to be systematically sequenced and controlled on the basis of predictable stimulus-response patterns. Behaviourist theory thus focuses on observable behaviours, the factors that relate to changes in behaviour, and the acquisition of new knowledge or skills that can be measured.

Early work in the behavioural theoretical tradition revealed that stimulus-response patterns could be significantly altered by associating new stimuli with stimuli that automatically produced predictable responses. For example, classical conditioning experiments carried out by Pavlov and his colleagues in the late 1800s and early 1900s revealed that the presentation of a piece of meat to a hungry dog resulted in an automatic salivation response. When a neutral stimulus, such as the ringing of a bell, was presented along with the meat over successive trials, it alone eventually triggered the salivation response in the dog. Through such experiments, behaviours previously

• Know theorists

thought to be automatic and reflexive, such as salivating, were shown to be learned responses. The careful observation and measurement techniques pioneered in these early experiments were particularly influential in later behavioural learning studies.

Critical of classical conditioning experiments that were limited to a relatively small set of behaviours, B. F. Skinner proposed a broader class of behaviours he referred to as *operant*, in that they operated in the environment and were not dependent on unconditioned stimuli such as food. **Operant conditioning** was formulated on the observation that painful and pleasurable consequences were reliable predictors of behaviour decrease and increase, respectively. Using animal and human subjects, Skinner's experiments established reliable laws of reinforcement, punishment, extinction, stimulus control, shaping, and discrimination, which came to be widely and successfully applied in many dimensions of educational practice.

Some Skinnerian concepts that are still evident in teaching practice today include the use of teaching machines to individualize instruction; programmed instruction and specific programs such as Direct Instruction System for Teaching Achievement and Remediation (DISTAR) (Becker & Englemann, 1978); the use of behavioural objectives, hierarchical analysis, and **task analysis** in instructional design; criterion-referenced assessment; and the use of praise, tangible rewards, behavioural contracts, charting and graphing behaviour changes, time-out procedures, and group-based contingencies for individual and classroom management (Lefrançois, 1988; Vander Zanden, 1980; Rosser & Nicholson, 1984; Slavin, 1988; Walberg & Haertel, 1992). Many of these concepts and their contemporary derivatives, are described in subsequent chapters of this text.

Despite the widespread applicability of universal laws of learning, behavioural theory has drawn substantial criticism. First, Lefrançois (1988) points out that teachers' use of behavioural principles is limited in that the most powerful reinforcers for many students are their own peers or their parents; thus, teacher use of grades or praise may be of lesser positive reinforcement value than is commonly supposed. A second area of concern is that behavioural principles are restricted to maintaining desirable behaviours that students already demonstrate, and offer no solution to the more pressing instructional problem of how to elicit a particular behaviour or response in the first place.

A third criticism, raised by Slavin (1988), concerns generalization of learning. Controlled behavioural management that is successfully introduced in a particular setting or environment does not automatically transfer to behavioural improvement in other settings. For example, student-attending behaviour might be improved in the Science class through the implementation of a behavioural contracting system in which the student earns so many points for in-class attention over a specified number of minutes. However, in the absence of a similar arrangement in the Social Studies class with a different teacher, it is highly unlikely that the student will demonstrate similar

◆ operant conditioning: broad class of behaviours that operate in an environment of instructional manipulations and outcome performance

◆ task analysis: the breaking down of a task into components and logically sequencing learning activities to master these subtasks

levels of improvement in attending behaviour. Simply dealing with the observable behaviour may be helpful for a student, or group of students, in a given classroom situation; however, if the efforts of the teacher do not lead to similar desirable behaviour in other settings, then the usefulness of this kind of effort is in question. Thus, the greatest limitation of behaviourist theory is that the responsibility for behaviour change rests mostly with the teacher, and consequently does little to encourage the student to use new learning independently. Cognitive theory, to which we turn now, offers an alternative way of viewing student learning and development, and places major emphasis on the importance of students becoming self-directive or self-regulatory in their learning.

◇ COGNITIVE PSYCHOLOGY AND THEORY

Over the last forty years, cognitive theory has provided the impetus for a renewed interest in the unobservable mental processes important to student learning and development. Neisser (1976) defines **cognition** as "the activity of knowing: the acquisition, organization, and the use of knowledge" (p. 1). This perspective, and its associated applications for teaching, are in sharp contrast to behavioural approaches. Behaviourism, as noted earlier, implicitly views all learners as being initially the same; differences in their behaviours are attributed to the fact that the environments and conditions individuals are exposed to are unique. Cognitive theorists, on the other hand, believe that individuals vary significantly in their learning, and that it is "the individual's pre-existing network of concepts, strategies, and understanding that makes experience meaningful" (Lefrançois, 1988, p. 54). In contrast to the behaviourist perspective, cognitive theory shifts the focus to "the relationships among external factors (e.g., instructional manipulations and outcome performance) and internal factors (e.g., learning processes, learning outcomes, and the existing knowledge and skill of the learner)" (Mayer, 1987, pp. 4-5).

◆ cognition: the process of acquiring, organizing, and using knowledge

This is not to suggest that one theoretical perspective cancels out the other, as each answers very different questions about student learning. Nevertheless, the voluminous research and educational applications literature generated by cognitive theory confirms its practical significance for teachers. Three theories in particular offer much promise in helping educators understand the unique learning and social needs of children with exceptionalities, and how these needs can be addressed in the inclusive classroom. These are: (1) information-processing theory; (2) developmental theory; and (3) sociocultural theory.) For an overview of the three theoretical domains, the leading theorists, and their associated key word descriptors, see Figure 3.1.) For the balance of this chapter, each theory will be briefly outlined, then discussed more specifically in terms of its contributions to our understanding of the learning needs of students who are exceptional.

Figure 3.1
Cognitive Theories for Educational Practice

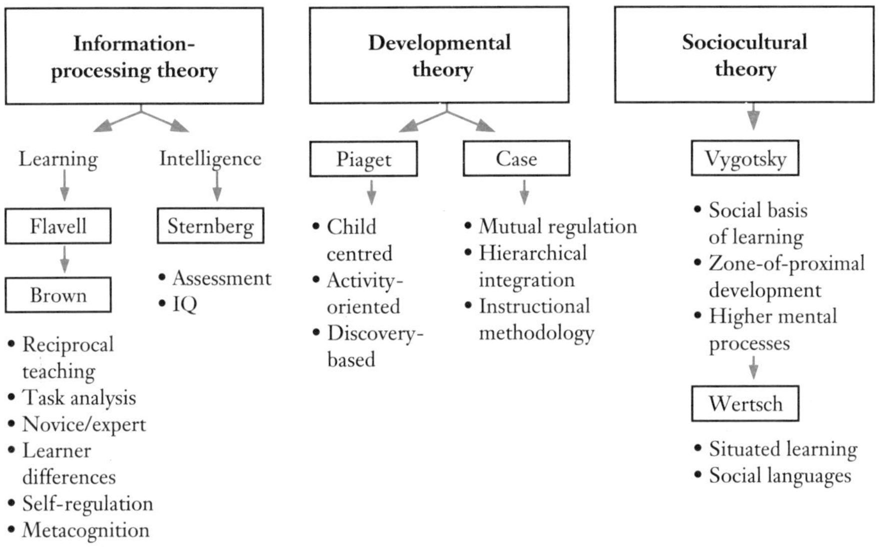

Information-processing theory	Developmental theory	Sociocultural theory

Information-processing theory → Learning, Intelligence

Learning → Flavell → Brown
- Reciprocal teaching
- Task analysis
- Novice/expert
- Learner differences
- Self-regulation
- Metacognition

Intelligence → Sternberg
- Assessment
- IQ

Developmental theory → Piaget, Case

Piaget →
- Child centred
- Activity-oriented
- Discovery-based

Case →
- Mutual regulation
- Hierarchical integration
- Instructional methodology

Sociocultural theory → Vygotsky
- Social basis of learning
- Zone-of-proximal development
- Higher mental processes

→ Wertsch
- Situated learning
- Social languages

◆ INFORMATION-PROCESSING THEORY

A computer metaphor is often used to describe the focus of information-processing theories. In essence, it is assumed that the human brain and the computer process information in similar ways, and that we can use much of the knowledge that has been derived from computer programming to generate hypotheses about how the brain functions. In the same way that computer programmers need to map out every single step for all operations—simple and complex—to achieve a desired output, information-processing theorists concentrate on mapping out all aspects associated with human cognitive performance. An understanding of how children process information and acquire new knowledge and skills is essential to the practice of instruction. Information-processing models have provided teachers with new ways of understanding the capacities and limitations of children for learning new information, skills, and attitudes. These characteristics, along with the rigour of information-processing methodology, make this theoretical approach especially attractive for educators.

Nevertheless, reservations have been expressed. Miller (1989) criticizes information-processing models on three fronts. First, the computer metaphor is too constricting a description of human processing, especially as it relates to areas such as memory. Second, unlike general models, information-processing models tend to be highly specific to a limited set of behaviours, as well as somewhat limited in describing changes in the relationships among several areas of behaviour, and in explaining the actual course of development. Third, information-processing models are relatively insensitive to contextual aspects of learning and behaviour; educational researchers using the information-processing framework have tended to ignore external factors affecting learning (e.g., teacher expectations/decision-making and class size/composition), internal factors (e.g., motivation and self-concept), and, more importantly, the interactive effects of these areas.

Two strands of investigation that currently dominate information-processing approaches to the study of school-age children are the *learning theories approach* and the *theories of intelligence approach*. The learning theories approach is widely used in several educational contexts, primarily for curriculum development purposes, the development of effective teaching strategies, and the determination of learning differences of students with exceptional needs.

INFORMATION PROCESSING AND LEARNING

Learning can be described as the process of taking in information and being able to access it in future situations when it might be useful. A student asked to describe a learning event from the past might recall studying for an exam, and be able to report on the success of the event by stating the mark received. As to how they absorbed the information required for the exam, most students would reply that they read the text and notes, and devised strategies to summarize important points and commit them to memory. This describes conscious learning that is carried out to achieve a specific goal, and underlines the fact that memory and attention to specific aspects of information play an important role in the learning process.

For many decades, cognitive learning theory and research focused on the areas of attention and memory. This research helped cognitive learning theorists describe the process by which information is either remembered or forgotten. Information processing in memory was extensively examined using the box model originally proposed by Broadbent (1958), and later modified by Atkinson and Shiffrin (1968). Research in this area typically involved an examination of all the processes by which sensory information is taken in, transformed, stored, retrieved, and used. *Sensory information* refers to what is taken in from the external world by the senses, in other words, seeing, hearing, smelling, tasting, and touching. The *box model* includes specific temporal-structural components of the memory system (i.e., sensory store, short-term store [STS], and long-term store [LTS]). The components (see Figure 3.2) associated with memory processes are typically mapped out in a series of boxes, and their respective size, location, and processes of interaction are the elements of central interest.

According to the box (or modal) model, processing begins when information from the external environment is entered into the infinite capacity sensory store through the senses. Unless the information is immediately processed (*attention*), decay results and information is lost. Further processing allows information to enter the limited capacity short-term store where the information is cycled (*rehearsal*) and, if left here, is also subject to decay.

Figure 3.2
Box Model of Memory

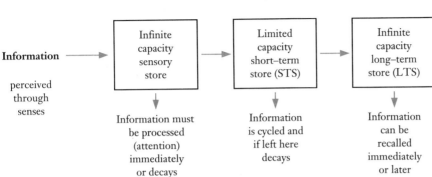

Information that enters the long-term store may be recalled immediately or at some later time; the capacity of the long-term store is considered to be infinite. Thus, retention is considered to relate directly to the amount of time items remained in the memory stores. Although processing of the items is included in the model, the central focus for several decades of research remained with the various structures and capacities of the memory stores.

Models of attention were similarly depicted as structural systems. Broadbent (1958) introduced the *filter theory model*, which assumes that only one stimulus can be perceived at a time. In the case of two competing bits of sensory information, while one of the items is immediately perceived, the other is held momentarily as an unanalyzed echo or image; perceptual analysis of the first item must be completed before echoes can be analyzed. The filter theory model suggests a blocking of irrelevant perceptual information by means of selective filtering, so that the physical properties of high information value concerning the event are attended to first. Later models challenged whether the information gets selected early or later on in perceptual analysis, and whether the selection is based on physical or meaningful information about the event.

Research and theory in the field of mental retardation and learning disability has been highly influenced by the box model (Ellis, 1970; Fisher & Zeamon, 1973). For example, early research in memory and exceptionality often involved a comparison of information-processing abilities of exceptional and nonexceptional children. The inferior memory performance of individuals who were identified as mentally retarded was widely attributed to a defective short-term memory store. Thus, the box model of memory resulted in a structural—or deficit—interpretation of observed memory performance limitations.

A major shift in the conceptualization of memory was advanced by Craik and Lockhart (1972) with the *levels of analysis memory model*, which placed major emphasis on the type and quality of processing an individual experienced while taking in new information. Contrasting the two models, Brown (1974) notes that in the box memory model "STS is a structural feature of the memory system. In a levels of analysis approach, processes subsumed under the heading STS in information processing models are seen as the result of deliberate strategic devices employed by the subject" (p. 58). Thus, research interest shifted to the examination of the strategies individuals used to facilitate memory performance, as well as the circumstances that led them to use one strategy over another.

The distinction between structural features and control processes subsequently gained prominence in the developmental literature (Brown, 1975), particularly that pertaining to children with exceptional needs (Butterfield & Belmont, 1975; Brown, 1974; Torgesen, 1978). According to Torgesen (1978), "the structural features have to do with the basic capacities of the system and perhaps how rapidly the processes are executed, while the control processes describe activities which the organism engages in to maximize the performance of a limited capacity system" (p. 61). When the distinction is applied to children who are exceptional, the structural features can be considered as either more or less permanent (e.g., disability or deficit), or developmentally determined. The *deficit approach* takes the view that there is some specific causal factor (e.g., genetic, neurological, brain damage) that is directly responsible for the impaired functioning of the individual. The *maturational lag perspective* emphasizes the fact that learning improves with age and maturity, and for students with learning disabilities limitations are typically apparent in only one or two subject areas, such as reading or math. In the latter case, the problem is considered structural in that the ability of the student to perform certain tasks is developmentally constrained. Gallagher (1966) attributes this to the notion of developmental imbalance, the assumption being that development has "lagged" behind in specific areas and manifests itself in an inability to perform certain tasks.

In contrast, control processes refer to any processes or strategies in the child's repertoire of resources that can be used in any learning or problem-solving situation. The utility of the distinction is advanced by Brown (1974), who points out that structural features are of interest to those who are concerned with the labelling (causal) or identification of children with special needs, whereas control processes are of interest to those who are more practically concerned with how to remedy the problem.

As contemporary concepts of memory became more widely known, there were a number of significant changes in the research. Brown and French (1979) drew attention to the division between research and the real-life needs and contexts of the people being studied, and others were quick to point out that the problem was particularly acute when applied to students with exceptional needs (Brooks & Baumeister, 1977; Gaylord-Ross, 1979). Research in cognitive learning and associated applications in IQ and achievement tests had produced little more than fairly accurate predictions of the school failure of students who were slow learners or learning disabled. In contrast to the overwhelming evidence concerning these students' deficiencies, little attention had been given to what capabilities they had, or what learning conditions and tasks worked best for them. Hence, cognitive learning studies moved out of the experimental laboratory and into everyday home and school environments.

During the 1970s, there was a proliferation of studies on the learning abilities of young children and children with exceptional learning needs. Information-processing theory played a prominent role in generating new questions important to the understanding of children's learning. One such question was how the processing capabilities and knowledge base of the child differed from those of the adult. Following a series of studies on memory in young children, Flavell (1970) found (1) that improved memory ability is characterized by the gradual accumulation of a repertoire of memory strategies and processes, and (2) that young children and children with learning difficulties have two major deficits that differentiate their memory abilities from those of adults. The first deficit is a **mediation deficiency**, which becomes apparent when a child is unable to use a memory-enhancing strategy, such as rehearsal, even when instructed to use it. In other words, training in how to rehearse items to be remembered does not improve memory performance. This implies a developmentally related structural limitation in the sense that the child is insufficiently mature to benefit from the induced mediating strategy (Brown, 1974). The second deficit is a **production deficiency,** which arises when a child who may have learned from previous instruction how to use the rehearsal strategy fails to spontaneously use it in situations where it could be effective. This deficiency can be alleviated by providing instruction and experience with tasks for which the rehearsal strategy is productive.

Two studies by Flavell, Beach, and Chinsky (1966), and Keeney, Cannizzo, and Flavell (1967) dealt with rehearsal as an organizational process. The results of the first study revealed that with increasing age (Kindergarten to Grade 6) there was greater recall and a greater amount of rehearsal. The second study examined the rehearsal performance of three groups of Grade 1 students. One group consisted of children who rarely or never rehearsed, whereas children in the other two groups were usual rehearsers. For the first ten trials, all children were instructed to rehearse, and subsequent recall was found to be similar for all groups. No instructions to rehearse were given on the second battery of trials. The results showed that the majority of non-rehearsers dropped their rehearsal activities, and, subsequently, their recall performance diminished; in contrast, all the usual rehearsers maintained their initial high-recall performance levels. Hence, the nonrehearsers were considered to have a production deficiency.

Related studies carried out by Brown and her associates (Brown, 1972; 1974; Brown, Campione, Bray, & Wilcox; 1974, Brown, Campione, & Murphy, 1974) demonstrated similar patterns in the memory abilities of students with moderate learning handicaps, and showed that such strategies could not only be learned but could also be retained over a lengthy period. These studies lent convincing support to the notion that memory-processing

◆ mediation deficiency: a developmentally related structural limitation or immaturity evidenced by a child's inability, despite adequate instruction, to use a strategy

◆ production deficiency: the inability to use a learning strategy spontaneously even when it is part of one's repertoire of strategies

differences between children, children with handicaps, and adults were not due to the structure of the memory system, but to the tendency to adopt (or not to adopt) the active rehearsal strategy.

In a similar vein, Chi (1976) criticized structural models of memory for their theoretical limitations. Following an exhaustive research review, she found no evidence to support the claim of structural theorists that STM capacity increases with age. There was, however, substantial evidence to suggest that the processing strategies used by adults are unavailable or deficient in children. Chi (1976) proposed that such deficits can be explained in terms of "the lack of proper control processes (or processing strategies), as well as an impoverished LTM knowledge base rather than a limitation in STM capacity" (p. 559). The importance of the knowledge base in explaining memory differences was later reaffirmed. Chi and Glaser's (1985) study concluded that a child's knowledge base might differ from an adult's in terms of the amount of information stored, the organization of that information, and the number and strength of pathways through that information. Moreover, as it would be anticipated, a limited LTM affects memory processing in terms of how new information is taken in, and how this information is recalled.

general

Another concept, introduced by Flavell (1970), relevant to differences in child and adult memory performance is **metamemory**. This term refers to individuals' self-knowledge about their own memory capabilities, the mnemonic requirements of different tasks, potential strategies for meeting task demands, and strategies for capitalizing on one's own capabilities. Thus, optimal **metamemory performance** involves selecting and assessing strategies most appropriate for carrying out a task (Fry & Lupart, 1987). A classic study of this phenomenon was carried out by Kreutzer, Leonard, and Flavell (1975), who used an interview approach to examine how children at different age levels (Kindergarten, Grades 1, 3, and 5) understood their own memory systems. Their findings revealed a developing awareness among subjects of many aspects relevant to improved memory performance. Even the youngest subjects correctly stated that more study time can improve recall on a list of items. Younger subjects were also aware that peers or adults could help them to remember information, and that memory could be cued by certain objects. For example, asked how they would remember to take their skates to school, most students were able to cite placing the skates by the door. Older students demonstrated a more sophisticated and thorough knowledge of memory performance including the understanding that memory varies across tasks and occasions; that the kinds of things one tries to remember can make a difference on recall; that people differ in memory ability; and that adults are better rememberers. In older children and especially adults, metamemory processes are automatically adopted in countless instances throughout the day, whereas the young child's options are both structurally and experientially limited.

The concept of metamemory was extended by the work of Brown and her colleagues (Brown, 1975; 1978; Baker & Brown, 1984; Brown, Bransford, Ferrara, & Campione, 1983) to the broader concept of

◆ metamemory: self-knowledge about memory capabilities

◆ metamemory performance: the selection and assessment of strategies that are most appropriate for carrying out a task

metacognition as consisting of (1) one's self-knowledge about learning in general, and one's own learning capabilities; and (2) one's ability to independently control and regulate cognitive abilities such as planning, monitoring, and checking. The first aspect, **metacognitive knowledge,** refers to the learner's self-knowledge about his or her cognitive abilities and resources. Table 3.1 shows that metacognitive knowledge in reading would entail students' perceptions of themselves as readers, including an awareness of the conditions and circumstances that promote reading ability (*intrapersonal competence*), and how this ability compares with others (*interpersonal competence*). Metacognitive knowledge also involves a knowledge of task variables. In reading, this might include such aspects as awareness of the purpose of a reading task, speed in carrying out the task and how this reflects on performance, or incentives and preferences associated with the reading activity.

◆ metacognition: awareness and self-regulation of basic learning strategies and executive processes that deal with planning, monitoring, and evaluation of one's learning

◆ metacognitive knowledge: self-knowledge about cognitive abilities and resources

Table 3.1
Metacognitive Knowledge in Reading

Person Variables
View as cognitive processor
Intra- and interpersonal competence

Task Variables
View of text (expectations, structure)
Nature of information
Task demands (criterial task)
Sensitivity (motivation, interest)
Decisions related to understanding and
  remembering (monitor, nature of
  difficulty)

Strategy Variables
Macro-procedures
  Notes
  Summaries

Outline
Underline
Map
Paraphrase
  Rehearse
  Elaborate
Re-read

Micro-procedures
  Check familiarity
  Reflect to recall definition of terms
  Visualize terms
  Relate concept to example, or example
    to concept

Interaction of Variables

Another aspect important to metacognition is the student's awareness of a variety of strategies that enhance reading activity. Questions a teacher might consider in assessing a student's metacognitive abilities in reading are provided in the sample Metacognitive Interview Guide prepared by Lupart and O'Brien (see Table 3.2).

The dimensions of metacognitive knowledge have been widely explored in the literature on reading comprehension, linguistics, memory, and attention, and in areas such as mathematics and science. As seen by Baker and Brown (1984), metacognitive knowledge is (1) something that can be described by an individual; (2) often fallible in the sense that young children especially may have faulty impressions of their own cognitive knowledge; and (3) relatively stable in the sense that one's knowledge base is a gradual accumulation built on new learning and experiences. Markman's (1977) research has shown that the knowledge component of metacognition seen in children's ability to accurately judge their own cognitive limitations, or to correctly describe the cognitive demands involved in a given task, does not appear until students reach upper elementary grades. This has important implications for classroom teaching in that learners must be aware of their own failures in performing learning tasks before adopting corrective or alternate strategies.

◆ **self-regulation**: aspect of metacognition in which a person actively and consciously utilizes more elaborate and effective learning strategies

The second aspect of metacognition, **self-regulation,** refers to the notion that the thinking of infants and young children, which is initially guided or mediated by adults, becomes increasingly more autonomous and independently controlled as the child grows older (Lupart, 1991). Thus, the learner is not simply a passive recipient of new knowledge, but rather is actively engaged in evaluating and guiding his or her own cognitive activity. According to Baker and Brown (1984), the regulation or control aspect of metacognitive knowledge is somewhat unstable in the sense that there is much variation in performance and behaviour from one situation or task to another.

Metacognition researchers have attempted to address two important questions: (1) What are the self-regulatory mechanisms used by an active learner during an ongoing attempt to solve problems? and (2) What are the instructional conditions that promote this kind of intellectual engagement? Research on exceptional students and metacognition has generated effective strategies to support student learning, and will be presented throughout this text in subsequent chapters. Some of the primary implications of metacognition for teachers in inclusive schools or classrooms are outlined in Table 3.3.

Current information processing theorists have moved from a quantitative, or skills-based, approach in the study of memory and attention, to an interest in strategies and metacognitive or executive processes involved in problem-solving and learning tasks. Siegler (1991) identifies four distinguishing characteristics of current information-processing theories:

1. A basic assumption that thinking is information processing.
2. An emphasis on the precise analysis of change mechanisms.
3. A focus on which processes are performed, in what order, and for how much time.
4. A belief that investigations of children's and adults' thinking can contribute to our understanding of the nature of cognitive development. (p. 63)

◆ **automaticity**: the ability to perform, behave, or process information subconsciously in a manner that facilitates learning and development

Aspect 4 implies that the mind of the child is fundamentally similar to that of the adult, notwithstanding key differences in the quantity and the organization of information, and in the **automaticity** of processing. The following section concerning information processing and intelligence will outline one of the current leading theories in this area.

Table 3.2
Metacognitive Interview Guide

I. PERSON VARIABLES
a. General Perceptions
1. What is reading?
2. How did you learn to read?
3. How does a teacher help you learn to read?

b. Motivation, Attitude and Perceptions
4. Do you like to read?
5. Are you a good reader?
6. What do you do that makes you a good/not-so-good reader?
7. How would you describe a really good reader?
8. How would you describe a poor reader?
9. What things does a person have to learn to be a good reader?
10. Why do you think some children have trouble learning to read?
11. Do you read at home?
12. How often?
13. When and where do you think that you read best?
14. Do you prefer to read out loud or to read to yourself?
15. Do you like to read out loud in front of the class?
16. What do you like/dislike about it?

II. TASK VARIABLES
a. Purpose: Reproduce or Recall
17. The other day I asked a girl to read a story to me and then to tell me what she had read. Before she started reading she asked me if I just wanted her to remember the general meaning or if I wanted her to remember all of the details of the story. Why do you think she asked me that?
18. Would it be easier for you to read to remember the general meaning or to read to remember all of the details?
19. How would that be easier?

b. Speed
20. Do only good readers read quickly or can poor readers read fast too?
21. Does reading fast help you or hurt you in remembering of the story?
22. When do you read slowly?
23. When do you read quickly?
24. What kind of a book do you read quickly?

25. Why do you think you read that kind of book quickly?
26. What kind of a book do you read slowly?
27. Why do you think you read that kind of book slowly?
28. Do you change your reading speed according to the kind of book you are reading?
29. How do you change it?
30. Do you know what 'skimming' means? (For negative response explain.)
31. Do you ever use skimming?
32. When do you use it?

c. Incentive and Preference
33. What kinds of books do you like to read?
34. What kind of book do you find most difficult to read?
35. What makes it difficult?
36. Do you ever stop reading a book?
37. What makes you stop?

d. Reading Mode: Oral or Silent
38. You said earlier that you prefer to … (response to question 13)
39. Which helps you to remember better, reading out loud or reading to yourself?
40. Which helps you to understand better?
41. What do you think it is important to do when you are reading out loud?
42. What do you think it is important to do when you are reading to yourself?

e. Prior Knowledge
43. A class is going to read a story about mining. Janet toured a coal mine while she was on vacation last summer. Do you think the story might be easier or harder for Janet to understand than for someone who has never seen a mine?
44. What would make it easier/harder?

III. STRATEGY VARIABLES
a. Recursive Operations
45. After you have read a story do you ever think about it again?
46. How do you think about it?
47. Do you ever repeat a story or part of a story to yourself after you have read it?
48. What kinds of things do you repeat?

b. Inferencing
49. Do you ever feel that you have more

ideas in your head about the story than what the author actually says?
50. How can that happen?

c. Prediction
51. Do you ever try to guess what will happen next in a story?
52. Does that help you to understand the story better?
53. How does that help/hinder you?
54. When you are reading along and you come to the bottom of a page do you ever know the first word that will be on the next page before you turn the page?
55. How can that happen?

d. Imagery
56. Do you make up pictures in your head while you read?
57. What kinds of pictures do you make up?
58. Do you understand better when you make up pictures?
59. How does that help/hinder you?

e. Projection
60. Do you ever see yourself in the stories you read?
61. Does that help/hinder your understanding of the story?

f. Monitoring
62. What do you do if you don't understand

a word while you are reading?
63. Have you ever come across a word which you could not pronounce when you are reading?
64. What do you do with such a word?
65. Does it make it difficult for you to understand what you are reading when this happens?
66. What do you do if you don't understand a whole sentence or a whole paragraph while you are reading?

Probes for Question 66 (67-69)
67. Do you ever go back and read a sentence or paragraph again?
68. Why do you do that?
69. Does it ever help?
70. Have you ever been reading to yourself and felt that even though you knew all of the words something did not make sense to you?
71. What do you do if this happens?
72. Have you ever been reading silently and discovered that you were thinking about something completely different, such as what happened at recess?
73. What do you do when that happens?
74. Do you ever ask yourself questions when you are reading?
75. What kinds of questions do you ask?

Source: (By Dr. Judy Lupart, University of Calgary; and Dr. Margaret O'Brien, Mount Saint Vincent University).

INFORMATION PROCESSING AND INTELLIGENCE

Robert Sternberg

Information-processing theory as it applies to the development of theories of intelligence is exemplified by the work of Robert Sternberg (1984a, 1984b, 1985), whose primary goal has been to provide an information-processing analysis of intelligence that would eliminate some of the limitations of traditional theories of intelligence based on IQ tests. **Intelligence (IQ) tests** have been widely debated (Kamin, 1974; Strenio, 1981; Gould, 1981; Snyderman & Rothman, 1987) and criticized for being culturally biased; for not directly measuring such critical capacities as the ability to learn and create; and for the fact that a single number fails to capture a quality as rich and complex as intelligence. On the other hand, IQ tests provide some unique virtues in that they predict with fair accuracy later school performance and provide a solid base from which to examine individual differences in cognitive functioning.

◆ intelligence (IQ) test: assessment device that attempts to measure intellectual and academic potential by comparing mental age to chronological age

Table 3.3
Metacognition: Implications for Teachers

Consciousness-Raising
1. Students need to become aware of their own thought processes.
2. Provide many opportunities to share ideas, feelings, and strategies concerning students' own cognitive activities.
3. Encourage students to evaluate their ongoing performance (problem detection) and respond appropriately (solve detected problems).

Self-Regulation
4. Encourage students to predict and plan.
5. Encourage students to check and monitor during task performance.
6. Encourage students to evaluate, reflect, and revise the performance/outcome relationship (reality testing).
7. Encourage active monitoring of one's own cognitive activities to achieve

recognized self or other imposed learning goals.

Teaching Strategies
8. Use direct teaching methods, including demonstration, modelling, defining, and explaining.
9. Provide explicit instructions for focusing students' attention on relevant features of the learning task.
10. Provide assistance only as far as necessary, with the goal of independent control or regulation over cognitive activities.
11. Learners of any age are more likely to take active control of their own cognitive endeavours when they are faced with tasks of intermediate difficulty.

Sternberg's (1984b, 1985) global theory of intelligence is unique to current theories of intelligence, in its attempt to apply aspects of intellectual functioning that have to do with the individual's ability to cope within the real world (including creativity) to the more traditional area of analytic reasoning. His triarchic theory of intelligence is composed of three subtheories (see Table 3.4). Three types of information-processing components (metacomponents, performance components, and knowledge-acquisition components) are incorporated into the **componential subtheory**, which is the primary mechanism for strategy construction and complex problem-solving.

Metacomponents play a key role in the development of intelligence in the sense that they are self-monitoring, and because they enable persons to learn from their own mistakes, the system improves with greater experience. Sternberg (1984) describes metacomponents as executive processes used in:

1. Deciding on what the problem to be solved is.
2. Selecting the lower-order components for task solution.
3. Selecting one or more representations or organizations for information.
4. Selecting a strategy for combining lower-order components.
5. Deciding how attentional resources will be deployed.
6. Monitoring the solution of a problem.
7. Sensitivity to and acting upon external feedback (p. 282).

Essentially, metacomponents deal with the planning, monitoring, and evaluation aspects of information processing.

An important distinction is made between *controlled* and *automatic processing*. McKeough (1991) describes the task of driving to the office to illustrate

◆ **componential subtheory:** a subtheory of Sternberg's triarchic theory of intelligence which refers to the use of information processing components for strategy construction and complex problem-solving

◆ **metacomponent:** an executive process that deals with planning, monitoring, and evaluation aspects of information processing

Table 3.4 Sternberg's Triarchic Theory		
Componential Subtheory	*Contextual Subtheory*	*Experiential Subtheory*
Metacomponents Performance components Knowledge-acquisition components	Adaptation Shaping	Novelty Automatization

the importance of these two modes of processing in individual problem-solving. The daily drive to the office is normally carried out with ease, having become automated to the degree that one can carry out the necessary procedures and operations of driving a car with minimal conscious thinking. If, however, an individual moves to a new city, this task becomes a novel learning situation, requiring conscious control. As McKeough explains it, "The operations used in the old procedure would be applied to the new set of facts, and the new information would be temporarily held in attention, while problem-solving operations manipulated it. Through these strategic operations, linkages would be forged among new items in the information store" (p. 3).

Sternberg (1984) points out that "[c]ontrolled information processing is hierarchical in nature, with the executive metacomponents consciously directing the nonexecutive performance and knowledge-acquisition components. Controlled processing is also of strictly limited capacity, primarily serial: but it has unlimited ability to call upon all of an individual's stored knowledge base" (p. 173). Thus, teachers can explicitly teach children problem-solving procedures conducive to efficient task performance, and thereby facilitate the expansion of the child's knowledge base.

A student with high componential intelligence might be described by her teacher as having strong analytical skills, an excellent memory, and the ability to earn consistently high scores on tests. These students tend to have well-developed verbal skills, and are often perceived by teachers to be gifted students. They are excellent consumers of curriculum knowledge, and can in later grades be effective in critical analysis. However, students with high componential intelligence may lack the flexibility and creativity needed to produce unique and original work, and they may not have the ability to select and shape their environment adaptively. The latter abilities are central to Sternberg's second dimension of the triarchic theory, contextual subtheory.

In Sternberg's own words, intelligence in context is "the purposive adaptation to, shaping of, and selection of real-world environments relevant to one's life" (1984, p. 271). The **contextual subtheory** refers to the notion that people are able to make adaptations in their environment in order to impose control over their lives. This involves the ability to effectively use practical or tacit knowledge derived from previous experience, and to shape the environment to suit personal needs. Students who are strong in this area have a talent for quickly assessing the "rules of the game" at school, for selecting

◆ **contextual subtheory:** a subtheory of Sternberg's triarchic theory of intelligence which refers to the ability to bring control to one's life by making adaptations in one's environment

courses and programs that make the most of their intellectual capabilities, and for rapidly acquiring and adaptively using tacit knowledge to fit any situation that is encountered. Moreover, they know when to abandon a situation that offers no beneficial returns; for example, a student who wants to be regarded as a good student will likely distance herself from friends who are negatively viewed by the teacher, and associate herself with a more positively regarded group. Sternberg contends that it is contextual intelligence, not IQ, that predicts job success (Trotter, 1986).

The third and last dimension of Sternberg's triarchic theory of intelligence, **experiential subtheory**, refers to the ability of an individual to learn from previous situations and use new learning in novel situations. According to Sternberg (1985), the core element operating here is _insight_, which can be achieved in three ways. **Selective encoding** refers to insights derived from sifting through information to focus on only the critical elements (the ability to "see the trees"). **Selective combination** is the kind of insight needed to piece together sufficient information to discern the larger picture (the ability to "see the forest").

The third type of insight, **selective comparison**, refers to the ability to perceive old information in a new way, or vice versa. Sternberg's (1981) studies confirm that this attribute is highly developed in gifted learners. Sternberg (1991) further indicates that rate and level of automatization are related to intellectual skill, and relating this to novelty, he comments: "Better ability to cope with novelty enables one to begin automatization of information processing sooner and perhaps more effectively. Better ability to automatize enables one to free more resources for novelty, and hence for dealing with new kinds and levels of experience." (p. 97). Hence, there are reciprocal benefits to the interaction of novelty and automatization through experience.

The ability to think creatively and to produce creative ideas is typically not addressed in general education classes, even though these abilities are often nurtured in programs for gifted students (Feldhusen & Treffinger, 1980; Davis, 1991). Inclusive education classes would seem an ideal context for introducing experiences that foster such thinking abilities. The undue emphasis on academic (or componential) intelligence can fail to prepare students for the workplace, where having creative ideas is what often results in the greatest success.

Sternberg's work has direct ramifications for advances in the assessment of intelligence, as well as strategic learning. He attempts to broaden traditional concepts of how children's learning and functioning is measured by applying the notions of adaptation to novelty and automatization of information processing. In contrast to traditional conceptions of intelligence, Sternberg adopts a more global perspective by considering the academic, experiential, and practical aspects of intellectual ability. Moreover, he contends there should be a closer correspondence between assessment materials and the instruction given. For example, Sternberg (1991) suggests that the triarchic test of intellectual skills he is currently developing can be used for

◆ experiential subtheory: a subtheory of Sternberg's triarchic theory of intelligence which refers to a person's ability to learn from past situations and to use new learning in new situations

◆ selective encoding: the ability to sift through information in order to focus on critical elements

◆ selective combination: the ability to piece together information in order to discern the larger picture

◆ selective comparison: the ability to perceive old information in a new way, or vice versa

pre- and post-test assessment of his instructional programs for teaching intellectual skills. His approach to assessment is centred on bringing the testing dimension and the teaching dimension into closer alliance—an emphasis that bodes well for inclusive education and its goal of meeting the needs of a more diverse group of students.

SUMMARY OF INFORMATION-PROCESSING THEORY

Information-processing theory has provided a framework for the generation of two branches of knowledge relevant to current educational practice— learning theories and theories of intelligence. The former strand is represented in the work of Flavell and Brown, and has evolved from early studies of memory and attention to an interest in metacognition, which concerns the learner's ability to identify and use activities and strategies to enhance understanding and performance in learning tasks. These abilities have been widely investigated, resulting in the development of effective teaching procedures, and in the delineation of learning differences in exceptional children. The application of information-processing theory to the study of intelligence has resulted in new ways of viewing intelligent behaviour, and has contributed significantly to new approaches and techniques for assessment of achievement and aptitude in general. The work in information-processing theory has shown that in addition to knowledge of a subject, knowing what you know and how well you know it is important (Leinhardt, 1992).

◆ DEVELOPMENTAL THEORY

Developmental theorists are interested in defining patterns or laws that explain the development of the mind—from the primitive understanding of the infant to the mature forms of thought seen in adults—and the mechanisms that account for this development. Our overview of cognitive developmental theory begins with Jean Piaget.

JEAN PIAGET

The father of developmental theory, Swiss psychologist Jean Piaget conducted intensive, observation-based studies of young children. His early work featured the "clinical interview," in which a child is asked to perform a task or solve a problem, and is then asked to give reasons for behaving in a particular way. Initially rejected by Western psychologists, who valued empirical research, Piaget's experimental methods found eventual widespread acceptance and acclaim.

In contrast to information-processing theory, Piaget (1971) proposed that all individuals follow a similar course of intellectual development, and that cognition in children differs qualitatively from adult cognition. According to Piaget, all cognitive growth is related to, and stems from, the existing knowledge base. When an individual takes in new information, it is interpreted through the existing knowledge structures. Learning is the process of combining new information with what the child already knows. Because one's experiences and perceptions are filtered and mediated through existing thought structures, the resulting representation is distorted, as opposed to forming an exact replica.

Young children have limited experiences, and their representational structures are immature in comparison with those of adults; consequently, their mental reality is qualitatively quite different. Piaget separates the conceptual and logical thought development of the child into four distinct stages (see Table 3.5). The ages given are approximate, and it is acknowledged that environment and genetic factors may cause variations. However, Piaget maintains that the *order* of stages is invariable: the child will not move on to a higher stage until all mental operations associated with a given stage have been organized and consolidated. Each stage of development is characterized by the emergence of new abilities, which constitute a major reorganization of the child's thinking. Development depends on the child's manipulation of, and active interaction with, the environment.

Table 3.5 Piaget's Stages of Cognitive Development		
Stage	**Approximate Age Range**	**Major Characteristics**
Sensorimotor	0 - 2 years	Child represents the world in terms of motor behaviour; learning involves coordination of motor activities with sensory inputs. Objects and people are differentiated from one another and recognized as permanent.
Preoperational	2 - 7 years	Language skills and the ability to use symbols to represent objects and events develops. Thinking is egocentric and perceptually based.
Concrete Operations	7 - 11 years	Logical thinking develops with manipulation of concrete objects. Classification and serialization according to weight or size is achieved. Understanding of numbers. Speech is less egocentric and more socialized.
Formal Operations	11 -15 years	Reasoning is based on hypotheses or propositions. Abstract and purely symbolic thinking emerges, and can be applied hypothetico-deductive reasoning (i.e., scientific inquiry). Relations need not be directly experienced for understanding.

◆ schemes: patterns of behaviour that are used to deal with specific kinds of information in a person's environment

The concept of **schemes** is basic to understanding how individuals organize their thinking and behaviour, and how thinking changes as the child grows. Schemes are the patterns of behaviour that are used to deal with specific kinds of information in an environment. The sensory and motor actions the infant engages in, such as sucking, grasping, or pushing, are examples of simple schemes. Furth (1969) suggests that these early schemes "include the organization of space and time, of causality, and most importantly, of permanent objects, among which is found the self" (p. 51). They are formed out of the child's interaction with the environment, and are gradually incorporated (developmentally) into operations in subsequent stages. Thus, an infant thinks and knows in terms of action sequences. As the child experiences play, or other problem-solving activities, these schemes become increasingly more complex and integrated. Following a course of progressive construction and reconstruction, the child's sense of reality becomes increasingly like that of an adult. The older child knows and thinks in terms of more symbolic representational forms or higher level representations, eventually resulting in the capacity for abstract and logical thought.

According to Piaget (1983), in the course of adapting to the environment, the mind builds cognitive structures to encode, interpret, transform, and organize external sensory input. Adaptation involves the invariant complementary processes of assimilation and accommodation. Ginsburg and Opper (1960) indicate that, "while organization and adaptation are inherited, they are not structures (like reflexes) but tendencies" (p. 19). Piaget saw intelligence as the process of adapting, and in the sense that intelligence emerges out of the activities one is engaged in, it is ever-changing. As Lefrançois (1988) describes it,

> If intelligence is the process of adapting, and if adaptation is the result of the interaction of assimilation and accommodation, then intelligence can be defined in terms of assimilation and accommodation. These processes are simply ways of interacting with the environment. They do not change from childhood to adulthood, hence they are referred to as invariant functions or, more often, as functional invariants (p. 182).

◆ assimilation: the process of incorporating a new experience and modifying it so that it fits into an existing physical or mental system of organization

Assimilation is the process of incorporating a new experience, and then filtering or modifying it so that it fits into an existing scheme of physical or mental systems of organization. This process is evident in a young infant's behaviour when the rattle he has been playing with drops onto the floor and his sister hands him a ball instead. The child will proceed to grasp, mouth, and bang it against the crib, using schemes developed in relation to the rattle. Essentially the child is using existing schemes to learn about his new toy.

◆ accommodation: the process of adjusting schemes — through discontinuity, transformation, and reorganization—to fit new information

Accommodation refers to a change in existing schemes to fit new information. If, for example, the infant had dropped a rattle that squeaks when pressed, he would most likely try to squeeze the ball. Of course, no squeak is heard, which leads the infant to try out other actions. Behaviour such as pushing the ball along the mattress produces a new consequence, and with continued activity a new scheme might result. Thus, accommodation involves discontinuity, transforming, and reorganizing existing structures.

When a child encounters a situation that cannot be fully interpreted by existing schemes, a state of **disequilibrium** is created. Accommodation and assimilation processes operate to reduce such imbalances by focusing on the stimuli that caused the disequilibrium, and by developing new schemes, or adapting old ones, until **equilibrium** is restored. Hyde (1970) defines equilibrium as "an internal regulatory (balancing) mechanism, an active mental process which operates outside the individual's awareness, but which is brought about by the child reflecting in an auto-regulatory sense on his own activities" (p. 25). Thus the invariant constant restructuring and changing of inward organization and assimilation, along with the outward accommodation, result in qualitative differences in the way the child experiences his or her environment throughout the developmental stages. Learning is dependent upon the process of equilibrium, and when disequilibrium is created, children have the opportunity to grow and develop.

A major educational implication of Piaget's constructivist theory is that learning is dependent on numerous and varied opportunities for concrete manipulations of materials and practical activities. Simply telling a child about a process or new concept is insufficient. The child should have numerous opportunities for relating school learning to real concrete objects and events. Schooling should be child-centred and based on a discovery-based learning approach, which emphasizes the effective physical arrangement of the learning context, and the provision of challenging materials and interesting problems to investigate. Furthermore, teaching strategies and materials should be consistent with the child's stage of intellectual development. Teachers need to be sensitive to the fact that children truly do have thinking limitations; they are not purposely giving an inaccurate response when, in the teacher's perception, all necessary clues have been given. Thus, the curriculum should reflect the same sequences of stages discovered by developmental researchers, a concept perhaps best illustrated through example.

Inhelder and Piaget (1964) examined children's ability to deal with multiple classification problems of the type shown in Figure 3.3. The task involves analyzing shape and colour dimensions to determine which of the choices along the bottom fit. A correct solution requires the individual to attend to the two dimensions together in classifying each object. Inhelder and Piaget (1964) found that children age 4–6 chose objects with two correct dimensions on only 15 percent of the problems. By the age of 9 or 10, most children were able to reliably select the correct figure. It was concluded, therefore, that younger children are developmentally capable of one-dimensional problem-solving, whereas older children are able to consider classes and relations together to solve the multiple classification problem.

A final educational implication of Piaget's theory is that the adoption of the developmental concept of children's learning would minimize the need for categorizing children, because instructional programming decisions

◆ **disequilibrium:** state of imbalance that results from an inability to use existing schemes to interpret a new situation

◆ **equilibrium:** state of balance in which a person uses accommodation and assimilation to increase development both quantitatively and qualitatively

Figure 3.3
Multiple Classification Matrix

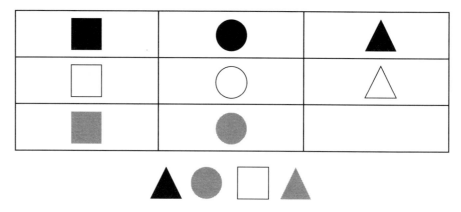

would be made on the basis of the individual child's level of intellectual functioning, not on the basis of characteristics associated with a given category such as learning disabilities.

ROBBIE CASE

Piaget's lack of interest in the instructional mechanisms that lead to advanced development stimulated a new line of inquiry, which is referred to as neo-Piagetian theory. Representative of this strand is the work of Robbie Case. Like Piaget, Case (1985, 1986) postulates four main stages of development, from birth to adulthood. However, Case's (1991) theory incorporates key concepts from information-processing theory and sociocultural theory, and differs from Piaget's with respect to: (1) the detail and arrangement of the structures within stages; (2) the transitional processes leading from one stage to the next; (3) the degree to which environment influences cognitive structures; (4) the nature of the structures.

Case's (1985) research is directed toward understanding the cognitive processes that enable the child to progress from one stage of intellectual development to the next. Central to this process is the concept of **regulation**. According to Case (1985), there are two kinds of regulation that are critical to cognitive development: (1) independent problem-solving and exploration activities with which the child becomes involved; and (2) socially mediated regulation such as the adult organization a teacher provides in the teaching/learning process in the form of imitation or mutual regulation. The development of *self-regulation* is achieved through the formation of executive control structures, which undergo qualitatively distinct transitions from the age of 4 months to 19 years.

101 – 107

◆ regulation: process in cognitive development in which a child's learning and environment is mediated by adults and the social system

The child is born with a natural propensity toward self-regulation, an innate processing ability Siegler (1991) describes as "the potential for setting goals, for formulating problem-solving strategies to meet the goals, and for integrating different problem solving strategies into more elaborate and effective strategies" (p. 74). Such goal sequences are organized in the form of cognitive structures. Structural development is contingent on four elementary information processes: schematic search, evaluation, retagging, and consolidation. As can be seen in Figure 3.4, these processes are operative in all of the general regulatory activities. Over a period of time, the child's cumulative experiences result in a hierarchical integration of existing mental structures, and in this process new structures are formed that are qualitatively distinct from the previous. Each new level of hierarchical integration that is achieved increases the child's capacity to handle higher-level goals. According to Case, the capacity for this hierarchic integration is regulated by an increase in working memory that occurs as a result of maturation and increased operational efficiency.

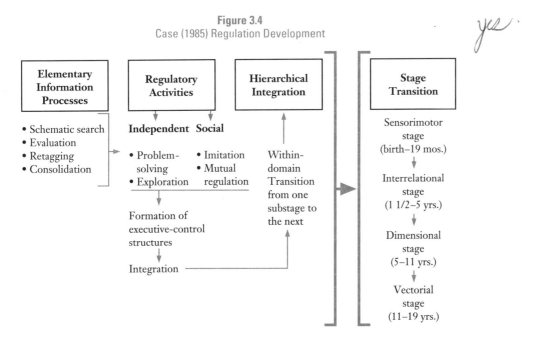

Figure 3.4
Case (1985) Regulation Development

A unique feature of Case's perspective is the incorporation of socially based forms of learning, which is central to the sociohistorical tradition. The concept of *mutual regulation* is defined by Case (1985) as "the active adaptation of the child and some other human being to each other's feelings, cognitions, or behaviors" (p. 269). Each society develops its own set of intellectual inventions necessary for higher-level problem-solving. Through means such as formalized schooling, the goal is to transfer the advanced knowledge structures of the society to the individual, thereby allowing him or her to function adequately and independently. Accordingly, Case (1985) asserts that there is a necessary relationship between the process of education and the process of development.

In Case's concept of the intellectual development of children, "instruction is considered a unique form of mutual regulation, in that the teacher plays an active role in facilitating the child's learning" (Lupart, 1991, p. 174). For Case (1991), the developmental perspective offers insight into the design of educational activities, appropriate to each developmental level, that will facilitate optimal and advanced learning. The instructional methodology Case (1991) recommends is based on three major steps. Step 1 involves the analysis and identification of the conceptual structures and developmental representations that are germane to conceptual understanding in a task domain. Step 2 is directed at specifying where, in the sequence, the child or instructional group is currently functioning. Finally, Step 3 involves building a series of conceptual bridges that link the child's level of understanding to more advanced levels in the developmental sequence. Through the implementation of this process of specific instructional intervention, the child is taught to successfully perform the task or solve the problem. The teaching/learning process, then, is a matter of creating the appropriate mapping of the task situation, and then tailoring instructional activities in such a way that the child moves from his or her current level of understanding to the level of conceptual understanding necessary for independent task performance.

Case and his colleagues (Case & McKeough, 1990; Case, 1992) carried out a number of research studies, within a variety of subject domains, in which an instructional intervention approach is used. To illustrate how the teacher might use the approach, let us consider a typical Grade 2 classroom. We know from previous research studies that children around age 6 are capable of conceptualizing numbers on a single linear dimension. Children of this age typically are able to count forward or backward, or to carry out simple addition and subtraction, enabling them to correctly figure out balance-beam problems of weight and distance from the fulcrum, or time-telling. Research has also shown that by the age of 8, children have the mental capacity to coordinate two numerical dimensions, which enables them to carry out new arithmetic operations such as incrementing in columns, or dealing with 10's and 1's. In a typical Grade 2 class, it is likely that students span these two developmental levels. Consequently, the teacher's knowledge of the developmental sequencing that precedes and follows the particular grade level can be used to adjust the instruction according to the individual's level of understanding. The shift from a one-dimensional focus to the coordination of two dimensions has been extensively researched by Case and his colleagues who found the same pattern occurring in a number of tasks over a variety of task domains.

SUMMARY OF DEVELOPMENTAL THEORY

Cognitive development among children is similar because there are universal laws of development that apply to all children. The mind of the child is different from the mind of the adult. Mental structures are constructed by the child in interaction with the environment, and there are four qualitatively distinct stages that all children pass through. Regulation is a critical developmental process that helps to explain how individuals move from one stage or substage of cognitive development to another. The concept of socially based mediation refers to the situation in which more experienced learners or adults assist the child in forming the necessary hierarchical integration to advance his or her thinking. Educational theorists have shown that substages within task domains can be effectively mapped out on the basis of normal developmental progression, and that these sequences can be used as the basis for instruction of atypical learners, as well as for curriculum design. Teachers adopting this theoretical perspective need to recognize that "learning is an active process of knowledge construction and sense-making by the student" (Leinhardt, 1992, p. 23).

◆ SOCIOCULTURAL THEORY

LEV VYGOTSKY – *yes!*

The final perspective, sociocultural theory, is best represented by the work of the Russian psychologist Lev Vygotsky, who sought to integrate historical, social, and psychological processes into a unified theory of human consciousness (Wertsch, 1991a). Western researchers were unaware of Vygotsky's work until the 1962 publication of the English translation of his major book, *Thought and Language* (originally published in 1934). The subsequent impact of his work is widely acknowledged in North America and throughout Europe, and there are currently many new translations and analyses of his work (Moll, 1990; Kozulin, 1990; Wertsch, 1991a, 1991b). Recent descriptions of Vygotsky's theory (Kozulin, 1990; Wertsch, 1991a) focus on a number of interlocking themes that include: (1) higher mental functions, (2) mediation, (3) the cultural origins of thinking, (4) the role of language, and (5) the zone of proximal development. We will examine each of these concepts briefly.

Higher Mental Functions

Vygotsky recognized two branches of higher mental functioning (Kozulin, 1990). The first group stems from the traditional avenues of psychological study such as logical memory, selective attention, and concept formation (lower functions). The second group consists of "the processes of mastering the external means of cultural development and cognition, e.g., language, writing, counting, and drawing" (Kozulin, 1990, p. 113). Vygotsky thus recognized the critical influence that formalized schooling has on the development of advanced thinking.

For Vygotsky, the higher functions are not merely an outgrowth of the lower functions, but are also qualitatively distinct from them. For example, he distinguishes between two forms of attention. The first form of attentional development relates to the "organic processes of growth, maturation, and development of the neurological apparatuses and functions of the child" (Vygotsky, 1981, p.193). This refers to the biological capacity of a child to sit up, or maintain eye contact with an adult for a lengthy period of time.

The second form, voluntary (or, in Western literature, intentional) attention, emerges out of social interaction with adults who "begin to use various stimuli and means to direct the child's attention and subordinate it to their control" (p. 194). These same means will gradually become self-controlled or self-regulated attentional processes, and the individual will be able to independently demonstrate voluntary attention. This concept is similar to the notion of metacognition described earlier in this chapter. The important distinction Vygotsky makes, however, is that higher psychological processes are first shared social functions that are later internalized by the individual. The implication for inclusive classroom teachers is to ensure that all students participate in and experience numerous cooperative and group learning activities with peers.

Mediation

◆ mediation: the use of technical/psychological tools or human relationships to bring about cognitive development

Mediation refers to the mediums through which we demonstrate and communicate our thoughts with others. Teachers use a variety of technical and abstract mediums in their classroom instructional activities—in a more direct sense they mediate the thinking of students in the classroom. Vygotsky identified three forms of mediation important to the development of thinking (Kozulin, 1990). The first form involves using a material or technical tool, such as a stick to obtain something that is out of reach. (A present-day example would be the computer.) The second form involves semiotic mediators or signs (e.g., language, math, maps, and literature)—those psychological tools that serve in "transforming natural impulses into higher mental processes" (Kozulin, 1990, p. 114). This form of mediation was of particular interest to Vygotsky, who wrote:

> Human behavior is distinguished by the very fact that man creates artificial signal stimuli, among which is the "great signaling capacity" of speech . . . but the fundamental and most general activity distinguishing man from animals, psychologically speaking, is *signification*, i.e., the creation and use of signs (1977, p. 62).

The third form of mediation important to the development of higher mental processes is the mediation that occurs through another person, as in the teacher/student relationship. Teachers mediate student learning in problem-solving activities, for example, through modelling, explaining, or instruction. Within the inclusive classroom environment, the teacher must be flexible in adjusting mediation activities to suit a diverse student population.

Cultural Origins of Thinking

Unique to Vygotsky's theory is the notion that all advanced forms of human thought are the products of culture, and thus it is this level of development that must be understood in order to understand the thinking of the individual. Accordingly, thinking belongs to groups as opposed to individuals, and is formed on the basis of the social and historical activities that constitute the culture. For Vygotsky, then, culture shapes basic cognitive functioning.

According to the *general genetic law of cultural development*, "any function in the child's cultural development appears twice, or on two planes. First it appears on the social plane, and then on the psychological plane. First it appears between people as an interpsychological category, and then within the child as an intrapsychological category" (Vygotsky, 1981 p. 163). Vygotsky argues that not only the *content* but also the *process and structure* of social thought are internalized by the individual. More importantly, he (1979) states "that the social dimension of consciousness is primary in time and in fact the individual dimension of consciousness is derivative and secondary, based on the social and construed exactly in its likeness." (p. 30). This underlines, once again, the importance of formal schooling and the primary role it plays in the transmission of the culture.

The Role of Language

Vygotsky (1986) describes the relationship between thought and language as a continuous back-and-forth process, irreducible to separate or component forms: "Thought is not merely expressed in words; it comes into existence through them" (p. 218). In other words, language shapes our thinking. Vygotsky also believed that language plays an important role in regulating an individual's behaviour. With increasing age, there is a qualitative transformation of the thinking of the child, associated with the three stages of language development, as proposed by Vygotsky (1986).

During the first year of life, the child's intellectual development proceeds independently from symbol-based language. **Social speech** is the first form of language development, and is evident up to about age 3. Meanings are learned within social contexts. The behaviours of the child are regulated through the speech of adults or significant others in the child's environment, and gradually the child begins to use words in an attempt to share and convey meaning in the social context. Speech and intelligence merge in the preschool years after the child has mastered the rudiments of spoken language.

The second level of language development, **egocentric speech,** is typically evident from ages 3 to 7, and undergoes marked structural and

◆ **social speech:** a child's first level of language development—evident up to age 3—in which meanings are learned in social contexts

◆ **egocentric speech:** a child's second level of language development—evident from ages 3 to 7—which is directly connected to thinking

functional qualities over this period of development. Early on, there is no difference between the child's social and egocentric speech, but at the end of this stage egocentric speech becomes much more distinctive in comparison with social forms of speech. Egocentric speech serves as a mental orientation for the individual, and is directly connected with the child's thinking; thus young children who are deeply involved in a problem-solving task will often verbalize the steps along the way to successful completion. As autonomous egocentric speech becomes more independent, it resembles social discourse less and less. Using the terms outlined previously, during this period the child's speech provides the means of transition from interpsychic (social) to intrapsychic (individualized) functioning.

The final stage of language development, **inner speech,** could be described as "thinking gone underground." This form of language becomes increasingly idiosyncratic and personalized, and is typically conceived as having disconnected and incomplete forms. It is this form of language that is associated with higher mental functioning. Gradually, the individual learns to use inner speech to gain self-conscious control (in Western literature, metacognitive or executive control) of mental processes, and to plan and direct thinking and learning.

♦ inner speech: a child's third—and final—level of language development, which is idiosyncratic, personalized, and associated with higher mental functioning

Zone of Proximal Development

A key area of interest for Vygotsky was understanding how formal instruction or training contributed to the development of higher levels of thinking, or, in essence, intelligence. In summarizing his views, Vygotsky (1963) wrote: "We must determine at least two levels of a child's development, otherwise we fail to find the correct relation between the course of development and potentiality for learning in each specific case" (p. 28). The first level Vygotsky refers to is the **zone of actual development,** which represents mental functions that have already been attained, and that serve to independently regulate the behaviour of the child. The second level, **zone of proximal development,** involves the learning potentiality that is achieved through the direction or guidance of adult teaching, modelling, demonstration, and so forth.

♦ zone of actual development: existing mental functions that serve to regulate a child's behaviour

♦ zone of proximal development: the distance between children's actual development and their potential for intellectual achievement

Unlike Western educators and psychologists, who use standardized tests to determine the accomplished learning of the child, Vygotsky was concerned with the direction of a child's thinking. To use an illustrative example, suppose a standardized mathematics test is administered to a Grade 3 class and two boys aged 8 achieve the same age score of 8 years. We could say that both students can deal with math activities to the same level as has been standardized for 8-year-olds. If, however, the teacher were to continue the assessment and assist each child through guided questioning and through providing partial clues, we might find that one boy achieves an age score of 12 and the other boy an age score of 9. Through this kind of mediated assistance, the teacher is able to target the areas the individual will next be able to accomplish independently.

The zone of proximal development is created in the dialogue between the teacher and student, and involves the joint accomplishment of learning tasks or problems that are too difficult for the child to carry out independently. American researchers Campione, Brown, Ferrara, and Bryant (1984) and Brown and Ferrara (1985), having conducted studies using the zone of proximal development concept, concluded that observations such as the child's willingness to participate with a teacher, the amount and type of assistance required for a variety of learning tasks, and the ability to transfer learning to new situations can contribute significantly to instructional intervention plans. Hence, the zone of proximal development appears to be a robust concept in the area of student learning, and is, therefore, of considerable importance to inclusive classroom teachers.

The width of the zone is a measure of the child's actual "development and potentiality for learning in each specific case" (Vygotsky, 1963, p. 28). Differing zone widths reflect differing potentials for intellectual development—and the wider the zone, the greater the intellectual potential. Thus, for Vygotsky, the teaching/learning process is a spiral-like process in which learning potential becomes realized through instruction, thereby creating new forms of thinking, which, in turn, become the starting place for estimating the next level of learning potential.

JAMES V. WERTSCH

The work of James Wertsch has been instrumental in breaking new ground through the development and extension of particular aspects of Vygotsky's theory, and the work of another Soviet theorist, Mikhail Bakhtin (1895-1975). Specifically, Wertsch (1991b) adopts a sociocultural approach aimed at creating "an account of human processes that recognizes the essential relationship between these processes and their cultural, historical, and institutional settings" (p. 6). This might involve, for example, analyzing the thinking of an Eskimo fisherman, or an 18th-century writer versus a 19th-century one, or Russians versus Canadians, or a student in a Newfoundland school. Put another way, sociocultural analysis involves the study of how the mental functions of a particular culture and/or institution are, at any given time in history, shaped out of, and at the same time impact on, the setting in which they occur (Wertsch, 1991a).

This perspective has been of minimal interest to mainstream Western psychologists, who have been traditionally more concerned with establishing universal laws of learning. However, recent work in the area of literacy, coupled with a renewed interest in cross-cultural research and its applications, has led to an increased appreciation for the notion that "cultural traditions and social practices, regulate, express, transform, and permute the human psyche, resulting less in psychic unity for humankind than in ethnic divergences in mind, self, and emotion" (Shweder, 1990, p. 1).

Wertsch (1979) comments that certain aspects of Vygotsky's theory have been misunderstood by Western researchers, partly due to inaccurate translations of his works, and possibly because some of Vygotsky's concepts have not been fully detailed, making them vulnerable to misinterpretation. Wertsch (1979) elaborates on Vygotsky's notion of the zone of proximal development and, more specifically, the child's movement toward self-regulation in parent-child interaction. He describes the parent as providing *other-regulation*, in the sense that his or her questions, comments, and directions constitute the initial means of regulation in the child's attempt to solve, for example, a picture-puzzle task. The transition from other-regulation to self-regulation is achieved in four levels:

1. The child develops enough of a sense of the task that he or she can begin to participate in a communicative context. Primary regulation is provided by the mother.
2. The child begins to recognize that the adult's talk is meaningfully connected to the task at hand; however, the talk/activity connection is not consistently interpreted. Although the child participates fully in the dialogue, his or her level of task understanding is still far removed from that of an adult.
3. The child takes over some of the strategic responsibility for completing the task. At this stage, the communication remains within the interpsychological plane, and the dyad comes to a common *situation definition*.
4. The child takes over complete responsibility for the problem-solving situation, and is able to complete the picture puzzle independently.

Wertsch observes that at the point at which a shift from other-regulated social control to self-regulation occurs, instances of egocentric speech are often evident. Interestingly, these utterances are similar to the regulatory statements of adults in the earlier stages. Egocentric speech, which for Wertsch serves as a self-regulatory function, is part of a transitional stage in the evolution from vocal to inner speech. Progression through the levels of the zone of proximal development is "largely the result of the child's effort to establish and maintain coherence between his/her own action and the adult's speech" (Wertsch, 1979, p. 20). Wertsch (1991) stresses the need to explore the implications of the concept of social languages (i.e., languages peculiar to specific disciplines or groups, such as professional jargon) for formal schooling.

SUMMARY OF SOCIOCULTURAL THEORY

In contrast to the traditional Western approach, which focuses on the individual and the search for universal laws of learning, sociocultural theory regards culture and the intellectual tools it produces as the primary elements that shape and make possible advanced cognitive development in the individual. As Leinhardt (1992) describes it, "Knowledge is a cultural artifact of human beings: we produce it, share it, and transform it as individuals and as groups. . . . knowledge is distributed among members of a group, and this distributed knowledge is greater than the knowledge possessed by any single member" (p. 23). (This idea is central to the "community of learners" concept detailed in Chapter 14.) The zone of proximal development helps to clarify the relationship between learning and development, and as well as articulate what constitutes successful teaching/learning situations. The importance of formal schooling to the development of cognitive ability is confirmed by historical and present-day studies of literacy and the sociocultural approach to thinking.

◆ SUMMARY

This chapter began with a discussion of the importance of theory in guiding the thinking and actions of inclusive education teachers as they attempt to meet a diversity of student learning needs in the classroom. The chapter next provided a brief overview of behaviourist theory, followed by a review of cognitive theories that have the greatest relevance for understanding the teaching and learning process, and the unique learning needs of exceptional students.

Information-processing theory offers a detailed and flexible system involving the analysis of specific learning tasks and learning/teaching strategies, the understanding of learner differences, and new concepts of intelligence. Developmental theory brings to education the important concept of qualitatively differing stages in a child's intellectual development, and the need for young children to have numerous direct experiences. Neo-Piagetian theory incorporates aspects from both the information-processing and sociocultural perspectives, and provides subject- or domain-specific analyses of the mechanisms involved in the developmental sequencing of abilities, which can be implemented in instructional programs.

The final domain, sociocultural theory, emphasizes the importance of culture and the intellectual tools it produces, with respect to advanced cognitive development and the contemporary knowledge bases that characterize modern society. A predominant theme in sociocultural theory is the centrality of language and literacy in the progression to higher mental processes; formal education and the interactive social basis of learning in the zone of proximal development are key elements in this developmental process. Sociocultural theory differs sharply from Western information-processing and developmental theories, which seek patterns or universal laws of mental development.

The ideas and concepts associated with the theories outlined above have important implications for transforming teaching and learning in the inclusive education classroom. These ideas are expanded upon in subsequent chapters.

QUESTIONS
◆◆◆◆◆◆◆◆◆◆◆◆◆◆

1. Based on information-processing theory, explain how the task-analysis approach could be used to teach addition with double digits.

2. Distinguish between the traditional assessment of aptitude and assessment based on sociocultural theory.

3. Discuss how knowledge of developmental theory can be useful in designing an appropriate curriculum for an exceptional student.

4. What is the significance of the relationship between educational psychology theory and inclusive education?

5. Differentiate between cognitive theory and behaviourist theory as it applies to inclusive education.

REFERENCES

Atkinson, R. C., & Shiffrin, R. M. (1968). Human memory: A proposed system and its control processes. In K. W. Spence & J. T. Spence (Eds.), *The psychology of learning and motivation: Advances in research and theory, Volume 2* (pp. 89-195). New York: Academic Press.

Baker, L., & Brown, A.L. (1984). Metacognitive skills in reading. In P. D. Pearson (Ed.), *Handbook of reading research* (pp. 353-394). New York: Longman.

Becker, W. C., & Englemann, S. (1978). Systems for basic instruction: Theory and applications. In A. C. Catania & T. A. Brigham (Eds.), *Handbook of applied behavioral analysis: Social and instructional processes* (pp. 325-377). New York: Irvington.

Broadbent, D. E. (1958). *Perception and human communication.* New York: Pergamon.

Brooks, P. H., & Baumeister, A. A. (1977). A plea for consideration of ecological validity in the experimental psychology of mental retardation: A guest editorial. *American Journal of Mental Deficiency, 81,* 407-416.

Brown, A. L. (1972). A rehearsal deficit in retardates' continuous short-term memory: Keeping track of variables that have few or many states. *Psychonomic Science, 29,* 373-376.

Brown, A. L. (1974). The role of strategic behavior in retardate memory. In N. R. Ellis (Ed.), *International review of research in mental retardation, Volume 7* (pp. 55-111). New York: Academic Press.

Brown, A. L. (1975). The development of memory: Knowing, knowing about knowing, and knowing how to know. In H. W. Reese (Ed.), *Advances in child development and behavior, Volume 10.* New York: Academic Press.

Brown, A. L. (1978). Knowing when, where and how to remember: A problem of metacognition. In R. Glaser (Ed.), *Advances in instructional psychology.* Hillsdale, NJ: Lawrence Erlbaum.

Brown, A.L., Bransford, J. D., Ferrara, R. A., & Campione, J. C. (1983). Learning, remembering, and understanding. In J. H. Flavell & E. M. Markman (Eds.), *Handbook of child psychology, Volume 1: Cognitive development* (pp. 77-168). New York: John Wiley.

Brown, A. L., Campione, J. C., Bray, N. W., & Wilcox, B. L. (1974). Keeping track of changing variables: Effects of rehearsal training and rehearsal prevention in normal and retarded adolescents. *Journal of Experimental Psychology, 78,* 446-453.

Brown, A.L., Campione, J. C., & Murphy, M. D. (1974). Keeping track of changing variables: Long-term retention of a trained rehearsal strategy by retarded adolescents. *American Journal of Mental Deficiency, 78,* 446-453.

Brown, A. L., & Ferrara, R. A. (1985). Diagnosing zones of proximal development. In J. V. Wertsch (Ed.), *Culture, communication, and cognition* (pp. 306-322). Cambridge: Cambridge University Press.

Brown, A. L., & French, L. A. (1979). The zone of potential development: Implications for intelligence testing in the year 2000. *Intelligence, 3,* 255-273.

Butterfield, E. C., & Belmont, J. M. (1975). Assessing and improving the executive cognitive functions of mentally retarded people. In I. Bialer & M. Sternlicht (Eds.), *Psychological issues in mental retardation.* Chicago: Aldine-Atherton.

Campione, J. C., Brown, A. L., Ferrara, R. A., & Bryant, N. R. (1984). The zone of proximal development: Implications for individual differences and learning. In B. Rogoff & J. V.

Wertsch (Eds.), *Children's learning in the "Zone of Proximal Development"* (pp. 77-91). San Francisco: Jossey-Bass.

Case, R. (1985). *Intellectual development: Birth to adulthood.* New York: Academic Press.

Case, R. (1986). The new stage theories in intellectual development: Why we need them—What they assert. In M. Perlmutter (Ed.), *Perspectives on intellectual development, Volume 19): Minnisota symposia on child psychology* (pp. 57-95). Hillsdale, NJ: Lawrence Erlbaum.

Case, R. (1991). *A developmental approach to the design of remedial instruction.* In A. McKeough & J. L. Lupart (Eds.), *Toward the practice of theory based instruction: Current cognitive theories and their educational promise* (pp. 117-147). Hillsdale, NJ: Lawrence Erlbaum.

Case, R. (1992). *The mind's staircase: Exploring the conceptual underpinnings of children's thought and knowledge.* Hillsdale, NJ: Lawrence Erlbaum.

Case, R., & McKeough, A. (1990). Schooling and the development of central conceptual structures. *International Journal of Education, 13*(8), 835-855.

Charles, D. C. (1987). The emergence of educational psychology. In J. A. Glover & R. R. Ronning (Eds.), *Historical foundations of educational psychology* (pp. 17-38). New York: Plenum.

Chi, M. T. H. (1976). Short-term memory limitations in children: Capacity or processing deficits? *Memory and Cognition, 4*(5), 559-572.

Chi, M. T. H., & Glaser, R. (1985). Problem-solving ability. In R.J. Sternberg (Ed.), *Human abilities: An information processing approach.* New York: W. H. Freeman.

Craik, F. I. M., & Lockhart, R. S. (1972). Levels of processing: A framework for memory research. *Journal of Verbal Learning and Verbal Behavior, 11,* 671-684.

Davis, G. A. (1991). Teaching creative thinking. In N. Colangelo & G. A. Davis (Eds.), *Handbook of gifted education* (pp. 236-244). Boston: Allyn & Bacon.

Ellis, N. R. (1970). Memory processes in retardates and normals. In N. R. Ellis (Ed.), *International review of research in mental retardation, Volume 4* (pp. 1-32). New York: Academic Press.

Feldhusen, J. F., and Treffinger, D. J. (1980). *Creative thinking and problem-solving in gifted education.* Dubuque: Kendall/Hunt.

Fisher, M. A., & Zeamon, D. (1973). An attention-retention theory of retardate discrimination learning. In N. R. Ellis (Ed.), *International review of research in mental retardation, Volume 6* (pp. 171-251). New York: Academic Press.

Flavell, J. H. (1970). Developmental studies of mediated memory. In H. Reese & L. Lipsitt (Eds.), *Advances in child development and behavior, Volume 5.* New York: Academic Press.

Flavell, J. H., Beach, D. R., & Chinsky, J. M. (1966). Spontaneous verbal rehearsal in a memory task as a function of age. *Child Development, 37,* 283-299.

Fry, P. S., & Lupart, J. L. (1987). *Cognitive processes in children's learning: Practical applications in educational practice and classroom management.* Springfield, IL: Charles C. Thomas.

Furth, H. G. (1969). *Piaget and knowledge: Theoretical foundations.* Englewood Cliffs, NJ: Prentice-Hall.

Gallagher, J. J. (1966). Children with developmental imbalances: A psychoeducational definition. In W. M. Cruickshank (Ed.), *The teacher of brain-injured children* (pp. 23-43). Syracuse, NY: Syracuse University Press.

Gaylord-Ross, R. J. (1979). Mental retardation research, ecological validity, and the delivery of longitudinal education programs. *The Journal of Special Education, 13,* 69-80.

Ginsburg, H., & Opper, S. (1960). *Piaget's theory of intellectual development: An introduction.* Englewood Cliffs, NJ: Prentice-Hall.

Gould, S. J. (1981). *The mismeasure of man.* New York, Norton.

Hilgard, E. R. (1987). Perspectives on educational psychology. In J. A. Glover & R. R. Ronning (Eds.), *Historical foundations of educational psychology* (pp. 415-424). New York: Plenum.

Hyde, D. M. G. (1970). *Piaget and conceptual development: With a cross cultural study of number and quantity.* London: Holt, Rinehart & Winston.

Inhelder, B., & Piaget, J. (1964). *The early growth of logic in the child: Classification and seriation.* London: Routledge.

Kamin, L. J. (1974). *The science and politics of IQ.* Potomac, MD: Lawrence Erlbaum.

Keeney, J. T., Cannizzo, S. R., & Flavell, J. H. (1967). Spontaneous and induced verbal rehearsal in a recall task. *Child Development, 38,* 953-966.

Kozulin, A. (1990). *Vygotsky's psychology: A biography of ideas.* Cambridge: Harvard University Press.

Kreutzer, M. A., Leonard, C., & Flavell, J. H. (1975). An interview study of children's knowledge about memory. *Monographs of the Society for Research in Child Development, 40,* (1, Serial No. 159).

Lefrancois, G. R. (1988). *Psychology for teaching* (6th ed.). Belmont, CA: Wadsworth.

Leinhardt, G. (1992, April). What research on learning tells us about teaching. *Educational Leadership,* 20-25.

Lupart, J. L. (1991). A theory, by any educational perspective, is still a theory. In A. McKeough & J. L. Lupart (Eds.), *Toward the practice of theory based instruction: Current cognitive theories and their educational promise* (pp. 148-182). Hillsdale, NJ: Lawrence Erlbaum.

Markham, E. M. (1977). Realizing that you don't understand: A preliminary investigation. *Child Development, 50,* 643-655.

Mayer, R. E. (1987). *Educational psychology: A cognitive approach.* Boston: Little, Brown.

McKeough, A. (1991). Three perspectives on learning and instruction. In A. McKeough & J. L. Lupart (Eds.), *Toward the practice of theory based instruction: Current cognitive theories and their educational promise* (pp. 1-14). Hillsdale, NJ: Lawrence Erlbaum.

Miller, P. H. (1989). *Theories of Developmental Psychology* (2nd ed.). New York: W.H. Freeman.

Moll, L. C. (Ed.). (1990). *Vygotsky and education: Instructional implications and applications of sociohistorical psychology.* Cambridge: Cambridge University Press.

Neisser, U. (1976). *Cognition and reality.* San Francisco: W. H. Freeman.

Piaget, J. (1971). The theory of stages in cognitive development. In D. R. Green, M. P. Ford, & G. B. Flamer (Eds.), *Measurement and Piaget.* New York: McGraw-Hill.

Piaget, J. (1983). Piaget's theory. In W. Kessen (Ed.), *Handbook of child psychology, Volume 1: History, theory, and methods* (4th ed.), P. H. Mussen (Series Ed.). New York: Wiley.

Rosser, R. A., & Nicholoson, G. I. (1984). *Educational psychology: Principles in practice.* Boston: Little, Brown..

Shweder, R. A. (1990). Cultural psychology—What is it? In J. W. Stigler, R. A. Shweder, & G. Herdt (Eds.), *Cultural psychology: Essays on comparative human development.* New York: Cambridge University Press.

Siegler, R. S. (1991). *Children's thinking* (2nd ed.). Englewood Cliffs, NJ: Prentice-Hall.

Slavin, R.E. (1988). *Educational psychology: Theory into practice.* (2nd ed.). Englewood Cliffs, NJ: Prentice-Hall.

Snyderman, M., and Rothman, S. (1987). Survey of expert opinion on intelligence and aptitude testing. *American Psychologist, 42,* 137-144.

Sternberg, R. J. (1981). A componential theory of intellectual giftedness. *Gifted Child Quarterly, 25,* 86-93.

Sternberg, R. J. (1984). *Mechanisms of cognitive development.* Prospect Heights, IL: Waveland Press.

Sternberg, R. J. (1984a). Mechanisms of cognitive development: A componential approach. In R. J. Sternberg (Ed.), *Mechanisms of cognitive development* (pp. 163-185). Prospect Heights, IL: Waveland Press.

Sternberg, R. J. (1984b). Toward a triarchic theory of human intelligence. *Behavioral and Brain Sciences, 7,* 269-287.

Sternberg, R. J. (1985). *Beyond IQ: A triarchic theory of human intelligence.* Cambridge: Cambridge University Press.

Sternberg, R. J. (1991). A triarchic model for teaching intellectual skills. In A. McKeough & J. L. Lupart (Eds.), *Toward the practice of theory based instruction: Current cognitive theories and their educational promise* (pp. 92-116). Hillsdale, NJ: Lawrence Erlbaum.

Strenio, A.J. (1981). *The testing trap.* New York: Rawson, Wade.

Torgeson, J. K. (1978). Performance of reading disabled children on serial memory tasks: A selective review of recent research. *Reading Research Quarterly, 14,* 57-87.

Trotter, R. J. (1986). Robert J. Sternberg: Three heads are better than one. *Psychology Today,* 56-62.

Vander Zanden, J. W. (1980). *Educational psychology: In theory and practice.* New York: Random House.

Vygotsky, L. S. (1963). Learning and mental development at school age. In J. Simon & B. Simon (Eds.), *Educational psychology in the U.S.S.R.* (pp. 21-34). Stanford, CA: Stanford University Press.

Vygotsky, L. S. (1977). The development of higher psychological functions. *Soviet Psychology, 15*(3), 60-91.

Vygotsky, L. S. (1979). Consciousness as a problem in the psychology of behavior. *Soviet Psychology, 17*(4), 3-35.

Vygotsky, L. S. (1981). The development of higher forms of attention in childhood. In J. V. Wertsch (Ed.), *The concept of activity in Soviet psychology* (pp. 187-240). Armonk, NY: M.E. Sharpe.

Vygotsky, L. S. (1986). *Thought and language.* Cambridge, MA: MIT Press.

Walberg, H. J., & Haertel, G. D. (1992). Educational psychology's first century. *Journal of Educational Psychology, 84,* 6-19.

Wertsch, J. V. (1979). The zone of proximal development: Some conceptual issues. In B. Rogoff & J. Wertsch (Eds.), *Children's learning in the "zone of proximal development"* (pp. 7-18). San Francisco: Jossey-Bass.

Wertsch, J. V. (1991a). The problem of meaning in a sociocultural approach to mind. In A. McKeough & J. L. Lupart (Eds.), *Toward the practice of theory based instruction: Current cognitive theories and their educational promise* (pp. 31-49). Hillsdale, NJ: Lawrence Erlbaum.

Wertsch, J. V. (1991b). *Voices of the mind: A sociocultural approach to mediated action.* Cambridge, MA: Harvard University Press.

STUDENTS WITH SPECIAL NEEDS

*I*n the past, the term exceptional children referred to children with learning and behaviour problems, physical, sensory, and health impairments, severe handicaps, and children with gifts and talents. These children were very often labelled, classified, categorized, and excluded from the mainstream of education. In contrast, the current use of the term exceptional children acknowledges the fact that all children are exceptional, each with unique strengths, weaknesses, and interests.

A NOTE FROM THE AUTHORS

This change in definition reflects the present paradigm shift in education discussed in Part 1. A common phenomenon associated with educational transformations is that, in the transitional phase, old concepts and standards coexist with new ones. For example, although the classroom-instructional-based assessment model is being increasingly used, the traditional clinical-diagnostic or diagnostic-prescriptive models of assessment are still widely practiced. Moreover, although many school districts are expanding the regular curriculum in order to account for student diversity, there is still widespread use of standard and unmodified school curriculums. Thus, although there is a paradigm shift in the assessment, instruction, and service delivery practices for students with diverse needs, the traditional paradigm still exists. In keeping with this reality, the two chapters in this section purposely blend the "old" with the "new."

Chapter 4 introduces the reader to the traditional categories of exceptional children, and then focuses on children with learning disabilities, mental retardation, behaviour disorders (emotional disturbance), and gifts and talents. We focus on children with these exceptional learning and behaviour characteristics because they represent a significant percentage of children who have been provided special education services over the past couple of decades, and who will be most likely integrated into mainstream classrooms in our present educational transition phase. The chapter moves from a categorical treatment of exceptional children to discuss children's learning and behavioural characteristics from an information-processing perspective, and then provides general instructional guidelines for accommodating these characteristics in inclusive classrooms.

Chapter 5 introduces the reader to ESL (English as a Second Language) students, who arguably represent the highest incidence of special-needs children in mainstream classrooms. Following a discussion of the historical background of immigration, this chapter focuses on the major concepts and issues relevant to multicultural education, and provides working guidelines and adaptations for second-language teaching in a multicultural context.

The underlying goals of this section are to promote tolerance of uniqueness and individuality, to reinforce the transactional view of learning, and to facilitate reflection about student diversity and inclusive education.

THE CLASSROOM: AN INCLUSIVE MOSAIC

CHAPTER 4

CHAPTER OBJECTIVES

To stress the student diversity in the inclusive classroom.

To provide an overview of the educational characteristics of students in an inclusive classroom.

To discuss definitions and issues relevant to inclusive education.

To overview the information-processing system and its relevance to the understanding and teaching of children and youth.

To present instructional suggestions for teachers of students with diverse educational needs.

Students in Inclusive Classrooms

One is a practical joker.
One gossips all the time.
One never combs his hair.
One never washes her hair.
One gets frustrated extremely easily.
One gets angry extremely easily.
One is like a little puppy dog who always follows you around.
One is emotional about everything.
One is quick and slow at the same time.
One is always cool.
One is always helpful.
One is always late.
One is always talking.
One is always laughing.
One is always slow to respond.
One is always messy and slow to clean.
One is always mumbling.
One is always first to raise her hand.
One has braces.
One shuffles along slowly.
One needs kid gloves all the time.
One needs to be involved or helping continually.
One needs firmness.
One needs flexibility and options at all times.
One loves music.
One loves electronics.
One loves reading.
One loves computers.
One loves her friends.
One hates snakes.
They are great kids who are all a joy (and a challenge) to teach.

Teachers in Inclusive Classrooms

They care about the students.
They are enthusiastic about teaching.
They work hard.
They put in long hours.
They know and love their subject areas.
They understand kids and the way they develop.
They are innovative and creative.
They are fair.
They are flexible.
They dress well.
They have high expectations.
They are always prepared.
They "pull-out" rather than "pour-in."
They are positive and optimistic.
They take risks.
They stretch, challenge, and motivate their students.
They are dedicated.

They have the ability to admit their mistakes.
They seem to love learning.
They go the "extra mile."
They are patient.
They have a sense of humour.
They are self-confident.
They are intelligent.
They understand the problems of their students.
They think and plan for weeks and months ahead.
They use teaching strategies that help develop, maintain, and remediate lower-order skills (knowledge acquisition and comprehension).
They use teaching strategies that engage the higher orders of intellectual activity (analysis, synthesis, evaluation).
They smile a lot.
They are great people who are all a joy (and a challenge) to work with.

⬦   ⬦   ⬦

⬦ INTRODUCTION

Today's regular classroom is a microcosm of Canadian society—a community of individuals with varied backgrounds, abilities, difficulties, interests, goals, and identities. Its representative nature can be attributed to a variety of social, political, economic, and educational policies that brought more students with diverse needs into the regular (or *inclusive*) classroom. Students with diverse needs are those who have difficulty maximizing their potential due to cognitive, emotional, physical, developmental, psychological, social, and/or environmental factors. These students require adaptive instruction and a differentiated curriculum to reach their potential.

As society becomes more diversified it also becomes more challenging to govern. This is also true of the inclusive classroom, where we can now expect to have a wider range of children to manage. In order to effectively manage this student diversity, teachers must be aware of the characteristics, strengths, and weaknesses of their individual students, and be able to provide effective instruction that is directed toward each student's learning needs (see Chapter 9 for further discussion). For example, some students might have difficulty processing information and need to be taught how to use efficient learning strategies independently; others might have difficulty initiating and maintaining satisfactory interpersonal relationships and require social-skill intervention; and still others might have physical and health-related difficulties that require particular environmental and instructional modifications.

In the last two decades, many children have been diagnosed and classified according to their mental, physical, sensory, health, social, and emotional characteristics. This practice has resulted in the categorizing and labelling of

many children according to their particular attributes. Once categorized and labelled, many students were placed into special classes and/or provided special programs. The most common categories of exceptional children are (for further reference, see Gearheart, Weishahn, & Gearheart, 1992; Heward & Orlanski, 1992; Schulz, Carpenter, & Turnbull, 1991; Winzer, 1989, 1990; Ysseldyke & Algozzine, 1990):

- Learning disabilities
- Mental retardation
- Behaviour disorders (emotional disturbance)
- Gifted and talented
- Visual impairments
- Hearing impairments
- Communication (speech and language) disorders
- Physical and health impairments
- Severe disabilities

Many educators consider categories to be meaningless when applied to educational planning and instruction. Stainback and Stainback (1984) point out that "categories often do not reflect the specific educational needs and interests of students in relation to such services. For example, some students categorized as visually handicapped may not need large-print books, while others who are not labelled visually impaired and thus are ineligible for large-print books could benefit from their use" (p. 105).

This chapter provides an overview of the educational characteristics of students in an inclusive classroom. We first examine students with learning disabilities, delayed cognitive skills, behavioural disorders, and advanced cognitive abilities, as well as definitional and conceptual issues relevant to these areas. Next we present an information-processing model of learning in order to: (1) select and discuss information-processing characteristics of children in the classroom; (2) address visual and hearing difficulties, communication problems, physical and health impairments, and severe handicaps that children may experience; and (3) provide instructional recommendations relevant to teaching children with these diverse educational characteristics.

◇ STUDENTS WITH LEARNING DISABILITIES

Many children who experience significant learning difficulties have a specific learning disability. Although learning problems have been linked to specific learning disabilities, there is no universally agreed-upon definition of the term *learning disability*. However, the definition most widely referenced is the one incorporated in the United States Public Law 94-142, or the Education for All Handicapped Children Act (1975). The definition reads:

> "Specific learning disability" means a disorder in one or more of the basic psychological processes involved in understanding or in using language spoken or written, which may manifest itself in an imperfect ability to listen, think, speak, read, write, spell, or do mathematical calculations. The term includes such conditions as perceptual handicaps, brain injury, minimal brain dysfunction, dyslexia, and developmental aphasia. This term does not include children who have learning problems which are primarily the result of visual, hearing, or motor handicaps, of mental retardation, of emotional disturbance, or of environmental, cultural, or economic disadvantage (Federal Register, 1981).

According to this definition, individuals with learning disabilities have difficulty processing information (i.e., attending to, memorizing, and/or perceiving information), and developing their learning and thinking skills. The definition also suggests that a learning disability is apparent if there is a significant discrepancy between the individual's potential for learning and his or her present level of achievement.

In the 1980s, the National Joint Committee on Learning Disabilities (NJLCD), representing a number of professional organizations involved with learning disabilities, proposed the following definition:

> "Learning disabilities" is a generic term that refers to a heterogeneous group of disorders manifested by significant difficulties in the acquisition and use of listening, speaking, reading, writing, reasoning, or mathematical abilities. These disorders are intrinsic to the individual and presumed to be due to central nervous system dysfunction. Even though a learning disability

may occur concomitantly with other handicapping conditions (e.g., sensory impairment, mental retardation, social and emotional disturbance) or environmental influences (e.g., cultural differences, or inappropriate instruction, psycholinguistic factors), it is not the direct result of those conditions or influences (NJCLD, 1987, p. 107).

This definition extends the federal concept of learning disability by indicating that a learning disability can be any one of a heterogeneous group of disorders or chronic problems. The definition also recognizes that learning disabilities may coincide with other handicapping conditions (i.e., an individual may have a behavioural disorder *in addition to* a learning disability).

Members of the Association for Children and Adults with Learning Disabilities (ACLD) did not totally endorse the NJCLD definition, because they believed that a learning disability selectively interferes with an individual's abilities, and also that it can vary with respect to manifestation and severity. Hence, the organization proposed the following definition:

> Specific learning disabilities is a chronic condition of presumed neurological origin which selectively interferes with the development, integration, and/ or demonstration of verbal and/or nonverbal abilities. Specific learning disabilities exist as a distinct handicapping condition in the presence of average to superior intelligence, adequate sensory and motor systems, and adequate learning opportunities. The condition varies in its manifestations and in degree of severity. Throughout life the condition can affect self-esteem, education, vocation, and/or daily living activities (ACLD, 1985, p. 2).

Unlike the federal and NJCLD definitions, which make reference to the information-processing causes of learning disabilities, this definition simply lists the various manifestations of learning disabilities, citing cause only in its assumption that these disabilities are intrinsic to the individual and presumably due to a dysfunction of the central nervous system (see Conte & Andrews, 1993 for further discussion regarding the definitions of learning disabilities).

The inability of educators to propose a universally accepted definition of learning disabilities has provoked much criticism. As Ysseldyke, Algozzine, and Epps (1983) state:

> From its inception, the classification of learning disabilities has been an ill-defined, poorly conceptualized, incredibly popular idea. There are millions of children who perform poorly in reading, writing, mathematics, listening, speaking, and other academic areas; significant numbers of students are failing to profit from their educational experiences, but no defendable system exists for classifying or categorizing these students; there are no defensible inclusionary and exclusionary principles. (p. 165)

In more specific terms, the major problems with our current definitions of learning disabilities are: (1) they focus on the *result* rather than the *cause* of learning difficulty; (2) they create ambiguity with respect to identification, e.g., failing to suggest *how much* discrepancy between an individual's potential and his or her achievement should be evident before identifying that person as learning disabled; (3) they focus on the underachievement of individuals with learning disabilities and ignore their strengths; and (4) they speculate as to the intrinsic and possible neurological basis of the learning problem and yet the medical and educational fields have not been able to validate this hypothesis.

It is possible that a single definition of learning disability may be infeasible because as Keogh (1987) notes, a learning disability is not a single condition but rather a group of related and overlapping conditions. Problems of etiology and identification aside, there *are* common elements in the definitions of learning disabilities that allow us to better understand the condition(s) and help us "see it" in our students.

What are specific diagnostic criteria?

Educators across Canada generally conceptualize learning disabilities in terms of features common to the earlier-described definitions. Thus, Canadian educators view a learning disability as any one of a mixed group of long-lasting disorders, which may be the result of a central nervous system dysfunction. These disorders may be evidenced by difficulties in one or more processes such as attention, concentration, perception, memory, reasoning, organization, planning, and problem-solving. The results are observable weaknesses in such areas as language arts, mathematics, and (sometimes) interpersonal relationships. If a student is underachieving relative to his or her potential, has had an adequate learning environment along with adequate motivational and learning opportunities, and has no primary, sensory, motor, or emotional problems, then a learning disability is considered to be the primary cause of the learning difficulty. Psychologists and educators further distinguish learning disabilities on the basis of severity; thus, a child may have a mild, moderate, or severe learning disability.

◇ STUDENTS WITH DELAYED COGNITIVE SKILLS

Within our schools are children who have significant difficulty functioning independently in the academic and social domains. They seem to learn very slowly, to forget information sooner than their peers, and to have problems integrating different pieces of information and applying this information from one situation to another. They also demonstrate delayed expressive and receptive language skills, and project relatively negative feelings about their abilities and potential.

In class 3 basic criteria for definition

In the past, children with delayed cognitive skills (mental retardation) were described as intellectually subnormal individuals who were incurable (Doll, 1941). Indeed, until the mid-1970s, mental retardation was solely identified through intellectual assessment. However, psychologists and educators have since expanded assessment to include adaptive behaviour, in recognition of the fact that intelligence tests are poor measures of adaptive ability, which is an important factor in assessing intelligence.

The definition most widely accepted by most authorities is the one adopted by the American Association on Mental Deficiency (AAMD), the major professional association in the field of mental retardation, which reads:

> Mental retardation refers to significantly subaverage general intellectual functioning resulting in or associated with concurrent impairments in adaptive behaviour and manifested during the developmental period. (Grossman, 1983, p. 11).

According to this definition, before an individual is considered to have mental retardation three criteria must be met: subaverage intellectual functioning, deficits in adaptive behaviour, and age of onset.

Subaverage intellectual functioning refers to below-average scores on a standardized intelligence test (e.g., the Wechsler Intelligence Scale for Children-Revised [WISC-R] or the Stanford-Binet Intelligence Test) that are at least two standard deviations below the mean (an IQ score of approximately 70 and below).

Deficits in adaptive behaviour are determined in relation to "the standards of maturation, learning, personal independence, and/or social responsibility that are expected for his or her age level and cultural group" (Grossman, 1983, p. 11). According to the AAMD definition of mental retardation, an individual who obtains a low score on an intelligence test, but demonstrates an ability to cope with the contextual and situational demands of his or her environment, should *not* be regarded as having mental retardation. In addition, there is a cultural/situational component that needs to be taken into account when assessing the adaptive behaviour of an individual. As Mercer and Lewis (1978) note, we must be aware that people operate in a number of different roles, in a variety of social contexts, and within a multicultural and pluralistic society. Hence, what is appropriate and adaptive in one culture and in one situation may or may not be appropriate in another culture and another situation. This factor needs to be considered before determining that someone's behaviour is unadaptive and due to mental retardation.

Scales commonly used to assess adaptive behaviour include the American Association on Mental Deficiency Adaptive Behaviour Scales and the Vineland Adaptive Behaviour Scales. These scales allow the examiner to assess adaptive behaviour in relation to a variety of domains such as independent functioning, physical development, money-handling, language development, and socialization (Lambert, Windmiller, Tharinger, & Cole, 1981). To reduce the risk of bias, it is sometimes recommended that more than one examiner and assessment scale be used. Moreover, because adaptive behaviour is developmental in nature, expectations of behaviour need to be considered in light of various age levels. During childhood, adaptive behaviour should be assessed in relation to sensorimotor, communication, self-help, and interpersonal skills. During childhood and adolescence, behavioural deficits may be seen in the individual's academic, reasoning, and social skills. During late adolescence, deficits in adaptive behaviour may be manifested through vocational and general social skills (Chinn, Drew, & Logan, 1979).

The *age of onset* aspect of the AAMD definition regards the manifestation of mental retardation during the developmental period, which means that the condition needs to be observed between conception and 18 years of age.

Mental retardation, like learning disability, is a heterogeneous condition due to the variety and severity of associated problems. Hence, students with mental retardation are often differentiated according to the dysfunctional severity of the intellectual and adaptive behaviour. The typical classifications are: profound mental retardation, severe mental retardation, moderate mental retardation (or trainable mental retardation), and mild mental retardation (or educable mental retardation).

Individuals with *profound mental retardation* typically score below 25 on standardized intelligence tests. In almost all cases, brain injury and physical handicaps are present (MacMillan, 1982), and communication ability, as well as motor development, is very limited. Individuals who have this condition make up about 1 percent of all persons diagnosed as having mental retardation and require care in a supervised setting. Individuals with *severe mental retardation* typically score between 25 and 40 on standardized intelligence tests. For this group, which constitutes about 3 percent of all persons with mental retardation, serious intellectual and adaptive behaviour deficits necessitate lifelong care. Most individuals with this condition can achieve minimal communication and self-help skills, and some may be able to acquire low-level vocational skills and work, under close supervision, in sheltered workshops. Individuals with *moderate mental retardation* generally score between 40 and 55 on standardized intelligence tests. This group makes up about 8 percent of persons with mental retardation. Individuals with moderate mental retardation have marked developmental delays, and often exhibit physical and motor difficulties. Typically, they can adjust reasonably well socially (e.g., learn how to cooperate and share with others, as well as respect others' property), achieve basic academic skills (usually to a Grade 3 to 5 level), and acquire semi-independent vocational skills.

Individuals with *mild mental retardation* account for about 85 to 90 percent of persons who have mental retardation. Slightly below average in terms of their developmental and self-help skills, many of these individuals come from lower-class, disadvantaged families. Individuals with mild mental retardation typically score between 55 and 70 on standardized intelligence tests, and are capable of achieving academic skills at advanced elementary grade levels and adaptive behaviour skills at an independent level.

Although the AAMD definition of mental retardation dominates the field, sociological perspectives regarding mental retardation should also be considered. As Sarason and Doris (1979) state, "The shifting definitions and management of mental retardation are not understandable in terms of the "essence" of the "condition" but rather in terms of changing social values and conditions" (p. 417). Thus, our thinking about mental retardation is embedded in the values, ideologies, and attitudes toward mental retardation in society at large (Ysseldyke & Algozzine, 1990). The concept of mental retardation as a sociological phenomenon is supported by Mercer (1973, 1981), who developed a system of multicultural pluralistic assessment (SOMPA) designed to eliminate cultural bias in intelligence testing by estimating a child's learning potential in light of his or her cultural and familial background.

◇ STUDENTS WITH BEHAVIOUR DISORDERS

Teachers in today's inclusive classrooms are likely to have children who behave in ways that depart significantly from social or cultural norms. The records may report that these children tend to show frustration when trying to reach their goals, have difficulty solving academic and social problems, have difficulty interacting with others, and tend to create discomfort for themselves and others around them. Most likely, they are children with behaviour disorders.

To date, there is no single accepted definition of behaviour disorder. Indeed, there is still debate among educators as to whether students who show marked and prolonged behaviour that is undesirable, inappropriate, and maladaptive have a behaviour disorder or an emotional disturbance. This reflects a split among professionals between those who ascribe behavioural problems to psychological or biopsychological pathology (e.g., phobia and depression), and those who prefer sociological explanations. The Council for Children with Behaviour Disorders (CCBD), it should be noted, has officially adopted the term *behaviour disorder* (1987).

The most widespread definition, articulated by the United States Office of Education and included in Public Law 94-142, uses the label "seriously emotionally disturbed," which according to United States federal law means:

1. a condition exhibiting one or more of the following characteristics over a long period of time and to a marked degree, which adversely affects educational performance:
   (a) An inability to learn which cannot be explained by intellectual, sensory, or health factors;
   (b) An inability to build or maintain satisfactory relationships with peers and teachers;
   (c) Inappropriate types of behaviour or feelings under normal circumstances;
   (d) A general pervasive mood of unhappiness or depression; or
   (e) A tendency to develop physical symptoms or fears associated with personal or school problems.
2. The term includes children who are schizophrenic. The term does not include children who are socially maladjusted, unless it is determined that they are seriously emotionally disturbed (Office of Federal National Archives and Records Administration, 1985).

The above definition identifies characteristic behaviours and emotions (e.g., inability to build or maintain satisfactory relationships, general pervasive mood of unhappiness), but it does not direct us with respect to the assessment of these characteristics. For example, how do we measure such terms as "satisfactory relationships" and "pervasive" (Heward & Orlansky, 1992)?

Despite the general lack of consensus about what constitutes behaviour disorders, they have certain recognizable features. First, behavioural disturbances and emotional crises can range from minor to severe, and from transitory to chronic. Teachers should, therefore, identify behavioural disorders according to their severity, frequency, and chronicity (duration). Moreover, they need to evaluate the behaviour in relation to the developmental level of the student, as well as social and cultural norms.

The two most common behaviours exhibited by children with behavioural disorders are aggressive/acting-out behaviour and social withdrawal (Heward & Orlansky, 1992), or, as they are sometimes referred to (respectively), *externalizing* and *internalizing behaviour disorders* (Achenbach & Edelbrock, 1978). *Aggressive* behaviour can take many forms—verbal abuse, vandalism, physical attacks (Heward & Orlansky, 1992), disturbing peers, talking back to teachers, displaying frustration, and refusing to work (Hutton, 1985). Children who exhibit aggressive behaviour tend to be disliked by their peers (Drabman & Paterson, 1981), and have difficulty making friends. Moreover, these children tend to be readily identified by their teachers because of the visibility of their acting-out behaviour in the classroom. Children who withdraw from others limit their social development. Some may show lack of interest in their lives, be unwilling to try new things, make self-deprecatory remarks, and give up easily. Some are fearful of things without reason (Heward & Orlansky, 1992), refrain from contact with others, and resist attempts by others to form positive relationships.

Many theories have been proposed to explain behaviour disorders. For example, some believe that a child's inborn temperament may predispose him or her to behavioural problems (Thomas & Chess, 1984), while others attribute behaviour disorders to internal psychological conflicts (Erikson, 1963), or behavioural, sociological, and/or ecological factors (Gearheart et al., 1992). Ecological models that emphasize child-environment interactions have gained the support of many teachers.

Children who exhibit behavioural disorders challenge teachers' authority and control in the classroom, and disrupt the learning and development of the other children in the class. If these disorders go untreated, some children may end up abusing drugs and alcohol, or even committing suicide. Suicide rates and drug use have increased steadily over the last two decades (Krug, 1983; Muse, 1990), particularly among students with behavioural disorders; (Hawton, 1986). Hence, there is a crucial need for all teachers to be aware of these issues so they can provide the necessary guidance and assistance.

◆ STUDENTS WITH ADVANCED COGNITIVE ABILITIES

Today's inclusive classroom is likely to include students who show precocity (remarkable early development) in areas such as language and mathematics;

demonstrate special abilities or accomplishments in a variety of areas; and/or reveal learning styles and strategies that facilitate accelerated learning. In comparison to their peers, these students may appear to be more intrinsically motivated, creative, self-confident, versatile, adaptive, task-committed, and/ or verbally expressive. While students who have been identified as having these advanced cognitive abilities have been frequently labelled "gifted" and "talented," there is lack of agreement about what constitutes giftedness and who should be considered as gifted and talented.

As defined by Marland [United States Commissioner of Education] (1972),

> Gifted and talented children are those identified by professionally qualified persons who by virtue of outstanding abilities are capable of high performance. These are children who require differentiated educational programs and services beyond those normally provided by the regular school program in order to realize their contribution to self and society.
>
> Children capable of high performance include those with demonstrated achievement and/or potential ability in any of the following areas:
>
> 1. General intellectual ability
> 2. Specific academic aptitude
> 3. Creative or productive thinking
> 4. Leadership ability
> 5. Visual and performing arts
> 6. Psychomotor ability. (p. 2)

For Renzulli (1978), this definition is problematic because it does not include motivational (task-commitment) factors; it represents the six categories of giftedness as being independent, thus ignoring the degree to which they overlap; and, lastly, it alerts professionals to consider many areas of high performance when, in practice, intelligence tests dominate the identification process. Hence, as Renzulli (1978) defines it,

> Giftedness consists of an interaction among three basic clusters of human traits—these clusters being above-average general abilities, high levels of task commitment, and high levels of creativity. Gifted and talented children are those possessing or capable of developing this composite set of traits and applying them to any potentially valuable area of human performance. Children who manifest or are capable of developing an interaction among the three clusters require a wide variety of educational opportunities and services that are not ordinarily provided through regular instructional programs. (p. 261)

As Renzulli (1978) notes, most educators identify and plan for only one type of giftedness: the *intellectually gifted*. Gifted children obtain scores on individually administered intelligence tests (usually the WISC-R or Stanford-Binet) that are typically two to three standard deviations above the mean. An intelligence score of 130 and above indicates that a student has general intellectual ability in the superior range. However, there is considerable debate as to whether intelligence tests measure giftedness, or even intelligence.

Intelligence tests typically differentiate individuals on the basis of the *quantity* of their performance, rather than on the *quality* of their performance, and therefore fail to tap the richness and complexity, as well as potential, of intellectual processing. Moreover, traditional measures of intelligence are based on the idea that intelligence is primarily unidimensional, whereas recent conceptualizations indicate that intelligence is *multidimensional*. For example, Gardner (1984) suggests that individuals possess "several intellectual competencies" (p. 699), and that people can vary in ability, potential, and achievement across what he proposes as seven basic intelligences: linguistic, logical-mathematical, musical, spatial, body kinesthetic, interpersonal, and intrapersonal. Sternberg (1984b) believes that traditional intelligence tests do not measure abilities that are more closely related to behaviour in the real world, and views intelligence as consisting of three types of behaviour: problem-solving ability, verbal ability, and social competence. According to these scholars, intelligence and giftedness is more varied and complex than what is measured by traditional intelligence tests.

A second issue to emerge from the Marland/Renzulli definitions is that both include creativity as an aspect of giftedness, but do not define it. While creativity generally refers to a process by which an individual brings new and different responses to a situation, there are varied opinions as to how creativity evolves and manifests itself. For example, Sternberg and Davidson (1983) believe that creative individuals have the ability to discover, express, and build upon new ideas because they have insight skills that allow them to more effectively and efficiently sift irrelevant from relevant information, combine relevant information in novel and productive ways, and relate new information with old information in new ways. Khatena (1976) views creativity as "the power of the imagination to break away from perceptual set so as to restructure ideas, thoughts, and feelings into novel and meaningful associate bonds" (p. 316). According to Torrance (1969), creative individuals differ from others in terms of their ability to respond to situations with greater flexibility, originality, elaboration, and fluency of ideas. These definitions of creativity provide us with some useful ways of understanding the construct. However, identifying creatively gifted children is difficult because there are so many variations among the definitions, and because reliable and valid measuring devices are unavailable. Therefore, although creativity is considered to be an aspect of giftedness, it remains elusive in terms of identification.

A third issue with respect to the definitions of giftedness is that they do not differentiate between giftedness and talent. Indeed, both definitions use the terms synonymously, which leads to conceptual ambiguity. According to Gagne (1985), giftedness and talent encompass completely separate ideas: "Giftedness corresponds to competence which is distinctly above average in one or more domains of ability. Talent refers to performance which is distinctly above average in one or more fields of human performance" (p. 108). She further notes that

> [t]his distinction implies, as a corollary, that every talented individual is necessarily gifted, although the inverse is not true; a gifted individual is not necessarily talented. Since it is a manifestation of giftedness in a particular field of activity, talent necessarily implies the presence of underlying abilities capable of explaining it. However, it can certainly happen, as is well illustrated in the case of underachieving children, that an individual shows himself to be gifted, that is the possessor of exceptional abilities, without having manifested his giftedness in any academic talent. (p. 108)

This distinction between giftedness and talent alerts educators to the possibility that individuals may be intellectually gifted, but not necessarily talented academically.

Finally, the Marland/Renzulli definitions do not specify whether *actual* above-average performance or *potential* above-average performance should be the criterion for determining giftedness. Demonstrated and potential achievement are considered to be equally valid for identifying children with advanced cognitive abilities. However, allowing both possibilities can lead to different identifications across different educational environments. For example, students who are assessed as demonstrating poor performance (i.e., low academic achievement) but high potential may be identified as gifted in some areas and not in others.

The two definitions and associated issues presented above reveal the complexities involved in defining giftedness. Within our multicultural and pluralistic country, different teachers and parents value and encourage different abilities and capacities. Our theorizing, research endeavours, and educational practices are influenced by this variance, which is evident, too, in the present definitions of giftedness. A theme that *is* emerging with some consistency across our country is *the importance of evaluating children's educational needs and making programming decisions according to their learning and behavioural characteristics*. As Hallahan and Kauffman (1988) put it, "Perhaps giftedness is not a fixed or absolute human characteristic—perhaps we should speak of people who exhibit *gifted behaviour* rather than of *gifted people*" (p. 418).

◆ STUDENTS' LEARNING AND BEHAVIOURAL CHARACTERISTICS: AN OVERVIEW

Students have educational characteristics that range from a large variety of learning and behavioural difficulties to a large variety of superior abilities and skills. Many of these characteristics are also associated with average students, who may not possess significant gifts or talents, or have learning disabilities, cognitive delays, and behaviour disorders.

Children with significant learning and behaviour problems are primarily characterized by mild to severe difficulties related to: (1) using strategies to acquire, retain, organize, elaborate, and express information; (2) reflecting upon and monitoring their learning; (3) developing fine and gross motor abilities; (4) attending to, perceiving, and discriminating information; (5) integrating information from auditory, visual, and tactile stimuli; (6) comprehending information from reading and listening; (7) reading and communicating; (8) reasoning and calculating; (9) interacting with others; (10) succeeding in academic and social tasks independently; (11) following rules and behaving normally; and (12) achieving academic standards in relation to their age, grade, and cultural group (Heward & Orlansky, 1992; Winzer, 1990; Ysseldyke & Algozzine, 1990).

Children with superior abilities and skills are primarily characterized by proficiencies related to: (1) thinking at high intellectual levels; (2) achieving academic skills beyond their age, grade, and cultural group; (3) acquiring, retaining, organizing, synthesizing, analyzing, elaborating, and expressing information; (4) attending to, perceiving, and discriminating information; (5) empathizing with others; (6) concentrating, persevering, and committing themselves to various tasks; (7) leading others in various domains; (8) moralizing with deep conviction; (9) creating ideas and products; and (10) being resourceful, flexible, and original in their behaviour (Heward & Orlansky, 1992; Winzer, 1990; Ysseldyke & Algozzine, 1990).

EDUCATIONAL IMPLICATIONS

Because of their diverse problems and talents, students with significant learning and behavioural difficulties, as well as students with superior skills and abilities, present various challenges to teachers of inclusive classrooms. Some salient needs of these students are:

- To have well-structured and organized learning environments, as well as unstructured and discovery learning experiences.
- To be taught how to control, regulate, monitor, and evaluate their own learning as effectively and efficiently as possible.
- To be provided academic programs that will not only develop and remediate specific academic skills but also enrich their abilities and interests.
- To have teachers who will make compensations, adaptations, and modifications in relation to the teaching-learning environment and in accordance with student individuality.
- To have teachers who will look at what their students *are* rather than what they *are not*.
- To be given opportunities to develop and strengthen their social competencies.
- To be taught strategies that can develop their ability to acquire, retain, organize, elaborate, generalize, transfer, and express information.
- To have teachers who are effective managers and who will minimize boredom, confusion, and frustration.

- To have opportunities to develop and strengthen leadership skills, creative and artistic abilities, and individual interests.
- To have teachers who will facilitate students' capabilities in self-initiated action, independent learning, thinking, problem-solving, and decision-making.

Strategies for meeting these educational challenges in inclusive classrooms are discussed later in this chapter, and much more comprehensively in the following chapters. Next we discuss current trends related to the categorizing and labelling of children.

◇ CURRENT TRENDS IN CATEGORIZING AND LABELLING

In the last couple of decades, the educational field has followed the *psychomedical model of assessment* under which children with abnormal learning and behavioural characteristics are diagnosed and classified, and then placed in settings that provide particular kinds of programming and instruction. This process involves the categorization and labelling of children. *Labelling* refers to the classifying of children based on their primary educational characteristic (e.g., learning disabled, mentally retarded, behaviour disordered, and gifted). As Ysseldyke and Algozzine (1990) note, "Labels are cues that help organize our knowledge, perceptions, and behaviour. They carry with them certain expectations—some good, some bad" (p. 89).

ADVANTAGES OF LABELLING

- Labelling helps professionals communicate with each other.
- Labelling allows parents, teachers, and advocacy groups to focus public attention on children with special educational needs.
- Labelling can establish eligibility for resources to meet the demands of children with learning and behavioural needs.
- Categories of special-needs students can serve as a basis for further diagnosis, treatment, and research, as well as facilitate educational organization and legislative policy-making.

DISADVANTAGES OF LABELLING

- Labelling and categorizing children stigmatizes and stereotypes them, and can therefore affect their self-image. Children may view themselves—or be perceived by others—as *being* behaviourally disordered or learning disabled, as opposed to simply *having* learning and/or behavioural difficulties.
- Labels can affect parents' and teachers' expectations regarding what a child can accomplish, or how a child can behave. A parent or a teacher

may underestimate or overestimate a child's potential and abilities, resulting in unsatisfied expectations and frustration.

♦ Labels may absolve people of responsibility. A parent or teacher may not be willing to deal with a child's academic or behavioural development in particular areas because the child has cognitive delays/advanced abilities and is therefore unable/able to learn on his or her own.

♦ Labelling can lead to inappropriate placement of children due to misdiagnosis. Children from cultural minority groups, for example, have been unfairly assessed as being intellectually or academically delayed, resulting in placement in special classrooms for the mentally retarded.

♦ Labelling most often identifies children as being different from others, which can lead to their exclusion from the everyday lifestyle of their peers.

♦ Labelling usually points out children's weaknesses instead of their strengths.

♦ Labelling increases the chances for children to be teased by their peers, which can lead to lowered self-image and peer rejection.

Labelling does *not* benefit instructional practice. Becker, Engelmann, and Thomas (1971) point out that "for the most part labels are not important. They rarely tell the teacher who can be taught in what way. One could put five or six labels on the same child and still not know what to teach him or how" (p. 436). The trend in educational practice today is toward labelling the learning and behavioural characteristics the child displays, rather than identifying the learning and behavioural characteristics the child displays and labelling the child. There is recognition, too, that intervention approaches are based not on the labels or categories of children but on the learning characteristics revealed by the children we serve.

In order to educate children effectively, teachers need to know both how children typically learn and behave, and how to meet the needs of children who exhibit both normal and abnormal learning and behavioural characteristics. The balance of this chapter first presents current perspectives on how children learn and process information, and then isolates and discusses the most prevailing cognitive and behavioural characteristics of children in an inclusive classroom setting.

◆ STUDENTS' LEARNING AND BEHAVIOUR: A COGNITIVE FRAMEWORK

Models for learning and behaviour can assist us in understanding how children learn and behave, as well as help us plan and modify the learning and teaching context in order to foster more effective learning and behavioural development. The cognitive-oriented model of learning and behaviour outlined below allows us to discuss the salient cognitive and behavioural characteristics of children in today's inclusive classrooms, as well as to provide suggestions for teaching in this context.

According to Jones, Palincsar, Ogle, and Carr (1987), there is consensus among many researchers and educators that learning is an active, strategic, planful, and constructive process. These authors note that there is increasing evidence that efficient learners strive to understand the meaning of academic and social tasks, and to regulate their performance on these tasks. Such learners are able to organize and interpret information that is poorly presented, and to appreciate the quality of their performance by linking new information to prior knowledge and experience. They also know when, how, and where to use particular skills, strategies, and knowledge, as well as how to monitor and control their own learning. In the process of learning, the efficient learner focuses his or her attention on a particular task, activates **prior knowledge**, assimilates and evaluates new ideas, consolidates what is learned, and then transfers and generalizes acquired information to other contexts and situations (Jones et al., 1987). This learning process is cyclical, interactive, and influenced by one's development, experience, and proficiency.

prior knowledge: knowledge that is already part of a person's cognition

The above conceptualization of learning contrasts with the traditional view of learning as a passive endeavour—"essentially a matter of responding to the information that was given" (Jones et al., 1987, p. 5). According to present educational theory, the performance of students can be improved by providing effective instruction; by making students more aware of their own goals, approaches, and strategies for learning; by teaching them how to better organize and link information they acquire; and by teaching them how to monitor and regulate their own performances.

◆ INFORMATION PROCESSING

Our understanding of how and why people vary in their learning has come largely from research based on cognitive development, and from information-processing theory (e.g., Case, 1978, 1984; Siegler, 1976, 1984; Sternberg, 1982, 1984b). Cognitive learning theorists and researchers of human memory (e.g., Atkinson & Shiffrin, 1968; Bransford, 1979) have helped us describe the process by which information is received and remembered. This theoretical perspective is known as the information-processing view of learning, memory, and cognitive development.

Information-processing theory presents learners as active processors, who attend to and select information from the environment; transform, reduce, and elaborate information; relate prior knowledge and experience with new information; and organize information in order to make it meaningful (Schunk, 1991). This process is illustrated in Figure 4.1. What follows is an overview of specific elements in the information-processing system.

INPUT AND SENSES

A person receives information from many environmental sources (e.g., visual, auditory, tactual, kinesthetic, gustatory, and olfactory stimuli) through his or her senses (i.e., vision, hearing, touch, movement, taste, and smell).

SENSORY REGISTER

The information that is received from the environment through our senses is stored for a very short time in the sensory register, where we perceive and attend to it for a fraction of a second. The sensory register helps us discern and focus our attention on new information. Perception is "not as straightforward as reception of stimuli; rather, it is influenced by our mental state, past experience, knowledge, motivation, and many other factors; *furthermore, we do not record the stimuli we perceive as we see or sense them, but as we know (or assume) they really are*" (Slavin, 1991, p. 132). Attention refers to the ability of an individual to notice details in the environment, to select important and relevant information, and to concentrate on particular tasks (Calfee, 1976).

Under Diff parts

SHORT-TERM MEMORY

After information is received, recognized, attended to, and assigned meaning, it is transferred to working or short-term memory (STM), where it is stored for a few seconds. STM has limited capacity in that only a small amount of information can be retained at any one time. The information that enters working memory can come from our sensory register and/or from acquired information that is stored in long-term memory. STM has a capacity of five to seven "bits" of information (Miller, 1956), which means we are able to consider only five to seven distinct things at a time (Slavin, 1991). Therefore, our ability to retain isolated bits of information depends on actively working with the information we receive.

Bold Face Italics

LONG-TERM MEMORY

In contrast to short-term memory, long-term memory (LTM) is where we permanently store information. LTR is thought to have unlimited capacity. Essentially, information that is actively engaged in STM is transferred to LTM if the individual believes that the information warrants later retrieval and use. Information that is irrelevant, or not actively attended to, or beyond the capacity of STM will not be transferred to LTM.

LTM comprises three types of memory: episodic memory, semantic memory, and procedural memory (Tulving, 1972, 1985). *Episodic memory* includes information associated with particular times and places, and comes from personal experience (e.g., remembering a particular date we had with someone, or remembering a party we attended). *Semantic memory* includes general information (e.g., facts, concepts, principles, learning strategies) that is not necessarily tied to any specific context. Semantic memory is organized in networks of connected ideas or relationships called **schema** (Anderson, 1985; Chang, 1986; Schank & Abelson, 1977). Schemas or semantic networks "allow us to organize our knowledge in such a way that we can retrieve information and effectively add new information to long term memory. They also assist us in determining the relationship among ideas" (Bos & Vaughn, 1991, pp. 54-55). *Procedural memory* refers to knowing *how* to do something (Cotten & Squire, 1980, cited in Slavin, 1991). Knowing how to remember information, study for tests, organize information, and reduce anxiety are examples of skills or strategies retained in procedural memory.

◆ schema: cognitive networks that facilitate the organization and retrieval of information

RESPONSE MECHANISMS

The effectiveness of a student's information processing can sometimes be indicated by the overt behaviours he or she demonstrates in academic and social tasks. Research on efficient or effective performance shows that people typically execute behaviours according to a sequence of planned elements (Bilodeau, 1966; Fitts & Posner, 1967). Effective learners tend to be goal-directed and able to select specific strategies to achieve desired outcomes. They tend to monitor their performance, make changes where necessary, and alter their performance to meet specific contextual demands. Behavioural responses not only indicate how individuals process information but also, to a degree, represent the learning style of an individual. It must also be remembered that our information processing and overt behaviours can also be affected by a variety of hereditary and environmental factors, as well as by such things as our communication ability, health, and physical state.

CONTROLLING VARIABLES

Specific elements in the information-processing system (e.g., perception, attention, STM, and LTM) are mediated by personal attributes, executive functioning (metacognition), developmental characteristics, and sociocultural experiences (see Figure 4.1).

Information processing is influenced by *personal attributes* in the sense that individual characteristics such as motivation, versatility, self-concept, introversion or extraversion, creativity, verbal ability, and general adjustment can affect how one processes information and performs within and across a variety of situations. To take the example of motivation, students sometimes need to be sold on the idea that classroom activities are meaningful. Motivation and coping ability come from student empowerment, which results from the acquisition of knowledge, skill, and self-responsibility for learning and behaviour. Motivating students involves allowing them opportunities to control and monitor their learning and behaviour. It also involves "creating a

Figure 4.1
An Information-Processing Model of Learning

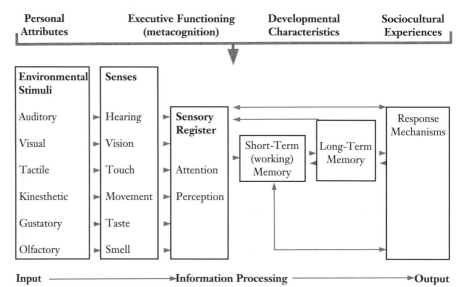

Cognitive = how do we learn (handwritten margin note)

Ital. (handwritten margin note)

Knowing why we do things (handwritten margin note)

Know how to info process (handwritten margin note)

setting in which students consider what they know and can do" (Marx & Winne, 1991, p. 160).

The learner's ability to regulate and coordinate his or her learning processes, known as *executive functioning* or *metacognitive functioning*, also impacts upon the information-processing system. Metacognition is knowledge or awareness about one's information processing. The two major dimensions of metacognition are *reflection* and *control or regulation* (Brown, 1980; Flavell, 1976). *Reflection* is an introspective dimension that involves knowing about one's cognitive activity, generally, the *why* of an action. This dimension is usually domain and task specific, as well as conscious and reportable. The *control* of information processing is an executive dimension that regulates *how* one accomplishes the act of perceiving, attending, and remembering. This dimension involves such things as planning, monitoring, and checking, and, like regulation, it is conscious and reportable.

Taking the two dimensions together, metacognition can be viewed as knowledge about, and the regulation of, information processing. When applied to a particular task, metacognition allows for the development and employment of learning strategies. Strategies are mechanisms, rules, or specific behaviours that enable an individual to complete a task or solve a problem in a means-end fashion; they emerge from one's reflection about the task, from one's knowledge about the task, and from one's experience related to the task.

Lastly, the information-processing model of learning indicates that such things as perception, attention, working memory, and long-term memory are affected by *developmental characteristics* and *sociocultural experiences* (Vygotsky, 1978). According to this aspect of the model, learning is a developmental and social activity, and therefore highly influenced by the "resources that learners bring to the learning environment" (Bos & Vaughn, 1991, p. 41).

We next use the information-processing model as a framework to: (1) discuss why and how children differ in their learning; (2) introduce and address conditions that account for student differences in learning and behaviour; and (3) offer suggestions for teaching children who have special learning needs.

◇ SPECIAL LEARNING CONDITIONS: AN INFORMATION-PROCESSING FRAMEWORK

Vision and hearing are the two major senses through which we receive and transmit information from the environment. Visual and hearing impairments, therefore, have significant impact on the quality of the information-processing system. These impairments vary in terms of cause and severity. Accordingly, the learning needs of visually and hearing-impaired children must be adapted to accommodate both the cause of the impairment and its degree of severity.

Visually impaired children currently make up the smallest group of exceptional children for whom special education services may be needed and provided. Most visually impaired (and many blind) students attend today's inclusive classrooms because the majority of legally blind children are able to make some use of print. The medical-legal definition of blindness states that

> a person shall be considered blind whose central visual acuity does not exceed 20/200 in the better eye with correcting lenses or whose visual acuity, if better than 20/200, has a limit in the central field of vision to such a degree that its widest diameter sub-trends an angle of no greater than 20 degrees, (Hardman, Drew, & Egan, 1987, p. 291).

Visual acuity refers to the ability to distinguish objects and discriminate details at a specified distance (Olson, 1992). **Central field of vision** refers to the ability to see things straight ahead and peripherally. According to the above definition, what a normally sighted person can clearly see at two hundred feet, a legally blind individual must view at twenty feet to make a similar visual distinction (Olson, 1992). Furthermore, a person with normal sight can see things within a range of 180 degrees, whereas someone with visual impairment does not have this range of sight. In education, blindness is considered to be a condition in which an individual's vision is so defective that he or she cannot be educated through the visual learning channel, but must instead be educated through the auditory and kinesthetic learning channels (i.e., reading and writing in braille).

Partially sighted individuals have limited distance vision, but can usually see objects, words, and materials with the aid of special lenses and magnifiers. Visual defects affect visual acuity and are indicated when an individual has significant difficulty perceiving and discriminating object forms, coordinating

◆ visual acuity: the ability to distinguish and discriminate objects at a specified distance

◆ central field of vision: the ability to see objects straight ahead and peripherally

◆ hyperopia: farsightedness

◆ myopia: nearsightedness

◆ astigmatism: uneven curvature of the cornea or lens resulting in blurred vision

his or her eyes on a single object, or seeing things in the outer field of vision. The most common disorders are *refractive disorders*, which cause blurred vision. These disorders include **hyperopia** (farsightedness), in which sight is clear at a distance but rays of light from near objects are not focused clearly; **myopia** (nearsightedness), in which rays of light from distant objects are not focused clearly, but sight is clear in proximity; and **astigmatism,** which causes blurred vision due to an uneven curvature of the cornea or lens. Except for extreme cases, all of these disorders can be aided with corrective lenses; children with refractive disorders are not, therefore, usually placed in special programs.

Children with visual impairments may show consistent difficulty in focusing on words on the blackboard, remembering things that are seen, and discerning relevant visual stimuli. Children with visual problems may also persistently lose their place when reading, skip lines, confuse letters that are similar in appearance, use their fingers for following a line while reading, and make copying mistakes. They also may show reduced motivation to explore their environment, have misconceptions about objects in the environment, and exhibit problems with space perception, spatial relations, abstract thinking, and social skills. Children who experience visual problems may, as well, complain about blurred or double vision and be seen rubbing their eyes, shutting or covering one eye, being sensitive to light, showing an unusual amount of squinting, blinking, eye-scratching, frowning, or facial distortion while reading or when doing other types of close work (National Society to Prevent Blindness, 1977).

Visual impairments can result from prenatal influences, systematic diseases, infections, accidents, poisoning, tumours, and a number of other causes (Olson, 1992). However, the leading causes of blindness (National Society to Prevent Blindness, 1980) are:

1. *Glaucoma.* Abnormally high blood pressure in the eye. If detected in its early stages, this condition can be treated through medication or with surgery.
2. *Detached retinas.* Impaired vision resulting from the retina tearing away from layers of tissue in the eye. Surgery can usually correct this condition.
3. *Optic nerve atrophy.* Degeneration of the optic nerve fibers.
4. *Retinopathy of prematurity.* Abnormal growth of blood vessels and scar tissue in the eye. This condition is most common in premature infants who require high levels of oxygen to survive.
5. *Diabetic retinopathy.* Impaired vision resulting from diabetes (a disorder of the circulatory system). Early detection can help the individual deal with the diabetes, thereby reducing the negative impact on the retina.
6. *Macular degeneration.* Deterioration of the central area of the retina (the macular area).
7. *Retinitis pigmentosa.* Gradual degeneration of the retina—the most common inherited retinal disorder. One of the first symptoms is difficulty

seeing at night, followed by a loss of peripheral vision. While in most cases this condition is not treatable, a small amount of central vision may be maintained.

Regular and special education teachers need to work together with visually impaired students in their classes. These students should be provided information through the nonvisual senses as much as possible, but they should also be given the full range of instructional experience. Generally, visually impaired students require a program of instruction that includes mobility training, socialization, and communication development. Heward and Orlansky (1992) note that "it is extremely important that, from an early age, visually impaired children be taught basic concepts that will familiarize them with their own bodies and their surroundings. For example, they must be taught that the place where the leg bends is called a knee and that rooms have walls, doors, windows, corners, and ceilings" (p. 363).

In terms of socialization and communication, Hatlen (1976, 1978) points out that visually impaired students should receive basic instruction in practical living skills (e.g., cooking, shopping, and personal hygiene), as well as be taught how to interact with strangers, how to to make socially appropriate gestures in conversation, and how to explain their visual impairments to others. Moreover, due to their reliance on the auditory learning channel for processing information, listening-skill development should be a major component of their educational program (Swallow & Conner, 1982). In addition, behavioural mannerisms (e.g., repetitive head-rolling and rocking) that can place visually impaired students at a social disadvantage should be addressed.

Teachers also need to be aware of the special adaptations and technology designed for visually impaired students. For example, some blind students require instruction in braille reading. **Braille** is a tactual system of reading and writing in which letters, words, and numbers are composed by an arrangement of raised dots. Most blind children are introduced to braille at an early age. Children usually learn to write braille with a braillewriter, a six-keyed device that looks like a typewriter. Older students are usually introduced to another writing device, the slate and stylus. This device punches out braille dots one at a time, from right to left. Less efficient than the braillewriter, the slate and stylus is also smaller and less costly, and has some note-taking advantages. Other forms of technology and special aids include:

1. *The Optacon.* An electric reading device that transforms regular print into vibrating letter configurations that are read tactually. Although the Optacon is not widely used by school children, it does allow some blind individuals to read regular print effectively.

2. *The Kurzweil Reading Machine.* A computer that can translate printed material into synthetic speech. This costly machine is not generally found in schools.

◆ braille: a tactual system of reading and writing in which letters, words, and numbers are composed by an arrangement of raised dots

3. *Laptop computers.* Portable computers on which students with visual impairments can take notes and complete tests and assignments at home.
4. *Special optical devices.* Special glasses, contact lenses, and magnifiers that help students with visual impairments read small print and see distant objects.

Hearing-impaired children make up another small group of exceptional children for whom special education services may be needed and provided; however, most hearing-impaired (and some deaf) students attend today's inclusive classrooms. Hearing impairments include all disorders of hearing, which can vary with respect to cause and severity. Outer- or middle-ear hearing problems (*conductive disorders*) are usually temporary and can be typically treated with medicine or surgery (e.g., **otitis media,** a middle-ear infection that can be treated with medicine). Inner-ear hearing problems (most often sensorineural disorders resulting from damage to the cochlea or auditory nerve, due to illness or disease) are usually permanent and uncorrectable.

◆ otitis media: inflammation of the middle ear

Children with hearing impairments often demonstrate behaviours that are indicative of their condition. They may, for example, show persistent inattentiveness in class, tilt their heads when listening, constantly ask for questions and statements to be repeated, and become overly dependent on using gestures to communicate. These children may also have difficulty remembering verbal information, following oral directions, answering questions, and repeating sentences. Additionally, children with hearing impairments may be reluctant to participate in oral activities, and may occasionally act out or become progressively withdrawn in social situations.

Hearing impairments include *deafness* and being *hard-of-hearing*, which Moores (1987) define in terms of degree of hearing loss:

> A 'deaf person' is one whose hearing is disabled to an extent (usually 70 dB or greater) that precludes the understanding of speech through the ear alone, without or with the use of a hearing aid. A 'hard-of-hearing' person is one whose hearing is disabled to an extent (usually 35 to 69 dB) that makes difficult, but does not preclude, the understanding of speech through the ear alone, without or with a hearing aid (p. 9).

Children who are born deaf (*congenital deafness*) do not learn speech and language spontaneously, and have educational needs that differ from those of children who acquire deafness after speech and language are well established (*adventitious hearing loss*). Intervention for the prelingually deaf child focuses on the acquisition of speech and language, whereas educational instruction for the postlingually deaf child focuses on the maintenance of speech and language skills (Heward & Orlansky, 1992).

According to Brown (1986), the major causes of hearing impairment are:

1. *Heredity.* Genetic factors (Vernon, 1987).
2. *Prematurity and complications of pregnancy.* Low birth weight and early delivery are more common among deaf children than among the general population (Heward & Orlansky, 1992).

3. *Maternal rubella* (German measles). Known to cause hearing impairments in developing children, particularly in the first trimester of a woman's pregnancy. Fortunately, effective vaccinations are available for rubella.
4. *Meningitis*. A bacterial or viral infection.
5. *Noise.* Repeated exposure to loud noises such as the amplified music at rock concerts.

Audiological assessment is usually done by an audiologist, who uses specialized audiometric procedures to assess one's ability to hear sounds at different levels of intensity and frequency. Hearing loss can range from mild to severe, and can cause a variety of academic and social problems. Hearing-impaired students do not, as a rule, perform as well as their normally hearing peers on standardized tests of reading and writing, and research indicates that they have difficulty acquiring language skills (Moores, 1987). The academic achievement of hearing-impaired students is closely related to the severity of their hearing impairment, the age at which their hearing loss occurred, their level of intelligence, the hearing status of their parents, and the socio-economic status of their family (Moores, 1985; Paul & Quigley, 1990). In terms of social and emotional functioning, Moores (1987) comments that "the evidence suggests that the social-emotional adjustment of the deaf is similar to that of the hearing, with great individual variation. Most deaf individuals cope with the reality of deafness as a life-long condition and lead normal, productive lives" (p. 180). However, because they exhibit language delays and a tendency to be passive participants in communication (McNally, Rose, & Quigley, 1987), hearing-impaired children need help in developing their ability to communicate with other students. Teachers can help their students in these areas by encouraging them to participate in conversations with their peers, and by exposing them to a variety of communication partners (Berko-Gleason, 1989).

Educational approaches available for teaching hearing-impaired children include the oral approach, the manual approach, and total communication.

The *oral approach* stresses the importance of understanding and using speech and language. Advocates believe that successful integration into the hearing world depends on the development of receptive language skills and the use of speech. Oral language and auditory training is emphasized in this approach, along with different methods that might be used to promote oral communication. Cued speech, for example, uses cues, such as hand signals, to help the hearing-impaired person identify sounds that cannot be distinguished in **speechreading**. The *manual approach* uses gestures for words, ideas, and concepts (sign-language method), as well as letters of the alphabet (finger-spelling method), to aid communication. Although several sign-language systems exist, American Sign Language (ASL) is the language of the deaf population in Canada. According to Wilbur (1987), ASL is a language with its own set of syntactic, semantic, and pragmatic rules. Finger spelling

◆ speechreading: the process of comprehending speech by observing the speaker's lips and facial expression

uses gestures to represent the twenty-six letters of the alphabet, and is often used with other methods of communication.

The *total communication* approach uses a variety of forms of communication to aid the development of speech and language. Advocates of total communication maintain that forms of manual communication (e.g., sign language and finger spelling), along with oral methods, facilitate a deaf person's integration into the hearing world better than the use of any one approach. Although total communication is the "predominant method of instruction in schools for the deaf" (Luterman, 1986, p. 263), there is debate among educators, parents, and researchers about the best way to teach deaf children.

◆ TEACHING CHILDREN WITH SENSORY IMPAIRMENTS

All children should be screened for sensory problems. This process can be aided by reviewing students' files for pertinent information, and by talking to parents about symptoms they may have observed, or about results they can share regarding current medical examinations. Children suspected of having visual or hearing problems should be referred to specialists inside the school (e.g., school nurse) or outside the school (e.g., audiologists and optometrists, who can examine auditory and visual functions respectively) for comprehensive ear and eye examinations. The initial referral may lead to more specialized referrals if preliminary screening indicates further examination. Teachers should monitor the referral process and be willing to work with specialists in designing intervention methods.

For children with sensory deficits, a collaborative team (i.e., classroom teacher, parents, resource teacher, language and speech specialists) should share the responsibility of designing program objectives and goals. Moreover, teachers of children with sensory deficits may need to adapt the classroom and modify their instruction to better meet the needs of these children.

ADAPTATIONS FOR STUDENTS WITH VISUAL IMPAIRMENTS

- ◆ Arrange seating so that students can interact easily with materials and be close to classroom activities.
- ◆ Ensure that students have adequate light but do not have to face glaring light, e.g., from a window (Pasanella & Volkmor, 1981).
- ◆ Provide desks or tabletops large enough for students to use specialized equipment (e.g., braille writers, cassette tape recorders, talking calculators) (Maron & Martinez, 1980).
- ◆ Familiarize students with the general layout of the room before placing them in the classroom, and orient them to main landmarks (e.g., teacher's desk, students' desks, storage areas, learning centres, material centres, bulletin boards and chalkboards, doorways, and other classroom equipment (Gearheart, Weishahn, & Gearheart, 1988), as well as to the gen-

eral school environment (e.g., lockers, bathrooms, cafeteria, and gymnasium).

◆ Develop students' academic and social independence by facilitating their ability to move around their environment, and by increasing their awareness of objects within the environment.

ADAPTATIONS FOR STUDENTS WITH HEARING IMPAIRMENTS

◆ Arrange seating so that students are not distracted by excessive classroom noise, and vary seating arrangements so that students get a chance to interact with all of their peers.

◆ Supplement teaching activities and assignments with visual materials.

◆ Speak very clearly and distinctly, and encourage students to watch the teacher's face.

◆ Become familiar with such things as hearing aids, auditory training programs, speechreading intervention, and manual communication procedures.

TEACHING CHILDREN WITH VISUAL IMPAIRMENTS

◆ Maintain curricular goals but be prepared to modify methods of instruction and materials. For example, incorporate hands-on learning whereby the student learns by doing; use concrete materials and manipulatives in teaching as much as possible; and allow students to explore and experience many of the concepts that are explained verbally.

◆ Supplement lessons that use visual explanations and directions with verbal explanations and directions.

◆ Reproduce material from the blackboard onto separate sheets of paper for student referral at his or her desk (Glazzard, 1980).

◆ Vary activities as much as possible (e.g., alternate visual activities with verbal activities), and allow students to take short breaks from activities that stress visual learning (Gearheart, Weishahn, & Gearheart, 1988).

◆ Use peer teaching or tutoring particularly in helping visually impaired students to comprehend information that is visually presented.

◆ Allow students extra time to complete assignments, and modify tests used to ascertain student achievement and knowledge attainment (e.g., design oral tests using tape-recorded question-and-answer formats).

◆ Develop critical listening skills because these do not automatically improve (Blankenship & Lilly, 1981).

◆ Become familiar with special equipment that can be used by visually handicapped students, and encourage students to use adaptive aids where necessary (Pasanella & Volkmor, 1981).

◆ Work closely with parents so that commitment, direction, and intervention is consistent and unified.

TEACHING CHILDREN WITH HEARING IMPAIRMENTS

- Develop "total communication" for hearing-impaired students by working with specialists to provide individualized instruction in speech reading, finger spelling, and sign language. Maintain face-to-face contact when speaking to hearing-impaired students. Reinforce good expression, maintain appropriate voice volume, and encourage students to speak in complete sentences (Reynolds & Birch, 1988).

- Encourage students who need to wear hearing aids to use them at all times and check them daily (Lewis & Doorlag, 1991).

- Use captioned films, supplementary pictures and diagrams, overhead projectors, and copies of teachers' notes for student referral (Reynolds & Birch, 1988).

- Use classmates as helpers. The helper or "buddy" can help the hearing-impaired student review notes and study for tests; orient the student to the class and school; and clarify concepts, ideas, and skills presented by the teacher.

- Explain concepts clearly, question students to ensure comprehension of presented information, watch for student fatigue, and monitor academic and social progress regularly (Lewis & Doorlag, 1991).

- Share lesson plans with the special teacher of the hearing-impaired student. This allows cooperative instructional relationships to be fostered and maintained, and special problems to be identified and systematically addressed.

- Work closely with parents so that commitment, direction, and intervention is consistent and unified.

◇TEACHING CHILDREN WITH ATTENTIONAL PROBLEMS

As noted before, the sensory register is the brief holding component of the information-processing system. This is where representations of incoming stimuli from the senses are maintained so that cognitive activities can start to be performed on them. The processes of perception and attention take place in the sensory registers, which seems to be a critical source of individual difference in cognitive development (Kramer, Piersel, & Glover, 1988), particularly with respect to *how much* information can be perceived and attended to (*capacity*), and *how long* an individual can perceive and attend to the information (*duration*) (Hunt, Frost, & Lunneburg, 1973).

Research suggests that the input capability and speed of processing among mildly retarded individuals may be shorter (Saccuzzo, Kerr, Marcus, & Brown, 1979) and poorer (Libkuman, Villiky, & Friedrich, 1980; Saccuzzo et al., 1979). Children with significant learning problems (i.e., learning disabled) have been characterized as having perceptual disorders and disorders of attention (short attention span, distractibility, preservation). Children with advanced cognitive development (i.e., gifted children) have been found to respond more rapidly and accurately than their peers to problems that require attention (Bockrath, 1981; Lajoie & Shore, 1986; Scruggs & Mastropieri, 1984). Moreover, Sternberg and Davidson (1983) conclude that a distinctive characteristic of intellectually gifted individuals is their *exceptional insight* ability. According to these authors, insight involves *selective encoding* (sifting out relevant information from irrelevant information), *selective combination* (combining isolated pieces of information into a unified whole that may or may not resemble its parts), and *selective comparison* (relating newly acquired information to information acquired in the past). Sternberg and Davidson (1983) contend that intellectually gifted individuals are not only quantitatively better than their peers in these aspects of insight, but also differ in their performance of insights, particularly in terms of originality and consequence. Thus, intellectually gifted children perceive and attend to information quantitatively and qualitatively better than their peers.

Attention is an important and necessary prerequisite to learning. For example, in order to develop reading comprehension skills, students need to attend to words, and, in order to do multiplication problems, they must attend to each step in the process. As prerequisite skills become routinized, information processing requires less conscious attention, and reading and mathematical problem-solving, for example, become more automatic (Schunk, 1991).

Many children with learning problems have attentional deficits. Specific problems are related to their inability to sustain their attention for long periods, as well as to their inability to focus on main ideas rather than on peripheral or irrelevant information (Loper, 1980). Problems in attention and concentration reduce the opportunity for learning and create gaps in the acquisition of knowledge and skills. For example, information that is not attended to, or is attended to poorly, will either not be stored in memory for later use, or will be badly encoded and have deleterious effects when used later. Students with attention and concentration problems often demonstrate behaviours indicative of these problems. For example, they may not be as alert as the other students, may fail to learn from listening or repetition, may show loss of interest in activities, may forget previously learned information, may misunderstand the meaning of words and gestures, and may be unable to sit still when engaged in academic activities.

INSTRUCTIONAL GUIDELINES

♦ Use visual and auditory cues and prompts to enhance students' ability to discriminate between various stimuli (Polloway, Patton, Payne, & Payne, 1989), e.g., teaching sight words by superimposing picture cues (Westling & Koorland, 1979).

♦ Use novel and varied instructional materials, and vary teacher presentations, student activities, and lesson formats.

♦ Encourage students to monitor their own attention and concentration.

- Provide meaningful, well-structured materials and activities that capture student interest.
- Design lessons that promote student involvement and active learning.
- Consistently and systematically check and monitor students' progress, and develop students' self-monitoring and checking skills.
- Have students explain concepts and skills in their own words, and stress that they are responsible for their own learning (Schunk, 1991).
- Use signals at the start of lessons, or at times of transition from one activity to another.

◆ TEACHING CHILDREN WITH PERCEPTUAL DEFICITS

Perception refers to the meaning an individual attaches to stimuli received through the senses. It involves recognizing, discriminating, and interpreting incoming information. Thus, children with perceptual difficulties have trouble recognizing, discriminating, interpreting, and attaching meaning to information they receive through their senses. According to Bruner, Goodnow, and Austin (1956), conceptualizing information (recognizing, discriminating, interpreting, attaching meaning) is done by placing the information in appropriate categories. Misperception, then, is a function of *improper categorization.*

Bruner et al. (1956) believe that categorization reduces the complexity of the environment, thereby allowing the individual to effectively process a wide variety of incoming stimuli. Categorization also allows an individual to recognize information cognitively in relation to classification (e.g., a chair is not only an object that has four legs, a seat, and a back but is also within a class of objects on which we can sit). Moreover, it allows the individual to relate bits of information, anticipate events, make inferences, and direct learning activity. For example, if students can recognize the context of a story and attach meaning to specific situations before reading the story, they are more likely to be able to recognize relevant details in the story, comprehend information in the story, relate isolated bits of information, and infer (as well as anticipate) events. Perception depends on the accessibility of the appropriate category, and on knowing what cues can be used to place information in proper categories (Lefrançois, 1988); it is thus dependent on an individual's past experience and knowledge, as well as on his or her ability to discriminate the cues of incoming stimuli.

Many children with learning problems show perceptual deficits (Hallahan, 1982). Indicators of perceptual difficulties include difficulty recognizing, discriminating, and matching shapes, letters, words, and sounds; difficulty scanning and drawing objects; persistent errors in written work; poor performance in tasks requiring speed, precision, and recall; weakness in sight vocabulary, sound blending, and oral reading; inability to learn from repetition; weak closure skills (e.g., filling in the end of sentences); difficulty recalling details or making inferences; problems with dimensions of space and time; difficulty isolating relevant details and ideas; difficulty in anticipating events; and poor planning skills.

INSTRUCTIONAL GUIDELINES

- Build on past learning by constantly relating new information and skills to prior knowledge and experience.
- Show children how individual parts or details make up the whole.
- Focus on activities that help students recognize objects, words, letters, sounds, etc., and have students describe and attend to the details.
- Provide scanning activities that give students practice at identifying missing elements.
- Focus on cause-and-effect relationships, inference-making, and sequencing skills.
- Use sentence and story completion exercises.
- Develop students' ability to identify problems, and discuss alternatives related to academic activities and social tasks (e.g., identify conflicts in stories or in social situations, and then discuss possible alternatives for resolving them).
- Use cues and prompts to help students recognize and discriminate details, and then develop students' ability to interpret information with reduced prompts and cues.
- Teach and reinforce planning skills and guide students toward evaluating their responses.
- Give students practice in reproducing or copying designs and patterns.
- Develop students' ability to classify and categorize information using semantic webs, organized outlines, flow-charting techniques, and linking strategies).
- Give students practice in matching objects, words, letters, numbers, and so forth.
- Develop students' sensitivity to environmental stimuli (sounds, smells, taste, touch, etc.).

◇ TEACHING CHILDREN WITH SHORT-TERM MEMORY PROBLEMS

As discussed earlier, information that is perceived and attended to is transferred to short-term (working) memory, where it is stored for a short time, *worked* on, and often related to information stored in long-term memory. Many children with learning problems demonstrate poor memory ability because they have deficient or inefficient strategies for remembering information (Borkowski & Buchel, 1983; Torgesen & Houck, 1980). Efficient learners automatically use rehearsal or chunking strategies to help them remember incoming information, whereas many children with significant learning problems either do not use these types of strategies or use them ineffectively (Bauer, 1977; Ellis, 1970; Spitz, 1966; Swanson, 1982; Torgesen & Greenstein, 1982).

Rehearsal involves such things as thinking about or saying information repeatedly, writing down information, visualizing information, and underlining or shadowing information in text. **Chunking** involves breaking information into subunits. For example, remembering the number 2566530 would be facilitated by arranging the number into subunits like 25, 66, 530, or 256, 6530. Thus, instead of trying to remember seven separate numbers, a student would need only to remember three or two groups of numbers (the latter resembling a telephone number). These strategies are important because the longer information remains in short-term memory, the greater its chances are for being transferred to long-term memory, where it can be retrieved for later use.

Researchers such as Ellis (1970), Spitz (1966), and Swanson (1982) discuss differences between children with significant learning problems and average-achieving students with respect to their ability to rehearse and chunk (organize) information to be memorized. They report that students with significant learning problems often fail to use these strategies, thereby reducing their capacity to remember information and transfer it to long-term memory. However, these researchers and others (Belmont & Butterfield, 1971; Schultz, 1983) note that once these children are instructed to use rehearsal and chunking strategies, their performance on memory tasks approximates the performance of children without significant learning problems.

INSTRUCTIONAL GUIDELINES

- Explain to students how they can profit from memorizing information.
- Reinforce the idea that memory strategies are designed to aid learning (Reid & Hresko, 1981).
- Show students how to label, group, cluster, and organize information into familiar patterns.
- Give students sufficient time to practice and apply memory strategies in order to increase the accuracy and speed of their information processing.
- Stop lessons periodically to give students a chance to chunk and rehearse the information presented to them.
- Facilitate students' independent regulation of memory strategies.
- Limit the amount of information students have to attend to at a particular time (Case, 1978).
- Use salient cues so that students do not have to cognitively search for cues to understand incoming information (Case, 1978).
- Use familiar terms where possible so that the processing of linguistic information does not overload working memory (Case, 1978).
- Use concrete examples and allow students to manipulate materials (Cohen & Bain, 1983).

◆ rehearsal: a learning strategy that facilitates the transfer of information to long-term memory storage

◆ chunking: grouping individual units of information into larger meaningful units in order to extend the limited capacity of short-term memory

◆ Provide opportunities for students to perform tasks using memory strategies within and across a variety of contexts.

◆ Use pictorials (visual aids) to help students memorize information, and develop students' ability to analyze information semantically (Schultz, 1983).

◇ TEACHING CHILDREN WITH LONG-TERM MEMORY PROBLEMS

Long-term memory is the part of the information system where information is permanently stored. Research in long-term memory, unlike that in short-term memory, has not shown significant differences between handicapped and nonhandicapped children in their rates of forgetting comparable material (Belmont, 1966; Klausmeier, Feldhusen, & Check, 1959). The major difference appears to be that handicapped learners have significant difficulty in transferring learning from one situation to another, and are limited in their use of cognitive strategies related to the organization, elaboration, regulation, retrieval, and evaluation of long-term information (this is why children with learning problems often have problems with conceptualization and abstraction). However, once handicapped learners are provided in-depth training and feedback regarding effective ways for organizing, elaborating, regulating, retrieving, and evaluating information, there is evidence that their performance becomes similar to that of their nonhandicapped peers (e.g., Borkowski & Cavanaugh, 1979; Hallahan, Kauffman, & Lloyd, 1985).

Whereas rehearsal and chunking strategies are efficient ways to store information in short-term memory, an efficient learner must use other processing techniques for storing information in long-term memory. Among these techniques are: (1) making information more meaningful by constructing mental images; (2) linking prior knowledge and experience with present content by creating analogies, paraphrasing information, applying principles to better assimilate new information, summarizing material, and constructing schemas; (3) transforming information from one form to another by grouping information according to taxonomic categories (semantic webbing); and (4) organizing and simplifying information in complex material by creating conceptual diagrams, outlining chapters students are required to read, and constructing a hierarchy or network of main ideas. Processing techniques can also help the individual retrieve information. For example, storing the names of the Great Lakes into long-term memory might be aided by using the first letter mnemonic: HOMES (H̲uron, O̲ntario, M̲ichigan, E̲rie, S̲uperior).

Information in long-term memory is stored by way of associative structures (i.e., information is linked) (Schunk, 1991), in both verbal and visual form (Paivio, 1971). We tend to remember information by interconnecting bits of information (concepts, general concepts, times, places, and events) through verbal procedures and visual pictures (images and scenes).

Children's ability to remember information appears to be a function of their capacity to employ processing strategies for interconnecting ideas in both verbal and visual forms.

INSTRUCTIONAL GUIDELINES

- Direct students' attention to the meaningfulness of presented information.
- Show students how, when, and where they can employ long-term memory strategies.
- Explain the specific and varied reasons for remembering information.
- Discuss and demonstrate how students can link prior knowledge and experience with current information.
- Set up brainstorming sessions with students and discuss how they can best remember information over an extended period.
- Teach students strategies that can help them organize, simplify, and elaborate upon information.
- Give students time to practice and apply long-term memory strategies.
- Provide advanced organizers in lessons. For example, direct students' attention to the most important concepts in the material to be learned.
- Show students different types of schemas or semantic networks that they can use to understand, retain, and recall ideas.
- Use analogies to link familiar material with unfamiliar material.

◆ ENHANCING STUDENTS' METACOGNITIVE ABILITIES

Specific processes (attention, perception, short- and long-term memory) are influenced by one's personal attributes (self-concept, expectation for success, perception of ability, and motivation), and coordinated by what has been called *executive functioning* or *metacognition* (discussed earlier in this chapter).

Students with learning and behaviour problems have lower levels of academic self-concept, self-efficacy, and motivation than their peers. They are also more likely to feel that their lives are controlled by outside forces rather than by their own efforts (Pearl & Bryan, 1979; Zigler, 1966). Moreover, they have been found to be deficient in metacognitive abilities.

Metacognition involves being aware of the strategies needed to perform tasks effectively and efficiently. It also involves being able to regulate, control, plan, monitor, and evaluate one's information processing. Many children with learning problems are inefficient or deficient in metacognitive abilities (e.g., predicting, planning, checking, monitoring) (see Hallahan, Kneedler, & Lloyd, 1983, for a review of this literature), whereas many average achieving and most gifted children tend to have average-to-superior metacognitive abilities (Sternberg, 1981; Wilson, 1985; Wong, 1982; Zimmerman, 1981).

INSTRUCTIONAL GUIDELINES

- Provide assignments that allow for a high success rate among students.
- Match academic and social tasks with students' learning needs.
- Clearly explain lessons and concepts.
- Provide sufficient time for students to practice and master skills.
- Consistently and systematically monitor and evaluate students' progress.
- Provide positive feedback for students and refrain from criticizing them.
- Stress and encourage flexible thinking and problem-solving.
- Help students understand and appreciate the relevance of what they are learning.
- Use real-life situations that are meaningful to the students.
- Focus on the *meaning* of ideas, not the *memorization* of ideas.
- Expose students (when and where appropriate) to content that is complex, sophisticated, and novel, and relate this content to students' past experience and knowledge.
- Have students practice analyzing and evaluating learned information.
- Guide students toward predicting and monitoring their comprehension.
- Provide training, practice, and feedback on the use of learning strategies.

◇ PROMOTING STUDENTS' SOCIAL AND COGNITIVE DEVELOPMENT IN THE CLASSROOM

As our model (see Figure 4.1) indicates, information processing is also influenced by developmental and sociocultural variables. According to the *developmental theory*, as students develop, their attention span and capacity for processing information (rehearsing, organizing, elaborating information, and self-regulating actions) increases, in conjunction with the expansion of their knowledge base. Additionally, as children get older, they better understand their memory abilities and limitations (Flavell, Friedrichs, & Hoyt, 1970), and are better able to monitor their memory performance (Wellman, 1977).

Piaget's (1952) *cognitive-developmental stage theory* describes the process of intellectual development as moving from concrete experience to abstract thought through four distinct stages: sensorimotor (birth to 2 years); preoperational (2 to 7 years); concrete operational (7 to 11 years); and formal operational (11 years to adulthood). In each stage, individuals gain new abilities that allow them to change and reorganize their thinking. According to Piaget, all children, whether gifted, average, or retarded, progress through these stages in an invariant order. However, recent research supports the view that progression within and between stages occurs more quickly for gifted children (Carter & Ormrod, 1982; Carter, 1985). Cognitive development, then, is determined by the relative efficiency of an individual's information processing strategies.

The enhancement of students' information processing through cognitive and metacognitive instruction should be programmed and sequenced in relation to the cognitive developmental level of the student, and in relation to the quality and quantity of knowledge/skills that the student has acquired. Strategies for improving students' perception, attention, and memory should be taught and practiced at each grade level, and in all content areas, with increasing complexity and sophistication (see Chapter 12.) Although children's abilities to select, maintain, and generalize information-processing strategies are relatively late in developing (Kendal, Borkowski, & Cavanaugh, 1980), young children can be trained to be strategic in their learning (Bray, Justice, Ferguson, & Simon, 1977).

The *sociocultural theory* of cognitive development (Vygotsky, 1978) makes us aware that learning is a social activity. Teachers need to be conscious of how culture and language influence knowledge acquisition, problem-solving, and decision-making. Learning can be enhanced by incorporating students' diverse cultural experiences in day-to-day teaching and learning interactions, and by openly discussing the process of learning. Social dialogue in the classroom allows teachers to promote meaningful discussions on cognitive and metacognitive development—and it allows students to express their thoughts about development and about how they approach learning (see Chapter 14.)

INSTRUCTIONAL GUIDELINES

- Facilitate cooperative learning and sharing in a context of mutual respect and appreciation for everyone's knowledge and background (Bos & Vaughn, 1991).
- Provide opportunities for students' cultural experiences to be expressed.
- Allow students to question, explore, and expose knowledge and processing limitations or misconceptions without fear of ridicule.
- Teach information-processing strategies in a consistent and systematic fashion.
- Instil in students an awareness of their role in the learning process.
- Be sensitive to students' social and cultural context.
- Adapt materials and adjust teaching to accommodate the cognitive and social needs of the students.
- Allow students to discuss how they have tried to solve academic and social difficulties.
- Incorporate cross-cultural sensitivity and the cognitive/metacognitive approach into teaching and learning.
- Give students opportunities to work in pairs and small groups in order to facilitate friendship-making and an appreciation of individual differences.
- Develop students' self-esteem and self-confidence by showing interest in their interests and pursuits, and by interacting with them inside and outside the classroom.

◆ STUDENT APPROACHES TO LEARNING

Response mechanisms are the internal and external ways students manifest their information processing. *Internal mechanisms* involve the cognitive strategies students use to, for example, organize and remember information, whereas *external mechanisms* are the overt behaviours students demonstrate when performing varied tasks. These behaviours are often indicative of how students process information. When students show preferred strategies across different situations (i.e., show preferred ways of doing things), they are reflecting their *style* or *approach to learning*.

Effective learners typically have a positive view of their own abilities, use efficient cognitive and metacognitive learning strategies, and take an active and independent approach to their learning. Children with learning problems typically have a negative perception of their abilities, use inefficient or deficient cognitive and metacognitive strategies, and take a passive and dependent approach to their learning. According to Biggs (1978, 1985, 1987), students tend to adopt one of three approaches or styles of learning.

The *surface approach* is reflected when students try to minimize their efforts in the learning process. They tend to limit their processing efforts to memorizing essential details that can be reproduced through rote learning and the use of rehearsal strategies. Typically, students who take this approach are interested in meeting only the minimal learning requirements; tend to be extrinsically motivated (seek external rewards); and tend to be dependent learners with low self-efficacy, low verbal ability, and an **external locus of control** (Schmeck, 1988).

The *deep approach* is reflected when a student has an intrinsic interest in the content to be learned, and is motivated by his or her search for personal meaning in learning. Students who take this approach to learning strive for academic competence. They typically (1) organize, synthesize, analyze, and evaluate information, as well as link present knowledge with prior knowledge and experience; (2) categorize and network concepts, as well as elaborate upon and abstract information; (3) are intrinsically motivated, creative, self-confident, and independent; and (4) have **internal locus of control** and high verbal ability (Schmeck, 1988).

The *achieving approach* is reflected when students are motivated to conform to situation expectations, and want to obtain high grades whether or not the material is interesting. These students tend to be good at organizing and scheduling their time and study, reasoning through analogies, relating information to personal experience, and transforming information into images and schemas. They also tend to be both intrinsically and extrinsically motivated, to be **field dependent**, and to have a well-defined self-concept and internal locus of control (Schmeck, 1988).

Teachers wishing to encourage their students to take a deep approach to learning might consider the following guidelines:

◆ Facilitate active, independent, and self-controlled learning.

external locus of control: the belief that outcomes are independent of how a person acts in a given situation

internal locus of control: the belief that outcomes result from a person's actions in a given situation

field dependent: cognitive style whereby an individual relies on—or is distracted by—the context in which an event occurs

- Arouse students' motivation for learning.
- Promote self-questioning and reflective thinking.
- Discourage students from being minimally involved in their learning.
- Encourage students to be meaningful learners.

◇ CHILDREN WITH COMMUNICATION DISORDERS

Children with communication disorders make up another group of exceptional children for whom special education services may be needed and provided. Most students with communication disorders as a primary diagnosis or secondary handicapping condition are educated in today's inclusive classrooms, and include children who have speech and language disorders. Some children with learning problems have speech and/or language impairments. Some researchers have estimated that one out of twenty children have some degree of language and speech problems, irrespective of cognitive development, family background, or presence of other exceptionalities (Reynolds & Birch, 1988).

SPEECH DISORDERS

A speech impairment is defined as

> a communication disorder, such as stuttering, impaired articulation, a language impairment, or voice impairment, which adversely affects a child's education performance. (Federal Register, 1981, pp. 42478-42479)

Associated with problems in oral expression, speech disorders are usually conspicuous and interfere with an individual's ability to effectively communicate with others. The three major types of speech disorders are articulation disorders, voice disorders, and fluency disorders (American Speech-Language-Hearing Association, 1982).

Children with *articulation disorders* often demonstrate one or more of the following types of speech errors: (1) *omission* of sounds (leaving out a sound, e.g., saying "oup" instead of "soup"); (2) *substitution* of sounds (replacing one sound for another, e.g., saying "thoup" instead of "soup"); (3) *addition* of sounds (adding a sound that normally does not occur, e.g., saying "ath*a*lete" instead of "athlete"); and (4) *distortion* of sounds (replacing an acceptable sound with a sound that does not exist).

Voice disorders are evident when the pitch, loudness, quality, resonance, and/or duration of an individual's speech differs from that of others of similar age, sex, and cultural group. The most common problems are associated with voice quality, and are typically characterized by speech that has excessive or reduced nasal quality, or by speech that is harsh, breathy, or hoarse. *Fluency disorders* are evident when the normal flow and rhythm of speech is disturbed with inappropriate blocks, pauses, hesitations, and/or repetitions of sounds, syllables, phrases, and/or words. The most common fluency disorder is stuttering.

LANGUAGE DISORDERS

Language disorders are associated with problems of comprehension and/or the use of spoken, written, and/or other symbol systems (American Speech-Language-Hearing Association, 1982). A language disorder may involve: (1) difficulties with phonology (learning and using the sound system of language, as well as the linguistic rules governing how sounds can be combined); (2) difficulties with morphology (learning and using linguistic rules that govern the structure of words, e.g., prefixes, suffixes, pluralizations, and verb tenses); (3) difficulties with syntax (learning and using the grammatical rules of language, i.e., problems in organizing and ordering words to form sentences); (4) difficulties with the content of language or semantics (problems understanding meanings of words, word combinations, and sentences); and (5) difficulties with the use of language in communication or pragmatics (i.e., problems with initiating conversation, maintaining dialogue, taking turns in communicative interactions, or adjusting language with respect to the specific context). It is also important to note that language and speech difficulties can interact and result in much more complex problems.

INSTRUCTIONAL GUIDELINES

- Be sensitive to speech and language situations that might be threatening to students.
- Be prepared and willing to work with speech pathologists and language specialists on program planning and intervention strategies.
- Develop students' language knowledge, skills, and use within and across various communicative contexts.
- Allow students to practice communication skills within naturally occurring routines and activities (e.g., class discussions, small group projects).
- Use behavioural principles, such as shaping, prompting, and reinforcement, in natural contexts (McCormick & Richard, forthcoming).
- Model appropriate speech and language skills.
- Provide a comfortable atmosphere that allows students to practice their communication skills without criticism.
- Expand vocabulary development in both speaking and writing contexts across curriculum areas.
- Modify activities and assignments that require complex language skills (e.g., provide instruction in shorter and less complex sentences).
- Allow students to write stories, tell stories, and read aloud in relaxed situations.
- Facilitate the social use of language.

◊ CHILDREN WITH PHYSICAL AND HEALTH IMPAIRMENTS

Some students have physical and health impairments that do not allow them to respond in ways that are expected of their peers. Children with physical disabilities (sometimes called *orthopedical impairments*) most often have disorders associated with their joints, skeleton, and muscles, which make it difficult to use their bodies. Children with health impairments have a disease or medical condition that interferes with their ability to lead a normal life.

The physical and health handicaps of children also vary with respect to severity. Physical and health impairments may be present from birth, or acquired during childhood, adolescence, or adulthood. Some children with physical or health impairments have secondary problems such as a learning disability, behavioural disorder, or communication disorder, and may demonstrate below- to above-average intelligence and/or academic achievement. Alternatively, children may be singularly disadvantaged by a physical or health impairment.

Children with physical and health impairments make up two other groups of exceptional children for whom special education services may be needed and provided. However, most children with physical and health impairments do attend today's inclusive classrooms. Physical and health impairments include a wide range of conditions affecting mobility and vitality, as well as learning and development.

PHYSICAL IMPAIRMENTS

A physical (orthopedic) impairment is defined as a condition that

> adversely affects a child's educational performance. The term includes impairments caused by a congenital anomaly (e.g., clubfoot, absence of some member, etc.), impairments caused by disease (e.g., poliomyelitis, bone tuberculosis, etc.), and impairments from other causes (e.g., cerebral palsy, amputations, and fractures or burns which cause contractures) (Federal Register, 1981, p. 42478).

The most serious and common physical impairments are outlined below. **Cerebral palsy** refers to dysfunction of the neurological motor system resulting from brain damage occurring before, during, or shortly after birth (Hardy, 1983). The most common forms are: (1) **spasticity,** involving excessive muscle tone and characterized by abrupt contractions of muscles or muscle groups; (2) **ataxia,** which affects the ability to coordinate body movements and control balance and equilibrium; (3) **athetosis,** a type of cerebral palsy characterized by slow repeated movements of the limbs; (4) **rigidity,** which is marked by rigid limbs; and (5) **tremor,** which is characterized by repetitive and rhythmic contractions of the muscles. All forms involve involuntary movements and can affect all four limbs (*quadriplegia*), an arm and leg on one side (*hemiplegia*), three limbs (*triplegia*), one limb (*monoplegia*) or just the legs (*paraplegia*).

- ◆ cerebral palsy: dysfunction of the neurological motor system resulting from congenital brain damage

- ◆ spasticity: a type of cerebral palsy characterized by abrupt contractions of muscles or muscle groups

- ◆ ataxia: a type of cerebral palsy characterized by loss of coordination or control over movements associated with balance and equilibrium

- ◆ athetosis: a type of cerebral palsy characterized by slow, repeated movements of the limbs

- ◆ rigidity: a type of cerebral palsy characterized by rigid limbs

- ◆ tremor: a type of cerebral palsy characterized by repetitive and rhythmic contractions of the muscles

Spina bifida is a birth defect of the spinal column in which the bones of the spine fail to close around the column of nerves it protects. The extent of the disability resulting from this condition can vary with respect to paralysis, sensation in the legs, and various degrees of bowel and bladder incontinence (Pieper, 1983).

Muscular dystrophy is a condition that causes progressive muscle weakness in children. It is inherited and terminal. The most common form is *Duchenne's muscular dystrophy*, which usually occurs between the child's first and sixth year and is characterized by a slow deterioration of muscles. Children with this form of dystrophy are usually confined to a wheelchair by late teens and are in a complete state of helplessness by adulthood. Individuals with this condition usually die due to pneumonia or heart failure.

Scoliosis refers to a lateral (side-to-side) curve in the spine that is absent in normal spines. It is associated with a prominent shoulder blade, poor posture, unlevel shoulders, and a flattening of the back (Bauer & Shea, 1989). This condition can result in impairment of motor function, and is often treated by the use of back braces and/or surgery to stabilize the back (Boos, Garlonski, MacEwen & Steg, 1984).

Osteogenesis imperfecta is a defect in the development of the bone structure. It is often called *brittle bones* because the bones break very easily due to the structural weakness. Children with this condition need to be in a protective environment, and are usually wheelchair-users.

Hip disorders involve congenital dislocation of the hip and leg. **Legg-Calvé-Perthes** disease is one of the most commonly found hip disorders in school-age children. It is characterized by the density of the femoral head (round end) of the thigh bone where it fits into the hip socket. Hip disorders are usually diagnosed before a child enters school and are often temporary problems which can be corrected by bracing, casting, or surgery (Gearheart et al., 1988).

Amputation of a limb may be the result of disease, infection, or a congenital condition. In most cases, children are fitted with an artificial limb (**prosthesis**).

◆ spina bifida: a congenital malformation of the spinal column

◆ muscular dystrophy: a disease in children that is characterized by a deterioration of the muscles

◆ scoliosis: lateral curvature of the spine

◆ osteogenesis imperfecta: a hereditary condition—sometimes called brittle bones—in which the bones fail to develop and break easily

◆ Legg-Calvé-Perthes: a hip disorder characterized by a change in the density of the femoral head (round end) of the thigh bone where it fits into the hip socket

◆ prosthesis: a functional device used to replace a missing body part

INSTRUCTIONAL GUIDELINES

◆ Modify the classroom and school according to students' needs (e.g., ramps for wheelchairs, lowered water fountains, widened classroom doors, lowered blackboards).

◆ Avoid overprotection, and provide opportunities for students to be involved in as many activities as possible so they can discover their own strengths and limitations.

◆ Become familiar with special equipment and learning aides (e.g., mechanics and maintenance of wheelchairs, prostheses, braces, crutches, reading and writing aides).

◆ Inform other students in the class about the physical impairments of their peers.

◆ Arrange and adjust appropriate seating and working areas for students.

◆ Allow extra time for students to complete assignments, and to move between classes or to various activities and events in the classroom and school.

◆ Be prepared and willing to collaborate with occupational therapists, physical therapists, psychologists, resource teachers, volunteers, and aides.

◆ Reinforce recommended treatment procedures for students regarding, for example, movement and posture.

◆ Be sensitive to the self-care, exercise, and social needs of the students.

◆ Refer students to counselling if they need more help in coping with their condition(s).

◆ Be prepared for students being absent from class for varying lengths of time, and be willing to assist those who require occasional hospital or homebound instruction.

◆ Provide space for and maintain special equipment needed by students.

◆ Develop classroom procedures for emergency situations. For example, assign specific students to assist peers with mobility problems.

HEALTH IMPAIRMENTS

Health impairments can be permanent, indefinite, or temporary, as well as mild (preventing a child from doing strenuous activities), moderate (interfering with the ability of a child to engage in many normal activities), or severe (immobilizing a child over a prolonged period of time).

Health impairments are defined as

> … limited strength, vitality or alertness, due to chronic or acute health problems such as a heart condition, tuberculosis, rheumatic fever, nephritis, asthma, sickle cell anemia, hemophilia, epilepsy, lead poisoning, leukemia, or diabetes, which adversely affect a child's educational performance. (Federal Register, 1981, pp. 3865-3866)

The most common and serious health impairments are outlined below.

Epilepsy is caused by abnormal electrical activity in the brain, which results in disturbances of movement, sensation, and behaviour. The two most common types of seizures are *absence* (formerly "petit mal") *seizure* and *generalized tonic-clonic* (formerly "grand mal") *seizure*. Children who have absence seizures may stare or blank out for a few seconds, a period in which they are unaware of things happening in their environment. Children who have generalized tonic-clonic seizures often experience strange sensations (called an *aura*) before a seizure, which is characterized by convulsive movements and unconsciousness lasting several minutes.

Cystic fibrosis is characterized by chronic pulmonary (lung) dysfunction and pancreatic deficiency. Children tend to experience chronic coughing

◆ **epilepsy:** an impairment of the nervous system characterized by recurrent and sudden disturbances of movement, sensation, and behaviour

◆ **cystic fibrosis:** a hereditary respiratory disease characterized by chronic pulmonary dysfunction and pancreatic deficiency

and have difficulty breathing. Although this is one of the most lethal child diseases, medical advances have increased patients' potential life span into adulthood (Schwachman, Kowalski, & Khaw, 1977).

Leukemia is a form of cancer in which white blood cells increase and upset the normal functioning of the blood. This condition is often fatal. Side-effects of treatment may include nausea, weight changes, fatigue, headaches, and emotional disturbances. During periods of remission, children are able to participate in all aspects of their educational program (Link, 1982).

Diabetes is an inherited disorder of metabolism indicated by excessive amounts of glucose in the blood and urine. Symptoms include general drowsiness and weakness, abnormal thirst, frequent urination, extreme hunger, and skin infections.

Allergies refer to sensitivity or low tolerance to various substances that usually do not cause problems for other people (Kuzemko, 1978). Reactions may include sneezing, nasal congestion, watering eyes, itching, coughing, and rashes. Children may also suffer various degrees of emotional stress.

Asthma is a condition that restricts breathing because of air-flow problems in and out of the lungs. Children go through periods of constricted breathing and experience wheezing coughs.

Acquired Immune Deficiency Syndrome (AIDS). This always fatal disease is arguably one of the most feared and misunderstood conditions that educators, families, and health professionals are facing. It is the result of the Human Immuno-deficiency Virus (HIV), which attacks and weakens the body's immune system. AIDS can be transmitted through blood-to-blood contact and through various sexual practices with people who have AIDS or carry the HIV virus, or it can be transmitted through transfusions of blood from carriers of the virus and from intravenous drug use with contaminated hypodermic needles. The disease can also be transmitted to babies through their mothers before or during birth. No cure (or vaccine) for AIDS exists as yet.

Although there are relatively fewer cases of AIDS in children than in adults, with only a small number of these children attending school, the number of infected children is expected to increase. This will require educators to be prepared to accommodate children with AIDS in their classrooms, to answer questions that are asked by students about AIDS, and to be sensitive to the developmental delays experienced by children with the disease (Barnes, 1986; Crocker, 1989; Epstein, Sharer, & Goudsmit, 1988; Kerr, 1990).

Kerr (1990) notes that schools are very important for educating youth about AIDS. However, AIDS education and teaching children with AIDS are controversial issues because AIDS education involves sex education and there is pressure from many members of the community to exclude infected children from classrooms (Church, Allen, & Stiehm, 1986). Some parents oppose the inclusion of sex education in the school curriculum. Others are fearful of the potential risks associated with having their children in the company of children with AIDS. Teachers must deal with these issues in their

◆ **leukemia:** a form of cancer involving the overproduction of white blood cells

◆ **diabetes:** a hereditary metabolic disorder characterized by excessive amounts of glucose in the blood and urine

◆ **allergy:** a hypersensitivity to certain substances in the environment

◆ **asthma:** a condition that restricts breathing because of air-flow problems in and out of the lungs

◆ **Acquired Immune Deficiency Syndrome (AIDS):** a fatal disease that attacks and weakens the body's immune system

instructional planning, as well as in their approach to AIDS education and to infected children. Moreover, they should be prepared to collaborate with counsellors and other specialists (thus providing broad-based support for children with AIDS and their parents); include children with AIDS in as many school activities as possible; and monitor their physical health and social-emotional development (Byers, 1989; Merina, 1989; Reed, 1988). Beyond local parent/teacher organizations and health agencies, the Canadian Public Health Association is a good source of information, with publications on AIDS (e.g., "AIDS: What Young Adults Should Know"), as well as videos and films (e.g., "AIDS, The New Facts of Life").

Sickle-cell anemia is an inherited disorder that affects the red blood cells and results in poor blood supply to tissues. This condition can result in severe pain in the abdomen, legs, and arms, as well as fatigue and dehydration. Children may experience difficulty at irregular intervals and have to be absent from school for medical treatment.

Hemophilia is a condition that results from poor blood-clotting ability—hence its name *"bleeder's disease."* In severe cases, orthopedic problems may result due to bleeding in the joints.

Arthritis is a chronic joint inflammation disorder resulting in stiffness and soreness of the joints.

Heart disease is most often a congenital condition detected immediately after birth. Problems are typically the result of defects in heart structure or functioning, and are treated through surgical methods and/or medication.

INSTRUCTIONAL GUIDELINES

- Treat children as normally as possible and avoid overprotection.
- Facilitate peer acceptance and understanding.
- Encourage social participation and student interaction.
- Be prepared to administer and monitor medications. Check school policies regarding the administration and monitoring of medication, obtain written consent forms from parents and doctors, and keep anecdotal records of drug dispensement.
- Make allowances and special modifications for students who have missed time in class (e.g., focus on short-term goals).
- Address misconceptions students might have about the health impairments of their peers (e.g., the misconception that seizures are painful to epileptics).
- Prepare yourself and your students to respond to the problems health-impaired students may experience (e.g., arrange a comfortable and protective place in the classroom for a student to have a tonic-clonic seizure).
- Monitor students' eating and exercise habits, and make restrictions or modifications where necessary.

◆ **sickle-cell anemia**: a hereditary disorder that affects the red blood cells and results in poor blood supply to tissues

◆ **hemophilia**: a hereditary blood disorder characterized by poor blood clotting

◆ **arthritis**: a chronic joint inflammation disorder

◆ **heart disease**: a congenital condition resulting from a deficiency in heart structure or functioning

◆ Be aware that some children with health impairments may experience psychological problems and need extra attention as well as counselling.

◆ Watch for signs that students are having difficulty coping in their day-to-day routines (e.g., lack of stamina, disorientation), and notify parents and medical personnel when necessary.

◆ If students have been absent from school, spend extra time or assign student peers to help orient them to current events, topics, concepts, and expectations.

◆ Provide rest periods and/or modified work schedules for students who are experiencing fatigue.

◆ Arrange student schedules in accordance with students' needs.

◆ Be willing to collaborate with others (e.g., specialists and parents) who are responsible for students' education and development.

◆ Become familiar with specialized equipment that students may need to use in the classroom.

◇ CHILDREN WITH SEVERE DISABILITIES

Children with severe disabilities have extreme deficiencies in cognitive functioning. They tend to display poor language skills; to have difficulty developing self-help skills; to lack social and vocational abilities; and to have limited physical mobility due to impaired physical and motor development. Coincidentally, like many other children, they can also be warm, caring, determined, likable, and humorous (Forest & Lusthaus, 1990). The Association for Persons with Severe Handicaps describes individuals with severe disabilities as

> individuals of all ages who require extensive ongoing support in more than one major life activity in order to participate in integrated community settings and to enjoy a quality of life that is available to citizens with fewer or no disabilities. Support may be required for life activities such as mobility, communication, self-care, and learning, as necessary for independent living, employment, and self-sufficiency (cited in Lindley, 1990, p. 1).

Most students with severe disabilities experience greater difficulty with skill acquisition, retention, generalization, and synthesis of information than do nondisabled individuals (Peterson, 1980). Thus, educators should take advantage of natural learning opportunities that occur each day to help students acquire important skills. Moreover, they should reinforce these skills by allowing frequent practice, and they should integrate diverse intervention methods into students' daily routines to help them synthesize and generalize their skills from one situation to another (Rainforth, York, & Macdonald, 1992). The best practices in the education of students with severe disabilities are: age-appropriate placements in community schools; integrated provision of services; social integration; transition planning; development of skills within appropriate community settings; functional curricular expectations;

systematic data-based instruction; home-school partnership; and systematic program evaluation (Williams, Fox, Thousand, & Fox, 1990).

A collaborative team approach (see Part 3) for integrating related services into educational programs for students with severe handicaps should be used in the community school so that each student's participation, achievement, contribution, and satisfaction in home and community life can be achieved (Rainforth et al., 1992).

INSTRUCTIONAL GUIDELINES

Although many children with severe disabilities have challenging learning and behavioural characteristics, every effort should be made to help these students develop their learning and thinking skills and function more independently (Bannerman, Sheldon, Sherman, & Harchick, 1990).

- Provide choice-making activities for students to help them function more independently (see Shevin & Klein, 1984).
- Use a variety of communication systems (sign language) and aids (communication boards) to help students receive and express information (Reichle & Keogh, 1986).
- Develop students' ability to select recreational and leisure activities (see Wehman, Renzaglia, & Bates, 1985).
- Promote belongingness and socially acceptable behaviour within integrated community settings (Forest & Lusthaus, 1990; Meyer & Evans, 1989).
- Develop students' vocational competencies to help them obtain and perform meaningful work (Brown, Evans, Weed, & Owen, 1987).

Children with severe disabilities should be educated in their community schools, which, compared to segregated placements, can better provide the motivation and the means to implement the above guidelines for teachers (Reynolds & Birch, 1988).

◆ CONCLUSION: CONCEPTUALIZING CANADIAN CLASSROOMS

Today's classrooms include students who have a variety of strengths, weaknesses, and needs with respect to their learning and development. Students with weaknesses and/or strengths beyond what is considered to be average are typically viewed as *exceptional*. Until recently, many of these students were removed from *regular* classrooms and placed in *special* classrooms. Because they tend to include rather than exclude exceptional students, today's regular classrooms are more appropriately called *inclusive* classrooms.

As our concept of regular classrooms has changed, so too has our concept of exceptional students. The past emphasis on categorizing and labelling children has given way to an emphasis on diagnosis and on prescribing for the special needs of all children.

This chapter has presented an overview of the concepts, issues, and educational concerns associated with the majority of children in inclusive classrooms. Children who experience second-culture and second-language challenges in inclusive classrooms are addressed in the following chapter. As we conclude this chapter, we offer these final words: "Congratulate yourself on selecting such an important area for your life's work. Know that it is possible to make a significant difference in the lives of children and youth in our public schools. Embrace the challenges that lie ahead; you will experience great personal and professional growth in addressing the challenges" (Rainforth et al., p. 252).

QUESTIONS
◆◆◆◆◆◆◆◆◆◆◆◆◆

1. Discuss some of the issues associated with children who have learning disabilities, delayed cognitive skills, behaviour disorders, and advanced cognitive abilities.

2. What are the advantages/disadvantages of labelling?

3. What are the major aspects of the information-processing system?

4. How does an understanding of the information-processing system help a teacher adapt instruction to meet the learning needs of his or her students?

5. Discuss how communication disorders and physical and health impairments can affect students' learning and behaviour.

REFERENCES

Achenback, T. M., & Edelbrock, C. S. (1978). The child-behaviour profile 2: Boys aged 12-16 and girls aged 6-11 and 12-16. *Journal of Consulting and Clinical Psychology, 41*, 223-233.

American Speech-Language-Hearing Association. (1982, November). Definitions: Communicative disorders and variations. *Asha*, 949-950.

Anderson, J. R. (1985). *Cognitive psychology and its implications* (2nd ed.). San Francisco, CA: W. H. Freeman.

Association for Children and Adults with Learning Disabilities (ACLD) Board of Directors. (1985). Definitions of the condition of specific learning disabilities. *ACLD News Briefs, 158*, 1-3.

Atkinson, R. C., & Shiffrin, R. M. (1968). Human memory: A proposed system and its component processes. In K. Spence & J. Spence (Eds.), *The psychology of learning and motivation, Volume 2*. New York: Academic Press.

Bannerman, D. J., Sheldon, J. B., Sherman, J. A., & Harchik, A. E. (1990). Balancing the right to habilitation with the right to personal liberties: The rights of people with developmental disabilities to eat too many doughnuts and take a nap. *Journal of Applied Behaviour Analysis, 23*, 78-89.

Barnes, D. M. (1986). Brain function decline in children with AIDS. *Science, 232*, 1196.

Bauer, A. M., & Shea, T. M. (1989). *Teaching exceptional students in your classroom*. Toronto: Allyn & Bacon.

Bauer, R. H. (1977). Memory processes in children with learning disabilities: Evidence for deficient rehearsal. *Journal of Experimental Child Psychology, 24*, 415-430.

Becker, W. C., Engelmann, S., & Thomas, D. R. (1971). *Teaching: A course in applied psychology*. Chicago: Science Research Associates.

Belmont, J. M. (1966). Long term memory in mental retardation. In N. R. Ellis (Ed.), *International review of research in mental retardation, Volume 1*. New York: Academic Press.

Belmont, J. M., & Butterfield, E. C. (1971). Learning strategies as determinants of memory deficiencies. *Cognitive Psychology, 2*, 411-420.

Berko-Gleason, J. (Ed.). (1989). *The development of language* (2nd ed.). Columbus, OH: Merrill.

Biggs, J. B. (1978). Individual and group differences in study process. *British Journal of Educational Psychology, 48*, 266-279.

Biggs, J. B. (1985). The role of metalearning in study processes. *British Journal of Educational Psychology, 55*, 185-212.

Biggs, J. B. (1987). *Student approaches to learning and studying*. Hawthorn, VIC: Australian Council for Educational Research.

Bilodeau, E. A. (1966). *Acquisition of skill*. New York: Academic Press.

Blankenship, C., & Lilly, M. S. (1981). *Mainstreaming students with learning and behaviour problems*. New York: Holt, Rinehart, & Winston.

Bockrath, D. A. (1981). The relationship between reaction time and both intelligence and achievement in normal, gifted, EMR, and ID populations. *Dissertation Abstracts International, 41*, (8-A) 3484.

Boos, M., Garlonski, R. M., MacEwen, G. D., & Steg, N. (1984). Orthopedic problems. In J. Fithian (Ed.), *Understanding the child with a chronic illness in the classroom*. Phoenix, AZ: Oryx Press.

Borkowski, J. G., & Buchel, F. P. (1983). Learning and memory strategies in the mentally retarded. In M. Pressley & J. R. Levin (Eds.), *Cognitive strategy research: Psychological foundations* (pp. 103-128). New York: Springer-Verlag.

Borkowski, J. G., & Cavanaugh, J. C. (1979). Maintenance and generalization of skills and strategies by the retarded. In N. R. Ellis (Ed.), *Handbook of mental deficiency: Psychological theory and research*. Hillsdale, NJ: Lawrence Erlbaum.

Bos, C. S., & Vaughn, S. (1991). *Strategies for teaching students with learning and behaviour problems* (2nd ed.). Toronto: Allyn & Bacon.

Bransford, J. D. (1979). *Human cognition: Learning, understanding, and remembering*. Belmont, CA: Wadsworth.

Bray, N. W., Justice, E. M., Ferguson, R. R., & Simon, D. L. (1977). Developmental changes in the effects of instructions on production deficient children. *Child Development, 48*, 1019-1026.

Brown, A. L. (1980). Metacognitive development and reading. In J. R. Spiro, B. C. Bruce, & W. F. Brewer (Eds.), *Theoretical issues in reading comprehension* (pp. 453-482). Hillsdale, NJ: Lawrence Erlbaum.

Brown, F., Evans, I., Weed, K., & Owen, V. (1987). Delineating functional competencies: A component model. *Journal of the Association for Persons with Severe Handicaps, 12*(2), 117-124.

Brown, S. C. (1986). Etiological trends, characteristics, and distributions. In A. N. Schildroth & M. A. Karchmer (Eds.), *Deaf children in America* (pp. 33-54). San Diego: College Hill.

Bruner, J. S., Goodnow, J. J., & Austin, G. A. (1956). *A study of thinking*. New York: John Wiley.

Byers, J. (1989). AIDS in children: Effects on neurological development and implications for the future. *The Journal of Special Education, 23*, 5-16.

Calfee, R. C. (1976). Sources of dependency in cognitive processes. In D. Klahr (Ed.), *Cognition and instruction*. Hillsdale, NJ: Lawrence Erlbaum.

Carter, K. R. (1985). Cognitive development of intellectually gifted: A Piagetian perspective. *Roeper Review, 17*, 183-185.

Carter, K. R., & Ormrod, J. E. (1982). Acquisition of formal operations by intellectually gifted children. *Gifted Child Quarterly, 26*, 110-114.

Case, R. (1974). Structures and strictures: Some fundamental limitations on the course of cognitive growth. *Cognitive Psychology, 6*, 544-573.

Case, R. (1978). A developmentally based theory and technology of instruction. *Review of Educational Research, 48*, 439-463.

Case, R. (1984). The process of stage transition: A neo-Piagetian view. In R. J. Sternberg (Ed.), *Mechanisms of cognitive development*. New York: W. H. Freeman.

Case, R. (1985). *Intellectual development: A systematic reinterpretation*. New York: Academic Press.

Chang, T. M. (1986). Semantic memory: Facts and models. *Psychological Bulletin, 99*, 199-220.

Chinn, P., Drew, C., & Logan, D. (1979). *Mental retardation: A life cycle approach*. St. Louis: C.V. Mosby.

Church, J. A., Allen, J. R., & Stiehm, E. R. (1986). New scarlett letter(s), pediatric AIDS. *Pediatrics, 77*, 423-427.

Cohen, R., & Bain, G. (1983). Memory in educable mentally retarded adults. Deficit in subject or experimenter? *Intelligence, 7*(3), 287-298.

Conte, R., & Andrews, J. (1993). Social skills in the context of learning disability definitions: A reply to Gresham and

Elliott and directions for the future. *Journal of Learning Disabilities*, Vol. 26, No. 3, 146–153.

Council for Children with Behaviour Disorders. (1987). Position paper on definition and identification of students with behaviour disorders. *Behaviour Disorders, 12*, 9-19.

Crocker, A. C. (Ed.). (1989). Developmental disabilities and HIV infection: A symposium on issues and public policy. *Mental Retardation, 27*(4), Special Issue.

Doll, E. (1941). The essentials of an inclusive concept of mental deficiency. *American Journal of Mental Deficiency, 46*, 214-219.

Drabman, R. S., & Patterson, J. (1981). Disruptive behaviour and the social standing of exceptional children. *Exceptional Education Quarterly, 1*, 45-55.

Education for All Handicapped Children Act (PL 94-142). (1975). 94th Congress.

Ellis, N. R. (1970). Memory processes in retardates and normals. In N. R. Ellis (Ed.), *International review of research in mental retardation, Volume 4* (pp. 1-32). New York: Academic Press.

Epstein, L. G., Sharer, L. R., & Goudsmit, J. (1988). Neurological and neuropathological features of human immune deficiency virus infection in children. *Annals of neurology, 23*, 19-23.

Federal Register. (1981). Washington, DC: U.S. Government Printing Office.

Fitts, P. M., & Posner, M. I. (1967). *Human performance*. Belmont, CA: Brooks/Cole.

Flavell, J. H. (1976). Metacognitive aspects of problem solving. In L. B. Resnick (Ed.), *The nature of intelligence*. Hillsdale, NJ: Lawrence Erlbaum.

Flavell, J. H., Friedrichs, A. G., & Hoyt, J. D. (1970). Developmental changes in memorization processes. *Cognitive Psychology, 1*, 324-340.

Forest, M., & Lusthaus, E. (1990). Everyone belongs with the MAPS Action Planning System. *Teaching Exceptional Children, 22*(4), 36-39.

Gagne, F. (1985). Giftedness and talent: Reexamining a reexamination of the definitions. *Gifted Child Quarterly, 29*, 103-111.

Gardner, H. (1984). Assessing intelligence: A comment on testing intelligence without IQ tests. *Phi Delta Kappa, 65*, 699-700.

Gearheart, B. R., Weishahn, M. W., & Gearheart, C. J. (1988). *The exceptional student in the regular classroom* (4th ed.). Toronto: Merrill.

Gearheart, B. R., Weishahn, M. W., & Gearheart, C. J. (1992). *The exceptional student in the regular classroom* (5th ed.). Toronto: Maxwell Macmillan Canada.

Glazzard, P. (1980). Adaptations for mainstreaming. *Teaching Exceptional Children, 11*, 101-104.

Grossman, H. (Ed.). (1983). *Manual on terminology and classification in mental retardation*. Washington, DC: American Association on Mental Deficiency.

Hallahan, D. P. (1982). Learning disabilities. In D. P. Hallahan & H. M. Kauffman (Eds.), *Exceptional children: Introduction to special education*. Englewood Cliffs, NJ: Prentice-Hall.

Hallahan, D. P., & Kauffman, J. M. (1988). *Exceptional children: Introduction to special education* (4th ed.). Englewood Cliffs, NJ: Prentice-Hall.

Hallahan, D. P., Kauffman, J. M., & Lloyd, J. W. (1985). *Introduction to learning disabilities* (2nd ed.). Englewood Cliffs, NJ: Prentice-Hall.

Hallahan, D. P., Kneedler, R. D., & Lloyd, J. W. (1983). Cognitive behaviour modification techniques for learning disabled children: Self-instruction and self-monitoring. In J. D. McKinney & L. Feagans (Eds.), *Current topics in learning disabilities*. Norwood, NJ: Ablex.

Hardman, M. L., Drew, C. J., & Egan, M. W. (1987). *Human exceptionality* (2nd ed.). Boston: Allyn & Bacon.

Hardy, J. C. (1983). *Cerebral palsy*. Englewood Cliffs, NJ: Prentice-Hall.

Hatlen, P. (1976). Priorities in education programs for visually handicapped children and youth. *Division for the Visually Handicapped Newsletter, Winter*, 8-11.

Hatlen, P. (1978). The role of the teacher of the visually impaired: A self definition. *Division for the Visually Handicapped Newsletter, Fall*, 5.

Hawton, K. (1986). *Suicide and attempted suicide among children and adolescents*. Beverly Hills, CA: Sage.

Heward, W. L., & Orlansky, M. D. (1992). *Exceptional children: An introductory survey of special education* (4th ed.). Toronto: Maxwell Macmillan Canada.

Hunt, E., Frost, N., & Lunneburg, C. (1973). Individual differences in cognition: A new approach to intelligence. In G. Bower (Ed.), *The psychology of learning and motivation*. New York: Academic Press.

Hutton, J. B. (1985). What reasons are given by teachers who refer problem behaviour students? *Psychology in the Schools, 22*, 79-82.

Jones, B. F., Palincsar, A., Ogle, D., & Carr, E. (1987). *Strategic teaching and learning: Cognitive instruction in the content areas*. Elmhurst, IL: North Central Regional Educational Laboratory.

Kendal, C. R., Borkowski, J. G., & Cavanaugh, J. C. (1980). Metamemory and the transfer of an interrogative strategy by EMR children. *Intelligence, 4*, 255-270.

Keogh, B. (1987). Learning disabilities: In defense of a construct. *Learning Disabilities Research, 3*(1), 4-9.

Kerr, D. (1990). Ryan White's death: A time to reflect. *Journal of School Health, 60*(5), 237-238.

Kerr, D. (1990). Aids-speak. *Journal of School Health, 60*(8), 431-432.

Khatena, J. (1976). Major directions in creativity research. In J. Gowan, J. Khatena, & P. Torrance (Eds.), *Educating the ablest*. Itasca, IL: Peacock.

Klausmeier, H. J., Feldhusen, J., & Check, J. (1959). *An analysis of learning efficiency in arithmetic of mentally retarded children in comparison with children of average and high intelligence*. Madison: University of Wisconsin Press.

Kramer, J. L., Piersel, W. C., & Glover, J. A. (1988). Cognitive and social development of mildly retarded children. In M. C. Wang, M. C. Reynolds, & H. J. Walberg (Eds.), *Handbook of special education research and practice, Volume 2: Mildly handicapped conditions*. Toronto: Pergamon.

Krug, R .S. (1983). Substance abuse. In C.E. Walker & McRoberts (Eds.), *Handbook of clinical child psychology* (pp. 853-879). New York: John Wiley.

Kuzemko, J. A. (1978). *Allergy in children*. Kent, England: Pitman Medical.

Lajoie, S. P., & Shore, B. M. (1986). Intelligence: The speed and accuracy trade off in high aptitude individuals. *Journal for the Education of the Gifted, 9*, 85-104.

Lambert, N., Windmiller, M., Tharinger, D., & Cole, L. (1981). *AAMD-ABS school edition*. Washington: American Association on Mental Deficiency.

Lefrançois, G. R. (1988). *Psychology for teaching* (6th ed.). Belmont, CA: Wadsworth.

Lewis, R. B., & Doorlag, D. H. (1991). *Teaching special students in the mainstream*. Toronto: Collier Macmillan.

Libkuman, T. M., Villiky, R. S., & Freidrich, D. D. (1980). Nonselective read-out from iconic memory in normal, borderline and retarded adolescents. *Intelligence, 4*, 363-369.

Lindley, L. (1990). Defining TASH: A mission statement. *TASH Newsletter, 16*(8),#1.

Link, M. P. (1982). Cancer in childhood. In E. Bleck & D. Nagel (Eds.), *Physically handicapped children: A medical atlas for teachers* (2nd ed.) (pp. 43-58). New York: Grune & Stratton.

Loper, A. B. (1980). Metacognitive development: Implications for cognitive training. *Exceptional Education Quarterly, 1,* 1-8.

Luterman, D. M. (Ed.). (1986). *Deafness in perspective.* San Diego: College Hill.

MacMillan, D. L. (1982). *Mental retardation in school and society* (2nd ed.). Boston: Little, Brown.

Marland, S. (1972). *Education of the gifted and talented.* Report to the Congress of the United States by the U.S. Commissioner of Education. Washington, DC: U.S. Government Printing Office.

Maron, S. S., & Martinez, D. H. (1980). Environmental alternatives for the visually handicapped. In J. W. Schifani, R. M. Anderson, & S. J. Odle (Eds.), *Implementing learning in the least restrictive environment* (pp. 149-198). Baltimore: University Park Press.

Marx, R. W., & Winne, P. H. (1991). Cognitive approaches to classroom motivation. In R. H. Short, L. L. Stewin, & S. J. H. McCann (Eds.), *Educational psychology: Canadian perspectives* (pp. 157-175). Toronto: Copp Clark Pitman.

McCormick, L., & Richard, N. (forthcoming). Designing an optimal learning environment. In L. McCormick & R.L. Schiefelbusch (Eds.), *Early language intervention* (2nd ed.). Columbus, OH: Merrill.

McNally, P., Rose, S., & Quigley, S. (1987). *Language learning practices with deaf children.* Boston: College Hill Press.

Mercer, J. R. (1973). *Labelling the mentally retarded.* Berkley, CA: University of California Press.

Mercer, J. R. (1981). Testing and assessment practices in multiethnic education. In J. A. Banks (Ed.), *Education in the 1980s: Multi-ethnic education* (pp. 93-104). Washington, DC: National Education Association.

Mercer, J. A., & Lewis, J. P. (1978). *System of multicultural pluralistic assessment: Parent interview manual.* New York: Psychological Corporation.

Merina, A. (1989). Is your school ready for AIDS? *NEA Today, 8*(5), 10-11.

Meyer, L. H., & Evans, I. M. (1989). *Non-aversive intervention for behaviour problems: A manual for home and community.* Baltimore, MD: Paul H. Brookes.

Miller, G. A. (1956). The magical number seven, plus or minus two: Some limits on our capacity for processing information. *Psychological Review, 63,* 81-97.

Moores, D. (1985). Educational programs and services for hearing impaired children: Issues and options. In F. Powell, T. Finitzo-Hieber, S. Friel-Patti, & D. Henderson (Eds.), *Education of the hearing impaired child* (pp. 3-20). San Diego: College Hill.

Moores, D. (1987). *Educating the deaf: Psychology, principles, and practices* (3rd ed.). Boston: Houghton-Mifflin.

Muse, N. J. (1990). *Depression and suicide in children and adolescents.* Austin TX: Pro-Ed.

National Joint Committee on Learning Disabilities. (1987). Learning disabilities: Issues on definition. *Journal of Learning Disabilities, 10*(2), 107-108.

National Society to Prevent Blindness. (1977). *Signs of possible eye trouble in children* (Pub.G-112). New York: Author.

National Society to Prevent Blindness. (1980). *Vision problems in the U.S.: A statistical analysis prepared by Operational Research Department, NSPB.* New York: Author.

Office of the Federal National Archives and Records Administration. (1985). *Code of federal regulations.* Washington, DC: Government Printing Office.

Olson, M. R. (1992). Visual disorders. In L.M. Bullock (Ed.), *Exceptionalities in children and youth.* Allyn & Bacon: Toronto.

Paivio, A. (1971). *Imagery and verbal processes.* New York: Holt, Rinehart & Winston.

Pasanella, A. L., & Volkmor, C. B. (1981). *Teaching handicapped students in the mainstream* (2nd ed.). Columbus, OH: Merrill.

Paul, P. V., & Quigley, S. P. (1990). *Education and deafness.* New York: Longman.

Pearl, R., & Bryan, J. (1979). Self-concept and locus of control of learning disabled children. *Journal of Clinical Child Psychology, 8,* 223-226.

Peterson, C. (1980). Support services. In B. Wilcox & R. York (Eds.), *Quality education for the severely handicapped: The federal investment* (pp. 136-163). Washington, DC: U.S. Department of Education, Office of Special Education and Rehabilitative Services.

Piaget, J. (1952). *The origins of intelligence in children.* New York: Basic Books.

Pieper, E. (1983). *The teacher and the child with spina bifida.* Chicago: Spina Bifida Association of America.

Polloway, E. A., Patton, J. R., Payne, J. S., & Payne, R. A. (1989). *Strategies for teaching learners with special needs* (4th ed.). Toronto: Merrill.

Rainforth, B., York, J., & Macdonald, C. (1992). *Collaborative teams for students with severe disabilities: Integrating therapy and educational services.* Toronto: Paul H. Brookes.

Reed, S. (1988). Children with AIDS: How schools are handling the crisis. Kappan Special Report. *Phi Delta Kappan, 19,* K1-K12.

Reichle, J., & Keogh, W. J. (1986). Communication instruction for learners with severe handicaps: Some unresolved issues. In R. H. Horner, L. H. Meyer, & H. D. B. Fredericks (Eds.), *Education of learners with severe handicaps: Exemplary service strategies* (pp. 189-219). Baltimore, MD: Paul H. Brookes.

Reid, D. K., & Hresko, W. P. (1981). *A cognitive approach to learning disabilities.* New York: McGraw-Hill.

Renzulli, J. S. (1978). What makes giftedness? Re-examining a definition. *Phi Delta Kappan, 60*(3), 180-184, 261.

Reynolds, M. C., & Birch, J. W. (1988). *Adaptive mainstreaming: A primer for teachers and principals* (3rd ed.). New York: Longman.

Saccuzzo, D. P., Kerr, M., Marcus, A., & Brown, R. (1979). Input capability and speed of processing in mental retardation. *Journal of Abnormal Psychology, 88,* 341-345.

Sarason, S. B., & Doris, J. (1979). *Educational handicap, public policy, and social history: A broadened perspective on mental retardation.* New York: Free Press.

Schank, R. C., & Abelson, R. (1977). *Scripts, plans, goals, and understanding.* Hillsdale, NJ: Lawrence Erlbaum.

Schmeck, R. R. (1988). Individual differences and learning strategies. In C. E. Weinstein, E. T. Goetz, & P. A. Alexander (Eds.), *Learning and study strategies: Issues in assessment, instruction and evaluation.* Toronto: Academic Press.

Schultz, E. E. (1983). Depth of processing by mentally retarded and MA matched non-retarded individuals. *American Journal of Mental Deficiency, 88*(3), 307-313.

Schulz, J., Carpenter, C., & Turnbull, A. (1991). *Mainstreaming exceptional students* (3rd ed.). Toronto: Allyn & Bacon.

Schunk, D. H. (1991). *Learning theories: An educational perspective.* Toronto: Collier MacMillan Canada.

Schwachman, H., Kowalski, M., & Khaw, K. T. (1977). Cystic fibrosis: A new outlook. *Medicine, 56,* 129-149.

Scruggs, T. E., & Mastropieri, M. A. (1984). How gifted students learn: Implications from recent research. *Roeper Review, 6,* 183-185.

Shevin, M., & Klein, N. K. (1984). The importance of choice making skills for students with severe disabilities. *The Journal of Association for Persons with Severe Handicaps, 9,* 159-166.

Siegler, R. S. (1976). Three aspects of cognitive development. *Cognitive Psychology, 8,* 481-520.

Siegler, R. S. (1984). Mechanisms of cognitive growth: Variation and selection. In R. J. Sternberg (Ed.), *Mechanisms of cognitive development.* New York: W. H. Freeman.

Slavin, R. E. (1991). *Educational psychology: Theory into practice (3rd ed).* Englewood Cliffs, NJ: Prentice-Hall.

Spitz, H. H. (1966). The role of input organizations in the learning and memory of mental retardates. In N. R. Ellis (Ed.), *International review of research on mental retardation.* New York: Academic Press.

Stainback, W., & Stainback, S. (1984). A rationale for the merger of special and regular education. *Exceptional Children, 51,*102-111.

Sternberg, R. J. (1981). A componential theory of intellectual giftedness. *Gifted Child Quarterly, 25,* 86-93.

Sternberg, R. J. (1982). A componential approach to intellectual development. In R. J. Sternberg (Ed.), *Advances in the psychology of human intelligence, Volume 1.* Hillsdale, NJ: Lawrence Erlbaum.

Sternberg, R. J. (1984a). Mechanisms of cognitive development: A componential approach. In R. J. Sternberg (Ed.), *Mechanisms of cognitive development.* New York: W. H. Freeman.

Sternberg, R. J. (1984b). Testing intelligence without IQ tests. *Phi Delta Kappan, 65,* 694-698.

Sternberg, R. J., & Davidson, J. E. (1983). Insight in the gifted. *Educational Psychologist, 18*(1), 51-57.

Swallow, R. M., & Conner, A. (1982). Aural reading. In S. S. Mangold (Ed.), *A teacher's guide to the special education needs of blind and visually handicapped children* (pp. 119-135). New York: American Foundation for the Blind.

Swanson, H. L. (1982). Strategies and constraints: A commentary. *Topics in Learning and Learning Disabilities, 2,* 79-81.

Thomas, A., & Chess, S. (1984). Genesis and evolution of behavioural disorders. From infancy to early adult life. *American Journal of Psychiatry, 141,* 1-9.

Torgesen, J. K., & Houck, D. G. (1980). Processing deficiencies of learning disabled children who perform poorly on the digit span test. *Journal of Educational Psychology, 72,* 141-160.

Torgesen, J. K., & Greenstein, J. J. (1982). Why do some learning disabled children have problems remembering? Does it make a difference? *Topics in Learning and Learning Disabilities, 2*(2), 54-61.

Torrance, E. P. (1969). Creative positives of disadvantaged children and youth. *Gifted Child Quarterly, 13,* 71-81.

Tulving, E. (1972). Episodic and semantic memory. In E. Tulving & W. Donaldson (Eds.), *Organization of memory.* New York: Academic Press.Tulving, E. (1985). How many memory systems are there? *American Psychologist, 40,* 385-398.

Vernon, M. (1987). The primary causes of deafness. In E. Mindel & M. Vernon (Eds.), *They grow in silence: Understanding deaf children and adults* (2nd ed.) (pp. 31-38). San Diego: College Hill.

Vygotsky, L. S. (1978). *Mind in society: The development of higher psychological processes.* Cambridge, MA: Harvard University Press.

Wehman, P., Renzaglia, A. M., & Bates, P. (1985). *Functional living skills for moderately and severely handicapped individuals.* Austin, TX: Pro-Ed.

Wellman, H. M. (1977). Tip of the tongue and feeling of knowing experiences: A developmental study of memory monitoring. *Child Development, 48,* 13-21.

Westling, D. L., & Koorland, M. A. (1979). Some considerations and tactics for improving discrimination learning. *Teaching Exceptional Children, 11*(3), 97-100.

Wilbur, R. (1987). *American sign language: Linguistic and applied dimensions* (2nd ed.). Boston: Little, Brown.

Williams, W., Fox, T. J., Thousand, J., & Fox, W. (1990). Level of acceptance and implementation of best practices in the education of students with severe handicaps in Vermont. *Education and Training in Mental Retardation, 25*(2), 120-131.

Wilson, D. W. (1985). Approving the problem solving behaviour of mathematically gifted children. *Dissertation Abstracts International, 45,* 831-851.

Winne, P. H., & Marx, R. W. (1989). A cognitive processing analysis of motivation within classroom tasks. In C. Ames & R. Ames (Eds.), *Research on motivation, Volume 3: Goals and cognitions* (pp. 223-257). San Diego, CA: Academic Press.

Winzer, M. A. (1989). *Closing the gap: Special learners in regular classrooms.* Toronto: Copp Clark Pitman.

Winzer, M. A. (1990). *Children with exceptionalities: A Canadian perspective.* Toronto: Prentice-Hall.

Wong, B. Y. L. (1982). Strategic behaviours in selecting retrieval cues in gifted, normal achieving and learning disabled children. *Journal of Learning Disabilities, 13,* 33-37.

Ysseldyke, J., & Algozzine, B. (1990). *Introduction to special education* (2nd ed.). Boston: Houghton-Mifflin.

Ysseldyke, J., Algozzine, B., & Epps, S. (1983). A logical and empirical analysis of current practice in classifying students as handicapped. *Exceptional Children, 50,* 160-166.

Zigler, E. (1966). Research on personality structure in the retardate. In N. R. Ellis (Ed.), *International review of research in mental retardation* (pp. 77-108). New York: Academic Press.

Zimmerman, B. L. (1981). Individual differences in intelligence and learning. *Dissertation Abstracts International, 42* (2-A), 625-626.

STUDENTS IN THE MAINSTREAM WHO FACE LINGUISTIC AND CULTURAL CHALLENGES

CHAPTER
5

CHAPTER OBJECTIVES

To introduce students to the major conceptual and critical issues relating to multicultural education.

To relate current multicultural education to the historical context of immigration into Canada.

To familiarize students with the major social-psychological terms and variables relating to cross-cultural communication and multicultural education.

To provide an introduction to the central concepts relating to second language learning and teaching within a multicultural context.

To provide some working guidelines for the regular classroom teacher as the basis for the inclusive education of immigrant students.

When Helen Horner looked at her class register the day before school started, she saw nothing unusual about the names—Tranh Ting, Chen Zenmin, Sofia Pironek, Luis Gonzales, Sally Little Bear, Sammy Wang, Suzie MacDonald … —twenty-four children, and if the past were any predictor of the present, at least half of them would speak a language other than English. Vietnamese, Chinese, Polish, Spanish, Sarcee—she would likely hear these languages tomorrow, but she might also hear Italian, Greek, German, Ukrainian, Russian, or, indeed, any language of the world.

She glanced again at the class list. Whatever ethnic background their names suggested, some of these children would speak English, at least enough to get by in the Grade 2 classroom. But many, she knew, would need a lot of help. Helen thought back to previous

years. Fifteen years ago, she would have had perhaps two or three children who did not speak English, probably francophone or native children, in a class of twenty or twenty-five students. Tomorrow she would find out for sure, but chances were good that twelve to fifteen children would need additional help in English, and they would come from any number of language and cultural backgrounds. Some would be able to speak English very well but would not know how to read or write English. Others would be able to speak a little English and read and write a little of the language as well. Still others would be true beginners, and all would be in the same classroom, along with a dozen or so children whose first language was English.

Fifteen years ago, she would have been very worried about having such a diverse population represented in her class. But over the years, as more and more children arrived needing language support and help in cultural adaptation, Helen had learned to cope. Although she felt the usual beginning-of-school-year anxieties, she no longer panicked in the face of ethnic and linguistic diversity. She had come to understand how to create a classroom environment that was welcoming to Tranh, Chen, Sofia, and indeed, to all the children who arrived there.

Helen's class is at Saint Monica's School, an inner-city school in a large western Canadian city, but it could be almost anywhere. The ethnic mix that characterizes her classroom—English speakers, French speakers, immigrants from around the world, Canadian-born children of immigrants, Native Canadians—is coming to characterize more and more classrooms across Canada. In fact, there are relatively few schools in the country whose student enrolments do not reflect Canada's ethnic diversity.

◇ INTRODUCTION

These facts of classroom life mean that all teachers are well advised to get as firm a grasp as they possibly can of the central issues in second-cultural and second-language education. No single chapter can cover all aspects of ESL education, and it is the central purpose here to provide a conceptual basis for classroom decision-making rather than a detailed inventory of teaching methods. The foundation for all multicultural education lies in gaining greater sensitivity to, and understanding about, the experiences of immigrants and other non-English-speaking cultural minorities.

MULTICULTURALISM: A HORIZONTAL OR A VERTICAL MOSAIC?

Most Canadians seem to be aware that theirs is a multicultural country in which people from different countries are encouraged to live with one another in a pluralist *mosaic* rather than, as south of the border, in a *melting pot*. The fundamental ideal of multiculturalism is that immigrants from other cultures may live in peace and harmony with all others in Canada while being free—indeed, encouraged—to maintain their original heritages and languages. The mere statement of a philosophy, however, does not guarantee its realization in practice, and recently many people have been arguing that multiculturalist policy—so *apparently* reasonable and generous to all—is in reality little more than a panacea that does more to camouflage the real issues of individual rights and freedoms than to ensure their existence (Moodley, 1983; Mallea, 1984; Wyatt, 1984).

Porter (1965) suggests that what Canada has is not a horizontal mosaic where cultural groups exist in a unifying and egalitarian pattern, but rather a **vertical mosaic** where cultures are ranked in hierarchical order, and where the "founding race" groups from Britain and France are clearly privileged over Aboriginal groups and other non-European immigrant groups who are both effectively suppressed and economically disadvantaged. A clear piece of evidence of such vertical structuring is that immigrants typically have access

[handwritten margin notes: "horizontal = good" "yes" "not good"]

◆ **vertical mosaic:** the hierarchical stratification of Canadian society in terms of ethnic groups

to only certain kinds of work in Canada. Our system of qualifications makes it difficult for any but those fully educated within the Canadian (or other "equivalent") system to enter professions such as law, medicine, or teaching; those fortunate to have at least one fluent official language inevitably find it easier than immigrants to find opportunities that enable them to take full advantage of their talents.

At the outset, then, it is important to be aware of the many dangers inherent in multiculturalism. One such danger is that by assuming we are all truly equal within our multicultural context we may well be blinding ourselves to the very real suffering, anger, and hostility felt by many of those pushed to the bottom of the vertical mosaic. A second danger is that by continually overemphasizing our rejection of the melting-pot model of immigration, which embodies the idea that immigrants should strive toward becoming indistinguishable from members of the majority culture into which they immigrate, both politicians and educators cause more fragmentation between groups than is either ideal or necessary. What emerges for those in the teaching profession from current observations about multiculturalism in Canada is that multicultural policy should be treated like all ideologies—with critical alertness rather than passive acceptance.

◆ HISTORICAL BACKGROUND: THE TREATMENT OF IMMIGRANTS IN CANADA

The pattern of contemporary treatment of immigrants in Canada is not simply a function of modern policies or societal reactions but has developed over the entire history of Canadian immigration. In explaining our current circumstances, many cultural historians emphasize the strong influence of *colonial* and *post-colonial* events, and it is here that we find the source of many attitudes and feelings that are still prevalent today.

COLONIALISM

Although Canada has never itself been a colonizing power, it has been the site of a long period of British colonization, and has been strongly affected by the parallel history of slavery both in the British empire and in the United States. Historically, colonialism was based on the domination and subsequent economic exploitation by whites of other populations. By the end of the 19th century, it was common to view whites as both biologically and culturally superior to other peoples. This idea is the starting point of modern racism (Rex, 1973).

Following the early expeditions of the European conquerors, two major phases of colonization can be identified (Tierney, 1982). In the first phase, up to the beginning of the 19th century, European conquerors populated their new colonies, simply removing territory from any indigenous people who might live there. These occupied lands were thought of as direct extensions of the colonizing countries. In this way, Canada, Australia, and New Zealand became the extended territories of a white commonwealth. Resistance by indigenous people, such as the Native Indians of North America, was suppressed through the superior power of the white settlers, and this generally resulted either in the annihilation of populations or in their removal and incarceration in reservations. Between the 17th and late 19th centuries, the population of Native Indians in North America was reduced from over two million to less than a quarter of a million.

The first period of colonization includes the era of slavery, during which it has been estimated by some that up to 150 million Africans were forcibly removed from their homelands. According to the ideology of the time,

> [b]lacks were classified as sub-human, as the biological inferiors of white 'races,' thus it was morally acceptable for them to be owned by white people, to be deprived of all freedoms, and for slavery to be a socially inherited status (Tierney, 1982, p. 17).

In our own time, it is important to understand how the entire history of colonization has affected both contemporary perceptions of races, nations, and regions, as well as the global economic order. Colonial history still provides the essential framework within which modern immigrants arrive at a country, only to find that they are viewed as being qualified to do only certain types of (generally menial) labour. The idea that colonialism is alive and well, if under a different guise, is an important one to consider when examining the history of various groups of immigrants to Canada.

Canadians have also recently been reminded that their own history is by no means free of overt expressions of hatred and suspicion toward others. In 1989, the Canadian-Japanese community received formal apology from the Canadian government for its placement, during the Second World War, of Japanese-Canadians in internment camps in central British Columbia. Vestiges of similar institutional reaction were to be found even during the Gulf War of 1991, when several Iraqi-Canadian citizens were harassed and made to feel like suspects. The recent use of the phrase "two founding races" (i.e. "English" and "French") in Canadian government documents is further evidence of how Canada views itself as fundamentally white Anglo-Saxon. Perhaps the most blatant manifestation of colonial racism in Canadian history concerns the treatment of Native children in missionary and residential schools. Historians have described the relentlessness with which officials and teachers went about their task of extinguishing both Native languages and cultures in order to satisfy their colonial objectives (Ashworth, 1979, pp. 20-25). Given these facts of Canadian history, it is hardly surprising that educational negotiations between provincial ministries of education and Native representatives are nowadays wrought with difficulty and cross-cultural suspicion. The historical instances of suppression and cultural extinction of Native people in Canada have left a legacy of poignant and perhaps insuperable cross-cultural problems in the area of language education.

IMMIGRANT CHILDREN

Ashworth (1979, 1988) provides us with sensitive insights into the lives of child immigrants and the children of immigrants to Canada, which help us better understand some of the feelings of members of minority groups. She summarizes the historical experiences of specific ethnic and racial groups in Canada, indicating that there are, in fact, many different histories of Canada tied to the experiences of particular groups in particular locations (1988, p. 1).

Black Canadians

The experiences of most black immigrants to Canada have their origin in slavery. From the 17th to 19th centuries, in the areas now known as Ontario, Quebec, New Brunswick, and Nova Scotia, slaves were traded to work on plantations. A later wave of blacks entered Canada in support of a British victory during the American Revolution. Known as the Black Loyalists, these emigrants from the United States were promised fair treatment and land, neither of which were forthcoming after their arrival in Canada. Those who stayed were forced to exist at the margins of white society and thus never became fully integrated.

In the early 19th century, groups of black immigrants attempted to settle in the Maritimes only to be confronted with an attempt in 1815 by Maritimers to legally ban all further such immigration. For most of their history up until the 20th century, blacks were educated in separate schools under religious jurisdiction, and it was not until the U.S. civil rights movement in the 1960s that such segregation was abandoned. The position of black immigrant children in the Maritimes and Ontario up until the end of segregation can be summarized as follows:

> For Black children in the Maritimes and Ontario, segregated schooling, coupled with poverty, resulted in an inadequate education. Youngsters dropped out of school or were forced to repeat grades. Those who were admitted to a public school often found themselves one, two or three years older than their white peers in the same grade. The combination of a poor education and the colour of their skin severely reduced employment opportunities for young Blacks and the poverty cycle was repeated from generation to generation (Ashworth, 1988, p. 5).

The current experiences of black immigrants to Canada are thus founded on a history of exploitation and racial segregation. The experience of blacks in eastern and central Canada have much in common with the experiences of Chinese immigrants in western Canada.

Chinese Canadians

Chinese immigrants first came to British Columbia in the mid-19th century to work as miners and railroad employees. By 1880, organized anti-Chinese groups had formed and petitions were delivered to Parliament in attempts to stem the tide of Chinese immigration. As in the case of Maritime blacks, there were efforts to segregate Chinese children from other children in the school system, and in 1904 a head tax of $500 was placed on each new Chinese immigrant, although certain classes of immigrants, such as diplomats and students, were able to obtain a later refund of the money. In 1923, a bill was passed in Victoria that disallowed any further Chinese immigration. It was not until 1947 that this ban was lifted, and not until 1967 that Chinese immigrants were given the same rights to landed immigrant status as immigrants from Europe. Thus, the contemporary experiences of Chinese Canadians, like those of blacks, are at least partly conditioned by a history of discrimination and oppression.

Other Groups

Other groups of children who have arrived in Canada over the past two centuries include those in Jewish, Mennonite, Doukhobor, Japanese, Vietnamese, Laotian, Latin-American, Ukrainian, and other European families. In many cases, the educational response in Canada has been more sensitive to other groups than it has to the Blacks and the Chinese, especially to those groups (e.g., the Ukrainians) that have maintained a strong culture and exerted political pressure for bilingual education.

Even the more favoured groups, however, have been in conflict with the majority culture. For example, in Montreal between the years 1870 and 1902, most Jews elected to pay taxes to the Protestant school board. In 1902, however, following years of such payments, the Protestant school board denied a scholarship won by a Jewish student on the grounds that his father was only a tenant and not an owner of property. A court supported this ruling, stating further that Jewish children whose parents were not owners (or "proprietors") of business property had no right even to enter Protestant schools. Although Jewish parents managed to overturn this ruling in 1903, they were still barred, solely on the basis of race, from sitting on governing boards of schools; taxation without representation was thus legalized. No Jewish teachers were hired in Montreal until the year 1918.

More recent debates between the Jewish community and school boards have concerned the less contentious issue of the right of Jewish children in schools to avoid Christian observances. The earlier history of discrimination in Canada, however, is still part of contemporary Jewish consciousness. From a historical perspective, then, immigrant children in Canada have had to face resistance to the idea that their own cultural backgrounds are of equal value with those of children from the majority culture. Until quite recently, the predominant mode of response to children from minority groups has been to assimilate them into the majority culture.

◆ SOCIAL PSYCHOLOGY OF IMMIGRATION

As established in the previous section, there are significant historical dimensions to be taken into account when attempting to explain contemporary feelings and attitudes of immigrant groups. The historical dimension is just one of many significant variables that contribute to the interactions of teachers, students, and administrators in schools. We now turn to consider several models that will help us to understand how historical forces combine with social and psychological variables to influence the interactions of individuals in educational settings.

CULTURE AS A MULTIVARIATE PHENOMENON

Anyone attempting to define "culture," or describe how culture relates to language and behaviour, faces a *multivariate* challenge. The term "multivariate" is used in psychology to refer to situations where related behaviours, thoughts, or reactions can be explained only by looking at a number of different potential causes that overlap and cannot be considered in isolation from one another. Take, for example, the complex relationship between culture and language. It is clear that the two are closely related, but it is equally clear that they are not synonymous. In Belgium, for example, an individual may speak either French or Flemish and yet still refer to his or her cultural identity as "Belgian." At the same time, however, language *can* be used by groups as the most important defining characteristic of their cultures. For example, the protection of the French language in Quebec has become the focal point of separatist tendencies in that province.

Ital.

Although language can on occasion be viewed as the cement that binds a culture together, it cannot be viewed as the *only* thing that does this. Besides viewing themselves in terms of a national cultural identity (e.g., "Belgian" or "Canadian"), individuals may use more global labels ("Western" or "Eastern," or "Muslim" or "Christian") or less global labels ("Manitoban," "cub scout," or "television addict") to refer to their cultural orientations.

Implicit in these many levels of potential cultural identification is the fact that individuals naturally belong to many (and often overlapping) cultural groups. An individual might describe her cultural identity in the following terms: "female," "Catholic," "having Polish immigrant parents," "Canadian," "athlete," "university student," "heavy metal fanatic." Moreover, our cultural identities, in addition to being *overlapping*, must also be *dynamic* in nature. They are, in fact, dynamic in two important ways. In the first place, our cultural profiles change over time—the above individual will not always be a university student or, possibly, a heavy metal fanatic—and, in the second place, individuals are likely to respond differently to questions about their cultural identity, depending on the *social context*.

A simple example of the latter kind of dynamism might be found in the responses of a mixed group of Canadians watching the Olympics on television. A Polish-Catholic-Canadian, for example, might feel strong patriotic support for the Polish athletes in the competition, even when competing against Canadians. In events where no Polish athletes are competing, however, this same individual is likely to switch allegiance to Canada. Such switches of allegiance are both common and natural, depending as they do on perceptions about what cultural characteristics are most relevant on given occasions. In short, we all have many different cultural identities, which we are able to display and distribute across different social contexts.

"IN" VERSUS "OUT" GROUPS

As a normal part of their upbringing, members of all societies learn that some people are to be liked and trusted—to be "included"— while others are to be avoided and "excluded." The reasons for inclusion or exclusion include race, skin colour, religion, economic status, and language, and, just like feelings about cultural membership, they may change across differing contexts. Brewer and Campbell (1976) argue that the formation of "in" and "out" groups is common to all human societies. From a social-psychological perspective, belonging to in-groups enhances feelings of identity and solidarity among individuals within the group, whereas exclusion from in-groups may result in feelings of rejection and insecurity.

In trying to understand how such dynamics may underlie behaviour in schools and classrooms, it is important to realize that almost any feature, or combination of features, may be singled out as the source of exclusion. Experience in schools, however, tells us that some features, such as visible attributes like skin colour, facial characteristics, and manner of speaking, are much more likely to be chosen than others. While a single feature may be identified by in-group members as the basis for rejection of out-group members in the first instance, there soon develops a complex of features that serves to reinforce rejection of others. Another important thing to realize here is that the feelings and judgments relating to exclusion can be passed on *subconsciously*. In particular, parents pass on their own attitudes and prejudices to children, not so much consciously as through behaviours and reactions that are used as a model by their children.

RACISM: LEVELS AND TYPES

◆ racism: the use of racial characteristics as a basis for judgment and discrimination

Like culture, *race* is a complex term whose precise meaning continues to be a controversial matter. In the educational context, however, it is important to note that the related term **racism** covers a variety of behaviours, some more covert than others. We may *all* behave in a racist manner on given occasions, and some would argue even more strongly that all members of the dominant white Anglo-Saxon culture are unavoidably racist because of their acceptance of, and participation in, the vertical mosaic. Racism exists, then, at many different levels and not just in the overt forms typically reported in the media. Brislin (1981) has usefully categorized some of the levels of racism as follows.

Redneck Racism

According to Brislin, this type of racism appears not just in the southern United States, where the term was first coined during the civil rights confrontations of the 1960s, but "all over the world" (p. 45). *Redneck racism* consists of the belief that certain people (sharing racial characteristics) are inferior by definition, are not worthy of decent treatment, and are incapable of advanced standards of civilization that rednecks believe they themselves reflect. Examples of the extremes of this level of racism are the Ku Klux Klan and certain anti-semitic gangs of "punks" and "skin heads."

[handwritten: ~inferior]

Symbolic Racism

Symbolic racism is a more common form of racism, which adheres to the belief that individuals in other groups are "interfering with" or "getting in the way of" members of an in-group. Evidence of this type of racism comes to light in surveys asking people to agree or disagree with statements such as, "Over the past few years [name of racial group] have gotten more economically than they deserve" (Brislin, p. 46). Individuals who are not racist in the overt redneck way may well respond in the affirmative to statements such as these. In addition, persons who are not overtly racist as a rule may become so if they perceive themselves to be threatened, for example, by the competition of outsiders for jobs or by outsiders taking up residence in close proximity.

[handwritten: → interferes]

Tokenism

More difficult to recognize than symbolic racism, *tokenism* is a form of racism which may be unconscious, but which individuals reveal through their behaviours. A study by Dutton (1976) found that subjects who had shown willingness to donate a small amount of money to an out-group were much less willing to devote any time to social interaction with members of this outgroup; in other words, they offered a "token," which allowed them to feel self-satisfied about their lack of open prejudice. The presentation of such tokens often makes us feel that we have "done enough" to show that we have nothing but positive feelings toward outsiders, although we may still harbour subconscious desires to exclude them from our own social groups.

[handwritten: → offered a "token" instead of spending time w/ them.]

Arm's-length Prejudice

Arm's-length prejudice is a type of context-specific behaviour. Individuals who are able to interact positively with people of colour in some situations, may in another social setting keep those same people at arm's length (Brislin,

[handwritten: — able to interact w/ races in certain circumstances.]

1981, p. 47; Triandis & Davis, 1965). In other words, individuals can be very fickle in deciding membership of in-groups and out-groups, as we saw in the earlier example of supporting different nationalities while watching the Olympic Games. Sometimes the reasons for such erratic behaviour have to do less with benign attributes, such as team membership, and more to do with race, colour, or class.

PREJUDICE AND ATTRIBUTION

In a classic investigation of the nature of prejudice, Allport (1954) defines (ethnic) **prejudice** as:

> an antipathy based upon a faulty and inflexible generalization. It may be felt or expressed. It may be directed toward a group as a whole, or toward an individual because he is a member of that group. (p. 10)

◆ **prejudice:** a feeling or expression of judgment about others based on unfair and faulty overgeneralization

◆ **attribution:** the interpretation one person gives to the behaviour of another

The term **attribution,** which is closely related to prejudice, refers to our everyday interpretations of the causes of behaviour in others. We need to explain the behaviour of others (partly to guard our own self-concepts), and thus we tend to *attribute* causes to the behaviour of others.

It does not require a great stretch of the imagination to see how the social phenomena of prejudice and attribution are closely related. An example might be given of a member of one culture labelling as "hostile" or "snobbish" the behaviour of out-group members at a social gathering who are huddling together, speaking another language, and apparently refusing to eat any of the food provided. Of course, such attributions about the behaviour of others can be quite unfounded. The out-group in the above example might well be feeling threatened by their lack of familiarity with the proceedings, and may, indeed, be thinking much the same about the hosts as they think about their guests. Once formed, attributions are typically used to prejudge others from the same cultural out-group, and, as we have already seen, are often used to justify and reinforce the lines of demarcation between social groups. Attribution is a normal social-psychological process, which is quite harmless when we make small and correctable errors in judgments about friends. It becomes extremely dangerous, though, when overgeneralizations or judgments made about individuals lead to opinions and prejudices about larger cultural groups, and to decisions to exclude or to deal with entire cultural groups in a negative manner.

IMMIGRATION AND THE CULTURAL DISTANCE MODEL

A convenient way of thinking about the problems and challenges faced by immigrant families in Canada, and about the subsequent effects of immigrant experiences on academic and social success in schooling, is in terms of a model of *cultural distance.* In this model, increased distance between immigrant students and Canadian society and its values leads to the prediction of higher levels of difficulty and failure in adaptation to the new culture, while greater proximity to the culture and values of the host society leads to the prediction of success. Mainstream teachers have perhaps the greatest opportunities of all for minimizing feelings of cultural distance in classrooms, and so this model, if it is interpreted with sensitivity and good judgment, provides a particularly useful analytic framework .

In presenting a distance model of cultural interaction, Schumann (1978) divides the factors that may affect the progress of immigrants in learning a second language into two general types—*social* and *psychological*. (See Table 5.1.)

Table 5.1

Characteristics Used to Measure Cultural Distance

		Tending to minimize distance	—	Tending to maximize distance
		1	2	3
	Degree of dominance	Nondominant		Dominance or subordination
Social Factors	Integration strategy	Assimilation	Acculturation	Preservation
	Degree of enclosure	Low	Medium	High
	Intended length of stay	Long-stay	Medium-stay or "unsure"	Short-stay
	Ego-perme-ability	Flexible ego boundaries	—	Rigid ego boundaries
Psychological Factors	Tolerance for ambiguity	High	—	Low
	Self-esteem	High confidence and feeling of self-worth	—	Low confidence and feeling of self-worth

Source: Shumann, 1978.

Social variables are held to affect the degree and quality of contact between persons from different cultures who speak different languages.

Social Variables

Degree of Dominance

If one of the cultural groups is in some way(s) dominant over the other (by way of political, technical, or economic advancement, for example), then this will tend to increase social distance between them and to minimize second-cultural learning. Within this category, immigrants can be classified into three groups—*dominant*, *nondominant*, and *subordinate*—where a state of approximate equality (i.e., a state of nondominance of either culture) reduces social distance and encourages cross-cultural learning, and where distance is increased in the case of reciprocal dominant-subordinate circumstances. It is important to note that this distancing works both ways. Oil company employees from North America working in Middle East countries in which they have clear technical and economic superiority are no more likely to learn much about Arabic culture or language than are suppressed Indians of the American southwest likely to immerse themselves in Anglo-centric language and culture.

Integration Strategy

Schumann (1978) suggests that there are three basic strategies adopted by immigrants to a new country—*assimilation*, *preservation*, and *acculturation*. If a second-language group assimilates into a new culture, such as Canada, then members of the group effectively give up all memory of their own cultural and linguistic background. The motivation behind **assimilation** is to become "undetectably different" in the new society by adopting its lifestyle and values completely. Obviously, such a strategy is likely to minimize social distance and to maximize both contact between the given groups and second-language learning. If a group maintains a self-preserving strategy **(preservation),** then it keeps to its own lifestyles and systematically reduces opportunities for cross-cultural contact (e.g., the Hutterites in Canada). This, of course, increases distance and minimizes opportunities or motivation for second-language learning. If a group chooses the middle road, **acculturation,** then it maintains some of its traditional beliefs, values, and customs, while adapting in other ways to the new culture. This yields various degrees of contact and language learning. In a multicultural society such as Canada's, balanced acculturation is considered to foster the optimal minimization of cross-cultural distance.

◆ **cultural assimilation:** the process of becoming similar to—and ultimately identical with—members of a different cultural group

◆ **preservation:** the process by which members of an immigrant cultural group protect their own interests and identity

◆ **acculturation:** the process by which members of an immigrant cultural group maintain some of their beliefs, values, and customs, while adapting in other ways to the new culture

Degree of Enclosure

Some immigrant groups completely share the educational, religious, and professional institutions of the host society. Other groups, in contrast, establish their own churches, schools, and professional organizations, and can thus be said to be more enclosed, increasing social distance. This factor is likely, of course, to be correlated both with integration strategy (see above) and with the group's overall size and **cohesiveness.**

◆ cohesiveness: the extent to which a cultural group reinforces its own norms and social networks

Intended Length of Residence

Not surprisingly, immigrants are much more likely to make a commitment to a second culture when they know that they are going to stay in a country for some time. Indeed, it has been found that *intention* to stay is itself a crucial factor in language learning, whether or not a given immigrant is later obliged to return home unexpectedly. Belief that length of residence will be long tends to reduce social distance and to increase cross-cultural contact and second-language learning.

In the case of "all individuals being equal," the above social factors are held to apply to various immigrant groups. All things, however, are not equal between individuals, and Schumann (1978) holds that the above variables interact with variations in the psychology of individuals.

Psychological Variables

Ego-Permeability

Following Guiora (1972), the term *language ego* has been used to parallel the Freudian concept of "body ego" to refer to individuals' sense of the boundaries of their language. In children, these boundaries are permeable and less rigid than they are in adults, making language learning easier and less inhibited. In a rather comic experiment, Guiora (1972), together with some other experimenters, tested for the presence of **ego-permeability** in adults by giving them varying amounts of alcohol to drink. They found that after about one-and-a-half ounces, their subjects' second language pronunciation improved, although in the three-ounce condition of the experiment, they began to do worse again. Within the model, greater ego-permeability suggests that psychological distance will be reduced and learning thereby enhanced.

◆ ego-permeability: the extent to which a person is open to challenge and change

Tolerance for Ambiguity

Following Cohen (1977), Schumann (1978) suggests that some individuals are better than others at accepting the ambiguity of the world around them. Many individuals stop attending to messages that are unclear or that necessitate a great deal of interpretation. Greater tolerance for ambiguity, then, is associated with greater comprehension ability in a second language.

Self-Esteem

Second-language research has found that learners' levels of self-esteem can be used to predict learning success or failure. Not surprisingly, then, it is believed that individual immigrants who feel secure and who manage to maintain or improve their levels of self-esteem throughout the immigration process both seek more contacts and learn more language skills in their second cultures.

CULTURE SHOCK

◆ culture shock: the complex of feelings and reactions that typically occur when a person moves from one culture to another

At some point in their adaptation, all members of immigrant families are likely to experience **culture shock i**n one form or another, especially when the cultural distance measures mentioned earlier are high. In an attempt to explain why it is that most people are destined to experience some kind of shock when they travel from their own to another culture, Bock (1970) wrote that

> [c]ulture, in its broadest sense, is what makes you a stranger when you are away from home. It includes all those beliefs and expectations about how people should speak and act which have become a kind of second nature to you as a result of social learning. When you are with members of a group who share your culture, you do not have to think about it, for you are all viewing the world in pretty much the same way and you all know, in general terms, what to expect of one another. However, direct exposure to an alien society usually produces a disturbing feeling of disorientation and helplessness that is called 'culture shock' (p. ix).

People who have never been immigrants have experienced these feelings of "disorientation and helplessness" in another culture at one time or another, and even vacationers are likely to experience milder forms of disorientation and culture shock when in a foreign country.

But the differences between the immigrant to Canada and the tourist in a foreign country are many. First, unlike tourists, immigrants are generally committed to a long stay in the foreign culture, perhaps to the rest of their lives, and this is something over which they typically have no control. Some immigrants who are refugees from violent political conditions strongly desire to, and actually do, return to their home countries when the political climate has stabilized. Believing they will eventually return home, such immigrants often experience less culture shock than do others who have no chance of returning. In keeping with the distance model, however, immigrants who believe they will soon leave Canada will likely absorb much less of the language and culture than will those who are committed to stay for a longer period. Second, unlike the case of the tourist, modifications are not going to be made for the immigrant in either language or diet. Third, many immigrants are totally unprepared for the Canadian winter climate, either in practical or psychological terms; for an immigrant who has grown up near the equator, the Canadian winter can have a deeply depressing effect upon the spirits.

Finally, there are three clear psychological effects associated with culture shock that deserve to be mentioned. First, immigrants are very likely to experience a great deal of fatigue due to the increased load placed on their information processing by the vast array of new sensations and perceptions they experience in their new surroundings. As a result, many immigrant children appear to *withdraw* during the early stages of their adaptation, a natural response that serves to protect them from greater mental stress and tiredness (withdrawal, should not therefore, be automatically equated with "laziness" or with some reluctance to participate in classroom life).

Second, culture shock often involves a *diminished sense of self*. Typically, a child moving from one country to another loses many of the friends and relations who have become part of their everyday lives, and who have contributed to their identity—to how they see themselves. The resulting loss in sense of secure social identity is especially severe in cases where the whole family must also undergo a drop in prestige due to the sudden absence of professional opportunities equal in status to those in their first culture.

Third, as Furnham and Bochner (1986) point out, following Bowlby (1961), immigration often brings about *feelings of loss of culture* much like those feelings of loss experienced by individuals following the death of a close family member. Immigrants, then, often go through periods of profound grief during their period of adaptation into a new culture. Recognition of the above psychological effects should help teachers to avoid hasty or stereotypical responses to the complex behaviours of immigrants experiencing culture shock.

◆ THE NATURE OF SECOND-LANGUAGE LEARNING

Second-language learning has been the focus of a great deal of research over the past few decades, and the field of inquiry has been influenced by each of the theoretical orientations introduced in the third chapter—although there has been a recent trend away from information-processing approaches and toward those founded in sociocultural theories.

LANGUAGE ACQUISITION FROM THREE COGNITIVE PERSPECTIVES

Cognitive theories of language acquisition hold that language acquisition is part of the child's more general cognitive development. These theories are especially interesting in the study of first-language acquisition, where language learning can be seen to run a parallel course with other significant kinds of cognitive development. For second-language acquisition, the relationship between other forms of cognitive development and language is less clear, simply because most second-language learning is superimposed on cognitive structures that are already established. This is especially true of theories that postulate parallels between cognitive and linguistic achievement.

Information Processing

Although the details of information-processing models of language acquisition are highly technical and beyond the scope of this chapter, they are worthy of some brief discussion. Current information-processing models of language acquisition are based on the principles of **parallel distributed processing (PDP),** and presuppose no innate structures other than a "processor" or learning mechanism. As its name suggests, PDP refers to the brain's ability to process a multitude of stimuli *in parallel*, or simultaneously, rather than in sequence. This means that processing cannot be of any simple stimulus-response kind.

◆ parallel distributed processing (PDP): assumption in information-processing theory that the brain conducts distinct processes in parallel

Bates and MacWhinney (1987) propose an information-processing model called the **competition model,** based on the assumption that a number of different language forms may compete as stimuli to represent a particular meaning. For example, for the young learner of English as a first language, both *ran* and *runned* are possible representatives of the past tense of the verb *run*. Most children, in fact, use both forms at some time during their development. Eventually, however, they learn to use *ran* simply because it is the correct, adult form and the one they hear more frequently. In this way, children come to learn the language they hear: the correct forms eventually "win" the competition between adult and immature forms because they get more air time.

◆ competition model: a theoretical model founded on the idea that different language forms may be processed by the brain in parallel, and therefore in competition with each other

This model of acquisition may have some relevance to second-language learning. In the early stages of acquisition, the new language is a jumble of noise, in which few words are discernible. Gradually, learners begin to recognize an increasing number of individual words until some understanding of the intended meaning begins to register. As they turn their attention to form, they will for a time overgeneralize and produce forms not unlike the child's *runned*. Eventually, however, the correct form will dominate for the simple reason that it "wins out" in the competition between correct and incorrect forms. It is important to note, however, that if the learner is in an environment of other non-native speakers, the competition between incorrect and correct forms may be stiff and the correct form may take longer to win.

Developmental Theory

Understanding why second-language learners make the errors they do is central to formulating any reasonable theory of second-language acquisition. Information processing offers one perspective, but there are others that must be considered.

◆ interlanguage: the series of systematic stages involved in the learning of a second language

<u>Interlanguage</u> theory is a developmental theory in the sense that it attempts to describe the changing rule system that governs the learner's progression toward error-free speech. In fact, interlanguage theory would question whether overgeneralizations such as *runned*, *goed*, or *mouses* should even be considered as errors. According to Corder (1967) and Selinker (1969), and many other subsequent theorists, these types of errors should be viewed as

natural results of viable language systems that second-language learners develop en route to full acquisition. These systems, which Selinker (1969) called *interlanguages*, can be looked at as forms of "transitional competence" (Nemser, 1971; McLaughlin, 1987), and also perhaps as transitional "dialects" of English that ESL learners speak at given stages of their learning. The central point is that, like children learning their first language, second-language learners appear to go through identifiable stages associated with different approximate *grammars* of the language. According to interlanguage theory, these systematic approximations provide useful intermediary frameworks for second-language learners to consolidate what they already know in the second language, and to build new hypotheses about what they do not yet know.

Interlanguage theory has especially important implications for how language *errors* are treated in the second-language classroom. Behaviourist theory held that language was "a set of learned habits," and that second-language learners typically incorporate the habits of their first language into the learning of their second language. Subtractive bilingualism involved treating these habits as errors to be eradicated through *extinguishing* memory of the first language. Typical examples of such errors made by second-language learners might be the German speaker's utterance of "Very vell" for "Very well," or the Japanese speaker's "Brack fries" for "Black flies" (English speakers, of course, make just the same kinds of odd-sounding mistakes when they attempt to learn other languages.)

There are good reasons for the above kinds of phonological errors when we look at the other languages in question. German has no "w" sound at all, and so what German speakers of English as a second language typically do is to use the nearest sound to the "w" in their own language, which is "v." In the case of Japanese speakers, the pronunciation in English of both "l" and "r" as "r" results from the fact that in Japanese these two sounds are never used to distinguish between the meanings of two otherwise identical words. Thus, whereas in English, native speakers can detect the difference in meaning between the two words *right* and *light* on the basis of the audible distinction between the "r" and the "l," the Japanese speaker finds this distinction difficult to hear and especially to produce. What both the German and Japanese speakers are doing is replacing English sounds with the ones that are closest to those in their own first languages.

Extending characteristics of first languages to second languages, known as **language interference,** is closely tied to a process long recognized by psychologists called *normalization*, or the tendency to process almost everything in terms of our own background knowledge and expectations (i.e., schemata). As the theory of interlanguage demonstrates, however, there is good reason to question whether these kinds of interferences should be treated as errors at all.

There is one crucial difference between the interlanguage systems of second-language learners and the interim systems of child first-language learners.

◆ language interference: the effect that the first language has on the pronunciation or organization of expressions in the second language

◆ **fossilization:** a process in which second-language learners halt their learning due to an exhaustion of motivation

At some point(s) second-language learners *fossilize* their second language— that is, they decide for whatever reason that "enough is enough." **Fossilization** generally occurs only when an individual language learner has reached a stage at which his or her English is sufficient for most communication. At this point, language learners may, even if aware of certain defects such as imperfect accent, decide that there is little point trying to sound exactly like native English speakers.

Sociocultural Theory

Sociocultural theories of language acquisition attempt to account for social as well as cognitive influences on children's learning of language. One such theory, commonly known as *social interaction theory*, holds that children's language acquisition is governed by the interaction of a number of different physical, linguistic, and social factors. This theory is especially useful in understanding individual differences because it accounts for the fact that children differ in physical and cognitive abilities, and in the social environment in which they live.

It has long been recognized that environment plays a central role in language acquisition. Vygotsky (1962) emphasized the interaction of children with the environment in the learning of language. He believed that language stimulates conceptual growth and that both language and conceptual growth depend on children's interaction with objects in their environment. He also emphasized the point that adults and older children stimulate language development in a variety of ways as they interact with younger language learners in different social situations.

To be effective, this stimulation should occur within the *zone of proximal development,* which Vygotsky defined as the distance between a child's actual level of development and the level at which they could function with adult assistance (see also Chapter 3). Vygotsky's emphasis on the role of the adult— whether parent, teacher, or friend—in the child's conceptual and linguistic development is consistent with current theorists who emphasize the contribution to children's language learning.

In recent years, researchers have paid a great deal of attention to the role that caregivers' talk plays in the child's linguistic accomplishments. In adapting their speech to make themselves understandable to young children, caregivers provide the *comprehensible input* that is essential to both first- and second-language learning. It has been suggested that infants learn to control their vocal apparatus by watching their mothers as they make the exaggerated sounds of baby talk (Field, Woodson, Greenberg, & Cohen 1982, cited in Piper, T., 1993). Interaction continues to play an important role as infants grow older and begin to babble. Social interactionists believe that one of the ways in which children acquire the ability to express their intentions and meanings is through the interaction that occurs during the babbling period. Caregivers tend to treat their children's speech, even if it is incomprehensi-

ble, as intentional and meaningful, and by doing so they engage in the negotiation of meaning that is central to communication.

For understanding second-language learners, social interaction theory is
particularly appealing. This is true for two reasons. First, social interaction
theory recognizes that language learning is not the sole responsibility of the
learner. Responsibility is shared by all those with whom learners come into
contact, that is, those who provide the linguistic input or the data base from
which they learn. Social interactionists remind us that unless that input is
comprehensible to the learner, it is useless and learning will not occur. Placing immigrant children who speak no English into a classroom where
English is the only language spoken, and where there is no or little attempt
made to make that language understandable, will do little to foster language
growth.

Second, social interaction theory recognizes that children's success at
learning additional languages rests in large part on the environment in which
they must learn them. For example, the experience of anglophone children
learning French in federally funded immersion programs is fundamentally
different from the experience of an immigrant child in an English-speaking
classroom. In the first case, children are supported in their endeavour by
school and the community, and at the end of the school day they return to
their homes and a native language that receives full familial and community
support. Immigrant children, on the other hand, are often viewed as "problems" by the school and community in which they live, are supported in very
limited ways, and at the end of the day return to their homes and a native language that is not valued at all outside the family. A theory that is broader in
scope than information-processing or developmental theories is necessary to
recognize and account for the differences in learning that result from the
qualitative differences between the language-learning experiences of immersion children and those of immigrant children.

COMMUNICATIVE COMPETENCE IN A SECOND LANGUAGE

One of the most powerful ideas in second-language education over the past
decade has been the idea that communicating in a second language involves
many types of knowledge, including those related to both information processing and to the sociocultural context. It has long been recognized that in
some sense, everyone who speaks and understands a language "knows the
rules" of that language. Of course, this does not mean that they can state
them on request, any more than they can exactly quote the rules of the road
to which they conform while driving. What knowing the grammar of a language means for most people is knowing how to *follow* and *behave according to*
a set of rules, rather than knowing how to articulate these rules in great
detail.

But even a secure knowledge of how to follow grammatical rules does not
guarantee effective communication, as is shown in the following exchange

between a teacher and a 9-year-old. *Teacher:* "Late again, Than? What on earth have you been up to this time?" *Than:* "Yes, I am. But I have not been digging for worms today." While Than's response is perfectly grammatical, it demonstrates that he understands neither an idiom in English (i.e, an expression where the words do not literally reflect the meaning, as in "what on earth?") nor the mood or intention of his teacher, whose utterance might express anything ranging from mild amusement to extreme frustration. While Than demonstrates good *grammatical* English, then, he does not give similar evidence of good *communicative* English.

What are the crucial abilities that a fluent speaker of any language—be it first or second—needs? Savignon (1982) provides a convenient analysis of **communicative competence** by proposing four types of abilities: grammatical competence (discussed above), discourse competence, strategic competence and sociolinguistic competence (1982, pp. 45-47).

- communicative competence: theory that communication requires knowledge about grammar, society, discourse, and strategies

Discourse Competence

One additional feature of grammatical competence is that it may be restricted to knowledge of the rules by which sentences are formed, rather than including knowledge about how paragraphs or longer textual units fit together. *Discourse competence* refers to the abilities needed to manage the patterns of these larger units. It is the competence by which language-users are able to detect the topics of conversations, and to follow the complex descriptions and arguments that take shape in longer utterances comprising groups of sentences. Children need to acquire this form of competence very early on in schooling if they are to cope later with complex academic texts.

Strategic Competence

Strategic competence covers an important class of strategies that can be acquired and used by second-language learners in order to help them make up for missed pieces of information, or to check that things have been fully comprehended. Examples of the successful use of such strategies occur when second-language learners are able to ask native speakers of English to repeat something they have said, or to define a particular word, or to write something down for them. Such routines naturally involve conscious politeness on the part of the language learner and include using phrases such as "Thank you," "Could you please say that slower for me?" "Excuse me, I don't understand," and so on.

Children can be encouraged to use the above strategies both in and out of class. If they are successful, they will often be responded to with what is sometimes referred to as **foreigner talk.** Foreigner talk is a form of English that good communicators reserve especially for such occasions. It may be slower, it may have deliberately greater clarity at the beginning and ends of

- foreigner talk: a specialized kind of language that native speakers of the language use to facilitate foreigners' comprehension

words, and it may contain simple choices of words that the speaker believes the second-language learner will readily understand.

Sociolinguistic Competence

Sociolinguistic competence refers to the ability of children and adults to take social context into account during communicative interaction. It includes knowledge, for example, about how to talk to teachers or employers, as opposed to friends, and also knowledge and understanding about other people's moods and intentions, their roles, and their purposes in given situations. Such abilities are also often referred to as being *pragmatic* in character.

Most Canadian ESL teachers now work within the framework of *communicative competence*, which can be also used as a basis for work with ESL students in the mainstream. An essential characteristic of the communicative approach to ESL is that language is treated *holistically* —like first-language learners, second-language learners need to be aware of many things besides grammar. Children can build sociolinguistic competence in English as a second language only if learning tasks demand more than the strict decoding of textual information or completing exercises in grammar.

◆ ESL IN THE MAINSTREAM: PREPARATION AND PRACTICE

This chapter has so far been devoted to describing the historical facts that shaped Canada's current attitudes toward its multicultural population, and to describing some of the social-psychological variables that are known to affect second-language learning. In the following section, we look briefly at the programming options available to ESL children in Canadian schools, as well as at the teaching approaches they are likely to encounter. We begin with a list of definitions of terms currently in use, and conclude with suggestions for teachers to apply in the mainstream (inclusive) classroom.

SOME KEY EDUCATIONAL LABELS

ESL

In Canadian schools, the most familiar term relating to the education of students from other cultures is the term "English as a Second Language" or **ESL.** In Quebec, the equivalent term is **FSL** for "French as a Second Language."

Several things are worth noting about the term *ESL*. First, although the word *second* is used, it is often the case that official Canadian languages are third, fourth, or even higher-numbered languages for students. For this reason, the largest organization in the world for foreign language education is called TESOL, which stands for "Teachers of English as a Second or Other Language." Second, it is important to realize that in many cases it is *only*

◆ ESL: English as a second language

◆ FSL: French as a second language

language that underlies these students' special needs; they do not necessarily have some special learning problem, and, just like students born in Canada, they cover the entire range of abilities.

One frequent and alarming report from teachers in the field continues to be that ESL students are being "dumped" into special education classes designed to help students with specific learning, reading, or other academic problems. Sometimes this dumping takes place simply because school administrators cannot think what else to do with the children. In the worst cases, ESL students are inappropriately labelled as "learning disabled" or "dyslexic," which can severely erode their self-esteem, as well as impair their academic and social progress

The use of English-based tests and assessment techniques also threatens ESL students with inappropriate labelling since these are not only grounded in English language but also in the cultural norms of English-speaking societies. Well-informed school boards now make educational assessments of ESL students by using interpreters and by checking carefully for evidence of cultural insensitivity and bias in assessment materials and techniques.

EFL

◆ EFL: English as a foreign language

EFL or "English as a Foreign Language" shares much with ESL. The essential difference between EFL and ESL is that while ESL concentrates on the needs of immigrants for whom a second (or other additional) language is a means of survival in a new culture, EFL covers the education of those learning English for mainly academic or social purposes within their own first-cultural education systems. From the perspectives of teaching and learning, the most important distinction is that whereas ESL generally involves some degree of *immersion* (i.e., placement of students in situations where they have to survive in the second language without recourse to the first), EFL generally involves more attention to grammar, structure, and translation, and students have all sorts of opportunities for communicating with each other in their first language. On this basis, classroom approaches developed for ESL and EFL reflect significantly different educational adaptations to the types of motivation involved in language learning.

ESD

◆ ESD: English as a second dialect

ESD refers to students for whom English is a second dialect. In Canada, the term is generally used to describe the linguistic situation of Native students who have grown up in a mixed linguistic setting in which, for example, Cree and English are spoken. The educational problems faced by these students are sometimes even more severe than those faced by a learner who is approaching a second language for the first time. A consensus is growing among educators in Canada and elsewhere that a secure grasp of *one* language provides the optimal basis for *all* subsequent cognitive development. When languages become confused with each other during development, what sometimes happens is that children become *semilingual*—that is, fully fluent in neither of the languages to which they are exposed. **Semilingualism** has an especially negative impact on academic learning, and also brings with it a lack of cultural security, which compounds and reinforces the educational problems that are due to language per se.

◆ semilingualism: the state of knowing two languages only to a limited extent

LEP

LEP stands for "Limited English Proficiency," a term used mainly in the United States as a catch-all term for children whose proficiency in English is not sufficient to the demands of schooling. These children may have English either as their second language or dialect.

◆ LEP: limited English proficiency

PRESL

PRESL, standing for "Preschool English as a Second Language," reflects the growing realization that the sooner children can securely establish the language of the school, the better are their later chances of attaining advanced levels of literacy and schooling. Critics have recently argued that preschool education should concentrate first and foremost on establishing children's *first* languages (i.e., the languages they speak at home). In New York and California, programs in Spanish for Hispanic preschoolers have met with great success. At the level of preschool education, then, the current trend is toward the early establishment of the first language (or "mother tongue"), followed by the gradual merging of English during the early school years.

◆ PRESL: preschool English as a second language

WHAT HAPPENS TO ESL STUDENTS IN CANADIAN SCHOOLS?

It is apparent that quite different choices about programming for ESL students are made by different school districts across Canada, and also that any one district may contain several types of programs. These differences are due to many factors, including the general prevailing philosophy about the education of immigrants, the number of ESL students to be served, available space and funding, availability of transport, and local regulations (Ashworth, 1988, p. 78). Several key types of programs can be identified, however, that serve as the basis for selection.

Self-Contained Programs

This type of program is generally reserved for new Canadians having little or no English. It can be in the form of a full "reception class" (sometimes taking in new immigrants throughout the school year) in which the students spend all day in the same group with a qualified ESL specialist teacher. In a

Wang He and Wang Xinhua

Wang He and his sister Wang Xinhua arrived in Vancouver in June 1989 from Hong Kong. A few weeks after arrival, they went to the Public School Board's Reception Centre, where their level of English proficiency was assessed. Thirteen-year-old Wang He was found to have sufficient English to go into a mainstream class with some ESL support. His sister, aged 8, however, was judged to require additional language training. In September, she was sent to a reception class for half days. Fortunately, because this school system had so many ESL pupils, Wang Xinhua's reception class was held in the same school as her mainstream class. By Christmas, she was able to cope in the mainstream full-time.

◆◆◆◆◆◆

◆ **half-day reception class:** reception class but one in which students spend half their time in regular classes

◆ **reception class:** an ESL (FSL) class in which students spend all their time in a specialized language class

half-day reception class, students may be bused to a central ESL class for half of the day, while returning to their regular schools for the other half.

Withdrawal Programs

In the second type of program, the school sets up a special resource room for ESL students that serves as a **reception class** for new students, as a place where all teachers may find help and special materials, and as a place where ESL students can be withdrawn from the mainstream to work on a one-to-one basis either with their teachers or with other English-speaking students within a "buddy system." Sometimes there are sufficient funds to support one full-time teacher to manage the withdrawal program, while in some school districts itinerant teachers serve several schools at prearranged times of the school day.

Transitional Programs

This type of programming is generally used for upper elementary or secondary students, and is designed to bridge the gap between language and curriculum content. Classes attempt to ensure coverage of the regular school curriculum, while the language is modified to help ESL students grasp the central concepts. In this way, ESL students are treated as having special academic needs and helped through clear definition of the specific areas of difficulty they may be experiencing.

Thuy

Thuy (pronounced "Twee") is a 9-year-old girl from Vietnam. Every morning she arrives at her Calgary school where she is a student in Grade 4. She has been in Canada for only a few months, but her English is good enough for coping with most of the Elementary curriculum. She does have some difficulty with her writing, however, so her teacher sends her each day to work for an hour with an ESL teacher in a small room off the library. The ESL teacher helps Thuy with her class assignments, providing supplementary materials when necessary. Her main role is to assist both the child and teacher by providing individualized instruction. Thuy is learning that her first language is not a liability and that ESL is a challenge that she can meet. Although Thuy is making great progress, she will probably need the additional help for more than a few months, and it will be available for as long as she needs it.

◆◆◆◆◆◆

Wang He

Wang He was assigned to a junior high school in Vancouver following his original language assessment. After a few weeks, his teachers reported that he was doing well in math and science but that he was experiencing some difficulty in his English and Social Studies classes. The ESL teacher, after consulting with the English and Social Studies teachers, and having interviewed him, decided that Wang He would benefit more from transitional classes in these subjects than from traditional ESL classes. While his communicative abilities in English were good, he was having trouble with the more abstract language typical of high-school textbooks and discussions. If Wang He is typical, he will spend one year or less in these classes.

◆◆◆◆◆◆

Jan

Jan ("Yan") is from the Netherlands. He attends Kindergarten in Halifax. For a few hours each week, he is withdrawn from his regular classroom to spend time with an itinerant ESL teacher, but for most of each school day he sits at his desk trying to understand what is going on around him. Sometimes, he comprehends enough to participate but a good part of the time he has very little idea of what the teacher or the other children are saying or what is expected of him. Because the itinerant ESL teacher has to see over a hundred children a week, she has little time to spend with Jan. His Kindergarten teacher has thirty children to deal with, and so she doesn't have much time for Jan either. Both teachers have asked for additional ESL support, but have been told that the budget simply will not allow it. All they can do is hope that Jan will somehow survive the experience and will learn English by osmosis.

◆◆◆◆◆◆

Mainstreaming

Finally, in mainstreaming (without prior placement in other types of programs) students are simply put directly into the mainstream, where it is believed they will learn by "osmosis" (Ashworth, 1988, pp. 77-84).

Each of the above program types has its advantages and disadvantages. While the self-contained class guarantees intensive training in English, it segregates students from the rest of the school. While the withdrawal class ensures immediate socialization in the school, some ESL immigrants are simply not ready for this. While the transitional class gives the ESL student the chance to experience academic success, it is often taught by teachers insufficiently prepared in given content areas, which may mean that students are denied academic credits they may have received if they had stayed in the mainstream class. The fourth type of programming, however, continues to provoke the greatest controversy. With younger children, mainstreaming *may* sometimes be educationally justified should there be adequate language support in the classroom, such as that provided by a teaching assistant who is able to work with children individually. The danger of this last kind of programming lies in the fine line that exists between it and *submersion*, a topic taken up below.

Immersion versus Submersion

Placement of students directly into the mainstream **(submersion)** has especially dangerous consequences for older children, since it is these students who face by far the greatest challenges of academic learning. Placement of this type by no means guarantees that children are properly *included* in what is going on. A child aged 9 or more who enters a Canadian school for the first time is confronted with what must seem an overwhelming and impossible task, namely, to learn both the English language at a level of sophistication sufficient to talk, read, and write about almost anything, and, further, to learn the vast amount of information contained in the school curriculum. ESL students, unlike others, must acquire language and conceptual content at one and the same time.

It has long been thought that the ideal situation of learning both a language and academic content together is to be found in **immersion** classrooms. It is this model of language education, pioneered in Canadian English-French programs, that many administrators have in mind when making direct placements of ESL students into the mainstream. But some have argued that students so placed are not so much *immersed* as they are *submersed* (Genesee, 1979; Piper, D., 1985). It is important for teachers to recognize the clear differences between these two approaches, as well as their emotional and educational consequences.

The idea of language immersion is that children learn a second language naturally, while at the same time learning curriculum content. In general, early immersion classes, in which, for example, an anglophone child learns school content in an exclusively French-speaking class, merge with a combination of first-language instruction and second-language maintenance classes in high schools. This mode of bilingual education has met with continuing success, and it has been used as an *analogy* to justify submersion. Some administrators believe that if students are "dipped" into the waters of the second language, and required to speak only this language in schooling they will be forced to pick it up in the same way as children do in immersion. The key difference, of course, is that rather than being carefully and sensitively "dipped," submersed ESL students are literally pushed into the water and left to sink or swim. Unfortunately, much more sinking than swimming seems to occur: the sight of ESL learners sitting in the back-row seats of mainstream classes, understanding little of what is going on and yearning for some specific help with English, is a poignant and ubiquitous one in Canadian schools.

The negative effects of submersion occur for three key reasons. First, whereas in immersion a young child continues to receive reinforcement and support for using her first language out of class, both in her peer group and family, the submersed student is unable to count on such support—she may speak Portuguese, for instance, but only to a few other students outside the classroom and in a way that will naturally exclude her from other student

◆ submersion: the placement of ESL students directly into regular classrooms before they are sufficiently prepared

◆ immersion: a language learning situation in which students are totally surrounded by the second language they are learning

Lucky Luciano

"Salvatore Lucania ... entered New York schools at the age of 9 and learned English the way his father did. In Salvatore's own words: 'All the other kids in my class was like little babies but they could talk English and I didn't know what the —— they was sayin.' Maybe that's why I fought so hard to get outta school, out into the streets where a lotta people spoke Sicilian-Italian and they knew what I was sayin' and I could understand them. I picked up my English on the streets. That's the one thing I regret in my life more than anythin' else, that my grammar is lousy and I don't have too many good words and I talk with a New York accent'" (Gosch et al., 1974, p. 13).

"Salvatore Lucania was certainly no burden on the American taxpayer, and he learned everything that the streets had to teach him. After some independent study spent extorting money from young school kids for protection, he moved to group work—taking over unions by strong-arm methods. Having established his qualifications, he graduated to the Mafia and rose to the top, becoming known to the world as Lucky Luciano" (Mohan, 1982, p. 11).

groups. In addition, her first language is not an official language of Canada, and so she will likely be encouraged to lose her first language, along with all of its cultural associations. For obvious reasons, the submersion of students in language arts or secondary English classes has been referred to as **subtractive bilingualism,** a term (following Lambert, 1977) that is opposed to **additive bilingualism,** which is characteristic of immersion programming that encourages children to add a second (official) language to their first. Submersion as opposed to immersion, then, is likely to have negative effects both upon the motivation levels and the levels of academic success of those subjected to it.

♦ subtractive bilingualism: a form of second-language education that attempts to deny or minimize the importance of students' first cultures

♦ additive bilingualism: a form of second-language education that values the language and learning related to the students' first cultures

A second reason that the analogy between immersion and submersion breaks down has to do with the likely socioeconomic differences between the families of students in either group (Swain, 1983). While students enrolled in French immersion programs, for instance, typically come from secure middle-class homes, immigrant language learners tend (although not exclusively) to come from families lower down the socioeconomic scale.

Third, there are some clear distinctions between what actually happens in classrooms to students when they are submersed as opposed to immersed.

The distinction is particularly clear in the case of language arts or English classes. In many of these classes, especially at the junior-high and high-school levels, the focus is often on literature and language in literature. This violates one of the most basic principles of immersion language teaching, namely, that the language be taught *indirectly* through concentration on the content it is used to express. Focusing directly on language at such a sophisticated level does little to help the English or the general confidence levels of students still struggling with their second language at a rudimentary level.

In conclusion, submersion bears little resemblance to immersion. At its worst, submersion reflects nothing less than institutional discrimination against ESL children, since it both causes them emotional trauma and denies them the basic human right of language education. Times, moreover, have changed, and whereas a century ago it may well have been possible for Canadian pioneers from southern Europe or the Ukraine to pick up sufficient English for their work and their social lives without formal instruction, the demands of today's education systems mean that students not receiving sensitive and well-organized instruction in English are likely to be denied many of the opportunities that they deserve, and that Canada's economic future demands they have.

LAYING THE GROUNDWORK

Most of the above programming options require ESL children to spend all or part of the day in the mainstream classroom. In order for mainstreaming to be a successful language learning experience for these children, teachers need to be aware of certain aspects of ESL theory and practice that directly underlie educational adaptations in the mainstream classroom. Without some commitment and sensitivity on the part of mainstream teachers toward the issues so far raised, ESL students, as has happened so often in the past, will likely be collectively dismissed as a "problem" outside the teacher's area of responsibility. If this scenario is to be avoided, an initial sequence of thinking about ESL students—one that ensures they are properly treated within the overall context of educating for individual differences—needs to become habitual in the minds of administrators and teachers.

The Least Restrictive Environment for ESL Students

The first and most fundamental question in our initial sequence of thinking is that of whether a given ESL student *should* be placed in the mainstream classroom as a whole. Other readings in this book underscore the challenges connected with establishing the *least restrictive environment* for each student, within an overall framework of ensuring equality of opportunity for all students in mainstream classrooms. A least restrictive environment for ESL students is one in which they have at least sufficient English for basic academic survival in a classroom.

If a student shows no evidence of being able to follow basic instructions or respond to very simple questions about classroom activities, then it is most likely that he or she has been improperly placed (submersed), and that a mainstream teacher's first efforts should be directed toward persuading the school administration to ensure that student's placement in a special setting for at least part of the day (see programming options above). Arguing for replacement of students depends heavily on a teacher's abilities to negotiate, and to become an *advocate* for individual ESL students. Mainstream teachers who are unsuccessful in achieving such replacement are faced with the very undesirable situation of submersion, and their best efforts must then be directed toward damage control.

Thinking About the Class as a Whole

Second comes the question of how to ensure the most positive environment for ESL students within the context of mainstream classroom interaction as a whole. There can be little hope of academic progress for these students in classes where they are treated as members of out-groups, or, worse, where they are confronted by various levels of implicit or explicit racism.

The most effective way of dealing with this is to do as much as possible to ensure that all students in the mainstream are properly prepared to interact positively with each other, and to become actively involved in helping each other learn. In order to achieve such an egalitarian and cooperative atmosphere, teachers have to model appropriate attitudes and behaviour, as well as discuss with all students some of the central principles by which their mainstream classes must operate.

Special Considerations for Native Canadian Students

There is a growing realization among educators that many Native students have special language needs due to their particular cultural background (see ESD, above). Until recently, little has been done to ensure that Native cultures and their place in Canadian history are adequately reflected in school curricula. One of the surest ways to enhance the learning of many Native students is to include their own history and culture into regular school content.

Klesner (1987) further points out that there is a need to match instructional strategies to the particular learning styles of Native students. As she puts it:

> Native Indian children from a healthy home environment exhibit extremely desirable qualities as learners when first entering school. They come from a rich, supportive web of kinship; they are trained for self-reliance and autonomy; they are strong visual and kinesthetic learners; they are encouraged to engage in close, direct observational learning of the world around them; they have respect for the wisdom of their elders (1987, p. 4).

Unlike many immigrant children, who are used to strict, highly directive teacher-centred classroom approaches, Native children are far more likely to benefit from student-centred approaches, together with close monitoring of individual progress. These students are often highly responsive to visual and tactile educational materials that allow them to experience things in different ways, and that foster discussion and interaction with their teachers.

Native students, just like all other students referred to here, ultimately have to become comfortable with a variety of modes of discourse and ways of teaching and learning. In the initial stages of specialized language work, however, given the additional cultural distance felt by Native students—a distance associated with their continuing cultural subordination following the colonial invasion of their territories—teachers need to work especially hard to ensure that these students are fully included and integrated in their classrooms; this is inseparable from presenting subject matter about their lives, and from introducing modes of teacher-student interaction that respect their more experiential and sensory ways of learning.

PUTTING IT ALL TOGETHER

When everything is going well, a mainstream classroom might be compared to a well-sounding orchestra. Just like a musical group, the mainstream classroom has many parts and many players whose activities are ideally coordinated within an organic whole. The teacher's role is to ensure that everyone knows what they are supposed to be doing, that they are cooperating with each other to achieve their various objectives, and that, where possible, they are contributing to each other's learning.

If certain conditions can be met—proper placement of ESL students in a positive learning context—the next challenge concerns adapting materials and teaching methods to the needs of ESL students. This may seem the greatest challenge of all for the hard-pressed mainstream teacher, but adherence to one basic principle may simplify the whole task of adaptation for individual students. *Good materials that are clearly organized, clearly explained, and clearly expressed and presented in English are of benefit to all students.* It turns out, indeed, that many of the materials and approaches that have been developed separately for regular students and for ESL students are potentially of mutual benefit to both these and other subgroups in the mainstream.

Recommendations: At the Level of the Whole Class

At the beginning of the life of any mainstream class containing ESL students, it is a good idea to have a frank and open discussion with all the students about the challenges ESL students face, about the reasons they are in the class, about the help and encouragement they need, and the many positive opportunities for learning that the presence of individuals from different cultural backgrounds provides. Below are some further ideas about what to plan for and what to include in the initial and continuing open class discussions, while at the same time refraining from placing undue pressure on ESL students.

Sharing Experiences

ESL students, even if they speak only in rudimentary English, should be given the chance to tell other members of the class about their own experiences, about some of the differences between Canada and where they come from, and about learning English. It is important, however, to ensure that they are given the opportunity, not forced, to talk about themselves. Once a permissive climate has been established, allow all students opportunities to question each other about their cultural backgrounds. As an alternative in cases where ESL students are not yet at a point where they feel confident enough to express themselves fully, teachers can mention aspects of the students' experiences and culture that they have related to them. It is a good idea while doing this to make constant checks for approval from the ESL students themselves. This approach has the added advantage of modeling for all students the kinds of sensitivity and interest required by good cross-cultural communicators.

Involving Cognition and Affect

Make sure that class discussion includes *feelings* as well as *knowledge* about various aspects of cultural group membership. Encouraging students to think about the challenges and feelings faced by immigrants to Canada, and about the relations between immigration and the general formation of in-groups and out-groups in society, will help preclude some of the potential negative consequences of such group alignments. In making a multi-ethnic mainstream classroom run smoothly, teachers must, in a sense, take on the roles of "social psychologist" and "cross-cultural negotiator" (see also Piper, 1984, 1988). They also have to encourage the adoption of these roles by students.

Viewing the Classroom as a Microcosm of Society

Encourage students to view the mainstream classroom as a microcosm of Canadian society in general, and to recognize that the consequences of classroom hostilities, just as at the societal level, are negative not only in terms of reducing social harmony but also at the *economic* level. Remind students of the consequences for the Canadian economy of *not* ensuring full ESL rights for immigrants (e.g., severely limiting the development of skills necessary for economic competition). The main point is to stress the interdependency of communicative competence and the individual and national economies.

Direct Experience of What It Is Like to Be an ESL Student

An activity that has been successfully used to support class discussions about ESL and multi-ethnicity is that of having ESL students teach the rest of the class some part of their own first language(s)—the numbers from 1 to 20, for example. This provides a very direct way of forcing other students to recognize some of the challenges of surviving in a second-language environment, not to mention the need for good humour and ego-permeability when attempting to pronounce a second language in public.

Speaking Normal English

When addressing a multi-ethnic class as a whole, do not change the nature of the English you speak. Be particularly careful not to change vocabulary and intonation patterns in ways that you would for children younger than the students in your class. Good "teacher talk," however, may include some useful repetitions and clarifications or paraphrases of ideas when you see that ESL students (or other students) may not have fully grasped the meaning. Avoid turning away from ESL students while writing on the blackboard— these students benefit from the additional information about the language given in your lip movements and facial expressions. Also make sure that you start and finish off words clearly, without overenunciating; this kind of clarification makes it easier for ESL students to discern the boundaries of significant chunks of information within the continuous flow of sounds they hear.

Recommendations: At the Level of Groups

As you will know from other areas of teacher preparation or classroom experience, having students work together in groups can have all sorts of advantages. In addition to learning academic content, working in groups leads to incidental learning (including learning about learning itself), and, in the case of groups comprising students from different ethnic and social backgrounds, learning about cultures and individuality.

Working in smaller groups also allows students with individual needs to experience the feelings, attention, and acceptance of others, and increases the likelihood of individual contributions to discussion or to whatever other activities are selected. In addition, restructuring of group members on different occasions ensures that all class members get to know each other better and to learn about each other's individual differences.

Creative group work requires teachers' constant monitoring, and involves carefully choosing and describing activities that are likely to lead to positive cooperation and learning. Below are some ideas that a mainstream teacher might use to facilitate the progress of ESL students and their peers.

Mixed-Language Groups

Select small groups of students (three to six is ideal) that include native English speakers and at least one ESL student. Assign worksheets to each group based on the academic content to be covered, and assign specific roles to students within groups. These roles can be various and should differ for individual students on different occasions. They include the following: a *reader*, who reads aloud a given text section to the rest of the group; a *questioner*, who asks questions on the worksheet at appropriate times before, during, or after the reading of each subsection of text; a *scribe*, whose duty is to take notes of the answers given to the questions; and a *translator*, who finds and gives answers to questions about the meaning of words or phrases that may be difficult. At the conclusion of the reading and the oral questions and answers, each group should provide written answers to the questions. Assigning equal marks to all members of each group for the resulting written work will underscore the cooperative nature of the group.

One good way of ending small-group sessions is to add to those above the role of *reporter*, a student who will read out or otherwise represent a group's worksheet answers to the entire class. A teacher can encourage (but not pressure) ESL students to assume this role, which provides a good opportunity for the enhancement of self-esteem.

There are several advantages to the above general approach to academic learning. First, the academic task is broken down into manageable chunks. Second, ESL students (who may be assigned any of the roles) are able to practise English in a supportive environment. Third, *all* students can benefit from the special attention given to language and, through this, central terms and concepts related to the activity.

Cultural Learning in Groups

As well as acting as a framework for the synthesis of ideas, a small group can be used as a springboard for exploring individual differences. This approach is especially appropriate when it comes to questions of value, such as those at the core of the Social Studies or the English curriculum, where it is educationally worthwhile to have students discover their different opinions and to explore the cultural sources of such opinions. Many types of stimuli might be used, ranging from photographs to journal articles that express particular points of view. The contrasting ideas generated in small-group activities can become the source of discussion about **cultural relativity,** which refers to the view that most of the world's ideas, whether expressed in literature, journalism, or art, are strongly affected by the cultural milieux in which they were developed.

◆ cultural relativity: the notion that all ideas and perceptions are particular to the cultures in which they are developed and experienced

Working in Pairs

Putting students to work in the smallest possible groups—pairs—also has several advantages. The most common dyad is the buddy system, in which ESL students are paired with English-speaking partners. Dyadic pairings give students a good opportunity to develop friendships through such interaction, as well as provide a more intimate working context in which the chances of failure-related stress are reduced. The danger of such relationships—that they may become one-sided and encourage dependency on the part of ESL students—can be avoided through vigilance and occasional re-pairing. By constant monitoring and informing other teachers, home-room teachers can play a valuable role in ensuring that optimal pairings are established and maintained as long as is possible in the mainstream.

A particularly useful technique provides pairs with materials of the "battleship" variety, where one student, for instance, is given a problem to be solved and the second student is given some form of data that is needed for the solution of the problem. This technique can be adapted to almost any kind of curriculum material and level of work. The particular advantage of this kind of activity is that ESL students are forced to communicate effectively in order to complete the given task. Presentation of several problems in which the roles alternate between the pair members ensures practice in both speaking and listening, in addition to cooperative learning.

Pairs are also very useful units in cases where English-speaking students may strongly need to review materials, or where they have not yet fully grasped a given topic or concept. There is no better way of learning the fine distinctions between what you know, what you don't know, and what you need to know than by trying to teach something to someone else. In the paired ESL-English-speaker dyad, then, it could be argued that there exist opportunities that are of advantage to *both* members of the pair.

Recommendations: At the Level of Individual Students

If there is one most important point in this chapter, it is that if a teacher can enhance the self-esteem and self-confidence of an immigrant ESL student, then linguistic, communicative, and academic success will surely follow. One rather amazing statistic about second-language learning is that, in global terms, *most* people (estimates are as high as 80 percent) speak at least two languages: monolingualism is not the norm. This strongly suggests that if the situation is right and sufficient motivation is present, there is little to prevent successful second-language learning from taking place. Thus, we place great stress on teachers working to enhance self-esteem and motivation, on the one hand, and on providing optimal classroom environments where the natural processes of second-language learning can take hold.

Involvement Beyond the Classroom and School

In enhancing ESL students' self-esteem, as with other groups of special-needs students, teachers must first and foremost demonstrate that they care about individuals' progress. This inevitably means going beyond the role of classroom instructor, and it is perhaps outside regular classroom hours that teachers can best demonstrate that they are interested and empathetic partners in the processes of immigration. Simply asking students during breaks, or on encounters outside the classroom, how they are doing and what problems they are facing will help raise their self-esteem.

One further important measure of a good mainstream teacher is how he or she communicates with the parents of immigrant students. Extra effort is sometimes required to ensure that immigrant parents turn up at parent meetings. If at all possible, it is beneficial to all concerned if teachers can meet with both ESL students and their parents at the beginning of the school year, or whenever the children start their classes. As a natural part of the immigration process, immigrant parents often feel isolated from the school or other institutional systems in Canada, and immigrants from nondemocratic countries may, not surprisingly, view schools and teachers with suspicion. In order for individual students to make optimal progress in our schools, it is essential that the educational enterprise be seen as one that is shared by schools and families. Doing all you can to involve immigrant parents in a process with which they are likely to be unfamiliar, then, is one important way to enhance security and progress in ESL students.

Constant Monitoring of Classroom Progress

When students are working individually on classroom assignments, perhaps the most useful role for a teacher to adopt vis-à-vis ESL students is that of a *roving resource*. ESL students often experience problems in completing an assignment due to some particular language difficulty—perhaps even one misunderstood word. They should, of course, be encouraged to use dictionaries and similar reference materials, but dictionary definitions may at times be insufficient. A good example can be found in idioms, such as "to look a gift-horse in the mouth," which have no literal translation. In cases such as these, the teacher can provide individual students with either simple explanations or, even better, examples of such usage. "To look a gift-horse in the mouth" might be illustrated by a student's refusing another student's help on an assignment.

Use of English-Language Knowledge

As we have pointed out, specialist ESL teachers are trained to identify particular aspects of language structure for which mainstream teachers are not normally responsible. At the core of English (or any other language), however, lies the *sound system*, and just about all native speakers of English have at least some intuition about sounds that are crucial for understanding the language.

In discussing the difficulties German and Japanese speakers have in detecting crucial differences between sounds such as "w" and "v" or "l" and "r," we gave examples of pairs of words that show how these differences are tied to differences in meaning in English. Such pairs of words are often called **minimal pairs** since they differ (minimally) in only one sound, while contrasting in their two meanings. Examples of such pairs in English abound, ranging from *rat* vs. *bat* (contrasting in meaning by way of the distinction in sounds between "r" and "b" at the beginnings of the words) to *ruler* vs. *rumor* (contrasting meaning through the distinction in sounds between "l" and "m" in the middle of the words) to *bat* vs. *back* (contrasting meaning through sound at the ends of the words). When an ESL student has a particular problem with a word, either in spoken or written form, presentation of a suitable minimal pair to distinguish the target word from others that the student may know is sometimes very productive.

◆ minimal pairs: a pair of words that differ in meaning while differing in only one individual sound

English speakers also have reserves of knowledge about how to pronounce English sounds, some of which are especially challenging for groups speaking particular first languages. For Chinese students, to give an example, the English sounds at the beginning of the words *think* or *then* are particularly difficult since they simply do not occur in Mandarin or Cantonese dialects. However, a mainstream teacher can—by inserting the tongue between the teeth and forcing air through the resulting complex obstruction—demonstrate the sound to Chinese ESL students. In addition to this kind of phonological aid, mainstream teachers can introduce to ESL students visual aids that stimulate the forging of associations between language and the world around them.

◆ TWO FINAL CRITICAL QUESTIONS ABOUT ESL EDUCATION

Like the United States and Great Britain, Canada currently makes substantial provisions for its immigrants to learn English. In addition to the various types of school programs reviewed earlier, every major English-speaking city in Canada has programs for adult ESL learners at the college level, while Canada Manpower and school-board extension programs provide further opportunities for immigrants to learn English. However, the continuing presence of submersion in Canadian schools, and of many house-bound adults who learn little or no English, suggests there is still much work to be done.

The future of ESL education in Canada greatly depends on the answers to two questions. The first of these is: *Should as much funding as immigrants require to learn English be provided or should the present system, which limits funding periods following the date of immigration or the start of schooling, continue?* Jurisdictions across Canada differ slightly in their provisions, but the financial support that a given school receives for the education of each ESL student is generally limited to a two-year period following the date of immigration.

This question deserves careful attention for three reasons. First, many learners—especially immigrant teenagers—need much more than two years' support. Second, since Canada is a country with two official languages, and French- or English-speaking minorities have the right to receive education in their first languages or have their children attend immersion programs, there would appear to be a greater right to become "officially" rather than "unofficially" bilingual. Should it be the case that in an egalitarian multicultural Canada greater opportunities exist for official bilingualism than for the acquisition of a second language needed for social and economic survival? Third, full recognition of the relations between language, citizenship, and human rights contained in the Canadian Constitution and the Charter of Rights and Freedoms leads one to conclude that second-language education for immigrants must be a "right" since, without incorporating this right, no educational provision can be said to guarantee anything like the equality of educational or vocational opportunity supposedly available to all citizens.

The second question pertinent to the future of ESL education in Canada is: *Why is it that while Canadian English-speaking students continue to receive academic credit for learning such additional languages as Spanish, German, or Russian (in addition to French) while they study in schools, ESL students receive no such direct credit for learning* their *second language?* We continue to expect ESL students to learn English as a "price" they have to pay to succeed in the Canadian school system. This fact, despite our pretensions to equality in education, puts ESL students at an immediate and permanent disadvantage. It is no wonder that so many ESL students leave school, at the first opportunity, without a secure academic background with which to compete. Is it possible, then, that we could (and should) start moving to a system in which the challenges faced by ESL students—and the huge strides they typically make—are recognized, and in which they are allowed to compete on an equal basis in schooling?

These two final questions should compel the attention of all Canadian teachers as we reach a point in many cities where schools contain more students for whom English is a second language than for whom it is a first. This short review chapter has attempted to provide teachers with a basis on which to proceed in their multi-ethnic classes. Some readers may choose to pursue the matter of ESL education in the mainstream further by registering in one of the many specialist ESL courses now offered in Canadian universities. The specialist knowledge acquired in such courses, together with sensitivity to the issues raised in this chapter, is the best guarantee against the continuing unfairness in our education systems to immigrant students.

◆ SUMMARY

The position taken in this chapter has been that it is cultural sensitivity and empathy that lie at the core of multicultural and second-language education, rather than any particular techniques taken in isolation. Accordingly, the chapter concentrated on aspects of knowledge that will help teachers understand the experiences and feelings of immigrant students in their search for cultural identity and educational success.

We looked first at some key topics in the social psychology of immigration, noting the centrality of in- and out-group behaviour in cultural interaction. The issue of racism was addressed, and several levels were described, as were the closely related processes of prejudice and attribution. The section concluded with a presentation of the model of cultural distance, in which central social and psychological influences on immigrants' motivation to integrate and to learn were described. The related issue of culture shock was also discussed.

The next section, on aspects of second-language learning, began by relating the area to the three major cognitive perspectives introduced at the beginning of the book: information processing, developmental theory, and sociocultural theory. This was followed by a review of the influential framework of communicative competence, which broadens our understanding of the many significant types of ability that underlie successful language performance.

Next, we looked at how education systems typically treat ESL students. Key labels were introduced, as were the principal types of programming found in Canadian schools. The chapter ended with a discussion of what "least restrictive environment" means for ESL students, and with recommendations for improving educational practice.

QUESTIONS
◆◆◆◆◆◆◆◆◆◆◆◆◆

1. What are some critical issues related to multicultural education?

2. Discuss some of the social-psychological dimensions that influence the interactions of individuals in educational settings.

3. How has second-language learning been influenced by cognitive, developmental, and sociocultural theories?

4. What crucial abilities does a fluent speaker of any language require?

5. How can a teacher facilitate the inclusive education of immigrant students?

REFERENCES

Allport, G. W. (1954). *The nature of prejudice*. New York: Addison-Wesley.

Ashworth, M. (1979). *The forces which shaped them*. Vancouver: New Star Books.

Ashworth, M. (1988). *Blessed with bilingual brains: Education of immigrant children with English as a second language*. Vancouver: Pacific Educational Press.

Bates, E., & MacWhinney, B. (1987). Competition, variation, and language learning. In MacWhinney (Ed.), *Mechanisms of language acquisition*. Hillsdale, NJ: Lawrence Erlbaum.

Bock, P. K. (1970). *Culture shock: A reader in modern cultural anthropology*. New York: Alfred A. Knopf.

Brewer, M., & Campbell, D. (1976). *Ethnocentrism and intergroup attitudes: East African evidence*. New York: Wiley/Halsted.

Brislin, R. W. (1981). *Cross-cultural encounters: Face-to-face interaction*. New York: Pergamon.

Cohen, A. (1977). Successful second-language speakers: A review of research literature. *Balshanut Shimushit, 1*, 3-21.

Corder, S. P. (1967). The significance of learners' errors. *International Review of Applied Linguistics, 4*, 161-169.

Dutton, D. (1976). Tokenism, reverse discrimination, and egalitarianism in interracial behavior. *Journal of Social Psychology, 32*, 93-107.

Field, T., Woodson, R., Greenberg, R., & Cohen, D. (1982). Discrimination and imitation of facial expressions by neonates. *Science, 218*, 179-181.

Genesee, F. (1979). Schools, bilingualism, and multiculturalism. In A. McLeod (Ed.), *Multiculturalism, Bilingualism and Canadian Institutions*. Toronto: University of Toronto Press.

Guiora, A. Z. (1972). Construct validity and transpositional research: Toward an empirical study of psychoanalytic concepts. *Comprehensive Psychiatry, 13*, 139-150.

Klesner, M. (1987). *Language arts for Native Indian students*. Victoria, BC: Province of British Columbia Curriculum Development Branch.

Mallea, J. R. (1984) Introduction: Cultural diversity and Canadian education. In J. R. Mallea & J. C. Young (Eds.), *Cultural diversity and Canadian education: Issues and innovations*. Ottawa: Carleton University Press.

McLaughlin, B. (1987). *Theories of second-language learning*. London: Edward Arnold.

Mohan, B. (1981). *Language content and the interactive principle*. Vancouver: TEAL Conference Proceedings.

Moodley, K. A. (1983). Canadian multiculturalism as ideology. *Ethnic and Racial Studies, 6*, 320-331.

Nemser, W. (1971). Approximative systems of foreign language learners. *International Review of Applied Linguistics, 9*, 115-123.

Piper, D. (1984). ESL classroom dynamics: Towards a discourse processing interpretation. *TESL Canada Journal, 2*, 41-52 .

Piper, D. (1985). Perspectives from Canada: Language submersion in the high school English classroom: Some causes for concern. *English Education, 17*, 102-107 .

Piper, D. (1988). Critical pedagogy, teacher preparation and the semantics of race. *Canadian Ethnic Studies, 20*, 112-128.

Piper, Terry (1993). *Language for all our children*. Columbus, OH: Merrill.

Porter, J. (1965). *The vertical mosaic*. Toronto: University of Toronto Press.

Rex, J. (1973). *Race, colonialism and the city*. London, Routledge and Kegan Paul.

Savignon, S. J. (1982). *Communicative competence: Theory and classroom practice*. Reading, MA: Addison-Wesley.

Schumann, J. H. (1978). Social and psychological factors in second language acquisition. In J. C. Richards (Ed.), *Understanding second and foreign language learning: Issues and approaches*. Rowley, MA: Newbury House.

Selinker, L. (1969). Language transfer. *General Linguistics, 9*, 67-92 .

Swain, M. (1983). Home-school language switching. In J. W. Oller & P. A. Richard-Amato (Eds.), *Methods that work*. Rowley, MA: Newbury House.

Tierney, J. (1982). Race, colonialism and migration. In *Race, migration and schooling*, J. Tierney (Ed.). London: Holt, Rinehart & Winston.

Triandis, H., & Davis, E. (1965). Race and belief as determinants of behavioral intentions. *Journal of Personality and Social Psychology, 2*, 715-727.

Vygotsky, L.S. (1962). *Thought and language*. Cambridge, MA: M.I.T. Press.

Wyatt, J. (1984). Implications of multiculturalism for curriculum. In S. Shapson & V. D'Oyley (Eds.), *Bilingual and multicultural education: Canadian perspectives*. Clevedon: Multilingual Matters.

THE SCHOOL-HOME PARTNERSHIP

*I*n Canada, there has been a growing widespread adoption of activities that encourage professional collegiality and cooperation between regular and special educators who are attempting to meet the diverse and challenging needs of children in today's schools. In addition, there has been increasing support for the view that parents are important and useful collaborators in the educational process. This trend reflects a movement toward professional and parental partnerships, and a pattern of thinking and practice that is very important for initiating and sustaining inclusive teaming within a unified educational system. True partnership exists when people with equal status work together towards common goals. Partnership in the educational field can result from open communication, mutual trust, and respect between teachers and parents, as well as a cooperative working environments where teachers and members of the community can share in educational planning, decision-making, and evaluation.

Before educational partnership can occur, however, the school environment must adapt to the challenges of student diversity in ways that will be examined in the following two chapters.

Over the next decade, we will witness significant changes in educational policy and practice that

A NOTE FROM THE AUTHORS

will affect the school-home partnership. The overall purpose of Part 3 is to introduce the reader to the salient issues that concern this partnership, and to provide informaion that will enhance relationships among school professionals, as well as communication between teachers and families.

Chapter 6 defines and outlines the concept of inclusive teaming; discusses the growing field of educational consultation and collaboration; examines the changing roles and responsibilities of regular and special educators, as well as support service professionals, in meeting the diverse needs of students; and discusses professional preparation programs in the context of inclusive education and teaming.

Chapter 7 considers parental reactions to their child's exceptionality; reviews the major issues that parents of exceptional children face; provides an overview of the complexity of today's families and the multiple roles that parents of exceptional children have to assume; discusses some of the benefits that parents can bring to the home-school partnership, as well as the various avenues that are open for their involvement; and lastly, offers a number of ways in which teachers can promote information sharing between school and home.

INCLUSIVE TEAMING

CHAPTER

6

CHAPTER OBJECTIVES

To outline the limitations of the traditional special education approach.

To examine the implications of inclusive teaming for teacher education and professional development.

To describe changing roles and responsibilities of the inclusive education support members with respect to a unified system of education.

To review the inclusive teaming principles reflected by school organization, educational policies, and funding systems.

To stress the importance of a nonhierarchical approach to consultation and support of classroom teachers for inclusive education service delivery.

Mrs. Jones had looked forward to her first year as a Grade 3 teacher in the local public school system. The year passed so quickly, it seemed impossible that it was June already. Looking back, she realized that the enthusiasm with which she had started the year was lost entirely. For one thing, the class was larger than she had expected, with a total of thirty-two students. Moreover, the school had adopted an inclusive education policy that year, and there were three students with exceptional learning needs in the classroom, including a student with learning difficulties, another student with behavioural problems, and a highly able student.

Mrs. Jones had noticed these three early on in the school year, and had made out referral forms to initiate assessment. Certainly, her own background in teaching

exceptional children was very limited, with just the one half-course from her university program. Nevertheless, it was helpful to refer to suggestions in the course text and notes, and she was able to implement some of the them. Indeed, it was a good thing that she had kept this information, because it took much longer than she had anticipated for the referrals to be addressed. Even though the referral was made in early October, the actual assessments didn't take place until January and February. And this was provided for only two of the students, since gifted students were assessed only if the child was experiencing severe difficulty in the school program.

Mrs. Jones remembered how frustrated she had been at the program planning meetings for the two youngsters. The parents were invited to meet with the professional assessment group, which included the principal, the school psychologist, the speech therapist, and the district social worker. One of the strongest impressions that remained with Mrs. Jones was the feeling of intimidation and anxiety at meeting with the "experts," and in such a formalized context. Although she met briefly with the school psychologist after he completed his assessments, her only interaction with the others was when they had come to the classroom to fetch the students for individualized assessment.

As each member summarized the assessment results, several questions came to Mrs. Jones's mind, and yet she did not pose them. For one thing, some of the terms and abbreviations used, like ADD and DSM 111 and CBM, were unfamiliar to her, and she didn't want to seem ill-informed or, worse yet, incompetent. For another thing, the purpose of the meeting was to determine an individualized program plan for Rick—the student with learning disabilities—and she did not see how much of the information being reported could be useful to her in the classroom. Somehow she had thought that the "specialists" would tell her how to work more effectively with the students in the classroom. In the end, it was she who agonized a week and a half preparing two individualized education programs, terrified of misinterpreting the assessment findings.

Since the formal meeting, Mrs. Jones was less at ease talking to her principal, Mr. Pope, even though she had always found him to be helpful and supportive in

the past when she had raised concerns or problems. For some time after the meeting she avoided him—until her growing frustration erupted in an emotional outburst at the recent staff meeting. She felt embarrassed afterward and was relieved when Mr. Pope came to her classroom the next day and asked her to express her concerns. To her surprise, he thanked her for being open and frank about her experiences and assured her that she was perfectly justified in feeling frustrated. He informed her that he, too, was concerned about the current student services program, and that he was reviewing the literature to come up with a school-based model that would be more compatible for effective inclusive education. Moreover, he indicated that he would initiate a review of the referral process, and that he would be implementing a new "inclusive teaming" concept the following year, which would be based on the collaborative professional development of school staff and the involvement of parents.

Although the concept was new to Mrs. Jones, she was impressed by the idea of shared responsibility for all students in the school. Working collaboratively with administration, the special education teacher, and her colleagues would both challenge her and offer greater opportunity for professional growth and development. Even though she did not feel completely satisfied about having met the needs of her special students this past year, she resolved to share her journal notes and observations with the Grade 4 teacher who would be responsible for these students in his class next year.

◆ INTRODUCTION

◆ service delivery: method by which education is provided to students in the educational system

◆ inclusive teaming: process in which professionals and parents share information and expertise in order to reach common goals supporting students with exceptional needs

The needs of students with exceptionalities are varied and complex. As illustrated in the opening vignette, traditional systems of **service delivery** for students with exceptional learning needs do not appear to be working. Efforts to manage human and material resources effectively within an inclusive system have been blocked because the historical development of special education services in Canada and the United States has been based primarily on a categorical, segregated system. The creation of a unified system of service delivery involves eliminating services based on categorical affiliation, and reorganizing of educational supports and services that address the learning needs and potentialities of all students.

This chapter reviews a new approach to serving the needs of all students called **inclusive teaming**. This approach attempts to redefine the roles and responsibilities of the regular and special educator, in particular, in the planning and decision-making processes necessary to ensure the effective imple-mentation of inclusive education. The changing roles of professional support staff, such as psychologists and social workers will also be discussed—but first we consider the limitations of the traditional approach to service delivery for students with exceptional learning needs.

◆ WHY THE SPECIAL EDUCATION APPROACH ISN'T WORKING

As described in Chapter 2, Canada's provinces and territories have adopted a wide range of service delivery and funding policies, backed with new laws and revised school acts, that attempt to address the fundamental issues emerging out of the process of progressive inclusion. The power of progressive inclu-sion philosophy can be seen in the fact that every province and territory has made major revisions to existing school acts in the past ten years, and most school districts, having articulated a conceptual shift in this direction, have made attempts to integrate or mainstream students with exceptional needs.

Despite these changes, most school systems continue to use a **special education approach** to serving the needs of students with exceptional learn-ing differences. (Figure 6.1 depicts the general framework in which most sys-tems operate.) Under this approach, provincial and territorial departments of special education allocate special funding to serve these students, and school systems typically follow a five-step process, beginning with identification of students with exceptional needs, and ending with individual programming in special education classes or with part-time individualized assistance in or out-side of the regular classroom. Unfortunately, there are a number of funda-mental flaws inherent in the special education approach that negate—or run counter to—the building of a unified system of inclusive education.

◆ special education approach: a five-step model of service delivery that leads to tradi-tional category-based pro-grams/interventions and student placement alterna-tives

Figure 6.1
Traditional Special Education Approach

Referral ▸ Testing ▸ Labelling ▸ Placement ▸ Programming

First and foremost, the special education model is a static one. Huge bureaucratic structures and complicated professional staff deployment pro-cedures have been built up to support a system that has grown substantially over the past twenty years. Accompanying the increase in numbers of stu-dents being referred has been an increase in the number of specially trained professionals needed to carry out the assessments, as well as administrative procedures and policies required to justify additional funding requests and to ensure accurate placement decisions. Student needs may be minimal and consequently require only slight modification, or they may be multifold and complex, requiring substantial attention. A static special education approach, however, is used in *every* case of student referral, thus precluding quick intervention in the case of students whose needs are relatively minimal.

The second failing of the special education approach is the fact that the period between referral and programming is often excessively long, bound up as it is in a one-way pattern of formalized steps and procedures. Students who are having difficulty in regular class placements often face a considerable waiting period before they are seen by the various professionals involved in assessment procedures, and if the results do not support a diagnosis of exceptional learning needs the student usually has no choice but to remain within the regular classroom. For parents, this can be a frustrating and disenchanting experience. Figure 6.2 shows one mother's depiction of the special education approach in its treatment of students who are intellectually gifted.

Figure 6.2

Parent Perspective of Gifted " Special Education" Approach

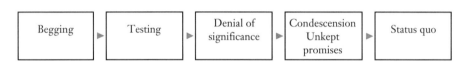

But even when the testing results do identify exceptional learning needs, it may still be several months before these needs are addressed because most placement decisions require input from teachers, administrators, parents, and other professionals involved in assessment. Furthermore, once the referral is made, classroom responsibility for serving the individual needs of the student is passed on from the regular teacher to special education; although it may take several months for a referral to be fully processed, the child is left in a kind of limbo in the regular classroom.

The third problem with the special education approach is that the roles and responsibilities of the professionals and parents are rigidly aligned with the appropriate steps in the special education box system. Classroom teachers are responsible for initiating the referral, while other professionals carry out assessment and diagnosis. Special education consultants are typically called upon to provide intervention recommendations, and to formulate the individual educational programs. Administrators are responsible for conceiving and providing special education alternatives in the school, and for scheduling the program-placement meeting for each student deemed to require special education assistance. Parents have the right to disagree with the recommendations made by the school, in which case they may prefer to leave the child in the regular-class placement, send the child to another school, seek out an appropriate private school, or, in some provinces, appeal to a higher authority.

The above system is both costly and labour-intensive. Even though the adults who participate in the process may have a wealth of expertise and insight to contribute to the formulation of a suitable individualized educational plan, there is typically insufficient time in a special education framework to explore this prospect; consequently, the decision-making is largely left up to the designated professionals. Moreover, a hierarchy of decision-making authority is well established in most school systems, such that in situations of dispute administration can refer to the rules and regulations in order to quash any proposal that runs counter to the school's recommendations.

The final flaw inherent in the special education approach to serving students with exceptional needs is that the school (or the system) can provide assistance only for those students who have been successfully processed through the five boxes. If a school does not offer a gifted program, for example, it is highly unlikely that administration will support a referral from the classroom teacher who has observed that a student shows particular ability or talent in one or more areas. A similar dilemma is evident for ESL students, students who are underachieving, students who create behaviour problems in the class, students who have a personality clash with the teacher, students whose problems at home are interfering with their ability to achieve at school, and so on. In the majority of instances, the individual child must be failing significantly before the special education approach is initiated.

The key factor for creating effective inclusive schooling lies in the recognition that there are formal and informal means of meeting the needs of exceptional students in the regular classroom. Traditional special education approaches have concentrated almost entirely on formal means of serving students, with the bulk of resources and personnel tied to the first four boxes depicted in Figure 6.1. The unfortunate reality is that no matter how sophisticated and comprehensive a diagnosis or assessment may be, what makes a difference for the individual student *is what happens in the classroom environment day by day.*

Properly orchestrated, daily interaction in the classroom can offer multiple opportunities for individual student potential to be realized. School resources need to be redeployed, therefore, to ensure that the in-class *experiences* of the child meet his or her unique learning needs. In other words, inclusive schooling depends first and foremost on what happens in the fifth box of the traditional special educational approach—programming for individual learning needs (see Figure 6.3)

Figure 6.3

Inclusive Education

In order to effect the differential emphasis needed to support inclusive schooling, there needs to be a dramatic shift from formal special education approaches to the ongoing informal and formal means of programming for full actualization of student potential in the regular classroom. Underlying this shift is the process of inclusive teaming, which is described in the following section.

◇ INCLUSIVE TEAMING: A SUPPORT SYSTEM FOR GENERAL CLASSROOM TEACHERS

Inclusive teaming is a process that is geared toward improving schools from within (Barth, 1990). Inclusive teaming is flexible, collaborative, supportive, nonhierarchical, and primarily designed to provide support to the classroom teacher in meeting the needs of all children in the inclusive classroom. Both informal and formal means are used to effect creative problem-solving when a student's needs are not being fully met, and the process begins as soon as a problem is recognized. Awareness of a problem might stem from a variety of sources, including the teacher's classroom observations, a request from a child's parents, or from the observations of other students or professionals in the school. At all times the focus of inclusive teaming is to provide school and classroom experiences that will enable all students to achieve to the full extent of their capabilities. The two fundamental components of effective inclusive teaming are *collaboration* and *consultation*.

COLLABORATION

The ultimate goal of inclusive teaming is the creation of a collaborative school. This component of inclusive teaming is centred on the professional relationships in the school, particularly between teachers and administrators. Smith and Scott (1990) characterize collaborative schools in the following terms: (1) The quality of education is mainly a function of what happens at the school site; (2) Collegiality and continuous improvement are professional norms that foster effective instruction; (3) Classroom teachers have a professional responsibility for the instructional process, and are accountable for its outcomes ; (4) Administrators and teachers work together, using a wide range of practices and structures to effect school improvement; and (5) teachers are involved in decisions regarding school goals and the means for achieving these.

It is inappropriate to expect regular teachers to accomplish inclusive education on their own, or to expect that any single individual will have all the expertise and talent that successful inclusive education requires. Schools are only beginning to recognize that the first important step toward effective inclusive education is to reverse the isolation that is predominant in many schools, and to seek out new forms of collaboration and support networking between parents, administrators, teachers, and other specialists (Morsink, Thomas & Correa, 1991; Stainback & Stainback, 1990; Porter & Collicott, 1992). Inclusive teaming teachers must be committed to the concept and perceived benefits of inclusive education, while receiving assistance from divisional and ancillary support services that are founded on a philosophy of collaborative professional development.

Collaboration refers to any mutual effort to plan, implement, or evaluate educational programs for a student or students (Morsink, Thomas, & Correa, 1991). For example, a teacher working with a hearing-impaired student who has cerebral palsy might collaborate with a specialist in hearing impairment, a speech therapist, an occupational therapist, and the student's parents to develop an individualized program to implement in the classroom. Tied to the notion of collaboration is the recognition that teachers and support professionals have varied experiential backgrounds, interests, talents, and areas of expertise, and that opportunities for sharing of expertise need to be built into the ongoing professional development of all school staff. Professional development is a process in which there is continuous growth of the entire school system in meeting the needs of all students, and a process to which all teachers and school staff have a responsibility to contribute. Schools need to develop better systems of recognizing and nurturing good teachers, and, beyond that, what is recognized as successful effective teaching needs to be demonstrated, modelled, or in some way shared with other teachers. In the period of transition from a special education approach to service delivery toward an inclusive teaming approach, the expertise that has been traditionally relegated to special education professionals will be transferred to the inclusive classroom. This transition will be facilitated primarily through consultation among regular classroom teachers, special educators, and support personnel in the school and district.

CONSULTATION

Idol (1990) describes the classroom consultation process as encompassing both the scientific and artful dimensions. She defines these bases respectively as:

> the content or knowledge base the consultant brings to the consulting process … In education, this knowledge is usually comprised of a wide span of content pertaining to technical teaching interventions, materials modifications, and child management strategies (p. 5).

> the way in which the consultant works with consultees in solving the problem. This base is often referred to as the process skills of consultation. It is a demonstrable knowledge of how to bring about effective decision making, how to solve problems with others, and how to interact and communicate effectively with others (p. 5).

The primary goal of classroom consultation is to help regular classroom teachers accommodate students who have exceptional learning needs in the classroom. Consultation occurs when a team member with the greatest understanding of a particular issue shares his or her knowledge or skill "by explaining or carrying out actions that demonstrate this knowledge"

(Morsink et al., 1991, p. 5). Inclusive teaming is not limited to the formal interactions and procedures that are carried out by a designated team of professionals in a given school or district. Expertise is instead tapped from the best available source. For example, a teacher with several years experience in gifted education might be asked to meet with school staff to suggest methods of differentiated instruction to meet the needs of advanced students in all classrooms. The individual who does the consulting is chosen on the basis of the specific situation and the kind of expertise that is required.

Heron and Harris (1993) point out that the "consultation process can be initiated by a consultant (e.g., the principal, supervisor, or resource teacher) who might observe that a school-related problem needs attention, or by a consultee (general education teacher, parent, or student) who might seek additional assistance with problem resolution" (p. 1). According to the inclusive teaming concept advanced in this text, the roles of consultant and consultee are not exclusive to any one professional group but can be served by any person—teacher, principal, psychologist, therapist, or special educator.

Merging, through inclusive teaming, the professional expertise of experienced classroom teachers with that of the special education teacher and resource specialist will create new opportunities for professional development, and provide support for teachers without professional preparation or experience in working with students who have exceptional learning needs. In order to meet the increasing diversity of student needs in the regular classroom, teachers will have to broaden their knowledge base by adopting new strategies and skills, and by implementing them on an individual, small-group, or whole-class basis.

Instruction that has been developed and implemented in traditional special education programs has been largely carried out by special education-trained teachers. These professionals have a different kind of expertise that can be effectively incorporated into inclusive classrooms. Porter and Collicott (1992) suggest that transferring this expertise might involve a specialist working alongside the inclusive classroom teacher until necessary adaptations are incorporated and the classroom teacher feels confident about meeting the child's needs independently. Or it might involve gathering and synthesizing information on student achievement and behaviour, and determining whether additional assessment is required. Alternatively, it might involve modelling and assisting classroom teachers in using new strategies that promote the inclusion of all students. Smith and Scott (1990) have examined the various means by which teachers and support professionals collaborate in promoting cooperative professional development. Some of the better known models include peer observation, peer coaching, mentor teacher programs, teaching centres in which expert teachers train other teachers, and teacher support teams.

INCLUSIVE TEAMING

Morsink et al. (1991) provide a useful set of definitions to describe the various aspects of interactive teaming. *Teaming* refers to the process in which two or more persons (professionals and parents) share information and expertise in order to meet a common goal. For example, when parents meet with the teacher to discuss improving their child's ability to organize and record homework assignments, they are engaged in teaming. The *interactive team*, the parents and teacher in the above example, are involved in a mutual or reciprocal effort toward the achievement of a specific goal. Inclusive teams may be spontaneously formed as the need for a particular goal becomes evident, or may be formally scheduled to address a concern of common interest to a number of professionals or parents.

The classroom teacher is seen to be the primary professional in the inclusive education process, and resources and school expertise must be realigned and organized in order to support the teacher's efforts to serve the needs of students at both ends of the learning continuum. While some students, particularly low-incidence, high-needs learners, may require partial, or possibly full-time support (eg., a full-time teaching aide), to ensure maximal development of learning potential in the regular classroom, every effort is directed toward preventive strategies (Wilson, 1989) that will eliminate the need for special-class or segregated placements. The inclusive teaming approach further recognizes the valuable contributions that parents and the community at large can provide to enrich and support effective inclusive education in the school (Turnbull & Turnbull, 1990; Shea & Bauer, 1991).

While emphasis in the past was on the group meeting and planning functions of the consultative team, the present view of inclusive teaming focuses on the immediate availability of services to effect programming changes that are student-centred. Instead of concentrating on identification and assessment to select those students who meet exceptionality criteria, inclusive teaming channels its efforts into supporting all students— with or without exceptional learning needs—in inclusive classrooms.

Many proponents of inclusive schooling believe that long-term implementation will ultimately result in the **neverstreaming** system of service delivery proposed by Slavin et al. (1991). These authors suggest that early, intensive intervention can be a powerful means of preventing school failure and the debilitating social stigmatization that segregated special classes and the labelling of exceptional students creates. Providing teachers with the resources needed to support all students in the regular classroom both focuses the definition of service needs and ensures professional development for all teachers and school staff.

In many current school systems, student service teams are predominantly made up of support staff, including psychologists, speech therapists, social workers, administrators, and special education personnel. Assessment and placement decisions are often determined with limited input from, and consultation with, teachers and parents. The inclusive teaming concept reverses

◆ neverstreaming: system of service delivery that combines the practices of prevention and early, intensive, and continuing intervention for at-risk students

the traditional special education approach by shifting the primary responsibility for learners with exceptional needs from the outside professional group (support services) to the regular classroom teacher, with support team members being held jointly responsible for what goes on in the classroom. The following sections review major trends in the changing roles of students, teachers, and other professionals who play a critical role in the success of inclusive teaming and inclusive schooling.

◇ NEW ROLES FOR CLASSROOM TEACHERS

Inclusive education has provided the impetus for major changes in the traditional roles and responsibilities of both regular and special education teachers. West and Brown (1987) point out that three major trends have been established to accommodate the inclusive education of students with exceptional needs in the regular classroom. The first two trends—the formation of regular teacher-based assistance teams to collaboratively resolve students' learning and behavioural problems (Chalfant, Pysh, & Moultrice, 1979), and the creation of adaptive learning environments in regular classrooms (Wang, 1983; Wang & Birch, 1984)—have resulted in direct changes in the role of the regular classroom teacher. The third trend—the collaborative consultation of regular and special education teachers in formulating instructional programs and strategies for learners with special needs (Heron & Harris, 1993; Idol, Paolucci-Whitcomb, & Nevin, 1986; Idol-Macstas, 1983)—affects role changes for both regular and special education teachers. In the following segments, we examine the particular elements involved in this transition.

THE CHANGING ROLE OF THE REGULAR TEACHER

Before we delineate the contemporary roles and expectations for regular classroom teachers in the inclusive education process, it is useful to examine the traditional roles of the regular teacher:

1. Plan instruction.
2. Arrange physical learning environments.
3. Establish productive social climates.
4. Organize students into working groups ….
5. Present instruction using methods suited to topics and students.
6. Manage students, materials, and activities.
7. Communicate effectively with students.
8. Maintain class control.
9. Evaluate student progress.
10. Report student progress to parents and administrators (Charles & Malian, 1980, p. 31).

Placing of students with exceptional needs in inclusive classrooms requires an expansion of these traditional roles, with greater emphasis given to serving the educational, social, and behavioural aspects of student development. The emerging role of the regular classroom teacher in the inclusive classroom context has been widely considered (Morsink et al., 1991; Wood, 1992; Salend, 1990; Idol, 1993; Lewis & Doorlag, 1991), and seven major dimensions are outlined below:

NO

1. *Provision of a supportive learning environment for all students.* This entails the creation of a welcoming classroom environment in which student diversity is respected, and in which the unique characteristics of all students are acknowledged. The teacher is instrumental in promoting acceptance and facilitating positive interaction among all class members.

2. *Assessing learner needs and instructional goals.* The classroom teacher is responsible for gathering information concerning individual learning needs through a variety of means, including observation, curriculum-based assessment, and formal assessment. Individual goals that are realistic, appropriate, and measurable must be formulated and synthesized with the more general goals for subgroups of students or the entire class.

3. *Planning instructional interventions.* Teachers must consider a variety of activities, strategies, and procedures that will accommodate the spectrum of individual learning needs in the classroom. Sufficient variety, differen-

tiation, and flexibility in classroom activities must be planned to ensure that the learning, physical, and social needs of each student are provided.

4. *Utilizing available resources.* Teachers need to be aware of the human and material resources available in the classroom, school, and community that can enhance and enrich classroom instruction. This dimension includes an awareness of the potential support that can be provided through collaboration with available support professionals and families, and a familiarity with the technical and material aids that may be used to enhance students' learning potential.

5. *Implementing and adapting instruction.* Teachers are responsible for the implementation of a variety of teaching methods and approaches that will ensure appropriate instruction for all students in the classroom. This dimension includes adapting classroom materials, organizing and scheduling to incorporate the assistance of support professionals, volunteers, and parents, and using a variety of individualized, small-group, and whole class instructional formats.

6. *Classroom management.* Techniques and skills for effective classroom management must be selected, used, and monitored to ensure that individual and class learning goals are accomplished. Student interactions that promote individual coping strategies and appropriate classroom behaviour must be encouraged and developed.

7. *Evaluation of student progress and learning.* Teachers are responsible for organizing and monitoring individual student progress through the systematic collection and recording of classroom data. Information must be analyzed and synthesized in such a way that it can inform the on-going instructional programming, and contribute to the development of new learning goals, which the teacher can convey to students, parents, and other support professionals.

Effective inclusive classrooms will depend not only on specific changes in a teacher's role description but also on the evolution of the student from *reproductive thinker* to *autonomous thinker*, and a parallel shift in teachers from *directive thinking* to *facilitative thinking* (see Alberta Education, 1990, and Tables 6.1 and 6.2).

Murray (1991) suggests that teachers build individual instructional programming needs into lesson designs that allow for **multi-level instruction**. The teacher can accommodate differential student learning needs by presenting a variety of instructional formats, and by providing students with alternative forms of demonstrating their understanding of the lessons. This might entail using augmenting equipment such as a tape recorder or computer, providing modified materials, or combining small-group, whole-class teaching with more student-to-student collaboration and peer support.

Murray (1991) further stresses the need for teachers to incorporate into the classroom life experiences that will be meaningful for all class participants, and to provide the essential transfer of learning for students with exceptional learning needs. It is also important for students with exceptional

◆ multi-level instruction: the use of various task presentation and response formats to accommodate students' differing learning styles and abilities

Table 6.1
The Changing Role of the Student

Reproductive Thinker	Autonomous Thinker
◆ reproducing knowledge	◆ creating and discovering
◆ passive recipient	◆ active decision-maker
◆ convergent, rule-abiding	◆ divergent, steps outside of rules to create original ideas
◆ information narrowly focused	◆ information broadly focused and inter-related
◆ one right answer	◆ multiple solutions
◆ mistakes are flaws	◆ mistakes are learning devices
◆ external evaluation and direction	◆ self-evaluation, self-direction
◆ individualistic, competitive	◆ collaborative

Table 6.2
The Changing Role of the Teacher

Directive Thinking	Facilitative Thinking
◆ provision of knowledge	◆ construction of knowledge
◆ disseminator	◆ mediator, collaborator
◆ content focus	◆ process focus
◆ information narrowly focused	◆ information broadly focused and inter-related
◆ general student assessment based on common standards	◆ assessment of student as an individual learner
◆ common instruction	◆ accommodation of learner differences

needs to have experiences that highlight their particular abilities. A teacher can be an important mediator in helping other students in the class recognize that people learn in different ways, and that the contributions and successes of all classroom members are important. A final and very important role for the teacher is to monitor and promote the exceptional student's independence; by demonstrating independence, a child with a disability can motivate other students to similarly help themselves.

The role of the classroom teacher can be significantly enhanced through interaction with others professionals within the school. A report on integration (New Brunswick Department of Education, 1988) provides a number of recommendations concerning the needs of regular classroom teachers and their collaboration with support professionals in the successful inclusion of students with exceptional needs in the classroom. These include:

◆ Support from personnel in identifying and observing students with special instructional needs.

- Support from specialist teachers, who can assist in determining the extent of learning needs or delays.
- Support from specialist teachers in devising classroom strategies and alternative educational programs designed for special-needs individuals.
- Assistance in determining appropriate expectations or goals for exceptional students.
- Encouragement for regular teachers as team participants in implementing individual education programs (p. 12).

Overall, the current role of the inclusive classroom teacher is to assume primary responsibility for all students in the inclusive classroom, including responsibility for the implementation of educational intervention decisions. Given that few classroom teachers have the professional training and experience needed to teach students with exceptional learning needs, it is essential that teachers work closely with special education personnel and support service staff to develop effective strategies that can be introduced into the classroom. Inclusive teaming through consultation and collaboration is the most flexible and effective means of providing this support for classroom teachers as their role in this transition develops.

THE CHANGING ROLE OF THE SPECIAL EDUCATION TEACHER

NO

Special education teachers have expressed concern regarding their role in schools where inclusion has been effected. As special education classrooms are being closed down, what is to become of the teachers associated with them? A major concern on the part of special educators and advocates who have worked so diligently to build educational provisions for students with exceptional needs is that the resources, knowledge base, and experience will be lost as students move into inclusive classrooms.

Another major problem associated with the transformation of roles and responsibilities of both regular classroom teachers and special education teachers concerns the traditional mutual isolation of these roles. Referring to the common practice in English universities, Wright (1989) points out that special training programs do not prepare teachers for regular-class teaching. In Canada, regular training programs and special training programs are similarly bifurcated. Indeed, specially trained teachers may be assigned directly to special-class teaching positions and continue throughout their careers as specialist teachers. Special education teachers are often uncomfortable with the challenges that regular classroom teaching presents, and, similarly, regular teachers are resistant to the prospect of serving increasing numbers of exceptional children in their classrooms.

It is clear that special and regular classroom teaching expertise must converge if effective inclusive education is to occur. The contemporary role of the special educator is seen as a catalyst for inclusive teaming, and as an essential component in successful transition.

For the purposes of the present discussion, the term *special educator* refers to any professional who has background training, expertise, and/or experience in addressing the learning needs of exceptional students.

Special Educator as Support Facilitator

An important change in the traditional role of special educators has been seen in the shift in emphasis from specialized teaching of exceptional students to the special education teacher's function as support facilitator (Stainback, Stainback, & Harris, 1989). Special educators, who have traditionally been the key professionals involved in progressive inclusive education efforts, are in an ideal position to extend this role to include responsibility for identifying and organizing support systems that aid both the inclusive classroom teacher and students with exceptional learning needs. Moreover, the special educator becomes an active facilitator in ensuring that such supports are adopted and used by the inclusive classroom teacher.

No

In order to be effective in this role, the special teacher must have a thorough knowledge of available support options, and be able to mediate resources and strategies that ensure maximal support for inclusive education. For example, an effective but underused resource like peer support can be initiated by the special educator through a student peer collaboration program, which is typically planned on the basis of academic or social-emotional goals for one or more children (Maheady, Sacca, & Harper, 1988). Student peers can be effective agents of in-class problem-solving, and can do much to ensure that all students in the classroom are recognized and respected for their unique contributions.

Other role changes for the special teacher, suggested by Porter and Collicot (1992), include responsibility for collaboration with school and district staff, parents, students, and outside agencies; program development; monitoring; and personal professional development. These aspects will be considered in the following sections.

Special Educator as Consultant

Johnson, Pugach, and Hammitte (1988) note that the recent theoretical shift to an emphasis on the consultative aspects of the special educator's role is not being realized in practice—not even when teachers have been specially trained to carry out this service.

yes

From the perspective of this text, the specific role of the special educator as consultant can be defined as

> [a] school-based individual with special education training and expertise who interacts collaboratively with within-school and within-division personnel to facilitate and support the classroom teacher in meeting the needs of exceptional students in the regular classroom.

A large-scale survey of consultation practice in U.S. departments of education (West & Brown, 1987) revealed major discrepancies in current practice, and results indicated a critical need for improved policies and leadership in this area. Out of this data, eleven competency areas pertinent to effective consultation practice by special educators were identified:

1. Technical skills associated with effective teaching.
2. Collaboration competencies involved in generating effective solutions or responses to identified problems or issues.
3. General consultation skills.
4. Communication skills.
5. Ability to develop rapport.
6. Peer education/in-service.
7. Interpersonal skills.
8. Problem-solving skills.
9. Team support skills.
10. Interviewing skills.
11. Ability to identify need for and to provide consultation (p. 48).

NO

Few states have certification requirements that include consultation as a responsibility of direct service providers such as **resource teachers** and special education teachers, or of support staff such as school psychologists and

◆ resource teacher: teacher with specialized training as a special educator who mediates support services for classroom teachers

educational diagnosticians (West & Brown, 1987). In a similar vein, even though such collaboration may be happening in Canadian schools as an adaptive response to the inclusive education movement, most provinces and territories do not have certification-based systems of special education service delivery, thus leaving the potential benefits of a school-based consultant model for special education teachers largely untapped.

yes

As we look ahead to the next century, it is readily apparent that improved approaches to consultation and collaboration in the schools will be essential to ensure that all students achieve their full potential in the inclusive classroom. Success will be contingent on the building of effective partnerships between regular teachers and special educators.

SPECIAL EDUCATOR AS PARTNER WITH REGULAR TEACHER

The role played by the special educator in collaboration with classroom teachers is a supportive one. Although the inclusive classroom situation may seem overwhelming at first, particularly for new or inexperienced teachers, it offers a means for shared problem-solving, and encourages the classroom teacher to adopt strategies that may be effective not only for the individual student, but for a large portion of the class. Through collaborating with special education teachers, classroom teachers will eventually be able to initiate strategies on their own—a process referred to in the literature as *teacher empowerment* (West, 1990).

The new and modified roles that we have outlined will require changes in pre-service, in-service, and graduate programs. In order for classroom teachers to become full partners in the inclusive education process, they will need to become better informed about aspects that are critical in providing for the individual needs of students. Teachers involved in the Manitoba collaborative teaching model (Freeze, Bravi, & Rampaul, 1989) cite the particular need for: "(i) improved pre-service teacher education with respect to mainstreamed handicapped students, (ii) continuing professional development of in-service teachers and administrators, and (iii) a consultative-collaborative in-service support services model designed to provide support to teachers in the classroom and increase teacher expertise" (p. 74). In addition, a common basis for communication and understanding between regular and special education teachers must be established (Johnson et al., 1988).

The Manitoba collaborative teaching model evaluation (Freeze et al., 1989) indicates a preference for two types of professional development to assist teachers in their inclusive education efforts in the classroom: "(i) more consulting time with resource teachers and other specialists, and (ii) a series of in-service professional development sessions" (p. 74). Balshaw (1989) suggests that in-service activities should be directly related to the concerns of the participants, and, most importantly, to the needs of regular classroom teachers. There should be opportunities for school members to collaborate and plan in-service activities that have practical relevance for the classroom, and, at the same time, are oriented toward merging theory and practice. Through a variety of formats—including workshops and discussions, curriculum and materials development, peer coaching, and in-class piloting of new approaches and materials—the school can work toward the implementation of informed, planned change, and, ultimately, total school or divisional development.

The successful development of inclusive teaming in schools depends on a systematic and organized approach to detecting, developing, and tapping the expertise and commitment of all school staff members. With schools being restructured to accommodate increasing numbers of students with special needs, regular teachers must familiarize themselves with the areas of expertise provided by the various supportive disciplines. The next section discusses the contributions that each of the related disciplines may provide in helping teachers deal with the unique learning needs of their exceptional students.

✧ ROLES OF SUPPORT PROFESSIONALS

Effective inclusive education depends on the development of innovative and efficient ways of working and communicating with members of supportive disciplines who are involved in service provision for children with special needs. West (1990) suggests that the two crucial areas for change are: "(a) from a specialized programs/services orientation to a school-wide or systems perspective in educating all children; and (b) from an "*expert* orientation to a truly collaborative, shared decision-making and problem solving role" (p. 31).

The inclusive perspective, while recognizing the expertise of the various professional support staff, at the same time recognizes that educators are the front-line professionals who work with students daily, and that it is their understanding of particular learner needs that is most critical in effecting significant change for students. Thus, input from professional support staff should be directed toward the contextual factors that support or hinder the individual child's progress in the classroom.

The effort to establish more effective communication between classroom teachers and professional support staff is embodied in the **transdisciplinary model,** defined by Gast and Wolery (1985) as: "an education model that effectively integrates goals and objectives from various disciplines and professions.... The integration begins in the assessment process and extends through direct programming effort" (p. 481). The transdisciplinary model was developed to address the need for multi-disciplinary input, and the reality that the everyday provision for the child is often the responsibility of one person. Thus, the emphasis for the transdisciplinary team is on providing and sharing expertise, and, through consultation, helping the inclusive education teacher maximize students' learning potential.

The trend in schools today is toward an adapted transdisciplinary model of service delivery. The fact that multidisciplinary teaming is becoming

◆ transdisciplinary model: an education intervention model characterized by collaborative information exchange, planning, and implementation

General

increasingly school-based and student-centred has sparked efforts to ensure that all teachers in the school share in the decision-making process. Most important is the recognition that educational personnel are the key professionals in the multidisciplinary teaming process, and that whether or not students develop to their maximum potential depends largely on the quality and degree of support available to the classroom teacher.

The adapted multidisciplinary model represents a significant shift in emphasis for the contributing disciplines, in that there is an increasing expectation for the assessments and recommendations to be "classroom friendly." In other words, teachers are becoming much more vocal about the kinds of information that will best help them serve student needs. Assessment reports have been criticized for containing excessive jargon and for straying from classroom concerns. Teachers benefit most from the assessments of support service professionals when time is allocated to classroom observation and there are opportunities for discussion and questions.

No

Services for children with special needs have been closely tied to formalized systems that are organized according to the five-step special education approach described earlier in this chapter. As schools develop the informal and collaborative practices that will become the foundation for effective inclusive schooling, it will be important to create new forms of interaction and involvement of support professionals. Freed from the rigid boundaries of a five-step special education approach, the professional distance that is perceived by many classroom teachers may be reduced or eliminated. In order for this to happen, however, the philosophy and function of inclusive teaming will have to be clearly articulated for support professionals who are called upon to participate. If members of the school staff have a clear picture of their own roles and expectations vis-à-vis inclusive education, it may well prevent some of the confusion and distrust that is often reported by parents and support service professionals. The primary responsibility for ensuring this kind of unity in the school lies with school administrators.

ADMINISTRATORS

yes

The direction and leadership of school administrators is one of the most critical features of successful inclusive schools. The responsibilities of the principal-as-administrator include staffing and organization of programs and services in the school; close communication and representation of school goals and needs; and liaison with the network of support professionals who work within and outside the central administrative offices (New Brunswick Department of Education, 1988). Particular duties of the principal are also channelled into directing, coordinating, and evaluating the total school program. More specifically, Muir (1986) suggests that "[p]rincipals must be able to play a coordinating role related to time scheduling, delegating respective staff responsibilities, and leadership based on knowledge of exceptional children's needs" (p. 19).

Hewitt (1989) stresses the importance of school district supervisors recognizing the fact that the evolution of the inclusive program is unique for every school. He argues that the principal must have the freedom to tailor general district policies in ways complementary to the school operation, and that when the circumstances warrant it, the principal must be able to make immediate changes without having to wade through a lake of policy guidelines. Schools must instead be given the responsibility and trust necessary for effective inclusion, not as a "top-down" directive but through a carefully planned and orchestrated process that empowers teachers to use their professional training and judgment in ensuring that the common philosophy of the school is known and practiced by all its members. This "bottom-up" approach to school change and professional development will depend on the professional leadership and modelling provided by the principal, as well as on the support provided by inclusive teaming.

Wood (1992) notes that principals, [b]ecause of their dual roles of instructional leader and building administrator … are central to the implementation and maintenance of effective collaborative arrangements among and between staff members" (p. 86). In discussing the development of collaborative schools, Smith and Scott (1990) stress the need for the principal to be available on a regular basis to consult with school staff on matters ranging from instructional strategies to resolution of student issues. Beyond simple verbal encouragement, the principal can foster effective collaboration by revising schedules to accommodate collaborative activities such as mentoring, coaching, peer observation, planning, and problem-solving; by funding collaboration-based projects; and by providing systematic professional development training sessions, and post-session opportunities to practice new strategies; and by allowing adequate resources.

SCHOOL PSYCHOLOGIST

The school psychologist has traditionally been an active contributor to the assessment and placement decision-making team in categorical special education classrooms. School psychologist training programs have emphasized the development of expertise in the administration and interpretation of standardized psychological and intelligence tests.

In a national survey of the roles and functions of school psychologists in the U.S., Benson and Hughes (1985) found that 50 percent of school psychologist time was taken up in assessment activities; 20 percent of the time in consultation; and 30 percent of the time was collectively used in counselling students and parents, in-service, administrative activities, research, and program evaluation. Hestick (1987) noted that psychologists who work with exceptional students are spending increasing amounts of time in consultation with parents, teachers, and other professionals, in counselling activities, and in crisis intervention.

Public Law 94-142 [U.S.] (1977) defines psychological services as including:

(i) Administering psychological and educational tests and other assessment procedures;

(ii) Interpreting assessment results;

(iii) Obtaining, integrating, and interpreting information about child behavior and conditions relating to learning;

(iv) Consulting with other staff members in planning school programs to meet the special needs of children as indicated by psychological tests, interviews, and behavioral evaluations; and

(v) Planning and managing a program of psychological services, including psychological counseling for children and parents (p. 121a.13 paragraph 8).

The expertise of the school psychologist can be a valuable resource for the successful inclusive school. Watson (1985) points out that the primary contribution of the school psychologist is to represent to the inclusive education team the unique combination of a student's strengths, weaknesses, personality structure, and aptitudes.

In Canada, psychologists must take specialized certification examinations, must undergo a required number of hours of clinical supervision, and, in most provinces, must have a graduate degree at the Ph.D. level. Certification qualifies the psychologist to assess the cognitive and emotional functioning of students. A future trend for Canadian school systems would be the de-emphasis of testing and increased attention to the emotional and behavioural support needs of exceptional students.

SPEECH AND LANGUAGE CLINICIAN

Information concerning the speech and language abilities of students can be provided by the speech and language clinician. As is the case for many disciplines involved in service delivery for children with exceptional learning needs, the role of the **speech/language pathologist** has undergone considerable change over the past twenty years. Numerous factors such as inclusive education policies, changing public attitudes, and research developments indicating important links between language acquisition and learning have all been instrumental in carving out a more primary role for the speech/language clinician within the school setting.

◆ speech/language pathologist: a clinical specialist trained to diagnose and remediate speech and language disorders

For example, services that were once provided solely in a hospital setting or community clinic are now being offered on a regular basis at the school; indeed, many school systems have at least one speech/language clinician employed as part of the professional service delivery team. This is an important development because it grows out of a recognition that a child's language difficulties interact in major ways with the kind of classroom and schooling experiences that occur daily. The incorporation of speech/language pathologist services into the school can ensure a more ecologically valid assessment and intervention framework than has been possible through clinic-based intervention services.

The particular functions that a speech/language pathologist might perform in the school setting include:

◆ Direct service—including identification, assessment, and intervention—for communication-impaired children.
◆ Input into the development of an individual program plan (IEP).
◆ Consultation with and support of regular classroom teachers and parents.
◆ Provision of in-service education on adaptive strategies that could be implemented within the regular classroom.
◆ Participation on the supportive services team and planning committees.

It is well recognized that speech and language problems can have a significant impact on school performance, and that communication problems can also interfere significantly with social development (Wiig, 1984). If students with speech/language disorders are to reach their full learning potential, policies and funding structures must be developed to complement the needs of children at all age levels. Services must be varied and flexible enough to accommodate the wide scope of communication problems, which are often easily remediable if appropriate service is available at the right time. As Dr. Helen Ilott (1990) suggests, the focus should be not on determining whether health or education should provide funding and direction for speech/language services, but rather on addressing three important questions: What are the speech-language service needs of children? How can these needs be met? How can we accommodate professionals in administrative structures to facilitate service to children?" (p. 5)

Speech/language pathologists in Canada have provincial and national professional associations that provide leadership in maintaining and defining professional standards and training requirements. Specialized programs are available (highly competitive in most universities due to enrolment limits), and most speech/language pathologists have completed graduate-level training and have undergone a rigorous supervised clinical practicum.

SOCIAL WORKER

The social problems that are commonplace in society today have placed tremendous pressure on the schools. School-age children who are physically, psychologically, or sexually abused, or who suffer from the emotional effects of being in dysfunctional families where there is alcohol/drug abuse or marriage disintegration, present an ever-increasing challenge for teachers and school support staff.

The social worker plays a key role in linking educational personnel and the family, and in ensuring that supportive resources in the community are accessed. One of the important functions the social worker provides is the compilation of a social history that takes into account the student's educational, psychological, and medical history. This holistic overview, which is based on student records and parent/student interviews, is developed to enable maximum coordination of educational services with other community and social service agencies (Schloss & Sedlak, 1986; Watson, 1985). The social worker can facilitate stronger school-home ties by:

◆ Providing counselling for families and students, and conveying information about the effects of family and living circumstances on student performance in school.

◆ Observing student behaviour and interaction in nonschool settings, and participating on student referral teams to ensure that the family resources and needs are taken into consideration in program planning and decision-making.

◆ Assisting families in crisis, alerting school personnel to such special circumstances, and supporting teachers in helping the child cope at school.

◆ Serving as advocate for the family or pupil by representing their interests in matters of controversy or confrontation with the school.

In addition to the above activities, the social worker should have a thorough knowledge of the various service resources in the community, and should be prepared to assist schools in making referrals and helping families to access these services. Through a process of information exchange and liaison, the social worker can be highly instrumental in coordinating family

Teachers learning lessons of violence

It's been two years since she lost a 12-year-old student to prostitution, but Donna Steffes still feels a yawning emptiness inside.

It doesn't matter that the girl had violently pushed and shoved her teacher in the supposed safe sanctuary of a Grade 6 classroom.

"I feel like a failure," Steffes says quietly. "It hurt me most that I hadn't been able to touch her life even though I spent a lot of time trying to understand. She's probably lost. She may not even be alive."

The 30-year-old Steffes is not a social worker, not a child care worker, not a psychiatrist. She is one teacher among hundreds forced to deal with the reality that is life for many of today's kids.

And in the six years of trying to teach her kids at St. Monica elementary/junior high school, at 235 18th Ave. S.W., the traditional Three Rs, her body has been battered and bit at by kids who often come from dysfunctional families.

"They don't like to be cornered so they strike out," Steffes says. "Sometimes I feel like I have to crack the whip like a lion tamer."

Her feelings are not unusual. Dr. Mary Jo Williams, co-ordinator of professional development for the Alberta Teachers' Association, says there have been more cases of teachers being assaulted in the last five years than ever before.

"There are drugs, tensions on the playgrounds," says Williams. "Inner city schools, in particular, have teachers worried about safety."

The strain is showing. The number of teachers on long-term disability (under the Alberta School Employees Benefit Plan which does not include Calgary teachers) has jumped by 81 per cent in the last five years. Of those, up to half can be linked to job stress.

The crisis has forced the ATA and the Alberta School Trustees' Association to set up a committee to try to resolve a problem costing them more than $1.5 million per month in disability insurance premiums.

Officials worry about losing good teachers and say the problems are being dumped on the schools because society refuses to spend money to tackle poverty, child abuse and immigration.

They say education is in crisis because society is and, as one weary teacher puts it, schools are being asked to "salvage the wreckage of parents who don't care."

Steffes knows some of the kids who leave school will end up selling their bodies or drugs, or joining a gang.

"If you don't have the skills to get a job and haven't had a stable home environment—some of these kids have been to 25 different schools in six years —what else can they do?"

At the same time, growing numbers of immigrants are entering schools with inadequate English skills.

In Steffes' class, just six of her 28 students are Canadian born — and for several of those six, English is still a second language at home.

This year, Steffes' class is bright and healthy. She admits it's a relief.

Source: *Calgary Herald*, June 23, 1990.

support services, and in maintaining communication of student needs and progress between home, school, and community agencies.

Training programs for social workers are provided at the undergraduate and graduate levels in Canadian universities. Programs typically concentrate on family dynamics and community/social behaviour. As social workers become more closely aligned with the schools, the need to refine traditional programs is underscored. For example, in the United States, guidelines that relate specifically to the necessary standards for social work services in the schools have been established (National Association of Social Workers, 1978). This trend will no doubt be followed in Canada, as social and emotional behavioural problems involving families and students continue to escalate and have an effect on school performance and achievement.

GUIDANCE COUNSELLOR

School counsellors can play a critical role in supporting the inclusive education efforts of the school. An important function of the guidance counsellor is to provide, following a cumulative synthesis of the relevant day-to-day experiences and observations of teachers and peers, summary information about the student's adjustment in the school context. McCann (1987) suggests that the school counsellor can provide direct support to classroom teachers by helping students with exceptional needs to develop positive self-concepts and to express their emotions constructively, and by supporting parents as they help their children cope with matters of peer acceptance and interaction.

The specific role of the guidance counsellor includes organizing and planning the guidance program; direct individual and group student counselling; consulting support and assistance with parents, teachers, and administrators; and the integration of community resources. With respect to inclusive education, this role might be expanded to include an advocacy function, in addition to service as coordinator/consultant for the student with exceptional needs. McCann (1987) emphasizes that such a role change must be coupled with specialized training (including both theoretical and practical experience in special education), cautioning that "[o]ur concerns and good intentions, without the necessary knowledge and skills, are potentially dangerous" (p. 7).

Professional preparation of school guidance counsellors in Canada is offered through post-baccalaureate diploma programs, or through graduate programs in educational psychology. Emphasis is given to counselling theory, personal and social development, developing communication skills and strategies, and practicum opportunities for application in educational settings. In concert with recent inclusive education developments, information about students with special needs, and about relevant counselling strategies, is being incorporated into many current programs.

PHYSICAL AND OCCUPATIONAL THERAPIST

Students who have physical disabilities associated with fine and gross motor coordination are assisted in adapting to their educational environment through the services provided by physical and occupational therapists. Much of the work of these professionals involves providing adaptive therapy through exercise, massage, and hydrotherapy, and assisting in securing and using prosthetic devices such as artificial limb and braces, as well as adaptive equipment and classroom materials. In addition, physical and occupational therapists serve as consultants and physical-service mediators for associated professionals, such as nurses, doctors, and teachers, to ensure that the physical needs of the students are properly assessed, and to monitor the coordination of team efforts to provide maximal support for the functional adaptation of the child within the school context.

yes

The expertise of the physical therapist is focused on the assessment and training of the lower extremities and large muscles, whereas the occupational therapist deals with upper-body and fine motor needs (Gearheart, Weishahn, & Gearheart, 1988). The occupational therapist is concerned with the development and/or restorative functions of the upper-body extremities and fine motor skills that are important in school performance. Physical therapists work closely with physicians to correct or prevent the motor-performance problems of students resulting from physical defects, diseases, or injuries (Heron & Harris, 1982). Direct assistance to students would include therapeutic procedures such as heat treatments, massage, exercises to increase motor function and range, and posture improvement (Gloeckler & Simpson, 1988; Heron & Harris, 1982).

yes

Mather and Weinstein (1988) note that primary therapy goals are to provide appropriate recreational and functional experiences that will facilitate adaptive interaction in the child's environment, to supply and expand an adaptive skills repertoire; and to promote independent functioning. The occupational therapist works collaboratively with the classroom teacher by suggesting developmentally appropriate activities for individuals or small groups, and by proposing ways to use classroom resources to increase physical, psychological, and cognitive growth. Program implementation and integration may be incorporated into everyday classroom activities such as handwriting, using scissors, matching shapes and colours, fitting together puzzle pieces, buttoning clothes and tying shoes, and wrist rotation and extension (Heron & Harris, 1982; Mather & Weinstein, 1988). Mather and Weinstein (1988) refer to the interactive teaming between teacher and therapist as a system of "role release" that occurs as a result of mutual problem-solving, case conferences, shared observations, and record-keeping. Specialized training programs in physical and occupational therapy are offered at the baccalaureate level at a number of Canadian universities.

PARAPROFESSIONAL

NO

White (1988) and Fimian, Fafard, and Howell (1984) note that the role of the paraprofessional, traditionally seen as one that freed the classroom teacher from all of the noninstructional duties, has undergone a subtle shift from housekeeper to greater involvement in the instructional role. While the extent of paraprofessional involvement in classroom instruction is still a matter of debate, it is increasingly acknowledged that as the inclusive classroom teacher becomes more like program manager, paraprofessional support can be put to more effective use.

Some of the typical activities that paraprofessionals might perform in the inclusive classroom include: preparation of teaching materials and resources; tutorial assistance; monitoring of behavioural management programs; scheduling; small group and individual instruction; clerical duties; and out-of-class supervision. According to White (1988), paraprofessionals can substantially reduce the pupil-teacher ratio in inclusive classrooms, and through flexible organization can provide more opportunity for individual and small-group instruction. Collaborative monitoring, problem-solving, and instructional planning can contribute to a more complete assessment of student progress, and the special talents and strengths of the paraprofessional can augment those of the classroom teacher. Moreover, daily collaboration of teacher and paraprofessional provides for mutual emotional support.

The paraprofessional can also be an effective liaison with special services outside the classroom, and help to maintain the continuity and communication necessary for effective integration of all special service provisions. Other noninstructional tasks, such as materials preparation and helping students into outside wear, can further help to relieve the classroom teacher. Finally, paraprofessionals who are involved with inclusive classrooms on a daily basis can be effective community support advocates.

Over the past twenty years, the changing role of the paraprofessional has prompted the allocation of additional funding, the development of better training programs, and, finally, clarification and change in the role responsibilities and job descriptions (Fimian et al., 1984). These developments have progressed at different rates, and there is wide variation in their degree of implementation across different school systems. However, this trend, which is quite evident in the United States, will no doubt become more apparent in Canadian systems as educators begin to reassess and restructure their schools with a view to maximizing the contributions of their human resources.

◆ INCLUSIVE TEAMING: COORDINATION OF SERVICES

A school system based on inclusive teaming through collaborative consultation requires a rethinking of typical service delivery systems. At the present time, many schools are bound by a cumbersome model of referral, assessment, and program-placement systems that requires extensive support staff involvement, along with hours of meeting time. Such activities are a tremendous drain on the school's financial and human resources. Moreover, because many of the personnel involved (e.g., special education consultants, school psychologists, speech and language clinicians) are employed at a system level, it is often difficult to hold the consultation meeting, or have the necessary supportive services in place, when actually needed.

In inclusive schools, therefore, it will be important to organize for immediate service delivery, planning, and problem-solving resources at the school level. The new *Journal of Educational and Psychological Consultation* is specifically geared to the development of a scientific understanding of consultation, and provides practical strategies to increase the effectiveness and efficiency of consultation involving individuals and organizations.

INNOVATIONS IN SERVICE DELIVERY

Leadership in school innovation and change through inclusive teaming and collaborative consultation has been predominantly carried out in the United States. The elements and foundations that guide similar movements in Canada will need to reflect educational policy and procedures that are implemented at the provincial, as opposed to the federal, jurisdictional level.

Moreover, it must be recognized that each province has its own distinct history of service delivery for exceptional students.

Csapo and Goguen (1989) indicate that all provinces are sensitive to the problems and issues regarding service provision for students with special needs, and that many innovative developments have been implemented. What follows is a discussion of four of these developments, beginning with the Freeze et al. (1989) **consultative-collaborative model** for serving students with exceptional needs in the regular classroom. This model, which has been developed and implemented in the province of Manitoba over the past fifteen years, operates in conjunction with the University of Manitoba one-year post-baccalaureate resource teacher training program.

In the consultative-collaborative model, special education delivery services are framed within six operative levels, beginning with the *classroom teacher*. The remaining levels include the *teacher team* (organized according to subject areas, particular streams or programs, disciplines, and/or special interests); *resource teacher* (who has specialized training as a special educator and mediates support services to the classroom teacher); *in-school support services team* (serving on a case-by-case basis and typically involving an administrator, a counsellor, a resource teacher, and classroom teachers); *divisional support services team* (comprising clinical specialists, specialized programs, the Department of Education, university and private consultants, and contracted services); and *ancillary support services* (indirect community-based support services).

Consistent in many ways with the concept of inclusive teaming, the consultative-collaborative model attempts to merge the best of special education and classroom teaching experience. Aside from enhancing professional development, the foremost goal is to serve the majority of learners with special needs in the regular classroom. The developers of the model deliberately underplayed the use of categories and labels, focusing instead on supporting classroom teachers as they attempt to deliver ecologically sound instructional and behavioural procedures that will meet the learning needs of all students in the classroom. Assessment procedures are geared to the classroom situation, and data- and curriculum-based procedures are used to assist the classroom teacher in developing and implementing instructional programs. Instructional programs and procedures are, where possible, delivered on a systemic basis (i.e., targeted for whole-class or group implementation, as opposed to an individual child with learning problems). The individual learning needs of the child are the focus of collaborative problem-solving, and instructional strategies are revised accordingly when necessary.

A *second* example of innovation with respect to inclusive education can be seen in New Brunswick, where legislation, in place since 1986, directs schools to provide integrated school programs for all students. Gordon Porter and his colleagues (Porter & Richler, 1991; Porter & Collicott, 1992) have become leading figures in designing and implementing changes that will ultimately create effective inclusive schools. Backed with legislation that

◆ consultative-collaborative model: a system of service delivery based on the collaboration of educational professionals in meeting the needs of all students in the general classroom was philosophically enabling for inclusive education, Porter and his colleagues began with the recognition that the classroom teacher was the primary professional involved in making inclusive schooling work, and that the collective resources of the system had to be realigned to support all teachers in effectively carrying out this role. As a result, the traditional special education approach was abandoned and replaced by a new methods and resource (M&R) teacher role, which was designed to "provide immediate and direct assistance to regular class teachers in planning, implementing and monitoring programs to meet the individual needs of students with special needs" (Porter & Collicott, 1992, p. 190).

The duties included in the M&R teacher role are based on collaboration and consultation with teachers, parents, and other personnel and/or agencies to ensure student success in learning. Specific responsibilities include collaboration, liaison, program development, monitoring, and personal professional development. M&R teachers have primary responsibility "for providing direct and effective support to classroom teachers, with the goal of enabling *all* students to be meaningfully included in learning activities in regular classrooms" (Porter, 1991, p. 107). Secondary responsibility is given to direct service for exceptional students requiring individualized supports and services to participate in, and benefit from, regular classroom instruction. Porter and Collicott (1992) report that the present number of M&R teachers has increased to the present ratio of one teacher for every 150-200 students.

In addition to the direct support provided by M&R teachers, four key instructional initiatives were developed to address the need for staff development of regular teachers. The first instructional initiative involved developing multi-level strategies to assist teachers in planning a lesson for all students, while at the same time interweaving individual goals with the broader classroom content and instructional strategies (Collicott, 1991). Implementing this initiative, educators were required to formulate various presentation methods to address the different learning styles of students, to provide flexible alternative ways for students to express their understanding, and to adjust student evaluation procedures accordingly (Porter & Collicott, 1992).

Italics

The second instructional initiative was based on the cooperative learning approaches developed by Johnson, Johnson, and Holubec (1984) to create classroom environments in which the learning of all students is valued and enhanced. (This approach is described in Chapters 4 and 10.) The development of classroom teacher competency in using cooperative learning approaches was facilitated by workshops, modelling, peer coaching, and practice.

One of the most formidable challenges facing inclusive education teachers is dealing with the inevitable classroom management problems that result from bringing together students with diverse learning needs and behavioural patterns. This aspect was addressed in the third instructional initiative of the New Brunswick school district. A non-violent crisis intervention model was selected, and designated staff members received training and certification in the methods associated with this approach. These individuals provided within-district workshops for staff, and over a two-year period all teachers, bus drivers, librarians, teacher assistants, and district members who interact with students received the training. In this way, consistency in implementation strategies is ensured, and, as Porter and Collicott (1992) point out, the increased contact between members with varying roles in the system results in a greater mutual appreciation of the challenges associated with those roles.

The final instructional initiative was implemented to deal with **at-risk students,** particularly in light of the increasing dropout rates among junior and senior high-school students. Federal incentive grants were tapped by the New Brunswick project to develop two programs—the stay-in-school mentorship program and the peer-facilitator program. Under the first program, every junior and senior high school was provided with at least one **mentor** designated to work with a group of eight to ten students. Daily contacts centred on organizational and planning aspects of school life, and on providing emotional support. Mentors were responsible for liaising with teachers, student, and home to facilitate the student's success in achieving school goals; for making bimonthly home visits to review student study skills, and for limited involvement in academic tutoring as part of an overall remediation plan. The second program employed peer facilitators to recruit, orient, and train prospective student peer helpers to work with at-risk students in a peer partnership arrangement.

A *third* example of an innovative Canadian inclusive education program is outlined by Flynn and Innes (1992), who are Director of Education and Staff Development Consultant, respectively, for the Waterloo Region Catholic School Board in Ontario. Their efforts to develop inclusive schooling were based on the adoption, in 1985, of a new transformational leadership orientation, which focused on three main themes: "1) the curriculum of caring, 2) Catholic context as a gift, and 3) community involvement as an extension or enlargement of inclusive community" (Flynn & Innes, 1992, p. 203). The curriculum of caring was built on a common system of values that call for equity, justice, and fairness for all students. For the school system organization, this meant providing appropriate educational experiences that foster the respect and dignity of all students in their own community schools. The commitment to inclusive educational practice implicit in this orientation was more an issue of morality than it was an issue of law. Transformational leaders for each school were designated to articulate the new values, and to facilitate their adoption through the revamping of existing human resource systems and management processes.

The first step to bringing about system-wide commitment to inclusive education was to move system staff, as Flynn and Innes (1992) describe it, "to begin to look at the world of education differently and to move firmly and more intentionally to root our practices in what we said we stood for—our values" (p. 212). Inclusive education perspectives were articulated to various

◆ at risk: a term used to refer to students who are considered to be potential candidates for intervention programs due to poor achievement resulting from adverse intrinsic or extrinsic conditions

◆ mentor: person with special skills or knowledge who tutors less experienced learners in the domain(s) of interests

General

system staff groups by leading academics, government ministers, representatives of advocacy groups, and representatives from school jurisdictions that were incorporating similar changes in school-system values. In 1988, the Waterloo Region Catholic School Board system plan identified inclusion as its principle priority, and supporting activities and within-school discussions prompted increasing commitment to this philosophy.

Specific organizational restructuring involved, first of all, enlarging administrative council to include a staff development consultant and a public relations consultant, and making meetings open to all school and community members. This sent out a clear message that the traditional concentration of power and control in the administrative council was being replaced by an inclusive process. The second aspect of organizational change was to increase the interaction between supervisory officers and schools in order to ensure continuity of system transition. The third and final component was to significantly reduce the erroneous and time-consuming meetings of identification, placement, and review committees, which are required by law.

Also subject to organizational change—in more general terms—was staff development. The staff development department assumed a major role in rethinking teachers' roles as partners in a community of learners, who must be supported and guided by the inclusive values of the system. Flynn and Innes (1992) conclude that the initial reorganization results have confirmed their choice of direction, but acknowledge that the changes, however promising, are somewhat "scary because there isn't yet a framework that 'holds' all of this" (p. 217).

A *fourth* innovation and change in Canada is one that is being addressed at the school and classroom level. Cullen and Pratt (1992) address the issue of measuring and reporting progress in inclusive schools. They consider large-scale, norm-referenced testing and grading programs to be of limited value in determining the learning needs and styles needed to support students in inclusive classrooms. Instead, Cullen and Pratt (1992) recommend basing student evaluation plans on appropriate curriculum developed at the local level of education, while making any necessary adjustments to suit a particular student's needs. A particularly important aspect of student evaluation, for Cullen and Pratt (1992), is a partnership with parents that invites two-way communication about expectations and about the progress the child is making.

The educational innovations and approaches described above represent some of the various new directions that support inclusive education in Canada. Each approach has been developed with the goal of providing more effective instruction for all students in an inclusive education environment. Early indicators suggest that these and similar inclusive teaming programs not only improve service provision to students, but also foster the on-going professional development of classroom teachers and their associated professional colleagues.

◇ SUMMARY

In this chapter, we reviewed some of the major developments and trends that support a radical change in the way that teachers, parents, and professional support staff interact in order to promote inclusive education for all students. These developments have important implications for Canadian educators involved in teaching students with exceptional learning needs, as well as at-risk students. As the primary professionals in the inclusive schooling process, teachers will need to assume responsibility for supporting a greater diversity of student needs in the inclusive classroom.

The concept of inclusive teaming, which is founded on the practice of collaborative consultation and the efficient allocation of school and community resources, was depicted in this chapter as a promising and effective means of alternative service delivery for students.

Putting inclusive teaming into practice will require radical changes in school policies, organization, community resource allocation, funding structures, and teacher preparation and professional development. Critical to such change is redefining the roles and responsibilities of inclusive classroom teachers and special educators, who will work in partnership to create positive learning environments that serve to develop and nurture the learning potential of all students.

General

QUESTIONS
◆◆◆◆◆◆◆◆◆◆◆◆◆

1. In what ways are inclusive education principles reflected in the concept of inclusive teaming?

2. How does the inclusive teaming approach conceptualize the roles and responsibilities of the special education teacher and the regular classroom teacher?

3. Describe the consultative-collaborative teaming that might be most appropriate for a 6-year-old child with a specific learning disability and behaviour problems. Support your choices.

4. How can the regular classroom teacher ensure the success of students with exceptional needs in inclusive classrooms?

5. What overt and covert barriers may jeopardize the successful inclusion of students with exceptional needs in the regular classroom?

REFERENCES

Alberta Education. (1990). *Teaching thinking enhancing learning: A resource book for schools ECS to grade 12.* Edmonton, AB: Curriculum Branch.

Balshaw, M. (1989). Special schools and ordinary schools: It's not what you do, it's the way you do it. In D. Baker & K. Bovair (Eds.), *Making the special schools ordinary?* , Volume 1(pp. 46-60). London: Falmer.

Barth, R. S. (1990). *Improving schools from within: Teachers, parents, and principals can make the difference* (p. 209). San Francisco: Jossey-Bass.

Benson, A. J., & Hughes, J. (1985). Perceptions of role definition processes in school psychology: A national survey. *School Psychology Review, 11*(3), 221-228.

Chalfant, J. C., Pysh, M. V., & Moultrice, R. (1979). Teacher assistance teams: A model for within-building problem solving. *Learning Disability Quarterly, 2,* 85-96.

Charles, C. M. & Malian, I. M. (1980).*The special student: Practical help for the classroom teacher.* St. Louis, MO: Mosby.

Collicott, J. (1991). Implementing multi-level instruction: Strategies for classroom teachers. In G. L. Porter & D. Richler (Eds.), *Changing Canadian schools* (pp. 191-218). North York, ON: The Roeher Institute.

Csapo, M., & Goguen, L. (Eds.). (1989). *Special education across Canada: Issues and concerns for the 90s.* Vancouver: Centre for Human Development and Research.

Cullen, B., & Pratt, T. (1992). Measuring and reporting student progress. In S. Stainback & W. Stainback (Eds.), *Curriculum consideration in inclusive classrooms* (pp. 175-196). Baltimore, MD: Paul H. Brookes.

Fimian, M. J., Fafard, M. B., & Howell, K. W. (1984). *Managing human resources in special education.* New York: Praeger.

Flynn, G. J., & Innes, M. (1992). The Waterloo Region Catholic School System. In In R. Villa, J. Thousand, W. Stainback, & S. Stainback (Eds.), *Restructuring for caring and effective education: An administrative guide to creating heterogeneous schools* (pp. 201-217). Baltimore, MD: Paul H. Brookes.

Freeze, D. R., Bravi, G., & Rampaul, W. E. (1989). Special education in Manitoba: A consultative-collaborative services delivery model. In M. Csapo & L. Goguen (Eds.), *Special education across Canada* (pp. 47-80). Vancouver: Centre for Human Development and Research.

Gast, D. L., & Wolery, M. (1985). Severe developmental disabilities. In W. H. Berdine & A. E. Blackhurst (Eds.), *An introduction to special education* (2nd ed.) (pp. 481-482). Boston: Little, Brown.

Gearheart, B. R., Weishahn, M. W., & Gearheart, C. J. (1988). *The exceptional student in the regular classroom* (4th ed.). Columbus, OH: Charles E. Merrill.

Gloeckler, T., & Simpson, C. (1988). *Exceptional students in regular classrooms: Challenges, services, and methods.* Mountain View, CA: Mayfield.

Heron, T., & Harris, K. C. (1982). *The educational consultant.* Boston: Allyn & Bacon.

Heron, T., & Harris, K. C. (1993). *The educational consultant: Helping professionals, parents, and mainstreamed students* (3rd ed.). Austin, TX: Pro-ed.

Hestick, H. (1987). Roles and functions of the psychologist in special education. Eric Document 304 822.

Hewitt, J. (1989). The role of the principal: Integrating special education students. *Federation of Women Teachers' Associations of Ontario News, 7*(4), 14-19.

Idol, L. (1990). The scientific art of consultation. *Journal of educational and psychological consultation, 1*(1), 3-22.

Idol, L. (1993). *Special educator's consultation handbook* (2nd ed.). Austin, TX: Pro-ed.

Idol-Maestas, L. (1983). *Special educator's consultation handbook.* Rockville, MD: Aspen Systems.

Idol, L., Paolucci-Whitcomb, P., & Nevin, A. (1986). *Collaborative consultation.* Rockville, MD: Aspen Systems.

Ilott, H. G. (1990). Speech and language services: Whose responsibility?—When we ask the wrong question. Canadian C.E.C Newsletter, *Keeping in Touch,* June, 4-5.

Johnson, D., Johnson, R., & Holubec, E. (1984). *Cooperation in the classroom.* Edina, MN: Interaction.

Johnson, L. J., Pugach, M. C., & Hammitte, D. J. (1988). Barriers to effective special education consultation. *Remedial and Special Education, 9*(6), 41-47.

Lewis, R. B., & Doorlag, D. H. (1991). *Teaching special students in the mainstream* (3rd ed.). New York: Macmillan.

Maheady, L., Sacca, M., & Harper, G. (1988). Classwide peer tutoring with mildly handicapped high school students. *Exceptional Children, 55,* 52-59.

Mather, J. & Weinstein, E. (1988). Teachers and therapists: Evolution of a partnership in early intervention. *Topics in Early Childhood Special Education, 7*(4),1-9.

McCann, W. (1987). The school counsellor and special needs students. *New Brunswick Counsellor, 13* (1), 6–8.

Morsink, C. V., Thomas, C. C., & Correa, V. I. (1991). *Interactive teaming: Consultation and collaboration in special programs.* New York: Merrill.

Muir, R. (1986). Mainstreaming: A second look. *Journal of Education* (Nova Scotia), *399,* 19.

Murray, M. (1991). The role of the classroom teacher. In G. L. Porter & D. Richler (Eds.), *Changing Canadian schools* (pp. 173-189). North York, ON: The Roeher Institute.

National Association of Social Workers (1978). *NASW standards for social work services in schools.* Silver Springs, MD: author.

New Brunswick Department of Education (1988). *Working guidelines on integration.* Fredericton, NB: Student Services Branch.

Porter, G. L., & Collicott, J. (1992). New Brunswick School Districts 28 and 29: Mandates and strategies that promote inclusive schooling. In R. Villa, J. Thousand, W. Stainback, & S. Stainback (Eds.), *Restructuring for caring and effective education: An administrative guide to creating heterogeneous schools* (pp. 187-200). Baltimore, MD: Paul H. Brookes.

Porter, G. L., & Richler, D. (1991). *Changing Canadian schools.* North York, ON: The Roeher Institute.

Public Law 94-142. (1977). Federal Register, Department of Health, Education, and Welfare. Vol. 42, No. 163, 121a.13.

Salend, S. J. (1990). *Effective mainstreaming.* New York: Macmillan.

Schloss, P. J. & Sedlak, R. A. (1986). *Instructional methods for students with learning and behavior problems.* Boston: Allyn & Bacon.

Shea, T. M., & Bauer, A.M. (1991). *Parents and teachers of children with exceptionalities: A handbook for collaboration* (2nd ed.) Boston: Allyn & Bacon.

Slavin, R. E., Madden, N. A., Karweit, N. L., Dolan, L., Wasik, B. A., Shaw, A., Mainzer, K. L., & Haxby, B. (1991). Neverstreaming: Prevention and early intervention as an alternative to special education. *Journal of Learning Disabilities, 24,* 373-378.

Smith, S. C., & Scott, J. J. (1990). *The collaborative school: A work environment for effective instruction.* Eugene, OR: ERIC/EM School Management Digest Series, Number 33, ED 021 574.

Stainback, W., & Stainback, S. (Eds.). (1990). *Support networks for inclusive schooling: Interdependent integrated education.* Baltimore, MD: Paul H. Brookes.

Stainback, S. B., Stainback, W. C., & Harris, K. C. (1989). Support facilitation: An emerging role for special educators. *Teacher Education and Special Education,* 12(4), 148-153.

Turnbull, A. P., & Turnbull, H. R. III (1990). *Families, professionals, and exceptionality: A special partnership* (2nd ed.). Columbus, OH: Merrill.

Wang, M. C. (1983). *Provision of adaptive instruction: Implementation and effects.* Pittsburgh: University of Pittsburgh, Learning, Research and Development Center.

Wang, M. C., & Birch, J. W. (1984). Comparison of a full-time mainstream program and a resource room approach. *Exceptional Children,* 51(1), 33-40.

Watson, T. F. (1985). Pupil services—The team approach. Part I: The team. Part II: Record keeping. Paper presented at the Annual Meeting of the National Association of Social Workers, New Orleans.

West, J. F. (1990). Educational collaboration in the restructuring of schools. *Journal of Educational and Psychological Consultation,* 1(1), 23-40.

West, J. F., & Brown, P. A. (1987). State departments of education policies on consultation in special education: The state of the States. *Remedial and Special Education,* 8(3), 54-51.

White, R. (1988). Paraprofessionals in Special Education. In D. S. Marozas & May, D. C. (Eds.) *Issues and practices in special education.* New York: Longman.

Wiig, E.H. (1984). Language disabilities in adolescents: A question of cognitive strategies. *Topics in Language Disorders,* 4(2).

Wilson, A. K. (1989). Ontario's "Bill 82" in retrospect. In M. Csapo & L. Goguen (Eds.), *Special education across Canada* (pp. 81-92). Vancouver: Centre for Human Development and Research.

Wood, J. W. (1992). *Adapting instruction for mainstreamed and at-risk students* (2nd ed.). New York: Merrill.

Wright, M. (1989). INSET: The role of the special school. In D. Baker & K. Bovair (Eds.), *Making the special schools ordinary?* (pp. 150-163). London: Falmer.

FAMILIES AND SCHOOLS
IN PARTNERSHIP

CHAPTER OBJECTIVES

To understand the multiple roles and pressures on parents from a family systems perspective.

To specify the vital ingredients for, and mutual benefits of, a successful parent-teacher partnership.

To outline methods of information-sharing between parents and professionals.

To discuss the responsibilities of professionals in collaboration with parents.

To suggest possible levels of parent involvement in the educational process.

On the drive over to the school, Ed and Hilda CalfRobe discussed the points they wanted to raise, and the questions they wanted to ask Ms. Bows, their son Jake's Grade 5 teacher. They had attended every parent/teacher conference they had been invited to since Jake began school, and they felt they had a pretty good idea of Jake's learning strengths and needs. Nevertheless, they both felt somewhat uneasy about the pending meeting with Ms. Bows, since this was the first year Jake would be enrolled in an inclusive education program after spending three years in a segregated classroom for children with learning disabilities.

The CalfRobes had enjoyed working closely with the special-class teacher, Mr. Glen, communicating regularly and implementing at home any suggestions to help improve Jake's school performance. Mr. Glen had been particularly helpful in finding reading materials on pottery making—Jake's hobby—and they all worked

very hard for Jake to succeed as he had. Even though they were exhilarated when Mr. Glen discussed the school's recommendation to move Jake into a regular Grade 5 inclusive classroom last June, they were filled with more questions and concerns now that Jake had completed the first month in an inclusive classroom.

How would they know if Jake was working up to his potential? What if the other children would not accept Jake's cultural difference? With twenty-eight other children to serve would there be sufficient time for Ms. Bows to attend to Jake's individual learning needs? Would Jake's work be graded in comparison with all the other students? Mr. Glen had special training to teach students with learning disabilities; would someone without this background be able to teach Jake as well? Would the CalfRobes be able to support the school program at home as they had over the past three years? As these questions came to mind, Hilda

CalfRobe wrote them down to be certain that no concern would be overlooked.

Ms. Bows collected the samples of Jake's work over the month of September, and sat reflecting at her desk as she awaited the parent/teacher interview with Mr. and Mrs. CalfRobe. She had ten years of teaching experience—the past four with Grade 5—and had been both apprehensive and excited about participating in the first-year inclusive classroom project. The school principal, Mr. Brown, had approached her and four other teachers on staff last year to be involved in the first stage of the project, which was to be fully implemented over the next three years. Accepting the challenge, the five teachers had begun meeting regularly since last April, sharing their plans and ideas with Mr. Brown and Mr. Glen, the school resource teacher. It had been helpful to attend the spring course offered at the university, and they appreciated the offer from the instructor, Dr. Nelson, to contact her should they wish to discuss anything as they implemented the inclusive schooling project.

The workshop arranged by Mr. Brown and Mr. Glen for all school staff at the end of last year had been particularly useful, involving the team of five teachers and focusing on sharing the plans for the next year. On a personal level, Ms. Bows had been reassured, as she addressed the many questions and concerns raised by the other teachers, that the few months of reading and planning with the other team members had been productive. It was particularly reassuring when Mr. Harris announced at the end of that day that the rest of the teachers were delighted to have a team as prepared as they were, and that he and the others would be there to help out in any way possible.

Continuing with the planning over the summer, and meeting with Mr. Glen to discuss the background of each of the four children who were to be joining the class, had given Ms. Bows the extra confidence she needed to begin on a positive and optimistic note in September. That confidence soon evaporated as the first week of school got underway. By Friday she was feeling completely overwhelmed, wishing that she hadn't been so readily agreeable to participating in the project. Mr. Glen stopped by her classroom at the very moment she was feeling her lowest, and listened calmly as she reviewed her misgivings. "I'm not trained to work with students who have special needs." "I don't know how to assess or diagnose what their needs are."

"Just when I think I'm making some progress, one of them says something—or worse yet does something—to throw everything off balance again." "I've spent four hours every night this week trying to come up with strategies to make it work for all the students in the class, and it seems to me the whole thing is hopeless."

It had been a relief to say what was troubling her, and, as she thought back to the encounter, she silently thanked Mr. Glen for the umpteenth time for his reassurance and his help in targeting the immediate problem areas that day, and for his subsequent support in September. Perhaps the most valuable advice he had given her was to avoid thinking about what expertise she lacked in special education, and instead concentrate completely on the unique learning needs of the four students. This, he asserted, was her primary responsibility for the current teaching year.

As she sat there waiting for the CalfRobes to arrive, she suddenly realized that what Mr. Glen had said was true. Over the month of September, she had made numerous anecdotal records as she observed Jake in the classroom and out on the playground. She had prepared an academic profile of his performance in all subject areas, and despite the obvious difficulties he had with the language arts, he showed numerous strengths in other areas. His contributions to the classroom discussions in Social Studies and Science were particularly advanced, and he appeared to have an excellent background knowledge in these areas. On the social-emotional side, despite occasional lapses, Jake was generally easygoing and was well liked by his classmates.

Ms. Bows made a further note on her summary sheet to mention to the CalfRobes how Jake had been demonstrating increasing independence in his day-to-day work, and how well he had responded to the daily plan sheet that she had prepared especially for him. The plan sheet had been suggested by Dr. Nelson, whom she had contacted at the university after discussing the matter with Mr. Glen. In fact, Ms. Bows was hopeful that tonight she would be able to suggest a second phase of the daily plan, which would involve the CalfRobes in monitoring Jake's improvement in this area. Moreover, as Dr. Nelson had pointed out, having the parents review the daily plan sheet would facilitate home-school communication and allow any issues that arose to be noted on the day they occurred.

Hearing the knock on the door, Ms. Bows rose to greet the CalfRobes, confident that their warm smiles were indicative of their willingness to become partners in the inclusive classroom process.

◆ INTRODUCTION

The above vignette underscores the fact that in a successful **school-home partnership** the responses and feelings of both parents and teachers need to be considered. Recent literature suggests that school-home interaction is becoming increasingly collaborative and productive as its benefits are recognized by parents and teachers alike (Shea & Bauer, 1991; Turnbull & Turnbull, 1990). This partnership taps the two most important sources of influence on the child with exceptional needs: the parents, who have invested their time and energy in raising the child and who know the child best; and the educator, who has the professional preparation and experience needed to work effectively with all students.

The benefits of a collaborative partnership between parents and teachers are reciprocal. Parents can provide the teacher with relevant home information that is based on long-term experience. Teachers can use parental knowledge about a child to develop a personalized, individual educational program that can broaden their understanding of the student's learning needs. Moreover, an effective school-home partnership fosters parental support for school goals that are conveyed by the teacher (Shea & Bauer, 1991). When parents are actively involved with the school they gain knowledge of their children's learning abilities and needs, and can better appreciate the teacher's role in accommodating these.

When communicating with parents, the two most critical points for teachers to keep in mind are to be a *good listener* and to *avoid making judgments or blaming parents*. This caution is underlined by Tolan (1987), who asserts that "parents possess vital information professionals may not know, so that it is as important for professionals to listen and learn as to 'explain' and teach" (p. 187). Teachers can inform parents about the special needs and progress of the student at school, as well as about programming strategies that can be supported at home. With an understanding of the shared goals for the child, parents can provide extended educational experiences in the home. Moreover, as parents gain increased experience and competence in using supporting instructional and/or behavioural strategies in the home—and as they become familiar with the efforts and successes of other parents—they will no doubt benefit in terms of their own sense of self-worth (Shea & Bauer, 1991).

In an atmosphere of cooperation, there is less possibility of teachers and parents wasting valuable time and energy in confrontation or in placing blame, as both groups work together as partners in helping the child to learn and grow. *Collaboration* and *shared understanding of goals* underscore the desired partnership of parents and teachers in the successful inclusive school or classroom.

◆ school-home partnership: active collaboration and information exchange between families and school personnel

◆ AGENDA FOR CHANGE

The current view of the school-home partnership—particularly as it concerns parents of exceptional children—has been slow to develop, as the comments of Gorham (1975) testify:

> Although I have learned much, I am clearly one of the last generation of parents of handicapped children. We are parents who are either intimidated by professionals or angry with them or both; parents who are unreasonably awed by them, parents who intuitively know that we know our children better than the experts of any discipline and yet we persistently assume that the professional knows best; parents who carry so much attitudinal and emotional baggage around with us that we are unable to engage in any real dialogue with professionals—teachers, principals, physicians, psychologists— about our children (p. 521).

These remarks are in sharp contrast to those made by Judy Larson, the recipient of the 1986 "Teacher of the Year" award from the Council for Exceptional Children.

> Parents are a very important part of my classroom. They can make the difference between success or failure in the student's attempt to change behavior. The parents of my students are welcome to come into the class, telephone, or set up an appointment to discuss any problems regarding their children. Many times I find myself just listening to their concerns that don't have anything to do with the classroom. The wealth of information parents can provide to help the school staff in working with students can be very helpful. Each time a parent tries to assist in this manner, it renews my faith in the fact that parents do the very best they know how with the skills they have acquired (Larson, 1987).

As described in Chapter 2, over this century there have been significant changes and improvements in the educational service delivery for students with special needs. The role of parents in conjunction with schools has shifted significantly and positively along several dimensions. Turnbull and Turnbull (1990) provide a particularly useful analysis of key role changes that parents have assumed (or have been expected to assume) by educational professionals over the century. They note that views on parental roles have shifted from the very negative view of parents as instigators of their child's disability; to parents as advocacy-group participants; to parents as passive recipients of professional advice; to parents as at-home teachers; and, most recently, to parents as educational decision-makers.

While the impetus for changing the school-home partnership came primarily from parents and parent groups, schools are rapidly coming to recognize that working with parents and inviting their input can contribute significantly to overall program improvement. For example, the research of Nedler and Oralie (1979) shows that students in educational programs that emphasized parental involvement scored significantly higher than comparison groups on achievement tests and intelligence tests. Other research

(Rioux, 1978; Spencer, 1979) has clearly shown that direct parental involvement in the academic program can bring about positive changes in students' self-perceptions and their sense of control over their environment, as well as noteworthy improvement in academic performance.

A lingering problem with the parental role as currently defined is the tendency of educators to view parents solely in relation to the child with the disability. Often overlooked are other family considerations, such as the needs of other siblings and the increased demands that a child with disabilities or special learning needs places on parents. For example, children with severe physical and mental handicaps require substantially more assistance from parents (and for a longer period of time) than do children without exceptional learning needs. Activities such as feeding, toileting, catheterization, medication, lifting, bathing, dressing, and other physical needs are a major part of the daily routine for the parents of a child with severe physical handicaps. Such parents are often additionally burdened with expectations that they will participate in advocacy, political lobbying, and parent-as-teacher roles to ensure that their child is provided an appropriate education. In creating effective working partnerships with the home, therefore, schools must develop viable models that do not impose unrealistic expectations on parents. The following section describes some of the new directions that are being explored to overcome these problems.

◆ FAMILIES IN PERSPECTIVE

A promising development in recent years is the influence of **family systems theory** on school-home partnerships (Turnbull & Turnbull, 1990; Morsink, Thomas, & Correa, 1991; Shea & Bauer, 1991; Carter & McGoldrick, 1980). Consistent with the sociocultural theoretical perspective described in Chapter 3, family systems theory focuses on the complex interactions of four family subsystems: marital, sibling, parental, and extrafamilial (Carter & McGoldrick, 1980). The family system is a dynamic, ever-changing one, and its ability to function effectively "depends on how clearly the boundaries and rules of the family are defined and how cohesive and flexible the family is during life cycle changes" (Morsink et al., 1991, p. 250).

Change is also necessitated by numerous other dimensions within the larger society, with the rate of such change—and the resulting pressures brought to bear on families—being much greater today compared to previous times. Shea & Bauer (1991) contend that we can no longer continue to view the behaviour of family members on a strict cause-and-effect basis. What one family member does or needs may demand some reorganization within the family system, and consequently the roles, expectations, and attitudes of other family members will need to change as well. "Reorganization within the family affects other settings in which the child and other family members spend time, such as the school" (p. 4). For professionals who work

◆ family systems theory: a perspective that focuses on the dynamic and interactive patterns of family life and the impact of family characteristics, family life cycle, and family functions on the exceptional child

with parents of children with exceptional needs, it will be helpful to consider the student from the perspective of the family.

FAMILY CHARACTERISTICS

The birth of a child with a handicap affects all members of the family system, including parents, siblings, grandparents, and friends. Teachers and other professionals who become involved in the education of the child need to take into consideration the broader family system to ensure that interventions and expectations are appropriate. Based on their extensive work with parents and families of children with exceptional needs, Turnbull and Turnbull (1990) have proposed a conceptual framework drawing from family systems theory, which includes four major components: family characteristics, family inter-action, family functions, and family life cycle. The first component, *family characteristics*, includes consideration of the child's exceptionality; the makeup of the family in terms of size, socioeconomic status, and cultural background; personal features such as attitudes and health of family members; and partic-ular challenges such as drug abuse or unemployment.

The nature of the exceptionality—and family attitudes and reactions to it—has a substantial impact on the overall functioning of the family. Parental and family responses to the child's exceptional condition vary considerably, depending on the type of exceptionality, the stage at which the exceptional condition is evident, the severity of the condition, and the degree of impact it has on the normal functioning of the family as a whole. For example, Williams (1983) notes that the prospects for positive parental reaction to learning disability are much better than for more severe exceptionalities. In support of this, Bos and Vaughn (1988) suggest that: "When the child is iden-tified as learning disabled or emotionally handicapped, many parents feel relieved at first, hoping this identification will lead to solutions that will elim-inate the child's learning or behaviour problem" (p. 340).

Although it is often assumed that families with a child of exceptionally high intellectual ability are particularly favoured, according to Tolan (1987), "gifted children are at risk, and while a supportive home environment and the understanding of a few caring adults can minimize that risk, it is difficult to get support for gifted children in pain when the prevailing attitude (even among professionals who work with the gifted) is that gifted children are lucky, privileged and better off than anyone else" (p. 185).

In the case of severe handicap, sensory impairment, or severe multiple handicaps, the family must begin to deal with their feelings and cope with the immediate circumstances right from birth. Emotional reactions might include a sense of isolation, fear, and anxiety (Schuldt, 1975), and related anx-ieties including loss of self-esteem, shame, ambivalence, depression, self-sacrifice, and defensiveness (Roos, 1978).

Gargiulo (1985) describes three phases of parental reaction that are com-monly experienced after the birth of a child with single or multiple handicaps. In the primary phase, the most common response is one of overwhelming shock and disbelief, which is often associated with crying spells and feelings of numbness and helplessness. A typical defensive reaction is _denial_ of the handicap, which can be helpful in cushioning the impact of reality. This is eventually replaced by feelings of grief and depression as parents begin to contemplate an unknown future; at times, there may be a withdrawal response in which normal social affiliations are cut off. Such reactions, while understandable, can thwart the adjustment process if carried on for an extended period.

The second phase of parental reaction is characterized by feelings of ambivalence, guilt, anger, shame, and embarrassment as the family moves forward in the adjustment process. Gargiulo (1985) notes that the "child with disabilities is capable of intensifying the normal emotions of love and anger experienced by most parents toward their children" (p. 24). Negative feelings about the child produce immense guilt on the part of the parent, which can express itself in behaviours ranging from total self-sacrifice to total rejection—behaviours that may jeopardize other family interactions or have severe effects on the marital relationship.

The final or tertiary phase of parental reaction is characterized by a shift to bargaining, which might take the form of a silent vow to devote one's life to the church, or to refrain from drinking alcohol forever, if the child could just be cured. As time passes, there is a reduction of intense emotional response and anxiety, and, as the family participates in the day-to-day living experience, there comes a gradual adaptation and reorganization. It is noteworthy that parents may progress through the above phases of acceptance at markedly different rates—a factor that may be an additional source of stress on school-home interaction.

At the same time as they are experiencing emotional reactions, parents must deal with the numerous additional demands of attending to the daily caring and medical requirements necessitated by the exceptionality. As Kneedler, Hallahan, and Kauffman (1984) describe it, "In addition to dealing with their feelings and others' reactions, for parents there is the physically and emotionally draining task of everyday life with a handicapped child, with its incessant demands and no time off" (p. 343).

Children with severe emotional difficulties or **autism** can tax a family's resources in a somewhat different way. Many of these children require constant supervision to ensure that they do not physically harm themselves or others. Because their behaviours are unpredictable, it may be particularly stressful for families to include such children in everyday activities such as shopping or going on a picnic. Unfortunately, when a child with a severe emotional problem has a tantrum in public, observers are typically unsympathetic, blaming the parents for their lack of control over the child.

Teachers must be prepared to offer support to parents and families when needed. For families in which there is a child with severe single or multiple handicaps, the teacher might assist by telling parents about available

◆ autism: a severe behaviour disorder characterized by extreme self-absorption, withdrawal from reality, and an absence of social and communication skills

community services, or, more specifically, by suggesting behaviour management strategies that can be implemented at home. In the case of a child with a mild handicap, it is often not until the formal schooling years that a diagnosis of special learning needs is made or that a disability becomes apparent; at that time the teacher is most often the primary professional to whom parents will turn for assistance and information. Of course, the way teachers deal with all children who have exceptionalities can have a significant facilitative effect on the child's adjustment and acceptance in the classroom.

While most schools attempt to present information in a clear and open manner, parents may be uncertain of the reasons for their child being identified as different from his or her same-age peers. According to Sapon-Shevin (1987), "The literature[s] of giftedness and of retardation are both plagued by stereotyping and overgeneralization" (p. 182). Parents can interpret the school's labelling of the exceptional child in a number of ways, and this interpretation serves to guide their subsequent reactions and behaviour. Montgomery (1982), who has worked extensively with learning-disabled children, suggests that parents are primarily concerned with social acceptance and the child's future prospects. Of the social-acceptance issue, she notes that parents "are the initiators of their child's sense of self, and [they] are deluding themselves if they think their kids don't pick up on their feelings" (p. 116). Teachers can do much to help parents set realistic expectations for their child.

On the basis of her work with parents of gifted children, Tolan (1987) stresses the importance of informing parents not only about the individual child's needs but also about giftedness in general. A double dilemma for parents of gifted children is that they are often given the responsibility of choosing between special programming or continued regular-class placement when, as Colangelo and Dettman (1983) note, even the experts cannot agree on the benefits and disadvantages of one option over the other.

As emphasized in Chapter 5, children from culturally diverse families may hold different ideologies, values, and feelings, which will require teachers to place more emphasis on providing information, fostering a positive self-image, and encouraging a sense of belonging. Marion (1980, 1985) asserts that educators need to demonstrate an appreciation for the cultural and dialectical differences of the child, a process that may necessitate special teacher support and understanding; moreover, a child's religious affiliation might entail a special diet, rituals, and holiday celebrations.

Beyond considering the child with the exceptionality, it is important for teachers to be aware of the characteristics of the family as a whole. Turnbull and Turnbull (1990) suggest that factors such as family size and form, cultural background, socioeconomic status, and geographic location all affect the degree to which families are able to engage in school-home partnership.

Also important are the individual characteristics of each family member. The physical and mental health of family members has a direct bearing on the family's ability to understand the needs of the exceptional child and to cope with the associated demands and pressures—an ability that can be compromised, for example, by a family member who is engaged in substance abuse. Moreover, statistics indicate that the incidence of single-parent families is on the rise, and economic stresses, coupled with the additional demands of supporting a child with a disability, may seriously hamper school-home collaboration.

Each family is unique in the above respects, and it is the task of the teacher to anticipate this diversity; to seek out creative ways of tapping the strengths and resources of the family; and to cultivate the cooperation and collaboration that will form the basis of a successful school-home partnership.

THE MULTIPLE ROLES OF PARENTS

Parenting is a complex, dynamic process. Turnbull and Turnbull (1990) suggest that professionals working with children who have special needs be especially sensitive to the numerous family functions as they develop student intervention plans. Their family systems model delineates seven major categories: economic, daily care, recreation, socialization, affection, self-definition, and educational/vocational. For Heward, Dardig, and Rossett (1979), contemporary roles of parents include that of teacher, counsellor, behaviour manager, parent of nonhandicapped siblings, spouse, educator of significant others (e.g., relatives, storekeepers, neighbours) and school/community relations person.

Turnbull and Turnbull (1990) note that the developmental stages and transitions of the family life cycle, coupled with related changes in family functions and characteristics, can place additional stress on the family system—stress that can significantly affect the everyday life of the child with exceptional learning needs. Common events in the family system—e.g., the loss of a job, the major illness of a family member, an older sibling leaving home—necessitate adaptations and adjustments in family interactions.

Placing further stress on parents are concerns about the exceptional child—concerns about the child's social-emotional adjustment, about the availability of appropriate educational programs, about the child's prospects for adult independence, and about possible vocational options, to name a few. Many families experience the additional financial burden of having to provide drugs, special clothing, medical supplies, transportation, noninsured health/medical services, tuition/residence fees, attendant home care, and home modification to accommodate the special needs of their child. Not all families have sufficient resources, flexibility, and parenting skills to ensure that the needs and interests of the child are met.

In view of this, teachers who want to promote school-home collaboration should avoid overburdening the parent who has responded positively to such an invitation, while recognizing and accepting that some parents do not have the time to get involved with the teacher and the school.

Having focused on parental responses to a child with an exceptionality, we shift the discussion to consider parental response to the efforts of the schools and school-home partnerships.

FAMILY MEETS SCHOOL

Recent literature (Rizzo & Zabel, 1988; Kroth, 1985; Turnbull & Turnbull, 1990; Shea & Bauer, 1991) stresses the fact that families today are, in both style and structure, considerably different from those of fifty years ago. Marked increases in the number of two-income families and single-parent families present enormous challenges to schools as they attempt to communicate with and involve parents in their child's education program. In view of the complexity and multidimensionality of today's family structure, Rizzo and Zabel (1988) recommend that educators use a classification system of four general types of parents: involved parents, overwhelmed parents, unresponsive parents, and hostile parents.

The majority of parents would be classified as *involved parents*. These are parents who are interested, supportive, and actively involved in helping their child achieve to his or her potential. Parents who are eager to establish school-home partnerships will often become strong advocates for their own child and other exceptional children in the school. Teachers stand to benefit maximally by initiating partnerships with such parents.

Overwhelmed parents characteristically do not have the energy, resources, or possibly the know-how to become actively involved in their child's education. Parents become overwhelmed for a variety of reasons, including repeated unsuccessful attempts at dealing with their child's specific difficulties, or, even more likely, basic survival needs related to chronic economic stress, along with the associated behavioural and emotional responses that arise from circumstances such as being on welfare or living in crowded and substandard housing developments. Rizzo and Zabel (1988) suggest that the school's challenge in this case is to help the parents meet their family's basic needs so that they have sufficient energy left to deal with their child. For example, the teacher might provide the family with a listing of subsidized home-care services, which could free up time for parents to go to a social event, do some shopping, or even attend a parent-teacher meeting. Information about ways of coping more effectively with the child's needs at home, and about available community resources or services, would be of further benefit to these parents.

The last two categories of parents present the greatest challenge for teachers. The sometimes hard-to-recognize *unresponsive parents* may be too preoccupied with their careers or social involvements to attend to the child's needs, or may be intimidated by the school due to their own insecurities about being parents or about their lack of education. Cummings and Maddux (1983) note that some parents may be intimidated because they are members of a minority group (see Chapter 5 for a full discussion of related issues). For example, new immigrants to Canada often do not speak English; in this situ-

Italisized.

ation it is important to seek out interpreter resources for the initial parent-teacher meetings. The teacher's challenge with immigrant parents is to open up communication channels, devise means and options for them to become more involved, and familiarize them with the formal structure and culture of the school.

Hostile parents exhibit an extreme negativism toward the school. The hostility may be overtly or covertly expressed, and stems from a variety of circumstances ranging from bitter memories of their own schooling experiences to dissatisfaction with the diagnostic and/or interventive program or methods used for the child. A particularly difficult situation arises when these parents instil in their child their own negative feelings toward the school, thereby jeopardizing the teacher's efforts. Given the alarming rise of drug and alcohol abuse, teachers may occasionally have to deal with a parent's emotional lability, which is characterized by sharp mood swings ranging from complete despondency to aggressive outbursts or even physical attacks. In a hostile school-parent interaction, the teacher should adopt a calm and straightforward approach that focuses on defusing the conflict and engaging in active problem-solving to determine ways of accommodating the child's learning needs.

While by no means exhaustive, the above categories of parents can be useful in helping the inclusive education teacher appreciate (and anticipate) that each family has a unique configuration and, as such, will have unique responses to the school. As we have seen, the family system framework can provide a solid foundation for the inclusive education teacher to plan and promote an effective school-home partnership. However, past experience has shown that certain factors tend to work against the establishment of such partnerships. These will be briefly reviewed in the following section.

BARRIERS TO SCHOOL-HOME COLLABORATION AND POSSIBLE SOLUTIONS

Despite the fact that the *concept* of school-home partnership has emerged as a positive and mutually beneficial arrangement, the literature suggests that it will take time and much continued effort on the part of both families and teachers if they are to become true partners in education. A recent survey by Jowett and Baginsky (1988) revealed that many of the perceived barriers to school-home interaction were more teacher-related than parent-related; the study cited such factors as teachers not having time to develop these relationships; teachers not giving priority to this aspect of their work; and teachers having a general apprehension about working with parents and families. In another survey, Kaufman and Sexton (1983) found that in a sample of ninety-eight parents of gifted children, 45 percent had encountered a teacher whom they felt was unsympathetic to the special needs of their gifted child.

In the interests of improving school-home relations, Vaughn, Bos, Harrell, and Lasky (1988) recommend that schools adopt a framework that allows for varying levels of parental involvement, suggesting that "[v]ariables such as the severity of the child's handicapping condition, the age of the child, and the needs of the parents may best determine the type and level of parent involvement" (p. 89). Planning for improved school-home involvement requires an in-depth assessment of what both parties can realistically offer. For example, Shea and Bauer (1991) have developed a parent needs form, which surveys many of the common concerns expressed by parents of exceptional children, and which can be an effective means of establishing successful school-home partnerships. The survey should be written from the perspective of the parent. For example, a statement such as "I would like to know more about my child's exceptionality" might include the following response choices:

_____ I prefer to have written information.
_____ I prefer to observe my child in class and discuss observations following.
_____ I prefer individual parent/teacher meetings.
_____ I prefer formal presentations by school experts.
_____ I prefer to meet with parents of children with similar exceptional needs.

Each survey statement should include a blank space for the parent to fill in preferred options that have not been listed.

We conclude this section with some observations by Kroth (1985), who has had several years experience teaching and working with teachers and parents in the public schools:

1. There will never be enough money to do the things that need to be done.
2. Time will always be lacking for both parents and professionals to work toward desired goals.
3. Even with training programs already in place, there probably will never be enough trained personnel to satisfy parents or staff.
4. Parents of exceptional children are not a homogeneous group and should not be treated like one.
5. All parents of exceptional children have strengths to be used, and all have needs to be met (p.10).

Keeping these points in mind, the following section will focus on the strengths that parents bring to the school-home relationship.

◆ STRENGTHS PARENTS BRING TO SCHOOL-HOME PARTNERSHIPS

AUGMENTING SCHOOL PROGRAMS AT HOME

There is ample evidence to suggest that the participation of parents in promoting programs at home has far-reaching and positive effects. Parental support can take many forms: from nurturing the child's academic motivation, to implementing a behaviour management program, to promoting effective study strategies, to providing basic academic tutorial assistance. Often parents will approach the teacher for advice about a particular problem or concern they have observed in the home. This type of situation offers the teacher an ideal opportunity to develop collaborative approaches that will capitalize on parental desire to bring about positive changes for the child, and, under the guidance of the teacher, complement aspects of the child's functioning in the school program.

For example, the frequency with which parents have reported difficulty in managing their exceptional child's behaviour extremes has led Kaufman and Sexton (1983) to recommend that behaviour management techniques be given greater emphasis in schools. They further suggest that parents acquire intervention skills that will extend the benefits of such efforts. Research shows that parents can be successfully taught to use a variety of techniques for improved management of behaviour and adjustment problems (Evans & Evans, 1983; Swassing, 1984, 1987; Moore & Bailey, 1973).

Although programs vary according to the needs of the student and the resources available at home and school, a program implemented by Evans and Evans (1983) outlines the important components of behavioural change programs that teachers and parents could use. The first step involves the gathering of information to identify the exact problem. Although the teacher is the best source for observations about the day-to-day behavioural functioning of the child, other school professionals, such as counsellors or school psychologists, might be involved in this stage of the program. Once the focus has been determined, teachers and parents meet and collaborate in the development of procedures to deal with the problem. It is important that the response to behaviours is consistent at home and at school.

The second step involves program implementation in the home. Parents are typically asked to keep a daily behavioural log in which all instances of the specified behaviour are noted. After a set period, parents and teachers meet to review the program and procedures and make adjustments as required. If there are particular instances of difficulty in the implementation at home, teachers might invite parents into the classroom to observe procedures being used. Observations of effective behaviour management modelled by the classroom teacher can be confirmed in a followup discussion meeting and prepared for in-home implementation.

In some programs, a **token economy system** has been successfully used to involve parents directly in the management of their child's behaviour (Thompson & Fairchild, 1985). In this type of system, behaviour change is rewarded, for example, through the allocation of points that can be exchanged for some desirable activity such as watching television, attending a hockey game, or making a particular purchase. The parents, the student, and the teacher should all be involved in the planning and design of this system. Involving parents in this and other behaviour management approaches provides a consistent response to the child's behaviour at home and school,

◆ token economy system: a reward and cost program that encourages appropriate behaviours by bestowing or removing tokens, contingent on student response and fosters collaboration on selected goals for the child. A further benefit of this approach is that it facilitates open communication and ongoing dialogue between parents and teachers.

Parents can also contribute to the effectiveness of school programs by providing academic tutoring at home (Shapero and Forbes, 1981; Williams, 1983). The present need for services for exceptional students far outweighs the availability of professionals; parents can be instrumental in filling this gap. Training parents to work with their children also allows professionals more time to engage in activities other than working on a one-to-one basis with each child, thereby multiplying the overall effectiveness of professional input. Despite Bos and Vaughn's (1988) caution that parent in-home tutoring programs may, if parents lack the proper instructional skills, impose such pressures on the child so as to impede academic and social progress at home and at school, recent reports about these programs have been most encouraging.

In reviewing parent in-home tutoring programs, Jowett and Baginsky (1988) found that the areas of reading, math, home economics, computers, and preschool learning activities were most frequently pursued. The majority of the initiatives were on an ad hoc basis, with the primary impetus coming from the school. By far the most widespread direct involvement activity for parents of elementary school children was reading. Parental involvement takes a different form at the high-school level, with parents being increasingly invited to contribute their particular expertise in areas that relate directly to the school curriculum; the most popular areas in this regard are career education and work experience.

There are many specific examples in the literature of useful methods that facilitate parents' ability to assist in their child's academic and social development at home (Nystul, 1987; Strickland & Taylor, 1989; Shapero & Forbes, 1981). For example, Strickland and Taylor (1989) discuss the advantages and importance of family storybook reading and how this type of activity, when practiced regularly in the home, supports literacy development. Parents can positively augment school programs by providing enrichment experiences for their child, such as trips to the local museum, historic-based holidays, or regular visits to the public library. In a similar vein, Bos and Vaughn (1988) suggest that summer programs can be a valuable extension of schooling.

◆ positive parenting princi-ples: procedures followed by parents to create mutual learning and sharing experi-ences between themselves and their children

In the social development area, Nystul (1987) provides an excellent overview of a parent-centred approach to counselling emotionally disturbed children. By receiving small-group or individual instruction in **positive parenting principles**, and key instruction in creating a positive environment at home, parents learn to take on an active role in the child's therapy program. This approach emphasizes greater understanding of the child's motivation and perspective in discerning the factors behind the child's misbehaviour. The resulting continuity in the home and school program can expedite the rehabilitation process.

In summary, teachers must explore the pros and cons of involving parents in home-based programs. As Williams (1983) puts it, educators must learn to "balance the fact that parents are powerful teachers and models in their own right against the dangers of burdening them with a job they may have few skills for, undermining their important nurturing function" (p. 505).

PARENTS AS VOLUNTEERS IN SCHOOL

Many schools have implemented, or have considered implementing, parent volunteer programs. This type of parental involvement is one of the most common means of fostering school-home collaboration, and the literature suggests that such programs can provide many positive results for both parents and teachers.

For example, parent volunteers who assist in the classroom and are introduced to present-day instructional programs and materials can positively apply this knowledge to their exceptional child. In addition, day-to-day association with the school can increase parents' understanding of their own child's perceptions of the school environment and their place within it, and perhaps provide a more realistic sense of the problems faced by other exceptional students.

For the teacher, the potential help from a well-planned, well-organized parent volunteer program is immeasurable. Activities such as helping children to select library books, assisting students with individual research projects, or listening to a youngster read aloud can save hours of the teacher's time to devote to professional duties. Other nonteaching tasks such as lunchroom supervision, equipment or school materials repair, assisting students with winter outerwear, and organizing art materials can substantially reduce teacher preparation time. Parents who are unable to devote their time during the school day can participate in activities such as telephoning parents, sewing costumes or art aprons, or saving materials that can be recycled for classroom use. To maximize parental support, the school should devise a master list of possible activities, using as a reference listings suggested in the literature (Shea & Bauer, 1991; Berger, 1981).

Heron and Harris (1982) suggest that using parent volunteers for teaching tasks can reduce the teacher-student ratio in the classroom, thus freeing up the teacher's time for the more needy students. The benefits of this type of involvement were seen during a summer school program for children with learning disabilities at the University of Alberta (Lupart & Mulcahy, 1978). Children from rural communities stayed in the university residence with their parents for a three-week period and attended a remedial program during the day. Assessment was carried out and the master teacher planned individualized programs for each student. Parents were invited to volunteer their time to work with other children in the program, and to help carry out the learning goals that had been established for each child. Not only did the program benefit from parental participation, but the parents themselves came to realize that the children had just as much—sometimes more—difficulty than their own child; by helping another child with his or her learning difficulties, parents gained a better understanding of their own child's learning problems.

The current trend toward inclusive education within the general classroom underscores the need for parental assistance in the classroom. In a study that examined the impact of different forms of parental assistance, Thomas (1985) assessed classes with no parent involvement, classes with traditional parent involvement, and classes with room management (RM). Under room management, in a set period during the day, parents were designated specific roles such as individual helper, which involved working on a particular teaching activity with an individual child. Other parent roles included an activity manager, who was responsible for engaging other students in group instructional activities, and another individual who performed a wide variety of tasks—e.g., setting up equipment and cleaning up spills— that kept the individual helper and the activity manager free of distraction. All of these roles allowed the teacher to focus instructional time on individuals who most required assistance. Thomas (1985) found that engagement levels (the degree to which students were on task or demonstrating relevant behaviours) and individual teaching time were doubled using the RM procedures.

PARENTS AS PARTICIPANTS IN PARENT GROUPS

As an alternative to becoming involved at the school level, parents can join a local or national association for parents in specific areas of exceptionality. (The major Canadian parent associations are listed in Appendix 7.1.) Organizations such as the Learning Disabilities Association of Canada (LDAC) provide parents with a variety of services, including information services, regular meetings, conferences, and summer camps for children. A teacher can help interested parents by informing them about local or nation-wide associations, in which, it should be further noted, many teachers and other professionals have memberships.

Commenting on the impact of parent groups, Dessent (1987) points out that while schools can ignore the suggestions of teachers, educational psychologists, and other professionals in the educational system, they cannot ignore input from the very people they are paid to serve. Indeed, many of the special education services that are currently available to exceptional students in Canada are the direct result of the appeals to school boards and governments that were made by local parent associations. Dessent (1987) cautions, however, that this kind of organized lobbying can lead to an adverse situation in which special education policy "is being formed around parental choice and parental pressure rather than any overriding educational or ethical principles" (p. 140). There must be a reasonable balance between the parental desire to push for first-class educational services and the professional experience and expertise needed to facilitate this goal.

Another option that teachers might suggest to parents is participation in parent education and/or parent training programs, which are available in many local communities. Programs can range from informal, teacher-initiated discussion groups to formal courses in which parents are taught various skills. A detailed discussion of these programs is offered later in this chapter.

No .

PARENTS AS ADVOCATES

Legislative Advocacy

Advocacy as it appears in the United States is defined and explained by Davis (1980) as

> [a] program in which agencies or individuals, serving mostly as volunteers, act on behalf of the interests of others, e.g., child advocates. Generally the major goal of an advocacy program is to ensure that the rights of a particular individual or group are protected. As a result of federal and state legislation and litigation in recent years, advocacy programs for the handicapped are developed at a rapid rate. Advocates for the handicapped frequently function in such areas as school placement, housing discrimination, vocational placement and barrier-free access to public buildings (p. 8).

1. School placement
(2) Housing discrimination.
3. Vocational placement
4. Barrier-free access
*   to public buildings*

Parental advocacy was highly influential in the development of U.S. federal legislation, known as the Education for All Handicapped Children Act (Public Law 94-142), which was passed in 1975. PL 94-142 has had considerable impact on the Canadian context. Bunch (1984) notes that since 1969 six provinces had taken measures to mandate special education services for all children. Ontario's Bill 82, for example, clearly specifies the rights of parents and contains a number of concepts that parallel those encompassed in PL 94-142. It is disappointing to note, then, that parental involvement in educational matters such as decision-making, program implementation, and advocacy for improved programs is not widely practiced in Canadian communities (Mitchell, 1983).

General.

This problem is underlined by recent U.S. surveys which suggest that legislative action to encourage parents of children with exceptional learning needs to become more involved with the schools may not be enough. For example, McKinney and Hocutt (1982) compared the involvement of parents who had learning-disabled children with that of parents of nonexceptional students, using a questionnaire in combination with a structured interview. They found that the two groups were relatively similar with respect to involvement in educational matters. The major factor distinguishing them was the involvement of the former group in the development of the Individual Education Program (IEP). Disappointingly, it was revealed that these parents were minimally involved in IEP development, with one quarter of the sample being unable even to recall the document. While the intent of PL-142 was to encourage parent participation in developing acceptable programs for children with exceptional needs, the actual implementation is still far off the mark.

The above findings were similar to those of Vaughn et al. (1988), who carried out an in-depth investigation of parent participation in the initial placement/IEP conference in light of the mandated involvement—PL-142—in the United States. Twenty-six conferences of parents of students with learning disabilities were observed. Observational data included the time parents spent asking questions, commenting, and responding to other team members, as well as structured interviews. The authors found that parents asked few questions and responded little during the conferences, and, in the structured interview, indicated that they were satisfied with the conferences and had no further questions.

Public Law 94-142 was enacted to reaffirm the legitimate, if not essential, role of parents to participate fully in the education of their exceptional children. The above studies by McKinney and Hocutt (1982) and Vaughn et al. (1988) suggest that in the United States this goal is not being realized in practice. Perhaps Canadian educators and parents can learn from the U.S. experience by deferring legislative means to enable parent participation in the education of exceptional children and focusing instead on other productive channels for parental advocacy, such as the community advocacy approach described next.

Community Advocacy

The recent literature suggests a growing trend toward community advocacy (Miezio, 1983; Gallagher, 1983). Gallagher (1983) defines advocacy by parents of highly able children as "a set of activities designed to change the allocation of resources to improve opportunities for the education of gifted and talented students. Advocacy, then, seeks to modify existing financial or program patterns" (p. 1). Advocacy participants can be divided into clusters of interest groups such as advocacy through parenting, advocacy in the schools, or advocacy in the community (Gogel, 1983); whatever the makeup of the advocacy group, the major emphasis is on what Tannenbaum and Neuman (1980) and Nathan (1976) call *organized persuasion*.

The efforts of community advocates can be directed at the local, provincial, or national levels; advocacy within the latter two levels may be aligned with the broader goals of existing groups such as the Ontario Action for Bright Children or the Learning Disabilities Association of Canada. However, advocacy can take place wherever there is a group of people who are concerned about the advancement and improvement of educational provisions for students with exceptional learning needs.

It is hoped that as the philosophy of inclusive education is increasingly adopted by schools—and is better understood by parents and communities—that advocacy efforts will no longer be based on categorical designations, but rather on the recognition of a common goal: to provide educational experiences that will foster independence in students and allow them to reach their full learning potential.

PARENTS ON LOCAL ADVISORY COMMITTEES

Increased parental involvement in the schools has led educators to reassess the many ways that parents might contribute to school activities and programming. Most school districts in Canada have a long history of electing parents as school board members or school trustees who are responsible for monitoring district policy and finances. Another way of encouraging parent input, which is currently being adopted in numerous schools and school districts, is through the invited participation of parents on local advisory committees.

Mayer (1982) recommends that local advisory committees have a balanced membership that represents different geographic areas, different types of exceptionality, and different types of expertise. These committees normally include parents, administrators, and educational and community professionals, and all participants need to work collaboratively in developing school policy or a specified mission. The local advisory committee should maintain a high level of positive visibility in the school district, and communicate regularly with both educators and the general public. Committee members should be prepared to attend meetings, to represent the views of the community, and to become actively involved in committee work.

Jowett and Baginsky (1988) undertook a major survey of parental involvement in education in England and Wales. Questionnaires were sent to all local education authorities (LEAs), and school visits and case studies of particular developments in some of the districts were included in their analyses. The information they gathered provides an excellent overview of some of the obstacles—as well as the benefits—of involving parents in the schools. Major benefits noted by primary and secondary teachers included:

- Improves parents' understanding of schools and education.
- Improves pupils' attainments.
- Allows parents to share the knowledge of their own children with the teaching staff.
- Allows parents to learn from the teaching staff how to help their children.
- Develops "open" schools that are resources in the community.
- Makes schools more sensitive to local needs and opinions (p. 42).

Major obstacles included:
- Teaching staff who do not have time to develop this work.
- Parents who are apprehensive about schools.
- Teaching staff who do not give priority to this aspect of their work.
- Teachers who are apprehensive about working with parents.
- Parents who do not have time available for involvement (p. 44).

Obstacles notwithstanding, local advisory committees can be an effective resource for creating school-home partnerships. Teachers can facilitate the establishment of local advisory committees by bringing together interested parents and school members to discuss the possibility of forming this type of committee.

◆ INFORMATION SHARING: THE EVOLUTION OF THE TEACHER'S ROLE

A necessary prerequisite to healthy parent-teacher interaction is the sharing of information about the child's learning and academic progress. This exchange is particularly important when students with exceptional learning needs are involved. Over the past twenty years, we have seen a significant evolution in the special education teacher's approach to sharing information with parents.

In a recent study, McCarney (1986) examined the preferred types of communication for parents and teachers of emotionally disturbed students. The study found that parents and teachers differed significantly on ten out of twenty possible communication means. Parents and teachers were in agreement in their preference for three forms of communication: parent-teacher conferences at school, phone calls from teacher to parent, and phone calls from parent to teacher. Similarly, both groups rated parent-group meetings, Parent-Teacher Association (PTA) meetings, and parent-teacher meetings other than those held at school or home as being the least preferred means of communication. The most notable items of disagreement were parents' preference for open house at school and report cards, and teachers' preference for parent-teacher conferences, which include other professionals, and individual educational program-planning meetings. The result of this and other studies has been a shift from one-way school-home communication toward two-way communication systems in today's schools.

ONE-WAY VERSUS TWO-WAY INFORMATION SYSTEMS

Teachers have traditionally used report cards and the like to inform parents and document their child's academic performance. Such practice allows for only minimal family interaction, which can result in unnecessary misunderstanding due to unanswered questions on the part of concerned parents. For example, Sapon-Shevin (1987), in describing the implications of information sharing with respect to the concerns of parents of gifted students, notes that

> [w]hen professionals inform parents that their child is "gifted," they share bits and pieces of professional terminology and jargon; how much or how little they convey to parents and the accuracy of what they share and what parents take away with them, may have a significant effect on parent's understanding, perceptions, attitudes toward and expectations for their child (p. 182).

It is important that teachers become sensitive to parents' information needs. This can be facilitated through two-way information sharing.

Edge, Strenecky, and Mour (1978) argue that two-way information systems are preferable to one-way systems in that they foster interactive participation by parent and teacher, and help in the development of constructive educational programs. Edge et al. (1978) point out that information sharing gives teachers the benefit of parents' insights into their child's learning potential, as well as input concerning the child's attitudes, behaviour at home versus school, motivations, and interests. Such information can help the teacher to better individualize the student program and thus accommodate to the particular **learning style** of the child. As parents become more familiar with the teaching procedures and learning goals specified for their child, they can enhance and complement the educational program by providing consistency at home.

◆ learning style: cognitive style of learning (reflective, impulsive, abstract, representational, concrete) and the preferred sense of modality (visual, auditory, tactile, cross-modal)

In a similar vein, Jowett and Baginsky (1988) recommend that the two-way communication approach include such activities as involving parents in developing homework policy; inviting parents to curriculum meetings hosted by the various department heads in a given school; holding PTA meetings and seminars; scheduling consultation meetings with parents to coincide with the issuing of student reports; and having parents check and sign homework timetables and/or diaries. Eby and Smutny (1990) further suggest that the school host monthly or quarterly meetings, for parents as well as the larger community, that focus on new ideas and critical feedback on programs that are in place.

yes

TEACHERS AS INFORMATION SHARERS AND FACILITATORS

The present-day role of the teacher in information sharing has evolved well beyond even that of the two-way information system. Today's teacher not only promotes parental input, but works as a facilitator, mediator, and resource person to connect parents with other professionals and resources that may be of support to the special-needs child. A teacher might initiate any number of actions, from providing information about a new grant system to fund tutors for disabled students, to suggesting the need for an in-depth reading assessment, to setting up a parent education program on behaviour management techniques, to putting parents in contact with a local parent group. This level of information sharing between parents and teachers would make them true partners in education.

◆ WHERE DOES A TEACHER START?

Following an extensive review of the research on parents and families of gifted children, Colangelo and Dettman (1983) concluded that despite the fact that parents desire greater involvement in the education of their children, "the schools have not always provided direction for participation; when such direction has been provided, it has not been specific enough to be fruit-ful" (p. 25). It is sometimes a frightening prospect for a teacher to accept increased parent interaction and involvement. Schools, districts, and counties vary considerably with respect to tradition, attitudes, and willingness to explore new ways of interacting with parents. Some teachers are fortunate to be part of a system that has traditionally adopted a philosophy of openness and invitation to parents. In this case, a working partnership with parents of exceptional children should be relatively easy to establish. On the other hand, if the school or system has a policy of strict regulation of (and limited access to) school records, as well as minimal parental involvement, then a teacher will need to thoroughly assess options for initiating information sharing with parents. The following section presents some of the options currently available to teachers and schools.

◆ SCHOOL-HOME COMMUNICATION POSSIBILITIES

TEACHERS INITIATING PARENT CONTACT

There are many simple methods teachers can use to signal to parents their interest in creating a system of information sharing and establishing a working liaison.

Newsletter

Class and school newsletters can be used as a general means of establishing contact with parents, and may be a particularly effective way for a new or inexperienced teacher to inform parents about major programs and approaches being used in the class, or to provide tips to parents (Imber, Imber, & Rothstein, 1979). Other information might include scheduled events, sample work of students, notice board, program descriptions, or, as Cummings and Maddux (1983) suggest, items of interest about parents.

Telephone

A quick and direct way of sharing information is to simply telephone the parent. If the teacher has a concern about a child, a phone call to the parents can help to confirm or dispel this concern while at the same time provide the first step toward the planning of a personal meeting or parent-teacher conference. Cummings and Maddux (1983) recommend telephone contact with parents who are either too busy or too unmotivated to attend parent-teacher meetings; teachers should make a followup call to inform parents about how their suggestions have been incorporated.

Effective and creative use of the telephone to increase parental interaction with the school has been reported in the literature. Heron and Axelrod (1976), for example, implemented a word-recognition program with inner-city school children and were able to show significant gains in progress for those students whose parents were daily reinforced by phone calls in which they were praised for assisting with their child's word-recognition assignments, as well as by feedback on the previous day's performance.

Another creative method of using the telephone, as reported by Bittle (1975), involved installing a telephone answering service at the school for use in a research project to improve student performance on spelling tests. By providing the student with a spelling word list and making this list available to parents via recorded telephone messages, the percentage of students obtaining perfect scores in spelling was significantly higher than when spelling word lists alone were used. Heron and Harris (1982) note that telephone answering systems are relatively inexpensive to install and maintain; are reliable in that the taped information can be accessed directly by parents without the mediation of the students; and are flexible because parents—especially working parents—can use them at their own convenience.

Notes, Letters, Diaries, and Logs

Written feedback to parents is a more traditional form of communication, often taking the form of a report card or letter to parents. Instead of expressing the negative aspects of the child's involvement at school, written feedback can be more positively used, for example, to praise the student's progress in a home-school behaviour-improvement project, or to denote achievement in the form of an award certificate. Written notes can provide a permanent record of student performance, and can serve as a basis for parents to initiate comment or relay information to the school.

yes

In cases where teachers would like to involve parents in particular behavioural or academic goals, a behavioural card system, a home-school note program, or a shared daily log system might be implemented. Imber et al. (1979) found that sending teacher praise notes home and having parents respond in a positive and consistent manner resulted in improved academic performance by their children. Parent acknowledgement of the child's accomplishments at school and praise delivered in front of family members can be a powerful incentive for repeat performance.

Before implementing a card or note system of parent-school communication, parents and teachers should meet to establish procedures (e.g., how often a note will be sent, what type of ratings or points are required to receive a reward), guidelines, and specific goals of the program. Table 7.1 exemplifies a daily progress card that can be used cooperatively by parents and teachers to help the child improve on predetermined academic and/or behavioural goals. Alternatively, Carpenter, Fathers, Lewis, and Privett (1988) describe a diary system that was used by support teachers for severely handicapped students who were being integrated into regular classrooms. Daily summaries of the child's activities were written up and sent home to parents, thus giving them ongoing knowledge that possibly could not have been provided by a severely disabled child. Regular teachers may choose to adapt and use this system as a means of promoting parental involvement.

Table 7.1 Daily Progress Card	
Student: _____	Date: _____
SUBJECT & TASK	EVALUATION
	Completed
	Accuracy
	Behaviour
	Completed
	Accuracy
	Behaviour
	Completed
	Accuracy
	Behaviour
	Completed
	Accuracy
	Behaviour
	TOTAL
COMMENTS	

Involving Involved Parents

NO

Cummings and Maddux (1983) suggest having involved parents talk to other parents who have not responded to the teacher's attempts. Involved parents can be very influential in assuring reluctant or apathetic parents that the school is interested in their child and willing to listen to their concerns. Parents who have been directly involved in the classroom, and who have a familiarity with the child's work, are recommended for this type of project.

Special Parents' Day

Cummings and Maddux (1983) further suggest that teachers set aside a day each week to honour an individual student's parent or parents. This could take the form of a Parent of the Week program in which the parents are invited to some special recognition activity; alternatively, such days could focus on the unique talents, hobbies, or careers of the parents being honoured. The central message to be communicated through these kind of activities is how important parents are to a child's success.

PARENT-TEACHER CONFERENCES

Parents and teachers have reported mixed feelings about parent-teacher conferences, ranging from fear and anxiety to anticipation at the prospect of working together to help the child. Given the fact that parent-teacher conferences are standard practice in most schools, negative attitudes on either side must be addressed.

Heward and Orlansky (1984) suggest that the successful parent conference is one that is carefully prepared and organized. The goal is to provide a means of exchange for both parent and teacher to collaborate in the development of the student at home and at school. Without considerable planning for this type of exchange, conferences can easily be reduced to the level of a social visit. In a major study by Dembinski and Mauser (1977), members of a parent group suggested how professionals might improve communication with parents:

yes

- Be straightforward with parents and avoid educational jargon.
- Involve both parents where possible.
- Provide reading material to help the parent better understand the child's problem.
- Present and review all written reports concerning the child.
- Contact other professionals who are also working with the child.
- Provide concrete and relevant advice on handling management and learning problems.

Teachers who are inexperienced in conducting parent conferences, or who are meeting a parent for the first time, might consider using the form shown in Figure 7.1 to structure the interview time. The type of information that can be elicited using this form will give the teacher a working knowledge of the student's unique family system, which can be important in the development of personalized learning. Teachers can find specific guidelines for conducting parent-teacher conferences in a number of sources (Turnbull & Turnbull, 1990; Kroth, 1985; Gallagher, 1979; Faas, 1980; Heward & Orlansky, 1984), and the following list provides a summary of these, as well as additional suggestions.

Planning the Conference

- The inexperienced teacher can role-play an interview with more experienced colleagues prior to the conference.

Figure 7.1
Parent Conference Summary Sheet

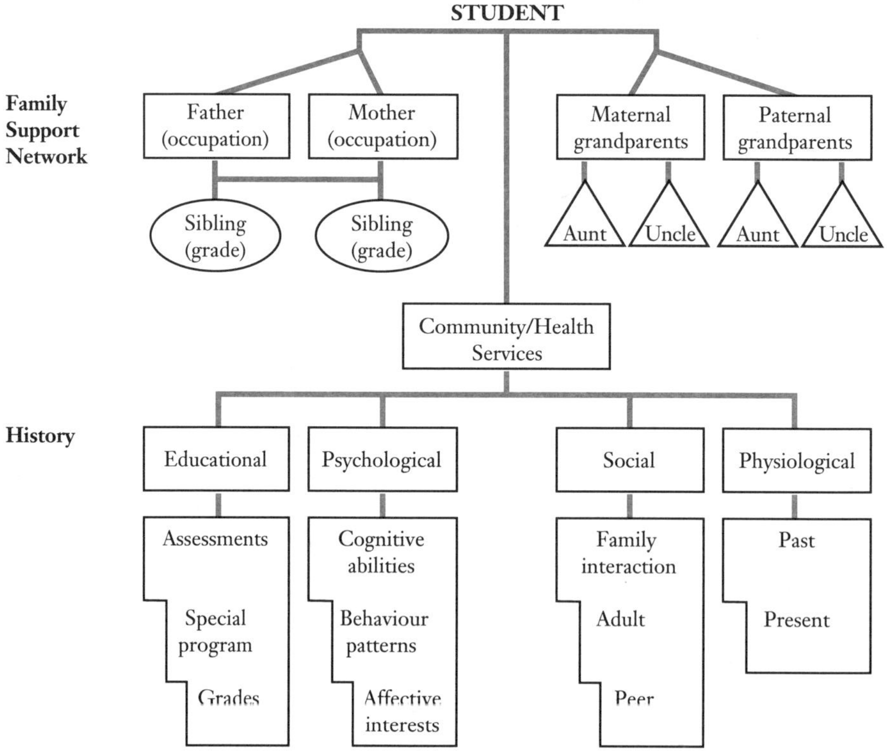

- Collect samples of the student's work to exemplify best, worst, and most characteristic performance.
- Assemble informal and formal assessments, as well as written reports, concerning the child.
- Review cumulative records as well as records or anecdotal notes from previous conferences.
- Have a written plan for discussion. This could be set out to include areas of strength; areas that have shown improvement; areas that require more attention; specific questions for parents concerning the child's behaviour and performance at home; and suggestions for helping the child.
- Schedule conferences well ahead of time, requesting both parents to attend, and indicate the amount of time available to them.
- If several conferences are scheduled, provide seating for waiting parents, and plan for interim time of approximately five minutes to make notes about the completed conference and to prepare for the next conference.

Conducting the Conference

- Start the meeting with a few minutes of casual conversation to create an easy, open atmosphere.
- Indicate the general areas that you wish to cover and begin as planned.
- Avoid jargon; speak in a clear, concise manner.
- Restrict note-taking to a minimum, but record all major plans and actions to be carried out.
- Give parents the opportunity to look at all work samples, assessment results, and written reports, and invite questions that may arise from these.
- Listen carefully to the parent, accepting the expression of feelings, attitudes, and ideas; refrain from judging parents or showing disapproval of their comments.
- Give positive feedback and encouragement to parents and convey your desire to have this active interest in the child's school experience continue.
- Avoid comparing the child to other classmates, especially older brothers or sisters.
- Take time at the end of the conference to summarize the discussion and review plans for specific and cooperative action to be taken by both parent and teacher.
- Establish plans and times for followup communication or further meetings.

No

Followup and Evaluation

- Immediately following the conference, fill out main points mentioned by parents, as well as pertinent summary notes.
- Review predetermined conference objectives and evaluate whether the goals have been met.
- Consider possible ways to improve the effectiveness of interactions, and jot ideas down in preparation for future meetings.
- Make sure that the appropriate teachers or school personnel are informed of plans or decisions resulting from the conference.
- Begin to carry out plans and provide feedback to parents as progress is noted, or if alterations in plans are necessary.

No

STEPS IN ESTABLISHING A VOLUNTEER PROGRAM

Teachers who are interested in establishing a volunteer program need to consider a number of factors. Programs can vary in their design and scope. They can be initiated by the individual teacher, or they might be part of a larger school or school division-based program. Teachers with limited experience should restrict initial programs to only one or two areas, and perhaps limit their hours of operation to a modest portion of the day or week. On the other hand, schools and school districts that are planning—or have already operationalized—large-scale programs for parents and paraprofessionals should implement proper in-service orientation, obtain adequate support from school administrators, and maintain proper and continuing supervision on the part of the teacher or the educational consultant. Precautions such as these are critical to the ultimate success of the program.

Step 1: Establish Program Goals

Before implementing a parent-volunteer program, the teacher/school should determine the design and goals of the program. Once established, these goals, along with a working model for program implementation and scheduling, should be reviewed and approved by school administrators.

Step 2: Inviting Parents to Volunteer

yes

Volunteers can be solicited by the teacher in a number of ways. Ideally, the entire school staff should be involved, perhaps through contributing suggestions for volunteers at a school staff meeting. Often the individual teacher sends an invitation to all parents requesting volunteer assistance. The parent volunteer invitation, exemplified in Appendix 7.2, should include a brief statement of the need and value of parental assistance, and list a wide variety of activities that can be undertaken in the classroom, and for those parents who are unavailable during the school day, a listing of tasks and activities that can be carried out in the home. Examples of alternative forms appear in Shea and Bauer (1991) and Berger (1981).

Table 7.2 Planning Card System	
Individual Session Plan	
Tutor:	
Student:	
Date:	Time:
Exercise(s):	Materials:
Comments:	

Step 3: Organization and Scheduling

In organizing and scheduling times and materials, the teacher should draw up a master timetable that lists parents' names and volunteer times. For programs that concentrate on tutorial work with individual students, a planning card system (see Table 7.2 on previous page) can be used to inform parents of concepts that will be covered. For programs that comprise a number of volunteer tasks and volunteers, the teacher could use a large blackboard to indicate tasks to be completed.

PARENTAL COUNSELLING

It is difficult to sort out where the role of the teacher ends and the role of the counsellor begins in interaction with parents of special-needs children. In alerting parents to the special learning needs of their child, it is sometimes necessary for the teacher to assume a dual role of teacher/counsellor. Shapero and Forbes (1981), who undertook a review of the literature on programs for parents of learning-disabled children, found that counselling approaches were typically **educational**, **interpretive**, or **habilitative**. They found that studies based on the latter two dimensions were generally more positive, and that the use of praise and **maternal counselling**, used in conjunction with academic tutoring, were significant factors in improving students' school performance.

Bos and Vaughn (1988) note the importance of communication skills in working with parents and colleagues, and yet there is typically little formal training of this sort provided in teacher preparation programs. Despite their lack of formal training in counselling, teachers can make a significant contribution to the goals of parental counselling as outlined by Gargiulo (1985), Stewart (1986), and Dettman and Colangelo (1980).

For example, Dettman and Colangelo (1980), in their discussion of counselling parents of gifted children, describe three different approaches that can be adopted in a teacher/counsellor role. The *parent-centred approach* focuses primarily on the motivation and resources of the parent, while the *school-centred approach* finds its emphasis in school-based long-term programs that benefit large numbers of gifted students. The *partnership approach* is described as the most effective and promising in that it "synthesizes the influences and resources of the home and school, [and] requires active participation from both parents and counsellors" (p. 159). The fact that parent and teacher are actively involved in joint decision-making in the educational planning process is of ultimate benefit to the gifted child, who receives clear and consistent messages at home and at school. In contrast, Stewart (1986) suggests that the counselling needs of parents of mildly and moderately handicapped children focus on such aspects as "information about their child, the nature and degree of the handicap, educational planning, and future prognosis" (p. 142).

- ◆ educational counselling: counselling approach that centres on the provision of information to parents

- ◆ interpretive counselling: counselling approach in which parents are shown how to interpret the behaviours of their child

- ◆ habilitative counselling: counselling approach in which professionals inform parents about habilitative home activities and behaviour management training, and in which the child's academic achievement is de-emphasized

- ◆ maternal counselling: a problem-solving approach for mothers of hearing-disabled children

The literature recommends that teachers undertake counselling only when parents indicate a readiness for it. Bos and Vaughn (1988) provide the following principles for establishing effective communication with parents who *are* ready for counselling:

♦ *Acceptance.* Convey to parents that what they are saying is valued.

♦ *Effective listening.* Active listening for *real content* and *feeling* in the parent's message, with periodic restatement for mutual clarification.

♦ *Effective questioning.* Use open questions such as who, what, when, where, and why to foster full responding on the part of the parent.

♦ *Providing encouragement.* Look for positive anecdotes or feedback to use in parent meetings, and try to open and close the session with such items.

♦ *Stay directed.* Follow the lead of the parents and stay focused on issues relating to the child's school performance. If more serious matters are revealed, teachers should urge parents to pursue the services of professionally trained counsellors.

♦ *Develop a working alliance.* Teachers can facilitate the school-home partnership by regular positive information exchange with parents and other professionals regarding the progress of the student (adapted from pp. 341-343).

No

Gargiulo (1985) points out common practices that can be barriers to the development of effective helping relationships; the more serious ones include advice-giving, moralizing, ridiculing, sarcasm, scolding, and threatening, and should be avoided in all cases.

PARENT EDUCATION PROGRAMS

♦ parent education: training programs that range from formal courses in child development and parenting skills to informal discussions about parental participation in a child's education

The goal of **parent education** is to extend parents' knowledge of their child's learning problem, as well as to convey the school's role in the education of the child (Hardman, Egan, & Landau, 1981). For parents who desire school counsel and consultation in helping to cope with the many challenges a child with exceptional needs presents, educators might consider initiating an informal parent education program to specifically address these concerns. The cooperative planning of a parent and school advisory board can ensure that the selection of topics is relevant. Kroth (1985) suggests that a parent education program might include such topics as classroom policies, procedures, and techniques; grading procedures; specialists and their role; related outside agencies as resources; and possibly a session on how parents can become active participants in the education process. The delivery method for such programs can vary substantially, from a seminar format to a local educational television production.

Advisory board members may choose to involve parents directly by creating, as Hardman et al. (1981) suggest, a menu of topical choices to be ranked in order of preference by all interested parents in the school community. Hardman et al. (1981, p. 37) further suggest that choices be provided

from three categories: (1) understanding your exceptional child; (2) the school curriculum; and (3) community services available.

According to Cummings and Maddux (1983), parent education groups can be particularly helpful for parents who are intimidated by parent-teacher conferences or IEP meetings. (These may be uneducated parents or parents of minority groups or parents who do not speak English well.) The authors recommend that educational films, knowledgeable speakers, and panel discussions be used at parent education meetings to inform parents of their part in the educational decision-making process; complimentary coffee might be served after the meeting to promote informal exchange between teachers and parents. It is critical that teachers and other school staff avoid professional jargon, which can be intimidating to parents. Cummings and Maddux (1983) further suggest that parents who have extensive knowledge about their own child's exceptionality be invited to share their expertise by speaking to parent groups and in-service meetings; another possibility might be to involve these experienced parents as consultants to work with parents of children with similar learning needs.

An innovative approach to parent education has been initiated at the University of Calgary through a continuing education course entitled **Parents and Gifted Education (PAGE)** (Lupart, 1990), which is intended for parents of gifted children. Various local experts in the field cover such topics as resources for parents and children, advocacy, assessing individual needs, and choosing the best school for your child. Through such programs parents can receive information about their own child, as well as a summary or overview of the present status of various issues that are pertinent to the area of gifted education. Karnes and Karnes (1982) suggest that it may be advantageous for parents of gifted students to form a discussion group, or a local chapter of a regional or national organization committed to gifted education, that will keep them informed about program possibilities and enable them to participate effectively with educators in the formulation and implementation of plans for gifted education.

◆ Parents and Gifted Education (PAGE): approach to parent education adopted at the University of Calgary, in which gifted parents request and review information pertinent to gifted education

PARENT TRAINING PROGRAMS

Hardman, Egan, and Landau (1981) define **parent training** as "specifically developing functional skills in parents through a variety of training techniques … [including] such areas as communication skills between parent and child, managing and motivating appropriate behaviour and other related skills" (p. 37). Parents of exceptional children have been taught to cope more effectively with their child's problems through various means, including in-depth instruction on how to carry out home teaching, as in the Portage Project in the United States (Cameron, 1989); training in the use of behaviour modification techniques (McLoughlin, 1982); and instruction using commercially prepared parent training kits such as the Systematic Training for Effective Parenting (STEP) kit developed by Dinkmeyer and McKay

◆ parent training: developing functional parenting skills in parents through a variety of training techniques

(1976). A few relevant examples will serve to illustrate the typical format and benefits of various parent training programs.

McLoughlin (1982) conducted a study to ascertain the advantages and disadvantages of using parents as behavioural change agents in working with their behaviourally disordered children. He found that there is ample evidence to support parent training programs that are directed at children who have a variety of academic, social, and behavioural difficulties. While acknowledging that more research is needed in this area, McLoughlin (1982) recommends that parent training programs continue to be offered, especially since service demands in behaviour modification greatly exceed service supply. Moreover, he notes that "[o]nce parents can assume the role of behavioural modifiers, they may become the primary, continuous, and inexpensive treatment personnel" (p. 833).

Wolf (1987) describes a workshop program for parents that helped parents become more knowledgeable about their gifted children, provided them with skills for working effectively with school personnel, and increased their advocacy for gifted education. The workshops varied from intensive two-and-a-half-hour sessions to full-day workshops based on discussion, anecdote review, and role-playing activities. Results were positive in that parents felt they were better informed about their child; were more positive about interacting with school personnel; and were generally more satisfied with their child's educational service. Wolf (1987) concludes that increased attention needs to be given to the provision of parent training programs, and that a workshop-based approach can be particularly effective in this regard.

As an example of commercially prepared training programs, the Systematic Training for Effective Parenting (STEP) by Dinkmeyer and McKay (1976) provides nine topical study sessions that are designed for groups of ten to twenty parents. The overall objectives of the program are to foster parent-child relationships that promote responsibility, self-reliance, cooperation, mutual respect, and self-esteem. Parents are provided with handbooks containing readings and exercises that are associated with each of the nine topics. After listening to cassette recordings of family interactions that relate to the principle of the session topic, parents are invited to discuss their reactions and experiences. The nine topics that are dealt with in the program are:

1. Understanding children's behaviour and misbehaviour.
2. Understanding how children use emotions to involve parents.
3. Encouragement.
4. Communication: listening.
5. Communication: exploring alternatives and expressing ideas and feelings to children.
6. Developing responsibility.
7. Decision-making for parents.
8. The family meeting.
9. Developing confidence and using potential.

Whatever means a school or school district may choose for their parent training programs, the major focus of all such programs is to teach small groups of parents selected problem-solving skills in a straightforward, hands-on manner. Kroth (1985), a noted expert in this area, suggests that the advantages of parent training groups are fourfold:

1. Parents benefit by the realization that others have problems similar to their own.
2. The opportunity to convey and discuss intense reactions or emotions resulting from the knowledge of the child's handicap can help to diffuse such stresses.
3. Advice that is given by others facing problems similar to the individual parent may be more readily adopted than that of professionals or other authorities.
4. Group training sessions serve to maximize the time of group leaders (pp. 165–168).

 yes.

Schools can decide either to establish their own parent training program(s) or to use one of the many available commercial training kits. In the former event Stephens (1977) provides the following guidelines:

1. Use a consistent theoretical model.
2. Determine parental skills to be mastered in advance.
3. Allow for varying rates of learning by parents.
4. Employ a systematic and functional approach.
5. Provide followup (p. 425).

◆ SUMMARY

This chapter has provided a review of a number of options that are available for both parents and teachers who are interested in establishing effective parent-teacher partnerships. It should be clear to the reader that the general trend is toward closer ties between the school and home, and that many options for involvement exist. The benefits of school-home partnerships have been well documented, and in the event that no such partnership is in place, the teacher should be encouraged to initiate one. The following lists for parents and teachers provide a review of the major points of discussion in this chapter. The first set might be a helpful resource for teachers who have been approached by a parent looking for information about home-school collaboration.

SUMMARY POINTS FOR PARENTS OF STUDENTS WHO ARE EXCEPTIONAL

◆ Make clear to the teacher the extent of your willingness to become involved with the school.

- If you wish to have better understanding of your child's special learning needs, approach the teacher for advice on how to obtain such information.
- If you are not satisfied with the progress of your child, request an interview with the teacher, and write out a list of your concerns for review at the meeting.
- Ask the teacher for advice concerning home-based followup of educational or behaviour management programs, and request assistance regarding materials and teaching procedures before implementing such a program.
- If you are interested in the general improvement of educational services in your child's school, consider volunteering your help or sitting on a parent advisory committee.
- Consider joining a local parent group or parent training program in order to meet and share experiences with other parents who have children with similar learning needs and/or behavioural problems, as well as to learn functional skills to manage such problems.
- Be aware of the rights of the child to receive the best education program possible, and act on behalf of the child to ensure that the school is providing this.

SUMMARY POINTS FOR TEACHERS OF STUDENTS WITH EXCEPTIONAL NEEDS

- Be aware of the parental perspective and appreciate the extra demands that a child with special learning needs may bring.
- Avoid labelling parents as "overly concerned" or "busybodies"; this only serves to create barriers to school-home relations.
- Convey your willingness to establish a school-home partnership with parents through promotion of two-way communication.
- Become familiar with school and community resources that may be helpful to the parent, and make this information available to them.
- Critically assess the level of school-parent interaction at your school and work toward the continued development of such interaction.
- Consider initiating parent contact through use of newsletters, telephone, notes, diaries, letters, or logs.
- Make the most of parent/teacher conferences by careful planning; by paying attention, during the conference, to conference goals and parent ideas, attitudes, and feelings; and by incorporating followup and evaluation procedures.
- Be prepared not only to inform parents about their child's problems, but to help them cope with their emotional reactions as well.
- Support school or parent efforts to establish parent education and parent training programs.

QUESTIONS
◆◆◆◆◆◆◆◆◆◆◆◆◆

1. What are the benefits of a successful school-home partnership?

2. How might a teacher encourage a reluctant parent to participate as a team member in his or her child's education?

3. Suggest school procedures and activities in which parents could be involved.

4. "School-home collaboration may be adversely affected by the complexity of today's families." Discuss.

5. How does the family systems perspective affect school approaches to programming for children with exceptional needs?

◇ APPENDIX 7.1

CANADIAN PARENT ASSOCIATIONS

The Association for the Gifted-Canada (TAG)
The University of Calgary
Department of Educational Psychology
2500 University Drive N.W.
Calgary, AB. T2N 1N4

Association of Visual Language Interpreters of
Canada (AULIC)
House 144
11337-61 Avenue
Edmonton, AB. T6H 1M3

Autism Society Canada
Suite 2, 20 College Street
Toronto, ON. M5G 1K2

Canadian Association for Adult Education
29 Prince Arthur Avenue
Toronto, ON. M5R 1B2

Canadian Association for Community Living
Kinsmen Building
York University
North York, ON. M3J 1P3

Canadian Association for Young Children
83 Baker Ave.
Richmond Hill, ON. L4C 1X5

Canadian Cerebral Palsy Association
880 Wellington Street
Suite 612, City Centre
Ottawa, ON. K1R 6K7

Canadian Council for Exceptional Children
#750, 2 Robert Speck Parkway
Mississauga, ON. L4Z 1H8

Canadian Cystic Fibrosis Foundation
2221 Yonge Street
Suite 601
Toronto, ON. M4S 2B4

Canadian Diabetes Association
78 Bond Street
Toronto, ON. M5B 2J8

Canadian Down's Syndrome Society
Box 52027
Edmonton Trail RPO
Calgary, AB. T2E 8K9

Canadian Hard of Hearing Association (CHHA)
2435 Holly Lane
Suite 205
Ottawa, ON. K1V 7P2

Canadian Home & School & Parent-Teacher
 Federation
323 Chapel Street
Ottawa, ON. K1N 7Z2

Canadian Mental Health Association
North Central Region
9th Floor, 10050-112 Street
Edmonton, AB. T5K 2J1

Canadian National Institute for the Blind
1929 Bayview Avenue
Toronto, ON. M4G 3E8

Canadian Paraplegic Association
Suite 201
1500 Don Mills Road
Toronto, ON. M3B 3K4

Epilepsy Canada
P.O. Box 1560
Station C
Montreal, PQ. H2L 4K8

Learning Disabilities Association of Canada
323 Chapel Street
Ottawa, ON. K1N 7Z2

National Educational Association of
Disabled Students
Carleton University
44th Floor, Unicentre
Ottawa, ON. K1S 5B6

◆ APPENDIX 7.2

PARENT VOLUNTEER INVITATION

(Name Of School) Volunteer Form

Student Name: ————————   Date: ————————

Parent/Guardian: ————————   Phone: ————————

Meaningful parental involvement is a vital part of the fabric of public education, with numerous benefits for parents, staff, and, most importantly, the students. Please consider helping at our school as we value your participation in activities and projects. Listed below are topics and activities generally believed to be of interest to parents. We invite you to check all those areas in which you wish to volunteer.

Instruct at Our School

Tutor Students
———— learning/remedial tasks   ———— bicultural/bilingual education
———— math lab   ———— science lab

Instruct Class
———— individual   ———— small group
———— large group

Develop Lesson Plans
———— lesson content   ———— reference material
———— instructional method   ———— student grouping

Prepare Materials
———— worksheets   ———— flashcards
———— drills   ———— displays
———— prepare/operate audio-visual equipment
———— organize learning centres
———— grading (quizzes, assignments, record-keeping)

Support Our School

Raise Funds
———— telephoning   ———— lobbying
———— project organization

Assist Directly
———— construction/repairs   ———— library
———— housekeeping   ———— administer tests
———— clerical (typing, sorting mail, attendance, inventories)

Supervise
———— field trips   ———— lunchroom
———— playground

Be a Resource
———— poetry appreciation   ———— music
———— arts and crafts   ———— horticulture
———— cooking   ———— carpentry
———— homemaking   ———— career information
———— other

Be Involved Politically
———— writing letters   ———— advocacy
———— lobbying (local, regional, provincial, federal)

Help with Social/Cultural Events
———— assemblies   ———— concerts
———— dances   ———— sports days
———— dinners   ———— holiday celebrations

Instruct At Home
Tutor
———— make and use learning activities
———— make instructional materials (games, puppets, charts)
———— problem-solving   ———— behaviour management
———— record-keeping   ———— home-study/homework materials

Do Summer Reading Projects
———— material to read over summer
———— weekly assignments

Use Resource Centres
———— check out games/materials for home use

Construct Idea Lists
———— conversion of home activities into learning experiences
———— cut out/catalogue pictures for instruction
———— assemble book lists

Be an Advisor
Curriculum
———— review curriculum materials/plans

Budget
———— budget allocations/program choices
———— plan/organize fund-raising

Personnel
———— screening of paraprofessionals

Parent Activities
———— coordinate parent-volunteer program
———— type and amount of involvement
———— monitoring/evaluation of parent programs

Be a Committee Member

_____ career education   _____ educational innovations

_____ athletic programming   _____ public relations

_____ school transportation   _____ work-study programs

_____ parent support group   _____ student-teacher relations

_____ extra-curricular activities

Educate Parents

Attend Workshops/Symposiums

_____ child development   _____ stress management

_____ sex education   _____ parenting skills

_____ nutrition   _____ family relations

_____ communication skills   _____ home safety

_____ training program in observation

_____ social problems (drug/alcohol abuse, family violence)

Attend Education Classes

_____ adult studies   _____ vocational/business training

_____ General Education Development

Join Field Trips

_____ museums   _____ industries

_____ legislature

Construct Materials

_____ newsletters   _____ professional resources

_____ texts/articles

Other topics and activities of interest to me are: _____

Preferred time:

_____ daily   _____ once per week   _____ twice per month

_____ once per month _____ other

	Morning	Afternoon	Evening
Monday	_____	_____	_____
Tuesday	_____	_____	_____
Wednesday	_____	_____	_____
Thursday	_____	_____	_____
Friday	_____	_____	_____
Weekends	_____	_____	_____

Your comments, concerns, and questions are welcome.

Thank you!

REFERENCES

Berger, E. H. (1981). *Parents as partners in education: The school and home working together.* St. Louis, MO: C. V. Mosby.

Bittle, R. G. (1975). Improving parent-teacher communication through recorded telephone messages. *Journal of Educational Research, 69*, 87-95.

Bos, C. S., & Vaughn, S. (1988). *Strategies for teaching students with learning and behaviour problems.* Boston: Allyn & Bacon.

Bunch, G. (1984). Special education in Canada: An overview. In D. D. Hammill, N. R. Barel, & G. O. Bunch (Eds.), *Teaching children with learning and behaviour problems* (Canadian edition). Toronto: Allyn & Bacon.

Cameron, R. (1989). Teaching parents to teach children: The Portage approach to special needs. In N. Jones (Ed.), *Special educational needs review* (pp. 82-96). London: Falmer.

Carpenter, B., Fathers, J., Lewis, A., & Privett, R. (1988). Integration: the Coleshill experience. *British Journal of Special Education, 15*, 119-121.

Carter, E.A., & McGoldrick, M. (Eds.). (1980). *The family life cycle: A framework for family therapy.* New York: Gardner Press.

Colangelo, N., & Dettman, D. F. (1983). A review of research on parents and families of gifted children. *Exceptional Children, 50*, 20-27.

Cummings, R., & Maddux, C. D. (1983). How to get parents involved in your program. *Academic Therapy, 19*, 227-233.

Davis, W. E. (1980). *Educator's resource guide to special education.* Boston: Allyn & Bacon.

Dembinski, R. J., & Mauser, A. J. (1977). What parents of the learning disabled really want from professionals. *Journal of Learning Disabilities, 10*, 578-584.

Dessent, T. (1987). *Making the ordinary school special.* London: Falmer.

Dettman, D. F., & Colangelo, N. (1980). A functional model for counseling parents of gifted students. *Gifted Child Quarterly, 24*, 158-161.

Dinkmeyer, D., & McKay, G. P. (1976). *Systematic training for effective parenting.* Circle Pines, MN: American Guidance Service.

Eby, J. W., & Smutny, J. F. (1990). *A thoughtful overview of gifted education.* New York: Longman.

Edge, D. , Strenecky, B. J., & Mour, S. I. (Eds.). (1978). *Parenting learning problem children: The professional educator's perspective.* Columbus, OH: NCEMMH, The Ohio State University.

Evans, W. H., & Evans, S. S. (1983). Using parents in behaviour management. *Academic Therapy, 19*, 37-41.

Faas, L. A. (1980). *Children with learning problems: A handbook for teachers.* Boston: Houghton Mifflin.

Gallagher, J. J. (1983). A model of advocacy for gifted education. In J. J. Gallagher, S. N. Kaplan, & I. S. Sato (Eds.), *Promoting the education of the gifted/talented: Strategies for advocacy* (pp. 1-10). Ventura, CA: Ventura County Superintendent of Schools Office.

Gallagher, P. A. (1979). *Teaching students with behaviour disorders: Techniques for classroom instruction.* Denver: Love Publishing.

Gargiulo, R. M. (1985). *Working with parents of exceptional children: A guide for professionals.* Boston: Houghton Mifflin.

Gogel, E. M. (1983). Community advocacy: Advocacy through parenting, advocacy in the schools, or advocacy in the community. In J. J. Gallagher, S. N. Kaplan, & I. S. Sato (Eds.), *Promoting the education of the gifted/talented: Strategies for advocacy* (pp. 27-36). Ventura, CA: Ventura County Superintendent of Schools Office.

Gorham, K. A. A. (1975). A lost generation of parents. *Exceptional Children, 41*, 521-525.

Hardman, M. L., Egan, M. W., & Landau, E. D. (1981). *What will we do in the morning?: The exceptional student in the regular classroom.* Dubuque, IA: W. C. Brown.

Heron, T. E. , & Axelrod, S. (1976). Effectiveness of feedback to mothers concerning their children's word recognition performance. *Reading Improvement, 13*(2), 74-81.

Heron, T. E., & Harris, K. C. (1982). *The educational consultant: Helping professionals, parents and mainstreamed students.* Boston: Allyn & Bacon.

Heward, W. L., Dardig, J. C., & Rossett, A. (1979). *Working with parents of handicapped children.* Columbus, OH: Merrill.

Heward, W. L., & Orlansky, M. D. (1984). *Exceptional children: An introductory survey of special education* (2nd ed.). Columbus, OH: Merrill.

Imber, S. C., Imber, R. R., & Rothstein, C. (1979). Modifying independent work habits: An effective teacher-parent communication program. *Exceptional Children, 46*(3), 218-221.

Jowett, S., & Baginsky, M. (1988). Parents and education: A survey of their involvement and a discussion of some issues. *Educational Research, 30*, 36-45.

Karnes, F. A., & Karnes, M. R. (1982). Parents and schools: Educating gifted and talented children. *The Elementary School Journal, 82*, 236-248.

Kaufman, F. A., & Sexton, D. (1983). Some implications for home-school linkages. *Roeper Review, September*, 49-51.

Kneedler, R. D., Hallahan, D. P., & Kauffman, J. M. (1984). *Special education for today.* Englewood Cliffs, NJ: Prentice-Hall.

Kroth, R. L. (1985). *Communicating with parents of exceptional children: Improving parent-teacher relationships* (2nd ed.). Denver, CO: Love Publishing.

Larson, J. (1987) An inside look at the 1986 Clarissa H. Hug teacher of the year: An interview with Judy Larson. *Teaching Exceptional Children, 19*, 37-39.

Lupart, J. (1990). Parents and gifted education (PAGE): A program for parents of gifted children. *Agate, 4*(2), 16-20

Lupart, J., & Mulcahy, R. (1978). Optimizing learning for the full year: A summer school program for children with learning difficulties. *The New Horizon, 12*, 27-29.

Marion, R. L. (1980). Communicating with parents of culturally diverse exceptional children. *Exceptional Children, 46*, 616-623.

Marion, R. L. (1985). Working with parents of the disadvantaged or culturally different gifted. *Roeper Review Symposia Series, No. 1*, 25-27.

Mayer, C. L. (1982). *Educational administration and special education: A handbook for school administrators.* Boston: Allyn & Bacon.

McCarney, S. B. (1986). Preferred types of communication indicated by parents and teachers of emotionally disturbed students. *Behavioural Disorders, February*, 118-123.

McKinney, J. D., & Hocutt, A. M. (1982). Public school involvement of parents of learning-disabled children and average achievers. *Exceptional Education Quarterly, August*, 64-73.

McLoughlin, C. S. (1982). Procedures and problems in behavioural training for parents. *Perceptual and Motor Skills, 55*, 827-838.

Miezio, P. M. (1983). *Parenting children with disabilities: A professional source for physicians and guide for parents.* New York: Marcel Dekker.

Mitchell, D. R. (1983). International trends in special education. *Canadian Journal on Mental Retardation*, 33, 6-13.

Montgomery, E. (1982). To parents of children with learning disabilities ... Some insights from a teacher's perspective. *The Journal of School Health*, *52*, 116-117.

Moore, B. L., & Bailey, H. (1973). Social punishment in the modification of a pre-school child's "autistic-like" behaviour with a mother as therapist. *Journal of Applied Behaviour Analysis*, *6*, 497-507.

Morsink, C. V., Thomas, C. C., & Correa, V. I. (1991). *Interactive teaming: Consultation and collaboration in special programs*. New York: Merrill.

Nathan, C. (1976). Constructive ways to work with the establishment: How "organized persuasion" works for the gifted in public education. In K. Coffey, G. Ginsberg, C. Lockhart, D. McCartney, C. Nathan, & K. Wood, *Parents speak: On gifted and talented children* (pp. 17-25). Ventura, CA: Ventura County Superintendent of Schools Office.

Nedler, S. E., & Oralie, D. M. (1979). *Working with parents: Guidelines for early childhood and elementary teachers*. Belmont, CA: Wadsworth.

Nystul, M. (1987). Strategies for parent-centered counseling of the young. *The Creative Child and Adult Quarterly*, *12*, 103-110.

Rioux, J. W. (1978). Parents and educator—A forced or natural partnership? *The Directive Teacher*, *1* (Fall).

Rizzo, J. V., & Zabel, R. H. (1988). *Educating children and adolescents with behavioural disorders: An integrative approach*. Boston: Allyn & Bacon.

Roos, P. (1978). Parents of mentally retarded children: Misunderstood and mistreated. In A. P. Turnbull & H. R. Turnbull III (Eds.), *Parents speak out: Views from the other side of the two-way mirror*. Columbus, OH: Merrill..

Sapon-Shevin, M. (1987). Parenting: Points of view. *Roeper Review*, *9*, 180-184.

Schuldt, M. (1975). "I'll never do that." *Exceptional Parent*, *5*, 6-10.

Shapero, S., & Forbes, R. H. (1981). A review of involvement programs for parents of learning disabled children. *Journal of Learning Disabilities*, *14*(9), 499-504.

Shea, T. M., & Bauer, A. M. (1991). *Parents and teachers of children with exceptionalities: A handbook for collaboration* (2nd ed.). Boston: Allyn and Bacon.

Spencer, T. L. (1979, March). *Parent involvement in education: Practical applications of research*. Bloomington, IN: Phi Delta Kappa, 1.

Stephens, T. M. (1977). *Teaching skills to children with learning and behaviour disorders*. Columbus, OH: Merrill.

Stewart, J. C. (1986). *Counseling parents of exceptional children* (2nd ed.). Columbus, OH: Merrill.

Strickland, D. S., & Taylor, D. (1989). Family storybook reading: Implications for children, families, and curriculum. In D. S. Strickland & L. M. Morrow (Eds.), *Emerging literacy: Young children learn to read and write*. Newark, DE: International Reading Association.

Swassing, C. S. (1984). Helping your child adjust to junior high school: A home-school contingency plan. *The Pointer*, *29*, 4-7.

Tannenbaum. A. J., & Neuman, E. (1980). *Reaching out: Advocacy for the gifted and talented*. American Association for Gifted Children. New York: College Press.

Thomas, G. (1985). Room management in mainstream education. *Educational Research*, *27*, 186-191.

Thompson, C. L., & Fairchild, T. (1985). A home-school token economy plan. *Elementary School Guidance & Counseling*, *December*, 141-146.

Tolan, S. S. (1987). Parents and "Professionals": A question of priorities. *Roeper Review*, *9*, 184-187.

Turnbull, A. P., & Turnbull, H. R. III(1990). *Families, professionals, and exceptionality: A special partnership* (2nd ed.) Columbus, OH: Merrill.

Vaughn, S., Bos, C. S., Harrell, J. E., & Lasky, B. A. (1988). Parent participation in the initial placement/ IEP Conference ten years after mandated involvement. *Journal of Learning Disabilities*, *21*, 82-89.

Williams, E. (1983). The family. In C. R. Smith (Ed.), *Learning disabilities: The interaction of learner, task and setting*. Boston: Little, Brown.

Wolf, J. S. (1987). Workshops for parents of the gifted. *Roeper Review*, *9*, 243-246.

PREPARATION FOR TEACHING AND LEARNING

PART 4

A NOTE FROM THE AUTHORS

As we have pointed out, the merger of regular and special education requires educators to consult and collaborate with one another, and adapt instruction to meet the diverse needs of students in the mainstream. The purpose of this section is to present information about adaptive instruction and to provide educators with a resource for teaching and student learning in an inclusive classroom. An important aspect of adaptive instruction is the ability of the teacher to make complex judgments throughout the day about students' learning and behaviour and to collect and record information about students' academic and social performance and progress. Chapter 8 discusses these aspects of adaptive instruction, and presents a model that can guide teachers toward making effective decisions.

Adaptive instruction also requires teachers to accommodate students' needs, to provide effective instruction, and to deal with various types of behaviour. Chapter 9 discusses these management issues within the context of teaching. Chapter 10 discusses students' skills and difficulties with respect to word identification, oral language, reading, writing, spelling, and mathematics, and presents teaching suggestions for improving students' abilities in these domains. In addition, this chapter describes and critiques the most common approaches used to develop students' academic competence in the above curricular areas, with reference to the theoretical affiliations of these approaches.

Finally, in Chapter 11, we examine program planning in terms of curriculum requirements; selecting, monitoring, and evaluating teachers' materials and instructional programs; recording and reporting program progress; and designing educational programs.

THE CHANGING FACE OF ASSESSMENT

*No But read anyways.
diff - formative/summ*

CHAPTER OBJECTIVES

To determine when it is appropriate and necessary to begin an extensive assessment process.

To differentiate between the purpose and usefulness of maintaining teacher-directed and student-directed information collections.

To identify a number of information-collection techniques.

To identify some guidelines for obtaining parental permission, storing and maintaining information, and sharing information with other professionals.

To develop a frame of reference to interpret assessment information, and to use it for multiple purposes such as instructional planning and reporting to parents.

Interview Segment (no instruction occurring)

Q: When you need to write a word that you can't spell, what can you do to figure it out?
A: Sound it out.
Q: Yes, you can sound it out. What is another way?
A: Take it apart.
Q: What do you mean by "take it apart"?

Notes on a Work Sample Interview (sample completed with teacher assistance)

Ms. Bannon prepared a series of exercises in which she printed letters that Kelly previously had been forming incorrectly. She also included others that were shaped correctly. Kelly was asked to find the letters that were printed correctly and the ones that needed to be changed. In addition, Ms. Bannon asked Kelly to com-

plete a printing exercise. After Kelly finished, he was asked to find the letters he thought were well formed (his best letters) and those he thought could be improved.

In examining Kelly's efforts, Ms. Bannon noted that he was able to identify the majority of his intentional printing errors; however, Kelly still had difficulty identifying several incorrectly printed capital letters and the letter "t" in lowercase form. After completing the assigned printing exercise, Kelly was able to identify those letters he had printed "the best," explaining his response in terms of appropriate spacing, form, shape, and height. For example, in considering a lower-case "p" he explained that it was "good, because the tail is below the line and the head is on it." Ms. Bannon noted that he continued to have some difficulty printing upper-case letters (Y, U, and J) and that further work was needed when making "z," as it continued to take a variety of forms, including "≤" and "≥." Ms. Bannon observed that Kelly's printing is continuing to improve, although his hand becomes "tired" easily, as he finds holding a pencil awkward. Kelly continues to make "A," "f" and "t" from the bottom up rather than starting at the top of the letter and printing down.

◇ INTRODUCTION

Recently three general questions have been asked about educational practice for students with special needs: (1) Where should teachers meet students who require support?; (2) How often should they meet with them?; and (3) What kind of instruction should they provide during such meetings? The proposed solutions to these problems will change as the 21st century begins, yet patterns of practice are emerging now. First, the meeting place of teacher and exceptional student is likely to be, for at least part of the school day, the regular classroom. Second, although the frequency of contact with students who have special needs will vary, in the most cases it will be daily given that these students will be members of the regular classroom. Finally, while reservations may be expressed by classroom teachers about providing instruction to students with special needs (Anderson & Bachor, 1990), a commonly held conviction is that exceptional individuals should be given every opportunity to learn the subject matter that is taught to their nonexceptional peers (Gartner, & Lipsky, 1987; Stainback, Stainback, Courtnage, & Jaben, 1985; Thomson, Ward, & Gow, 1988).

As a consequence of the above shifts in the location for instruction, the frequency of contact, and the scope of the curriculum, assessment practices are being reviewed and revamped (Bachor, 1990; Reason, Farrell, & Mittler, 1990). The repercussion of this shift in assessment is that the future evaluation of students with special needs will probably have little resemblance to past practices. It will become more formative and less summative; that is, the primary purpose of collecting information will be to help in making ongoing instructional decisions (formative) rather than reaching conclusions about what has been learned (summative). When necessary, the formative approach to assessment will be supplemented with other information that will be required to place the abilities of individuals with special needs in perspective, and to make decisions such as establishing priority when allocating extraordinary services.

The vignettes provided at the outset of this chapter reflect some of the changes that are occurring in evaluation practices and are illustrative of the assessment techniques presented in the following pages. The procedures shown in the vignettes are ones that teachers can use to collect information on any student in their classroom. As well as these two techniques of interviewing and obtaining work samples, other forms of information collection are discussed, along with methods to interpret the obtained results. Evaluation (or assessment) is viewed from the perspective of the regular classroom

No.
but read it
anyways.
-italitized

teacher and the school-based resource teacher working cooperatively as they strive to retain the special-needs student in a classroom with other students who are approximately the same age. *Assessment* consists of measurement, judgment, and decision-making (Wilson & Rees, 1990).

In this context, *measurement* is the process of information collection. In our daily life, any number of things are measured regularly, such as determining a child's height, pouring a cup of milk for a recipe, or choosing the correct size of shoe to buy. When measuring, we apply a standard of comparison that may be implicit or explicit. It is important to know, for example, if we have added enough milk to a particular dish—where the standard to be met is the amount suggested in the recipe—as that part of the dinner may fail.

When applied to the classroom, further considerations arise. First, the nature of the information (what is measured) can be diverse. A teacher may observe and record classroom performance. He or she could interview students about what problem-solving techniques they use in completing a mathematics assignment or in writing a composition. Students may be asked to examine their expectations and accomplishments to monitor how and what they learn. Alternatively, they could be asked to take a test as an indication of their achievement. Second, the accuracy of the obtained classroom information is often uncertain. Compared to determining a child's height, it is much more difficult to measure how someone is learning, or even *what* someone has learned. Thus, measurement specialists have been proposing standards of technical adequacy to assist in this area (Bachor and Crealock, 1986).

As an illustration of some of the things that need to be considered when checking technical adequacy, take the example of a couple purchasing curtains for a window in their residence. Before making the purchases, they measure the window. To ensure that the curtains will fit properly, they measure both the height and width of the window a second time. This second check, which is to determine the accuracy of measurement, is known as completing a *test-retest reliability check;* the objective is to ensure that the obtained measurement is the same on two or more occasions. If they were to measure the top and bottom of the window (or the two sides) to ensure they were the same size, they would be conducting a check for *internal consistency*; this time the purpose would be to determine if a window is the same size across its entirety. While minor differences in measurement would likely not affect the size of curtain purchases, it would influence their choice if they were to replace the window itself.

Validity can be understood in the context as well. If the couple wanted curtains for the bedroom window but measured the bathroom window instead, they may have reliable measurement in that it could be accurate; however, the probability of buying the correct size of curtain would be small, especially if the windows were different sizes. Similarly, when assessing a student, precautions must be taken to ensure that measurement is reliable and valid. A teacher wishing to measure whether some students understand a component of mathematics—division for example—might have them read instructions from the textbook. How well they read and understand the instructions could influence the probability of obtaining a reasonable measure of their knowledge of the operation of division. The measure may be reliable, but there is a chance that it will be invalid.

To assist us further in this regard, fair-test practices are currently being developed for use in Canada and should be available in 1993 (Joint Advisory Committee, 1993). Meanwhile, the standards for quality and fairness proposed for use in the United States can be applied in Canada (ETS, 1987). These standards can be helpful when establishing local policies on confidentiality of information or when checking the technical quality of tests prior to administering them. Maintaining student confidentiality is increasingly important as teachers become aware of the implications of the emphasis on individual rights advanced in the Canadian Charter of Rights and Freedoms (Section 1). Guidelines to ensure confidentiality are provided later in this chapter.

Once information collection is completed, the next task is to make judgments about the results. Judgments in the classroom are complicated by the fact that classrooms are dynamic and ever changing—that is, as students interact with teachers and their peers, they change as they learn. As educators, our goal is to encourage this growth and our assessment practices need to reflect this goal. Issues about expectations (or standards) will need to be raised.

Consider, for example, three questions that could be raised by a Grade 3 teacher. She or he will want to have a notion of the normally expected variations that occur in a child, such as, (1) What kind of behaviour is reasonable to expect at this age?; (2) When should multiplication facts be acquired?; or (3) When should a carefully crafted paragraph be expected? To help make decisions as to what standards to set, and to ensure some degree of uniformity across classrooms, provincial guidelines (such as the benchmarks recently developed for Ontario, or the primary program guidelines associated with the Year 2000 program in British Columbia), local curriculum guides, and **scope and sequence charts** continue to be developed. Such standards are useful approximations of the range of performance that might be found in any classroom.

◆ scope and sequence chart: a series of short descriptions of expected learning outcomes for a student at a specific age or stage of development

Finally, decisions must be reached about whether student performance is acceptable or unacceptable—in other words, have the set standards been met? Such decisions are analogous to those discussed in the example given earlier of preparing a recipe. The amount of liquid that must be added to most dishes is variable. Similarly, there is a range of student progress and teachers must decide whether the progress of a particular student falls within an acceptable range. If it does, then the challenge of teaching remains one of trying to find ways to help the student continue to progress.

When expectations are either exceeded or unmet, the issue becomes more complex. Should the student receive extraordinary assistance? Can the classroom teacher provide this service unaided, or is some collaboration with

yes?
#all terms

other professionals necessary? How long should this assistance be continued? When should it be extended, expanded, or stopped? The nature and scope of the completed evaluation will vary depending on the concern that is to be addressed. Teachers may find the decision-making model presented later in this chapter useful in planning their assessment. Before considering this model and some currently employed assessment techniques, a short overview of past practice will help to place assessment in context.

◆ REFLECTING ON PAST PRACTICE

To illustrate the changing face of assessment, an extreme-case scenario of past assessment practices will be painted. During the late 1960s and for most of the next decade, diagnostic assessment of students with special needs was often divorced from instructional planning. With some exceptions, the primary purpose of such assessment was to provide information to be used in making classification and placement decisions. Under this rubric, individualized **formal assessment** was often completed by specialists who were typically school psychologists. They administered a test (or a series of tests) that was usually **norm-referenced** rather than **criterion-referenced**. The content of these tests was directed at students' feelings, beliefs, attainment, and ability levels. In addition, these specialists might have completed some classroom observation and interviewed the teacher to determine whether the obversed behaviour was typical. They then scored the tests, interpreted the results, and reached conclusions about the assessed students' competency, and, generally in consultation with other involved professionals, determined where schooling would take place. In large part, the placement decision ended formal assessment. Although instructional recommendations were sometimes included, the primary purpose was **classification** and **placement**, not instructional planning.

Under this extreme scenario, parents contributed little, either to collecting information or to determining their child's subsequent schooling. Children were typically not allowed any comment on their future, and although teachers took part in placement meetings, they had only a small voice in the final decision. For the most part, instructional planning was not considered before placement had occurred. When students were moved to a new classroom or school, receiving teachers often did not meet their new students until after the placement had taken place; in such cases, specialist case workers may have travelled to the various receiving schools to explain the program that was to be provided.

Fortunately, the above case is a caricature of previous assessment practice. The model on which it is based has been criticized (Hirshosen & McGuigan, 1984; Singer, Palfrey, Butler, & Walker, 1989; Ysseldyke, 1987). Further, teachers have questioned the planning value or instructional utility of **decontextualized assessment** (Hilliard, 1989; Reid & Hresko, 1980). Concerns over the need for a link between evaluation and instruction will

◆ **formal assessment:** standardized evaluation measures such as intelligence tests

◆ **norm-referenced tests:** a form of testing in which the standard of comparison is the performance of other students

◆ **criterion-referenced test:** a form of testing in which students are evaluated on the basis of their ability to meet a particular standard

◆ **classification:** the determination of whether a student conforms to a particular label

◆ **placement:** the determination of where a student with special needs is to receive special education services

◆ **decontextualized assessment:** assessment in which the measurements taken do not parallel what is occurring in the classroom

require teachers to take a more active role in assessment, to put assessment into perspective, and to scrutinize their own practice.

◆ SCHOOL-BASED PROBLEMS THAT REQUIRE ASSESSMENT

Over the course of a school year, a number of problems related to what and how students learn have assessment implications. Some problems will be solved readily, whereas others will require more thought. In each case, the assessment procedures that are adopted will need to be adjusted to reflect the nature of the problem to be solved. Described below are the most common situations, ranging from daily occurrences in which subjective judgments must be made, to more complex episodes that require comprehensive evaluations.

ONGOING DECISIONS *general*

⋇ Know informal.

Many daily decisions require quick judgments to permit successful instruction to continue. Illustrations range from trying to decide how much material to present in a lesson, to noting that a child requires assistance in learning how to use a dictionary. Many of these daily instructional adjustments are made subjectively, otherwise the entire day would be consumed by assessment. Comfort with such decisions increases with teaching experience as the store of internalized situation-specific knowledge increases. Other decisions are better made by less subjective means. For example, the beginning teacher may feel uncomfortable determining the pace of instruction for a child with learning problems, and may want to collect information before making this decision. Some of the information-collection techniques suggested later in this chapter would be helpful in these circumstances.

Daily decisions should be subject to continual review and modification as new information emerges. For example, consider the following hypothetical problem. Two children, who are good friends, find it difficult to continue working together since they prefer to socialize with one another. In this case, solution-finding is an appropriate goal. The children may be asked to propose solutions and to evaluate them; for example, one young child might note, "I can't sit by her because we like to talk and play and I don't do my work. I think we should be in different groups." A temporary separation may provide a simple solution; further assessment would be of minimal benefit, unless the problem re-emerged in the new group or the two children continued to visit despite being separated. If children are unable to find a solution themselves, the teacher may assist them in identifying the issues that are interfering with learning. Alternatively, the problem may be brought as a general issue, rather than a specific case, to the entire class. Employing questions (e.g., "What happens when friends work in the same group and talk to each other?") will allow the whole class to propose and discuss solutions.

While the teacher does not complete a thorough evaluation in the above example, assessment does take place. The two children are asked to self-appraise, to complete their own evaluation of the problem, and to propose a solution. In addition, the teacher evaluates to see if the proposed solution is effective by observing the children as they work in their new groups. The teacher could also document some of the following things about this situation, which could be used to write a report card or to encourage further self-appraisal in the children. First, the incident could be recorded by following the procedures for incident recording to help determine if this is a recurring pattern of behaviour. Second, the teacher may record how the conflict is resolved (to note social development), and comment on the degree to which the children are learning to assume responsibility for their actions. Third, each child may be encouraged to record his or her own solution in a personal notebook; subsequently (a few weeks to a few months), they could revisit their solutions and ask themselves if they would still choose this kind of solution, given a similar problem, or whether they would propose a different course of action. This third type of assessment can become an important component of children learning to evaluate their solutions.

The situations discussed above have several things in common that make an informal approach to assessment appropriate. First, the information collected is not intended to be kept for long periods of time. Second, the decisions that are made can be readily reviewed and revised. Not all classroom decisions, however, are a result of the ongoing daily interactions among students and teachers. Some issues are "high stakes" in that they have long-term consequences. There are at least three problems that can be considered high stakes: (1) retention (extending a program, repeating a grade or course); (2) classification and placement; and (3) program modification (instructional planning).

◆ informal assessment: flexible evaluation measures such as teacher-prepared tests/checklists, classroom observations, and student self-evaluations

HIGH-STAKES DECISIONS *general what*

One of the most difficult high-stakes decisions is recommending that a student repeat a course or spend an additional year in a particular level of program. The trend in education is to seek alternatives to retention where possible. When a retention decision is made, however, it should be based on series of evaluations. Both formal and informal assessment likely will be completed before such a decision is made.

The issues discussed to this point could apply equally to exceptional and nonexceptional students. The following three high-stakes decisions, though, are made only for students who have been identified as having special needs: (1) classifying students as having special needs; (2) determining an alternative placement in a special program; (3) and/or planning an individual educational program (IEP). Decisions are typically made by a team of professionals referred to variously as a teacher support team, a mainstreaming team, an inclusive team, or a school-based team.

The first two decisions are currently the subject of much debate (Reynolds, 1989; Ysseldyke, 1983, 1987; Wiederholt, 1989). Questions like "Who should be eligible to receive special services?" and "Is classification valid?" mark this discussion. On a more immediate basis, however, teachers are still being asked to participate in meetings where classification and placement decisions are made. Assessment relating to these decisions is comprehensive and typically includes both formal and informal assessment. The third decision involves planning alternative programs for students who have been identified as requiring extraordinary services. Classroom teachers participate in planning instructional programs for students who are currently residing in their classrooms. Following the steps of the decision-making model outlined below should be of assistance in such planning.

◆ EMPLOYING A DECISION-MAKING MODEL

As an example of a set of procedures that have been formulated to involve teachers in assessment of students with special needs (Bachor & Crealock, 1986; Humphries & Wilson, 1986), a revision of the decision-making model proposed by Bachor and Crealock (1986) is given in Figure 8.1. The general

Figure 8.1

A Decision–Making Model for Use in the Classroom

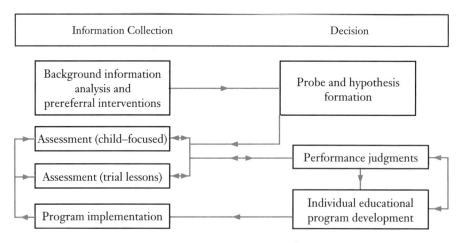

purpose of employing the decision-making model is to develop, when necessary, a long-term instructional plan for students who are experiencing learning problems. Implementing the model involves the completion of several interrelated steps.

The first two steps of the model (*background information analysis* and *implementing prereferral interventions*) are typically completed simultaneously. The purpose is to review what has been completed thus far for the student and to determine if any further steps are necessary. It is important to recognize that the model will not be applied fully to all individuals. For some students, the application will end with the conclusion of the second step. Two decisions are possible: (1) the decision that the current program is effective and, therefore, that further action is unnecessary; or (2) the decision to introduce supplemental assistance to the child without completing further assessment.

In completing the first step, if it is appropriate to do so, **prereferral interventions** are introduced (Pugach & Johnson, 1989). The prereferral phase gives regular classroom teachers the opportunity to work with resource teachers (or other specialists) to find solutions to problems, thus avoiding classification and placement. During this period, regular classroom teachers may also refine the manner in which they work with students who have special needs. Alternatively, the involved teachers may be already implementing as complete a program as is possible within the context of the regular classroom; in such cases, additional evaluation and review will be necessary.

If further steps of the decision-making model are to be followed, the records should be sorted into historical and current information. Current information is usually the most useful when planning instruction, although older material can illuminate complexity and duration of the problem. Information on how the student has been taught, and with what subject-specific materials, can be of additional use.

In moving to the second step, information (including the results of prereferral interventions) is grouped around probes or hypotheses. *Probes* are stated when the supporting documentation is limited, but there is reason to suspect that further investigation is merited. This subjective decision is what teachers refer to as "going on gut feeling," where they are relying on their accumulated knowledge to delve into whatever they have noted. *Hypotheses* are stated when the supporting information is more extensive. Hypotheses are guesses about a student that are supported by two or more pieces of evidence that the teacher wishes to advance as the starting point of further assessment. Information collected to support hypotheses should come from different assessors, or should be collected by one person using different modes (interviewing, observing, testing, teaching), representing a range of student response types (listening, writing, reading, copying, talking, making), and preferably covering a span of time rather than a single day.

The next cluster of steps is also completed together since the purpose is to complete as much assessment as is necessary to prepare an individual educational plan. *Child-based assessment* can consist of a variety of assessment techniques, including information collection (e.g., having the student engage in self-appraisal) or standardized tests that meet the standards established for fair-test practices described earlier in this chapter.

In addition to evaluating the child, *trial lessons* are conducted. The purpose in conducting trial lessons is to evaluate whether any suggested instructional method or material is likely to work with a group of students. A teacher might begin by selecting a teaching method such as strategy instruction

◆ prereferral intervention: steps that are taken prior to referring a student for formal intervention

(Palincsar, David, Winn, & Stevens, 1991), or some material that is to be incorporated into a series of lessons, such as a linguistic reading series or base-ten blocks. The selected method or material is then taught, and, at pre-selected points in the lesson, the teacher determines whether instruction was successful. The criterion of success is whether the student can demonstrate instructional mastery after the instructional period. At a minimum, information should be collected before instruction begins and immediately after it has been completed; it may also be useful to collect information while lessons are taking place. Depending on what is being taught, it may be helpful to obtain another estimate of instructional success a week to three weeks subsequent to instruction. Curriculum-based assessment (see "Collecting Information" section) is one technique that can be used to evaluate the success of trial lessons.

While assessing the child and conducting trial lessons can be done simultaneously, in some cases it will be appropriate to complete these two steps separately. For example, determining how a student responds to instruction could be of the highest priority when the student to be assessed is fearful of being evaluated. If sufficient information is already available, it may even be unnecessary to complete child-based assessment; performance judgments can be based on this information and on trial lessons.

The final step of the decision-making model is to *write and implement* an *individual educational plan.* Included in the IEP is a record of the student's present performance, which is based on information derived from the assessment completed in the previous steps. Long-term instructional goals and objectives are also stated. These goals are based on what the student needs to learn during the instructional period over which the IEP will be implemented—typically one year. Finally, the instructional plan is implemented. During this period, assessment does not end. Lessons are evaluated using the procedures of curriculum-based assessment and performance judgments are made regularly.

CASE STUDY

Prereferral and Background Information

Ratna is a 13-year-old Grade 6 student for whom English is a second language. She is approximately one year older than her peers and is taller and heavier than most of her classmates. Her teacher has requested assistance in facilitating her language development and in encouraging her to participate more in the classroom.

Ratna has been in Canada for three years, the first two of which she was enrolled in a class for immigrants. Last year she transferred to her current elementary school, enrolling in a Grade 5 program. For part of the year, Ratna received assistance from an English as a Second Language (ESL) teacher. During this four-month period, Ratna was withdrawn from class three days per week to receive instruction with a small group of four other students. The instructional material was simplified to meet the needs of all five recipients, and to help Ratna with her grammar and oral expression. While such instruction did help her build additional basic language skills, it did not help her to comprehend nuances such as conversational idioms; nor did it enable her to grasp textual material she needed to know in order to participate in ongoing classroom instruction.

At the start of Grade 6, Ratna no longer received ESL instruction. Her exposure to English remains limited, as Punjabi is the language of choice at home. Her family activities are directed toward fulfilling domestic responsibilities and participating in religious events. Partly because of her cultural and family background, Ratna seldom engages herself wholeheartedly in class activities, especially if they are playful. She is generally very quiet in school and is reportedly cooperative and attentive during class.

According to her background information, Ratna had completed part of the Canadian Test of Basic Skills (Hieronymous, Lindquist, Hoover, & King-Shaw, 1990) during her Grade 5 year. While this test meets technical adequacy criteria for use in Canada, there are some limitations that should be kept in mind when using it (Anderson, forthcoming). For example, it would be questionable to administer the Canadian Test of Basic Skills to someone who does not speak English well and use it as a measure of general achievement, because it would be unclear what was being measured—the ability to read and understand English or comprehension of the content area. In Ratna's case, only the vocabulary (**grade equivalent (GE) score**, 2.0) and comprehension (grade equivalent score, 5.5) subtests were administered in order to estimate reading level. In addition, scores were available from an unpublished informal reading inventory on which Ratna scored a grade equivalent of 3.0 on word recognition and of 4.0 on comprehension.

◆ grade equivalent (GE) score: a score that is calculated and used to project a student's average performance for a particular grade

During the prereferral consultation, the resource teacher and the classroom teacher introduced language development activities that were designed to increase vocabulary and reading fluency. Specifically, they introduced two techniques based on ideas both teachers agreed could be successfully maintained in the regular classroom. First, they encouraged Ratna to compile a list of words she knew, along with their meaning, in a card file that served as a personalized dictionary. As Ratna learned words, she would add a brief definition and use this new information to write a sentence. The purpose in developing the personal dictionary was twofold: Ratna would build confidence as she saw her vocabulary growing, and she would have a handy personal reference to check word use. Second, they paired Ratna with a "reading buddy," both to practice reading and to encourage a friendship to develop between the two students. Ratna and her reading buddy took turns listening to each other read and talking about what they had read; practiced repeated readings (Samuels, 1979), i.e., reading the same story several times to increase fluency; and built a number of story ladders (Dolch, 1945), selecting books around a single theme or category, such as fashion or oceanography.

The difficulty of the reading material increased as Ratna's fluency, vocabulary, and comprehension improved.

After a few months of these interventions, Ratna was still not progressing as well as her classroom teacher wanted. She talked to her reading buddy but remained very quiet in the classroom, speaking only when asked a direct question. While her classroom performance had improved, her oral language and reading had not reached the desired standard. Thus, the resource room teacher and the classroom teacher decided that additional intervention was necessary.

Probe and Hypothesis Formation

One probe and two hypotheses were stated. The classroom teacher, in co-operation with the resource teacher, began to maintain a dossier on Ratna that served as a main source of information for statements one and three, which are hypotheses. The second statement, a probe, is based on Ratna's self-report during interviews.

1. Based on her performance in classroom over the past three months, as illustrated in her dossier, her previous informal inventory, and CTBS results, Ratna appears to have a poor vocabulary and reads word by word.
2. Based on her continued extensive use of Punjabi at home and her cultural background, Ratna may still be translating from Punjabi to English and may feel uncomfortable speaking in class, both of which may influence her willingness to take part in classroom discussion.
3. Based on work sample analysis of tape-recorded reading and her inability to retell main ideas from longer stories, Ratna varies in her comprehension of instructional materials; she may lack the appropriate comprehension strategies to understand both fiction and nonfiction.

Assessment

On the basis of the classroom information available for Ratna, the assessment conducted by the resource teacher consisted of a teacher-prepared test, an interview, a re-analysis of the dossier, and a series of trial lessons. The major focus of this assessment was threefold: (1) to confirm the evidence that had been accumulated on how Ratna read; (2) to determine, through an interview, if Ratna was translating; (3) to ascertain if Ratna could learn, remember, and apply instructional strategies to improve her comprehension and increase her rate of participation in class.

Judgments

The collected information, previous probes, and hypotheses were classified into one of four categories: capable (can do above level of expectation, competent); characteristic (typical of what the student can do); acquiring (what the student is learning); and unknown (the student is unable to do at this time).

1. *Capable*. Ratna can spell words that are judged to be one to two levels above her current grade level. She has a number of strategies that she applies when a word is unfamiliar to her; her phonetic skills are especially good in assisting her to construct possible spelling options.
2. *Characteristic*. Ratna can write short stories or nonfiction paragraphs when the structure to be followed is clear. Her question-answering follows the same pattern, as she often incorporates the question statement into her responses. Ratna can read materials at grade level as long as they are thirty to fifty words in length. Her reading strategy has improved, but she still reverts to word-by-word reading when faced with more difficult subject-specific words or with longer passages.
3. *Acquiring*. Ratna is learning some strategies to assist her in understanding text; for example, she has been practicing **RAP**—R (read) A (analyze) P (paraphrase). Ratna is translating from Punjabi to English, which is slowing her understanding.

    ◆ RAP (Read, Analyze, Paraphrase): strategy used to help learners understand the key ideas in a story

4. *Unknown*. Ratna seems to continue to be uncomfortable talking in class, speaking only when asked a direct question and then giving only a minimal answer. Ratna appears to lack the vocabulary and reading strategies needed to comprehend long passages.

No

Individual Education Program and Program Implementation

An IEP was developed for Ratna that was implemented in both the regular classroom and the resource room. In the first case, the classroom and the resource teacher continued to work together to encourage Ratna to take part in classroom activities. The reading buddy program was continued and expanded so that Ratna read with small groups of three to four children at least twice per week. In addition, Ratna was provided with instruction in the resource room in which simulated discussions around themes currently being explored in the regular classroom were modelled and practiced. Ratna also was taught additional strategies to improve her comprehension, fluency, and vocabulary.

◆ *Sample Annual Goal*. Ratna will increase her reading comprehension to a beginning Grade 7 level.
◆ *Instructional Objective 1*. Given a three-hundred-word passage at the mid Grade 6 level of difficulty, Ratna will be able to use a selected learning strategy to identify the key ideas in the paragraph.
◆ *Instructional Objective 2*. Given a one-thousand-word passage at the end of Grade 6 difficulty, Ratna will be able to apply at least two different learning strategies to comprehend subject-specific text.

CONCLUSION

Using the decision-making model permits the teacher (in cooperation with other involved professionals) to plan instruction, based on a combination of child-based and lesson-based information, for students who need extraordinary support. The balance of the chapter places this model in a larger context by showing the reader how to establish a dossier and a portfolio (teacher directed collection of information), and by presenting some ideas for collecting and evaluating information.

◇ ESTABLISHING A PORTFOLIO AND A DOSSIER

In this section, two types of collections (ways of managing information) are discussed. Both portfolios and dossiers are employed to gather information using formal or informal measures, although profiles are mainly informal whereas dossiers contain a mixture of both types of information.

◆ portfolio: material chosen by students that reflects their ongoing academic achievement

A **portfolio**, profile, or process-folio (Wolf, Bixby, Glenn, & Gardiner, 1991) is a joint project between a teacher and a student—a parent may be minimally involved—that includes information chosen by the student, under the guidance of the teacher, plus a series of statements of continuing reflection about that material. More specifically:

◆ The teacher collaborates with the student (and, possibly, parent) to select *idea-outcomes* (products that represent what has been learned) across *learning descriptors* (reference sets, instructional goals, or any other listing of the material to be learned) on an ongoing basis.

◆ The teacher and the student (the parent may, in some cases, contribute ideas) choose samples of these idea-outcomes (e.g., writing samples, a tape of best reading, and so forth) based on criteria developed jointly with or by the teacher (e.g., things the student is proud about, wants to improve, or wants to show to his or her parent).

◆ The student periodically revisits his or her documentation of this ongoing work. With each evaluation, students are encouraged to examine the portfolio (state whether they would like to burn it, save it, revise it, or publish it), and to reflect on its contents (reasons as to why an item should be burned, saved, revised, or published).

In collecting information for a portfolio, a description of learning episodes is obtained, which can serve as "a context where students can learn to regard assessment as an occasion for learning" (Wolf, Bixby, Glenn, & Gardiner, 1991, p. 57). A sample portfolio entry is shown in Table 8.1.

◆ dossier: a teacher-directed, cumulative, and representative record of student attainment and learning

A **dossier** is a teacher-directed, cumulative, and representative record of student attainment and learning (inquiring, risk-taking, etc.), which contains three types of information. The first type is *medical* (history of childhood illnesses, special medical regime to be followed while in school, and so forth). The second kind of information that appears in the dossier is *ecological*, that

Table 8.1
Entry in Portfolio with Accompanying Comments

"Responsibility"

The word responsible mean to me that I have to take care of thing I have to listen to my parents and I have to do it right. The things I have to be responsible around my house is taking out the garbage water the plants and the grass. My parent's want's me to be responsible because when I grow older and I get a job I might lose it because I am imresponsible or I might have a bad accident because I am imresponsible.

October

Sharma L.: I included this work in my file because I want to show my parents when they come to the school. I am learn to be responsible.

Teacher comment: The piece of work is a good example of the improvement Sharma is showing in his writing. He is learning to write in complete paragraphs and to develop an idea.

March

Sharma L.: Burn it! I left endings off words and did not spell some words right. I am glad that I am learning to see my mistakes.

Teacher comment: Sharma has learned a great deal about the use of English over the last few months. His sentences are better formed and his spelling has improved greatly! Good job, Sharma!

is, material that is accumulated about the student's interactions in a number of contexts. Ecological material can include records of family interviews, descriptions of the student's in-class and schoolyard behaviour, and other important interpersonal information. The third type of material found is *educational* and includes standard test results, photocopies of student-selected work from the portfolio, and work samples selected by the teacher.

GETTING READY

Establishing either a profile or a dossier will not necessarily lead to better instructional planning, evaluation, and reporting, or to student self-appraisal and goal-setting. To accomplish these two objectives, the teacher needs to have stated them as intentional and purposeful outcomes of developing a profile and dossier. Thus, the teacher must be the manager of the collected information and use it to judge student progress.

The manner in which the portfolio and dossier are used will depend on whether their intended audience also functions as direct contributors to the accumulation of information. The role of parents is primarily that of an audience, since they typically comment *after* information has been collected (e.g., at a parent-teacher or child-parent-teacher conference). Parents can contribute to the interpretation of information in both the profile and the dossier: (1) by discussing the representative and exemplary information, and commenting on those aspects of their child's performance that they value or that they have noticed at home; and (2) by offering suggestions for short- and long-term instructional goals that they want to reinforce at home or ones that they would appreciate seeing further improvement in at school. For students and colleagues, usage changes only slightly since both groups can be direct contributors as well as the intended audience.

The benefits of the portfolio for students have been discussed. For colleagues and other professionals, both portfolios and dossiers can be used (1) to report evidence of student accomplishment or intervention success; and (2) as part of the information base needed to make high-stakes decisions. Finally, classroom teachers will find several in-class applications, including reporting to parents and encouraging student self-appraisal.

GUIDELINES FOR PERMISSION, MATERIAL INCLUSION, DOCUMENTATION, AND STORAGE

Careful thought must be given to determining the material that is to be included in a dossier. Clear documentation of this information is also necessary in order to facilitate later interpretation. Of additional benefit are guidelines to ensure secure storage, as well as policies to determine the circumstances under which material can be removed from a dossier. District-wide guidelines and policies, while helpful, are not essential, although school staff may find it useful to agree on common standards. Since the portfolio is student-selected, the guidelines for selection, documentation, and storage will differ slightly from those established for the dossier.

Permission

A first step to begin assessment is to decide whether parental permission is needed to establish the portfolio and the dossier. When the material placed in a portfolio or dossier has been drawn from the classroom and used with students themselves or shared with parents, obtaining parental permission is unnecessary. However, both as a courtesy, and to strengthen communication with parents, informing them that these documents have been established is advisable. This can be accomplished readily, at the outset of the school year, by sending a newsletter home. In this newsletter, the concept of each document could be briefly explained, as well as how it will be compiled. Including (fictitious) examples of material might also be appreciated. At the same time, it would be useful to describe the purpose of encouraging student self-appraisal in the portfolio, especially for parents who are resistant to the idea of students testing themselves.

The issue of permission becomes more complex when the obtained information concerns a student with special needs, or when the material is to be employed as evidence of intervention success or to reach high-stakes decisions. In such cases, parental permission is recommended, and may even be required by law.

Material Inclusion in a Dossier

In preparing a dossier on a student, the teacher (or other professional who is soliciting or choosing information) should select a range of material that reflects what the student can do under a variety of teaching and learning conditions. A minimum of two different types of evidence should be represented in the dossier: products that are typical (*representative*) of the student's current work and products that the teacher considers to be the best available (*exemplary*). Both representative and exemplary estimates of performance can be obtained over an arbitrary period, either during instruction on a particular theme (unit, module, etc.) or learning strategy, or directly following it. For example, the teacher may collect all the compositions completed during the last three weeks of October, during which time narrative strategies for writing were taught and practiced. Compositions that are selected for dossier inclusion should be vetted to ensure that they reflect what that individual can do currently. Specific inclusion criteria will vary as a function of the student's age and the domain in question. For the example of narrative writing, possible selection standards can include manuscript length, style, content variation, technical knowledge (such as the rules of grammar), and audience awareness. The same standards can be applied to selection exemplary compositions, although the weighting of the selection standards will probably need to be modified when the best work is chosen.

In addition to obtaining information that is representative and exemplary, a second goal is to include a range of products (e.g., a writing sample, a videotape of a puppet show, or an audiotape of a student reading a story of his or her choice) or observations (e.g., notes on a student's behaviour as he or she took part in a role-playing activity) from varying domains (academic, social, etc.). The number of products to be examined and the time span over which samples are drawn and then compared will vary considerably; however, the goal should be to obtain as broad an information base as is feasible. At the very least, three criteria should be met. First, the products must have been completed over different periods of the school year; a reasonable target is to strive for three to five samples of work completed in different terms of the year. Second, information should be obtained systematically. To ensure this, the teacher will need to obtain the same amount of information on each child across the same range of tasks. In doing so, both structured and unstructured learning conditions need to be represented in the dossier. For example, the samples retained from the more structured academic domains of mathematics, science, and reading should be similar in number to those retained from the more unstructured activities of free time, group problem-solving, or other cooperative and competitive situations in which, for example, skills in artistic endeavours such as painting or dancing can be observed. Third, to the extent that it is possible to do so when sampling continuous performance (which is always changing) the obtained information must be fair and accurate—a criterion that is of particular importance (and complexity) when students with special needs are concerned.

Material Inclusion in a Portfolio

The guidelines for material inclusion in a portfolio will vary from those proposed for a dossier, especially with respect to fairness and accuracy. The goal is to have students pick material that they believe represents their efforts. Students should be encouraged to select three types of sample performance across subject matter: products that the student feels are representative; two senses of exemplary (the best example of work for the period, and the work that the student most liked or enjoyed completing; and areas of modification (two or three things that the student would like to change or feels he or she needs to improve). This typology could be applied to the material inclusion suggestions outlined in Table 8.2.

Material Documentation in a Dossier

Dossier selections should be identified as completely as possible to show how information was collected, taking into consideration ongoing classroom activities. The following are examples of identifiers that will assist in later interpretation: (1) the date that product was completed or the date the observation was made; (2) the age, grade, and name of the student; (3) the name of observer or person who requested the product be completed; and (4) the conditions under which the estimate was taken (e.g., "Sheila wrote this paragraph on friendship directly after receiving instruction in novel methods of starting and ending paragraphs; she was provided assistance in spelling when she requested it").

NO

Table 8.2 Types of Material Found in Portfolios	
Types of Material	*Rationale for Inclusion*
initial drafts	to review and note changes in thinking and products (can range from first attempts at science experiments to notes from a story or essay)
final products	to allow comparison with drafts to see changes in planning, idea development, and language employed
self-appraisals	to encourage reflection over time
photographs, videotapes, or audiotapes	to record performances that would otherwise be lost; reflects psychomotor and affective development
records of subject-specific completion	to highlight a product (a record of stories or novels read, mathematical concepts applied, etc.)
records of unexpected performance	to note unusual efforts that may signal further change

Material Documentation in a Portfolio

Documentation in a portfolio for student-selected material need not be as comprehensive as for teacher-selected material. Students can be encouraged to identify their work by noting the date on which they completed the work, and by commenting on why they selected the item for inclusion; later students can revisit items, as suggested earlier, to re-evaluate their entries.

Material Storage, Security, and Removal

Since the purpose of the portfolio is to facilitate student self-evaluation and/ or goal-setting, this file should be kept in the classroom where students have easy access to it. The exact location of the dossier will vary depending on grade level and established school policy. In general, elementary teachers should maintain the dossier in their classrooms, especially if children spend a large percentage of their time with one teacher. For high-school teachers, subject-specialists may wish to keep separate samples of student work; however, to allow a more complete picture of an individual's progress to be determined, one teacher (the person who has the most frequent long-term contact with the student) should maintain a complete dossier. For students who are being considered for, or are receiving, extraordinary support services—such as counselling or specialized instruction—teachers should maintain an additional photocopy of selected information, which can be subjected to work sample analysis.

There are two considerations relating to safekeeping dossiers. First, materials like formal (standardized) test results need to be kept in a secure, central location to ensure confidentiality of records; for most dossier information, placement in a locked filing cabinet in the classroom is sufficient. Second, a school or district-wide policy on the removal of material from dossiers will need to be established. Informal assessment information that is representative of student accomplishment should be retained for at least twelve months but no more than sixteen months, resulting in a gradual elimination of historical information sets, with each new teacher omitting information on a systematic basis.

A different policy will be needed for formal assessment information. At present, most standardized test results are retained indefinitely; however, often it is only the cover sheet of tests that are kept, which is of little assistance to anyone planning an instructional intervention or examining how a student addressed a particular task. Completed standardized test-answer booklets (along with at least one copy of the test questions) should, therefore, be retained for a period of three years, allowing professionals to examine a student's recurring patterns of performance across time and over other similar tests.

◇ COLLECTING AND ASSESSING INFORMATION

The information-collection techniques described in this section are designed for teacher use and should, therefore, be used primarily to place information in a dossier rather than in a portfolio. From the perspective of this chapter, the person responsible for managing the collection of information for inclusion in the dossier—and, to a lesser extent (in cooperation with the student), the portfolio—is the classroom teacher. When a special-needs student is being assessed, the classroom teacher is assisted in dossier management and information collection by a resource teacher and, depending on the support services under consideration, other professionals.

OBSERVATION TECHNIQUES

Observation can range from recording how long a single student works on a particular assignment to noting the manner in which a group of children play together at recess. Differing techniques might be employed depending on whether the classroom teacher is observing selectively, or whether another person has been invited to record a child or a group of children engaged in some activity. Ideally, a second person should be present in the classroom, either to teach the class while the classroom teacher observes, or to complete the observation. To make this possible, at least periodically, teachers can use "buddy teachers" to exchange observation periods, or, more typically, complete observation in cooperation with the resource teacher.

Regardless of how observation is conducted, the purpose of completing this assessment technique is to attain a systematic, representative, fair, and accurate estimate of student's behaviour. Bachor and Crealock (1986) suggested that the probability of obtaining such estimates is increased by answering two general questions: (1) What important persons and places are involved in the situation to be observed?; and (2) What kind of behaviour is important in the context in which the student is being taught? While these questions are best asked before observation begins, if this is not possible they can be asked during, or after, an initial set of observations has been conducted.

The teacher should also keep in mind, when conducting classroom observations, that *signs* and *signals*—that which is observed—may have more than one meaning, and, moreover, may be only temporary, lasting a few hours or days. The two basic techniques involved in conducting a classroom observation are detailed below.

Analyzing Techniques

Two techniques are useful when a descriptive account of behaviour is desired. Preparing a *continuous chronologue* is helpful if the goal is to obtain a fairly complete description of what students are doing. When the behaviour of interest is recurrent yet infrequent, a technique known as *incident recording* can be of benefit.

Continuous Chronologues

The purpose of completing a continuous chronologue is to provide a descriptive summary of the student's actions in his or her classroom environment. This technique is time-consuming, if done properly, but it does yield a picture of variations in behaviour across curriculum areas. Thus, it should be used selectively when a more intensive examination of behaviour is desired. Students should be observed in those subject matters in which they are most likely to excel and display their most positive attributes, as well as in those subject matters in which they most need to improve. If possible, it is useful to observe students at varying times of the day for two to three weeks in order to obtain as complete a picture of their general pattern of behaviour as possible. Such sampling behaviour also increases the chances that the obtained estimate will represent typical rather than atypical performance.

When completing a continuous chronologue, it is important to apply the principles presented earlier in this chapter for material documentation. A sample continuous chronologue is shown in Table 8.3. In addition to recording what the student does, it sometimes is helpful to note the *context* in which the behaviour occurs, such as noting that "Larry" is working independently on all aspects of the assignment as opposed to focusing on one segment of the task (e.g., using his ruler to calculate as a problem-solving strategy). Noting the context for behaviour, however, should be limited in scope to avoid prejudging a student or to prevent overgeneralization.

In analyzing the completed record, the teacher can look for consistencies and inconsistencies across the sampled areas of performance. Checks can be stated in question form, and can range from the amount of time taken to how the person is approaching the task at hand. For example, a teacher might ask the following question: Does Larry differ in the amount of time he spends working on mathematics as compared to the amount of time he spends working on social studies? This simple check may reveal that a student spends more time on a particular subject because less effective learning strategies are employed.

Incident Recording

In recording incidents (see Table 8.4), the same descriptive procedures used for completing continuous chronologues can be applied. The only difference

Table 8.3			
A Sample Continuous Chronologue			

Student's Name: Larry   Date: May 2, 1990
Name of Observer: Mr. Looker   Time Observed: Below
Setting and Type(s) of Activity Observed: Mathematics, a cooperative activity where problems are to be completed independently but where problem-solving strategies can be brainstormed. Larry is part of a group of five children that have been assigned to work together.

Time	Setting	Behaviours Display	Interpretations (interferences or comments)
10:10	group seatwork	discussion of how to approach all problems Larry listening to discussion	
10:13		Larry begins work on problems independently	
10:15		talking to a group member	topic of discussion unclear
10:20		reading in textbook and using ruler as a calculator	
10:23		still working on problems independently	others are discussing strategies
10:26		reading textbook	seems to be on task but has only completed one-half the problems that his neighbours have

Table 8.4	
A Sample Incident Record Form	

Student's Name: _____   Date: _____
Name of Observer: _____   Time Observed: _____

Setting and Type(s) of Activity Observed: _____
Incident: _____

is that instead of recording continuous behaviour, specific incidents are noted as stand-alone data. If the incident reoccurs, another record is prepared. Thus, a cumulative record of incidents emerges, which can be examined for commonalities, related themes, or common participants.

Recording Techniques: Counting Behaviour

The principles that apply to analyzing behaviour also are germane to counting it. Prior to recording, it is useful to observe the student for a short period to ensure that the behaviour of concern is displayed on a regular basis. As a first step, define as precisely as possible the behaviour to be observed. This process—called *pinpointing*—makes it possible for the same types of occur-

know

rences to be noted during each observation period. There are three common methods of quantifying behaviour: event recording, duration recording, and interval recording.

Event Recording

When the behaviour is of short duration (one to three seconds) and occurs frequently (at least once every two to five minutes), event recording may be employed. In event recording, the behaviour to be observed is pinpointed and the frequency with which it occurs is noted. With this technique, more than one behaviour can be counted at once by keeping separate tallies for each. An example of event recording is given in Table 8.5.

Table 8.5
Event Recording

Date: November 21, 1990
Observer: Mr. Looker
Pinpoint: Tapping pencil on desk
Day 1, Observation period, Reading seatwork, 9:00 am. to 9:30 am.

***** ***** *****
***** ***

Observation period, Social Studies group project, 11:30 am. to 11:45 am.

***** ***** ***

Observation period, Paper-pencil drawing, 2:15 pm. to 2:30 pm.

***** ***** ****

Total tapping on Day 1: 47 taps; average per minute of observation is approximately 0.78.
Pinpoint: Throwing paper wads
Day 1, Observation period, 9:00 am. to 9:30 am.
///// ///// ///// ////
Observation period, 11:30 am. to 11:45 am.
///// ///// ///// ///// ///// ///// ///// /
Observation period, 2:15 pm. to 2:30 pm.
///
Total throwing on Day 1: 63 throws; average per minute of observation is approximately 1.05.

Duration Recording

If the purpose is to note the amount of time a person engages in a more continuous task, such as completing an assignment, duration recording is an appropriate choice. The observer simply records the number of minutes a student spends working in a given period, as illustrated in Table 8.6. The simplest procedure is to note both the time the observation started and the time it concluded. Subtract these figures to obtain the total time observed. Then subtract total time from the elapsed time, which is the amount of time the student actually spends on task. The most convenient way to record elapsed time is with a stopwatch. As a crude rule of thumb, a criterion of approximately 80 percent of total time spent on task has been found to be a necessary standard to ensure that the student's learning opportunities are maximized.

Interval Recording

This procedure allows the observer to estimate the degree to which inter-action occurs between individuals and the percentage of time spent on task. Typically, an interval of between ten seconds is specified and a plus or a minus is recorded for each interval period, depending on whether the person is on-task or not. The 80 percent rule can be applied to this score system as it was to duration recording. The interaction between individuals in the class can be noted to estimate the nature of the feedback a student is receiving. If the comment is a positive one, the plus or minus is circled; if it is a negative one, a slash is drawn through the plus or minus. An example of interval recording is provided in Figure 8.2.

Table 8.6
Duration Recording

Date: November 1, 1990
Observer: Mr. Looker
Pinpoint: Wandering around the room; any movement by the student away from her desk for which she cannot state a purpose
Day 1, Observation period, Group brainstorming for composition, 9:00 am. to 9:30 am.
   10 minutes, 30 seconds off task
Observation period, Individual seatwork in Science, 11:30 am. to 11:45 am.
   7 minutes, 10 seconds off task
Observation period, Individual work in student choice, 2:15 pm. to 2:30 pm.
   9 minutes, 45 seconds off task
Total time wandering on Day 1: 27 minutes, 25 seconds; average per minute of observation is approximately 0.45.

Figure 8.2

Interval Recording

Date: November 1, 1990
Observer: Mr. Looker
Pinpoint: Time on task, any portion of a 10-second interval spent following teacher insructions or engaged in self-directed school work.

+	+	+	–	+	+	+	+	–	–	+	+	–	–	–	+	+	+
–	–	+	+	+	+	+	+	+	–	+	+	–	–	–	–	+	+
+	+	+	+	+	+	+	+	–	–	–	–	–	–	–	+	+	+
+	+	+	–	+	+	+	+	–	–	+	+	+	–	–	+	+	+

Total time observed, 12 minutes; time on task (47 out of 72 intervals) is approximately 65 percent.

Comparative Observation

In recording behaviour, it often is useful to maintain a running comparison with other students in the class. Comparative observation is a technique whereby teachers compare the performance of a student or students with a sample of other students in the class. The sample should consist of two to four students who fall into three groupings: above-average, average, and below-average. The teacher compares the manner in which each of the groups approached the assignment, looking for differences in such factors as task persistence and thinking-skill effectiveness. Any of the previously described methods of analyzing or counting behaviour can be employed in making this comparison.

INTERVIEWING PROCEDURES —what are ; differences. 317-320 know what they are

italized terms.

It is often helpful to estimate how a child or adolescent feels or thinks about a general situation or some particular topic. Interviewing provides an opportunity to ask a set of questions that will reveal in considerable detail students' general or specific beliefs, and how they think their way through a limited set of problems. When interviewing, remember that neither feelings nor thoughts can be observed directly; evaluators must instead infer that the information collected is representative or exemplary.

Two different approaches can be taken to interviewing. If the purpose of the interview is to determine how a student feels about schooling, questions can focus on his or her beliefs (a *general interview*). If the objective is to obtain an estimate of thinking skills, questions can centre on problem-finding and solution-seeking (a *procedural interview*). During both interviews, students should be encouraged to consider how they believe they learn and how they feel about school. A *comparative interview* can be used to observe differences in performance and strategy across a group of students.

General Interviews

All interviews must be planned so that the questions asked match the purpose for interviewing. Sattler (1988) points out that the relationship between the interviewer and the interviewee is not reciprocal. The interviewer determines the nature of the questions asked during the interview, and decides when to ask additional questions to clarify an answer (and when to accept what was stated originally as a sufficient explanation). As a rule of thumb, in interviewing the goal is to make explicit "what might be left unstated in ordinary conversation" (Sattler, 1988, p. 401).

The first step in conducting an interview is to gain the trust of the person being interviewed. A friendly manner, coupled with questions that are neutral or of interest to the interviewee, will be helpful in this respect. It is also important for the interviewer to seek clarification and extra details when questioning at this stage; the individual being interviewed will be reassured by the interviewer's interest and by the fact that his or her answers are being accepted. Finally, as early as possible, the structure around which the interview will be held should be established. Structuring statements can be used at any time during the interview to initiate, conclude, or establish a direction. For example, an interview with a student who is having difficulty reading might begin with: "Your teacher has been [if the resource teacher is interviewing] or I have been [if the classroom teacher is interviewing] concerned about how you are reading. To start, we are going to talk about your likes and dislikes."

Throughout the interview, there are three procedural considerations that merit attention. First, leading questions should be avoided. Queries like "Don't you think that he/she has some good points?" or "Mr. 'X' can't be all bad, can he?" call for a specific conclusion rather than the student's opinion. Second, questions that can be answered yes or no (e.g., "Do you like (arithmetic, sports, your dad)?" should also be avoided. Third, questions should be asked one at a time rather than grouped together (e.g., "How are you doing in arithmetic, reading, and science?"). Table 8.7 provides sample questions that can be used as prototypes for a general interview.

Table 8.7
General Interview Questions

Leisure-time Topics
What do you like to do after school?
Tell me about your favourite (television show, sport, game, etc.)
Tell me about your _____ team. What position do you play?
I don't know how to play _____. Could you explain it to me?
What are the names of your friends? What do you like to do together?
Tell me about something special that you like to do.
Family-related Topics
Tell me something about your family.
So you have a pet _____. Does it (do they) have a name (have names)?
What do you like to do with your _____ (mother, father, brother, or sister)?
School-related Topics
How far do you live from school?
Tell me about how you get to school each day.
What do you like to do when you are at school?
What subjects do you like best?
When you have homework, what do you do?
If you could change three things in school, what would they be? How would you change _____?

Procedural Interviews

The purpose of procedural interviews is to obtain descriptions of the various types of thinking-skill knowledge and deployment used by students. Such interviews can be conducted in three separate phases. First, students can be asked to explain how they plan to do any task. Second, they can be interviewed while completing a preselected standardized assignment similar to classroom-based activities. In this type of interview, students can be asked to explain the procedures they use to solve a particular problem; this commonly employed interviewing technique has been termed *think-aloud protocols* (Lawson & Rice, 1987; Simon, 1975, 1978). Third, students can be questioned about their performance on a completed assignment. Table 8.8 lists some procedural interview questions, which will need to be adapted for variation in interview content. Lupart (1990) suggests that these questions be parcelled around four clusters—factors related to the person, the task, the strategy, and the stance. These components can be examined in terms of their affect on the student's planning and execution.

Table 8.8
Procedural Interview Questions

1. *Questions about the person*
Are you a good _____? What does your answer tell you (your teacher, your parents, your friends) about your _____?
Who is a good _____? How do you know _____?
What would you like to change about the way you _____?
Do you _____ at home? What do you _____?

2a. *Questions about the writing task*
What has to be in a good (well-crafted) story (essay, notes, journal)?
You are going to write a story (an essay, some notes, a journal). Is there anything else you need to know?

2b. *Questions about the reading task*
I want you to read this story and after you have finished, you are to tell it to me. Is there anything else you need to know?
Why did you pick (select) that book (novel, set of essays, reference)?

2c. *Questions about the task of doing mathematics or science*
I want you to read this set of problems and after you have finished, is there anything you need to know to complete them?
You are going to conduct (build, explain, demonstrate) an experiment (a number, an equation, a fraction). Is there anything else you need to know?

3. *Questions about the strategy*
What do you do to _____?
How are you doing _____?
If you have difficulty, what do you do?
Are there any changes you would like to make?
What did you do when you were doing _____?

4. *Questions about the stance*
If you were to do _____ for yourself or _____ when it was put on the bulletin board at the front of the room, would you do anything differently?
Here is the word _____. How would you (spell it, determine its meaning) if it were part of _____?
Do you approach _____ differently when you have to read/write longer versus shorter answers? (If yes) How? (If no) Could you explain what you do?

Source: Lupart (1990).

Comparative Interviews

Comparative interviews are a variation on general and procedures interviews. The purpose in conducting them is to discover where one student stands relative to another one, thus determining if there is a great deal of variation across a group of students in terms of how they approach a task. Building a set of expectations in this way can reveal, for example, if a solution strategy in mathematics is found only when interviewing students who have difficulty or if it is common across students. Comparative interviews should be conducted with students who have different levels of subject-matter expertise, thereby allowing the teacher to observe differences in actual performance or strategy. As with comparative observation, it is useful to compare across two to four students who fall into the three performance groupings.

WORK SAMPLE ANALYSIS

The purpose of work sample analysis is to collect work that students do in the classroom and use it systematically in evaluating them. It is important to collect samples on a single theme within a subject matter (so that comparisons can be made over time), and to document material clearly to allow interpretation after a few weeks or months have passed. The following steps can be taken in work sample analysis:

1. For each assignment examined, note the date that it was completed, the age and grade of the student, the type of assignment, and, if known, the conditions under which the student worked (e.g., Audrey wrote the paragraph directly after instruction in paragraph construction. She was provided assistance in spelling upon request).

2. Divide the assignment into logical units of analysis (e.g., an algorithm used in an addition question). Then, describe the acceptable performance patterns (what the student can do) and unacceptable performance patterns (what he or she is judged as being unable to do). Note the number of times any acceptable or unacceptable performance pattern occurs and express it as a ratio of the total.

3. Repeat Steps 1 and 2 for three to five assignments that have been completed over a period of one to five weeks. The knowledge, skills, or abilities to be examined must be repeated in some form across selected assignments.

4. Look for commonalities across all work sample analyses. List skills present (abilities or skills mastered by individual); skills absent (abilities or skills at grade- or age-level standards but not yet mastered by the individual); and weaknesses (errors of omission or commission that should have been remediated at an earlier age or grade).

5. Compare observations of skills present, skills absent, and weaknesses to expectations set for students (use curriculum guides or other locally established standards to determine what the student is expected to learn). Use these to develop further instruction, such as trial lessons.

DESIGNING TRIAL LESSONS

Trial lessons are carefully chosen lessons that are controlled for the amount of material presented and the difficulty level chosen. The purpose in conducting trial lessons is to evaluate whether a suggested instructional method or material is likely to work with an individual or a group of students. The criterion of success is whether the student can prove mastery of the taught curriculum after the instructional period.

Curriculum-based assessment (CBA) can be used to evaluate the success of trial lessons. To apply CBA to trial lessons, the following steps should be completed. First, a series of lesson-relevant, short, simple measures based on the objectives of the lesson that has been taught are developed. Second, these parallel measures are administered approximately three to five times over the course of one to two weeks. Third, students' performance data are graphed and analyzed to decide the appropriateness of the recommended instructional program.

Another technique to evaluate trial lessons is to make use of the procedural interviews described earlier. The stages of the interview can follow the three separate phases of a trial lesson, with students being asked to explain (1) how they plan to do a task (*before* instruction); (2) the procedures they are using (*during* instruction); and (3) how well they did (*after* instruction). This procedure can be repeated in two or three days to check the student's memory of instruction.

WORKING WITH THE STUDENT AS A CO-INVESTIGATOR

Treating the student as a co-investigator in evaluation is an essential component of the portfolio. In using portfolios, students are expected to participate fully in assessment, and are provided with access to the results of such evaluation (Nixon, 1990). Student self-evaluation is also encouraged for dossiers, although providing full access to the results is not.

Potentially one of the most helpful sources of information is the student's self-report. In examining their background, some students are able to add insights into how they learned in the past. Others, however, either do not remember or lack the descriptive skills necessary to provide self-report information on learner background. Students can further be asked to self-observe and to note their planning and task-relevant procedures. The various forms of self-evaluation should be limited to the following general statements of purpose: (1) to improve instructional delivery; and (2) to act as guidance for the enhancement of self-directed learning to increase the acquisition, memory, and application of strategies (applied to any domain) and/or knowledge. Some questions that mark such self-report are given in Tables 8.7 and 8.8.

Miller (1991) argues that self-appraisal can be used to accomplish two goals related to the question, "How are you doing at ———?" The first goal area is student assessment of the probability of overall success. Miller (1991) proposes three types of productive self-assessment: prejudging, inferred self-assessment, and specific self-assessment. In *prejudging*, the student estimates the probability of success before starting an assignment, then revisits his or her rating after completion to evaluate the prediction. In using *inferred self-assessment*, the student comments on the difficulty level of a task while completing it, or makes observations about specific concerns he or she might have. In using *specific self-assessment*, the student is asked to image traffic lights to evaluate performance (red light, incorrect; yellow light, uncertain; green light, correct) after completing a task.

The second goal area is student assessment of the task or strategy, for which Miller (1991) suggests two useful forms of self-assessment: task assessing and self-monitoring. In *task assessing*, the student "sizes up" a task in order to figure out how to approach it, as well as to determine whether she or he has the necessary skills or knowledge to accomplish it. When *self-monitoring*, the student makes a series of ongoing evaluations that can range from self-support ("I'm doing all right") to evaluative ("I don't think I completely understood this last paragraph, so I had better reread it")

OTHER EVALUATION TECHNIQUES

In addition to the techniques described above, there are at least three other types of assessment information that can be collected: commercially available instruments, teacher-prepared tests/measures, and curriculum-based assessment (CBA).

Commercially Available Instruments

The teacher who wishes to use commercially available instruments faces a multiplicity of choices. In choosing to use any test, check list, rating scale, or other instrument, he or she must carefully review it before and after administering it. Before administering the measure, the principles of fair-testing practice must be applied. To review, the measure should be checked for at least three factors: (1) content validity and bias in method (Is the information familiar to my students? Is it presented in a format with which my students have had prior experience?); (2) internal consistency reliability (Are the same things being measured on all sections of the instrument or across the entire measure?); and (3) clarity of procedures (Can students make sense out of the instructions? Are they likely to be mislead? Can I follow the administration procedures? Am I completely familiar with the administrative procedures?). In addition, it is worthwhile to check to see if there is a published review of the proposed measurement device; two sources of these reviews are books on assessment by Salvia and Ysseldyke (1991) and Conoley and Kramer (forthcoming).

Teacher-Prepared Tests and Measures

A common evaluation procedure employed by teachers is to develop their own tests to assess student performance. A number of books provide guidance to teachers in preparing classroom tests, including directions on preparing short-answer, multiple-choice, essay and true-false test items (Board of Education for the City of Etobicoke Writing Committee, 1987; Gronlund & Linn, 1990; Popham, 1990). In addition, teachers are beginning to prepare their own diagnostic measures for use with students who have special needs. Before undertaking such a task, however, the teacher should have solid test-construction skills of the kind referred to above. Finally, a thorough knowledge of fair-testing practices is essential, as these principles must be applied to all developed tests.

Curriculum-based Assessment

Curriculum-based assessment (CBA) is a relatively recent addition to the teacher's set of measurement tools. This type of measurement was originally designed to enable teachers to construct short curriculum-relevant measures that could serve as quick probes on student knowledge (Deno, 1985; Fuchs, Deno, & Mirkin, 1984) (see Salvia and Hughes [1990] for the expanded version of CBA).

As initially proposed, there are two main versions of CBA. In the version suggested by Fuchs and her colleagues (Fuchs & Fuchs, 1986; Fuchs, Fuchs, Benowitz, & Barringer, 1987), a pool of domain-referenced items is constructed to match annual goals and instructional objectives. Items called probes are then sampled from the item pool and administered to students to monitor instructional effectiveness. In the version suggested by Deno and his associates (Deno, Marston, & Mirkin, 1982; Wesson, Fuchs, Tindal, Mirkin & Deno, 1986), quick probes are used to estimate performance (e.g., the number of words read correctly from a basal reader in one minute. For both of the above techniques, the teacher administers to students three to five test items to check their understanding. The key difference between the two approaches is that a pool of items is developed in only one. While this extra step is time-consuming at first, it will probably save effort later in the year. It typically does not take test-wise students long to realize the same questions are being asked of all individuals, and then to memorize the items rather than to study the content. Developing a domain of items should prevent the overuse of particular items, thus increasing the chance that accurate probes will be made.

MAKING SENSE OF RESULTS

This final section of this chapter provides guidelines for making sense of descriptive assessment information and for interpreting the results. Readers seeking guidance on interpreting test scores can refer to Bachor and Crealock (1986) or Salvia and Ysseldyke (1991).

Guidelines for Reading and Making Sense of Assessment Information

Scores may be included in this frame of reference, but they must be put into perspective, that is, seen as a component of examining learning and teaching and accompanied by sufficient information to make them meaningful. For example, reporting that a student received a score of 100 out of a possible 150 points on a science exam is not particularly useful when the goal is to plan instruction. At a minimum, what is needed is a description of the item content, or a listing of items (or groups of item types), as well as a more detailed report on the number correct/incorrect.

Begin by reading the information you have accumulated over time in order to build a general impression. While reading, arrange the documents in chronological order and organize according to your reason for examining the information (e.g., writing a report or preparing an IEP). Once you have gained an overall impression, check the reasonableness and accuracy of the gathered information. Does the data seem to make sense? How representative are the performances collected? Are they fair estimates? Are there notes, reports, and the like that contain (or appear to contain) errors? Call into question such measures. Correct errors if possible, and eliminate information that is faulty (unless it can be readily checked) or not germane to your objective.

Next, classify each remaining document in the file as either historical or current (to reflect the recency of the available information) and as either measurement-based or judgment-based (to indicate the degree to which inferences have been made). Applying these relative criteria to the available information, four classifications of information emerge: historical judgments, current judgments, historical measurements, and current measurements. These classifications are subjective and are not immutable. As a crude rule of thumb, classroom information that is older than three months is historical, as are standardized educational measures that are older than one year.

The next step is to classify the information into preliminary groups of common elements that describe the conditions of assessment, that is, how information was previously collected (interviewing, observing, testing, teaching, and what response the student was required to employ (listen, write, read, copy, talk, make). Also, if possible, note whether the student has been working independently or with assistance from an adult, a classmate, or a group of children working cooperatively.

After identifying common themes, use the classified information to make judgments. These determinations vary depending on why the information is being reviewed. A minimum of three judgments need to be made over the course of the school year: judgment about the extent of evidence required, judgment about acceptability, and judgment about degree of proficiency.

Judgment about the extent of evidence required involves the key question, Have I accumulated the kind and amount of evidence needed to make further judgments?, and is the final cautionary note before the teacher moves on to making decisions about students. *Judgment about acceptability* involves the key question, Is progress satisfactory or unsatisfactory? *Judgment about degree of proficiency* can be facilitated by grouping pertinent information into four clusters: (1) capable (can do above level of expectation, competent); (2) characteristic (typical of what the student can do); (3) acquiring (what the student is learning); and (4) unknown (at this time, the student is unable to do 'X').

A final judgment may be made about the nature of reporting, if this was a purpose in completing assessment. Three questions need to be addressed here: How complete should the presented report be and what should it cover (number of domains, extent of coverage, etc.)? What form should the report take (oral or written)? What is the timing of the delivery of the report (e.g., before, after, or during a conference with other colleagues and/or parents)? Further analysis may be helpful when purpose is to prepare an instructional plan for a student. To permit such instructional planning, the judgments made about proficiency can be compared to expectations set for students in curriculum guides or by locally established standards.

Cautions in Interpreting Results

Both portfolios and dossiers may be subject to limitations similar to those established for rating scales (Nixon, 1990), which may result in selection and interpretation errors. The following issues should be considered when analyzing collected information.

Factors influencing assessment accuracy

Estimation is a necessary component of making use of information-collection techniques. If one administers, for example, a series of questions related to reading or writing, what is measured is only an approximation of what the student knows. Even if the goal is to establish the presumably more straightforward task of measuring a student's arithmetic procedural knowledge, estimation is necessary (Bachor, 1991).

A review of the process of evaluation will help to illustrate the need for estimation. We set out to measure what students know, how they learn and think, and whether our instructional procedures are effective. Because direct observation of these factors is impossible, we employ a variety of techniques (interviews, work sample analysis, trial lessons, etc.) to estimate what we want to know. What is assessed is observed as a form of behaviour, and since this behaviour is only a sample of what might have been obtained, what a person did at that time can only be estimated.

Variability in estimates may also occur as a function of content knowledge or required task-specific skill. Changing the task slightly may lead to increased effort and content knowledge or skill, resulting in a different assessment of what a person can do. Whether completed with groups or individuals, assessment always requires estimation and is subject to error. Thus, the application of any single assessment technique, regardless of its inherent validity, can never result in more than a situation-specific estimate of what a student can do.

Factors influencing assessment fairness

If the reliance on situation-specific estimates is eliminated, a new problem emerges: how to compare fairly across learners who are attempting different tasks. This problem has been raised in relation to classroom assessment as well. Traub (1990) recommends that standardized tasks or procedures be used in all assessment. Making comparisons across learners may not seem necessary if the purpose of assessment is to monitor the acquisition of individual thinking skills or to evaluate the effectiveness of individual instruction. According to Traub (1990), however, comparison using normative information will be necessary at some point to ensure fairness in reporting procedures and decision-making.

Other interpretive errors

In addition to accuracy and fairness issues, Nuttall & Goldstein (1984) list four errors in judgment a teacher can make when reading assessment information: halo effects, leniency or severity effects, central tendency error, and sampling information from a restricted range.

Halo effects occur when teachers' judgments reflect what they think the student's overall performance is likely to be, rather than how they actually performed in a specific context (Nuttall & Goldstein, 1984). This error often derives from thinking that a student will do well because he or she has always done so in the past. What is judged is expectation rather than actual performance. Halo effects may also occur when only "best effort" materials are selected for inclusion in a portfolio, excluding products that may be more typical or that may suggest the need for improvement. A third form of the halo effect may occur if a set of material completed under one condition (e.g., directly after receiving instruction with teacher or peer assistance) is assumed to be typical of performance across condition statements. The judgment that work completed with assistance is indicative of successful instruction overlooks the fact that students sometimes perform well with teacher-support but need further practice to allow them to become independent learners.

Leniency or *severity effects* occur when judgments are made about student performance that are not warranted by the collected information. Leniency effects can occur when a teacher wants a particular student to do well, and judges as acceptable an assignment that, in fact, fails to meet the desired standard; the reverse occurs with severity effects, when too harsh a judgment is made.

The *central tendency error* occurs when teachers ignore information or work that reflects extremes in student performance in favour of typical selections. A teacher might justify this course of action by saying, "He must have had a bad day when doing this assignment," or, "This must be a fluke—it's too good to be her work."

Sampling information from a restricted range occurs when performance is sought that reflects a restricted range of learning and teaching conditions. If there are several products that match one condition, the teacher may be biased (i.e., overwhelmed) by the obtained information. As a result of this error, a student who is being judged as to his or her mathematics may be classified as unacceptable and characteristic (typical of what the student can do) when his or her work represents performance with respect to reading only.

◆ CONCLUSION

In this chapter, assessment has been examined from the perspective of the classroom teacher and the nature of the decisions that are made over the course of the school year. We recommended throughout that assessment procedures be modified to suit the teacher's specific purpose. The student may be a pivotal part of the evaluation—especially when the goal is to help him or her become a more effective learner—or, in other cases, a major source of information that is teacher-directed in its use. The chapter concluded with a discussion of information-collection techniques and assessment procedures, in which the principles of fair assessment and good judgment were stressed.

QUESTIONS
◆◆◆◆◆◆◆◆◆◆◆◆◆◆

1. What is the difference between measurement, judgment, and decision-making, and how do all these concepts relate to assessment?

2. What are some high-stakes problems for the teacher?

3. What are the salient components of an effective decision-making model for educational planning?

4. What is the difference between a portfolio and a dossier, and how can they be used to help the teacher in the assessment process?

5. What are some information-collection and evaluation techniques?

REFERENCES

Anderson, J. (forthcoming). The Canadian test of basic skills, 1990. In J. C. Conoley & J. J. Kramer (Eds.), *The mental measurement yearbook*. Lincoln, NE: Buros Institute of Mental Measurements.

Anderson, J., & Bachor, D. (1990). Integrating special needs students: A survey of constituents in one school district. *Canadian Journal of Special Education, 6*, 101-120.

Bachor, D. (1990). Towards improving assessment of students with special needs: Expanding the data base to include classroom performance. *The Alberta Journal of Educational Research, 36*, 65-77.

Bachor, D. (1991). Thinking skills, strategic behaviour and arithmetic word problems: Research, assessment and instruction. In R. F. Mulcahy, J. Andrews, & R. Short (Eds.), *Thinking for a change: Recent perspectives and directions* (pp. 137-160). New York: Praeger.

Bachor, D., & Anderson, J. O. (1990). *Assessment practices in the primary program: Description of observed practices, functional factors, and recommendations as to some general principles*. Victoria: Province of British Columbia, Ministry of Education.

Bachor, D., & Crealock, C. (1986). *Instructional strategies for students with special needs*. Scarborough, ON: Prentice-Hall.

Board of Education for the City of Etobicoke Writing Committee (1987). *Making the grade: Evaluating student progress*. Scarborough, ON: Prentice-Hall.

Conoley, J. C., & Kramer, J. J. (forthcoming) (Eds.), *The mental measurement yearbook*. Lincoln, NE: Buros Institute of Mental Measurements.

Deno, S. L. (1985). Curriculum-based assessment: The emerging alternative. *Exceptional Children, 52*, 219-232.

Deno, S. L., Marston, D., & Mirkin, P. (1982). Valid measurement procedures for continuous evaluation of written expression. *Exceptional Children, 48*, 368-376.

Dolch, E. W. (1945). *A manual for remedial reading*. Champaign, IL: Garrard Press.

ETS. (1987). *ETS standards for quality and fairness*. Princeton, NJ: Educational Testing Service.

Fuchs, L. S., Deno, S., & Mirkin, P. (1984). The effects of frequent curriculum-based measurement and evaluation on pedagogy, student achievement, and student awareness of learning. *American Educational Research Journal, 21*, 449-460.

Fuchs, L. S., & Fuchs, D. (1986). Curriculum-based assessment of progress towards long-term and short-term goals. *Journal of Special Education, 20*, 69-82.

Fuchs, D., Fuchs, L. S., Benowitz, S., & Barringer, K. (1987). Norm-referenced tests: Are they valid for use with handicapped students? *Exceptional Children, 54*, 263-271.

Gartner, A., & Lipsky, D. K. (1987). Beyond special education: Toward a quality system for all students. *Harvard Educational Review, 57*, 367-395.

Gronlund, N. E., & Linn, R. L. (1990). *Measurement and evaluation in teaching* (6th ed.). New York: Macmillan.

Hilliard III, A. G. (1989). Back to Binet: The case against the use of IQ tests in the schools. *Diagnostique, 14*, 125-135.

Hieronymous, A. N., Lindquist, E. F., Hoover, H. D., & King-Shaw, E. M. (1990). *Canadian test of basic skills*. Toronto: Nelson Canada.

Hirshosen, A., & McGuigan, C. (1984). Something isn't always better than nothing: On the use of educational and psychological tests. *B. C. Journal of Special Education, 8*, 99-106.

Humphries, T. W., & Wilson, A. K. (1986). An instructional-based model for assessing learning disabilities. *Canadian Journal of Special Education, 2*, 55-66.

Joint Advisory Committee (1993). Code of fair assessment practices for education in Canada. Edmonton: Joint Advisory Committee. (Draft Available from Joint Advisory Committee, Centre for Research in Applied Measurement and Evaluation, 3-104 Education Building North, University of Alberta, Edmonton, Alberta, T6G 2G5).

Lawson, M., J. & Rice, D. N. (1987). Solving word problems: A detailed analysis using think aloud data. In J. Bergeron, N. Herscovics, & C. Kieran (Eds.), *Proceedings of the Eleventh Conference of the International Group for the Psychology of Mathematics Education, Volume 2* (pp. 170-176). Montreal: PME.

Lupart, J. L. (1990). An in-depth assessment model for gifted/learning disabled students. *Canadian Journal of Special Education, 6*, 1-14.

Miller, M. (1991). Self-assessment as a specific strategy for teaching the gifted learning disabled. *Journal for the Education of the Gifted, 14*, 178-188.

Nixon, N. (1990). Assessment issues in relation to experience-based learning on placements within courses. In C. Bell & D. Harris (Eds.), *World yearbook of education 1990: Assessment and evaluation* (pp. 81-111). London: Kogan Page.

Nuttall, D., & Goldstein, H. (1984). Profiles and graded tests: The technical issues. In J. Mortinare (Ed.), *Profiles in action* (pp. 5-15). London: Further Education Unit.

Palincsar, A. S., David, Y. M., Winn, J. A., & Stevens, D. D. (1991). Examining the context of strategy instruction. *Remedial and Special Education, 12*(3), 43-53.

Popham, W. J. (1990). *Modern educational measurement: A practitioner's perspective* (2nd ed.). Englewood Cliffs: Prentice-Hall.

Pugach, M. C., & Johnson, L. J. (1989). The challenge of implementing collaboration between general and special education. *Exceptional Children, 56*, 232-235.

Reason, R., Farrell, P., & Mittler, P. (1990). Changes in assessment. In N. Entwistle (Ed.), *Handbook of educational ideas and practices* (pp. 1023-1034). London: Routledge.

Reid, D. K., & Hresko, W. P. (1980). Thinking about thinking about it in that way: Test data and instruction. *Exceptional Education Quarterly, 1*(3), 47-57.

Reynolds, M. (1989). An historical perspective: The delivery of special education to mildly disabled and at-risk students. *Remedial and Special Education, 10*(6), 7-11.

Salvia, J. & Hughes, C. (1990). *Curriculum-based assessment: Testing what is taught*. New York: Macmillan.

Salvia, J. & Ysseldyke, J (1988). *Assessment in special and remedial education* (5th ed.). Boston: Houghton-Mifflin.

Samuels, S. J. (1979). The method of repeated readings. *The Reading Teacher, 29*, 403-408.

Sattler, J. (1988). *Assessment of Children* (3rd ed.). San Diego: Jerome M. Sattler.

Simon, H. A. (1975). The functional equivalence of problem solving skills. *Cognitive Psychology, 7*, 268-288.

Simon, H. A. (1978). Information-processing theory of human problem solving skills. In W. Estes (Ed.), *Handbook of learning and cognitive processes, Volume 5* (pp. 271-295). Hillsdale, NJ: Lawrence Erlbaum.

Singer, J. D., Palfrey, J. S., Butler, J., A. & Walker, D. K. (1989). Variation in special education classification across school districts: How does where you live affect what you are labeled? *American Educational Research Journal, 26,* 261-281.

Stainback, W., Stainback, S., Courtnage, L., & Jaben, T. (1985). Facilitating mainstreaming by modifying the mainstream. *Exceptional Children, 52,* 144-152.

Thomson, G. O. B., Ward, J., & Gow, L. (1988). The education of children with special needs: A cross-cultural perspective. *European Journal of Special Needs Education, 3,* 125-137.

Traub, R. E. (1990). Assessment in the classroom: What is the role of research? *The Alberta Journal of Educational Research, 36,* 85-91.

Wesson, C., Fuchs, L., Tindal, G., Mirkin, P., & Deno, S. L. (1986). Facilitating the efficiency of on-going curriculum-based measurement. *Teacher Education and Special Education, 9,* 166-173.

Wiederholt, J. L. (1989). Restructuring special education services: The past, present, and future. *Learning Disabilities Quarterly, 12,* 181-191.

Wilson, R. J., & Rees, R. (1990). Ecology of assessment: Evaluation in educational settings. *Canadian Journal of Education, 15,* 215-228.

Wolf, D., Bixby, J., Glenn, J., & Gardiner, H. (1991). To use their minds well: Investigating new forms of student assessment. In G. Grant (Ed.), *Review of Educational Research, Volume 17* (pp. 31-74.) Washington: American Educational Research Association.

Ysseldyke, J. E. (1983). Current practices in making psycho-educational decisions about learning disabled students. *Journal of Learning Disabilities, 16,* 226-233.

Ysseldyke, J. E. (1987). Classification of handicapped students. In M. C. Wang, M. C. Reynolds, & H. J. Walberg (Eds.), *Handbook of special education: Research and practice, Volume 1* (pp. 253-271). Oxford: Pergamon.

CLASSROOM MANAGEMENT WITHIN THE CONTEXT OF TEACHING: *A HOLISTIC PERSPECTIVE*

CHAPTER
9

CHAPTER OBJECTIVES

To provide a conceptual framework for understanding the nature of classroom management.

To review an appropriate approach and style of teaching and managing.

To note various learning and behavioural needs of students.

To describe ways of arranging the classroom and establishing classroom climate.

To discuss the important instructional factors, lesson planning components, and administrative functions related to classroom management.

To overview administrative functions related to classroom management.

To outline the development of classroom rules and routines.

To describe the salient aspects of behaviouristic management.

To recommend ways of dealing with specific behavioural problems.

As you walk into the classroom, there is a poster on the wall with the words "Classroom Rules." The rules listed on the poster are based on the three Rs: Respect, Reasonableness, and Responsibility. The three Rs serve as a basis for the school's rules as a whole. Part of the blackboard is used to remind students of their homework for that day. In addition, each student has a "binder reminder" that travels between the home and the school as a way of reminding students and their parents of homework and other activities. There is a good feeling in this classroom because everybody seems to get along and enjoy what they are doing.

There are thirty-three students in Mrs. Jones's classroom. Collectively, these students appear to be very active and excited about being in school. Individually, they present many different interests, behavioural tendencies, psychosocial needs, and academic abilities. For example, Samantha loves to talk to her friends and likes to arrange for recess activities before the day has even formally begun; Meagan is shy, withdrawn, and sometimes argumentative; Michael needs to have everything repeated to him and is often off task; Andrew is easily distractible; Sylvia is very bright and creative, and likes to make up her own stories to read to the class rather than use the books that are assigned for oral reading; Scott is nervous with strangers and has a low self-concept; Joel is very cooperative and likes to be a group leader; and Tony is always seeking attention.

Mrs. Jones likes her students to be actively involved in the learning process. She routinely uses cooperative group activities, encourages students to discuss task-related things among themselves, and wants them to solve their own problems, with a little guidance from her when needed. Mrs. Jones favours a whole language approach to teaching. She encourages her students to write about their own experiences, or about topics of their choice, and to develop their writing and reading abilities by practicing various skills across a variety of tasks and subject areas. She guides them into taking a strategic approach to their learning, and provides remedial instruction in areas that prove to be difficult. For example, reading and writing are a source of frustration for Mark, yet he does well in math and loves to recite poems and tell stories in class.

Mrs. Jones modifies Mark's program to allow for his successful participation. She is very conscious of the specialized help that Mark needs, and tries to attend to his needs as best she can. Since she has thirty-two other students (many of whom also need specialized attention), individualized programming and instruction is very difficult to plan and provide. Mrs. Jones arranges for student teachers from a local university to have their practicum experience in her classroom. In return for her supervisory duties and responsibilities, as well as her mentoring, these student teachers provide continual and specifically designed instruction for Mark and many of the other students who require curricular modifications, remediation, and/or enrichment. She also arranges for the resource (special education) teachers within the school to work cooperatively with her each day, particularly when she is initiating and/or developing new concepts in language arts or math.

Moreover, Mrs. Jones organizes and orchestrates a daily parent volunteer program. Volunteer parents come into the classroom at specified times each day and assist students in a number of areas. Parents may join cooperative groups as active participants, mediate reciprocal teaching in reading, tutor individual students, and/or monitor students' assignment work, provide feedback, and record student performance and progress under the direction of Mrs. Jones. Additionally, many of the students participate in individually tailored home-reading programs with their parents. For example, Mark brings home a book and an accompany-

ing cassette tape of a story. After listening and reading silently with the tape, he tells his parents about the story.

The students in Mrs. Jones's class seem to know her expectations concerning their behaviour. She consistently tells them about the good things she observes them doing (e.g., showing respect and concern for others, helping each other find solutions to problems, being patient when wanting attention), and about the "not so good" things (e.g., disturbing classmates who are doing an assigned task, teasing each other, name-calling, excluding others from group activities, being disrespectful towards others).

She also gets her students to reflect upon their own behaviour and actions. For example, the other day, Allan, preoccupied with his own interests, was making it difficult for the other children to hear Mrs. Jones's directions for a cooperative group exercise. Upon noticing this behaviour, Mrs. Jones first got the attention of the class and then (supportively and nonjudgmentally) said to Allan that his disruptive behaviour during small-group instruction made it difficult for people to hear the directions. "When we can't hear the directions, will we know what to do?" she asked him. He replied no, and she continued, "Is there a time when focusing on your interests is an appropriate thing to do?" To this question, Allan provided some alternative times that this activity would be appropriate, and chose an alternative plan for dealing with his personal interests the next time instructions were given to cooperative groups. Everyone in the class, including Allan, seemed approving of this brief problem-solving discussion between Mrs. Jones and Allan.

Mrs. Jones likes to focus her students' attention on their own thinking processes and challenge them to consider the adequacy of their responses. She helps all her students see that there are alternative behaviours and actions, and tries to instil within them the idea that they are competent and able to change. According to Mrs. Jones, mistakes are acceptable: they are fixable, and we can all learn from them. Mrs. Jones also reinforces and rewards her students' appropriate behaviours with such things as "Happy Face" charts and the provision of privileges to individuals and/or groups. Sometimes, she has had to make contracts with some of her students and deal with them more privately and therapeutically.

All in all, Mrs. Jones shows courtesy and empathy for her students, and is able to promote positive and respectful interactions. She also provides active, interesting, and meaningful learning experiences for her students, and is able to effectively manage various levels of behavioural disturbances from students in ways that do not interfere with the learning and behaviour of other students. Once again, there is a good feeling in this classroom.

If teachers teach, they also manage behaviour through actions. If teaching and managing are viewed as one, the overall process of teaching is likely to be more coherent, more reinforcing and more sustaining for teachers and students in the long run (Kameenui & Simmons, 1990, p. 469).

◇ INTRODUCTION

We view classroom management as a comprehensive and holistic enterprise rather than as an operation of isolated skills or parts. From our perspective, classroom management refers to the orchestration of classroom life so that all children can maximize their learning potential. We conceptualize classroom management as having three major interactive facets: *proactive*, *supportive*, and *reactive*. Proactive classroom management involves doing things that promote successful learning and appropriate behaviour and, by and large, prevent misbehaviour from occurring. Supportive classroom management involves the use of effective instructional procedures that maintain and facilitate successful learning and appropriate behaviour. Reactive classroom management consists of the methods that teachers use to change unsuccessful learning and misbehaviour into successful learning and appropriate behaviour. While some teachers may concentrate on a single facet of classroom management, effective teachers in inclusive classrooms use aspects of all three facets simultaneously and interchangeably throughout the school day. In other words, teachers need to constantly arrange classroom activities to keep students interested in learning, select and use effective instructional skills to increase the probability that students will learn, and correct or rechannel students' behaviour toward more acceptable behaviour.

◇ CLASSROOM MANAGEMENT FROM A THEORETICAL PERSPECTIVE

In this chapter, we examine the three facets of classroom management and their elements (see Table 9.1). These elements represent an integration of the cognitive, sociocultural, developmental, and behavioural perspectives on student learning, and thus they include a melding of the following views about classroom management: children need to be offered models of behaviour; the teacher and student need to communicate their ideas to each other; students need to be shown ways that will foster their ability to control and reflect upon their actions; students should be provided activities that match their developmental level and encourage them to explore their environment and construct knowledge; and students should be given sufficient order in their classrooms so that their learning can be reasonably structured and regulated.

Table 9.1		
The Facets and Elements of Classroom Management		
Proactive	*Supportive*	*Reactive*
Metacognitive approach to teaching	Instructional factors	Problem-solving
Mediational style of teaching	Lesson planning	Behaviouristic management
Accommodating students' needs	Administrative functions	Dealing with specific behavioural problems
Arranging the classroom environment	Rules and routines	
Establishing classroom climate		

The current literature on classroom management (Brophy, 1983; Doyle, 1986; Good, 1983; Jones & Jones, 1986) suggests that the facets and elements referred to above are centrally involved in the process of teaching. Therefore, along with being a holistic enterprise, we consider classroom management as a major part of classroom teaching. The overall purpose of this chapter is to present and discuss proactive, supportive, and reactive ways of achieving effective classroom management through the process of teaching. We begin with the first major facet and its elements of classroom management.

◆ PROACTIVE CLASSROOM MANAGEMENT

As mentioned above, proactive classroom management refers to things a teacher can do to minimize behaviour problems and to increase the chances that successful learning and appropriate behaviour will take place. This facet of classroom management has specifically to do with (1) teaching; (2) accommodating students' needs; and (3) establishing classroom environment and climate.

APPROACH AND STYLE OF TEACHING

There is no one correct way of managing a classroom. Teachers' approaches and styles of teaching and managing are influenced by their values and beliefs about how students should learn and behave. One teacher states her philosophy as follows:

> I believe that the teacher has the primary responsibility for developing students' knowledge. Students need to know many things and there isn't a lot of time to waste. Students should be rewarded for their good work and be penalized for lack of effort and poor work. I believe that teachers should tell students what they are expected to learn and how they are expected to behave in very simple and clear ways.

Another teacher states an alternative philosophy:

> I believe that the responsibility for learning lies primarily within the learner. Students need to know how to learn many things and understand the importance of their learning and behaviour. I believe that classroom behaviour should be discussed with my students so we can learn to respect each other and share and work together.

The above comments reflect two different sets of beliefs and values with respect to teaching and student learning and behaviour. It could be argued that the first teacher values the product of learning over the process of learning, and views students as passive rather than active learners. Moreover, this teacher favours a direct and didactic approach to teaching, and would appear to use extrinsic reinforcements to motivate students to learn. The second teacher values the process of learning over the product of learning, and views students as active rather than passive learners. Furthermore, this teacher favours an interactive approach to teaching, and would appear to use an intrinsic approach to motivation.

Traditional ideas about classroom management are based on the assumption that students are passive learners and dependent on teachers for controlling their learning and behaviour. Traditional approaches to classroom management have been partially based on the idea that classes consist of students with homogeneous learning styles, goals, and abilities, as well as common educational needs. Contemporary ideas about classroom management are based on the view that students are active learners and should be guided toward being independent with respect to their learning and behaviour. Contemporary approaches to classroom management are based on the idea that classes consist of students with heterogeneous learning styles, goals, and abilities, as well as varied educational needs—and that every attempt should be made to accommodate these differences and needs through flexible arrangements and shared responsibilities of school personnel and students.

Teachers who manage classrooms successfully have an approach and style of teaching that guides students to regulate their own learning and behaviour. Effective classroom managers believe that learning is, among other things, an active and organized process that requires students to be decision-makers, problem-solvers, and adaptive in their day-to-day performance encounters. Successful managers and teachers realize that school environments are unique and have changing demands that require students to develop adaptive strategies, as they attempt to resolve continually emerging problems. These teachers are aware that mere *content knowledge* (declarative knowledge) is not sufficient to meet the unique demands of changing contexts. More attention has to be given instead to developing *process knowledge* (procedural and conditional knowledge), which allows learners to know when, where, and how to use their skills.

Unfortunately, traditional education settings too often emphasize content knowledge to the exclusion of process knowledge. Acquiring facts and information often overrides making sense of new information and providing an opportunity to decide what can be done with it. There is a pressing need to develop within students the ability to independently and cooperatively adapt their thought processes to meet their contextual demands. To attain this ability, students need to develop their process knowledge, which we refer to as **metacognitive empowerment**. In order for students to develop metacognitive empowerment, teachers need to be able and willing to adopt a *metacognitive approach* and *mediational style of teaching* (discussed in the following two sections). For either approach or style to work, teachers must build positive and respectful interactions with students. According to Jones and Jones (1986), before teachers can foster such interactions with their students, "we [teachers] must be willing to encourage and even systematically seek students' feedback. We must be willing to become involved in openly discussing our own and the students' reactions to how the classroom is operating."

◆ metacognitive empowerment: the ability of individuals to reflect on and control their learning and behaviour

The Metacognitive Approach to Teaching

know what

Teaching doesn't just involve *what* one teaches. It also involves *how* one teaches. For example, teachers who are able to demonstrate to their students that they are liked and appreciated for who they are can positively influence their students' academic achievement and affective states (Brophy & Evertson, 1976; Norman & Harris, 1981). How teachers do this is by being warm and friendly and displaying empathy and positive regard for their students (Truax & Tatum, 1966). However, teachers also need to be firm with their students occasionally and set realistic limits for their behaviour. "Warmth and concern can exist side by side with firmness. Indeed, effective teaching involves blending these vital ingredients" (Jones & Jones, 1986, p. 87). Effective teachers are able to develop an open and trustworthy relationship with their students and convey to their students that they are willing and eager to help them in the learning process (Conger & Petersen, 1984; Purkey & Novak, 1984). Teachers accomplish this by involving students in open discussion regarding their day-to-day learning and behavioural encounters, and by facilitating a problem-solving approach toward goal attainment and conflict resolution.

A *metacognitive approach to teaching* is evident when teachers: (1) show an interest in how their students acquire and process information; (2) are aware of the levels of difficulty associated with the tasks they give their students;

(3) know their students' approaches to assigned tasks and ways to teach them to be more efficient and effective with these tasks; (4) support and promote within their students an active, independent, self-confident, and meaningful approach to learning; and (5) are able to monitor the effectiveness of their teaching, as well as their students' learning, and make modifications when and where it is necessary.

Teachers who take a metacognitive approach to teaching also try to foster their students' potential for decision-making, problem-solving, and creative thinking and learning, and to help students clarify their academic and social goals. Such teachers tend to be good listeners and to appreciate the views of their students, as they guide them toward evaluating the merits and limitations of their opinions and approaches with respect to their learning and behaviour.

The Mediational Style of Teaching — *know what* — 5 *mechanisms*

A *mediational style of teaching* is evident when a teacher focuses on the process of learning rather than just content and skills. According to Haywood (1987), mediators provide information to students that allows them to make links between prior information and present learning; ask questions of their students rather than give them answers; foster their students' ability to ask questions; guide their students' learning by arranging and directing sequences of learning experiences in a developmental fashion; build confidence within their students by communicating belief in their competence as learners and thinkers; focus their attention on the students' learning and thinking processes and try to empower them to be active, independent, and thoughtful learners and thinkers.

Haywood (1987) isolates five frequently used mechanisms of mediational teaching: (1) **process questioning** whereby students' attention is focused on their own learning and thinking processes. For example, if a child is rigid or inflexible in his or her approach to a task, or is having difficulty performing a task, a teacher might ask, "How else could you do that?" or "What must you do first, and how could you find out what to do next?" instead of showing or telling the student what to do; (2) **bridging** whereby teachers encourage students to modify, extend, or try different approaches for solving problems or completing tasks. This teaching mechanism attempts to help students generalize and transfer their learning and thinking strategies from one situational context to another. For example, students taught to use a particular strategy for improving their reading comprehension—e.g., RAP: R (read) A (analyze) P (paraphrase)—would be encouraged to apply this strategy to another context (bridge the strategy). In this example, a teacher might ask his or her students, "How could we use the RAP strategy to help us comprehend the information we get while watching a film?" To which students might reply, "Let's change the "R" to "L" for *Listen*." Thus, the RAP strategy becomes a LAP strategy when the context is changed from reading to

◆ process questioning: a form of questioning in which students' attention is focused on their own learning and thinking processes

◆ bridging: getting students to generalize and transfer their learning from one situation to another

listening; (3) *challenging of responses* whereby teachers encourage their students to justify their responses in order to develop their critical thinking capabilities. For example: "Yes, you are right, it could be that way. Perhaps you could look at it another way and find an even better way of doing it, " or "Yes, that's right. How did you know that should be the answer? Why is it better than this one?" "Could you tell me how you thought about and found your answer?"; (4) *teaching about rules* whereby the teacher attempts to further generalize the students' learning and thinking approaches. For example, after imparting some important information to students, the teacher might ask, "What could we do to help us remember this information?" and "Could we use this approach with other types of information?"; and (5) *emphasizing systematic and sequential learning and thinking strategies*, whereby the teacher encourages students to be strategic in their learning and thinking, and reinforces the concept that decision-making, problem-solving, and learning are often dependent on the efficient and effective use of learning and thinking strategies.

What follows is a sample of good mediational phrases from Haywood, Brooks, and Bruns (1986) that can be used in the classroom:

- What do you need to do next?
- Tell me how you did that.
- What do you think would happen if _____?
- When have you done something like this before?
- How would you feel if _____?
- Stop and look carefully at what you are doing.
- What do you think the problem is?
- Can you think of another way we could do this?
- Why is this one better than that one?
- Where have you done this before to help you solve a problem?
- Let's make a plan so we don't miss anything.
- How can you find out?
- How is _____ different (like) _____?

Adopting a mediational style of teaching requires teachers to accept and encourage open dialogue and active learning within the classroom (see Chapter 14 for further discussion on shared communication in the classroom). At certain times and in certain situations, a more direct and structured approach may be the most appropriate style of teaching to exercise. However, from our perspective, teachers should use the mediational style of teaching when trying to help students be active, self-responsible, and independent problem-solvers and decision-makers. This style of teaching reflects a proactive and preventative approach to classroom management, as opposed to a controlling and remedial approach. Various authors and researchers (Brophy, 1982; DeLuke & Knoblock, 1987; Jones & Jones, 1986; Smith, 1983) have proposed a number of skills that we believe characterize a mediational style of teaching:

- Discussing issues and/or important matters regarding student behaviour as soon as possible after the behaviour occurs.
- Providing direct feedback to students about their behaviour rather than informing parents and other teachers about it.
- Speaking courteously and respectfully to students.
- Making nonverbal messages congruent with verbal messages.
- Expressing personal feelings with students privately by using informal "I" messages rather than formal third-person messages. For example, instead of saying, "You are always talking when I am talking," or "We should always allow others to express themselves before we begin talking," a teacher might better say, "I get frustrated when someone else is talking when I am talking."
- Providing specific, descriptive, and nonjudgmental feedback to students.
- Providing consistent praise to students that is contingent on specific and desired behaviours, as well as appropriate for the situation and particular individual.
- Emphasizing the positive behaviours students exhibit instead of focusing on the areas in which students need to improve or adjust.
- Demonstrating empathic, nonjudgmental listening so that students are encouraged to express their views and feelings openly and freely.
- Modelling behaviours that are congruent with the teacher's goals for teaching and student learning.
- Guiding students toward solving problems or resolving misbehaviour independently.
- Monitoring students regularly so that potential problems can be dealt with before they escalate into disruption.
- Helping students manage their problems rather than threatening them with some form of punishment.

We now turn to the second major element of proactive management—the accommodation of student needs.

ACCOMMODATING STUDENTS' NEEDS

All students have a need to be socially accepted (Dreikers, 1968), and to experience a sense of competence and control in their endeavours if they are to develop a positive feeling about themselves (Coopersmith, 1967). Students also have a need for self-exploration and meaningful participation in school and community. They need to experience positive social interaction with peers and adults, and be provided with opportunities for achievement (Dorman, 1981; Lipsitz, 1984). Students need to feel comfortable in the school environment and have time in their school day to relax. They also need to feel safe and secure; to experience a sense of belonging and affection from those that are around them; to be given a chance to express and develop their potentials, capacities, and talents; and to have all of their physiological needs met (Maslow, 1968). All students need to be actively and meaningfully involved in the learning process (De Charms, 1976; Rotter, 1966; White, 1959), to experience success in their academic endeavours, and to be provided with well-organized environments that balance structure with flexibility.

All students, moreover, have strengths and weaknesses. Students with gifts and talents are sometimes perceived as being nonconforming, dominant, snobbish, egocentric, "off the wall," stubborn, or defiant, while children with learning disabilities and behavioural disturbances can be perceived as being awkward, emotionally unstable, impulsive, inattentive, or slow to learn. However, all of these students also have very positive academic and social characteristics, which teachers can build upon through the provision of enrichment activities.

Within inclusive classrooms, teachers are likely to find students who are task-committed and academically successful, and who value school work; students who are continually looking for teacher support, encouragement, and help, who are reluctant learners, and who value friendships over school work; and students who are aggressive and disruptive, who reject school work, and who have difficulty getting along with others (Good & Power, 1976). Although all students have common needs, students with particular learning and behavioural styles, abilities, and difficulties have specific needs. Understanding these needs can help teachers plan and prepare for more effective classroom management.

Students with advanced cognitive abilities need opportunities to foster their creativity, develop their leadership capabilities, enrich their academic achievement, and extend their intellectual-processing abilities. According to a study by Kerry (1981), many children with advanced cognitive abilities who find the work assigned to them to be too easy, and therefore, boring, may display disruptive behaviour. Sometimes these children dominate classroom discussions because of their interest in a topic, or they might attempt to correct the work of their teachers and peers or disturb others because they have finished their work ahead of time. Behaviours that many teachers consider problematic among these children include the tendency to be inattentive to others and interrupt them when they are talking; to be argumentative about doing tasks they perceive as being trivial; to be critical or bossy; and to display high energy, which can lead to disorganized work habits (Whitmore, 1979).

Some students with advanced cognitive abilities need to be given freedom as well as direction to maximize their development, while others require more structure in order to pursue and maximize their potential. Some might need assistance in defining their goals, expanding their interests, accomplishing their objectives, and developing their talents. Moreover, although many gifted students have excellent social skills, some need help in relating to significant others (i.e., peers, teachers, parents).

Delisle, Whitmore, and Ambrose (1987) suggest that the major causes of behaviour problems among students with advanced cognitive abilities are: (1) a need to behave as they feel "regular" children behave; (2) a need to prove to significant others that they are not as smart as teachers and parents believe they are; and (3) a need to convey their feeling that the type of curriculum and instruction they are receiving is inappropriate. According to Feldhusen and Wyman (1980), the basic needs of these students include: (1) a need to develop their basic skills and concepts to their maximum potential; (2) a need to be provided learning activities that accommodate their achievement level and learning pace; (3) a need to develop their convergent and divergent thinking abilities, as well as their creative talents, spatial abilities, verbal abilities, independence, self-direction, and discipline in learning; (4) a need to foster their higher-level goals and aspirations; (5) a need to promote their self-awareness, interests, and imagination; and (6) a need to have access to information about diverse topics, and to be stimulated in their reading, studying, and performance endeavours.

Students with learning disabilities tend to be average to bright learners who have difficulties performing in one or more school subjects. Because they have the capability to do well in some areas and learn things quickly and easily, their failure to learn in other areas and not meet the expectations of their teachers and others can be perplexing for all concerned.

Information-processing difficulties (see Chapter 3) may cause many of these children to underachieve in such areas as reading, writing, and arithmetic. Many students with learning disabilities are characterized as being hyperactive, inattentive, inflexible, distractible, and unorganized, all of which can lead to behaviour problems. Learning-disabled students may also have difficulty interacting with others, either because they fail to understand messages given by others or communicate their views inadequately.

The more critical needs of students with learning disabilities include: (1) a need to develop their organization skills; (2) a need to improve their concentration and attention; (3) a need to foster greater self-control; (4) a need to increase their academic self-concept; (5) a need to develop their learning strategies; (6) a need to facilitate a more active and independent approach to their learning; (7) a need to strengthen their ability to make, maintain, and continue positive personal relationships with peers and adults; and (8) a need to develop greater communicative competence.

Students with behaviour disorders create discomfort for themselves and for those around them. They have been described by their teachers as incorrigible, aggressive, withdrawn, disruptive, and antagonistic. Children with significant behavioural disturbances demonstrate prolonged behaviour that is undesirable, inappropriate, and maladaptive. Although most students with behaviour disorders have adequate intelligence, they often have difficulties in learning, relating to others, and demonstrating appropriate behaviours and feelings.

Children with behavioural disorders may exhibit a wide range of inappropriate classroom behaviours that are related to the aforementioned difficulties. For example, with respect to relating to others, some children may be highly selective in their relationships; may be in conflict with or withdraw from others; may resist attempts from others to foster more positive forms of relationships; and may be generally uncooperative, defiant, and/or disobedient. With respect to their difficulty in learning, some children may have specific difficulties in reading, math, or other subjects; may make self-deprecatory remarks; and may push help away and/or refuse to do work and take care of their materials. With respect to their inability to properly convey their feelings, many children with behaviour disorders have trouble making and keeping friends. This aggravates an already low self-esteem, which can leave many of these students not only friendless but also unwilling to take risks in social settings or allow others to help them.

The major needs of students with behaviour disorders include: (1) a need to foster positive interpersonal relationships; (2) a need for greater awareness of their emotions and conflicts; (3) a need to enhance personal coping skills; (4) a need to increase their motivation to learn new skills; (5) a need to promote a greater willingness to try new tasks; (6) a need to develop a positive self-concept; and (7) a need to develop a greater degree of personal responsibility and accountability.

Students with significant cognitive delays have below-average intelligence and deficits in adaptive behaviour. Most students with significant cognitive delays have difficulty acquiring basic academic skills at grade-level expectation and difficulty applying these skills to their day-to-day activities. Their delayed academic development can be due to deficits in attention, memory, and the ability to transfer information from one context to another, or it can be the result of particular difficulties related to abstract reasoning, decision-making, and problem-solving. Because of their slower rate of learning and difficulties in reasoning, many of these students demonstrate more problem behaviours than their peers in the regular classroom. For example, they may not follow directions efficiently or start and finish assignments on time, and they may say or do inappropriate things that cause them to be rejected or ignored by their regular classroom peers. Their socialization skills tend to be underdeveloped, making it difficult for them to interact with same-age peers (aside from the fact that their interests and play abilities are often more commensurate with those of younger children).

The major needs of students with significant cognitive delays include: (1) a need to develop basic academic skills; (2) a need to improve their ability to interact with others; (3) a need to enhance speech and language skills; (4) a need to develop information-processing strategies; (5) a need to advance their organizational and self-management skills; (6) a need to develop self-concept; and (7) a need to strengthen their ability to conceptualize and generalize information.

Students from diverse cultural backgrounds have customs, values, and language that differ from those found in their classroom and school (see Chapter 5). Because of their different backgrounds and experiences, they tend to demonstrate behaviours that are at variance with those of their peers. Some may have significant difficulty understanding and speaking English, while others may have difficulty with academic instruction and learning because of different entry-level skills, values, approaches to learning, and/or experiences with respect to classroom rules, routines, and expectations.

The major needs of students who are not from the dominant culture are: (1) a need to secure their own self-identity and develop their self-concept; (2) a need to express their views and problems related to cultural integration; (3) a need to develop their communication skills and language competence; and (4) a need to strengthen social interaction.

To sum up, classroom management requires teachers to adopt an approach to teaching that accommodates their students' particular needs and styles of learning, and at the same time satisfies the common needs of all students for such things as a sense of safety, belonging, and achievement, and meaningful learning experiences that empower them to become independent decision-makers and problem-solvers to the best of their abilities.

The third and last major element of proactive classroom management—establishing the classroom environment and climate—is discussed in the following section.

ESTABLISHING THE CLASSROOM ENVIRONMENT AND CLIMATE

Before teaching ever starts, teachers can increase the likelihood of successful learning and decrease that of behavioural problems by paying attention to the physical environment of the classroom. The classroom should be pleasant in appearance and conducive to the teaching and learning process. Moreover, teachers should arrange the classroom with respect to their preferred learning formats and the distinctive properties of classrooms.

Learning Formats — *differentiate btwn 6 formats*

According to Mercer and Mercer (1985), there are six general learning formats: (1) large-group instruction, (2) small-group instruction, (3) one-to-one instruction, (4) independent learning, (5) collaborative learning, and (6) peer teaching.

Large-group instruction is the traditional learning format and is most appropriate when the teacher wants to address the entire class. Teachers typically use this format of teaching when teaching curriculum subjects like math, social studies, and science. Large-group instruction is also used as a way to orchestrate interactive communication with all of the class members.

Small-group instruction is used when a teacher wants to have more focused discussion with the students and be able to provide specific feedback. Small groups usually consist of three to six students. Teachers very often group students according to common areas of academic strength and weakness in order to accommodate their learning needs more directly. Grouping arrangements allow for greater peer interaction, more efficient student management, and better use of instructional time. For example, a teacher could use the first ten to fifteen minutes of a sixty-minute academic period to provide information to the entire class about a particular concept. Following this, he or she could divide the class into a number of small groups and assign them distinctive goals and objectives related to the information provided to the large group.

One-to-one instruction allows the teacher to work individually with students. Through this arrangement, the teacher can make specific lesson plans and instructional modifications for the individual student, and can more closely monitor his or her progress as well as provide specific feedback. The arrangement of one-to-one instruction depends on the ability of teachers to successfully group other students in order to provide the opportunity and time for individualized instruction. Teachers who are able to arrange for professional aides, parent volunteers, or collaborative teaching can also plan for this type of learning format in a consistent manner.

Independent learning is used when students need to work on particular skills and can do this without much assistance. For example, students could be given time to study spelling independently using a strategy they have been previously taught and can employ proficiently.

Collaborative learning occurs when students work cooperatively toward completing an academic or social task. Students will typically need to be taught how to work cooperatively in groups by their teacher in order to ensure successful interactions and task completion (see Johnson & Johnson, 1986, for further discussion on cooperative learning).

Peer teaching takes place when students who have competence in particular skills teach—under the supervision and guidance of the teacher—other students who have difficulty with those skills (Delquadri, Greenwood, Whorton, Carta, & Hall, 1986; Fowler, 1986). This learning format can be practiced not only inside but outside the classroom as students help students of other grade levels in particular areas. Teachers who want to use this format

◆ peer teaching: instruction of one student by another in a structured situation in which materials are well planned and organized

need to spend significant amounts of time teaching students how to plan their lessons for other students and how to provide support and corrective feedback. However, many teachers have found this time to be well spent. As noted by Jones and Jones (1986), peer teaching can instil in students the idea that offering help is a positive and rewarding behaviour, as well as give them a greater understanding of individual differences in learning.

Distinctive Properties of Classrooms — *know what are* · *multi etc.* · *predic etc.*

According to Doyle (1986), classroom settings have distinctive properties that influence the behaviour of both students and teachers. These elements include: *multidimensionality*, which refers to the enormous variety of events and tasks that take place in classrooms; *simultaneity*, which refers to the fact that many things happen at once in classrooms that must be monitored by the teacher (e.g., individual seatwork, group projects, requests for assistance, interruptions, and class discussions); *immediacy*, which refers to the rapid pace of classroom events that results in teachers having little time to reflect before acting; *unpredictability*, which refers to the fact that distractions and unexpected events often occur in classrooms, making it difficult sometimes for the teacher to anticipate how planned activities will turn out on particular days; *publicness*, which stresses that classrooms are public places in which the activities of the teacher are witnessed by students; and *history*, which emphasizes the considerable amount of time teachers and students spend together—time during which events occur that can shape the norms of behaviour throughout the entire term.

Doyle (1986) suggests that if teachers can anticipate these factors, and if they are aware of their students' needs, then they can organize the classroom accordingly. For example, a teacher who knows that he or she is going to arrange a variety of events and tasks that need to be monitored, who anticipates a good deal of movement and interaction in the classroom, might consider a room arrangement like the one presented in Figure 9.1. This room arrangement is flexible enough to allow for various learning formats, with areas for both active interaction and independent work. The classroom space is designed to maximize teacher control and student comfort, to facilitate student movement in the classroom, and to minimize potential distractions.

Classroom research conducted over the past twenty years has provided detailed information about how successful teachers organize their classrooms. Key assumptions regarding effective classroom management are that effective managers provide good organization, planning, scheduling, and instruction (Brophy, 1983). One sign that effective management is in place is when students are comfortable in the classroom environment, and know where they are supposed to be and what they are supposed to do (Arlin, 1979).

According to Gray (cited in Polloway, Patton, Payne, & Payne, 1989), teachers should consider the following when designing their classrooms.

Figure 9.1

Example of a Room Arrangement

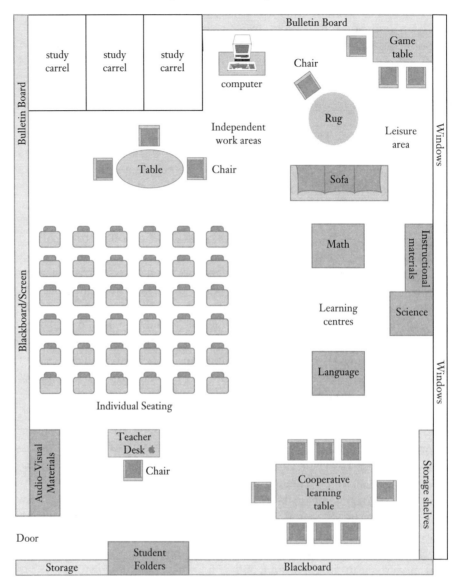

First, the physical setting should allow for student comfort; thus, chairs, tables, desks, and classroom materials need to be provided that are appropriate for the age and physical needs of the students. Second, students should be given space to be alone and away from group activities, as well as space to socialize with others. Third, the classroom environment should be flexible and manipulable in order to meet the changing needs of students. Fourth, the environment should be created by both the students and the teacher so that both can identify the classroom as belonging to them. Fifth, the classroom should be arranged so that there are a variety of seating and work areas to accommodate various academic and social tasks, as well as students' needs.

Not only do teachers need to organize their classrooms to meet the needs and demands of an inclusive classroom, but they also have to be organized themselves in order to establish and maintain order. Kounin's (1970) and others' (Brophy & Evertson, 1976; Good & Grouws, 1977) investigations related to classroom management have revealed that effective classroom managers deal with problems quickly before they become major disturbances. They are able to do this because they frequently monitor the classroom and let the students know that they are continually aware of what is happening in the classroom (Kounin characterizes this teacher behaviour as "withitness").

Effective classroom managers are also able to do more than one thing at a time. For example, when providing individual attention to one student, they are also able to monitor other students and groups of students. Furthermore, when they provide instruction and direction to one group of students they are able to deal with individual problems, questions, and concerns at the same time (Kounin characterizes this teacher behaviour as an "overlapping" technique). Effective managers are well prepared for teaching, and can provide instruction smoothly and continuously without confusion or uncertainty. They are able to deal with minor disturbances of individual students with such techniques as nonverbal signalling, eye contact, or proximity control (moving close to the student who is misbehaving) without disrupting the entire class.

Along with organizing the classroom, the teacher also has to establish and maintain a classroom atmosphere that allows for shared responsibility, recognizes and accepts individual needs and differences, accommodates the increasing complexity of the student population, encourages social interaction and integration, and promotes open dialogue and active learning. In other words, the teacher must establish a classroom climate in which students feel happy and are excited about learning.

Classroom Climate

According to Wayson and Lasley (1984) and Costa (1991), teachers can establish and maintain a positive classroom atmosphere by: (1) clarifying teaching goals and developing students' ability to establish their own learning goals; (2) fostering students' alternative thinking so they can deal more efficiently with their academic and social problems; (3) developing their students' ability to understand and empathize with the ideas and feelings of others; (4) giving students practice in expressing their views and feelings; (5) facilitating their students' abilities to reflect on and evaluate their behaviours; (6) encouraging students to apply their skills and knowledge across a variety of domains and situations; (7) allowing students to try different ways of doing things in order to maximize their creativity, curiosity, and enjoyment; and (8) promoting positive values.

In order to accomplish the above suggestions, teachers need to create stress-free environments. Stress can come from peer rejection, conflict with peers, parents and teachers, doing poorly in school, having difficulty in expressing thoughts and opinions, receiving bad marks, trying to maintain high grades, and from changing classrooms (e.g., moving from a regular classroom to a resource room) (D'Aurora & Fimian, 1988; Hiebert, 1992). Stress can result in affective symptoms such as anxiety, insecurity, and anger; somatic symptoms such as dizziness and stomach upset; and behavioural symptoms like fighting, crying, and isolating oneself from peers (D'Auroras & Fimian, 1988).

In order to help children in stressful situations, it is important for teachers to develop their students' ability to cope effectively with stressful events. Teachers can help reduce stress by: (1) placing demands on students that do not exceed their ability to cope; (2) establishing reasonable and predictable classroom routines and rules; (3) presenting well-organized lessons; (4) using cooperative learning approaches; (5) being flexible and responsive to learner characteristics; (6) helping children set realistic goals regarding their learning and achievement; and (7) providing positive feedback to students in order to enhance their self-concept and internal locus of control (D'Aurora & Fimian, 1988; Dougherty & Deck, 1984).

Hiebert (1988) notes that increasing coping resources is an important means of controlling or preventing stress. He suggests that when teachers address students' coping resources, they begin by assessing the students' perceptions of the demands they are facing (e.g., the types of situations that the child finds demanding). Next, the teacher should try to determine how the child attempts to deal with the situation, and to discover his or her perception of how well the coping strategy works. Teaching the student better skills (strategies) for coping with the situation would be the next step (Hiebert, 1992). Improving students' ability to cope with various stressors is similar to the strategy approaches we have recommended for developing students' ability to cope with various academic and social tasks. All of these approaches involve teachers informing students directly about what strategies are, how they work, why they are useful, and when and where they should be used (Paris & Oka, 1986).

◇ SUPPORTIVE CLASSROOM MANAGEMENT

As noted earlier, supportive classroom management involves doing things that promote and maintain successful learning and appropriate behaviour. From our perspective, the major elements of this facet are (1) the instructional factors and skills embedded in the teacher's lesson planning and teaching; (2) lesson planning itself; and (3) the administrative components of classroom management.

CRITICAL INSTRUCTIONAL FACTORS   *what are they*

Christenson, Ysseldyke, and Thurlow (1989) provide an overview of many important factors related to teaching children with special learning and behavioural needs. In this section, we present some of these factors, as well as teacher behaviours that can help facilitate and maintain a secure, democratic, empowering, and positive classroom environment. For now, we turn our attention to the following nine important instructional factors.

(1) Select appropriate learning tasks and match with students. In order for teachers to maintain students' motivation to learn, they must give students tasks that are meaningful and commensurate with their abilities. Students need to be provided academic tasks that they can understand and successfully complete. When assigning tasks, teachers need to articulate clearly goals, objectives, and performance standards so that students know what is expected of them and why it is important for them to complete the task. The goals, objectives, and standards·of performance associated with the task or activity should be designed according to the characteristics and needs of the students. Performance expectations, for example, should be related to the student's ability levels. Furthermore, the activities or specific learning tasks need to be appropriate for the learner; for example, some students might be given tasks that are concrete and functional in nature, whereas other students may be given tasks that are more conceptual and abstract.

(2) Follow systematic instructional procedures. Effective teachers typically follow the *demonstration-prompt-practice* model of instruction, in which they review previously learned concepts and skills; explain and show students the information and skills they need to perform successfully; provide opportunities for students to practice the skills under their supervision; give feedback to students regarding their performance; note and correct errors; and allow students time to practice the skills independently. It is also important for teachers to explain to students how they can apply these skills to their learning tasks. Rosenshine and Stevens (1986) recommend that teachers follow six fundamental steps when adopting the demonstrate-prompt-practice instructional sequence:

- ◆ Review, check previous day's work (reteach if necessary).
- ◆ Present new content/skills.
- ◆ Guide student practice (and check for understanding).   *no*
- ◆ Feedback and correctives (and reteach if necessary).
- ◆ Independent student practice.
- ◆ Weekly and monthly reviews (p. 379).

(3) Provide sufficient time for students to engage themselves in their learning. Another important consideration is the amount of time students have to be actively involved in their learning. When students are given time to do activities related to the concepts being presented by the teacher, and allowed sufficient time to ask questions, respond to questions, and engage themselves with various learning tasks, learning and achievement increases. However,

research suggests that students spend a relatively small amount of time during the school day engaged in academics (Fisher & Berliner, 1985; Haynes & Jenkins, 1986). Ysseldyke and Christenson (1987) found in one of their studies that learning-disabled students and their nonhandicapped peers spent less than thirty minutes of a ninety-minute instructional period actively responding to academic tasks.

Teachers can increase student engagement several ways. First, they should try to present information in a relatively brisk fashion, and in a way that maintains student interest and motivation; during this presentation phase, students should be given many opportunities to ask and answer lesson-related questions. Second, teachers should alternate between presenting information to students and giving them activities related to this information within their instructional time. For example, during the first few minutes of the lesson, teachers could review basic information from the previous class and then provide additional information related to concept and skill development of some area for the next ten to fifteen minutes. Following this phase, students could be given related tasks to complete while the teacher monitors their performance; these tasks should be designed so that students can achieve a high success rate within a relatively short period. Teachers could then repeat the sequence by providing more information, either individually or by group according to student needs, and then further opportunities for student response, practice, and feedback. Other ways to maximize engaged time and allow students to be active in their learning include the use of choral responding (all students respond in unison to questions asked by the teacher), peer tutoring, and cooperative learning procedures.

(4) Monitor student progress and performance. Effective teachers promote and maintain active student participation in their learning by monitoring their students' performance. Monitoring allows teachers to spot student errors and to make modifications to their lesson planning and teaching in accordance with students' development and needs. Student learning increases when teachers monitor their students actively and frequently (Good & Brophy, 1978; Hawley & Rosenholtz, 1984). It is important for teachers to discover how students approach learning tasks and what strategies they use to complete the assigned tasks, so that they can adjust their lesson planning and teaching accordingly (Good, 1983; Rosenshine & Stevens, 1986).

(5) Evaluate student progress and performance. The evaluation of student and teacher performance allows teachers to make educational decisions about their teaching and about their students' learning. In evaluating student performance, teachers should determine whether students fulfilled the objectives of the lesson and (if so) how they did so, with respect to, for example, speed, accuracy, style, and manner. In evaluating student performance, teachers should re-examine the quality and pace of their instruction, the materials and activities that were used (e.g., were they related to students' interests, needs, and strengths?), and the appropriateness of their goals and objectives.

(6) Maintain and generalize students' learning. Effective learning requires students not only to acquire skills and knowledge but also to apply skills and knowledge across a variety of situations and contexts. For students to know how to do this, they must be taught how to maintain and generalize their learning. Teachers can achieve this goal by providing their students with opportunities to practice their skills and to apply their knowledge across a variety of tasks, situations, and contexts.

(7) Communicate with students in ways that promote a positive self-concept. Ginott (1971) stresses the need for teachers to convey to students "sane messages" that address situations rather than a student's character and personality. For example, if a student is disrupting the class by talking loudly to peers while the teacher is trying to instruct the class, the teacher should deliver a sane message like, "I am talking to the class and everyone needs to listen," rather than judging the child's character by saying, "You are being rude. You always seem to be talking when you should be listening." Ginott (1972) further encourages teachers to speak objectively and respectfully to students, to model the behaviour they expect from their students, and to show appreciation for their efforts.

(8) Help students make good behavioural choices. Glasser (1969, 1977) believes that good behaviour results from good choices and that bad behaviour results from bad choices. Teachers can help students make better choices by reinforcing students' responsibility for their own behaviour, and by ensuring that natural consequences follow from whatever behaviour a student chooses.

Glasser advocates the use of regular classroom meetings in which students can engage in whole-class discussions about topics that are relevant to them. The major purpose of these meetings is to debate and resolve problems that emerge from the discussion. Glasser has proposed three different types of meetings:

- *Social problem-solving meetings* in which students attempt to solve problems that arise from people living and working together in the school setting.
- *Open-ended meetings* in which students discuss matters related to the school curriculum and their learning activities.
- *Educational-diagnostic meetings* in which students discuss issues related to their cognitive development.

The classroom meetings proposed by Glasser should be held daily for at least thirty minutes. Students should be free to express their opinions without fear of judgment. The teacher's role is to guide the discussion, help students present problems and issues, keep students on topic, and encourage everyone to participate and contribute to problem-solving. The underlying purpose of these meetings is to stress students' responsibility for their behaviour, and to provide an avenue for the teacher and students to discuss appropriate alternative behaviours for various situations.

(9) Emphasize student effort and self-control. Many students do not feel that they control their learning, attributing their successes and failures either to chance or to the actions of their teachers (Dweck, 1986). Teachers must continually and systematically reinforce feelings of self-confidence in their students by showing them strategies that can help them gain control of their learning and encourage them to take responsibility for their performance. As students become more adept in using their own strategies as part of the learning process, they will begin to realize that they can control their achievement outcomes through their own efforts (Borkowski, Johnson, & Reid, 1987; McCombs, 1982; Wittrock, 1986).

LESSON PLANNING — generally a question but not specific pts

Lesson planning allows teachers to examine and reflect on their teaching practice in a continual and systematic fashion, as well as providing a foundation for instructional improvement. Having provided a basis for effective instructional planning, we now present an overview of the factors involved in drawing up a lesson plan (see Table 9.2 for a sample plan):

1. Teachers need to consider their teaching goals and specifically determine what the intentions of the lesson are with respect to students' learning.

2. Teachers need to design objectives for the lesson that are meaningful and relevant to students. These objectives should be clearly presented so that the students can understand the teacher's expectations, and they should be commensurate with students' developmental level, range of abilities, specific needs, and general goals of the lesson. Objectives may be highly specific (e.g., related to particular academic skills such as adding numbers, decoding words, etc.) or more general and complex (e.g., related to analyzing, synthesizing, and evaluating information) (see Gronlund, 1985 and Mager, 1975).

3. Teachers should focus on the tasks and activities that will be assigned to the students. Teachers should consider whether the tasks relate to the goal(s) and objective(s) of the lesson; whether doing these tasks will allow students to reach the level of performance that has been set; whether students will be able to obtain a high enough success rate to promote interest, motivation, and learning; and whether there is sufficient time within the lesson to allow students to practice the skills and complete the task.

4. Teachers need to consider how they are going to introduce the content of the lesson (i.e., explain to students the purpose of the lesson and show them the relevancy of the lesson to their learning and development).

5. Teachers need to consider how they can promote a positive, cooperative, and supportive atmosphere.

6. Teachers need to consider how often and how well they will be able to monitor their students' performance, and whether they are allowing suf-

ficient amount of time for students to seek clarification, pose questions, and to ask/answer questions.

7. Teachers need to encourage the development and use of learning strategies.

8. Teachers need to consider how they can accommodate their students' variant needs and abilities.

9. Teachers need to focus attention on how they might model desired behaviours, personalize the learning, and foster students' active participation in the lesson.

10. Teachers need to evaluate the effectiveness of the lesson with respect to its goals and objectives, and provide feedback to students regarding their performance.

11. Teachers should conclude their lesson (provide closure) by discussing with their students one or more of the salient goals and objectives of the lesson.

Table 9.2

An Example of a Lesson Plan for Elementary Students

Goals for Learning

1. To facilitate a risk-free environment in the class, our goal is for the children to consistently encourage each other to participate, e.g., through body language, actions, and words.

2. That the children see the benefit of encouraging good behaviour, and know what "encourage" means.

Statement of Objectives

1.1 Students will be able to state what the lion and the mouse "did" and "said" that encouraged the other animal.

1.2 Students will be able to name and/or model what encouraging participation "looks like" and "sounds like."

2.1 Each child will be able to tell a partner how and why encouragement helped the lion escape.

2.2 Each child will be able to tell a partner about a time when he or she was encouraged and how it felt.

2.3 Students will be able to tell when it would be helpful to encourage each other in this class.

2.4 In their reflection logs, each student will be able to define "encourage," either by completing the sentence frame, "To encourage means to ———," or by drawing a picture representing encouragement.

Materials

◆ Five value statements are printed on the board. Some examples: "It feels nice when someone helps you finish a difficult job"; "It feels bad when someone calls you a nasty name."

◆ Two pieces of tagboard (60 cm. x 90 cm.) divided in half with a capital T. One chart is titled "The Lion," the other "The Mouse." Above both Ts are icons that symbolize what each animal *did* and *said*.

◆ VCR and "The Lion and the Mouse" animated video.

◆ T-chart—primary chart paper, divided in half, with icons at the top that symbolize "What do we see?" and "What do we hear?" when someone is encouraging behaviour.

◆ Reflection books.

Procedure

Instructional Skill		Learning Strategies
	The children will be in the big room, on the carpeted meeting area.	
engaging learners	Ask students to raise their hands if they agree with each value statement as it is read from the board. Teachers and students will take turns reading the statements.	questioning
accommodating readers/nonreaders		using prior experience
verbal/visual presentation	Print the word "encourage" on the board. Help the class sound it out. Explain that the word means "to give courage." Talk about how saying nice things or helping others gives people courage.	
demonstration	Demonstrate some words that an encouraging person might use, and write these on the board. For example, "Good idea," "Great!" Demonstrate some actions that encourage by modelling; for example, Barb pats Jody on the back (gently), and Jody smiles at Barb.	defining
modelling		aid comprehension
	Tell the class they are going to see a video called "The Lion and the Mouse." Ask if anyone has seen it before. If someone has, ask him or her to tell the class what the story was about. If no one has seen it, or if the student's explanation is incomplete, say that it is a fable, which teaches a lesson. Ask who the characters will be.	linking past information with present learning
		questioning to encourage prediction
sharing the purpose of the lesson	Tell the students, "You will watch 'The Lion and the Mouse' to see how encouragement can be helpful. Then we're going to fill in this chart about what we saw the lion and the mouse do and say that was encouraging." The teacher will point to the appropriate icons when she says "do" and "say."	
	After viewing the video, do the above.	

developing a positive, cooperative, and supportive atmosphere	After providing enough examples, tell the students to form pairs by pointing to students beside them and have them face each other knee to knee. Walk among the groups encouraging quiet voices and helping reluctant participants. Encourage students to tell each other how encouragement helped the lion escape, and why it helped. Select a few pairs to report to the class.	encouraging active and shared learning
Active Participation	Ask students to tell their partner about a time when they were encouraged and how it felt.	making connections to prior experience
visual/verbal cues to accommodate readers/nonreaders	Draw an ear and eye on the T-chart. Tell the students that the T-chart will help them remember things that they can do to encourage each other to participate when they are working together. Ask the students to tell what things listed as encouragement on the lion and mouse chart could be used by them to encourage each other, and enter their answers on the T-chart.	introducing the T-chart as an organizing strategy
active participation (role-playing)	Tell students to think of other encouraging behaviours that are not yet listed on the T-chart. Ask students to model their examples so that everyone can see or hear the behaviour in order to decide whether it belongs on the T-chart.	idea generating
personalizing the learning	Ask students to think to themselves for a minute about when it would be helpful to encourage each other in the class. Give time for reflection, and then listen to their ideas.	reflection and control of ideas
accommodating different abilities and styles providing closure evaluation and feedback	Have the students return to their desks to either complete the sentence frame, "To encourage means to _____" or draw a picture representing encouragement in their reflection books. Those who finish before recess will share their reflections with a teacher or a classmate. The teachers will look at all the books and comment positively by the next lesson.	

Note: Many of the ideas presented in this table were contributed by Barb Cowles and Jody Oetter.

We now turn our attention to some important administrative functions of supportive classroom management before concluding this section with a discussion of the ways in which an effective manager begins the school year.

ADMINISTRATIVE FUNCTIONS

Scheduling ← Know

Scheduling is one of the most difficult aspects of managing an inclusive classroom. It is the foundation of classroom organization and student learning. Teachers not only have to schedule their instructional time but also have to keep track of students moving in and out of the classroom (e.g., a student going to a resource room). They are also responsible for developing the schedules of special personnel who might be coming into the classroom to help particular students, and/or the schedules of personnel who work regularly in the classroom (e.g., teachers' aides and/or parent volunteers). Although schedules will differ across situations, Gallagher (1979) and Bos and Vaughn (1988) provide some guidance for preparing classroom schedules:

♦ Provide daily schedules for students and personnel working in the classroom.
♦ Provide schedules for personnel outside the classroom (e.g., resource teachers).
♦ Plan ahead and anticipate students' needs.
♦ Schedule time to communicate with special teachers and personnel working with individual students in the classroom (e.g., reading specialists, psychologists, speech/language pathologists).
♦ Keep track of time needed to cover different subject areas.
♦ Keep to routines as much as possible, particularly for children with learning problems.
♦ Organize for transitional times (e.g., when students arrive and leave the classroom, or when instruction changes from one subject area to another).
♦ Plan time to provide students with feedback and evaluation.
♦ Establish expectations in advance so that students know what is going to happen.
♦ Plan time for direct instruction, group work, and independent study.
♦ Be relatively consistent in scheduling yet flexible enough to meet the changing demands of your students.
♦ Schedule work for students that can be done within class time.

Record-Keeping — more in depth

An effective system of record-keeping allows teachers to monitor their students' progress, as well as manage and monitor their own instruction. Records are essential for teacher accountability and for demonstrating program effectiveness. Record-keeping allows teachers to know whether their lessons are working, to evaluate their efforts, and to make modifications to their teaching to better meet the needs of their students. Good record-keeping also allows the teacher to discuss more clearly and comprehensively the progress of students with their students, as well as with parents, teachers' aides, auxiliary personnel, administrators, and other teachers. According to Lund, Schnaps, and Bijou (1983), a basic recording system should (1) be manageable for the teacher and his or her aides; (2) be able to communicate the comparable performance of a child from one day to another; (3) be flexible enough to apply to all areas of the curriculum; (4) be consistent with lesson goals and objectives; and (5) be simple enough to continually record and display.

A number of specific techniques have been created for recording data (see Howell, Kaplan, & O'Connell, 1979). Record-keeping can be accomplished through the use of anecdotal logs, charts, and graphs. Regardless of the procedure used, teachers should try to use methods that are simple and efficient; try to get aides as well as students to participate in the recording process; and record only information that represents the critical elements of the learning event (Guerin & Maier, 1983). It is also important to observe and record the *process* of learning along with the *product* of learning (Bos & Vaughn, 1988). This can be done by asking students to explain how they are doing in completing tasks, and by monitoring their approach to tasks. Teachers' records should thus reflect not only *what* students are accomplishing in their learning but also *how* they are accomplishing the task, as well as how they are generalizing and applying the knowledge and skill (see Tables 9.3, 9.4, and 9.5 for examples of records).

Table 9.3
Record and Evaluation of the Lesson Plan

Date: _____

Subject: _____

Critical Components   *Rating*

	Very Good (1)	Good (2)	Satisfactory (3)	Needs Improvement (4)
1. Goals				
2. Objectives				
3. Tasks, activities, materials				
4. Introduction of lesson				
5. Classroom climate				
6. Student participation				
7. Accommodation of students' needs				
8. Modelling				
9. Feedback				
10. Closure				

Overall preparation

Table 9.4 Anecdotal Record: Students' Group Work Behaviours			
Date	*Student*	*Observation*	*Planned Intervention*
Nov. 2	Barb	Interrupts others	Discuss with Barb and show her how interrupting interferes with good communication
Nov. 3	Tom	Compliments others	Acknowledge this positive behaviour and reinforce the use of this behaviour with other students
Nov. 4	Jenna	Makes good suggestions to group members	Talk to Jenna and other students about the importance of providing suggestions to group planning and discussion

Grading *yes*

Grading is important because it communicates to the reader how well a student is doing in their learning. However, grading in inclusive classrooms is a difficult enterprise because students have different competency levels, and because there are a number of dimensions that can be and should be evaluated, such as academic progress, social skill development, and effort. Generally, the literature (e.g., Carpenter, 1985; Gronlund, 1981; Kohl, 1982; Terwilliger, 1977) suggests that more than one method of grading should be employed so that information can be conveyed in various formats (e.g., a checklist or pass-fail method for indicating whether or not a student has attained minimal standards, or the use of letter grades to indicate relative standing), and that grades should be brief but informative so that the message one is attempting to give can be clearly understood.

For mainstreamed remedial and handicapped students, Carpenter (1985) recommends the following grading adaptations: (1) grading should be based on measures, such as checklists, that reflect how well a student is doing with respect to clearly defined objectives; (2) grades should reflect mastery and progress of students in relation to their past performance and level of ability; (3) grades should be differentiated according to the areas of assessment (e.g., a grade for effort, a separate grade for progress, etc.); (4) grading should involve the participation of students whenever feasible so that they can more clearly appreciate their progress; (5) grading should be frequent so that

Table 9.5
Record of Written Language

Date: _____

Assignment: _____

Rating Scale: 1 (Very Good) 2 (Good) 3 (Satisfactory) 4 (Needs Improvement)
Writing Components

Student	Punctua-tion	Capitali-zation	Sentence Structure	Vocabulary	Organiza-tion	Spelling
Joan	1	1	2	3	3	4
Roy	3	3	4	1	4	3
Anne	4	4	4	3	3	3
Lauren	3	3	3	2	2	2
Tom	2	2	1	1	1	2
Sherry	3	3	3	4	3	4

students can be afforded more opportunity to know how they are doing; (6) grading symbols should be accompanied with both written and oral communication so that parents and others can more fully appreciate the quality and nature of the student's progress; and (7) grading should not only involve the regular classroom teacher but also include the input of the special education teacher, teachers' aides, and others involved in the student's program.

According to Kindsvatter (1969), school grades have a number of shortcomings:

1. They are variable, subjective, contaminated, even capricious.
2. They create a condition of unfair competition.
3. They reflect an aristocratic rather than democratic attitude.
4. They preoccupy students and their parents.
5. They deny the psychological principle of individual differences.
6. They tend to influence teaching in the direction of memorization at the expense of concept formation and creativity.
7. They encourage student dependency (p. 331).

The following are suggestions for alternative grading systems that can be used by the regular classroom teacher.

- Grades can be based on the goals recorded in a student's IEP (Cohen, 1983; Kinnison, Hayes, & Acord, 1981). A student's grade might reflect the number of objectives and goals achieved within a particular period, as well as the level of mastery demonstrated with respect to them; for example, a student who achieved 80 percent mastery in a particular objective might receive a B in that specific area, depending on the teacher's decision about performance standards.

- Instead of letter grades, teachers might provide descriptive comments with respect to a particular student's development in a certain area (Salend, 1990). For example, if the focus has been on developing social competence, a teacher could provide a detailed description of the types of social skills the student has acquired, the quality of social interaction that he or she has demonstrated, and/or the student's ability to identify and solve social problems independently.

- Rather than using one grade to reflect a student's progress in a particular subject area, many grades can be assigned to reflect the varying abilities and skills associated with mastery in a particular subject area (Kinnison, Hayes, & Acord, 1981). Instead of assigning a grade of 60 percent or a C in math, specific components related to the math exercises and the student's performance during the term could be isolated and graded. For example, although a student may not have completely mastered single-digit division (60 percent mastery), ability to follow a sequenced procedure is excellent (A), conceptual understanding is good (B), and effort and attitude is very good (B+).

- In some areas, a student's competency may not be best expressed by distinctive levels (such as grades) but through a system that acknowledges a minimal standard of performance or competency as satisfactory and sufficient (Bellanca & Kirschenbaum, 1976). In the pass-fail system, performance is not measured in comparison with those of a student's peers, but rather on the basis of how well the student did on a particular task. For example, a student who completed a class project in accordance with all of the basic requirements could be awarded a P (for pass), whereas a student who did not do this could be awarded a F (for failure); in the latter case, the teacher would carefully explain to the student all of the requirements needed to achieve a passing grade.

- For students who are receiving special assistance from others shared grading can be undertaken (Kinnison, Hayes, & Acord, 1981). This entails collaboratively reporting the observations and assessments of teachers' aides, resource teachers, and other involved personnel. Shared grading reflects a wider range of perceptions and therefore more clearly and adequately represent a student's performance across a variety of situations.

A student's process of learning and achievement can be evaluated and recorded along with the product of his or her learning achievement. A student's approach to learning, learning style, and learning strategies could be assessed and reported through descriptive comments, letter or percentage grades, a pass-fail system, or through some combination of these.

By now, the reader should appreciate that supportive classroom management is a complex and multidimensional process. We conclude this section by suggesting ways in which a teacher might most effectively begin the school year.

GETTING STARTED   no

The effective management process starts before the school year begins. As previously noted, teachers need to consider their style and approach to teaching, as well as the needs of their students. Additionally, specific instructional methodologies have to be considered along with such things as the organization of the classroom, instructional materials and equipment, student grouping, scheduling, record-keeping, and grading. As Emmer, Evertson, and Anderson (1980) comment, "Educators have long assumed that what happens in a classroom during the early days of the year sets the stage for the entire year."

Emmer et al. (1980) conducted a study in which they compared how effective managers and less effective managers began the school year. On the first day, effective teachers taught students what they needed to know about using the room, but did not overload them with information (e.g., procedures for using the bathroom, pencil sharpener, and water fountain). Effective teachers also monitored their students closely, introduced procedures and content gradually, provided enjoyable activities for students to engage in, and explained and reminded students of the classroom rules throughout the first week of school. Although effective teachers considered content to be important, they initially stressed socialization in the classroom, and if disruptive behaviour occurred it was stopped immediately. In contrast, less effective managers did not have adequate procedures for classroom organization and socialization, did not use rules as cues for appropriate behaviour, and did not effectively monitor their class. Unsure about their teacher's expectations, some children chose to "push the limits" and behave inappropriately.

The fact that more effective managers seem to have a better sense of how their students perceive the classroom was revealed in this study by the way these teachers related to their students' immediate needs (e.g., teaching procedures for using the bathroom or certain areas in the classroom), by the way they eased their students' entry into school life, and by the way they provided a warm and secure classroom environment. Effective managers met the needs of their students by considering attention span in lesson design, providing reasonable work standards and high rates of success in assigned activities, and relating content to students' interests and background. Effective managers also coped better with constraints (lack of materials, frequent interruptions, late arrival of students, etc.), whereas less effective managers had poorer coping strategies and did not anticipate problems well. In terms of personal characteristics, effective managers tended to have better affective skills, particularly with respect to listening and expressing feelings.

One way in which the effective manager organizes and maintains a classroom atmosphere that is conducive to student cooperation, active learning, and communication is to discuss with students his or her expectations for performance and to collectively develop rules and routines.

Rules and Routines

Rules are typically intended to promote positive interpersonal relationships, to maximize instructional effectiveness, to regulate positive student behaviour, and to minimize classroom problems. The quality of rule-setting can determine what will happen in the classroom for the entire school year. Rule-setting informs students about what can happen in the classroom and helps them understand the teacher's approach and his or her expectations for behaviour (Doyle, 1986).

Rules should be easy to understand and follow, well explained, and frequently repeated, especially at the beginning of the school year. No one set of rules is better than another. Rules are developed in accordance with the values and expectations of learning and behaviour. These values and expectations are derived from the experiences and perceptions of both teachers and students within the school and community context. They need to be clarified and discussed between teachers and students in order for them to be appreciated and followed. Due to the varied values and expectations of teachers and students, rules are also variable. However, there are guidelines for implementing rules that apply to all contexts.

- Involve students in rule selection.
- Explain and discuss rules with students.
- Avoid the use of too many rules.
- Provide practice for students to follow rules.
- Present clear expectations regarding students' behaviour.
- Provide feedback to students regarding their following of rules.
- Write and express rules in a positive manner (e.g., "Walk in the hall," not "Don't run").

◆ REACTIVE CLASSROOM MANAGEMENT

In this section, we present an overview of approaches that can be used to assist students in altering their behaviour when other methods have failed. The *problem-solving approach* to misbehaviour is congruent with the metacognitive approach and mediational style of teaching because it emphasizes the student's active involvement in the behaviour change process. The *behaviouristic approach* is incongruent with our orientation because it emphasizes conditions external to the student in the learning process rather than internal events and processes; however, it may be effective for students who require

highly structured procedures and special assistance in controlling their behaviour (Jones & Jones, 1986). We will conclude this section by discussing specific ways in which the teacher can deal with particular forms of misbehaviour that periodically arise in school environments.

PROBLEM-SOLVING APPROACH TO MISBEHAVIOUR

Teachers who use a problem-solving approach in dealing with student misbehaviour believe that it is important for students to control their own behaviour. They believe that it is important for students to examine their own behaviour, identify the reasons for conflicts when they arise, recognize that there are alternative ways for dealing with their conflicts (other than misbehaving), appreciate the consequences for their actions, and assume ownership and responsibility for the way they behave. Teachers who take a problem-solving approach to student misbehaviour also assume that students *want* to be self-controlling, responsible, and involved in their behavioural development.

In order to develop self-responsible behaviour, students need to be given opportunities to be actively involved in the problem-solving and decision-making process, which means that teachers need to develop and model these skills, as well as provide experiences and time for their students to acquire and practice them. If teachers assume all the responsibility for their students' behaviour, students cannot be expected to become self-controlling and self-responsible. A problem-solving approach to classroom problems provides students with strategies for solving problems and resolving conflicts, and enables them to be more independent.

Although there are many methods designed to help students resolve problems and take responsibility for their behaviour (e.g., Gordon, 1974; Maple, 1977), the following procedure is based on Glasser's (1969) model and Haywood's (1987) mediational approach.

1. Inappropriate behaviour has to be identified by the teacher.
2. The teacher needs to describe this behaviour to the student so that the student knows what he or she did. The misbehaviour should be specifically, clearly, and objectively described, using effective and empathic communication skills. The teacher should focus on the problem and encourage the student to clarify the problem in his or her own words. Identifying the problem behaviour, describing the behaviour, and encouraging students to focus their attention on the problem improves teachers' observational skills, provides good modelling for students, increases students' awareness that problem behaviour is occurring, and neutralizes any negative emotions associated with the misbehaviour.
3. The teacher should try to help the student determine whether the behaviour is desirable and whether it needs to be changed. This can be facilitated by discussing with students the advantages and disadvantages of their behaviour as well as the consequences of their behaviour. This discussion should be conducted in an objective, nonjudgmental, and nonthreatening manner, so that it is understood that the behaviour is being evaluated, not the student.
4. Alternative behaviours need to be discussed with students. The teacher should first attempt to elicit from the student what actions could be taken to solve the problem and/or what approaches could be used to deal more effectively with the situation. If the student cannot think of some possible solutions, the teacher should offer some ideas for him or her to consider. This step focuses attention on thinking and problem-solving, and engages the active participation of students in the process. It helps the teacher see the perspective of students, and it signals to students that the teacher sees them as competent and able to take responsibility for their actions.
5. The teacher needs to guide the student toward making a behavioural choice and commitment to a plan for dealing with the particular conflict and behavioural disturbance. At this stage, the teacher should clarify the behavioural choice and plan for problem resolution, so that there is clear understanding and direction.
6. After the student has practiced the plan and behavioural change, the teacher should provide praise if the student was successful in his or her efforts.
7. If the student fails to follow an agreed-upon plan or has difficulty making a behavioural change, the teacher should not punish or criticize the stu-

dent, but rather designate more time to discuss with the student why the plan is failing, and to make further modifications where necessary.

This seven-step problem-solving approach is exemplified by the following:

Situation: Susan doesn't start on tasks within an expected amount of time, which leads to her disturbing others around her. This eventually results in other students getting off task and in Susan not completing her tasks.

Steps 1 and 2: Identify and Describe Misbehaviour

Teacher: Susan, I see that you are having trouble getting started on the math problems, and that you are bothering some other students. What do you think the problem is?

Susan: I don't know what to do.

Teacher: O.K., Susan, you have identified a problem you are having. Is there any classroom rule you are breaking?

Susan: Well, I guess I shouldn't be bugging Terry and Samantha.

Teacher: Good, Susan, you have pointed out two problems. One problem is that you are having difficulty doing the math questions, and the other problem is that you are disturbing others around you.

Step 3: Discuss Advantages and Disadvantages of Behaviour

Teacher: What do you think will happen if you don't start working and continue to bother the students around you?

Susan: I won't get my work done and I'll get in trouble.

Step 4: Elicit/Provide Alternatives

Teacher: What do you think you could do about these problems?

Susan: I don't know. I don't know how to do these math questions.

Teacher: Well, if you have difficulty understanding what to do, I could help you.

Susan: I don't think I can get any of these right.

Teacher: After I give you and the rest of the students these math questions, what do you think you should try to do?

Susan: Well, I guess I could try to do the first one. And when I have trouble, I could ask you for help.

Teacher: How do you think you should ask for my help?

Susan: I should raise my hand and wait for you to come.

Teacher: What should you try to do while you wait for me?

Susan: I should try to keep quiet and not bother others.

Steps 4 and 5: Make A Choice/Plan

Teacher: Good, Susan. Why don't you try to do the first math question, and when you are finished raise your hand and I will come over and check it and help you with any problem you might have.

Susan: O.K., I'll try the first one and raise my hand when I need help.

not on dialogue.

but 7 steps are what he trains teachers to do ⌣ practical

Steps 6 and 7: Provide Praise and Followup

Susan: (after trying one question, raising her hand and being approached by the teacher) Could you see if I'm doing this right?

Teacher: I like that you did some work before you asked for my help. I also liked that you raised your hand and did not bother anyone else. A really great effort, Susan.

Susan: I'm really not sure about these math questions.

Teacher: Susan, you made a very good start. In a couple of minutes, after I see Richard, I would like to spend a few minutes with you and show you some ways that might help you do these questions. Why don't you do this for now, and I'll be right back.

Susan: O.K., thanks.

BEHAVIOURISTIC MANAGEMENT

The behavioural approach to managing behaviour involves systematic procedures for changing behaviour. Behaviourism is a theoretical orientation in psychology that emphasizes the environment in learning and instruction. Discovering the relationship between the environment and observable behaviour is the major goal of the behaviourist. Applied to learning and behaviour, the behaviourist is interested in understanding how different conditions in the student's classroom environment determine both the quantity and quality of a student's learning and behaviour. Factors such as self-concept, locus of control, and self-efficacy are not emphasized because, to the behaviourist, these affective characteristics are not clearly observable.

The cognitive approach, which we have emphasized in this book, focuses on the events and processes that take place within the individual (e.g., receiving, processing, storing, retrieving, and applying information). From our perspective, the active role the student takes in his or her learning and behaviour, rather than the environment, is the key variable in the learning and behaving process. However, some students need carefully structured environments and specific reinforcement procedures to help them control their behaviour and prepare and develop their ability to respond to the expectations of the teacher and the classroom.

Basic Assumptions

Behaviourists believe that all behaviour is learned and can therefore be changed by changing learning and environmental conditions. Behaviourists also believe that behaviour that is immediately followed by a reward will occur more frequently, that behaviour followed by aversive consequences will occur less often, and that behaviour that is no longer reinforced will stop occurring. From this perspective, in order to provide appropriate interventions for students to develop more desirable skills or eliminate undesirable behaviours, the behaviour needs to be specifically defined, observable, and measurable. Furthermore, in order to successfully implement a behavioural program and monitor its effectiveness, information (data) about the behaviour needs to be effectively collected and recorded.

Data Collection

Teachers often describe the behaviour of their students in general terms. For example, they might characterize a student as being aggressive or disruptive. However, in order to better understand and collect information about a behaviour, teachers need to be much more specific in their descriptions. For example, one student might be described as aggressive because he or she pushes, shoves, and hits other students; another student might be described as disruptive because he leaves his seat without permission, talks aloud, and does not follow directions.

Depending on the type of behaviour, a teacher needs to observe and record it across a variety of dimensions, such as: the number of times a behaviour occurs; the proportion of time a behaviour occurs; the length of time a behaviour occurs (duration); the shape of a behaviour (what it looks like); the strength or force of a behaviour (e.g., makes holes in his or her paper with a pencil); and where a behaviour occurs (locus). When recording behaviour, a teacher needs to decide which is more important—the number of times a behaviour occurs or the duration of the behaviour.

Recording Behaviour

Recording the number of times a behaviour occurs can be easily done by tallying the number of times a behaviour is demonstrated by a student. For example, if a student is hitting his or her peers, a teacher should tally how many times this occurs. The teacher should also consider recording the behaviour in relation to time and context—i.e., recording not only the number of times a student hits another in a single day but also such things as time of day, location, and conditions that might have precipitated the behaviour.

Recording duration of behaviour can be easily done by timing the student's behaviour every time it occurs, or by timing the behaviour at certain intervals (e.g., every minute). For example, if a student is leaving his or her seat without permission, the important factor might not be the number of times this occurs, but rather the amount of time the student is absent from his or her seat.

Graphing Behaviour

The record of behaviour can be displayed using bar graphs and/or line graphs. Typically, the times that the behaviour is observed is recorded on the horizontal axis of the graph, while the number of times the behaviour occurred (or the percentage of time that it occurred) is recorded on the vertical axis. Graphs provide a base from which an intervention approach for altering the behaviour can begin. After establishing a baseline with respect to the behaviour, the next step is to design and implement intervention approaches and reinforcement procedures.

BEHAVIOURAL APPROACHES AND REINFORCEMENT PROCEDURES

The first step in designing and implementing a behavioural approach to altering a student's behaviour is to formulate a behavioural objective. The behavioural objective should identify the student(s), isolate the behaviour that is to be the area of focus, specify the conditions related to the behaviour, and provide an estimate of the standard of performance that is expected of the student (Mager, 1975); for example: *John will raise his hand to answer questions—once given a nonverbal cue (raised index finger) by the teacher, eight out of ten times during math class.*

The next step is to provide intervention strategies. A common method of increasing desirable student behaviour is to use positive reinforcement. Natural reinforcers include smiles, handshakes, thank-yous, and praise that can be used by teachers to show students that their behaviour is appropriate and acceptable. Less natural reinforcers include such things as tangibles (foods, sweets, drinks), tokens (which can be collected and then later exchanged for rewards such as free time or toys), and desirable activities that can be earned through appropriate behaviour. Reinforcers may need to be changed if original ones do not work.

Before describing a few common behavioural approaches, we should note that regardless of the approach used, teachers should concentrate on one behaviour at a time, clearly inform students about the approach and the expectations for their performance, introduce the approach step by step, allow practice time, provide feedback to the students about their behaviour when using reinforcers, and be consistent when implementing the approach.

Contingency Contracting

Contracts are written or oral negotiated agreements that are established cooperatively between the teacher and student (Olsen, 1982). Contracts outline the specific responsibilities of each individual that are *contingent* upon the behaviours specified in the agreement. Essentially, contracts describe the behaviour that is expected to be performed by the student and the reward that the teacher is expected to give the student upon the performance of that behaviour. A sample behaviour contract is shown in Table 9.6.

According to Fagen and Hill (1977), the process for teacher-student contracting has four main steps:

Table 9.6
A Behaviour Contract

IF *I can play cooperatively at recess for fifteen minutes each day of the week*

THEN *I can be the leader of my class group the following week.*

_____ _____ _____

Date   Student's name   Teacher's name

Additional Comments:

_____

_____

_____

_____

1. *Planning for the student conference.* In this step, the teacher isolates the undesirable behaviour through observation and recording, and considers ways to discuss the behaviour with the student.
2. *Exploration with the student.* Here the teacher discusses his or her concern about the behaviour with the student and listens to the student's views. An agreement between the teacher and the student is negotiated through discussion of specific behaviours to be changed, rewards for the student's efforts, and responsibilities of both the student and the teacher.
3. *Establishing the contract.* In this step, the actual terms of the contract are specified and drawn up, including information about the desirable behaviour to be performed, the people involved and their responsibilities, criteria for reward, and consequences for not performing the desirable behaviour. The contract is typically finalized with signatures.
4. *Reviewing and revising.* This is a followup and feedback phase in which the student's progress is evaluated and, if necessary, modifications are made.

Homme, Csanyi, Gonzales, and Rechs (cited in Blankenship & Lilly, 1981) recommend that contracts reward frequently and with small amounts; reward accomplishment rather than obedience; reward the behaviour as soon as it occurs; be expressed in terms that are clear, fair, honest, and positive; and be used systematically (p. 235).

Token Economies

A token system is a method by which reinforcement is programmed through the use of tangible objects or symbols, which are given by the teacher to the student in exchange for a privilege, activity, or reward. Tokens may include things such as points, chips, special cards, and homemade bills (Fagen, 1986). The use of tokens in the classroom, like the use of a monetary reward system in the work world, rewards people for their performance. If tokens are used to facilitate the performance of desired behaviours by students, the teacher needs to explain clearly to students what behaviours will be reinforced, as well as how the tokens can be earned and exchanged for rewards (Gallagher, 1979).

Group Contingencies

When misbehaviour in classrooms is demonstrated by a group of students, contingencies are applied to all members of a group, with rewards and consequences depending on the total performance of the group. All of the students in the group must work together to receive a reward they will all share equally. When students in a group are responsible for one another's behaviour, peer pressure is likely to occur. If managed well, this type of procedure can foster cooperative learning and behaviour; however, if it is mismanaged, students in the group who have difficulty meeting a particular standard of behaviour, and thus prevent other members from gaining a reward for their own behaviour, may be subject to peer harassment and criticism.

To avoid negative peer pressure and promote peer cooperation, teachers should: (1) ensure that the initial performance standard needed to receive a reward can be reached by all members of the group, and then gradually raise the standard; (2) encourage everyone to participate; and (3) emphasize rewards for appropriate behaviour rather than punishment for misbehaviour (Kauffman, Pullen, & Akers, 1988).

Self-Management

One of the major problems with behavioural approaches is that the procedures, schedules of reinforcement, and monitoring/delivery of the approaches are primarily under the control of the teacher. Thus, the shift from undesirable to desirable behaviour tends not to generalize and transfer to other situations and environmental contexts. As we have stressed throughout this chapter, the best way to manage students' behaviour is to allow students to be actively involved in the learning process and to develop independent control of their own learning and behaviour. Having students monitor and record their own behaviour, referred to as self-management, has been effective in a variety of settings with exceptional children (McLaughlin, Krappman, & Welsh, 1985).

Self-management: (1) allows students to focus on specific behaviours; (2) allows students to become more aware of their own behaviour and involves them in the behaviour change; (3) enables students to be responsible for their behaviour in nonschool situations and environments; (4) gives teachers more time to do other tasks; and (5) can foster self-determination in students (Frith & Armstrong, 1986).

Frith and Armstrong (1986) and Salend (1983) provide some important steps and considerations involved in teaching students the specifics of a self-managed program:

◆ *Define and explain the behaviour explicitly.* In order to observe and record a behaviour, the behaviour has to be precisely defined. The effect of the behaviour on the student and others should also be explained and discussed.

◆ *Simplify behaviour counting and recording.* Students need to be shown an easy way of counting and recording their behaviour to ensure procedural understanding and accuracy.

◆ *Use time limits.* Students should not be expected to spend an excessive amount of time counting and recording their behaviour. Therefore, the teacher should establish definite time intervals for counting and recording behaviour.

◆ *Introduce the process as early as possible.* Students should be introduced to _not bulleted_ self-management procedures as early as possible, so that they assume responsibility for and control over their behaviour.

◆ *Provide demonstration.* The teacher should provide examples of the target behaviour, emphasizing to students the important features that characterize the behaviour to be changed.

◆ *Guide toward differentiation.* The teacher should develop students' ability to differentiate the target behaviour to be changed from other occurring behaviours. The students should also have the opportunity to present examples of the target behaviour.

◆ *Role-play and feedback.* The student and teacher should role-play the intervention—and the teacher needs to give the student feedback about his or her use of the self-monitoring and self-recording system.

◆ *Practice the process.* Students should be provided sufficient amount of time to practice the self-management system under the supervision of the teacher.

◆ *Provide assessment and followup.* After students have engaged themselves in the self-management process, the teacher should evaluate their efforts and achievements and make changes where necessary.

Teachers can involve parents in the classroom management process by clearly explaining to them the approach and style of teaching, the ways of accommodating students' abilities, needs, and interests, as well as the methods for dealing with students' development in learning and behaviour. Communicating regularly with parents may facilitate more cooperative planning and intervention whereby parents may adapt to the home some of the principles and procedures used in the classroom. When teachers and parents use similar behaviour management procedures, the child will be able to adjust much more easily to the conditions and expectations at both home and school.

The two case studies presented in Appendixes 9.1 and 9.2 exemplify many of the behaviouristic techniques discussed in this chapter. Appendix 9.1 depicts the use of various behaviouristic methods (e.g., data collection, graphing, and reinforcement procedures) at the elementary level, while Appendix 9.2 demonstrates the use of behavioural procedures at the secondary level.

MANAGING SPECIFIC BEHAVIOURAL PROBLEMS

Inappropriate student behaviour needs to be dealt with quickly and correctly so that it does not escalate. According to Dreikers (1968; Dreikers & Cassel, 1972; Dreikers, Grunwold, & Pepper, 1982), students are responsible for their behaviour and can choose to behave or misbehave. They are social beings who want to belong. Some students misbehave because they have the mistaken belief that it will get them the recognition they seek. Thus, modifying students' behaviour must involve modifying their motivation, which is tied to four mistaken goals: *attention-getting*, *power-seeking*, *revenge-seeking*, and *the desire to be left alone*.

Students who try to attract recognition by getting others to pay attention to them are, in fact, seeking proof of acceptance. If students who need recognition do not get it through attention-getting behaviour, they will try to get it through power struggles. Basically, students with this mistaken goal believe that a teacher who does not let them do what they want to do does not approve of them. If students are unsuccessful in their power struggles, they may seek revenge to attain the recognition they desire. Students with this mistaken goal believe that the only alternative is to retaliate, because only by hurting others (as they have been hurt) can they gain status. Most often, these students lack feelings of self-worth, and if their revenge-seeking behaviours do not get them the recognition they want, they may strive to be left alone. At this level, students anticipate defeat and avoid situations and people, holding on to the mistaken belief that if they are left alone, nobody will know how hopeless they are.

Considering misbehaviour in light of mistaken goals can help teachers understand what motivates students' behaviour. Dreikers (1968) suggests that teachers first observe their students' behaviour to determine mistaken goals. Next, they should confront the students about their motives by asking them: *Do you want special attention from me? Do you want to be your own boss? Do you want to hurt others? Do you want to be left alone?* in an empathic manner. Once they understand their students' expectations about their own behaviour, they can apply corrective procedures. We now apply some ideas of Dreikers and his colleagues in our consideration of students who *show off*, *rebel*, *bully*, and *quit*.

Students Who Show Off

Students who show off typically need reassurance that they are liked and respected. According to Dreikers' model, their actions are driven by the mistaken goal of attention-getting. Teachers must be careful not to reward attention-getting behaviour. Instead, they should focus on making students aware that only their demonstration of successful learning and appropriate behaviour will bring them recognition.

Students Who Rebel

Students who fight authority and want people to do things their way are power-seekers. According to Dreikers' model, getting into power struggles with these students can lead to more rebellious forms of behaviour. Instead, teachers should withdraw from their authority position and calmly and objectively discuss more appropriate ways to behave. Ultimately, teachers need to show students that they can get recognition by acting responsibly, rather than by being argumentative and disruptive.

Students Who Bully

The hostile and vindictive student is often secretly crying out for help. However, these students are difficult to deal with because they are hurting and care little about the consequences of their behaviour. The teacher's initial concern is to defuse the situation by adopting a calm approach. The teacher should then discuss with the student the causes of his or her hostility, as well as ways of dealing with it besides hitting, fighting, and so forth. Alternative ways of behaving need to be explored with the student, encouraged, reinforced, and praised.

Students Who Quit

Some students have experienced so much failure that they feel totally inadequate and powerless, and see no reason to try any more. They give up easily and tend to withdraw from others. Dreikers believes that teachers who give up on these students serve to reinforce their inadequacy and seclusion. Instead, teachers need to give them continual encouragement and support, in addition to showing them successful and appropriate ways of learning and behaving.

Some General Considerations for Dealing with Misbehaviour

When dealing with misbehaviour, teachers should try to eliminate the problem promptly, with minimal distraction of other students. Minor disruptions can often be stopped by making eye contact with the student, gesturing to the student, and/or by moving close to the student. These teacher behaviours are generally interpreted by students as cues to change their behaviour. Serious behaviour problems such as rudeness and defiance should be dealt with as privately as possible so the student is not embarrassed in front of his or her peers. Additionally, teachers should constantly acknowledge the positive behaviours that students demonstrate, rather than focusing on negative behaviours to the exclusion of all else. Finally, teachers need to practice applying the concepts and procedures presented in this chapter, which will enable them to better employ different methods across various situations.

◇ CONCLUSION

We conclude this chapter with a review of the major points and a classroom management checklist that teachers can use to identify and modify areas that may be the source of classroom problems:

1. Classroom management refers to the orchestration of classroom life so that all children can maximize their learning potential.

2. Classroom management is a comprehensive and holistic enterprise that has three major interactive facets: proactive management, supportive management, and reactive management.

3. Teachers should try to empower their students to understand and control their own behaviour.

4. Teachers who take a metacognitive approach to teaching are interested in fostering their students' ability to control and monitor their own learning and behaviour.

5. Teachers who have a mediational style of teaching model decision-making processes and skills so that their students can learn ways to solve problems independently and satisfy their goals.

6. Students have both common and unique needs that must be accommodated so that classrooms can run smoothly and meaningful learning can take place.

7. Classroom settings have distinctive properties that can influence classroom arrangement and lesson planning.

8. Students must be provided structure as well as opportunities for freedom and exploration.

9. Successful classroom management requires both the teacher and the classroom to be organized.

10. It is important for teachers to develop their students' ability to cope effectively with stress.

11. Successful teaching results in effective classroom management. The critical aspects of successful teaching are: (a) selecting appropriate learning

tasks and matching them with students; (b) following systematic instructional procedures; (c) providing sufficient time for students to engage themselves in their learning; (d) monitoring and evaluating student progress and performance; and (e) maintaining and generalizing students' learning.

12. Effective instruction promotes procedural and conditional knowledge, along with acquired knowledge, through active learning and open dialogue.

13. Student grouping, scheduling, record-keeping, and grading are necessary and important aspects of classroom management.

14. Effective classroom managers are well prepared at the beginning of the school year.

15. Some children require highly structured behaviouristic programs (e.g., contingency contracting and token economies) to help them adjust to their learning environment. However, these methods should be used only after the teacher has created a comfortable classroom environment; has established classroom rules and routines; has employed effective instructional procedures; and has involved students in meaningful learning experiences. Furthermore, behaviouristic approaches should be replaced as soon as possible with less externally controlled approaches that encourage and facilitate self-competence and self-control.

16. Successful teachers and managers are effective collaborators and coordinators.

17. Some students misbehave due to mistaken goals.

A CLASSROOM MANAGEMENT CHECKLIST

Proactive Classroom Management

Yes   No   Teacher demonstrates courtesy, respect, and empathy for students.

Yes   No   Teacher guides students toward regulating and controlling their own behaviour.

Yes   No   Teacher develops students' ability to be independent decision-makers, creative thinkers, and problem-solvers, and to be adaptive in their day-to-day performance encounters.

Yes   No   Teacher focuses equally on process knowledge and content knowledge.

Yes   No   Teacher promotes positive and respectful interactions with students.

Yes   No   Teacher values the views and perspectives of students.

Yes   No   Teacher shows willingness to help students with their learning and behaviour.

Yes   No   Teacher allows opportunities for students to have open discussion regarding classroom procedures and day-to-day activities.

Yes   No   Teacher sets realistic limits for students' behaviour.

Yes   No   Teacher evaluates and helps improve students' strategies for and approaches to learning.

Yes   No   Teacher clearly presents and explains academic and social goals.

Yes   No   Teacher effectively listens to students.

Yes   No   Teacher challenges and bridges students' responses and uses process questioning.

Yes   No   Teacher demonstrates and develops systematic and sequential learning strategies.

Yes   No   Teacher provides descriptive and nonjudgmental feedback to students with respect to learning and behaviour.

Yes   No   Teacher models behaviours that are considered to be appropriate for students to demonstrate.

Yes   No   Teacher gives clear and concise directions.

Yes   No   Teacher incorporates all of the senses in teaching and learning encounters.

Yes   No   Teacher prepares schedules and checklists for students.

Yes   No   Teacher gives time to students for independent study and relaxation.

Yes   No   Teacher arranges the classroom in a way that allows for free movement and multipurpose activities.

Yes   No   Teacher uses materials, desks, chairs, and tables that are appropriate for the physical needs and age of students.

Yes   No   Teacher deals with problems quickly.

Yes   No   Teacher gives assignments that are interesting and challenging.

Yes   No   Teacher gives sufficient time to students to practice and apply skills and knowledge.

Yes   No   Teacher develops students' ability to develop strategies for dealing with stressful situations.

Supportive Classroom Management

Yes   No   Teacher carefully selects learning tasks and matches them with students.

Yes   No   Teacher follows systematic instructional procedures.

Yes   No   Teacher provides enough time for students to engage themselves in learning.

Yes   No   Teacher continually monitors and evaluates students' progress and performance.

Yes   No   Teacher maintains and generalizes students' learning.

Yes   No   Teacher prepares specific goals and objectives for lessons.

Yes   No   Teacher promotes the use of learning strategies with students.

Yes   No   Teachers show relevance of learning to students.

Yes   No   Teachers continually involve students in the process of learning.

Yes   No   Teachers model for their students.

Yes   No   Teachers provide opportunities for students to practice concepts and skills.

Yes   No   Teacher prepares schedules for classroom aides and auxiliary personnel.

Yes   No   Teacher discusses roles and expectations for aides and auxiliary personnel.

Yes   No   Teacher make aides and auxiliary personnel feel welcome and comfortable in the classroom.

Yes   No   Teacher records performance of students with respect to the process and product of their learning.

Yes   No   Teacher uses alternative grading procedures for students.

Yes   No   Teacher and classroom are prepared for first week of school.

Yes   No   Teacher creates, discusses, and reviews rules and routines with students.

Yes   No   Teacher fosters and maintains communication with parents regarding students' learning and behaviour.

Reactive Classroom Management

Yes   No   Teacher tries problem-solving approaches with students.

Yes   No   Teacher meets academic and social needs of students.

Yes   No   Teacher identifies and praises desirable behaviour of students.

Yes   No   Teacher has reasonable expectations for students' behaviour.

Yes   No   Teacher allows students to express their views and opinions.

Yes   No   Teacher provides lessons that are meaningful and interesting.

Yes   No   Teacher provides activities and assignments that allow students to be successful.

Yes   No   Teacher gives clear directions, objectives, and goals to students.

Yes   No   Teacher effectively creates and practices rules and routines.

Yes   No   Teacher discusses reasonable consequences for students' behaviour.

Yes   No   Teacher gives sufficient feedback to students about their learning and behaviour.

Yes   No   Teacher observes and specifically defines misbehaviour.

Yes   No   Teacher collects and records information on the number of times and/or the duration of time an undesirable behaviour occurs.

Yes   No   Teacher graphs behavioural occurrence and shows and discusses it with students, parents, and involved personnel.

Yes   No   Teacher selects a behavioural method to deal with the behaviour and explains this method to students.

Yes   No   Teacher selects reinforcement procedures and discusses them with students.

Yes   No   Teacher guides students toward self-monitoring, self-recording, and self-managing their own behaviour.

Yes   No   Teacher explains behavioural approaches used with the students to parents, aides, and auxiliary personnel.

Yes   No   Teacher informs the student, parents, aides, and auxiliary personnel about the student's progress in learning and behaviour.

Yes   No   Teachers consider and deal with students' mistaken beliefs.

QUESTIONS
◆◆◆◆◆◆◆◆◆◆◆◆◆

1. Describe the metacognitive approach to teaching and the mediational style of teaching.

2. Distinguish between proactive, supportive, and reactive classroom management, and point out the salient elements of each.

3. What are some basic learning formats, and how can teachers create comfortable classroom environments?

4. List some factors to consider at the beginning of the school year with respect to classroom management.

5. Suggest differences between a problem-solving approach to misbehaviour and behaviouristic management.

APPENDIX 9.1

CONTROLLING OUT-OF-SEAT BEHAVIOUR: AN ELEMENTARY CASE STUDY*

Khristian is a Grade 2 student. Assessment found that his oral reading skills were quite good, but his comprehension level was low. During intervention sessions, Khristian's program has included strategies, such as predicting and retelling, to increase comprehension level. However, after only a few sessions of working with Khristian, it was noted that he tends to be off task during oral story reading, and appears to have a difficult time staying in his seat during shared story experiences. After several cues to have Khristian return to his seat, or cues to bring him back to attend to the group activities, it became clear that the out-of-seat behaviour was an important key to the comprehension problems that Khristian was experiencing. For this reason, it was decided that the behaviour should be decreased in order to allow a closer focus on Khristian's comprehension problems, and to work intensely with the predicting and retelling strategies that appeared to be improving his comprehension level.

Description of Behaviour

NO

In the small-group setting, Khristian's out-of-seat behaviour appears to begin as soon as he even slightly loses attention while listening to a story being read. It is probably not uncommon for most students to become inattentive for seconds during a listening activity; however, most students realize they have become distracted and try to pick up on the activity at hand. In Khristian's case, he loses his focus and almost unconsciously leaves his seat to look at something hanging on the wall, or his shoelace, or his marker box (which is now left on a separate table due to earlier distractions), or any other stimuli that catches his attention the second he goes off task. This behaviour is not long in duration, as Khristian leaves his seat only for a few seconds—the problem lies in the frequency of the behaviour occurrence.

Even though it appears that Khristian's out-of-seat behaviour stems from an attention difficulty, I feel that getting him to control his out-of-seat behaviour is the most appropriate place for him to start. Once the out-of-seat behaviour is controlled, perhaps we can begin to focus on some attention strategies, such as self-talk and self-monitoring, that Khristian could use to keep focused and on task during listening activities.

I initially checked to see if Khristian's getting out of his seat has something to do with his feelings about the small group and the activity of reading stories together. When I ask if he likes the group, Khristian replies that he likes

---

* We would like to acknowledge Gloria Yusishen, who contributed many of the ideas presented in this case study.

the stories that we read in class and wants to be in the small group. This reply and my own observation of Khristian's participation in discussion and writing activities has convinced me that his out-of-seat behaviour does not stem from the actual activities of the small group. He appears to enjoy himself during the activities and also enjoys the other students in the small group. The out-of-seat behaviour does not appear to be an attention-seeking behaviour. Khristian is very quiet when out of his seat, as if entirely focused on something else. Khristian does not ask irrelevant questions or make silly remarks during the activity. He does not bother other students or the teacher (directly). Also, Khristian does not require extra attention or cuing to stay on task during writing activities. He sincerely seems to have a difficult time staying focused during listening and group discussion activities, which in turn affects his comprehension.

It has become evident through discussion with Khristian that he is unaware of his out-of-seat behaviour. When asked, he cannot tell me the last time he got up or how many times he has left his seat. When asked if he thinks he gets out of his seat too much his reply is that he does not think so. For this reason, Khristian and I have agreed that he should be the record-keeper of his out-of-seat behaviour, with cues from me for him to record initially, in order to see if, in fact, he does get out of his seat too much. This is also to be done by myself to see if the behaviour is truly high in occurrence or if I just seem to notice it more with Khristian. An important note is that this activity is to be done *after* initial baseline data was collected. (Khristian was not aware of the focus on the behaviour during the time of baseline data collection.)

The results of the recording confirm that decreasing the out-of-seat behaviour should be pursued. Khristian also agrees that he gets out of his seat a lot. As stated, Khristian should be given strategies to stay on task and focused during listening activities, but, to begin, getting him to stay seated during listening activities (teacher reading a story) will reinforce these strategies. For this reason, the following behavioural objective has been designed to help Khristian monitor and decrease his out-of-seat behaviour.

Behavioural Objective

Given a thirty-minute period consisting of group discussion and shared story experiences, Khristian will not leave his seat without teacher permission for three consecutive thirty-minute periods.

Data Collection

Khristian loses focus and leaves his seat several times during the shared story experience. The students are in the small group for one hour, approximately thirty minutes of which is spent reading a story and looking at important parts, such as rhyming and unfamiliar words, as well as predicting and retelling parts of the story. It was during this time that event recording for the frequency of occurrence and duration of Khristian's out-of-seat behaviour was done for baseline data collection. I believe it is important to take more than one baseline collection in order to get a more accurate picture of the frequency of a certain behaviour. A number of factors could affect (and give a distorted picture of) a student's behaviour on any given day. A second collection of baseline data may provide a more accurate picture of the occurrence of this behaviour.

The following chart was used to record the occurrence of out-of-seat behaviour.

Date	Start time	End time	Notation of occurrences	Total occurrences	Duration (seconds)
Oct. 22	1:30	2:00	‖‖ ‖‖	9	9, 12, 14, 8, 6, 7, 1, 5, 20, 11, 13 (12.7 average)
Oct. 24	1:30	2:00	‖‖ ‖‖ ‖	11	23, 12, 14, 15, 11, 7, 9, 7, 11, 16, 18 (10.9 average)

(A similar chart was used for intervention checking excluding duration.) From the baseline data, it is evident that the frequency of this behaviour is what constitutes the undesirable behaviour. Duration of this behaviour is very short, usually consisting of only ten to twelve seconds while Khristian goes to examine something on the floor that he has noticed, or gets off his chair to look underneath the seat.

Graph

The following graph shows the baseline data collections done October 22 and October 24. Also shown on this graph is Khristian's collection of his own out-of-seat behaviour on October 29. It is interesting to note that the behaviour decreased when he was monitoring himself, but not as significantly as one would think. Frequently during this collection, Khristian would not notice that he had left his seat, and only after he was cued to sit down would he mark the occurrence. This implies that Khristian definitely needs a strategy to monitor his behaviour when he goes off task. The results for when the self-monitoring questioning strategy was used are also shown for November 5, 7, and 12.

Figure 9.A2

Frequency of Khristian's Out-of-Seat Behaviour

Date of 30-Minute Sessions

Procedural Implementation

After the initial self-monitoring of the behaviour, Khristian agreed that he got out of his seat several times during the story. When asked if he saw the other students getting out of their seats during the story, he replied that he did not. We came to a mutual agreement that he was getting out of his seat too many times during the story, without asking permission. Khristian agreed to take part in trying to decrease this behaviour during story time.

In order to effectively decrease this behaviour, Khristian had to become aware that he was, in fact, getting out of his seat. Khristian was given a self-monitoring strategy in which he was to ask himself the following three questions:

1. Why do I want to get out of my seat?
2. Should I be getting out of my seat right now?
3. What should I do if I have to get out of my seat?

Combined with this strategy was the following technique. Whenever Khristian did get out of his seat without asking permission, he would be asked the following three questions:

1. Why are you out of your seat?
2. Should you be out of your seat right now?
3. What should you do if you think you must get out of your seat?

This was a very teacher-initiated strategy, but necessary initially in order to bring to Khristian's attention that he had left his seat. It also allowed for me to model self-monitoring questions to Khristian, which he was to use on his own. The questions were asked very quietly and subtly, without using a negative tone, in order to get Khristian to feel in control of the situation and avoid making him feel like he was being "picked" on. This also prevented significant group interruption.

In order to implement these strategies, I discussed the plan with Khristian privately. Since I wanted Khristian to take control of his own actions and be responsible for them, I asked how he felt about the questions he was to ask himself. Khristian thought that the questions would help him to stay seated and help him to remember to ask permission before getting up. He also thought it was good that I was going to help him to remember the questions by asking him them if he did get out of his seat. I stressed that when I asked the questions, they were not in order to give him "heck," but to remind him of the plan.

We went through the questions verbally. I read the question and gave an answer for each one. I then asked Khristian to read the questions and provide verbal answers for them. We looked at several examples to give Khristian an idea of when the questions should be asked, and to build transfer into the strategy. For example, I asked Khristian, "What if you saw an eraser on the floor over by the door? Would you get out of your seat during the story and go get it?" Khristian replied, "No, because I might miss something happening in the story." I added, "or I might have to stop reading until you returned," then asked, "What could you do instead of getting up?" Khristian replied, "I could wait until after the story and then go get it." Since I wanted to reinforce *asking* to leave his seat, I asked, "When the story was over would you just get up and go?" Khristian said, "No, I should ask you before I go get it." Other examples were given for a variety of settings and situations, such as tying his shoelace, looking at a picture on the wall, looking at the mobiles in the room, reading the chalkboard in his classroom, or looking underneath the table or his chair. Incorporating the strategy questions in our discussion of these different situations was done to ensure that Khristian had a clear idea of what the questions were to be used for.

Throughout the implementation process, it had to be kept in mind that this student was only in Grade 2, and although he seemed to understand the procedure, I had to expect to use teacher-directed questions frequently for the first few sessions. This became part of the implementation process in that the teacher-directed questions became a modelling situation for Khristian. It was anticipated that as the self-monitoring strategy was used, the out-of-seat behaviour (without permission) would decrease and, therefore, I would not have to ask Khristian the three teacher-directed questions; as the self-monitoring increased, the teacher monitoring would decrease.

Reinforcement Procedures

A strength that has been mentioned several times throughout Khristian's assessment, IEP, and daily lesson evaluation is his strong ability in drawing. It was decided that allowing him a five-minute period per session to draw and colour, if his out-of-seat behaviour decreased, would work as an excellent extrinsic reward. By choosing this ability as a reinforcement for Khristian, I am not only allowing him to do something he thoroughly enjoys, but I am also building on his strengths; this allows Khristian to be in a win-win situation, as he becomes motivated to stay in his seat and also is allowed to show success through his drawing. I also verbally praise Khristian and make sure I use his in-seat behaviour to point out to others in the group how well he is listening to the story and staying on task. Also I tell Khristian to "give himself a pat on the back" when he does a good job during the session; this will become an internal reinforcement, which will help Khristian take ownership for his success.

Record of Results

It appears from the graph that with both teacher-directed and self-monitored intervention, the out-of-seat behaviour is decreasing. The amount of the decrease is not substantial, however, the intervention strategy has been carried out only for three thirty-minute sessions. The results show a decrease from eleven to eight occurrences over the time Khristian was observed for baseline data to the session where Khristian collected data for his behaviour. This perhaps indicates that simply bringing the behaviour to Khristian's attention was an effective start. The strategy itself was not implemented until the following week, which shows a decrease of one occurrence. However, during the next session the behaviour increased by one. It may be that Khristian was more involved in the story and the activity going on around him than with the fact that his behaviour was being monitored. Also, on this occasion there was a visitor in the group, which may have thrown Khristian off slightly. The November 12 session resulted in a further decrease, bringing the number of occurrences to six in a thirty-minute session.

It appears that in order to eliminate the behaviour entirely, several sessions will be required in which Khristian is given immediate feedback for using the self-monitoring questions. At first, the possibility of observing and praising Khristian immediately seemed remote, for if the strategy was being used there would be no sign that Khristian was about to get up. However, on four occasions I have observed Khristian start to rise from his seat and then sit down quickly. It is at such times that Khristian applies the strategy for out-of-seat behaviour. Observing these actions makes it possible for me to offer immediate positive reinforcement for application of the strategies.

I believe that the self-monitoring strategies will allow for Khristian to obtain success and decrease his out-of-seat behaviour. By self-monitoring his own behaviour, Khristian is in control of his own actions and knows what the consequences will be. He likes to be able to draw for five minutes at the end of the session, and is definitely motivated to stay seated during shared story experiences. It appears that after the three thirty-minute sessions, Khristian is well aware of the procedure and use of the strategies. He knows the questions well and recognizes what he has done almost immediately when I begin to ask the questions. I believe that this is a successful start to the implementation of the program in that the first important step was to make Khristian aware of the behaviour itself. This new awareness should aid Khristian in self-monitoring the actual occurrence of physically leaving his seat. In this respect, the intervention strategy should gradually become exclusively a self-monitoring procedure that Khristian can apply in any listening situation.

◇ A P P E N D I X   9 . 2

CONTROLLING LOUD REMARKS: A SECONDARY CASE EXAMPLE[*]

Periodically, John likes to remind everyone, through excessively loud verbalizations, of his presence in the classroom. He frequently enters class using a loud and boisterous tone of voice in speaking to another classmate or in making general remarks. While his manner of classroom entry can be tolerated, such loud verbalizations are inappropriate during the course of the English 13 class period. In responding to a teacher or classmate during class in an excessively loud tone of voice, John disrupts the class by directing other students' attention to him and whomever he is addressing.

While John has exhibited several other behaviours that are not age-appropriate, his loud attention-seeking comments are the most bothersome in terms of classroom disruptions. Since disrupted classroom activities affect the quality of instruction, as well as the performance and attention of the entire class, decreasing John's inappropriately loud comments is a highly desirable behavioural change. In addition, it is hypothesized that some of John's additional secondary inappropriate behaviours may be modified or eliminated as well.

Description of Behaviour

John's inappropriate behaviours include: (1) excessively loud remarks that are topic-related; (2) excessively loud remarks that are unrelated to a task and could be categorized as impertinent or "smart"; (3) attention-seeking through loud remarks; (4) being easily distracted from a task by other students' deliberate or inadvertent attempts; (5) inattentive behaviour when directions or instructions are given in verbal or written form; (6) goading of other students through sarcasm; (7) work not completed; (8) rapid and ineffectual completion of tasks.

In 1982, John, age 7, and his family came to Canada from Vietnam. He has been enrolled in the Canadian school system since Grade 1. According to WISC-R results, John's overall level of intellectual functioning falls in the average range. All available reports in John's cumulative records indicate very low skills in all aspects of reading and writing. He has been previously described as having low attention, especially when activities involve reading and writing. John's language difficulties are further documented by results of the Peabody Picture Vocabulary Test, which indicated a discrepancy between his receptive word knowledge (he scored in the borderline range) and expressive word knowledge (he scored in the mid-average range). Previous teachers reported that John has difficulty comprehending concepts and vocabulary in the regular classroom. While some teachers have attributed John's poor read-

* We would like to acknowledge Diana Lamb, who contributed many of the ideas presented in this case study.

ing and writing skills to English as a Second Language, others have asserted that this should not be a factor after nine years in Canada.

In terms of John's academic work, reports repeatedly emphasize the need for increased vocabulary knowledge and word-attack skills to increase John's reading comprehension. It is likely that if John's reading comprehension improved, his written expression would also show improvement as he increased his knowledge of words with which to express himself. Therefore, a behavioural objective that addresses John's frustration, which is exhibited by inappropriate behaviours in connection with reading or writing, seems to be in order.

Behavioural Objective

In an English 13 class (sixty-five minutes), John will learn to control his inappropriately loud remarks from making several loud comments per class period to making two or less loud comments during the total class time period over a time span of five weeks.

Data Collection

Baseline data on John's inappropriate off-task behaviour was collected during the week of October 21-28, for a total of five days, four of which were consecutive. The chart kept on John's behaviour during this period is reproduced in the figure entitled "Frequency of Inappropriately Loud Speaking-Out Behaviour." From past observations, it was evident that frequency rather than the duration of the inappropriate behaviour was the primary concern. That is, John's off-task behaviour was never long in duration, but it did seem to be frequent, which proved a distraction to other students and the teacher. Therefore, the chart details the frequency in five-minute increments over a sixty-minute period. The English 13 periods are sixty-five minutes in length, but, in fairness to John, at least five minutes of this time needed to be allowed for arriving, settling in, and preparing to leave.

In addition to charting the frequency of John's off-task behaviour, I also kept a brief anecdotal record of the particular class assignments for the day, because I thought the nature of the assignments might be related to the inappropriate behaviour.

In relation to the class work being done, John was behaving inappropriately primarily when he was required to engage in a writing activity or during oral discussions. Interestingly, although the majority of John's inappropriate behaviour was not comprised of loud remarks, these remarks were the most disruptive to the class as a whole. Other inappropriate behaviours exhibited included: (1) looking at pictures in his novel during reading time; (2) talking to other students; (3) leaving his seat to walk around the classroom; (4) answering questions directed at other students; (5) daydreaming; (6) fidgeting with another student's property; (7) making sarcastic remarks, to one student in

Frequency of Inappropriately Loud Speaking-Out Behaviour

Date	Frequency											
	5	10	15	20	25	30	35	40	45	50	55	60
October 21					x	x				x	x	x
October 22				x	x				x	x		
October 23	x	x				x			x	x		x
October 24			x				x		x			
October 28	x			x	x			x			x	x

Recorded in 5-minute increments during a 60-minute LD IV English 13 class over a 5-day span.

particular; (8) asking irrelevant questions; and (9) making irrelevant comments ("irrelevant" is defined here as unrelated to the topic except in some exaggerated form).

In examining the scatter of the frequency of inappropriate behaviours on the chart, a pattern of time between behaviour emissions began to emerge. It appeared that John was able to sustain on-task attention for periods of approximately fifteen to twenty minutes only. This had possible implications for changing activities after fifteen minutes and/or the reinforcement of appropriate behaviour, through praise or attention, at approximate fifteen-minute intervals in order to motivate John to continue to stay on task.

A brief summary of the classroom activities during the baseline period of October 22-28 follows:

October 21:   oral and silent reading of class novel, assigned novel questions for completion.

October 22:   video and oral reading of class novel.

October 23:   essay writing on assigned topic.

October 24:   essay completion, silent reading of assigned short story.

October 28:   written summary of novel's chapter and synopses, oral reading of novel, assigned questions on the novel.

It would seem that when John is able to read silently, or listen to others as they read orally, his disruptive speaking-out behaviour decreases, the data for October 22 and 24 suggests. Students are not required to read orally but many do not seem to mind doing so. John does not volunteer to read and has refused to read when asked, which is understandable considering his vocabulary difficulties.

On October 21, 23, and 28, the majority of the class period was taken up with written work. As previously hypothesized, John's speaking out became more frequent on these occasions. He has not yet completed the essay assignment of October 23, despite several reminders.

Procedural Implementation

The three strategies I implemented during the intervention period were contingency contracting, shaping, and reinforcement.

My aim was to attempt to reduce the number of excessively loud comments made by John, because this was not acceptable classroom behaviour and it was disturbing to others in the classroom. In order to implement the contingency contract, I had an informal conversation with John in which we discussed how he felt about his reading and writing skills and what he would like to be able to accomplish during the period of time I was in the English 13 class. John felt that his reading was satisfactory but that he sometimes did not know the meanings of words. When asked if he used a dictionary, his response was that it had too many meanings and was confusing.

John said he did not like to write because he could not think of what to say and the process (i.e., putting his ideas on paper) was too long. I pointed out that he would be expected to do a lot of writing in high school and that perhaps we could work on increasing his writing output for part of the period, followed by an activity John would like to engage in for the final ten to fifteen minutes of class. John agreed that he would try this, and chose reading as an activity he would like to engage in for the remainder of the class time.

I did not specifically discuss John's disrupting and excessively loud comments for three reasons. First, John knows his behaviour is inappropriate. Second, I wanted a commitment from John to become more involved in taking charge of his work. Third, I felt that the loud comments were related to his frustration with school work; therefore, it seemed more appropriate to work on the cause (poor writing) as opposed to the symptom (speaking out).

Since the data seemed to indicate that John's average attention span was approximately fifteen minutes, I used shaping and reinforcement of behaviours at fifteen-minute intervals. As the fifteen-minute interval approached, I would make a point of praising John verbally for work completed or moving close to him and smiling as I surveyed his work. If John showed signs of being distracted before the fifteen-minute period elapsed, I would ask him how his work was progressing and help him solve any work-related problems that had arisen. In this way, I hoped to reinforce John's appropriate classroom behaviour—attending quietly to a task rather than gaining attention through loud remarks.

In lessening John's loud comments, my intention was also to increase his work productivity and hence the amount of time he spent on a task. I actually began by asking John if he could time how long he spent on a task before he tired. I chose a ten-minute period as a starting point because I knew John was capable of fifteen minutes' sustained attention. By beginning below his baseline attention span, I hoped to provide John with success and thus intrinsic motivation to increase his attention time. While timing himself may have been a mild distraction, it provided John with a short break and hopefully with a sense of breaking his task into short time periods so that he could actually see what he was able to accomplish. On the first day of intervention we began with blocks of ten-minute work periods, and each day we increased the work period by five minutes. Given more time, I think I would have extended the time increases weekly rather than daily because it would have given John more adjustment time. By the time John had calculated his time spent on a task, it was close to the fifteen-minute limit I had established for myself in terms of providing praise and attention. This seemed to work well as a device for continuing to keep John on task.

Reinforcement Procedures

John's choice of final ten- to fifteen-minute activities following the successful completion of an agreed-upon number of daily work-time blocks was free reading of classroom magazines. This extrinsic reinforcement was a consequence of the contingency contract technique that was implemented. Additional methods of reinforcement included praise, attention, close proximity, and smiling. While these methods are basically extrinsically reinforcing, it was hoped John would also gain intrinsic reinforcement from the satisfaction of being positively rewarded. Timing himself during prescribed work blocks was a type of reinforcement as well in that it gave John a sense of accomplishment and control over what he was doing, as he could see the results of his efforts within the time period. It was hoped that this sense of accomplishment would transfer to a more intrinsic motivation to work.

Record of Results

While results of the intervention period were less than dramatic, I think that the intervention did show some success. On the first day of intervention, John worked for two ten-minute blocks of time on a writing assignment. For John to spend even twenty minutes of an entire period on his written work was out of the ordinary. He did make loud remarks, but their frequency was less than before intervention. On the second day of intervention, John's periods of sustained work were increased to fifteen-minute blocks, and he showed the same number of loud remark responses as he had during the previous day's ten-minute blocks. I felt this was an accomplishment in terms of sustained work output and attention. His loud comments did not increase, although his attention to task time did. On the third day of intervention, we maintained the previous day's fifteen-minute time periods because I wanted to see if an extra day would provide John with more practice and modify his

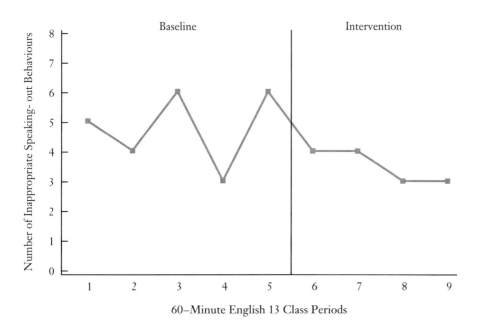

Figure 9.B1

Number of Inappropriate Loud Speaking-Out Behaviours
Before and During Intervention

speaking out. Indeed, John did speak out one less time than on the previous day. On the fourth day, I increased his attention to task time to periods of twenty minutes. His speaking-out responses remained at the same level as the previous day. Again, I feel this was an accomplishment, as attention time but not speaking-out time increased.

In retrospect, rather than giving John a few choices of free-time activities as a reward, I think I would try to involve him more by having *him* think of appropriate activities. Involving John in the planning would give him more responsibility and control over his decision-making, and perhaps more incentive to work at remaining on task, thereby reducing his speaking out.

In continuing the intervention, I would likely keep the work-time blocks unchanged for several days until I began to see a lessening of excessive speaking-out behaviour. I think this would be a good indicator that John was able to sustain attention and was ready for longer time periods. In terms of the type of written work in which John was engaged, I think there would have to be a readjustment of work-time blocks. This would be particularly appropriate in lengthy writing assignments such as essay writing, in which case I think it would be both practical and beneficial to break the essay into tasks of an introduction, body, and conclusion, and decide with John how much time per period should be devoted to each essay task. This strategy would likely keep John from being overwhelmed and would enable him to see an accomplishment after each stage.

As John's writing skills are very poor, I feel this type of intervention should ideally be carried out for an entire semester. John needs constant monitoring, feedback, and reinforcement vis-à-vis his writing efforts. Writing has been a problem throughout John's schooling, and will not be changed during the course of a few weeks. John needs sustained attention and remediation over the course of months, not only to build his writing skills but also to motivate him intrinsically to begin taking responsibility for his learning.

REFERENCES

Arlin, M. (1979). Teacher transitions can disrupt time flow in classrooms. *American Educational Research, 16*, 42-56.

Bellanca, J. A., & Kirschenbaum, H. (1976). An overview of grading alternatives. In S. B. Simon & J. A. Bellanca (Eds.), *Grading the grading myths: Primer of alternatives to grades and marks*. Washington, DC: Association for Supervision and Curriculum Development.

Blankenship, C., & Lilly, M. S. (1981). *Mainstreaming students with learning and behaviour problems*. New York: Holt, Rinehart & Winston.

Borkowski, J. G., Johnson, M. B., & Reid, M. K. (1987). Metacognition, motivation, and controlled performance. In S. J. Ceci (Ed.), *Handbook of cognitive, social, and neurological aspects of learning disabilities, Volume 2*. Hillsdale, NJ: Lawrence Erlbaum.

Bos, C. S., & Vaughn, S. (1988). *Strategies for teaching students with learning and behaviour problems*. Toronto: Allyn & Bacon.

Brophy, J. E. (1982). Classroom management and learning. *American Education*, 20-23.

Brophy, J. E. (1983). Classroom organization and management. *The Elementary School Journal, 83*(4), 265-286.

Brophy, J. E., & Evertson, C. (1976). *Learning from teaching: A developmental perspective*. Boston: Allyn & Bacon.

Brophy, J. E., & Putman, J. (1979). Classroom management in the elementary grades. In D. Duke (Ed.), *Classroom management: The 78th yearbook of the National Society for the Study of Education, Part 2*. Chicago: University of Chicago Press.

Carpenter, D. (1985). Grading handicapped pupils: Review and position statement. *Remedial and Special Education, 6*(4), 54-59.

Christenson, S. L., Ysseldyke, J. E., & Thurlow, M. L. (1989). Critical instructional factors for students with mild handicaps: An integrative review. *Remedial and Special Education, 10*(5), 21-31.

Cohen, S. B. (1983). Assigning report card grades to the mainstreamed child. *Teaching Exceptional Children, 15*, 86-89.

Conger, J., & Petersen, A. (1984). *Adolescence and youth: Psychological development in a changing world* (3rd ed.). New York: Harper Row.

Coopersmith, S. (1967). *The antecedents of self-esteem*. San Francisco: W. H. Freeman.

Costa, A. L. ((1991). The school as a home for the mind: A climate for thinking. In R. Mulcahy, J. Andrews, & R. Short (Eds.), *Enhancing learning and thinking*. New York: Praeger.

D'Aurora, D. L., & Fimian, M. J. (1988). Dimensions of life and school stress experienced by young people. *Psychology in the Schools, 25*, 44-53.

De Charms, R. (1976). *Enhancing motivation*. New York: Irvington.

Delisle, J. R., Whitmore, J. R., & Ambrose, R. P. (1987). Preventing discipline problems with gifted students. *Teaching Exceptional Children*, 32-38.

Delquadri, J., Greenwood, C. R., Whorton, D., Carta, J. J., & Hall, R. V. (1986). Classwide peer tutoring. *Exceptional Children, 52*(6), 535-542.

DeLuke, S. V., & Knoblock, P. (1987). Teaching behaviour as preventative discipline. *Teaching Exceptional Children*, 18-24.

Dorman, G. (1981). *Middle grades assessment program*. Chapel Hill, NC: Centre for Early Adolescence.

Dougherty, A. M., & Deck, M. D. (1984). Helping teachers to help children cope with stress. *Journal of Humanistic Education and Development, 23*, 36-54.

Doyle, W. (1986). Classroom organization and management. In M. C. Wittrock (Ed.), *Handbook of research on teaching* (3rd ed.) (pp. 392-431). New York: Macmillan.

Dreikers, R. (1968). *Psychology in the classroom* (2nd ed.). New York: Harper Row.

Dreikers, R., & Cassel, P. (1972). *Discipline without tears*. New York: Hawthorn Books.

Dreikers, R., Grunwold, B., & Pepper, F. (1982). *Maintaining sanity in the classroom: Classroom management techniques* (2nd ed.). New York: Harper Row.

Dweck, C. S. (1986). Motivational processes affecting learning. *American Psychologist, 41*, 1040-1048.

Emmer, E. T., Evertson, C. M., & Anderson, L. M. (1980). Effective classroom management at the beginning of the school year. *The Elementary School Journal, 80*(5), 219-231.

Fagen, S. A. (1986). Least intensive intervention for classroom behaviour problems. *The Pointer, 31*(1), 21-28.

Fagen, S., & Hill, J. (1977). *Behaviour management: A competency based manual for in-service training*. Washington, DC: Psychoeducational Resources.

Feldhusen, J. F., & Wyman, A. R. (1980). Super Saturday: Design and implementation of Purdue's special program for gifted children. *Gifted Child Quarterly, 24*, 15-21.

Feuerstein, R. (1977). Mediated learning experience: A theoretical basis for cognitive modifiability during adolescence. In P. Mittler (Ed.), *Research to practice in mental retardation, Volume 2*. Baltimore: University Park.

Fisher, C. W., & Berliner, D. C. (Eds.) (1985). *Perspectives on instructional time*. New York: Longman.

Fowler, S. A. (1986). Peer-monitoring and self-monitoring: Alternatives to traditional teacher management. *Exceptional Children, 52*(6), 573-582.

Frith, G. H., & Armstrong, S. W. (1986). Self-monitoring for behaviour disordered students. *Teaching Exceptional Children*, 144-148.

Gallagher, P. A. (1979). *Teaching students with behaviour disorders: Techniques for classroom instruction*. Denver: Love Publishing.

Ginott, H. (1971). *Teacher and child*. New York: Macmillan.

Glasser, W. (1969). *Schools without failure*. New York: Harper and Row.

Glasser, W. (1977). Ten steps to good discipline. *Today's Education, 66*, 61-63.

Good, T. L. (1983). Classroom research: A decade of progress. *Educational Psychologist, 18*(3), 127-144.

Good, T. L., & Brophy, J. (1978). *Looking in classrooms* (2nd ed.). New York: Harper Row.

Good, T. L., & Grouws, D. (1977). Teaching effects: A process product study in fourth grade mathematics. *Journal of Teacher Education, 28*, 49-54.

Good, T. L., & Power, C. (1976). Designing successful classroom environments for different types of students. *Journal of Curriculum Studies, 8*, 47-52.

Gordon, T. (1974). *Teacher effectiveness training*. New York: Wyden.

Gronlund, H. E. (1981). *Measurement and evaluation in teaching* (4th ed.). New York: Macmillan.

Gronlund, N. E. (1985). *Stating behavioural objectives for classroom instruction* (3rd ed.). New York: Macmillan.

Guerin, G. R., & Maier, A. S. (1983). *Informal assessment in education*. Palo Alto, CA: Mayfield.

Hawley, W. D., & Rosenholtz, S.J. (1984). Effective teaching. *Peabody Journal of Education, 61*(4), 15-52.

Haynes, M. C., & Jenkins, J. R. (1986). Reading instruction in special education resource rooms. *American Educational Research Journal, 23,* 161-190.

Haywood, H. C. (1987). A mediational teaching style. *The Thinking Teacher, 4*(1), 1-6.

Haywood, H. C., Brooks, P., & Burns, S. (1986). Stimulating cognitive development at developmental levels: A tested non-remedial pre-school curriculum for pre-schoolers and older retarded children. In M. Schwebel & C. Maher (Eds.), *Facilitating cognitive development: Principles, practices and programs* (pp. 127-147). New York: Haworth Press.

Hiebert, B. (1988). Dealing with stress. In M. Wideen, P. Holbourn, & I. Andrews (Eds.), *Becoming a teacher.* Toronto: Kagan & Woo.

Hiebert, B. (1992). Nature and treatment of stress-related problems in schools. In R. Short, L. Stewin, & S. McCann (Eds.), *Educational Psychology in Canada.* Toronto: Copp Clark Pitman.

Howell, K. W., Kaplan, J. S., & O'Connell, C. Y. (1979). *Evaluating exceptional children: A task analysis approach.* Columbus, OH: Merrill.

Johnson, D. W., & Johnson, R. T. (1986). Mainstreaming and cooperative learning strategies. *Exceptional Children, 52,* 553-561.

Jones, V., & Jones, L. (1986). *Comprehensive classroom management: Creating positive learning environments* (2nd ed.). Toronto: Allyn & Bacon.

Kameenui, E. J., & Simmons, D. C. (1990). *Designing instructional strategies: The prevention of academic learning problems.* Columbus, OH: Merrill.

Kauffman, J. M., Pullen, P. L., & Akers, E. (1988). Classroom management: Teacher-child-peer relationships. In E. L. Meyen, G. A. Vergason, & R. J. Whelan (Eds.), *Effective instructional strategies for exceptional children* (pp. 32-44). Denver: Love Publishing.

Kerry, T. (1981). Teachers' class management problems with bright pupils. *The Exceptional Child, 28*(3), 199-205.

Kindsvatter, R. (1969). Guidelines for better grading. *Clearing House, 43*(6), 331-334.

Kinnison, L. R., Hayes, C., & Acord, J. (1981). Evaluating student progress in mainstream classes. *Teaching Exceptional Children, 13,* 97-99.

Kohl, H. (1982). The all-American report card is a loser. *Learning, 10*(9), 47, 49-50.

Kounin, J. (1970). *Discipline and group management in classrooms.* New York: Holt, Rinehart & Winston.

Lipsitz, J. (1984). *Successful schools for young adolescents.* New Brunswick, NJ: Transaction.

Lund, K. A., Schnaps, L., & Bijou, S. W. (1983). Let's take another look at record keeping. *Teaching Exceptional Children, 15,* 155-159.

Mager, R. F. (1975). *Preparing instructional objectives.* Belmont, CA: Fearon.

Maple, F. (1977). *Shared decision making.* Beverly Hills, CA: Sage.

Maslow, A. (1968). *Toward a psychology of being.* New York: D. Van Nostrand.

McCombs, B. L. (1982). Transitioning learning strategies research into practice: Focus on the student in technical training. *Journal of Instructional Development, 5,* 10-17.

McLaughlin, T. F., Krappman, V. F., & Welsh, J. M. (1985). The effects of self-recording for on-task behaviour of behaviourally disordered special education students. *Remedial and Special Education, 6*(4), 42-45.

Mercer, C. D., & Mercer, A. R. (1985). *Teaching students with learning problems* (2nd ed.). Columbus, OH: Merrill.

Norman, J., & Harris, M. (1981). *The private life of the American teenager.* New York: Rawson, Wade.

Olsen, J. (1982). Treatment perspectives. In B. Algozzine (Ed.), *Problem behaviour management educators' resource service.* Rockville, MD: Aspen.

Paris, S. G., & Oka, E. R. (1986). Self-regulated learning among exceptional children. *Exceptional Children, 53*(2), 103-108.

Polloway, E.A., Patton, J. R., Payne, J. S., & Payne, R. A. (1989). *Strategies for teaching learners with special needs* (4th ed.). Columbus, OH: Merrill.

Purkey, W., & Novak, J. (1984). *Inviting school success: A self-concept approach to teaching and learning* (2nd. ed.). Belmont, CA: Wadsworth.

Rosenshine, B., & Stevens, R. (1986). Teaching functions. In M. C. Wittrock (Ed.), *Handbook of research on teaching* (3rd ed.) (pp. 376-391). New York: Macmillan.

Rotter, J. (1966). Generalized expectancies for internal vs. external control of reinforcement. *Psychological Monographs, 80.*

Salend, S. J. (1983). Classroom design adaptations for mainstreamed settings: Making least the restrictive environment less restrictive. *Journal of Special Education, 20,* 51-57.

Salend, S. J. (1990). *Effective mainstreaming.* New York: Macmillan.

Smith, C. (1983). *Learning disabilities: The interaction of learner, task and setting.* Boston: Little, Brown.

Terwilliger, J. S. (1977). Assigning grades: Philosophical issues and practical recommendations. *Journal of Research and Development in Education, 10*(3), 21-39.

Truax, C., & Tatum, C. (1966). An extension from the effective psychotherapeutic model to constructive personality change in pre-school children. *Childhood Education, 42,* 456-462.

Wayson, W., & Lasley, T. (1984). Climates for excellence: Schools that foster self-discipline. *Phi Delta Kappan,* 419-421.

White, R. (1959). Motivation reconsidered: The concept of competence. *Psychological Review, 66,* 297-333.

Whitmore, J. R. (1979). Discipline and the mentally gifted child. *Roeper Review, 2*(2), 42-46.

Wittrock, M. C. (1986). Students' thought processes. In M. C. Wittrock (Ed.), *Handbook of research on teaching* (3rd ed.) (pp. 297-314). New York: Macmillan.

Ysseldyke, J. E., & Christenson, S. L. (1987). Evaluating students' instructional environments. *Remedial and Special Education, 8*(3), 17-24.

INDIVIDUALIZING THE CURRICULUM: *A CLOSER LOOK AT ACADEMIC SKILLS, STUDENT DIFFICULTIES, AND INSTRUCTIONAL METHODS*

→ refer to 460 to what you need to pay attn to
→ know approaches ; critiques.
→ essentially all of it

CHAPTER OBJECTIVES

To identify academic skills and common difficulties related to word identification, oral language, reading, writing, spelling, and mathematics.

To present instructional methods for developing the above curricular areas.

To provide a critique of the instructional methods used to develop the curricular areas under discussion.

To identify formal and informal procedures for assessing students' performance with respect to the curricular areas under discussion.

To relate instructional approaches to major theoretical perspectives on learning.

Ten-year-old David moved to Canada from Israel with his family in September 1988. His parents immediately enrolled him in a private Hebrew day school, hoping that having Hebrew as his first language would help David succeed in the new school. David's school records from Israel were not available, and the Hebrew school obtained little information from David's parents about his previous school performance. Within the first month, David's parents were contacted by the school and told that David was exhibiting a range of learning and behaviour problems that the school had no expertise in dealing with. David had considerable difficulty sitting through an entire lesson, refused to participate in reading activities, and was often aggressive toward other students when placed in a small-group learning situation. It was recommended that David be trans-

ferred to the public system, where he would be provided special services.

David had to be bused to his public school, where he made friends with other students and learned about Canadian culture and what were considered acceptable and unacceptable behaviours in Canada. Soon David began to complain to his parents that he wasn't learning anything. He told them he wanted to learn how to read like the other students, and wanted to know when the school was going to teach him how to read. A short time after David voiced these concerns to his parents, he started to exhibit behaviour problems at school, pushing and hitting children with little provocation.

David's parents were asked to come to the school, where they were informed of David's increased aggression. They told the teachers about David's complaints that he was not being taught how to read. David's teacher, Mrs. Johnson, showed them the basal readers and workbooks that she was using. She said that the other children were doing very well in learning to read, but that David did not seem interested. It seemed to her that David was not learning to read because he had chosen not to learn. David's parents then revealed David's school history, telling Mrs. Johnson that David had always had learning difficulties, even before they moved to Canada. In Israel, he had been in special education classes in Grade 2 and Grade 3, and at the time of their move to Canada, he had just started to learn to read Hebrew. David's parents had hoped that moving to Canada would give David an edge over the other children in the Hebrew school because he was orally fluent in Hebrew. It had upset them to learn that David was having the same kind of learning problems in Canada that he had had in Israel.

Mrs. Johnson told David's parents that she believed a thorough assessment needed to be conducted to determine how David learned best. She suggested that the school psychologist and the resource teacher be part of the assessment team. David's parents agreed to her proposal, and immediately following the interview the resource teacher became involved.

The resource teacher observed David in the classroom. She noticed that he often joined in class discussions during science and social studies lessons, and that his oral contributions were always on topic and relevant. It was apparent that David had a very limited English vocabulary and would sometimes substitute a Hebrew word for an English word. The words he most often mixed up were "and," "but," and "with." David did not apply himself to individual work or assignments; he would either start talking to (distracting) another child in the class, look at pictures in science books, or work on puzzles.

When she assessed his reading, the resource teacher found that David had many prereading skills. He could recognize and reproduce most of the English letters but had difficulty matching letters with sounds. He was unable to read any of the words on a pre-primer sight-word reading list, but on one of the reading subtests that the resource teacher administered, he scored very high. This subtest (The Woodcock Reading Mastery Visual-Auditory subtest) pairs visual icons with words. For example, a line with a flag on it represents the word "horse," while two parallel lines represents the word "house." David was able to "read" the longest passage, which uses thirty-five different icons, without making any mistakes.

The school psychologist conducted an intellectual assessment of David, using language-free measures. He found that David had excellent nonverbal problem-solving skills, and he was able to solve highly complex nonverbal analogies that most adults would have had difficulty achieving. This assessment indicated that David had very strong visual discrimination skills. After careful analysis of their results, the resource teacher and psychologist concluded that David would have great difficulty learning to read using a phonics approach. The most appropriate reading program for David would have to take advantage of David's strong visual discrimination skills. They recommended that Mrs. Johnson try a rebus reading program, which incorporates the pairing of words with visual icons. They also suggested that Mrs. Johnson use a language-experience approach, which would allow David's oral contributions to discussions to be translated into written words; the icons that had already been taught could be paired with David's written words.

Mrs. Johnson initiated David into the Bridge Reading Series, a rebus reading program. This series includes fifty small readers, a pocket chart, and individual words matched with icons that can be placed in the pocket chart. Initially sight words are matched with symbols. For example the word "my" is represented by a square with two hands on either side in the books. The icons are gradually eliminated, leaving only the written words. The pocket chart, the paired words, and icons also support a language-experience approach.

Mrs. Johnson trained a tutor in the use of the Bridge Reading Series, and arranged for her to spend an hour every day working with David. While guiding class discussions, Mrs. Johnson would use the pocket chart to record David's ideas. Later in the day David would re-read the words in the chart to Mrs. Johnson and copy them down in his notebook. He seemed to enjoy this method, and reported to his parents that he was finally learning to read. He would often bring the readers home to share with his family. As well, his aggressiveness toward other students decreased dramatically. When his reading was reassessed, six months after the program had been initiated, David was able to read most of the sight words on the Grade 1 reading list and some of the words on the Grade 2 list. He told his teacher that he was feeling very pleased with himself.

*[handwritten note, top right:] * . while reading keep in mind the 3 criteria*

❖ INTRODUCTION

Currently, there are three distinct yet overlapping educational positions on how children can be best taught. As reviewed in Chapter 3, McKeough (1991) points out that some educators view the learner as a social being, and emphasize language development and inquiry methods of teaching. A second group of educators view the learner as an active processor of information, and emphasize problem-solving development and strategy teaching. Finally, a third group of educators view the learner as a developing child, and emphasize natural development and systematic teaching. Although some teachers tend to favour one educational position over the others, most effective teachers incorporate all three perspectives into their daily teaching, particularly with the emergence and growth of inclusive classrooms.

THE ACTIVE-PROCESSOR PERSPECTIVE

According to the information-processing model, how we learn and think is related to how we represent and process information. This perspective emphasizes the development of students' cognitive and metacognitive processes and focuses on the role of learning and thinking strategies. The active-processor perspective stresses the process rather than the product of learning. For example, proponents of this perspective recognize that skilled reading, writing, and math performance require, among other things, the ability to conceptualize, analyze, organize, and synthesize information. Moreover, they emphasize the need for students to be able to control and regulate reading, writing, and mathematical skills.

[handwritten note, right margin:] Theoretical. 4 prespectives .

As discussed in Chapter 4, information-processing theory suggests that teachers should facilitate the development of students' cognitive and meta-cognitive processing in order for them to be better able to reflect upon and regulate their own learning and thinking. Furthermore, students' strategies and approaches to learning should be developed in such a way as to promote independent and active decision-making and problem-solving (see Chapters 9 and 12 for further discussion).

THE DEVELOPING-CHILD PERSPECTIVE

According to the developmental model, students' learning and thinking evolves over time in a systematic fashion. Supporters of this theoretical orientation view students as active constructors of their knowledge. Moreover, they believe that students approach learning and thinking tasks with cognitive structures (*schemes*) that change over time as the students incorporate (*assimilate*) new experiences and change (*accommodate*) the way they think (Piaget, 1970). In addition, proponents of the developmental model believe that students' learning progresses along identifiable stages, and that their learning and thinking skills are hierarchically integrated (McKeough, 1991).

Developmental theory suggests that teachers should provide for their students age-appropriate experiences and tasks that allow them to both use and build upon the knowledge and skills they already possess. Moreover, instruction needs to be child-centred as well as activity-oriented and discovery-based (see Chapter 3 for further discussion).

THE SOCIAL-BEING PERSPECTIVE

According to the sociocultural model, students are social beings who develop their learning and thinking capabilities through interactive communication with members of their culture (see Chapter 3). According to this model, language plays the most central role in learning (Wertsch, 1989) and culture plays a significant role in shaping students' thinking.

Sociocultural theory suggests that teachers should mediate their students' learning and thinking by providing good models and by embedding the curriculum within the sociocultural context. More specifically, teachers should provide learning environments in which students can share and discuss their experiences and abilities to mutual benefit; in which the focus is on the interaction of speaking and listening as well as reading and writing; and in which there is a balance between individual and social learning.

THE TRADITIONAL PERSPECTIVE

differentiate this from others.

One other frequently cited education perspective is the behavioural perspective. As we have pointed out in other chapters, behaviourism emphasizes the role of the environment in learning and instruction. Proponents of the behaviourist approach stress the importance of the functional relationship between the environment and student behaviour. The teacher who follows the behavioural model is interested in understanding how different conditions in the classroom determine both the quantity and quality of learning. Dominant up until the last couple of decades, this model views the student as a passive learner who can be shaped and developed through external means (see Chapter 9).

Behavioural theory suggests that teachers should assess students' specific skills, as they relate to particular tasks, and develop those skills. Proponents of this perspective believe that learning and thinking can be enhanced by providing students more experience and practice with academic and social tasks. Thus, the theory focuses on the analysis of the task rather than on the analysis of the student (Lerner, 1985). Teachers who follow this model emphasize direct instruction and sequential skills in their teaching because, according to this model, learning involves the acquisition of skills that are dependent on experiences in the environment. Moreover, because behavioural theory proposes that all learning is the result of behavioural consequences, teachers who adopt this model typically use principles of operant conditioning (applying/withholding rewards and punishments to increase/

extinguish behaviours) in their teaching. In other words, they put into practice the behaviourist tenet—that it is possible to predict and control behaviour—by reinforcing students who demonstrate or approach expected behaviour.

MEETING THE NEEDS OF STUDENTS IN THE INCLUSIVE CLASSROOM: AN ECLECTIC PERSPECTIVE

According to the once-dominant behavioural model, students were passive learners. We now view students as independent, active, and creative learners and decision-makers. Similarly, teachers were once considered to be disseminators of information whose job was to ensure that students received and mastered information that was appropriate for their age group. Today, we view teachers as active mediators and collaborators, as well as efficient managers who identify students' needs and accommodate student differences. Moreover, we have become much more child-centred and socially conscious than in the past. Thus, current learning and instructional principles more closely correspond with the information-processing, developmental, and sociocultural models of learning and instruction than with the behavioural model of learning and instruction.

Regardless of the favoured orientation, however, rigid alliance with only one of the above models of learning will not allow teachers to adequately meet the needs of all students in the inclusive classroom. As noted in previous chapters, students in today's inclusive classrooms have *interindividual differences* in abilities and needs (i.e., abilities and needs that vary *across* students). Hence, teachers can expect to have students in their classrooms who, for example, need remediation, practice, and direct instruction with respect to particular skills and subskills. Teachers will also have students who have needs in the areas of self-control or who need to be provided with much more opportunity to share and discuss their ideas and experiences. Students in today's inclusive classrooms also have *intraindividual* differences in abilities and needs (abilities and needs that vary *within* students). For example, a student who needs remediation, practice, and direct instruction in mathematics might also need development of self-control in reading. Thus, in establishing a lesson plan, teachers need to consider both interindividual and intraindividual differences in their students' needs and abilities.

In this chapter, we discuss (1) academic skills and student difficulties as they relate to word identification, oral language, reading, writing, spelling, and mathematics; (2) instructional methods that can be used in these areas; (3) benefits and limitations of the instructional methods described; and (4) ways of assessing students' level of performance in each of the above-mentioned curricular areas.

Although we treat curricular areas separately in this chapter, it should be pointed out that there has been an increasing instructional preference to integrate them (see Goodman, Goodman, & Hood, 1989; Harste, 1990;

Rhodes & Dudley-Marling, 1988 for further discussion). The whole language approach stresses the need for teachers to use authentic literature and to provide students with reading and writing experiences that are embedded in meaningful situations (Bos & Vaughn, 1991). Teachers can promote the holistic and constructive nature of learning and development by relating instruction and skill development in word identification, reading, and oral language to writing, spelling, and mathematics.

◇ ACADEMIC SKILLS AND COMMON DIFFICULTIES RELATED TO WORD IDENTIFICATION

Word identification, which is critically important to effective reading and writing, involves vocabulary development, sight-word recognition, and phonic analysis. Academic skills with which it is associated include: (1) discerning multiple meanings of words and knowing their interrelationships; (2) using context clues to understand words; (3) knowing the meanings of words rapidly and automatically; (4) being able to learn words independently (e.g., knowing how to use a dictionary); (5) being able to build upon words to form new words (e.g., using suffixes and affixes); (6) recognizing words immediately and automatically; (7) decoding unfamiliar words; and (8) being able to discriminate letters and words visually and auditorily.

With respect to word identification, students commonly have difficulty: (1) with phonic rules; (2) differentiating between letters as well as words; (3) associating letters with letter sounds; (4) applying phonetic-analysis techniques; (5) recognizing words automatically; (6) building and retaining vocabulary; (7) associating the meaning of the word with the word; and (8) relating spoken language with written material.

IMPLICATIONS FOR TEACHING

- Build networks of words through the use of themes and topics to promote purposefulness and meaningfulness in vocabulary development and instruction (Duin & Graves, 1987).
- Expose students to words more frequently to foster automatic use of words across several language contexts (Stahl & Fairbanks, 1986).
- Encourage students to notice new words inside and outside classroom activities (Duin & Graves, 1987).
- Include both definitional and contextual information about word meanings (Stahl & Fairbanks, 1986).
- Encourage students to use context clues, as well as their general language and world knowledge, to infer unknown word meanings (Sternberg, 1987).
- Begin by introducing vocabulary based on the senses (i.e., words that can be seen, heard, smelled, touched, and tasted) so that students can learn to associate words with concrete experiences (Wood, 1989).

♦ Promote active play and discussion (particularly with young children) with objects so that students have a purpose and an opportunity to name, describe, and discuss objects and activities with peers and teacher (Winzer, 1989).

♦ Teach dictionary skills and provide ways in which students can actively apply their new word and concepts (Donlan, 1975).

Table 10.1 shows how many of the above ideas can be incorporated into a unit plan for developing students' word identification skills.

ASSESSING LEVELS OF PERFORMANCE

While there are many commercially prepared tests that can help teachers evaluate students' ability in word identification (see Appendix 10.1), teachers can evaluate their students' vocabulary and word-attack skills with self-made informal tests. For example, teachers can construct their own word-recogni- *No* tion tests from the reading materials they use in the classroom, and create their own checklists for recording their students' sight vocabulary development and word-analysis skills and phonetic analysis skills (see Tables 10.2, 10.3 and 10.4).

◆ INSTRUCTIONAL METHODS FOR DEVELOPING WORD-IDENTIFICATION SKILLS

SIGHT-WORD APPROACH *-gist of this*

diff approaches allie themselves to comm practises

The sight-word (or whole word) approach to learning new words and building vocabulary is a method that enables students to "say" what a word is on the basis of remembering what it looks like; thus, when a child sees the word again, he or she recognizes it and "says" what it is. In order for this method to be successful, students need to be constantly exposed to the same words through reading, speaking, and writing. Words should be chosen from the curricular material (e.g., language-experience stories, basal series, workbook activities) that is being used.

Words can be taught using a variety of strategies. For example, a visual-imagery strategy can be used whereby students are guided toward making mental pictures of words (see Chapter 12); or words can be written on index cards and filed in containers (e.g., a shoe box) where students can easily reference them. Students should be encouraged to draw pictures that represent particular words and sentences or to write short stories that include these words in order to reinforce both word recognition and word meaning. Finally, words, definitions, and stories can be recorded on audiotapes to reinforce visual/verbal associations.

Table 10.1

Unit Overview: Developing Word-Identification Skills

Objectives	Time	Activities	Resources	Dates	Evaluation
Students will put a list of words relating to Hallowe'en in alphabetical order.	10:30 to 11:15	Students review the alphabet. Students cut out words from sheet and place them in order alphabetically on a plain piece of paper. Students glue down words once they are correctly in order alphabetically.	Alphabet to look at Hallowe'en word sheet Scissors Glue Blank paper	Begin: October 16/90 End: October 16/90	Did each student correctly place words in alphabetical order?
Students will observe & discuss short "a" vowel sounds and print words that have the same sound.	10:30 to 11:15	Show students picture with short "a" sound. Ask students to identify picture. Brainstorm for more words with short "a" sound and teacher records on chart paper. Students look at both similarities and differences of words. Students list ten words that have the same sound.	Vowel/picture flash-cards Colour paper & marker Hallowe'en phonics sheet—short "a" sound Pencil and eraser	Begin: October 17/90 End: October 17/90	Did students observe pictures and orally identify words with short "a" vowel sounds? Did each student list ten words with short "a" vowel sound?
Students will draw pictures of things that have the short "i" vowel sound.	10:30 to 11:15	Give example of short "i" vowel sound on the board (e.g., witch). Students brainstorm for words with short "i" sounds and teacher records on chart. Students draw eight things with short "i" sound and print word under picture. Provide feedback on vowel sound.	Chalk & blackboard Chart paper & markers Paper and pencils Crayons or markers Coloured markers	Begin: October 18/90 End: October 19/90	Did students sketch appropriate pictures of things with short "i" sound and print correct word under picture?

Objective	Time	Activity	Materials	Dates	Evaluation
Students will generate and print words with the long "o" vowel sound.	10:30 to 11:15	Read poem to students. Draw their attention to long "o" sounds of specific words in poem. Students generate more words with long "o" sounds. Students print 8 words with long "o" sound.	Driftwood/Dandelions; Three Ghostesses; Paper and pencils; Chart paper/markers	Begin: October 23/90; End: October 23/90	Did each student generate at least three words with the long "o" sound?
Students will correctly identify words that have short (a, e, i, o) and long "o" vowel sounds.	10:30 to 11:15	Students review charts of short and long vowel sounds. Students print Hallowe'en words given on the phonics sheet in the correct box. Students check words. Students play Vowel Bingo.	Hallowe'en phonics sheet; Chart paper with examples of short a, e, i, o and long o vowel sounds; Pencil and paper; Vowel Bingo Game	Begin: October 24/90; End: October 25/90	Did students write Hallowe'en words in the correct box?
Students will draw Hallowe'en pictures that begin with specified sounds.	10:30 to 11:15	Review initial consonant sounds using word cards (p, c, w, h, b, g, m, s, j). Brainstorm for Hallowe'en words that begin with these initial sounds. Students draw a Hallowe'en picture that begins with each of these sounds.	Hallowe'en phonics sheet to draw pictures; Words on flashcards; Paper and pencils; Crayons or markers	Begin: October 31/90; End: October 31/90	Did each student sketch an appropriate Hallowe'en picture for each sound?

Note: Developed with the assistance of Jan Avis.

Table 10.2
Record of Sight Vocabulary

Checklist

Date	Adam %	Kristian %	Kyle %
October 24	90%	100%	80%
October 31	100%	100%	90%
November 7	80%	90%	80%
November 14	100%	100%	100%
November 21	90%	90%	100%
November 28	100%	90%	90%

Note: Developed with the assistance of Gloria Yusishen.

Table 10.3
Extending Word-Analysis Skills

1. *Context Analysis*: using meaning of surrounding words or phrases
2. *Structural analysis*: the use of word parts like affixes and base words
3. *Phonic analysis*: the use of letter sounds within words

Checklist

Name _____
Date _____

| | *Strategies Used* | | |
	Context	Structural	Phonic	% Used
October 24	2	1	3	75% (3/4)
October 28		4		100%
November 4	2	3		100%
November 11	1	4		83% (5/6)
November 18	4	5		100%
November 25	1	4		86% (6/7)
			1	

Note: Developed with the assistance of Gloria Yusishen.

Critique

While the sight-word approach is successful with many students, students with short-term memory problems and/or visual perceptual difficulties will require some modification of lessons. For example, teachers can reduce the number of words to be learned, allow more practice sessions, and provide more frequent reinforcement. Students who are exposed only to this type of instruction usually have difficulty reading unfamiliar words, tend to use context clues rather than graphic cues, and often substitute familiar words for unfamiliar ones (Biemiller, 1970). Therefore, teachers may need to provide phonic instruction for some students in order to improve their ability to read unfamiliar words. (A major advantage of the sight-word approach is that it

Table 10.4
Phonetic-Analysis Skills

Evaluation Marks: S–Satisfactory I–Improving N–Needs Improvement U–Unsatisfactory N/A–Not applied	Alphabetical Order	Short "a" vowel	Short "i" vowel	Short "u" vowel	Short "o" vowel	Short "e" vowel	sl consonant blend	pl consonant blend	fl consonant blend	sp consonant blend	sw consonant blend	sc consonant blend	sm consonant blend	sn consonant blend	br consonant blend	cr consonant blend	gr consonant blend	fr consonant blend
	Nov. 1/90						Nov. 13/90			Nov. 20/90					Nov. 29/90			
Clayton	S	S	I	I	S	I	S	S	S	I	I	N/A	S	I	S	S	S	I
Lindsay	S	S	I	I	S		S	S	S	S	S	N/A	S	I	S	I	S	S
Justin	S	S	S	I	I		S	S	N	I	I	N/A	I	I	S	I	S	I

cont...
yes.

teaches students phonetically irregular words, such as "ghost.") Students with superior intellectual ability who have good short-term memory, visual and perceptual skills, as well as large vocabularies generally do not need sight-word instruction, but may be provided with exercises and activities that allow them to increase their vocabularies independently.

Due to its emphasis on the functional relationship between the environment (what the word looks like) and the students' behaviour (remembering the word), the sight-word approach is most closely associated with the behavioural perspective on learning.

PHONICS APPROACH *— know sense of this*

The purpose of the phonics approach is to have students learn the relationship between letters and sounds, and to teach them how to independently analyze and decode unfamiliar words by sounding them out. Students are typically taught consonant and vowel sounds, and the various ways to blend these sounds—e.g., digraphs (sh, ch, th, wh); initial consonant blends (pl, cr, st); final consonant blends (nd, ds); vowel combinations (ea, ow, ie); diphthongs (oy, au); prefixes (re, un); suffixes (ing, ed); and r-controlled vowels (er, ir, ur, ar).

Typically, phonics instruction is highly systematic and structured. The presentation of letters and letter combinations is generally followed by the presentation of words that contain the letters and letter combinations in order to reinforce the memory of letter sounds. Students recite the letters and words as the teacher underlines the letter(s) on the blackboard. Next, the teacher presents a variety of words to the students and has them identify the letters by enunciating the sound and pointing to the letter(s). This sequence may be followed by various practice activities aimed at reinforcing the recognition and sound of the letter(s). Finally, the teacher provides review activities that incorporate additional words containing the studied letter(s) (see Table 10.5 for an example of a lesson plan using the phonics approach).

Table 10.5 **A Lesson Plan Using the Phonics Approach**	
Subject: Language Arts	Date: November 20
Topic: Consonant blends	Time: 10:30 - 11:15
Purpose	1. To have students create new words with "s" consonant blends. 2. To develop student ability to identify "s" consonant blends.

Objectives

1. Given six examples of words on a worksheet and a pencil, the students will print five new words that begin with the consonant blend "sl" with 50% accuracy.

2. Given six examples of words on a worksheet and a pencil, the students will print five new words that begin with the consonant blend "sw" with 50% accuracy.

3. Given six examples of words on a worksheet and a pencil, the students will print five new words that begin with the consonant blend "sm" with 50% accuracy.

Materials

◆ Worksheet on consonant blends (sl, sw, sm) for Phonics Basic Skills Wordbook (page 51)

◆ Pencil/eraser

◆ Game (Space Race)—Blend Sounds sw, sl, st, sm

◆ Crepe-foam letters

Lesson

5 min.

1. Introduce lesson: Today we are going to create more words.

2. Write the word <u>side</u> on the board and tell the students that they are now going to create a different word by adding another letter to this word.

Ask the students:

(a) to listen to the word <u>slide</u> as you say it;

(b) to say the word <u>slide</u> (listen to the words as they say it);

(c) to tell what sound was added to <u>side</u> to <u>slide</u>.

15. min.

3. Pass out the crepe-foam letters to the students.

4. Have them build the word <u>side</u> and then <u>slide</u> with the letters.

5. Write the following words on the board one at a time and add an "l" to make new words that begin with the consonant blend "sl."

a) sap   b) seep

6. Have the students use their letters to build the words in #7 and #8.

7. Write the following words on the board one at a time and add a "s" to make new words that begin with the consonant blend "sl."

a) low
b) lip
c) lit

8. Write the following words on the board one at a time and add a "w" to make new words that begin with the consonant blend "sw."

a) sift
b) seep

[handwritten notes:] – no lesson plan – personal use only for information

9. Write the following words on the board one at a time and add a "s" to make new words that begin with the consonant blend "sw."

a) way
b) wing
c) well

10. Write the following words on the board one at a time and add a "m" to make new words that begin with the consonant blend "sm."

a) sash
b) sack

11. Write the following words on the board one at a time and add a "s" to make new words that begin with the consonant blend "sm."

a) mall
b) mile
c) mash

20 min.

12. Pass out the worksheet on consonant blends "sl," "sw," and "sm" and read the instructions to the students.

13. Teacher should only observe the students completing the worksheet as this is only practice of the skills taught in class.

14. Ask students what new consonant blend words they learned today.

15. Collect worksheets for analysis.

Evaluation

1. Did the students willingly and actively participate in the lesson?

2. Were the students able to identify the new words created by adding "s" to the beginning of another word?

3. Were the students able to identify the new words created by adding the letter "l" after the initial "s" of another word?

4. Were the students able to identify the new words created by adding the letter "w" after the initial "s" of another word?

5. Were the students able to identify the new words created by adding the letter "m" after the initial "s" of another word?

Note: Developed with the assistance of Jan Avis.

Polloway, Patton, Payne, and Payne (1989) provide guidelines for word-analysis (phonics) instruction, which include: (1) diagnose specific needs of students before teaching; (2) be certain that students are ready for phonics training (in terms of their visual and auditory discrimination ability, memory capability, and oral language development); (3) emphasize blending sounds when initiating the phonics program; (4) give students an opportunity to apply phonic skills to their reading material; (5) teach sounds in word contexts, not in isolation; (6) teach exceptions to rules only after students have learned and can generalize phonic generalizations that follow the rules; (7) guide students toward using context plus the initial consonant as their primary strategy for analyzing unknown words; (8) teach students sequential steps for decoding unknown words; (9) use a variety of reinforcement activities; and (10) teach phonics as only one part of a reading program.

Critique — Good; Bad ✳

Students learning through phonic approaches tend to have difficulty with irregular words that do not follow conventional phonetic rules, and usually attempt to read unfamiliar words by using graphic cues rather than context clues (Barr, 1975). Teachers are often required, therefore, to supplement phonics instruction with other methods of instruction, such as the sight-word approach. In addition, some students may find this approach to be overly structured and monotonous. Hence, teachers should monitor students' attitudes (as well as performance) and be prepared to make program modifications, such as reducing instructional time, creating more interesting and motivating exercises, providing game activities, and/or allowing students to work independently or in cooperative groups. The phonics approach can help students identify words and build their vocabulary independently, but tasks need to be carefully selected, sequenced, and consistently practiced. The crucial factor in this approach is teaching effectiveness.

The phonics approach stresses the importance of systematic learning experiences according to a child's stage of learning and development, and is, therefore, most closely related to the developing-child perspective on learning.

❖ ACADEMIC SKILLS AND COMMON DIFFICULTIES RELATED — yes TO ORAL LANGUAGE

In every classroom there is great variability in students' language backgrounds and experiences as well as oral-language skills. Classroom discussion is typically the primary way in which students express their opinions, convey their ideas, and become better known to others—it is also the primary way in which teachers guide, direct, and organize their students' activities (Glover, Ronning, & Bruning, 1990). Classroom discourse also gives teachers an opportunity to judge consistently and informally many of their students' academic and social competencies.

important.
pt. not impt.

Academic skills related to oral-language development include the ability to:

1. Follow directions.
2. Recognize nonverbal cues (e.g., facial expressions and postures) and respond appropriately.

3. Use language and its component skills of *phonology* (sound units of language); *morphology* (form of words and the rules that guide their use); *syntax* (use of words to make sentences); *semantics* (word meaning); and *pragmatics* (social use of language).
4. Construct narratives (e.g., describing one's experiences to others).
5. Discriminate sound patterns in order to understand oral expression.
6. Adjust communication in relation to audience (e.g., younger children), context (e.g., making friends), and responses.
7. Ask questions to clarify unclear messages.
8. Acquire, retain, and retrieve vocabulary.
9. Interpret messages from others.
10. De-centre (i.e., take another's viewpoint).
11. Initiate and sustain communication, as well as repair communication breakdown.
12. Understand and relate concepts.
13. Understand and use multiple word meanings and figurative language.
14. Understand a variety of perspectives.

The major difficulties children have with oral expression include: (1) discriminating sound patterns; (2) retrieving words to use in communication; (3) adjusting communication to the people with whom they are speaking; (4) processing information effectively in order to improve self-expression; (5) comprehending word meanings; (6) understanding the expression of others; (7) questioning in order to clarify messages; and (8) identifying and understanding various verbal and nonverbal cues.

IMPLICATIONS FOR TEACHING

Provide guidance and practice with respect to various aspects of social discourse. For example, if a student has difficulty requesting information, have him or her conduct interviews with different people for different purposes (e.g., to learn about an occupation), and in different ways (e.g., face-to-face, telephone, airmail). Role-playing and sending the child on errands to gather information about various things (e.g., clothing prices or lunch menus) (Speckman & Roth, 1984) are other examples of activities that can be used to facilitate social discourse.

◆ Encourage students to express themselves beyond yes-no responses (Glover et al. 1990).
◆ Frequently check students' understanding of what has been said and clarify any ambiguities (Petrosky, 1982).
◆ Develop students' ability to produce various speech sounds, to formulate words and sentences, to use correct grammatical and syntactical language patterns, and to demonstrate adequate spoken vocabulary (Wallace & Kauffman, 1978).
◆ Develop speaking vocabulary, teach students linguistic patterns, and provide guidance and practice related to formulating sentences (Alley, 1977).

- Teach language in context so that students learn how to apply language (Bos & Vaughn, 1991).
- Reinforce language learning by using intrinsic reinforcers and naturally occurring consequences (Holland, 1975).
- Develop vocabulary and concept use and knowledge by providing activities that allow students to continually practice language as a useful and functional tool (Bos & Vaughn, 1991).
- Provide students with concrete experiences to talk about, with the teacher providing interactive language modelling (Temple & Gillet, 1984).
- Improve students' performance on listening tasks by teaching them effective listening strategies across a variety of contexts (Pearson & Fielding, 1982).
- Provide speaking skills training whereby students are encouraged to think about what they are going to say, given practice in role-playing, evaluated and provided feedback by the teacher and peers, and offered suggestions for improving speaking behaviour (Alley & Deshler, 1979).
- Provide real-life social situations in which students can practice their oral communication skills (ordering from a menu, giving direction, introducing themselves, and asking for help) (Mandell & Gold, 1984).

ASSESSING LEVELS OF PERFORMANCE

There are a variety of formal (standardized) tests that teachers can use to evaluate their students' oral-expression strengths and weaknesses (see Appendix 10.1). By helping teachers find discrepancies between expected and actual student oral achievement, these measures allow for teachers to screen their students' abilities and disabilities as a first step toward more specific diagnosis and intervention planning. Informal methods that teachers can construct and use to evaluate their students' expressive language include observation checklists (see Table 10.6), rating scales (see Guerin & Maier, 1983; Hargrave & Poteet, 1980), interviews, and various language-sampling techniques (see Lee, 1974; Lee & Carter, 1971; Tyack & Gottsleben, 1974) (see Chapter 8 for further assessment ideas that can be applied to oral language).

◆ INSTRUCTIONAL METHODS FOR DEVELOPING ORAL LANGUAGE

LANGUAGE-EXPERIENCE APPROACH

The language-experience approach uses the natural environment to develop students' expressive language skills, and everyday experiences in the classroom to foster oral-language development (Cavallaro, 1983). The approach also uses children's own language patterns and experiences, and encourages

	Yes	No	Sometimes
Table 10.6 Oral Language: An Observation Checklist			

Name: _____
Date: _____

	Yes	No	Sometimes
1. Student speaks frequently.			
2. Student is difficult to understand.			
3. Student uses gestures as substitute for words.			
4. Student appears nervous when talking to others.			
5. Student pauses when speaking.			
6. Student repeats words when speaking.			
7. Student distorts sounds of words.			
8. Student omits sounds in words.			
9. Student initiates conversation with others.			
10. Student effectively terminates conversation with others.			
11. Student understands messages from others without difficulty.			
12. Student seeks clarification when needed.			
13. Student expresses feelings adequately.			
14. Student uses nonverbal cues effectively.			
15. Student demonstrates good vocabulary.			

them to express their own ideas and emotions (Winzer, 1989). Winzer (1989) notes that teachers who use this approach stimulate children's oral language through daily planned activities such as spoken poetry and prose reading, open discussions, and integrated reading and oral vocabulary lessons.

Critique −6 ⸮ B

The language-experience approach gives students who have second-language and multicultural backgrounds an opportunity to engage in open communication. The approach is also appropriate for students with above-average cognitive abilities because it allows them to participate in diverse discussion and fosters in them an appreciation for the ideas of others. Generally, this approach lends itself to individualized programming and instruction, and encourages teachers to be creative and flexible (Winzer, 1989), which is an advantage to all students.

The language-experience approach, given its emphasis on students' day-to-day language experiences and interactive communication in developing their expressive skills, is most closely associated with the social-being perspective on learning.

STRATEGIES APPROACH - know, not memory

The strategies approach uses plans and procedures to help students prepare for oral communication. For example, students might be taught oral report strategies to help them remember important aspects of oral communication. Two examples of strategies that can be taught to students to help them give oral reports are the LEEP and CHECK strategies developed by Deborah Hamilton, a resource teacher with the Calgary Public School Board. These two strategies isolate salient requirements—outlined below—for oral reporting that many children fail to implement and monitor. Once learned and practiced, LEEP and CHECK strategies can help students cue and monitor themselves when giving an oral presentation.

LEEP

L: Loud and Clear

E: Expression

E: Eye contact

P: Posture

CHECK

C: Check the audience—is everyone ready to listen?

H: Have eye contact with the audience

E: Expression

C: Clear talking

K: Keen to be heard (show that you are interested in what you are saying; be enthusiastic)

Critique - 6ʿβ .

The strategies approach can be effective for students who have ineffective or deficient expressive-language plans and procedures. However, some students may resist adopting and practicing the strategies they are taught because they initially interfere with performance, due to the extra processing demands on the student. Moreover, unless the strategies are carefully designed and taught in accordance with students' needs and abilities, students may fail to appreciate their benefit and consider strategy learning simply another difficult learning experience. Therefore, the teacher should ensure that students are able to perform all aspects of the strategy successfully, and that they understand its utility and limitations.

Strategy teaching can help students with behavioural and/or emotional problems monitor and control their behaviour and emotions (particularly if the strategy is tailored to deal with these aspects), as well as improve their oral-language abilities. Teachers should allow students with adequate to above-average ability in expressive/receptive language skills to create their own strategies and share them with other students.

The strategies approach, in stressing the process of learning and the importance of self-reflection and self-regulation in students' learning and thinking, is most closely related to the active-processor perspective on learning.

ENRICHMENT APPROACH

The enrichment approach enables students to increase their communication ability beyond what might be considered average expectations. Debate seminars, panel discussions, skits, small-group projects, and whole-class activities allow students to be creative in receiving and sending information (e.g., through the use of cameras, television, radio, and computers), to practice their expressional fluency and leadership skills, and to explore and communicate their thoughts and feelings.

Critique

The enrichment approach can be used with all students as a supplement to other programs and teaching methods, or it can be used as a primary method for students who excel beyond average expectations. This approach requires the teacher to be creative and organized, as well as supportive of active learning and open communication.

In emphasizing the process of learning over the product of learning, the enrichment approach is most closely related to the active-processor perspective on learning.

◇ ACADEMIC SKILLS AND COMMON DIFFICULTIES RELATED TO READING

Reading is the most important skill to master in school and is one of the most valued skills in society (Mulcahy et al., 1991). Reading is a complex process that involves seeing, perceiving, recognizing, comprehending, remembering, integrating, interpreting, and paraphrasing written information. To be effective readers, children need to be able to identify words; interpret words and events with respect to what they know (Glover et al., 1990); construct meaning from the text; be aware of their purpose for reading; attend to relevant aspects of the text (e.g., titles and illustrations); and draw upon past experiences. Reading is thus a holistic, interactive, and meaningful process that requires the reader to decode messages, to relate their ideas to those presented by the author of the text, and to construct personal meaning from the text.

Because of its complexity, there is no one way to teach reading. Some educators believe that reading is dependent on word-recognition and decoding skills, while others believe that it is dependent on the experience and knowledge of the reader. Although how reading should be taught is debatable (Swaby, 1984), there is considerable support for using varied and balanced approaches that develop decoding skills as well as cognitive and metacognitive reading skills.

General reasons for reading difficulties include: (1) poor language foundation; (2) anxiety associated with reading; (3) low self-concept and/or motivation with respect to reading; (4) low cognitive development; (5) lack of reading strategies; (6) underdeveloped vocabulary; (7) lack of enabling skills (e.g., word-attack and study skills); and (8) poor information-processing skills (e.g., short attention, perceptual deficits, and poor memory).

Academic skills associated with effective reading (beyond the word-identification skills discussed earlier) include the ability to:

1. Apply reading strategies to better comprehend the material.
2. Recall what has been read.
3. Generalize reading skills across subject areas.
4. Select and comprehend main ideas from written passages.
5. Monitor one's own reading.
6. Use text clues to better comprehend the material.
7. Draw conclusions and predict outcomes.
8. Organize and memorize information in reading passages.
9. Answer questions after reading with respect to main idea, details, and cause and effect.
10. Make inferences from what has been read.
11. Evaluate reading material.
12. Elaborate or modify what has been read.

Before choosing instructional methods, teachers should carefully analyze the strengths and weaknesses of their students' reading ability, prepare a list of goals and objectives, and consider using a variety of materials and activities. A wide range of reading goals and objectives are necessitated by the diversity of students' reading abilities. Teachers should also provide differential instruction and a variety of intervention methods to accommodate their students' various reading needs.

IMPLICATIONS FOR TEACHING

- Integrate different instructional methods. For example, supplement basal readers with language-experience and cognitive approaches.
- Expect that some students will excel in their reading and that others will experience significant difficulty. In either case, use methods that promote student success in reading.
- Encourage children to reflect on their language knowledge and use (Glover et al. 1990).
- Develop students' awareness of the different purposes for reading.
- Supplement instruction for visually impaired students with activities that use other modalities (e.g., listening to stories on tape) (Winzer, 1989).
- Begin reading programs at the student's level of language development and demonstrated language performance (Winzer, 1989).

ASSESSING LEVELS OF PERFORMANCE

Teachers can distinguish poor and good readers by administering standardized reading achievement tests, which can give them an overall picture of the students' level of reading performance (see Appendix 10.1) and identify those students who need further assessment. However, informal tests can be a much more valuable means of identifying students' particular strengths and weaknesses in reading, of establishing reading objectives and goals, of selecting reading programs, and of determining teaching methods and approaches (see Chapter 8 for other assessment ideas that can be applied to reading).

One of the most common ways of assessing a student's reading ability is to observe and evaluate informally as he or she reads aloud. Informal reading inventories that assess reading level, reading errors, reading fluency, word-attack skills, and reading comprehension can be constructed by the teacher (see Hammill, Bartel, & Bunch, 1984; Johnson, Kress, & Pilulski, 1987). Other methods include curriculum-based assessment as a way to measure reading progress that is linked to instruction (see Fuchs & Fuchs, 1984), miscue analysis of oral reading (Goodman, 1967), cloze procedures (Ekwall, 1981), daily observations, and oral interviews.

The curriculum-based method requires teachers to take continuous measures of students' performance on specific reading tasks and then to chart their reading behaviours as a means of analyzing changes over time (Deno, 1987). **Oral-miscue analysis** allows teachers to identify common errors students are making in their reading (see Collins & Smith, 1982, for typical comprehension errors), and can indicate the types of reading strategies they are using. The **cloze technique** is a method by which teachers can determine a student's ability to use context, semantic, and syntactic cues, as well as his or her capacity for using comprehension strategies (see Table 10.7). This approach requires teachers to construct short reading passages with omitted words replaced by blanks, which the student is expected to fill. Checklists and rating scales can be used whenever students are reading aloud, retelling stories, and practicing reading strategies (see Figure 10.1 and Tables 10.8 to 10.10). Observations might include students' ability to sequence information, to read critically, to comprehend main ideas, and so forth. Teachers can interview students, informally and periodically, to monitor and evaluate their attitudes toward reading, their reading interests, and their self-perceived reading problems. Moreover, teachers can construct checklists that record and monitor students' reading progress (see Tables 10.11 and 10.12).

◆ oral miscue analysis: a curriculum-based method used to identify common reading errors and reading strategies

◆ cloze technique: a curriculum-based method used to determine a student's ability to use context, semantic, and syntactic cues, as well as comprehension strategies

◆ INSTRUCTIONAL METHODS FOR DEVELOPING READING

STRATEGIES APPROACH

The strategies approach encourages students to identify the purpose of their reading, to ask questions of themselves while reading, to monitor their read-

Table 10.7

Example of Cloze Procedure

When Jenna came home from the Calgary Stampede she wanted to plan a garage sale that involved playing games and selling toys and candy. She had planned the ———— for two days and ———— for a very nice ———— to have the event. ———— had a friend of ———— help her. Jenna and Meagan ———— excited about their garage ———— and told all the ———— in the neighbourhood.

On Saturday Jenna and ———— were able to have ———— garage sale. They were able to ———— lots of money and ———— more toys and candy.

Figure 10.1

Oral Reading Checklist

Name: _____

Date: _____

	Yes	No	Sometimes
1. Reads slowly	✔		
2. Reads word by word	✔		
3. Mispronounces words			✔
4. Loses place while reading		✔	
5. Omits words		✔	
6. Ignores punctuation			✔
7. Guesses at word			✔
8. Likes reading			✔
9. Points to words while reading		✔	
10. Reads loudly	✔		

ing and comprehension, and to evaluate their information processing. Chapter 12 discusses strategies that can help students with each of these tasks.

Obtaining meaning from printed material requires the reader to be actively engaged in organizing new information, linking new information with previously learned information, and analyzing information. One strategy that can help students organize, monitor, and analyze relationships obtained from reading material is called **story mapping** (see Reutzel, 1986). A story map can be developed using the following procedure (Mulcahy, Marfo, Peat, & Andrews, 1987):

◆ story mapping: a reading strategy used to help students organize, monitor, and analyze relationships obtained from reading material

Table 10.8
Reading Rating Scale

Name: _____

| | Scale | (1) Excellent | (3) Needs Improvement |
| | | (2) Satisfactory | (4) Unsatisfactory |

Books

Academic Skills	Barney and the Trap	The Sea	Trouble in the Ark	What Did You Leave Behind
Applies reading strategies	1	1	2	1
Recalls what has been read	1	2	2	2
Generalizes reading	1	2	2	2
Comprehends main ideas	1	1	2	1
Self-monitors reading	2	1	2	1
Draws conclusion	2	1	1	2
Predicts outcomes	2	2	2	2
Makes inferences	2	2	2	1
Evaluates reading material	3	2	2	1
Elaborates and/or modifies what has been read	2	1	1	2

Table 10.9
Improve Comprehension by Retelling

Name: _____

Checklist

Week Ending	# of Sentences	% of Sentences Correct
November 7 Comments:	7	100% (7)
November 14 Comments:	3	66% (2)
November 21 Comments:	5	80% (4)
November 28 Comments:	2	100%

Note: Developed with the assistance of Gloria Yusishen.

1. After reading a selection, the teacher discusses with his or her students the main ideas, major events, and major characters of the story.
2. While discussing the salient features of the reading selection with the students, the teacher lists the ideas, events, and characters of the story on the blackboard.

Table 10.10
Improve Prediction Strategies

Name: _____

1. using text
2. using illustrations
3. using inference

Checklist

Date		Strategy Used		
	Text	Illustration	Inference	% Applied
November 12	1	1		100% (2)
November 14	2		1	75% (3/4)
November 18	1			
November 21	1			100%
November 26		2		100%
November 28	1 (famil-iar with story)			100%

Note: Developed with the assistance of Gloria Yusishen.

Table 10.11
Increasing Oral Reading

Name: _____

Checklist

Date	Story Title	Completed Independently
November 7		
Comments:	Feathers for Lunch	2 Assists
November 14 Comments:	Sheep in a Jeep	2 Assists
November 21 Comments:	Sheep in a Shop	4 Assists
November 28 Comments:	Sheep in a Jeep	1 Assist

Note: Developed with the assistance of Gloria Yusishen.

3. The main ideas are placed in a circle, square, or other shape in the centre of the "story map."
4. Lines projecting out of the central shape are drawn to fit the major events and characters listed in Step 2; these lines should be arranged symmetrically around the central shape.

Table 10.12
Building Confidence as a Reader

Name: _____

Checklist

Week Ending	Books in Class	Books at Home	Total
October 31	2	2	4
Comments:			
November 7	2	3	5
Comments:			
November 14	2	1	3
Comments:			
November 21	2	1	3
Comments:			
November 28	2	1	3
Comments:			

Other Information:

_____

_____

_____

_____

Note: Developed with the assistance of Gloria Yusishen.

5. Key words for the major concepts or events are attached to the lines that contain major events and characters. The events are typically ordered in a clockwise direction around the central shape containing the main idea.

6. Subevents and subconcepts are entered around the shape containing the main idea.

The shapes can be differentially ordered and coloured to enhance presentation (e.g., a red circle for main idea and blue squares for main events). As well, the story maps can be laminated or produced with construction paper to enable long-term use. Students can improve their comprehension across various reading materials by creating in their notebooks story maps of their own, which teachers can periodically review.

Story maps can also be used in group work productions in which differences between various groups' maps are discussed; as aids for book reports and creative writing exercises; as alternative ways to respond to essay-question exams; and as alternative test formats whereby students fill in blank map items.

know This

A second reading strategy is **K-W-L** (Carie & Ogle, 1987; Ogle, 1986), which stands for **K**now-**W**ant to know-**L**earned. This strategy directs students to brainstorm prior knowledge on the basis of titles, illustrations, or other related information (what we know), to generate questions (what we want to know), and then to read in order to answer questions (what we learned). A third strategy, **semantic mapping** (Heimlich & Pittleman, 1986) involves making webs or maps prior to reading in order to access, expand upon, and organize prior knowledge. Maps can be created after reading in order to synthesize new information with prior knowledge.

◆ K-W-L: a reading strategy in which students brainstorm prior knowledge (**k**now), generate questions (**w**ant to know), and read in order to answer questions (**l**earned)

◆ semantic mapping: a pre- or post-reading strategy in which webs or maps are used to access, expand upon, organize, and sythesize information

Critique

The strategies approach requires teachers to guide students toward independent strategy modification and evaluation. It also requires teachers to be aware of areas in which students need direct instruction; for example, a student who has difficulty drawing should be instructed in this area before advancing to story mapping. While the strategies approach can benefit students who have difficulty relating their prior ideas to the ideas presented in a text and/or who have difficulty organizing learned information, it must be remembered that many students have preferred ways of doing things and may resist or have difficulty adopting a particular strategic way of learning. This approach must, therefore, include instruction that develops students' awareness of when, where, and how to use strategies.

The strategies approach emphasizes the development of students' cognitive and metacognitive processes, as well as the importance of strategic learning and thinking; therefore, it is most closely related to the active-processor perspective on learning.

WHOLE LANGUAGE APPROACH *yes*

The whole language approach uses students' language experiences and students' reading interests to guide reading instruction (Goodman, 1986). Teachers who use this approach use a wide range of books and real-life problems, ideas, and themes to organize the curriculum (Salend, 1990). In addition, they typically integrate reading with writing instruction, take students on field trips, involve students in role-plays and discussions, and use learning centres more often than do teachers who follow other instructional methods. These teachers also stress meaning when it comes to reading and writing, accept and encourage risk-taking (Goodman & Goodman, 1982), and encourage students to help each other in their reading and writing (Watson & Crowley, 1988).

Butler (1987) cites ten common elements of whole language programs: (1) teachers and students sharing stories by reading aloud and through oral story telling; (2) large-group reading instruction, often employing "Big Books"; (3) time arranged for students to engage in silent reading;

(4) individualized reading instruction in which students interact more directly with the teacher; (5) guided reading in small groups in which the teacher evaluates and works on specific reading strategies; (6) language-experience activities; (7) large-group writing instruction in which the teacher demonstrates a strategy or activity that is then practiced by the students; (8) students engaged in all aspects of the writing process (planning, drafting, revising, editing, and publishing); (9) students sharing and discussing stories they have written or read; and (10) specific writing activities that relate to content area themes.

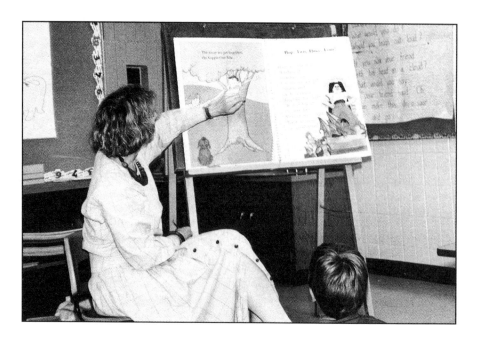

Critique

The whole language approach provides both functional and enriching language experiences for children, and is particularly beneficial for second-language students and gifted students because it exposes them to varied and meaningful materials and experiences. Children requiring more structured, sequenced, and analytic methods and materials, due to significant difficulties they have with such things as word-attack skills, on-task behaviour, and word recognition, may be accommodated by effective teaching and management procedures (see Chapter 9).

Because it focuses on authentic literature and meaningful language experiences, on students sharing and discussing their learning experiences, and on teachers integrating reading, writing, and oral language activities, the whole language approach is most closely related to the social-being perspective on learning.

LINGUISTIC APPROACH *know*

The linguistic approach focuses on students' oral language skills and the relationship of these skills to reading. The underlying assumption of this approach is that children need to understand that written symbols represent spoken words in order to learn to read effectively (Johnson & Moe, 1980). More specifically, the approach is based on the idea that English has an alphabetic code that can be mastered by the reader, and, furthermore, that language consists of patterns and contrasts that can be learned and analyzed. Teachers who use this approach are concerned with developing their students' ability to recognize printed words quickly and independently, and emphasize word-analysis approaches that focus on the sound elements and visual cues embedded in words. For example, they may present students with word families that share the same phonetic patterns (e.g., the *it* family—*bit, fit, hit, kit, lit, mit, nit, pit, sit,* and *wit),* so that they can learn sound and symbol correspondence (Salend, 1990).

Critique

While its highly analytic and systematic nature makes the linguistic approach a good choice for students who need structure, the approach places little stress on comprehension and would, therefore, need to be supplemented with methods that emphasize reading for meaning. Bos and Vaughn (1991) point out that "the linguistic approach has demonstrated its usefulness with students who are having difficulty developing sight vocabulary and learning phonic generalizations. Because of its highly controlled vocabulary, students are frequently able to experience success" (p. 116).

Stressing the need for teachers to provide systematic and structured learning experiences along identifiable developmental stages, the linguistic approach is most closely associated with the developing-child perspective on learning.

INDIVIDUALIZED APPROACH *know*

The individualized approach addresses the unique strengths, weaknesses, and interests of students, and involves: (1) determining reading objectives for individual students; (2) providing different reading materials and assignments for students according to their abilities and needs; (3) monitoring student progress and assisting students with, for example, language deficits, visual deficits, auditory deficits, attentional deficits, perceptual deficits, and affective deficits; (4) collecting and making available reading material in which students are interested; (4) allowing students time to work alone and to establish their own reading pace; (5) scheduling weekly student activities whereby students can share and discuss information they have learned, books they have read, difficulties they have encountered, and remedial strategies they have incorporated; and (6) recording student progress and making accommodations and modifications where necessary (Smith & Barrett, 1979).

Critique

The main advantages of the individualized approach are that it provides built-in motivation because the reading material is personally chosen; it does not focus on comparing children's reading ability; it allows students to read at their own rates; and it increases personal interaction between the teacher and the student (Mulcahy et al., 1991). The disadvantages of the approach are that it (1) requires a significant amount of time for collecting the reading material, for scheduling student conferences, for monitoring and ensuring that reading skills are mastered, and for record-keeping; and (2) lacks a sequential approach to skill development (Burns & Roe, 1980).

The individualized approach is highly child-centred in its emphasis on the need for teachers to provide for their students age-appropriate experiences and tasks that allow them to use and build upon the knowledge and skills they already possess; this approach is, therefore, most closely related to the developing-child perspective on learning.

LANGUAGE-EXPERIENCE APPROACH yes

The language-experience approach uses students' interests and hobbies as a basis for reading material and instruction. Teachers using this approach encourage students to think, discuss, and write about their personal experiences and emotions in order to make reading more meaningful and to establish closer links with familiar contexts and language patterns. Stories can be either individually created or composed by the entire class and then presented to other classes (e.g., readers' theatre). The teacher typically guides the students in creating and completing the story (e.g., leading discussion about the story's content and title, and attending to such things as sentence structure, organization, spelling, capitalization, and punctuation), and then provides activities to develop reading skills from the students' own stories (vocabulary development, sight-word recognition, word-attack skills, sentence composition, independent and creative expression, etc.).

Critique

The success of the language-experience approach depends on the teacher's efforts and abilities to ensure continuity in both language and reading development (Bachor & Crealock, 1986). Teachers who use this method tend to neglect specific reading skills (e.g., phonetic decoding, vocabulary analysis, sentence and paragraph reading, and visual/auditory blending and discrimination) that are important for most students who have reading difficulties.

Moreover, the language-experience approach lacks a developmental sequence, which is why it is often used by experienced teachers or by teachers who follow the outline of well-established developmental programs. However, this approach is particularly good for initiating reading instruction and for facilitating students' interest and participation in reading; thus it is especially appropriate for students who have low motivation for reading and for students who need opportunities to foster their creativity.

The language-experience approach can supplement or be used in conjunction with other approaches, or it can be used as a totally independent initial reading program. It can be used at all school levels and can assist students in seeing the relationship between reading and oral language. Moreover, it fosters greater interaction between teachers and students and can be used across all school subject areas.

The language-experience approach emphasizes the idea that students are social beings who develop their learning and thinking capabilities through interactive communication with members of their culture. This approach also stresses the need for teachers to provide learning environments that enhance the ability of students to talk about their experiences. Hence, it is most closely related to the social-being perspective on learning.

BASAL APPROACH ≠ mst common used

The basal reading approach, which is the most common method used to teach reading, provides students with various reading series materials that have self-contained teaching manuals, lesson plans, workbooks, skill-building activities, enrichment activities, and evaluation checklists and tests for each grade level. This approach offers teachers a structured and developmental reading program into which they can incorporate other ideas and methods for reading development. Teachers tend to like basals because they are structured, contain manuals that list objectives and activities, and are self-contained (Langone, 1986). They are designed for the average student but can be adapted to suit the needs of most students.

Critique

Basal reading series offer the teacher comprehensive, systematic, and sequenced coverage of almost all aspects of a reading program. Although they are very structured in format, they can be modified by the teacher to meet the individual needs of students. Furthermore, basals can be supplemented with other materials and methods in order to better adapt to students' needs. In themselves, basals are limited and inadequate for dealing with the unique difficulties and talents of students in integrated settings; tend to place too much emphasis on word learning and the use of workbooks, and not enough on the purpose of reading (Durkin, 1978); and often have unnatural vocabularies and syntax patterns (usually restricted to phonetically consistent and high-frequency sight words and to repetitive and simple sentence patterns). If children are to become good readers, they need early exposure to real books.

Based on the idea that learning progresses along identifiable stages and that learning and thinking skills are hierarchically integrated, the basal approach is most closely affiliated with the developing-child perspective on learning.

GROUP READING APPROACH

Various grouping methods can be used by teachers to meet the individual needs of students (Ekwall & Shanker, 1985). Students can be grouped according to their strengths and weaknesses so that the teacher can provide specific lessons for students who share common needs. Average and above-average readers sometimes have similar difficulties in reading and thus can be placed in the same group (Matthes, 1977). (This is important to remember because if students are placed according to their overall performance levels, teachers can end up with groups of good readers and groups of poor readers, which is not conducive to the development of positive self-concept, student interaction, and student cooperation.) Groups can also be formed on the basis of students' interests in reading, which can provide opportunities for students to share new learning among themselves. Tutorial grouping is another effective grouping format that brings together students with

particular abilities and disabilities and enables them to help each other with respect to reading development and practice (see Chapters 9 and 13).

Critique

Grouping according to ability level separates students and creates lowered self-esteem among students who have reading difficulties. It also compromises the teacher's ability to provide an equal amount of instructional time across all groups because students with more serious difficulties demand more time. Hence, the teacher should establish heterogeneous grouping arrangements.

Stressing the need for student interaction and for achieving a balance between individual and social learning, the group reading approach is most closely related to the social-being perspective on learning.

DISTAR READING PROGRAM — *prob. THE most-effective prgms.*

The Direct Instructional System for Teaching and Remediation (DISTAR) (Englemann & Bruner, 1974, 1975, 1984) is a remedial series aimed at systematically improving students' phonic skills. The program was originally developed for use with culturally disadvantaged children. Program design and instruction are carefully constructed and based on behavioural principles such as **prompting**, **discrimination learning**, **shaping**, and **reinforcement contingencies**. The DISTAR reading mastery program contains isolated drills and instructional reading activities. Instruction is typically given in small groups, for thirty-minute periods, each day of the week. Student performance is evaluated with criterion-referenced tests that are included in the program (Lerner, 1988).

Know terms.

- ◆ **prompting**: the eliciting of student responses when typical environmental conditions fail to produce the desired behaviour

- ◆ **discrimination learning**: a behavioural principle in which a person learns to respond to different environmental conditions and/or to similar stimuli

- ◆ **shaping**: the teaching of new skills by reinforcing successive approximations to the desired final behaviour

- ◆ **reinforcement contingency**: a behavioural principle in which behaviour is rewarded on the basis of an established condition

Critique

The major criticism of the DISTAR program is that it is too structured and lacks sufficient emphasis on the purpose of reading; additionally, it takes a long time for the teacher to complete the program. However, while the program is somewhat constraining in light of the variety of curricular objectives and goals in an inclusive classroom, it is a very good method for developing students' phonic skills in a clear and systematic manner.

With its emphasis on the analysis of the task over the analysis of the student, as well as on direct instruction and sequential skills, the DISTAR reading program is most closely related to the behavioural perspective on learning.

FERNALD'S READING TECHNIQUE   *Know it*

The aim of Fernald's technique (1988 [1943]) is for students to use all of their major learning modalities (visual, auditory, kinesthetic, and tactual) while developing their ability to read independently. The technique consists of four stages:

Stage 1. In this stage, the teacher writes words selected by the students on a blackboard or large piece of paper while the students watch. The students then trace the words until they can be correctly copied without looking. As the students trace the words, they say them aloud. Before moving on to the next stage, the students must be able to write the words correctly without looking at the copy. Teachers may have students incorporate the words into sentences and/or stories.

Stage 2. In this stage, the students no longer trace words, but should be able to learn new words by looking at, saying, and writing the words.

Stage 3. In this stage, students should be able to write new words, without the aid of the teacher, by looking at words in printed material.

Stage 4. At this stage, students should be able to learn new words simply by looking at them.

Critique

Fernald's technique is useful for students who have visual-perceptual difficulty and who need structured guidance in order to develop reading independence. However, it can be very time-consuming for both the student and the teacher (Bos & Vaughn, 1991).

Reflecting the view that students' learning progresses along identifiable stages and that learning and thinking skills are hierarchically integrated, Fernald's reading technique is most closely related to the developing-child perspective on learning.

GILLINGHAM-STILLMAN READING METHOD ‑used a/c+ in CBE

The Gillingham-Stillman (1960) approach is a detailed and systematic method of teaching reading that synthesizes writing, spelling, and reading. This system focuses on letter identification and sound-symbol associations, as students are guided by their teacher, in a consistent and systematic fashion, to identify and correctly name and pronounce letters and sounds of words. Students are then expected to trace the letters, copy the words, and finally write them from memory. This approach is particularly good for students who have difficulty following more general approaches of reading instruction, and who need structured and repetitive lessons.

Critique

The benefit of the Gillingham-Stillman method is that it provides a structured and effective way for students to develop phonic skills and for both teachers and students to monitor and evaluate students' developmental progress in writing, spelling, and reading. However, this approach de-emphasizes purposeful reading, requires training if it is to be used effectively, and significant commitment on the part of the teacher to implement it in an ongoing and consistent fashion.

The Gillingham-Stillman reading method emphasizes the role that teaching conditions have in determining the quantity and quality of students' learning, as well as the need for teachers to assess the specific skills related to particular tasks and develop those skills. This approach is, therefore, most closely affiliated with the behavioural perspective on learning.

NEUROLOGICAL IMPRESS METHOD OF READING

The purpose of the neurological impress method of reading is to improve reading fluency (Heckelman, 1969). The overall plan of this method is for the student and the teacher to read together for fifteen uninterrupted minutes each day of each week. The major goal is for the teacher to provide a model of fluency for the student to imitate. In this method, both the student and teacher read aloud. The teacher reads at the same speed as the student and points out words with a pen as they read. The movement of the pen should reinforce the smooth flow of reading, as should the teacher's reading aloud. Students are assisted with sounding out words that are new to them or causing them difficulty, and are immediately supplied the words if they are sight words. Before each reading session, problem words are reviewed and the student's progress is noted and discussed with respect to the previous session.

Critique

The neurological impress method is based on the theory that the auditory feedback from the reader's voice and the teacher's voice, when they are orally reading the same material, establishes a new learning process (Winzer, 1989). Although this method might improve students' fluency, oral expression, and confidence in their ability to read (Lorenz & Vockell, 1979), it should be supplemented with other programs aimed at improving word recognition and reading comprehension.

Reflecting the view that students' learning and thinking occurs over time in a systematic fashion and that learning progresses along identifiable stages, the neurological impress method of reading is most closely related to the developing-child perspective on learning.

used

RATE (Read And Then Evaluate) Program

The RATE program provides an opportunity for students to select, read, and evaluate reading materials. The teacher and student initially work together with respect to book selection and evaluation procedures. Later, students work independently at their own rate and evaluate books they read according to pre-established criteria. Group and class discussions are typically arranged by the teacher in order for students to share their recommendations and evaluations of the books they have read. This program is beneficial for more advanced readers, as well as for those who need to gain confidence in themselves as readers (Jamison & Shevitz, 1985).

Critique

Students' success with the RATE program depends on their level of motivation and satisfaction (Kranes, 1980). Although this program might help students gain confidence in their reading and provide a way for them to share their judgments about reading material (Bamberger, 1976), it should be supplemented with other methods, particularly for disabled readers. The program is generally beneficial for good readers because it encourages independent reading and evaluation.

The RATE program reflects the view that how we learn and think is related to how we represent and process information, as well as the belief that effective reading requires the ability to conceptualize, analyze, organize, synthesize, and evaluate information. Thus, this approach is most closely affiliated with the active-processor perspective on learning.

REBUS READING METHOD

Rebus reading is an appropriate method to use at the beginning stages of reading. This approach uses pictures in place of, or in conjunction with, certain words in sentences (see Figure 10.2). Rebus stories are created by the teacher, who types or writes by hand a story and provides picture cues for words. Students are often encouraged to make their own rebus sentences and stories, which can be collected and shared with their classmates. This method is effective in teaching high-frequency words and presenting them in meaningful contexts.

Figure 10.2
Example of Rebus Reading

The Gingerbread Boy

1. In a little yellow house up on a green hill, there lived a little old woman and a little old man.

2. She mixed some spicy gingerbread dough, and then she rolled it out.

3. Next, she cut it into the shape of a fine gingerbread boy.

4. She gave him raisins for eyes, and a wide smiling mouth.

Critique

Rebus reading is a good way to improve reading fluency and foster enjoyment in students who have a low sight-word vocabulary and struggle when reading.

With its emphasis on the relationship between stimulus (picture cues) and response (reading), and on the need for students to acquire word-identification skills in order to develop their reading, the rebus reading method is most closely related to the behavioural perspective on learning.

FUNCTIONAL APPROACH

The functional approach to reading stresses the relationship between observed student actions and words to read (Brown & Perlmuter, 1971). In this approach, teachers select words for instruction that are functional (i.e., words that an individual must know and read in order to function independently in the community) (Snell, 1983). According to Langone (1990), functional reading involves identifying and reading words, as well as performing related tasks, that are needed in a variety of real-life situations. For example, a teacher might organize words and reading in relation to grocery shopping and have students read words on a shopping list, as well as perform the task of reading while actually shopping so that the functionality aspect is emphasized and made real to the students.

Critique

The functional approach, which was designed to help students with low intellectual functioning and very low reading levels, actively involves students in their learning and clarifies for them the meaningfulness of reading.

Stressing the learning task over the learning process, the functional approach is most closely related to the behavioural perspective on learning.

DEFICIT APPROACH ˗ used

As discussed by Mulcahy et al. (1991), students with specific disabilities may require special assistance in reading. Strategies that can be used to compensate for various deficits are discussed below.

Visual-Perceptual Deficits

Students with visual-perceptual deficits might be provided a reading program that stresses phonetic analysis, due to its partial emphasis on auditory discrimination. Teachers might also use concrete manipulatives (e.g., wooden letters) or records and tapes as supplements to reading texts. Additionally, teachers might consider limiting visual activities to prevent attentional problems and keeping lessons short, clear, and familiar.

Auditory Deficits

Students with auditory deficits might be provided visual-imagery strategies to foster their reading skills. Teachers might need to keep students away from distracting noises when teaching reading and strengthen students' auditory skills by giving them appropriate auditory-discrimination activities.

Attention Deficits

Students with attention deficits might be provided self-instructional strategies in order to increase their attention and concentration. Teachers might need to free the environment of major distractions and use multiple reading methods and materials to maintain students' interest and attention.

Perceptual-Spatial Deficits

Students with perceptual-spatial deficits would probably benefit from multisensory approaches. Teachers might consider using cloze techniques (have students perform activities that require them to fill in missing letters and words) and special guiding markers to help their students orient themselves while reading.

Emotional Deficits

Students with emotional deficits might be provided with activities that help them develop a positive attitude and improve their confidence. Teachers should avoid comparing students' reading levels and performances and instead concentrate on matching reading activities with students' interest and ability.

Critique

The deficit approach targets specific disabilities and may benefit students who have particular weaknesses; however, given that studies have failed to show unequivocal benefits from using this approach, it should be balanced with methods that stress cognitive and social-cultural aspects of learning.

Child-centred in orientation and reflecting the view that students are active constructors of their knowledge, the deficit approach is most closely related to the developing-child perspective on learning.

ENRICHMENT APPROACH

The enrichment approach recognizes that some students need to be given reading activities that: (1) challenge and inspire them; (2) allow them to create and elaborate upon ideas; (3) encourage them to be active readers who can draw inferences, see relationships, come to conclusions, react critically to material, reorganize material, and so forth; (4) provide them opportunities to draw upon and use their experiences and abilities; and (5) foster their love of reading.

Critique

The enrichment approach is an appropriate supplemental approach for all students and particularly for very good readers who require greater challenges and opportunities for creativity. This approach stresses the process rather than the product of learning. Its proponents believe that skilled reading requires the ability to conceptualize, organize, and elaborate upon information. The enrichment approach also emphasizes the need for students to control and regulate their reading, and is thus most closely associated with the active-processor perspective on learning.

◆ ACADEMIC SKILLS AND COMMON DIFFICULTIES RELATED TO WRITING

Writing is an important part of everyday life both in and out of school. In school, students express their ideas in exams or essays. Outside school, we communicate our thoughts and feelings through letters and diaries. The quality of our writing reflects our intellectual and academic abilities, as well as our educational background and potential. The quality of our writing can affect not only how we perceive ourselves in these areas but also how others perceive us. Thus, students should be given opportunities to develop their writing in relation to a variety of purposes (e.g., social, recreational, creative, and occupational) (Graham & Harris, 1988).

The ability of an individual to express ideas meaningfully and accurately significantly increases the effectiveness of his or her communication. Since writing is a primary form of communication, it is a very important skill to master. Effective writing requires proficiency in a variety of areas, including handwriting (being able to form and space letters and words appropriately and consistently); written expression (being able to construct sentences and access an adequate fund of vocabulary to express ideas); and communication skills (facility in expressive and receptive language, spelling, and reading).

Effective writing also depends on the ability of the writer to: (1) have goals and objectives for writing; (2) access knowledge and information about various topics; (3) know who the audience will be as well as its expectations for the written material; (4) generate ideas in order to broaden content; (5) structure and organize information; (6) review, evaluate, and revise compositions; and (7) be aware of the writing process in order to self-monitor and improve his or her performance.

Many children have difficulty with writing because they lack one or more of the abilities mentioned above. Other problems associated with writing include low motivation and perception of ability, difficulty with topic selection (Graves, 1982), and an unclear purpose for writing (Shook, 1982).

Current theoretical and empirical work, in focusing on the cognitive processes of writing (Wong, 1991), emphasizes the planning, constructing, monitoring, evaluating, and revising stages of writing over the mechanical aspects of writing. Although handwriting, grammatical constructions, punctuation, and spelling are important skills to master, the current cognitive perspective in writing draws our attention to higher-order cognitive processes such as elaborating and revising.

IMPLICATIONS FOR TEACHING

- Provide students with excellent models of specific kinds of writing (Philips, 1986).
- Give students practice in writing for specific audiences. For example, get students to work in pairs, have them write for each other, and have them edit each other's writing by noting errors and commenting on how well meaning was communicated (Glover et al., 1990; Harris, 1986).
- Have students write about things they know so they don't have to struggle with gaps in knowledge (Glover et al., 1990).
- Provide opportunities for students to write and give frequent descriptive feedback (Applebee, 1984) and guidance as to how they can alter writing habits to achieve better results (Applebee, Langer, & Mullis, 1986).
- Provide opportunities for students to present their writing to various audiences, thereby enabling them to better appreciate their errors and to receive immediate feedback about the quality of their writing (Glover et al., 1990).
- Arrange teacher-student writing conferences to discuss the quality of the students' writing, the cognitive processes they used when writing, and the relationship of the writing processes to the quality of writing (Olson, Torrance, & Hildegard, 1985).
- Provide opportunities for children to work with microcomputers, particularly when editing and revising compositions (Sharples, 1985).
- Teach students how to plan and organize their writing. For example, provide students with a list of main topics, subtopics, and details. Show students how to make a skeletal outline and then structure the outline so that the students are cued as to which (and how many) topics and details should be included. Eventually, students can be guided toward creating their own topics and details, as well as developing and completing their own outline (Alley & Deshler, 1979; Mandell & Gold, 1984).
- Provide time each day for students to express their thoughts and opinions in daily journals. Teachers should respond daily in written form to encourage writing exchanges and engage students in the natural and purposeful use of language (Winzer, 1989).

◆ Use individual folders to facilitate the writing process and to foster independence in students (Bos, 1988).

◆ Give consideration to the student's motivation for writing (Dagenais & Beadle, 1984) and build in students a positive attitude toward writing (Alley & Deshler, 1979).

ASSESSING LEVELS OF PERFORMANCE

Although there are a variety of formal measures that can assist teachers in evaluating students' written expression and handwriting ability (see Appendix 10.1), informal measures of written expression (see Table 10.13) can provide even more valuable information. Guerin and Maier (1983), Weiner (1980), and Cramer (1982) have produced respectively: (a) a comprehensive checklist to evaluate students' knowledge about print conventions; (b) a diagnostic inventory of skills related to handwriting and written expression; and (c) a checklist for expository and narrative writing that examines such topics as quality of ideas and organization, selection of words, and structure of sentences and paragraphs. Teachers can either purchase evaluative measures or construct their own.

Table 10.13
Written Language: An Observation Checklist

Name: _____
Date: _____

	Yes	No	Sometimes
1. Provides appropriate spacing between letters and words.			
2. Maintains consistent letter size.			
3. Organizes information into main ideas and details.			
4. Makes spelling mistakes.			
5. Constructs adequate sentences.			
6. Generates lots of ideas.			
7. Understands different purposes for writing.			
8. Edits and revises compositions.			
9. Word selection is suitable and accurate.			
10. Transitions between paragraphs used.			

✧ INSTRUCTIONAL METHODS FOR DEVELOPING WRITING

PLANNING, WRITING, AND REVISING MODEL

The process of writing involves at least three stages: a prewriting (planning) stage, a drafting (writing) stage, and a rewriting (revising) stage. As discussed by Humes (1983), writers do not always begin with the planning stage and then move on to the writing and revising stages. Most writers take a non-linear approach to writing, moving back and forth among the stages.

According to Isaacson (1988), skilled writers explore their topic, consider what will be written and how it will be discussed, and make notes, diagrams, and pictures during the planning stage, whereas unskilled writers spend very little time considering the topic and make no plans or notes. During the writing stage, skilled writers tend to follow a learned model of written composition, keep their audience in mind, and frequently reread what they write, whereas unskilled writers follow more informal writing procedures, are overly concerned with the technical aspects of writing (e.g., spelling and punctuation), and stop writing only briefly and infrequently. During the revising stage, skilled writers typically edit and make content revisions and keep the audience in mind when rewriting, whereas unskilled writers tend to look only for surface errors, such as typos, and rewrite only to make the final copy look aesthetically better.

In the planning stage, students should be given opportunities to brainstorm and discuss interests, ideas, and possible writing topics in a comfortable and supportive classroom environment. At this stage, it is important that students be motivated to write. They also need to consider their purpose for writing and who the audience will be (Polloway et al., 1989). Teachers can facilitate the process by focusing students' attention on the creation of ideas rather than on the mechanical aspects of writing, and by having students actively engage in writing tasks (e.g., daily journal writing) without corrective feedback (Alley & Deschler, 1979).

Instruction during the writing stage should focus on both the creation and organization of ideas, as well as on mechanical aspects such as spelling, punctuation, and grammar (Polloway et al., 1989). At this stage, students should have abundant opportunities to write and should be given consistent, supportive, encouraging, and specific feedback with respect to their writing performance. Teachers should also focus on vocabulary, sentence, and paragraph development, and provide guided practice in these areas.

During the revising stage of the writing process, teachers should show students how to carefully review and revise what they have written, examining such things as spelling, punctuation, capitalization, sentence structure, semantics, and general appearance. Moreover, instruction should also be aimed at the review and revision of story content and organization. Krause (1983, p. 30) provides the following checklists:

Sentence Revision Checklist

1. Is my subject specific enough?
2. Do I need adjectives or other modifiers to create a better image?
3. Do I need adverbs or phrases to tell how, when, or where?
4. Have I used capital letters and punctuation marks correctly?
5. Do my subjects and verbs agree?

Paragraph Revision Checklist

1. Where is my most important sentence? Does it stand out?

2. Do all of my other sentences tell about the important sentence?

3 Can I combine some short sentences to make them sound better?

4. Are all my pronouns clear?

5. Do all of the verbs refer to the same time?

6. Is the first line indented? Does every sentence use proper capitalization and punctuation?

 ## Critique

Teachers should ensure that students consider whether their writing product addresses their original purpose for the writing task (Englert & Raphael, 1988) and guide them toward reviewing their work critically, with respect to such things as readability, style, organization, and word choices. Teachers might have students share their work to facilitate group learning and discussion, and/or form collaborative writing groups to promote the review and revision process in a peer-positive environment.

The planning, writing, revising model stresses the importance of the process of writing; emphasizes the creation and organization of ideas, as well as the checking and revising aspects of writing; and promotes active and independent decision-making and problem-solving. For these reasons, this approach is most closely related to the active-processor perspective on learning.

WRITE-TEACH APPROACH

Smith (1982) describes two roles of the writer: *author* and *secretary*. The author's role primarily involves the acquisition and organization of ideas, as well as the selection and arrangement of words and phrases to convey those ideas. The secretary's role is typically concerned with mechanical aspects such as spelling, punctuation, and grammar.

The write-teach approach to writing emphasizes the author's role in writing by stressing the creation and writing of ideas over the technical aspects of writing. Although form, structure, and mechanics are considered important, they are taught within the context of day-to-day writing activities. The most important goal for teachers who adopt the write-teach approach is to foster in their students a sense of enjoyment and purpose in writing.

Critique

Teachers who use the write-teach approach should provide for their students daily writing opportunities, which can take the form of daily journals, story compositions, and group writing projects. With its focus on the acquisition, organization, and application of ideas, and on the process of writing over the product of writing, the write-teach approach is most closely related to the active-processor perspective on learning.

ENRICHMENT APPROACH

The enrichment approach recognizes the need of some students to have instruction that goes beyond the educational curriculum in fostering their ability to write and communicate ideas. Some students might benefit from learning and practicing forms of writing such as exposition, argumentation, or narration, or from writing a document, doing research on a project, and writing articles for a journal or newspaper. Through selected groups, independent study, and/or special projects, students can plan writing products, organize materials and resources, discuss obstacles and problems, assume responsibility for themselves and others, develop higher-level thinking skills and questioning strategies, and present their ideas to their peers.

Critique

The enrichment approach would be a good supplement for any writing program. Teachers need to be highly organized and to monitor students' progress and products closely and consistently. Moreover, they should provide students with some direction and offer continual supportive and corrective feedback where appropriate.

Focusing on the development of higher-order cognitive skills, the enrichment approach is most closely associated with the active-processor perspective on learning.

WHOLE LANGUAGE APPROACH

As noted earlier, the whole language approach uses students' language experiences, as well as their reading and writing interests, to guide their writing development. Teachers typically integrate reading and writing, along with components of oral language, to promote students' language education. This approach stresses the need for teachers to provide opportunities for their students to participate in authentic writing each day.

Critique

The whole language approach supports the view that students should be involved in the entire process of writing, not just in isolated skills or parts. Englert (1992) points out that "writing reflects the social and cultural community of the classroom through the internalization of the audience's perspective." She further notes that "the interaction of authors and peers fuels literacy learning in another way. As authors and peers interact over texts, authors come to realize that there is a mismatch between written text and their intended meanings. When communication breakdowns occur, occasions are created for authors to expand the meanings of their texts and explore new strategies" (p. 169).

Viewing writing as a social enterprise, and supporting the development of writing through interactive communication with members of the community, the whole language approach is most closely related to the social-being perspective on learning.

STRATEGIES APPROACH

The strategies approach to writing encourages students to identify the purpose of their writing, to ask questions of themselves while writing, to monitor their writing, and to evaluate their information processing as it relates to their writing. There are a vast number of strategies that can help students with each of these tasks (see Chapter 12). Among these strategies are *semantic mapping* (the development of a web or map prior to writing to help organize the information to be presented in text), and *learning logs* (journals in which students can describe what and how they learn) (Vacca & Vacca, 1986).

Critique

The strategies approach can be of benefit to students who have difficulty organizing their ideas, as well as reflecting upon and regulating information-processing aspects related to writing (e.g., attention). Teachers who use this approach should: (1) adapt strategies to the needs, interests, and abilities of their students; (2) allow students generous practice time with the strategies; (3) relate the new strategic approach to the old approach; (4) use specific and concrete examples and tasks; (5) demonstrate the strategy across different areas; (6) discuss the purpose, value, and use of strategies; and (7) help students modify and develop their own strategies.

With its emphasis on the development of students' cognitive and meta-cognitive processes, and on the importance of learning and thinking strategies, the strategies approach is most closely affiliated with the active-processor perspective on learning.

MECHANICAL APPROACH

The mechanical approach stresses the secretarial role in the writing process. Typically, this method takes a skills approach to writing whereby students are given direct and systematic instruction with respect to capitalization, punctuation, vocabulary, spelling, sentence structure, and so forth. Following the acquisition of these skills, students are taught organizational strategies for sentence and paragraph writing and given activities related to such things as letter writing and note taking. Below we discuss another salient mechanical skill—handwriting.

Handwriting

Many children have handwriting difficulties. For example, some students have trouble with fine motor coordination while others have visual and perceptual problems and poor pencil grip. These problems can result in poor handwriting legibility, reduced speed and fluency of writing production, and low self-concept and motivation with respect to writing performance.

There is disagreement about how to teach handwriting. Some experts believe that only manuscript writing should be taught because it is easy to form the letters and resembles book print (Graham & Miller, 1980; Hagin, 1983), while others favour cursive writing because it allows for faster writing and reduces problems associated with spacing and reversals (Bos & Vaughn, 1991; Mercer & Mercer, 1985). Some experts suggest that cursive writing may be more appropriate to begin with, as it has rhythmic continuity and eliminates the need for students to learn another form of writing; but others argue that manuscript writing should precede cursive writing because it is thought to be much easier to learn.

Given that the above debate is unresolved, the decision of how to teach handwriting should be based on the particular needs of the students (i.e., the method with which they feel most comfortable), as well as on the philosophical and professional opinion of the teacher. Whatever the approach, handwriting instruction should be integrated into the total writing program so that students can appreciate the purpose of proper handwriting within the overarching goal of becoming a better communicator of ideas.

Generally, handwriting instruction should be individualized, well-planned, and direct. Moreover, students should practice handwriting within meaningful contexts and teachers should promote success and enthusiasm by fostering a pleasant atmosphere (Graham & Miller, 1980). Teachers should also impress upon students the importance of handwriting, provide them with continual and immediate feedback and reinforcement, and surround them with models of good writing (Bachor & Crealock, 1986).

The most effective approach to teaching handwriting is one in which the teacher is systematic and consistent, and in which the student is actively involved in the learning process. Teaching should include good modelling, demonstration, prompting, practice, corrective feedback, and positive reinforcement, while student learning should involve self-monitoring, self-regulation and self-reinforcement for successful performance. Meichenbaum and Goodman (1971) developed a program (also see Kosiewicz, Hallahan, Lloyd, & Graves, 1982) that incorporates these features and involves the following steps (Andrews, 1984):

1. Teacher models the particular task and the student observes.
2. The student performs the task and, along with the teacher, verbalizes the instructions.
3. The student performs the task and verbalizes the instructions alone.

4. The student performs the task while quietly whispering the instructions.
5. The student performs the task and self-instructs covertly (silently).

◇ ACADEMIC SKILLS AND COMMON DIFFICULTIES RELATED TO SPELLING

Spelling is an important academic skill that is very difficult to master. Inability to spell is frequently linked with illiteracy (Personkee & Yee, 1971) and can sometimes affect an individual's educational and occupational status. Spelling performance is linked to a student's abilities in a variety of areas, including linguistic competence, meta-language knowledge (knowledge about language), basic motor skills, visual and auditory readiness, automatic recall of letter formation, appreciation of letter-sound relationships, and memory.

The integrative complexities of cognitive and perceptual motor skills are not the only reasons why many students have difficulty spelling. Problems also emerge because the English language does not follow consistent rules with respect to spelling. The relation between spelling and spoken English cannot be described simply in terms of sounds represented by letters (Schwartz & Doehring, 1977), because spelling rules are governed by morphological, phonological, and orthographic patterns.

Poor spellers may have difficulty: (1) visualizing and recalling letter formations; (2) recognizing letter-sound relationships; (3) discriminating sounds; (4) identifying and sequencing letters; (5) associating and recalling sound-symbol correspondence; (6) memorizing letters, words, and rules; (7) integrating a visual motor response to words perceived auditorily; (8) decoding and pronouncing words; and (9) handwriting. Spelling is also a source of difficulty for children who lack appropriate strategies to aid their study and recall of words, or who have experienced so much failure that they feel inadequate to the task of improving their spelling skills.

The methods used to teach spelling are as diverse as the variables involved in spelling performance. Teachers need to be selective when choosing methods for their students. One viewpoint is that spelling requires visual comparisons and recall of word patterns (Hendrickson, 1967). A second viewpoint is that phonetics and spelling rules are critical to effective spelling (Block, 1972). A third perspective is that visual processing and phonetic knowledge and skills are equally important to effective spelling (Bradley & Bryant, 1980). Most researchers and educators support the view that there is an overlap of operations in spelling tasks, and that effective spelling requires phonetic, graphemic, syntactic, morphemic, semantic, and etymological resources. There is also general agreement that spelling instruction and remediation should consider the way a student processes information; should be easily understood by students; and should impress upon students the importance of spelling to their present and future needs.

IMPLICATIONS FOR TEACHING

◆ Have children keep a record of their own spelling performance through the use of charts and graphs (Bachor & Crealock, 1986).

◆ Give clear instructions, model appropriate spelling techniques, allow time for students to review previously learned words, and provide consistent reinforcement (Salend, 1990; Stowitschek & Jobes, 1977).

◆ Show students systematic ways of studying unknown spelling words (Graham, 1985).

◆ Structure spelling assignments for success, use interesting methods, activities, and games, and provide for meaningful practice (Henderson, 1985).

◆ Pre-test students to determine which words they do not know, teach them the words they misspelled, and then test them again (Graham, 1985).

◆ Use the whole-word approach to spelling (i.e., learning to spell by focusing on the entire word rather than on its parts), and allow students to correct their own spelling tests, under teacher supervision, immediately after taking the test (Graham, 1985).

◆ Address underlying problems related to spelling, such as handwriting skills, organization skills, visual-spatial problems, auditory discrimination, and memory (Bachor & Crealock, 1986).

◆ Teach students how to use a dictionary so that they can check their spelling (Graham & Miller, 1979).

◆ Teach students mnemonic devices (see Chapter 12) and configuration clues to cue them toward the correct spelling of words (Gloeckler & Simpson, 1988).

ASSESSING LEVELS OF PERFORMANCE

While a variety of norm-referenced tests are available that measure spelling ability (see Appendix 10.1), informal procedures can be created to identify particular strengths and weaknesses of students. Teachers can construct checklists and rating scales as ways of analyzing and recording spelling errors (e.g., vowel errors, reversal errors, substitution errors, blending errors, etc.) from tests and assignments (see Table 10.14). Teachers can also observe their students' daily work for spelling errors, monitor their students' pronunciation skills when giving oral responses, and evaluate students' spelling study habits. Moreover, teachers can interview and probe students regarding the approach and strategies they use for spelling (see Chapter 8 for further assessment ideas that can be applied to spelling).

Table 10.14 Error Analysis for Spelling		
Type of Error	*Error Example*	*Correct Form*
1. Omission of silent letter	-Her -for -mak -hom	-here -four -make -home
2. Substitution of letters	-well -dig -came -cawe -pat -rad	-will -big -come -cake -pet -red
2. Phonic equivalent	-Haf -coelr	-have -colour
3. Transposition (reversals)	-naem -soem -tow	-name -some -two
4. Omission of sounded letters	-thee -blck -wat	-three -black -want
5. Addition of letters	-goieng -funny	-going -fun

Note: Developed with the assistance of Jan Avis.

◈ INSTRUCTIONAL METHODS FOR DEVELOPING SPELLING

BASAL APPROACH

Spelling is traditionally taught through the use of spelling basal programs. Typically, basal programs have weekly lists of words for students to learn how to spell. At the beginning of the week, students are pre-tested on these words by the teacher. Following the pre-test, the teacher may introduce students to a theme unit from the basal program (single vowel words, *ing*-ending words, etc.), which is associated with the types of words contained in the word list. The middle part of the week is usually devoted to completing the various activities included in the students' workbooks that accompany the basal program. These activities might include such things as matching words to pictures, filling in missing letters of spelling words, using words to write sentences or complete crossword puzzles, and defining words. At the end of the week, students are usually given a spelling post-test by the teacher.

Critique

Although basal programs can be modified to meet individual needs, most teachers use the program as described above. A major drawback of this approach is that students may be provided words that do not match their reading level. In addition, students are not given the opportunity to choose their own words to study; the activities are uninspiring for many students and lack meaningfulness; and basal spelling programs do not lend themselves either to sufficient feedback by the teacher or to practice of the spelling words in other contexts.

Stressing the idea that students' learning and thinking occurs over time in a systematic fashion and that learning progresses along identifiable stages, the basal approach is most closely related to the developing-child perspective on learning.

DIRECT TEACHING

The purpose of the direct teaching method is to provide planned and systematic guidance for students with respect to their poor spelling performance. For example, if a student demonstrated poor spelling performance due to phonetic weaknesses, disorganized work habits, ineffective spelling strategies, and inconsistent self-monitoring, a spelling procedure such as the following could be *directly* taught to the student:

1. *Look at each word and sound it out.* This is done to reinforce the importance of decoding skills and phonetic analysis.
2. *Examine each word and write the word on a file card or in a notebook and check it.* This is done to reinforce attention to the studying task, facilitate self-monitoring, and enhance visual memory.
3. *Check the meaning of each word in a dictionary and write the meaning of the word on a file card or in a workbook.* This is done to reinforce the importance of knowing the meaning of a word and to give the student more experience in seeing words in other contexts.
4. *Spell the word out loud while looking at the word.* This is done to reinforce letter-sound correspondence.
5. *Write the word in a sentence.* This is done to make the task of spelling more meaningful.
6. *Write all of the spelling words from memory and check for accuracy. If correct, reward yourself. If some words are misspelled, repeat Steps 1 to 5.* This is done to facilitate self-evaluation and to foster active and independent involvement in the remediation process.

Critique

The major problem with the direct teaching approach is that it can be very time-consuming and difficult to maintain consistent monitoring and evaluation of student performance. Its primary strengths are that spelling instruction is designed to meet the specific needs of the student, and that chosen procedures can be undertaken by the student independently.

The direct teaching approach stresses the need for teachers to assess students' specific skills related to spelling and to develop those skills. With its emphasis on the analysis of the task over the analysis of the student, and its focus on direct instruction, this approach most closely relates to the behaviour perspective on learning.

MULTISENSORY METHOD

The multisensory approach, which has been successful with many students, attempts to strengthen and integrate the visual, auditory, kinesthetic, and tactile modalities. Fernald (1988 [1943]) presents the following recommendations for spelling remediation:

1. The words to be learned are written on the blackboard or on paper by the teacher.
2. The teacher pronounces each word clearly and distinctly, and then has students pronounce each word.
3. Students are given time to study each word.
4. After students have studied the words and are sure of their spelling, they write the words from memory at least twice.
5. Students are given writing activities that allow them to make use of the spelling words.
6. Students review words to maintain correct spelling.

Critique

A generally good approach to spelling for students who require attention to all senses, the multisensory method can also benefit students who need structured approaches. However, consistent monitoring and evaluation of students' spelling performance can be difficult for a teacher who has many students; moreover, this method assumes that one approach can meet all of the students' spelling needs.

Proponents of this child-centred approach believe that children's spelling can change over time as they incorporate new experiences and change the way they think. Thus, the multisensory method is most closely related to the developing-child perspective on learning.

RULE-GOVERNED APPROACH

The rule-governed approach can involve a variety of methods designed to teach students basic spelling rules. This approach assumes that knowledge of spelling rules can allow students to spell the vast majority of English words. Teachers using the approach often teach students spelling rules and patterns, discuss similarities and differences in words, practice the application of rules in the spelling of unfamiliar words, and learn exceptions to the rules (Salend, 1990).

Similar to the linguistic method used for learning sight words, teachers can focus on the patterns of whole words and use word families to help students generalize spelling patterns to other words (e.g., learning the *eat* family using words like *beat* and *heat*, and then applying the pattern to other words such as *meat*, *neat*, and *seat*) (Salend, 1990). Teachers might also use a phonetic method to teach rules in spelling, particularly as they apply to letter-and-sound relationships (e.g., r-controlled words, digraphs, diphthongs, and consonant blends).

Critique

The purpose of the rule-governed approach is to help students become better decoders. In order for students to understand and appreciate the purpose and importance of spelling across various contexts, teachers should supplement rule-governed approaches with methods that stress the meaningfulness of spelling.

Emphasizing the task, rather than the process of learning, as well as the teaching of sequential skills through direct instruction, the rule-governed approach is most closely related to the behavioural perspective on learning.

WORD-FREQUENCY APPROACH

The word-frequency approach is based on the idea that students learn to spell only those words that are used most often in written language; thus, words are selected for spelling instruction on the basis of frequency rather than on linguistic patterns (Lerner, 1988). According to some spelling authorities (e.g., Fitzgerald, 1951, 1955; Thomas, 1979), children in elementary school should only study words from a basic list of about 3,500 words. They further contend that because the most frequently used words do not follow spelling and phonics rules, students should not be taught patterns and rules (Lerner, 1988).

Thomas (1979) suggests that teachers use a test-study procedure in their spelling instructional approach, and recommends that teachers direct their students to study words to be learned in another context. His program includes a list of the 3,000 words most frequently written by students from Grades 2 to 8, as well as a list of the most commonly misspelled words in each of the elementary grades.

Critique

The word-frequency approach emphasizes a curriculum (list of target words) rather than a particular spelling method. The value of Thomas's (1979) test-study method rests with the idea that students should focus their efforts on learning how to spell words that they encounter most regularly and that cause them the most difficulty.

With its emphasis on the most commonly used words in the student's environment—and thus the role of the environment in learning—the word-frequency approach is most closely related to the behavioural perspective on learning.

METACOGNITIVE APPROACH

As Babbs and Moe (1983) suggest, the focus of the metacognitive approach is to help students plan, regulate, and monitor their spelling activities independently. The value of using this approach lies in developing students' knowledge and control of the spelling process. The following instructional sequence exemplifies a metacognitive approach to spelling:

1. The teacher develops students' awareness of the importance of spelling.
2. The teacher and the student establish objectives and goals for spelling.
3. The teacher and student focus on the particular demands related to the spelling task (e.g., attention, memorization, discrimination of letters and sounds, handwriting, studying, and practicing spelling in meaningful contexts).
4. The teacher and student devise a variety of plans and procedures for studying spelling words (e.g., visualizing the word, writing the word, examining word parts, thinking and writing the word in meaningful contexts, and monitoring the studying and spelling process).
5. The teacher and student choose and develop an effective spelling strategy.
6. The student and teacher monitor and evaluate the strategy's effectiveness in terms of spelling performance.
7. With help from the teacher, the student assumes greater responsibility for assessing spelling performance and for making modifications to the spelling strategy.
8. The student takes independent control of his or her spelling development (e.g., selecting words to study, selecting/modifying spelling strategies, monitoring and regulating spelling efforts, and evaluating spelling progress) under the supervision of the teacher.

Critique

The metacognitive approach encourages active and independent learning, although some students may require more structured guidance, as well as more language development. Emphasizing both the development of students' cognitive and metacognitive processes and the role of learning strategies, this approach is most closely associated with the active-processor perspective on learning.

MORPHOGRAPHIC SPELLING PROGRAM

The morphographic spelling program (Dixon & Englemann, 1976) is a carefully sequenced program that focuses on the development of spelling through the teaching of **morphemes**. The program encourages active participation of the students and provides for consistent feedback through the use of worksheets and summary charts.

◆ morpheme: the smallest meaningful unit of a language, whether a word or specific element such as a prefix or suffix

Critique

An example of the rule-governed approach discussed earlier, the morphographic spelling program stresses decoding over meaning and should, therefore, be supplemented with other methods. Stressing the learning task over the learning process, this spelling program is most closely related to the behavioural perspective on learning.

VISUAL-IMAGERY APPROACH

Some experts (e.g., Bradley, 1981; Durrel, 1980) recommend the visual-imagery spelling approach. Caban, Hambleton, Coffing, Conway, and Swaminathorp (1978) compared a visual-imagery approach to spelling with a "drill and practice" method and a "no direction" procedure. Grade 8 students in the visual-imagery group were taught to trace their spelling words on a "magic slate"—an opaque sheet on top of carbon paper. The students were instructed to form a visual image of each spelling word and to write the word on the slate while its correct spelling was in their view. The students were also instructed to check their spelling, erase the slate, and repeat this process with each word five times. The group of students using the visual-imagery approach to spelling scored higher than the comparative groups on followup spelling tests.

yes

Forest (1981) describes the visual-imagery method he once employed to help a student with a learning disability become a better speller. First, the student is asked to conjure up a mental picture of something to write on—a chalkboard or perhaps writing paper. The student is then asked to visualize (with eyes closed) himself or herself writing the letters of the word as they are called out by the teacher. The student is asked to try keep the image of the letters, but report to the teacher if they fade. If they fade, the letters are to be repeated. Once able to image the entire word, the student is asked to call off the letters backward as fast as he or she can, in order to verify that the whole word has been imaged. Then, at different times during the day, the student is asked to go back in his or her mind, see the word, and call off the letters either forward or backward. If at any time the student is unable to conjure up the image of the word, the original procedure is repeated.

Critique

Visual imagery has proven to be a very successful method for improving students' recall of words (see Chapter 12). Teachers who use this method need to show students how to image words, and should allow students frequent practice of visual imagery. Emphasizing the development of students' information processing, this approach is most closely related to the active-processor perspective on learning.

DEFICIT APPROACH

Spelling strategies and methods that can be used to compensate for various deficits are discussed below.

Visual-Perceptual Deficits

Students with visual-perceptual problems may benefit from a multisensory approach to spelling, which includes activities such as word matching, letter-and-word discrimination, word-part underlining (e.g., digraphs and consonant blends), and letter arranging and sequencing.

Visual-Memory Deficits

Children with visual memory problems might benefit from kinesthetic approaches to spelling as well as activities that develop visual-imagery and visual-discrimination skills.

Auditory-Perceptual Deficits

Children with auditory-perceptual problems might benefit from the Fernald (multisensory) spelling method, from spelling strategies that stress visualization, and from activities that attempt to strengthen their listening habits (e.g., identifying noises in the environment, picking out differences between pairs of words, and discriminating sounds, letters, and words with the use of record players and tape recorders).

Auditory-Memory Deficits

Students with auditory-memory problems might benefit from spelling methods that enable them to label, discriminate, recall, organize, and analyze spelling words (multisensory approach) and from activities that give them the opportunity to strengthen their listening skills (following directions, sequencing letters and words, etc.).

Critique

As noted earlier in this chapter, the deficit approach should be supplemented with other methods. Proponents of this child-centred approach believe that students' spelling ability can change over time as they incorporate new experiences and change the way they process information. Therefore, the deficit approach is most closely affiliated with the developing-child perspective on learning.

◇ ACADEMIC SKILLS AND COMMON DIFFICULTIES RELATED TO MATHEMATICS

Mathematics is a core curriculum subject and very much part of one's day-to-day life experiences (e.g., handling money, making change, comparative shopping). To be successful in mathematics, students require good concentration, attention, and memory, as well as adequate language skills and numerical reasoning ability.

Students can have problems with mathematics due to: (1) low interest and motivation; (2) lack of readiness for acquiring mathematical concepts and skills; (3) lack of parental support and guidance; (4) anxiety and distractibility; (5) poor concentration, attention, and memory; (6) reading problems; (7) perceptual-spatial problems; (8) problems with abstract, symbolic, and/or temporal thinking; (9) a poor foundation in arithmetic skills; (10) low self-concept; and (11) deficient and/or inefficient learning strategies.

The most important mathematical skills to master include numeration (the act of numbering), computation (the act of calculating), measurement, and problem-solving. Before teachers make program plans and choose teaching methods, they must determine goals and objectives for all of their students based on their students' needs, the educational curriculum, and the mathematical skills a person needs to function adequately in the community. Mathematics education involves the learning and application of computation skills, decision-making skills, and problem-solving skills. All students should ultimately learn how to deal with the typical mathematical problems they face in their day-to-day life experiences. Moreover, they should be taught mathematics in ways that reduce anxiety while promoting active and creative learning as well as enjoyment.

IMPLICATIONS FOR TEACHING

◆ Ensure that students can comprehend the reading and vocabulary level of the directions and word problems in commercial or teacher-made materials (Bachor & Crealock, 1986).

◆ Model math concepts and use concrete materials and manipulatives to illustrate concepts (Dunlap & Brennan, 1979).

- ◆ Construct self-correcting materials for students who are working independently so that they receive feedback about the correctness of their work (Mercer, Mercer, & Bott, 1984).

- ◆ Ensure that every student receives some teacher-directed instruction (Polloway et al., 1989).

- ◆ Give students opportunities to apply their acquired skills to other subject areas (Polloway et al., 1989).

- ◆ Relate new concepts to everyday situations in order to motivate students to learn (Bley & Thornton, 1981).

- ◆ Teach students essential math terminology (Salend, 1990) and have them develop and maintain a math dictionary (Bley & Thornton, 1981).

- ◆ Supplement verbal presentations and printed reading material with drawings and diagrams (Dunlap & McKnight, 1978).

- ◆ Teach math facts together rather than in isolation (Thornton, Tucker, Dossey, & Bazik, 1983).

- ◆ Use a variety of activities, such as flashcards and math sheets to promote automaticity of basic facts (Mastropieri & Scruggs, 1987).

- ◆ Conduct ongoing reviews and timed probes to evaluate mastery of previously learned skills (Thornton et al., 1983).

- ◆ Use cues (e.g., colour coding, bolding, and underlining) to discriminate computation signs (+, -, x), thereby helping students to reduce errors in computation (Salend, 1990).

- ◆ Develop math concepts by moving from concrete to abstract, and provide instruction and materials that are in accordance with students' language and cognitive development (Winzer, 1989).

- ◆ Provide opportunities for students to set their own goals for mathematics, thereby increasing their commitment to the goal (Fuchs, Bahr, & Rieth, 1989).

ASSESSING LEVELS OF PERFORMANCE

Information about a student's mathematical abilities can be ascertained through both formal and informal measures. Formal measures, which are readily available (see Appendix 10.1), assist teachers in discovering general areas of difficulty whereas informal measures help teachers discern specific problem areas. Teacher-made tests or informal mathematics assessments can include informal inventories and checklists. Additionally, teachers can observe their students' daily work in mathematics, examine their homework assignments, conduct error-pattern analysis (see Table 10.15) in their students' mathematical work, and provide oral interviews to assess their students' attitude and approach to mathematical computation and problem-solving (Underhill, Uprichard, & Heddens, 1980; Zigmond, Vallecorsa, & Silverman, 1983).

Table 10.15
Some Common Errors in Computation

Problem	Student Response	Type of Error
Count the number		
xxxxxx	8	Student does not understand number composition and one to one correspondence
6 + 8	12	Lacks computational skill
12 x 20	24	Missing zero
21 x 4	94	Computational error
24 - 10	34	Added instead of subtracted
142 + 5	192	Perceptual-spatial difficulty
17 + 19	26	Difficulty regrouping
7.24 x .82	583.68	Decimal in wrong place
432 x 36	2592 1296 27216	Improper alignment

◆ INSTRUCTIONAL METHODS FOR DEVELOPING MATHEMATICS

BASAL APPROACH

Most teachers use math texts and workbooks that are produced and/or recommended in school districts. These texts and workbooks usually correspond with the provincial curriculum and generally provide a good overview of skills, concepts, and activities for students of all grade levels as well as instructional ideas for the teacher. The major problem with the basal approach (the use of commercial programs and series) is that materials need to be modified in order to meet the unique needs of students.

The benefits of using modified curriculum materials (school district texts and workbooks) are: (1) all students are taught similar content; (2) skill development is usually presented in a sequential and comprehensive fashion, with some series providing real-life/hands-on activities (Polloway et al., 1989); and (3) costs associated with the purchase of special programs and materials can be reduced (Katsiyannis & Prillaman, 1990).

Critique

When using the basal approach, teachers should: (1) try to emphasize the functionality and realistic benefits of mathematics; (2) facilitate continuous success; (3) have students set their own learning objectives; (4) provide constant practice and feedback; (5) use a variety of activities and teaching tactics; (6) monitor student progress; (7) use self-correcting materials; and (8) sequence mathematical concepts in a developmental hierarchy (Ashlock, 1982; Sternberg & Mauser, 1975; Underhill et al., 1980). Teachers should also keep in mind the disadvantages of the basal approach, which include a lack of specific teaching strategies, review exercises, and assignments, as well as activities that are sometimes too complex for students to understand (Polloway et al., 1989).

Reflecting the view that students' learning progresses along identifiable stages and that their learning skills are hierarchically integrated, the basal approach is most closely related to the developing child perspective.

STRATEGIES APPROACH

One reason children have difficulty solving mathematical problems is that they lack a systematic plan for approaching and solving problems. The strategies approach helps students direct their processes of learning (e.g., attention, memory, and regulation) in mathematics. In this approach students learn to monitor and control their learning and thinking, and are encouraged to develop their information processing as it applies to mathematics.

One general model for problem-solving that could be taught to students and practiced with a variety of problems is outlined below:

1. *Study the problem.* Read the problem and find out what needs to be solved. Look for clue words and reread the problem if necessary.
2. *Activate background knowledge.* Compare the problem to other problems in one's experience, giving consideration to commonalities and differences.
3. *Organize the information.* Consider all of the facts presented in the problem and decide which facts are the most important to the solution.
4. *Make a plan.* Decide what steps and procedures need to be done in order to solve the problem (e.g., need to add these two numbers and then subtract this number).
5. *Activate plan.* Once the plan is decided upon and the procedures and operations selected, implement the plan.
6. *Monitor action plan.* While performing the procedures and operations, check and monitor your performance.
7. *Check answer.* Review the answer to see if it fits the problem and to ensure that the procedures and operations were correctly performed.

Critique

Teachers using a strategies approach should consider whether students can perform all of the steps and procedures involved in a particular strategy. For example, if a student has difficulty organizing information and selecting main ideas, he or she will have difficulty undertaking Step 3 above and will thus have problems using the strategy as a whole. Therefore, students need to acquire basic content knowledge and skills before problem-solving strategies can be efficiently used.

Emphasizing the development of student's cognitive/metacognitive processes and the role of strategies, the strategies approach is most closely related to the active-processor perspective on learning.

PRECISION TEACHING

Precision teaching emphasizes direct measurement of behaviour and daily monitoring of performance. Teachers who use this approach analyze students' daily behaviour and design instructional plans according to observed changes. This precise and systematic way of evaluating instructional intervention and curriculum (West, Young, & Spooner, 1990) has a framework consisting of seven basic elements: (1) the underlying principle that the student's behaviour is the best gauge for determining the effectiveness of instruction; (2) daily performance assessment; (3) consistent and systematic evaluation of the number of correct answers per minute; (4) a standard chart format or visual display that shows performance patterns; (5) ongoing description of behaviour; (6) analysis of teaching tactics on student learning; and (7) emphasis on developing appropriate behaviour (West et al., 1990).

Teachers who use precision teaching should follow these steps: (1) identify students' mathematical skill level; (2) analyze students' skill level in relation to criterion-level standard; (3) determine instructional tactic, e.g., if students need to acquire a skill give them specific instruction, and if their rate and accuracy of performance needs improvement, give them drills on a daily basis; (4) record students' drill-sheet scores on a chart to inform them of their progress and to facilitate instructional decisions; (5) maintain, reinforce, and generalize skills; and (6) advance skill level and develop further goals and objectives.

Critique

Precision teaching is highly structured and time-consuming. Moreover, it stresses the development of computational skills over problem-solving and decision-making skills, and should, therefore, be supplemented with methods that focus on the latter skills. However, it is an effective method for monitoring student performance frequently and regularly, and is thus helpful for making appropriate daily instructional adjustments.

With its emphasis on the learning task over the learning process, as well as on the need for direct instruction, the precision teaching approach is most closely associated with the behavioural perspective on learning.

FUNCTIONAL APPROACH

The functional approach to mathematics instruction identifies and empha-sizes basic skills that students need to know in order to function adequately outside the classroom and in the community at large (Bott, 1988). Some of these basic skills relate to such things as handling money and purchasing goods. Although the functional approach is most often used with junior-high and high-school students, the approach can be modified for younger stu-dents. Its essential aspects are described by Schwartz and Budd (1981) and Bos and Vaughn (1991) for whom the teaching sequence includes: (1) identi-fying for students how math is useful at home and on the job; (2) reviewing and practicing mathematical operations, as well as developing students' understanding of the choice of operations for solving problems; (3) promot-ing students' understanding of mathematical problems that are presented in realistic situations and identifying necessary and unnecessary information; (4) encouraging students to estimate their work; (5) having students do oper-ations necessary to solve the mathematical problem; (6) getting students to check their work; (7) facilitating students' skills at determining and interpret-ing the answer; and (8) providing students with opportunities to apply their developed skills to both teacher- and student-generated problems.

Critique

Many children with significant learning and behavioural problems graduate from school with little applied knowledge and understanding of mathemati-cal skills. Focusing instruction on the functional math skills necessary for sur-vival in the real world (Halpern, 1981) is an appropriate instructional plan for these students.

With its emphasis on the learning task and on the relationship between mathematical skills and the environment, the functional approach is most closely related to the behavioural perspective on learning.

DISTAR ARITHMETIC PROGRAM

The DISTAR arithmetic program (Corrective Mathematics) (Englemann & Carnine, 1981), a highly structured approach to teaching mathematics, con-sists of a carefully developed and sequenced program of lessons designed to introduce mathematical concepts and skills. Linguistic and perceptual cues are embedded in the instructional activities, which include diagnostic and achievement tests for the lesson units. The program also contains teachers' guides and student books, as well as specific instructional information for the teacher. In addition to direct teaching activities, the program also includes independent activities. Embedded in the program is a point system by which students can gain points for successful performance with the activities. The major objective throughout the program is for students to achieve criterion mastery as they perform the tasks without error and thereby accumulate points and rewards.

Critique

Although the DISTAR system has proven to be effective for teaching rote skills (Sedlak & Fitzmaurice, 1981), it does not sufficiently enable students to practice skills in situations relevant to their life experience (Sternberg & Fair, 1982). Moreover, the program does not give adequate attention to the development of mathematical concepts.

With its emphasis on the need for teachers to assess and develop students' mathematical skills, as well as on the use of rewards to increase students' acquisition of skills the DISTAR arithmetic program is most closely related to the behavioural perspective on learning.

COGNITIVE BEHAVIOUR MODIFICATION (CBM) SELF-INSTRUCTIONAL APPROACH

The self-instructional approach to teaching mathematics is primarily used to teach step-by-step math skills. The CBM self-instructional approach, which is derived from the work of Meichenbaum and his associates (Meichenbaum, 1977, 1980; Meichenbaum & Goodman, 1971), uses internal speech as a way for students to facilitate the problem-solving process. The self-instructional procedures developed by Leon and Pepe (1983) include modelling, self-reinforcement, feedback, coping instructions, and self-instructional dialogue. A general example of these procedures is delineated below:

1. The teacher models the skill (i.e., computation) by showing and verbalizing the steps in the process.
2. The teacher and student follow the steps in the process together.
3. The student goes through the process by himself or herself while the teacher observes.
4. The student gradually reduces overt verbalizations (about the process) and substitutes covert verbalizations while the teacher observes and provides feedback where necessary.
5. The student implements the self-instructional procedure independently and provides self-reinforcement.

Critique

Although the CBM self-instructional approach can foster student self-confidence (Andrews, 1984; Bornstein & Quevillon, 1976), in addition to intrinsic motivation, it can be time-consuming and difficult to monitor as well. Teachers who use this approach must adequately assess their students' present math strategies and modify the CBM method accordingly.

Stressing both the process and product of learning, as well as the role of both the learner and the environment in learning and instruction, the CBM self-instructional approach is related to both the active-processor and behavioural perspectives on learning.

DIRECT INSTRUCTION MATHEMATICS

The direct instruction mathematics program (Silbert, Carnine, & Stein, 1981) is a clear and organized approach to teaching mathematics. As discussed by Hammill and Bartel (1990), it is a highly comprehensive program that contains teaching suggestions, recommendations, and instructional examples and models with respect to specifying objectives, devising problem-solving strategies, determining and sequencing skills and subskills, selecting teaching procedures, designing formats, and providing for practice and review. The aim of instruction is to teach to criterion mastery (the program has its own criterion-referenced evaluation procedures).

Critique

Highly structured and teacher-controlled, the direct instruction mathematics program requires specific expectations and responses from students and is very analytical in terms of instruction and student evaluation. It provides detailed and coherent plans for the teacher and has proven a successful approach with some special-needs students (Gersten, 1985).

With its emphasis on direct instruction and the acquisition of skills, the direct instruction mathematics approach is most closely associated with the behavioural perspective on learning.

DEFICIT APPROACH

Instructional methods and strategies that can be used to assist students with various deficits are discussed below.

Memory Deficits

Teachers can help students with memory deficits by introducing them to grouping and organizing strategies to ease memory load, as well as to strategies designed to help them recall rules and apply them to problem-solving situations. Students should have plenty of time to learn and practice mathematical vocabulary, skills, and concepts.

Visual and Auditory Discrimination Deficits

Students with visual and auditory discrimination problems could benefit from exercises and activities that enable them to compare problems, evaluate similarities and differences between mathematical concepts, and discriminate mathematical operations.

Visual and Auditory Association Deficits

Students with visual and auditory association problems might benefit from intervention techniques such as practice in comparing and relating mathematical vocabulary, symbols, and operations; grouping objects according to particular properties; and associating numerical concepts.

Perceptual Motor Deficits

Students with perceptual motor problems could benefit from instruction that provides alternative ways to complete work (e.g., use of computers), practice with hand-eye activities, and opportunities to use manipulatives in order to learn mathematical concepts.

Spatial Awareness and Orientation Deficits

Students with spatial awareness and orientation problems could benefit from instruction that focuses on and provides practice with vocabulary related to their problem (e.g., inside, outside, above, below); measurement activities related to orientation; rules involving shape, symmetry, and order; operations requiring spatial manipulation; and concepts requiring the ability to recognize or use spatial associations.

Attention Deficits

Students with attention deficits might benefit from teachers who reduce distractions, provide organized and structured environments, and plan clear and specific lessons and mathematics assignments.

Critique

The deficit approach should be supplemented with other methods because assessment of students' modality preferences lacks clear reliability and validity, and because studies fail to show significant effect from tailoring instruction to students' processing strengths (Tarver & Dawson, 1978).

Proponents of this child-centred approach view students as active constructors of their knowledge, capable of developing their ability over time as they incorporate new experiences and change the way they process information. Thus, the deficit approach is most closely related to the developing-child perspective on learning.

• summary table of chpt

Pay attention to:

① • know what the methods are *in text.*

②• know what theoretical prespectives they're from

↳ know one from another ¿ difference.

③ what is good ¿ bad about them.

Table 10.16
Relating Teaching Methods or Approaches to Theoretical Perspectives

Methods and Approaches	Theoretical Perspective			
	Active Processor	Developing Child	Social Being	Behavioural
Sight Word				●
Phonics		●		
Strategies	●			
Language Experience			●	
Enrichment	●			
Whole Language			●	
Linguistic		●		
Individualized		●		
Basal		●		
Grouping			●	
DISTAR				●
Fernald		●		
Gillingham-Stillman				●
Neurological Impress		●		
Rate	●			
Rebus				●
Functional				●
Deficit		●		
Planning/Writing/Revising	●			
Write-Teach	●			
Mechanical				●
Direct				●
Multisensory		●		
Rule Governed				●
Word Frequency				●
Metacognitive	●			
Morphographic				●
Visual-Imagery	●			
Precision				●
Cognitive-Behaviour				●
Modification	●			

ENRICHMENT APPROACH

Students who have average to above-average ability in mathematics, and who achieve beyond grade-level expectations with respect to computation and problem-solving skills, require instruction that allows them to develop their creativity and skills in communication, organization, planning, decision-making, and critical thinking, in addition to nurturing their independent study. These students should be free to create new mathematical strategies to solve problems, to design mathematical games, to study mathematical concepts beyond what is presented in the curriculum, and to use and practice flexible, elaborative, original, imaginative, and inventive thinking. Specific teaching techniques might include: (1) planning student-teacher conferences on a regular basis to discuss possible endeavours; (2) small-group activities and experiences that enable students to share and discuss their individual projects, objectives, goals, and products; (3) independent study routines (e.g., students going to the library to do research pertaining to their endeavours); (4) using group problem-solving programs (e.g., Olympics of the Mind); and (5) decision-making activities, corresponding to real-life situations, in which students need to identify goals and conditions, examine alternatives, and try out and evaluate their actions.

Critique

Enrichment methods and activities can benefit all students by extending students' knowledge and experience from mathematical computation to mathematical problem-solving and decision-making. Before adopting the enrichment approach, teachers should ensure that students have acquired basic content and skills.

The enrichment approach emphasizes the process of learning over the product of learning. Its proponents believe that skilled math performance requires the ability to conceptualize, analyze, plan, organize, and evaluate information. Thus, this approach is most closely affiliated with the active-processor perspective on learning.

◆ CONCLUSION

Theoretical perspectives are very often embedded in teaching practice. Although teachers do not typically plan their instruction by referring to theories, their support for the salient conceptual elements of one or more theories can usually be inferred from the approaches and methods they use in their day-to-day teaching. The instructional methods and approaches presented in this chapter relate in a central way to one or more of the four perspectives discussed at the beginning of the chapter, and this relationship is depicted in Table 10.16. Although each approach is primarily associated with a single theoretical perspective, teachers may incorporate aspects of other theories into their teaching practice. For example, teachers who use the sight-word approach to develop their students' word identification typically focus on word-recognition tasks involving the use of flashcards and workbook activities—an instructional orientation that is most closely related to the behavioural perspective. However, these same teachers may also incorporate problem-solving and child-centred activities in a sociocultural context, which relate to the 'active-processor,' 'developing-child,' and 'social-being' perspectives respectively. Hence, although each approach tends to have a primary theoretical orientation, the practice of these approaches do not necessarily exclude other perspectives.

It was suggested at the beginning of this chapter that in order to better meet the diverse needs of students within inclusive classrooms, teachers must be flexible and eclectic in their choice of instructional approaches and methods.

The intention of this chapter was to inform the reader regarding teaching practices and show how they are related to theoretical perspectives in order to assist the reader with respect to educational decision-making.

QUESTIONS
◆◆◆◆◆◆◆◆◆◆◆◆◆

1. What are some academic skills and student difficulties related to word identification, oral language, reading, writing, spelling, and mathematics?

2. Describe some instructional methods for improving students' performance in the above curricular areas.

3. Name some assessment methods for evaluating students' ability in the curricular areas under discussion.

4. How are instructional methods related to theoretical orientations?

5. What instructional methods and approaches are most closely associated with the active-processor perspective on learning?

◆ APPENDIX 10.1

COMMON FORMAL TESTS

No from here
- only own ref

Word Identification

Test	Grade or Age Level	Content	Administration
Silent Reading Diagnostic Test (*Balow & Hoyt, 1970*)	2-6 grades	silent reading abilities, word recognition, word analysis	group administered
Botel Reading Inventory (*Follett, 1970*)	1 - 12 grades	word recognition, phonic skills, word opposites	individually administered
McCullough Word Analysis Tests (*McCullough, 1963*)	4 - 6 grades	phonetic analysis, discrimination and matching skills	individually administered
Doren Diagnostic Reading Tests of Word Recognition (*American Guidance Service, 1973*)	1 - 9 grades	letter and word recognition, phonetic analysis, sight words	individually or group administered
Roswell-Chall Diagnostic Reading Test of Word Analysis (Revised) (*Roswell, 1978*)	1 - 4 grades	phonetic analysis, syllabication, compound words, word recognition	individually administered
Phonetics Inventory Tests (*Houghton-Mifflin, 1972*)	1 - 9 grades	phonetic analysis	group administered

Oral Language

Test	Grade or Age Level	Content	Administration
Preschool Language Scale (*Zimmerman, Steiner, & Evatt, 1979*)	1- 8 years	expressive/ receptive skills	individually administered
Test of Adolescent Language—2 (TOAL-2) (*Hammill, Brown, Larsen, & Wiederholt, 1987*)	11 -18 years	expressive/ receptive skills (vocabulary and syntax)	individually administered

Test of Language Development—Intermediate (TOLD-I) (*Hammill & Newcomer, 1982*)	8 - 12 years	expressive language	individually administered
Test of Language Development—Primary (TOLD-P) (*Hammill & Newcomer, 1982*)	4 - 9 years	phonology, syntax, semantics, pragmatics	individually administered
Carrow Elicited Language Inventory (*Carrow-Woolfolk, 1974*)	3 - 8 years	grammar skills, verb analysis	individually administered
Clinical Evaluation of Language Function (CELF) (*Wiig & Semel, 1987*)	K - 12 grades	expressive-language skills (forms, content, use)	individually or group administered
Clinical Evaluation of Language Function (CELF) Screening Tests: Elementary Level and Advanced Level (*Semel & Wiig, 1987*)	K - 12 grades	language comprehension and expression	individually administered
Goldman-Fristoe Test of Articulation (*Goldman & Fristoe, 1972*)	above age 2	articulation (initial, medial, final speech sounds)	individually administered
"Let's Talk" Inventory for Functional Communication Skills (*Wiig, 1982*)	4 - 12 grades	pragmatic abilities for oral expression	individually administered
Test of Early Language Development (*Hresko, Reid, & Hammill, 1990*)	3 - 7 years	language use (content and form)	individually administered
Brigance: Diagnostic Inventory of Early Development (*Brigance, 1979*)	preschool - 7 years	variety of oral language skills (e.g., social speech, syntax, articulation of sounds)	individually administered
Multi-level Informal Language Inventory (*Goldsworthy, 1982*)	preschool - 7 years	overview of syntax and semantic development	individually administered
Reading			
Diagnostic Reading Scales (*Spache, 1981*)	1 - 8 grades	word recognition, phonics skills	individually administered

Durrell Analysis of Reading (*Durrell & Catterson, 1980*)	1 - 6 grades	vocabulary, spelling, phonic skills	individually administered
Gates-MacGinitie Reading Tests (*MacGinitie, 1978*)	ECS - 12 grades	vocabulary and comprehension	individually or group administered
Gates-McKillop-Horowitz Reading Diagnostic Tests (*Gates, McKillop, & Horowitz, 1981*)	1 - 6 grades	word recognition, word attack, oral reading, spelling skills	individually administered
Canadian Achievement Tests (*McGraw-Hill, 1978*)	ECS - 12 grades	pre-reading (i.e., listening for information, sound matching) and reading (phonics, vocabulary, comprehension)	group administered
Stanford Diagnostic Reading Test (*Karlson, Madden, & Gardner, 1977*)	1 - 12 grades	vocabulary, comprehension, rate of reading	individually or group administered
Canadian Test of Basic Skills (*Hieronymous, Lindquist, Hoover, & King, 1981*)	1 - 12 grades	vocabulary and reading comprehension	group administered
Brigance Diagnostic Inventory of Basic Skills (*Brigance, 1977*)	ECS - 6 grades	word recognition, vocabulary, comprehension	individually administered
Gray Oral Reading Test (*Gray & Robinson, 1967*)	1 - college grades	reading rate, accuracy, and comprehension	individually administered
Metropolitan Achievement Tests (*Prescott, Balow, Hogan, & Farr, 1980*)	ECS - 9 grades	word knowledge, word analysis, and comprehension	individually administered
Stanford Diagnostic Reading Test (*Karlsen, Madden, & Gardner, 1976*)	1 - 2 grades	vocabulary, word, sentence, and paragraph reading, comprehension	group administered
The Standard Reading Inventory (*McCracken, 1966*)	ECS - 7 grades	word recognition, oral and silent reading	individually administered

Woodcock Reading Mastery Tests (*Woodcock, 1973*)	1 - 12 grades	letter identification, word identification, word attack, word comprehension, passage comprehension	individually administered
Test of Reading Comprehension (*Brown, Hammill, & Wiederholt, 1978*)	1 - 12 grades	vocabulary, paragraph reading	individually or group administered
Classroom Reading Inventory (*Silvaroli, 1976*)	1 - 9 grades	reading capacity and level, word recognition	individually administered
Reading Placement Inventory (*Sucher & Allred, 1973*)	1 - 9 grades	word recognition, reading accuracy, comprehension	individually administered

Writing

Test of Written Language (TOWL) (*Hammill & Larsen, 1983*)	2 - 8 grades	vocabulary, spelling, word usage, style, handwriting	individually or group administered
Test of Adolescent Language (TOAL) (*Hammill, Brown, Larsen, & Weiderholt, 1980*)	7 - 12 grades	writing/vocabulary writing/grammar	individually or group administered
Metropolitan Achievement Tests (*Balow et al., 1979*)	ECS - 9 grades	punctuation, capitalization, grammar, spelling	group administered
Canadian Test of Basic Skills (*Hieronymous & King, 1973*)	1 - 8 grades	capitalization, punctuation	group administered
Test of Written English (*Anderson & Thompson, 1979*)	1 - 6 grades	capitalization, punctuation, paragraph writing	individually administered

Spelling

Peabody Individual Achievement Test (*Dunn & Markwardt, 1970*)	ECS - 12 grades	provides standard scores on letter and word identification skills	individually administered
Wide Range Achievement Test-R (*Jastak & Wilkinson, 1984*)	5 - adulthood ages	age norms on spelling ability	group administered

Canadian Test of Basic Skills (*Hieronymous et al., 1981*)	3 - 8 grades	common spelling errors (e.g., substitutions, omitted letters, and double letters)	group administered
Schonell Graded Word Spelling Tests (*Schonell, 1959*) *rev. 1965*	5 - 12 ages	"spelling quotients" related to spelling attainment	individually or group administered
Canadian Achievement Test (*McGraw-Hill, 1978*)	1 - 12 grades	measures common errors in areas of consonant phonemes/ graphemes, vowel phonemes/graphemes and morphemic units	group administered

Mathematics

Key-Math Diagnostic Arithmetic Test (*Connolly, Nachtman, & Pritcheft, 1979*)	ECS - 8 grades	math concepts, operations, and applications	individually administered
Canadian Achievement Test (*McGraw-Hill, 1983*)	ECS - 12 grades	concepts, computation, and application	group administered
Stanford Achievement Series in Arithmetic (*Kelly et al., 1964*)	1 - 10 grades	concepts and application	individually or group administered
Wide Range Achievement Test (*Jastak & Jastak, 1978*)	5 - adulthood ages	counting, number symbols, computation	individually administered
Metropolitan Achievement Tests - Arithmetic (*Durost et al., 1971*)	3 - 9 grades	computation and problem-solving skills	individually or group administered
Diagnostic Test of Arithmetic Strategies (*Ginsburg, 1983*)	1 - 6 grades	arithmetic calculations	individually or group administered
Pattern Recognition Skills Inventory (*Sternberg, 1976*)	5 - 10 ages	readiness and reasoning skills	individually administered
The Diagnostic Inventory of Basic Skills (*Brigance, 1977*)	ECS - 6 grades	concepts, operations, measurement	individually or group administered

The Diagnostic Inventory of Essential Skills (*Brigance, 1980*)	10 - 12 grades	numbers, fractions, decimals, percent, measurement, metrics, vocabulary	individually administered
Canadian Test of Basic Skills—Arithmetic (*Hieronymous et al., 1981*)	1 - 12 grades	concepts and problem-solving	individually or group administered
Stanford Diagnostic Mathematics Test (*Beatty, Madden, Gardiner, & Karlesen, 1984*)	1 - 12 grades	number system and numeration computation application	individually or group administered
The Diagnostic Mathematics Inventory (*Gessell, 1977*)	1 - 9 grades	concepts, operations, and applications	individually administered
Diagnostic Inventory of Early Development (*Brigance, 1978*)	pre-primary to primary	counting, numerals, money	individually administered
Test of Early Mathematical Abilities (*Ginsburg & Barody, 1983*)	4 - 9 ages	mathematical prerequisites	individually or group administered
Test of Mathematical Abilities (*Brown & McEntire, 1984*)	3 - 12 grades	vocabulary, computation, story problems, attitudes	group administered

REFERENCES

Alley, G. (1977). Grouping secondary learning disabled students. *Academic Therapy, 13*, 37-45.

Alley, G. R., & Deshler, D. (1979). *Teaching the learning disabled adolescent: Strategies and methods.* Denver: Love Publishing.

Andrews, J. (1984). *Exploration of study strategies used by spelling disabled children: A qualitative comparison of three teaching approaches.* Unpublished M. A. thesis, University of Alberta, Edmonton, AB.

Applebee, A. N. (1984). Writing and reasoning. *Review of Educational Research, 54*, 577-596.

Applebee, A. N., Langer, J. A., & Mullis, I. V. S. (1986). *Writing report cards.* Princeton, NJ: The Nation's Report Card, National Assessment of Educational Progress.

Ashlock, R. (1982). *Error patterns in computation: A semi-programmed approach* (3rd. ed.). Columbus, OH: Merrill.

Babbs, P. J., & Moe, A. J. (1983). Metacognition: A key for independent learning from text. *Reading Teacher, 36*(4), 422-426.

Bachor, D. G., & Crealock, C. (1986). *Instructional strategies for students with special needs.* Scarborough, ON: Prentice-Hall.

Bamberger, R. (1976). Literature and development in reading. In J.E. Merritt (Ed.), *New Horizons in reading.* Newark, DE: International Reading Association.

Barr, R. (1975). Influence of reading materials on response to printed words. *Journal of Reading Behaviour, 7*, 123-135.

Biemiller, A. (1970). Changes in the use of graphic and contextual information as functions of passage difficulty and reading achievement level. *Journal of Reading Behaviour, 11*, 308-318.

Bley, N. S., & Thornton, C. A. (1981). *Teaching mathematics to the learning disabled.* Rockville, MD: Aspen.

Block, J. (1972). Bur will they ever lern to spel korectly? *Educational Research, 14*, 171-178.

Bornstein, P. H., & Quevillon, R. P. (1976). The effects of a self-instructional package on overactive pre-school boys. *Journal of Applied Behaviour Analysis, 9*, 179-186.

Bos, C. S. (1988). Process-oriented writing: Instructional implications for mildly handicapped students. *Exceptional Children, 54*, 521-527.

Bos, C. S., & Vaughn, S. (1991). *Strategies for teaching students with learning and behaviour problems.* Boston: Allyn & Bacon.

Bott, D. A. (1988). Mathematics. In J. Wood (Ed.), *Mainstreaming: A practical guide for teachers* (pp. 7-21). Columbus, OH: Merrill.

Bradley, L. (1981). The organization of motor patterns for spelling: An effective remedial strategy for backward readers. *Developmental Medical Child Neurology, 23*, 83-91.

Bradley, L., & Bryant, P. E. (1980). Why children sometimes write words which they do not read. In U. Frith (Ed.), *Cognitive processes in spelling.* London: Academic Press.

Brown, L., & Perlmuter, L. (1971). Teaching functional reading to trainable level retarded students. *Education and Training for the Mentally Retarded, 6*, 74-84.

Burns, P. C., & Roe, B. D. (1980). *Teaching reading in today's elementary schools.* Boston: Houghton-Mifflin.

Butler, A. (1987). *Elements of whole language.* Crystal Lake, IL: Rigby Education.

Caban, J. P., Hambleton, R., Coffing, D. G., Conway, M. T., & Swaminathorp, H. (1978). Mental imagery as an approach to spelling instruction. *Journal of Experimental Education*, 15-21.

Carie, E. & Ogle, D. (1987). K-W-L plus: A strategy for comprehension and summary action. *Journal of Reading, 30*, 626-631.

Cavallaro, C. (1983). Language interventions in natural settings. *Teaching Exceptional Children, 16*, 65-70.

Collins, A., & Smith, E. (1982). Teaching the process of reading comprehension. In D. K. Detterman & R. J. Sternberg (Eds.), *How and how much can intelligence be increased?* Norwood, NJ: Ablex.

Cramer, R. A. (1982). Informal approaches to evaluate children's writing. In J. J. Pikvlski & T. Shannahan (Eds.), *Approaches to informal evaluation for reading.* Newark, DE: International Reading Association.

Dagenais, D. J., & Beadle, D. R. (1984). Written language: When and where to begin. *Topics in Language Disorders, 4*(2), 59-85.

Deno, S. L. (1987). Curriculum-based measurement. *Teaching Exceptional Children, 20*, 40-50.

Dixon, R., & Englemann, S. (1976). *Morphographic spelling.* Willowdale, ON: Science Research Association.

Donlan, D. (1975). Teaching words through sense impressions. *Language Arts, 52*, 1090-1093.

Duin, A. H., & Graves, M. F. (1987). Intensive vocabulary instruction as a pre-writing technique. *Reading Research Quarterly, 22*, 311-330.

Dunlap, W. P., & Brennan, A. H. (1979). Developing mental images of mathematical processes. *Learning Disability Quarterly, 2*(2), 89-96.

Dunlap, W. P., & McKnight, M. B. (1978). Vocabulary translations for conceptualizing math word problems. *The Reading Teacher, 32*, 183-189.

Durkin, D. (1978). *Teaching them to read* (3rd ed.). Boston: Allyn & Bacon.

Durrel, D. D. (1980). Letter name values in reading and spelling. *Reading Research Quarterly, 1*, 159-163.

Ekwall, E. E. (1981). *Locating and correcting reading difficulties* (3rd ed.). Columbus, OH: .

Ekwall, E. E., & Shanker, J. L. (1985). *Teaching reading in the elementary school.* Columbus, OH: Merrill.

Engelmann, S., & Bruner, E. (1974, 1975). *DISTAR reading.* Chicago: Science Research Associates.

Engelmann, S., & Bruner, E. (1984). *Reading mastery program: DISTAR.* Chicago: Science Research Associates.

Engelmann, S., & Carnine, D. (1981). *Corrective mathematics.* Chicago: Science Research Associates.

Englert, C. S. (1992). Writing instruction from a sociocultural perspective: The holistic, dialogic, and social enterprise of writing. *Journal of Learning Disabilities, 25*(3), 153-172.

Englert, C. S., & Raphael, T. E. (1988). Constructing well-formed prose: Process-structure and metacognitive knowledge. *Exceptional Children, 54*, 513-520.

Fernald, G. (1988). *Remedial techniques in basic school subjects.* Austin, TX: Pro-Ed (original work published in 1943).

Fitzgerald, J. (1951). *A basic life spelling vocabulary.* Milwaukee: Bruce Publishing.

Fitzgerald, J. (1955). Children's experiences in spelling. In V. Herrick & L. Jacobs (Eds.), *Children and the language arts* (Chapter 11). Englewood Cliffs, NJ: Prentice-Hall.

Forest, E. B. (1981). Visual imagery as an information processing strategy. *Journal of Learning Disabilities, 10*, 584-586.

Fuchs, L., & Fuchs, D. (1984). Curriculum-referenced assessment without measurement: How accurate for special education? *Remedial and Special Education, 5*(4), 29-32.

Fuchs, L. S., Bahr, C. M., & Rieth, H. J. (1989). Effects of goal structures and performance contingencies on the math performance of adolescents with learning disabilities. *Journal of Learning Disabilities, 22*, 554-560.

Gersten, R. (1985). Direct instruction with special education students: A review of evaluation research. *Journal of Special Education, 19*(1), 41-50.

Gillingham, A., & Stillman, H. (1960). *Remedial training for children with specific disability in reading, spelling, and penmanship.* Cambridge, MA: Educators' Publishing Service.

Gloeckler, T., & Simpson, C. (1988). *Exceptional students in regular classrooms: Challenges, services, and methods.* Mountain View, CA: Mayfield.

Glover, J. A., Ronning, R. R., & Bruning, R. H. (1990). *Cognitive psychology for teachers.* New York: MacMillan.

Goodman, K. (1967). Reading: A psycholinguistic guessing game. *Journal of Reading Specialist, 6*, 126-133.

Goodman, K. (1986). *What's whole in whole language?* Portsmouth, NH: Heinemann.

Goodman, K. S., & Goodman, Y. M. (1982). A whole language comprehension centred view of reading development. In L. Reed & S. Ward (Eds.), *Basic skills: Issues and choices, Volume 2* (pp. 125-134). St. Louis, MO: CEMREL.

Goodman, K. S., Goodman, Y. M., & Hood, W. J. (Eds.) (1989). *The whole language evaluation book.* Portsmouth, NH: Heinemann.

Graham, S. (1985). Evaluating spelling programs and materials. *Teaching Exceptional Children, 17*(4), 299-304.

Graham, S., & Harris, K. R. (1988). Instructional recommendations for teaching writing to exceptional students. *Exceptional Children, 54*, 506-512.

Graham, S., & Miller, L. (1980). Handwriting research and practice: A unified approach. *Focus on Exceptional Children, 13*(2), 5-16.

Graves, D. H. (1982). Break the welfare cycle: Let writers choose their topics. *A newsletter of the English composition board, University of Michigan. Eforums, 3*(2), 75.

Guerin, G. R., & Maier, A. S. (1983). *Informal assessment in education.* Palo Alto, CA: Mayfield.

Hagin, R. A. (1983). Write right or left: A practical approach to handwriting. *Journal of Learning Disabilities, 16*(5), 266-271.

Halpern, N. (1981). Mathematics for the learning disabled. *Journal of Learning Disabilities, 14*(9), 505-506.

Hammill, D. D., & Bartel, N. R. (1990). *Teaching students with learning and behaviour problems* (5th ed.). Toronto: Allyn & Bacon.

Hammill, D. D., Bartel, N. P., & Bunch, G. O. (1984). *Teaching children with learning disabilities (and/or) behaviour problems.* Boston, MA: Allyn & Bacon.

Hargrave, J. J., & Poteet, J. A. (1980). *Assessment in special education: The education evaluation.* Englewood Cliffs, NJ: Prentice-Hall.

Harris, J. (1986). A silent voice and absent ear: The role of the reader in theories of composing. *Dissertation Abstracts International, 47*, 08A (University Microfilms, No. 86-25, 625).

Harste, J. (1990). Jerry Harste speaks on reading and writing. *The Reading Teacher, 43*, 316-318.

Heckelman, R. G. (1969). A neurological impress method of remedial reading instruction. *Academic Therapy, 4*, 277-282.

Heimlich, J. E., & Pittleman, S. D. (1986). *Semantic mapping: Classroom applications.* Newark, DL: International Reading Association.

Henderson, E. (1985). *Teaching spelling.* Boston: Houghton-Mifflin.

Hendrickson, D. (1967). Spelling a visual skill. *Academic Therapy Quarterly, 3*, 39-42.

Holland, A. (1975). Language therapy for children: Some thoughts on context and content. *Journal of Speech and Hearing Disorders, 40*, 514-523.

Humes, A. (1983). Research on the composing process. *Review of Educational Research, 53*, 201-216.

Isaacson, S. L. (1988). Effective instruction in written language. In E. L. Meyen, G. A. Vergason, & R. J. Whelan (Eds.), *Effective instructional strategies for exceptional children* (pp. 288-306). Denver, CO: Love Publishing.

Jamison, P. J., & Shevitz, L. A. (1985). RATE: A reason to read. *Teaching Exceptional Children, 18*(1), 46-51.

Johnson, D. D., & Moe, A. J. (1980). Current approaches, Part 2. In P. Lamb & R. Arnold (Eds.), *Teaching reading: Foundations and strategies* (2nd ed.). Belmont, CA: Wadsworth.

Johnson, M., Kress, K., & Pikulski, J. (1987). *Informal reading inventories.* Newark, DE: International Reading Association.

Katsiyannis, A., & Prillaman, D. (1990). Teaching math using regular curricula. *Teaching Exceptional Children, 23*(1), 26-29.

Kosiewicz, M. M., Hallahan, D. P., Lloyd, J., & Graves, A. W. (1982). Effects of self-instruction and self-correction procedures on handwriting performance. *Learning Disability Quarterly, 5*, 71-78.

Kranes, J. E. (1980). *The hidden handicap.* New York: Simon & Schuster.

Krause, L. A. (1983). Teaching the second "R." *The Directive Teacher, 5*(1), 30.

Langone, J. (1986). *Teaching retarded learners: Curriculum and methods for improving instruction.* Boston: Allyn & Bacon.

Langone, J. (1990). *Teaching students with mild and moderate learning problems.* Toronto: Allyn & Bacon.

Lee, L. (1974). *Developmental sentence analysis.* Evanston, IL: Northwestern University Press.

Lee, L., & Carter, S. (1971). Developmental sentence scoring: A clinical procedure for estimating syntactic development in children's spontaneous speech. *Speech and Hearing Disorders, 36*, 315-341.

Leon, J. A., & Pepe, H. J. (1983). Self-instructional training: Cognitive behaviour modification for remediating arithmetic deficits. *Exceptional Children, 50*, 54-60.

Lerner, J. (1985). *Learning disabilities: Theories, diagnosis, and teaching strategies* (4th ed). Boston: Houghton-Mifflin.

Lerner, J. (1988). *Learning disabilities: Theories, diagnosis, and teaching strategies* (5th ed.). Boston: Houghton-Mifflin.

Lorenz, L., & Vockell, E. (1979). Using the neurological impress method with learning disabled readers. *Journal of Learning Disabilities, 12*, 420-422.

Mandell, C. J., & Gold, V. (1984). *Teaching handicapped students.* New York: West Publishing.

Mastropieri, M. A., & Scruggs, T. E. (1987). *Effective instruction for special education.* Boston: College-Hill.

Matthes, C. (1977). *How children are taught to read.* Lincoln, NE: Professional Educators' Publications.

McKeough, A. (1991). Three perspectives on learning and instruction. In A. McKeough & J. Lupart (Eds.), *Toward the practice of theory-based instruction: Current cognitive theories and their educational promise* (pp. 1-14). Hillsdale, NJ: Lawrence Erlbaum.

Mercer, C. D., & Mercer, A. R. (1985). *Teaching students with learning problems* (2nd ed.). Columbus, OH: Merrill.

Mercer, C. D., Mercer, A. R., & Bott, D. A. (1984). *Self-correcting learning materials for the classroom.* Columbus, OH: Merrill.

Meichenbaum, D. (1977). *Cognitive behaviour modification.* New York: Plenum.

Meichenbaum, D. (1980). A cognitive behavioural perspective on intelligence. *Intelligence, 4*, 271-283.

Meichenbaum, D., & Goodman, J. (1971). Training impulsive children to talk to themselves. *Journal of Abnormal Psychology*, 77, 115-126.

Mulcahy, R., Andrews, J., Janzen, H., French, C., French, F., Zingle, H. (1991). *Learning disabilities: A resource for teachers* (draft ed). University of Alberta, Edmonton, AB, Canada.

Mulcahy, R., Marfo, K., Peat, D., & Andrews, J. (1987). *SPELT: A strategies program for effective learning and thinking: A teacher's manual.* Cognitive Education Project: University of Alberta, Edmonton, AB.

Ogle, D. (1986). The K-W-L: A teaching model that develops active reading of expository text. *The Reading Teacher, 39,* 564-570.

Olson, D. R., Torrance, N., & Hildegard, A. (1985). *Literacy, language, and learning.* New York: Cambridge University Press.

Pearson, P. D., & Fielding, L. (1982). Research update: Listening comprehension. *Language Arts, 52,* 617-629.

Personkee, C., & Yee, A. H. (1971). *Comprehensive spelling instruction: Theory, research, and application.* Scranton Educational Publishers.

Petrosky, A. (1982). From story to essay: Reading and writing. *College Composition and Communication, 33,* 19-36.

Philips, L. M. (1986). *Using children's literature to foster written language development* (ERIC Document Reproduction Service, No. ED 276 027).

Piaget, J. (1970). *The science of education of the psychology of the child.* New York: Grossman.

Polloway, E. A., Patton, J. R., Payne, J. S., & Payne, R. A. (1989). *Strategies for teaching learners with special needs* (4th ed.). Toronto: Merrill.

Reutzel, D. R. (1986). Closing in on comprehension: The cloze story map. *The Reading Teacher,* 524-529.

Rhodes, L. K., & Dudley-Marling, C. (1988). *Readers and writers with a difference.* Portsmouth, NH: Heinemann.

Salend, S. J. (1990). *Effective mainstreaming.* New York: Macmillan.

Schwartz, S. E., & Budd, D. (1981). Mathematics for handicapped learners: A functional approach for adolescents. *Focus on Exceptional Children, 13*(7), 1-12.

Schwartz, S., & Doehring, D. A. (1977). The developmental study of children's ability to acquire knowledge of spelling patterns. *Developmental Psychology, 13,* 419-420.

Sedlak, R. A., & Fitzmaurice, A. M. (1981). Teaching arithmetic. In J. M. Kauffman & D. P. Hallahan (Eds.), *Handbook of special education* (pp. 475-490). Englewood Cliffs, NJ: Prentice-Hall.

Sharples, M. (1985). *Cognition, computers, and creative writing.* West Sussex, England: Ellis Norwood.

Shook, S. (1982). *The relationship between the written language of grade one and two children and their reading ability, IQ, and attitudes.* Unpublished M. A. thesis, University of Victoria, Victoria, BC.

Silbert, J., Carnine, D., & Stein, M. (1981). *Direct instruction mathematics.* Columbus, OH: Merrill.

Smith, F. (1982). *Writing and the writer.* New York: Holt, Rinehart & Winston.

Smith, R. J., & Barrett, T. C. (1979). *Teaching reading in middle grades.* Boston, MA: Addison-Wesley.

Snell, M. E. (1983). Functional reading. In M. E. Snell (Ed.), *Systematic instruction of the moderately and severely handicapped* (2nd ed.) (pp. 324-385). Columbus, OH: Merrill.

Speckman, J. J., & Roth, F. P. (1984). Intervention strategies for learning disabled children with oral communication disorders. *Learning Disability Quarterly,* 7, 7-18.

Stahl, S. A., & Fairbanks, M. M. (1986). The effects of vocabulary instruction: A model based meta-analysis. *Review of Reading Research, 56,* 72-110.

Sternberg, L., & Fair, G. W. (1982). Mathematics, programs and materials. In T. Miller & E. Davis (Eds.), *The mildly handicapped student* (pp. 345-366). New York: Grune & Stratton.

Sternberg, L., & Mauser, A. (1975). The LD child and mathematics. *Academic Therapy, 10,* 481-488.

Sternberg, R. J. (1987). Most vocabulary is learned from context. In M. G. McKeown & M. E. Curtis (Eds.), *The nature of vocabulary acquisition* (pp. 89-105). Hillsdale, NJ: Lawrence Erlbaum.

Stowitschek, C. E., & Jobes, N. K. (1977). Getting the bugs out of spelling: Or an alternative to the spelling bee. *Teaching Exceptional Children, 9,* 74-76.

Swaby, B. E. R. (1984). *Teaching and learning reading: A pragmatic approach.* Boston: Little, Brown.

Tarver, S., & Dawson, M. (1978). Modality preference and the teaching of reading: A review. *Journal of Learning Disabilities, 11,* 5-17.

Temple, C., & Gillet, J. W. (1984). *Language arts: Learning processes and teaching practices.* Boston: Little, Brown.

Thomas, V. (1979). *Teaching spelling.* Gage.

Thornton, C. A., Tucker, B. F., Dossey, J. A., & Bazik, E. F. (1983). *Teaching mathematics to children with special needs.* Menlo Park, CA: Addison-Wesley.

Tyack, D., & Gottsleben, R. (1974). *Language sampling, analysis, and training: A handbook for teachers and clinicians.* Palo Alto, CA: Consulting Psychologists' Press.

Underhill, R., Uprichard, A., & Heddens, J. (1980). *Diagnosing mathematical difficulties.* Columbus, OH: Merrill.

Vacca, R. T. & Vacca, A. L. (1986). *Content area reading* (2nd ed.). Boston: Little, Brown.

Wallace, G., & Kauffman, J. M. (1978). *Teaching children with learning problems.* Columbus, OH: Merrill.

Watson, D., & Crowley, P. (1988). How can we implement a whole language approach? In C. Weaver (Ed.), *Reading process and practice.* Portsmouth, NH: Heinemann.

Weiner, E .S. (1980). Diagnostic evaluation of writing skills. *Journal of Learning Disabilities, 13,* 48-53.

Wertsch, J. V. (1989). A sociocultural approach to mind. In W. Damon (Ed.), *Child development today and tomorrow* (pp. 14-33). San Francisco: Jossey-Bass.

West, R. P., Young, K. A., & Spooner, F. (1990). Precision teaching: An introduction. *Teaching Exceptional Children, 22*(3), 4-9.

Winzer, M. (1989). *Closing the gap: Special learners in regular classrooms.* Toronto: Copp Clark Pitman.

Wong, B. Y. L. (1991). Three conceptual perspectives on the connections between reading and writing processes. In A. McKeough & J. Lupart (Eds.), *Toward the practice of theory-based instruction: Current cognitive theories and their educational promise* (pp. 66-91). Hillsdale, NJ: Lawrence Erlbaum.

Wood, J. W. (1989). *Mainstreaming: A practical approach for teachers.* Toronto: Merrill.

Zigmond, N., Vallecorsa, A., & Silverman, R. (1983). *Assessment for instructional planning in special education.* Englewood Cliffs, NJ: Prentice-Hall.

PROGRAM PLANNING

CHAPTER
11

CHAPTER OBJECTIVES

To outline briefly curricular expectancies for all students.

To emphasize the importance of matching student needs with educational resources.

To discuss how to evaluate programs and materials.

To extend the reader's instructional repertoire for teaching basic subjects.

To underline the importance of interacting effectively with all members of the inclusive team in working with special-needs students.

Melinda, a happy, enthusiastic child, was very excited about moving from a French immersion class to an all-English class. After the first week of class, Melinda's mother, Mrs. Dane, made an appointment to see Melinda's new Grade 3 teacher, Mrs. Goertsky. She told Mrs. Goertsky that over the summer Melinda had been identified as having attention deficit disorder, although she was not hyperactive. Melinda had also experienced some difficulty learning to read and write in the French immersion program, which is why Mrs. Dane had transferred her to an all-English school. Mrs. Dane wanted Mrs. Goertsky to know about Melinda's difficulty because her daughter's attentional problems were not obvious.

After the appointment, Mrs. Goertsky made a point of observing Melinda carefully. Melinda was always very much attuned to and involved in any class discussion. She always raised her hand to speak, waited until she was called upon, and was always appropriate in her responses. Mrs. Goertsky did not see any evidence of Melinda's attentional problems when the class was involved in group discussions.

When the class was asked to do work individually, however, Mrs. Goertsky observed that, while Melinda would work quietly at her seat without disturbing others, she did not complete very much of her work. Asked to work on fifteen math problems, she would often finish no more than five. (Mrs. Goertsky often allowed her to take uncompleted problems home to work on with her mother.) Asked to write a story or short entry for her journal or to complete an exercise that included fill-in-the-blanks, Melinda would often sit quietly at her desk and not start the activity until Mrs. Goertsky came over and helped her begin the exercise. Mrs. Goertsky made a point of doing this frequently. Melinda seemed to appreciate the help, but she still had difficulty completing written assignments. She would write neatly and carefully, but, at the end of the forty-minute writing period, she would often have written only two sentences. Mrs. Goertsky was pleased that Melinda did not appear to be too discouraged with the amount that she had written.

For silent reading time, Melinda would always choose a Grade 3 reading-level book. When Mrs. Goertsky discussed the reading with her, Melinda was always able to talk about the story in general terms, but often failed to recall the details of the story. Melinda also avoided reading aloud to Mrs. Goertsky, saying that she preferred silent reading.

Toward the end of the first reporting period, Mrs. Goertsky had observed Melinda to be a very cooperative and friendly student, who participated well in group activities but needed a lot of teacher direction and support to complete her individualized work. Deciding that she needed more information about Melinda's reading, Mrs. Goertsky related her concerns about Melinda to the resource teacher. The resource teacher assessed Melinda's reading and found that, although Melinda actively sought to derive meaning from her reading (using pictures, cues, etc.), she was only reading at a beginning Grade 2 level.

Both teachers agreed that it was important for Melinda to improve her knowledge of oral and written English. First, they decided that Mrs. Goertsky should use webbing to introduce topics. Webbing would help all the students in the class to activate their prior knowledge of the subject and link new information with old, and it would be especially beneficial to Melinda in providing her with key vocabulary.

To assist Melinda with her individual work, Mrs. Goertsky began to ask her to verbalize what she thought she needed to do before she left the group to go to her desk. In this way, Melinda was encouraged to better attend to the directions that were provided to the whole class. Before beginning any writing assignments, Melinda was asked to discuss her ideas with another student and then make a web of the ideas. This strategy worked well with Melinda because she was very social and liked to talk a lot; some of her classmates were asked to use the same approach. In addition to these strategies, Mrs. Goertsky taught Melinda a problem-solving approach to help her when she had difficulties before asking for teacher assistance.

Melinda was encouraged to choose readers that were at her own level. As she was very friendly and liked to help others, she was allowed to read to the younger children in the school, an activity she really enjoyed.

Mrs. Goertsky and the resource teacher also read with Melinda individually a few times a week. During these times, both teachers would encourage her to think and talk about what she was going to read before she started, and to ask questions and talk about her reading as she was reading.

Melinda responded well to these interventions. She enjoyed the individual attention that she was receiving from the resource teacher and Mrs. Goertsky, and she liked to read with her Grade 1 buddy. She was beginning to initiate her work without individualized teacher help, and used the talking and webbing approach before starting writing assignments. But there was no quantitative increase in the amount she actually wrote. Melinda still did not complete her math work in class time, and continued to take her unfinished assignments home.

At the end of the first reporting period, Mrs. Dane came in for her parent-teacher interview. She told Mrs. Goertsky that although she was very pleased about Melinda's positive attitude, she found her daughter's approach to homework frustrating. Mrs. Dane explained, to Mrs. Goertsky's surprise, that she would often spend two hours nightly with Melinda working on her math assignments.

Mrs. Goertsky discussed the problem with the resource teacher, who told her that many students with attentional problems also had difficulty with task completion.

Mrs. Goertsky realized that she needed either to give Melinda more class time to complete her work, or to cut back on the amount of work that she required of her. She decided to reduce Melinda's math assignments by half and to encourage her to finish her work during school time. With respect to writing, because Melinda was asked to talk and web before starting to write, she would need more in-school time to complete her written assignments.

Her individualized program seemed to have positive effects on Melinda's academic achievement. Her reading improved, she completed all of her math work in class, and she continued to be an enthusiastic student. Although she still required considerable teacher support and cues to keep her on task when the class was working individually, Melinda was able to complete more of her written assignments. She was very proud that two of her stories were published in class that year.

◆ INTRODUCTION

In many provinces and territories of Canada, provincial/territorial legislation and the Canadian Charter of Rights and Freedoms have expanded the concept of placement of special-needs students to include provision for individual programs. In this chapter, we discuss programming for the special-needs student in terms of curriculum requirements; designing programs; selecting and evaluating materials; monitoring and evaluating programs; and recording and reporting educational progress to members of the inclusive team.

◆ CURRICULUM

Curricular scope and sequence charts, developed by the ministries of education at both the provincial and territorial levels, are available to all schools. These documents describe expected learning outcomes for students at a specific age or stage of development. For example, in several provinces, the specific mathematics competencies for numbers expected at the primary level include the following:

1. Understand and use associative property, communicative property, and identity property.
2. Do addition and subtraction facts to four digits with regrouping, multiplication facts to fifty, and division facts to fifty with remainders.
3. Count to 9999 and do place value to 9999.

   Competencies expected in the junior grades include:

1. Recite all multiplication tables.
2. Add, multiply, and divide using decimals, fractions, and mixed numbers.
3. Use factoring and prime numbers in multiplication.
4. Work with decimals to the tens of thousands.
5. Count to millions.
6. Count by ones through to tens.
7. Calculate place value to billions.
8. Express data as a percentage.
9. Find ratio of two sets.
10. List factors and multiples of numbers.
11. Convert between decimals, fractions, and percentages.
12. Write decimal numbers using powers to ten.
13. Round off numbers to specific place value.
14. Write sets of equivalent numbers.
15. Perform calculations on a series of operations.

   The program that is developed for each student is based on a match between individual strengths and weaknesses and the competencies defined in each area.

At the intermediate level, it is not unusual to find the curriculum emphasis in a subject like history to be on such topics as local community studies, native communities, the rebellion in Upper and Lower Canada, shaping the nation, the nation expands (1867-1914), and a changing society (1870-1920). In addition, there is an increasing focus at this level on cognitive skills, which would include focus, organize, locate, record, evaluate/assess, synthesize and conclude, apply, and communicate. These skills are expected to prepare students for the high-school curriculum, and subsequently for post-secondary school and employment.

In many schools, the paradigm shift from resource program to inclusive education (discussed at length in earlier chapters) has encouraged the integration of more students on a full-time basis. The inclusive team needs to be aware of the curriculum in each subject if it is to be effective in planning each student's educational program.

◆ PROGRAM DESIGN

A key aspect of programming is the individual education plan (IEP), which usually contains placement and personnel information, specific objectives that reflect the student's individual needs, time frames for meeting those objectives, and evaluation strategies (Bachor & Crealock, 1986) (see Table 11.1a and 11.1 b for sample IEPs). While the IEP is a guide and not a binding contract, it is important to indicate how and when its goals are to be reviewed. The IEP should be reviewed by year end at the latest, and sooner if the program is new and the match between the student's needs and the curriculum has still to be finalized, or if the school year is organized around two semesters, as illustrated in Table 11.1a.

Having addressed the basic concept of the IEP, we turn to more specific elements that are involved in successful programming, namely, remediation of reading, writing, and mathematics; homework and strategy training; behavioural approaches and social skills; and modifications to the program.

ACADEMIC SKILLS

Reading

Reading involves abilities in decoding, comprehension, and speed or rate of processing. Although all three skills are important, unless a student can decode the printed symbols into meaningful language, reading is impossible.

◆ Autoskill: a highly structured computer software program that identifies and provides training for various types of reading difficulties

Autoskill

Fiedorowicz (1986) developed a highly structured computerized program called **Autoskill**, which focuses on decoding (software packages on comprehension and mathematics are now being piloted in both Canada and the

Table 11.1a

Individual Educational Plan

Name: Naomi C.

Grade: 10

Time Period: September through January

Objectives:

1. To master the creative problem-solving (CPS) model; to apply its use in at least two subjects.
2. To become more outgoing in regular class.
3. To show your leadership by working with Nick in Grade 9 English (spend two, one-half hour sessions per week with him). Develop support experiences to complement "Who Has Seen the Wind."
4. Continue with narrative writing.

Person Responsible	*Time Period*	*Evaluation*
1. Mr. Smith (Resource teacher) Mrs. Haggerty (Science teacher) Mr. Szarbo (History teacher)	September to October 30 November to January	Teach and observe mastery of CPS Use of CPS in first-term assignments
2. Naomi Resource teacher	Throughout term	Self-evaluation Discussion with resource teacher
3. Naomi Miss Niri (Naomi's English teacher)	Throughout term	Naomi's knowledge of novel Monthly discussion of tutoring with Miss Niri
4. Naomi Mr. Smith (Resource) Miss Niri (Naomi's English teacher)	Throughout term	Observe development of writing

Signatures: _____   _____

                           Naomi   Teacher

Parents: _____   September 13, 1993

United States). The Autoskill program includes the identification of reading difficulties through computerized testing, profile analysis of different subtypes of reading difficulties, and subsequent training with programs specific to each of the three major reading disabilities identified. In addition, Autoskill features automaticity, attempts to integrate task- and process-oriented models, and includes an extensive record-keeping system for teachers.

The three reading subtypes identified in Autoskill are: Type O, which is characterized by problems in oral reading of words and syllables; type A, which indicates difficulties in auditory and visual matching of letters, syllables, and words; and type S, which indicates students who are poor in visual and auditory matching of syllables and words. The Autoskill program allows a teacher to specify the decoding problems of a special-needs student, and

Table 11.1b
Individual Educational Plan

Date: September 13, 1992
Pupil: Martha Smith   Male_____ /Female__x__
Date of Birth: 76/08/01   School: Banting High School

Grade Placement: 11
Curricular focus: English, advanced level
Minutes per week: 70 minutes

Current Educational Needs:

1. Share strengths, accomplishments, and potential with classmates.
2. Enhance natural leadership abilities.
3. Enhance abilities in dramatic skills.
4. Engage in intensive work in particular fields of expertise.

Responsibility for Educational needs: Needs 1, 3—Regular Teacher
                                        Needs 2, 4—Special Education
                                                    Teacher

Review: June 3, 1993

Signature: Principal: R. Allan
               Parent: K. Giles
               Special Education Teacher: M. Clarkson
               Regular Teacher: B. Willis

then to use behavioural principles in developing an IEP for that student. Remediation for each of the subgroups would involve the following:

1. A student with oral reading difficulties (Type O) would be presented with letter names (in both upper and lower case), followed by letter sounds, then consonant, vowel (CV) and vowel, consonant (VC) syllables up to consonant, vowel, consonant, consonant syllables (CVCC) such as *bilk*, and consonant vowel, consonant, consonant words (CVCC) such as *milk*.

2. If the student's difficulties were type A, the auditory-visual matching area, the program would begin with letter name and letter sounds, and again work through to consonant vowel, consonant, consonant words.

3. Students with visual matching problems (Type S) would begin with letter names but not include letter sounds. This program would also end with consonant, vowel, consonant, consonant words.

Fiedorowicz and Trites (1986) found that students with learning disabilities, after a two-and-a-half-month training period with the Autoskill program, gained approximately one grade level in word recognition and maintained this over a four-month period; the authors attribute this to the fact that each of the three reading subtypes were programmed to match the students' difficulties.

Phonics Teaching

A second strategy for mastering decoding has been proposed by Grossen and Carnine (1993), who suggest that a phonics approach in the first two years of reading instruction is better than a whole-word approach. While there are many phonics programs, these authors recommend the following steps for effective phonics teaching:

gen

1. Introduce letter-sound correspondence in isolation.
2. Teach students to blend sounds in real words.
3. Provide immediate feedback on oral reading errors.
4. Provide extensive practice.
5. Advance to sight-word approaches in order to consolidate phonics.

Cognitive Approaches

In addition to using Autoskill or teaching phonics programs to help students master decoding, cognitive approaches can have significant impact on students' reading development. An integral part of reading programs over the last decade, cognitive approaches focus on students' awareness and self-regulation of their own cognitive processes. The two guiding principles of these approaches are: (1) teaching the student *how* to learn as well as *what* to learn; and (2) teaching students to *think* like effective readers—to plan, check, and monitor themselves during learning, performance, and problem-solving.

yes

As was mentioned in Chapter 3, one of the most successful examples of the cognitive approach is *reciprocal teaching* (Palincsar & Brown, 1984), which involves the following four stages: (1) summarizing, in which students are asked to identify the essential aspects of the paragraph and/or unit in their own words; (2) questioning, in which students are asked to answer and ask questions of who, what, when, where, how, and why in order to understand their reading; (3) predicting what will come next, and (4) clarifying, in which the meaning is made clear, and the teacher shows the student how he or she can use context (e.g., getting the student to appreciate the importance of the second sentence for providing clues as to the meaning of the first sentence in the following example—"A worm's body is very flexible. It can twist and bend very easily").

Upon being introduced to the above four stages or strategies, students begin the following instructional sequence: (1) the teacher and the pupil read the passage silently ; (2) the teacher models the above four strategies; (3) the entire class reads a new passage; and (4) the students assume the teacher's role. This instructional sequence involves a shift from teacher to student responsibility, matching demands to ability, and diagnosing thinking skills. In the following example, "Laura" takes over the teacher's role (Palincsar & Brown, 1984).

Text: The second oldest form of salt production is mining. Unlike early methods that made the work extremely dangerous and difficult, today's methods use special machinery, and salt mining is easier and safer. The old expression, "back to the salt mine" no longer applies.

Laura: Name two words that often describe mining salt in the old days.

Kim: Back to the salt mines?

Laura: No. Angela?

Angela: Dangerous and difficult.

Laura: Correct. This is all about comparing the old mining of salt and today's mining of salt.

Teacher: Beautiful!

Laura: I have a prediction to make.

Teacher: Good.

Laura: I think it might tell when salt was first discovered, well, it might tell what salt is made of now and how it's made.

Teacher: O.K. Can we have another teacher? (p. 162)

In the above session, Laura has assumed more responsibility by leading discussions, summarizing important points, and predicting what will come next. Through reciprocal teaching, teachers come to realize that by giving as much control as possible to the students, they are making students responsible for some of their own learning, thereby enabling them to participate more effectively in their academic and behavioural decisions (Church, 1991).

One practical form of remediation as it pertains to reading involves the use of **readability indexes**. The best known of these, the **Fry Index**, entails choosing three one-hundred word passages at random from a text, counting the number of sentences and syllables in each passage, and then plotting the number of sentences against the number of syllables on a readability graph to determine the readability level (see Figure 11.1). It is not unusual in Grade 7 history to find that the readability level of four different texts ranges from Grade 6 through to college. Once the readability levels of various texts have been determined, students can be matched with texts on the basis of their reading ability (Fry, n.d.).

Another functional measure is to determine the speed at which a student can read. To accomplish this, the teacher has the student read out loud, and then compares his or her reading speed against median rates of reading for different grade levels, as shown in Table 11.2.

◆ **readability index**: an approach used to determine a text's level of difficulty

◆ **Fry Index**: a readability index in which the number of sentences and syllables of randomly chosen passages are charted on a readability graph to determine the readability level of the text

Table 11.2				
Median Rates of Reading (words per minute)				
Grade	2	4	6	8	12
Median Rate	86	155	206	237	251

Source: From Harris and Sipay (1980).

Figure 11.1

Graph for Estimating Readability

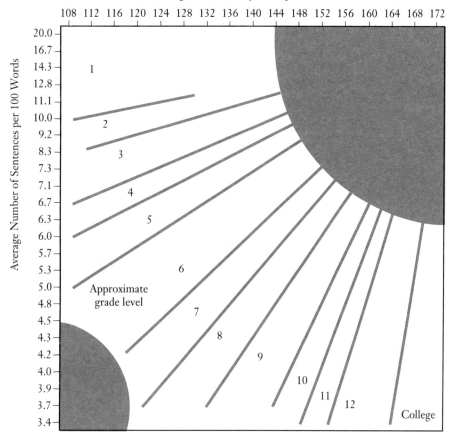

From Fry (n.d.).

One way to consistently build up reading speed is to have students read aloud for one minute every day, count the number of words read, and plot them on a graph. Indications of progress are motivating for the student, and the graph can be used as an assessment measure by the teacher.

Writing

Cognitive and Technical Approaches

Many special-needs students have difficulties with both technical and compositional aspects of writing. On the composition side, problems of quantity (too little) and quality are often evident. One approach to encouraging students to write more interesting stories is the **Grid Model** developed by

just this

♦ Grid Model: a cognitive approach to story writing in which story components are presented and developed in the form of a grid

Crealock (1993). The size of the grid should reflect the student's current level of writing. Across the top of the grid are basic components of the story (e.g., beginning, end, main character, plot, place, time, and so on). Along the vertical, students are asked to brainstorm specific content. For example, a grid may contain five horizontal story components, and ten specific vertical examples, which would yield a 5 x 10 grid. A frequently used grid is the 7 x 10, or the telephone grid, which allows random numbers and students' telephone numbers to be used simultaneously. The Grid Model involves developing the grid, listing random numbers, and then completing a worksheet that includes a specific formula for each student. Following that, students can work alone, in pairs, or in small groups. Using the example of the 5 x 5 grid, shown in Table 11.3, if the student's five random numbers were 45131, he or she would write a story in which the hero was Gretzky, the plot was passing science, the place was a car wash, the time was 2:30 p.m., and the animal was a toad. Although these elements are individually familiar, writing a narrative combining them effectively would demand a creative effort.

Table 11.3
The Grid Model

Main Character (Hero/Heroine)	Plot	Place	Time	Animal
1. Pete	1. mystery	1. car wash	1. spring	1. toad
2. Sam	2. solving sadness	2. Calabogi Hills	2. midnight	2. deer
3. My teacher	3. doing your job	3. back seat of a car	3. 2.30 p.m.	3. dog
4. Gretzky	4. romance	4. school	4. 2001	4. dinosaur
5. My girlfriend	5. passing science	5. Banff	5. 1914	5. worm

read

The Grid Model is one of several cognitive approaches to story writing, and is an example of process writing (Graves & Hansen, 1983). Another somewhat structured approach to narrative is found in Stein and Trabasso (1982), who present eight different types of stories:

1. A story with no structure.
2. A story that is basically a descriptive sequence, which may include a description of an object, place, character, and/or a sequence of events that a character may be involved in.
3. A story with an action sequence that has a chronological order.
4. A story with a reactive sequence (i.e., changes or events cause other changes in the story).
5. A story that contains simple and multiple episodes and an initiating event that is followed by a consequence. In this story, a goal may be either

stated or inferred, and there may be more than one simple episode. Complete and multiple episodes have beginnings, goals, and well-established characters.

6. A story with causal relations (e.g., between goals—and attempts to meet them—and consequences).
7. Stories with simple, complete, and multiple episodes that include characters, temporal relations, causal relations between goals and consequences, and efforts to achieve an appropriate ending.
8. A story that contains complete and multiple episodes in which obstacles are presented, as well as all of the features described in story types 1 to 7.

A second-level story would look something like this:

1. The old lady is old.
2. And her birthday is May 30.
3. She is very old.
4. And she has grey hair.
5. She lives in a small house.
6. The end.

As can be seen, the above narrative is basically a descriptive sequence with essentially simple sentences. A much more complex narrative would be one that involves simple, complete, and multiple episodes, as exemplified in the following:

1. One day Mrs. Smith was having a baby.
2. Mr. Smith didn't know what to do.
3. He had to find someone to stay with the kids.
4. So he called the grandparents.
5. And they came from Halifax and picked up the two kids, the dog, and the cat, and took them back to their home.
6. And the baby was born.
7. The family was happy with the new baby.

The preceding narrative is short and not very smoothly written, but it does include all the parts characteristic of the structural properties of the seventh level of the story grammar (McLurg, 1990).

The concept of story grammar is useful for remediation of various types. A teacher could increase the number of story elements, and try to slowly improve the quality of the narrative from the first to the eighth type. Teachers could also use story guides with software (Persons, The Missing Link, Macroclose) and involve students with scrambled stories, using either pen and pencil or computers.

The technical components of written work can be improved through either a computer or a pen-and-pencil approach. If the student is using a pen-and-pencil approach, each sentence should be written on one strip of paper. This allows the teacher to move the sentences around if the student has not organized them in proper sequence and/or move them to indicate to the student that he or she has not written enough to explain how the plot advanced from one aspect to another. Once the student has organized an effective story, he or she can work to correct each sentence technically before writing a final copy. If the student is using a word-processing program, the basic approach is the same, although the correction of technical aspects is expedited if the computer has a spelling, grammar, and/or punctuation check. Either of the above approaches tends to yield a longer, more creative product than does the instruction to "write an interesting story," without additional support (Bachor & Crealock, 1986).

Mathematics

Two essential components of remedial mathematics are drill and practice exercises, which help students in fluency areas, and more cognitively structured activities that address thinking and accuracy.

Drill-and-practice exercises are important if students are to establish *automaticity* and internalize basic facts, which is necessary if they are to solve problems without using too much working memory on basic computational elements. The concept of automaticity has been found to be integral to the basic structure of mathematical thinking. Several of the computer approaches to drill and practice (Semmel, Semmel, Gerber, & Karp, 1990) reflect a concern with devising software best suited to effective learning. Students often react best to fairly simple software packages when developing their essential mathematics skills. In fact, worksheets, not unlike the seatwork sheets used by many students, can be easily adapted to the computer. Teachers should use drill-and-practice materials that are sufficiently interesting to keep students on task when developing basic computational skills. One way of introducing fun into practice is to use card games and card tricks, as described by Golick (1973, 1986, 1987) and presented in Table 11.4.

Although drill-and-practice exercises are probably the core of any remedial program for special-needs students—from kindergarten to Grade 6, and even beyond in some cases—the more cognitively based approaches to remedial mathematics are also of benefit to the student. As discussed below, these approaches include teaching estimation, showing students relationships among numbers, and using problem solving and thinking skills to solve problems.

Estimation

With the introduction of calculators into the mathematics class, it is essential that students know how to estimate. Teaching estimation can involve: emphasizing to students the utility of rounding off so that they are working with tens rather than with units; encouraging students to estimate simply by counting the number of places in the addition or multiplication numbers; and giving consideration to metacognitive approaches. The latter approach

Table 11.4
Calculation Card

Procedure	Example
1. Student Behaviours	
a. Draw a card	Queen of Spades
(cards = own value)	Card Value = 12
Jack = 11, Queen = 12, King = 13)	
b. Multiply denomination x 2	12 x 2 = 24
c. Add 3	24 + 3 = 27
d. Multiply answer x 5	27 x 5 = 135
e. Add 1 if clubs, 2 if diamonds, 3 if	135 + 4 = 139
hearts, 4 if spades	
f. Say number aloud.	139!
2. Teacher Behaviours	
g. Subtract 15 from total	139 - 15 = 124
h. Last digit in new number = suit	4 = spades
i. First digits(s) = denomination	12 = queen
j. Say card chosen	Queen of Spades
3. Skills Supported:	
Adding	
Subtracting	
Multiplying	

Source: Adapted from Golick (1973).

is exemplified by the six different methods that Manang, Slemon, and Martin (1991) discovered when observing older students count by thinking aloud or problem-solving orally:

1. *Subarea method.* The student divides a design into x number of parts, counts the number of dots in each part, and adds or multiplies by x.
2. *Scanning method.* The student counts out a certain number, looks for other areas that contain about as many numbers, and then adds or multiplies.
3. *Count-and-add method.* The student counts as many numbers as possible, then adds across the design.
4. *Comparison strategy.* The student compares the design with others that he or she knows, which yields an approximate answer.
5. *Guessing method.* The student lacks an adequate strategy to bring to the problem but hopes that his or her guess is a reasonable estimate.
6. *Counting.* The student counts as many numbers as he or she can in the time allowed for finding the correct estimation.

Although students may prefer another strategy, it is better to teach the first or second for maximum effectiveness.

Teaching Number Relationships

Another way of encouraging students to work with numbers cognitively is to encourage them to see the relationships among numbers. An example would be the concept of doubles. Many students seem able to solve with relative ease problems that contain doubles. For most students, 6 + 6 = 12 is easier to solve than 5 + 7 = 12, even though both problems contain the same number of items. However, if students can be shown that 5 + 7 = 6 + 6 = 12, this interim step reduces the time required to find the correct answer. Another way of using number relationships is to show students how tens can work to their advantage. For example, expanding 9 + 6 to 10 + 5 = 15 seems to facilitate the problem-solving for students (Bachor & Crealock, 1986).

The nine times table enables students to explore number relationships in several ways. If the teacher writes out the multiplication table from 9 x 1 = 9 right through to $9 \times 10 = 90$ on a sheet or chalkboard, the following patterns become apparent:

1. As you advance through the nine times table, the tens are always increased by one and the units are always decreased by one.
2. The 10 trick, e.g., $9 \times 6 = (10 \times 6) - 6 = 54$.
3. The answer in the nine times table always adds up to nine (e.g., $9 \times 4 = 36$ and 3 + 6 = 9, $7 \times 9 = 63$ and 6 + 3 = 9, and so on).

The above approach to the nine times table not only facilitates computation but also gives the student a means of checking his or her answer.

The Problem-Solving Approach

Another way of introducing mathematics from a cognitive perspective is to show students how to use a problem-solving approach. Crealock (1981) uses a creative problem-solving approach that incorporates fact-finding, idea-finding, and solution-finding (see Figure 11.2). This approach is of particular benefit to older students who have not had success with drill and practice. Finally, a self-evaluation checklist, as shown in Table 11.5, can introduce metacognition into the program by prompting students to use cognitive skills as they work.

Homework

Homework for the special-needs learner has been an issue of debate over the past few decades, with some educators arguing that the daily academic routine is sufficiently demanding and that these students need time to relax, and to engage in sports and in other activities. Other educators have suggested that special-needs students require opportunities to develop social and physical skills to compensate for their poor academic skills. Recently, however, homework has come to be seen as a means of improving the quality of work

Figure 11.2

Cognitive Approach

Original problem: Mike went to visit a farm. He saw lots of animals running around. He counted 60 heads and 140 legs. The farm only had chickens and rabbits. How many of each kind of animal did he have?

Fact-finding	Idea-finding	Solution-finding

2 legs—chicken
 	
4 legs—rabbit
 	
140 legs all together
 	
60 animals all together
	1. 70 of each animal
	2. kill while counting
	3. count them as they go by
	4. divide them
	5. count the eggs
	6. stamp the chickens
	7. put a clamp on each animal
	8. tag them
	9. chicken—2 legs, 1 head
	10. 90 chickens
	11. 40 of each kind
	12. 30 of each kind
	13. 40 of one, 20 of other
	14. cut off heads & legs &
	    put in bag
	15. draw 60 circles (heads)
	— put 2 legs for each head
	— 20 legs left
	— put 2 more legs on as many
	    animals as possible
	16. get more rabbits
	17. kill some chickens
	18. half are chickens and
	    half are rabbits
	19. divide 60 heads into
	    140 feet
	20. try different numbers
	    until one works
	21. ask the farmer how many
	    he had
	22. ask the chickens how many
	    of them there are
	23. look at the rabbit chicken
	    foot ratio 4:2
		1. 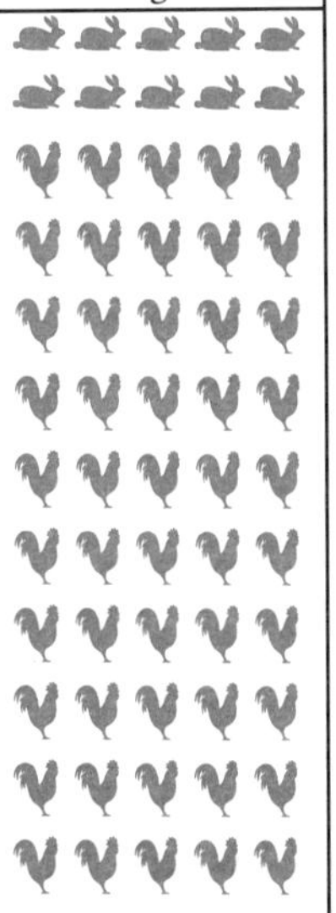
		
		10 rabbits
		50 chickens
		
		2. a form of trial
		   and error
		3. total animals = 60
		   chickens = x
		   rabbits = 60 - x
		$2x + 4(60 - x) = 140$ legs
		$2x + 240 - 4x = 140$
		$100 = 2x$
		$50 = x$
		
		∴ there are 50 chickens
		   and 10 rabbits

produced by special-needs students (Heller, Spooner, Anderson, & Mims, 1988).

The stages of learning include *acquisition*, *proficiency*, *maintenance*, and *transfer*. Mims, Harper, Armstrong, and Savage (1991) have developed a model that indicates how homework can be integrated into the IEP of each special-needs student. At the acquisition stage, special education teachers have primary responsibility for lesson planning and skills development, which may be taught in the regular and/or resource class, depending on the placement philosophy of the school. Once the student has acquired a skill with 80 to 90 percent accuracy, he or she must be given time to become

Table 11.5 Student Self-Evaluation on Learning Mathematics			
Question	Yes	Sometimes	No
1. Do I believe I can remember the multiplication tables?			
2. Do I use memory tricks?			
3. Do I organize on paper how I solve problems?			
4. Do I organize in my mind how I solve problems?			
5. Do I link what I already know to what I am learning?			
6. Do I keep practicing what I am learning until it is "overlearned"?			

Source: Adapted from "Adult Basic Literacy Assessment Kit," B.C. Ministry of Education, 1981.

proficient, to maintain accuracy, and to increase speed of response. At this point, drill, games, application, and homework are all needed.

Homework must be planned by both regular and resource teachers so that students have an opportunity to consolidate the goals of their IEPs. As discussed in detail in Chapter 7, parents need to be involved in decisions about materials required for homework completion, scheduled time and place, supervision of homework, positive atmosphere, noise level, and monitoring or help if needed. Following the proficiency stage, continued review is needed to support maintenance and transfer of skills. Intermittent review, timed drills, and modification may be applied as needed. Homework can support each stage of learning if assignments are matched to academic concept as well as to students' functional level and attention span. Finally, homework should be monitored continually by both parents and teachers, evaluated daily, and presented in a manner that is consistent with current teaching.

Strategy Training

◆ Herringbone method: a structured approach to note-taking that involves the charting of main idea, supporting detail, subdetails, and factual data

Many students need to practice study skills such as making daily classroom notes. This need can be met by using the **Herringbone method**, which asks (and answers) the basic who, why, where, when, how, and what questions (see Figure 11.3). The method addresses four aspects—main idea, supporting detail, subdetails, and specific facts—and provides students with a structure that helps them organize and code material so that it goes into long-term memory, where it can be retrieved later when needed for examinations or projects (see Chapter 12 for a full discussion of learning strategies).

Figure 11.3
The Herringbone Method

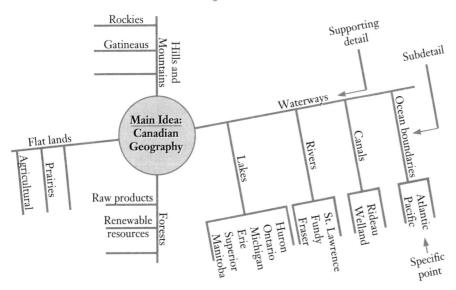

Summarizing, another skill that many students require (especially as they move into the intermediate and senior levels), involves the following essential steps (Gardner, Palmer, & Shallhorn, 1987):

1. Delete unnecessary information.
2. Delete redundant information.
3. Substitute a superordinate term for a list of terms, e.g., European countries for England, France, Portugal, etc.
4. Substitute a superordinate action for a list of examples of that action, e.g., exercise for jogging, tennis, biking, walking, etc.
5. Select or make up a topic sentence.

Classrooms that promote creative thinking and are characterized by: (1) good questioning techniques (i.e., ones that have no "right" answer and that call on students' general knowledge as well as factual material); (2) self-directed activities that allow the student to define his or her own problem; (3) openness and exploring of unusual ideas and hypotheses; (4) stimulating resources, both personal and concrete; (5) thinking time that allows students to try out several ideas mentally; and (6) reinforcement of mental and concrete ideas and projects, which includes praise and encouragement but not formal evaluation. To stimulate students' creativity and reinforce their understanding, a Grade 10 English teacher might, for example, arrange for the entire class to see a play that has been studied in class. Following the performance, the students might speak to artists, directors, prop managers, in order to understand their functions and thereby enhance their experience of the play.

BEHAVIOURAL SKILLS

Many students have behavioural as well as academic problems. Their IEPs should, therefore, reflect adjustment needs in the behavioural as well as academic, cognitive, and metacognitive areas. In the following two examples, behavioural principles were used to address adjustment needs. Crealock (1989), in observing students in regular and special education classes, found that they spent more time on task in the special education environment and more time engaged in socially active off-task behaviours in the regular class. A study by Solnick, Rincover, and Peterson (1977), which similarly employed behavioural principles, focused on the reinforcing and punishing effects of **time-out**. Used to reduce tantrums in young children, time-out initially caused an increase in negative behaviour. When the time-in environment was enriched, however, the time-out environment functioned as a punisher and the negative behaviour decreased.

◆ time-out: a behaviour management technique in which the opportunity for reinforcement is withdrawn for a specific amount of time contingent on appropriate behaviour

More recently, cognitive and metacognitive approaches to correct maladjusted behaviours have been used. Crealock (1991) employed a five-stage problem-solving model to teach a small group of at-risk adolescents how to solve social dilemmas. One problem was presented as follows: "It is Saturday night. Your friend Al comes up in a car and wants you to go out. Your father says, 'No, Al is a bad influence!' What do you do now?" The students worked through the problem by: (1) listing the facts involved; (2) brainstorming possible solutions; (3) selecting the best solution; and (4) developing an effective plan of action. Adopting this approach motivated these students, and their behaviour improved over a ten-week period.

Finally, Wong (1986) reviewed a series of experiments, using the metacognitive approach, in which students were taught to use mental checklists, self-perception/belief systems, self-esteem, self-verbalization, and self-instruction. The implications of Wong's findings for academic and behavioural interventions were promising, especially for students under age 8.

SOCIAL SKILLS

There is an increasing awareness of the importance in program planning of social skills that can be applied to both academic and personal areas (Gresham & Elliot, 1989). Armstrong and McPherson (1991) define social skills as those behaviours that promote successful interactions between exceptional students, their peers, and significant others. These skills include being kind and cooperative, showing interest in people, socializing often and effectively, and possessing the vocabulary and language skills required for appropriate expression of ideas.

For Pearl, Donahue, and Bryan (1986), planning for appropriate social behaviours is important because: (1) children's social experiences can influence not only their achievement but also their understanding of others' expectations for their behaviour; and (2) social adjustment is as critical a goal as academic adjustment. The direct teaching of social skills in the classroom is being seen as increasingly important (see Chapter 13 for a detailed discussion). Skills that should be taught can be registered on a checklist, as shown in Table 11.6.

Table 11.6 Teacher Observation Checklist				
Social Skills	No 1	So so 2	Yes 3	Comments
1. Student greeted the teacher appropriately upon entering the classroom.				
2. Student appeared to be relaxed and happy in class.				
3. Student listened and interacted appropriately with peers.				
4. Student seemed to be alert and motivated during classroom activities.				
5. Student expressed feelings and ideas appropriately.				
6. Student asked for help politely (appropriately).				
7. Student was willing to help others.				
8. Student worked well in group.				
9. Student seemed well liked by others.				

Source: Adapted from Noble (1990).

Earlier in this chapter, we discussed homework as it pertains to academic skill development. According to Armstrong and McPherson (1991), homework can also assist with the maintenance and generalization of social skills. For Heller et al. (1988), homework is characterized by the following components: previously acquired skills; planned extension of classwork; evaluation; part of IEP objectives; occurring outside school time; and teacher-directed. In class, structured social activities involve modelling, role-playing, and practice. However, actual social behaviours occur in other classes, at recess, during lunch hour, between classes, after school, and in the outside community. Therefore, it is necessary to assign homework on skills that apply to settings other than the classroom in which the skills program is being taught.

For example, referring to Table 11.7, "Anne" has difficulty initiating conversation with her peers. During social skills sessions, she practices with a peer but she rarely generalizes this skill outside the class. She is in the drama club, however, and part of her homework assignment is to initiate conversation with at least three other students each class. This will give her an opportunity to practice her communication skills. She is assigned similar homework following each weekly class, which is monitored by her parents, teachers, and peers. Although homework and social skills training is a new concept, in terms of maintenance and transfer, homework is probably more important for social skills than it is for academic work, especially as students get older and find social interaction to be increasingly important.

Table 11.7		
Sample of Social Skills Homework Form		

Name: Anne		Date: March 7
Grade: Grade 9		Date Completed: _____

Instructions:
You must initiate conversations with peers in your drama club, and have them, or someone else, write for you:
1. a description of the situation;
2. what you said; and
3. what the other person said (and did).

Behaviour: Initiate conversation at least three times this week with others in the drama club.

	What Happened	What You Said and Did	What the Other Person Said and Did
1.	_____	_____	_____
2.	_____	_____	_____
3.	_____	_____	_____
4.	_____	_____	_____
5.	_____	_____	_____

Signature of cooperating parent, teacher, or peer

_____

Source: Modification of form developed by Armstrong and McPherson (1991).

GENERAL PROGRAM MODIFICATION

The two major focuses of teaching in the classroom are social and academic development. An effective teacher is one who knows the subjects being taught, is organized, presents material clearly, is enthusiastic about teaching and students, informs students of the lesson and unit goals, and knows what to expect of each student. Below we discuss the following aspects of program modification: cooperative learning, subject exemption, altered work load, and summer school.

Cooperative Learning *- read through text .*

As suggested in Chapter 6, there is significant research and practical information to indicate that cooperative learning has advantages in both social and academic spheres. Parry (1990) offers the following suggestions for teachers who are just initiating cooperative learning:

1. Start slowly. At the outset, cooperative learning should be used at least once a week and then slowly increased. Both teachers and students need time to learn how to work together effectively.
2. Resist the urge to isolate students who are having difficulty integrating into groups. Students who are not accepted into any group may have to step out for a short time, but reintegrate them quickly since they probably need support and positive peer pressure more than do other students.
3. Allow time for processing with students after every cooperative lesson.
4. Begin with simple tasks. Once the students are comfortable with the process, they can be given more complex assignments.
5. If possible, work cooperatively with another teacher. It is essential to have a support system.
6. While the students are working in teams, set aside time to observe interaction.
7. Circulate around the room to offer encouragement to the group.
8. Keep an open mind about cooperative learning.
9. Have students as a group and/or individually assess their progress after each unit with checklists such as those presented in Figures 11.4 and 11.5.
10. Do not give up. The rewards that come as students work together effectively make your efforts well worthwhile.

Subject Exemption

Subject exemption is an option available to students in the intermediate and senior grades. The most frequent exemption is in French-language requirements. This exemption enables students with intellectual and language disabilities to attend resource programs without missing any of their regular class work. For students with physical handicaps—unless the course has been *NO* carefully adapted to their handicap—physical education is another possible exempt subject, as is mathematics for older students. While exemptions should never be granted without first carefully examining the possibility of adapting the course to meet the student's needs, when adaptation is not possible, exemption can have positive results.

Altered Work Load

At both the elementary and secondary levels, students with specific disabilities are sometimes excused from doing parts of their course work and/or *No* given altered forms of course work, which can be especially helpful when it

Figure 11.4
Wrap-up

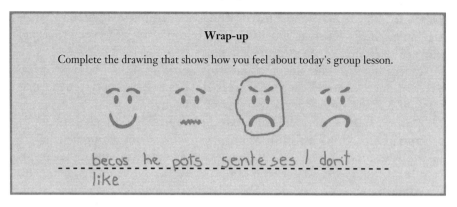

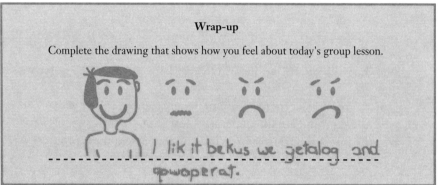

comes to evaluation and assessment. In addition, teachers may allow students with learning disabilities extra time to write in class, in the resource room, or in the guidance-counselling room. Students with problems in attention and distractibility may need to write exams in spaces where there are minimal distractions.

Summer School

For many students, nine to eleven weeks are too long to be away from school. This is especially true for students who have memory problems. Summer school offers courses like mathematics, French, and music at the secondary level, and skill-based subjects like reading and writing at the elementary level. By taking courses in the summer, students can maintain their level of skills, and either repeat a subject for higher grades and/or take a new subject that will lighten their load the following year. Summer school also allows students to maintain contact with peers.

Figure 11.5

Individual Evaluation

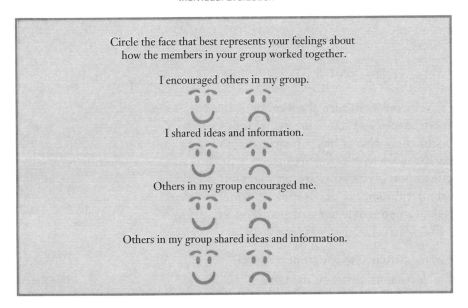

Adapted from Clarke & Wideman (1985, p. 25).

◆ SELECTION AND EVALUATION OF MATERIALS

The first issue in selecting materials is to match them to students' needs. For example, if a student's basic problem in reading is decoding, Autoskill, a highly structured computer program, would be an appropriate choice. Alternatively, the Fry test of readability could be applied to ensure that the level of reading material was commensurate with the student's reading ability.

A second key factor in selecting and evaluating materials is motivation. The popularity of computers is partly attributable to the motivation factor; students who will not do worksheets at their desks are often willing to attack the same material if it is programmed for them. Its high interest and low-reading demands make the Kropp (1980) series a good way to introduce students to reading for pleasure, and the Readers' Digest series—especially those books in large print—is another entertaining means of presenting a wide range of material.

Another important consideration in selecting material is matching materials to individual learning styles (Dunn & Dunn, 1978; Dunn, 1988; McCarthy, 1980). Teachers who adopt this approach look at students in terms of *when* they learn best (e.g., morning or afternoon, early or late in the week); *where* they learn best (e.g., a small, quiet space); and *how* they learn best. Teachers should also observe whether special-needs students have difficulty with bright lights versus dull lights; with fluorescent versus regular lights; with white noise (e.g., softly playing music) versus loud or noisy situations (e.g., rock music or other students); with studying early in the morning versus late at night, and so on. Students may also prefer to work individually, in dyads, or in small groups.

COMPUTERS — couple ques (2-3)
496 - 499

One of the most exciting developments in special education is the degree to which students can learn effectively with computers. Before purchasing a computer, the teacher should check that it has sufficient memory capacity (the rule of thumb is to buy hardware with as much capacity as is affordable). Another concern is selecting appropriate software packages—that is, ones that are affordable and that offer the special-needs student as much resource material as would an equivalent amount of paper-and-pencil materials. Questions that teachers need to ask when choosing software include:

1. Are the directions clear and matched to the student's level?
2. Is the program's reading level appropriate to the task?
3. How much teacher supervision is required?
4. How much eye-hand coordination is required?
5. Are a limited number of attempts allowed before an answer is given?

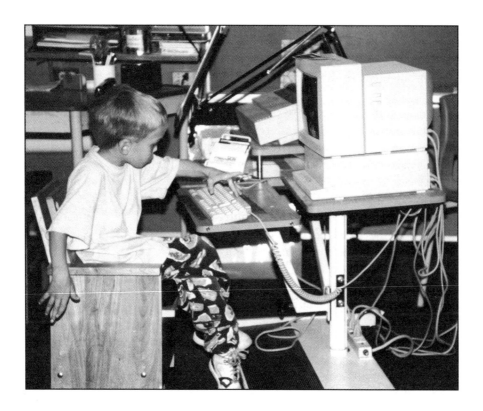

6. Does the program allow the student to exit, save what has been done, and return to the program later?
7. Does the program match the student's skill levels?
8. Can alternative input devices such as light pen, joy sticks, and graphic tablets be used?
9. Can the content be changed to allow the teacher to create lessons that are matched to students' needs?
10. Can the session length be adjusted to allow incremental training of attention?
11. Can the program collect data that the teacher and student can use to record ongoing progress?
12. Can the program speed be adjusted to allow fast programs that keep the child's attention while at the same time allowing him or her to be reflective? (Centre for Special Education Technology, 1989)

One computer writing program, designed to make secondary-school students in the mainstream independent, adopted the following objectives (McBride, 1989):

1. Hand in well-organized, neat assignments to classroom teachers.
2. Be independent in writing skills.
3. Improve writing skills.
4. Remove typical barriers associated with writing.
5. Improve attitude toward skills.
6. Transfer skills from the resource room to the regular classroom.
7. Use computer software as a vehicle for writing examinations in a resource room.

The above program involves collecting baseline data, learning to use a word processor, brainstorming, planning, writing a fast draft, proofreading sequence, graphics, publishing and assessment, and goal-setting for independent reading. As students achieve competency with the program, they can keep track of their development by asking for summaries of their writing, which provide a vocabulary index, maturity index, readability index, and recommendations for further improvement (McBride, 1989).

Computer remedial material has traditionally focused on drill and practice, offering little in the way of software with a built-in context. Bransford et al. (1988) looked at the issue of context in a study involving two groups of math-delayed children. For the first group—the experimental group—the authors isolated the sequence of frames shown in the first ten minutes of *Raiders of the Lost Ark* in order to develop a plan that would enable the children to understand measurement strategies. This group was shown the sequence of frames relevant to the problem received, whereas the second group—the comparison group—was taught with traditional instruction. When it came to problem-solving, the children who had received instruction in the context of *Raiders of the Lost Ark* performed better than the children who had received traditional instruction. The implication of this study is that despite the traditional drill-and-practice of most current software, teachers should make an effort to relate software to a context that is meaningful for students; for older students, this could involve writing personal programs that look at sports scores, clothing advertisements, and so on.

How effective is computer-assisted instruction (CAI)? Regosta (1982) conducted a study that showed CAI was effective because it followed good educational principles, not because there was some inherent value in working with computers themselves. She found that successful CAI is related to mastery learning, direct instruction, high academic learning time, adaptability and consistency of instruction, an orderly atmosphere with the experience of success in basic skills, the use of drill, and equal opportunity for all students to respond with a high degree of success. However, she cautioned researchers about pitting computers against straw men (i.e., comparing computer programs with inadequate traditional programs).

Computers have been found to be particularly effective in helping learning-disabled students master basic skills. In addition, computers have proven successful in developing the writing skills of hearing-impaired students. For example, in a recent study, Foster (1990) used telecommunication as a treatment mode with seven Canadian deaf students who were asked to write letters to seven American deaf students. He hypothesized that writing letters using computer technology would simulate speech more than would other writing tasks. After a six-month period of exchanging letters, the grammar of the average special-needs student showed an improvement that ranged from 100 to 200 percent.

An ongoing, collaborative study of computer technology by the Ontario Ministry of Education, Frontenac Board of Education, and Queen's University has produced the following results (Egnatoff, 1988).

1. Students are interested, confident, and competent in using the computer.
2. The computer is being used as a tool for both written and artistic expression. Drill and practice is available to students who need it, while others are using programs such as LOGO to increase their problem-solving skills.
3. Computer-driven projects have engaged the entire school rather than being programmed only for special classes.
4. Given adequate support, teachers are willing to adapt their teaching to the new technology.
5. The technical network gives students and teachers access to software and information across the school.
6. The role of the teacher has shifted from instructor to observer, learner, and coach.
7. Learning networks, be they pairs or task groups, have been effective in disseminating the learning experience.

Although the above findings are encouraging, it should be pointed out that the implementation of effective computer programs is being hampered by a reluctance on the part of teachers to accept technological innovations, as well as by their general lack of knowledge about how to use computers in the classroom (Collis, 1988). Further information about computer-assisted instruction is provided in Chapter 12.

◆ PROGRAM EVALUATION

CURRENT ISSUES

Recently there has been a movement at the federal level to introduce national education standards and nationwide testing systems. The School Achievement Indicator Program (SAIP) is a criterion-referenced assessment of the effectiveness of provincial programs, which is to be tested on a sample of 13- and 16-year-old students. The results will (1) indicate the percentage of students able to perform a particular skill or to demonstrate knowledge of specific content, and (2) allow for provincial and territorial comparisons. There are to be additional assessment programs in all provinces except Saskatchewan, New Brunswick (French), and Newfoundland as well as high-school diploma exams in all provinces but Saskatchewan, Ontario, New Brunswick (English), Nova Scotia, and Prince Edward Island (King & Peart, 1992).

There have been both positive and negative reactions to the above proposals. Critics of standardized testing argue that teachers will only teach to the test; teaching will become less flexible; actual achievement will not be measured; teaching and achievement on tests will not be appropriately linked; comparisons across boards and provinces will be unfair; and, finally, that standardized testing is a quick-fix solution. Advocates contend that standardized tests will provide data about the strengths and weaknesses of provincial programs; ensure a measure of accountability; be widely applicable; increase fairness in the university-admission process; and serve as a basis for resource allocation (McLean, 1990; Nagy & Traub, 1986; Rogers, 1991).

In a major study conducted by King and Peart (1992), over 14,000 Canadian teachers completed a questionnaire about their work and quality of life. Student effort was seen to be as "very important" by over 70 percent of teachers at every grade level. In the primary grades, the teaching of appropriate behaviour, social skills, and academic skills were seen to be of equal importance. In Grades 4 to 6, effort remained important, with somewhat more emphasis placed on testing, homework, notebooks, and class assignments; in these grades, group work, presentations, and projects as well as tests and assignments were evaluated. At the intermediate level (Grades 7 to 9), the majority of teachers still considered effort to be more important than achievement on tests and examinations, with most teachers evaluating students on the basis of both effort and ability.

At the senior level (Grades 10 to 12), achievement was seen to be most important for students who were college and university bound, but, even at this level, teachers still considered students' effort and feelings. For students who did not intend to go beyond Grade 12 and/or who had experienced frequent failures, approaches to evaluation played a significant role in encouraging them to remain in school, to feel good about themselves, to stay on task, and to develop academic and social skills. While the sample participants were primarily regular-class teachers, most commented positively on the inclusive classroom, although more in-service and resources were felt to be necessary. It is our belief that program evaluation at all levels—for all students—is necessary.

Checklists

Checklists are an effective way for students, peers, teachers, and parents each to be informed of daily and weekly progress. Checklists may centre on group evaluation (see Table 11.8) or completed work (see Table 11.9), or they may be aimed at individual activities such as note-taking, as shown in Table 11.10. Another type of checklist might record behavioural problems (see Table 11.11) (see Chapter 8 for a full discussion of tracking behaviours). Any of these checklists can be drawn up for single children, groups of children, or the entire class. Having student information in checklist form enables teachers to summarize changes over time with relative ease.

FORMATIVE EVALUATION ˙ read

Students can undertake much of the required formative evaluation of their work. Formative evaluation is more significant than summative evaluation in that it allows the teacher to make minor (and sometimes major) alterations to the program before the student has been unsuccessful for a long period. For example, a student who is having problems in Grade 5 mathematics should be assessed regularly, as shown in Table 11.12; it may be that the student has difficulty reading word problems, in which case the reading level would have to be adjusted.

If the student's difficulty is not with achievement, but rather with attitude, the teacher must assess whether he or she is working effectively in class. If not, the teacher can alter the program by, for example, placing the child in a different group—if group work is involved—or working with the entire class on group dynamics. An example of the latter option would be to brainstorm support techniques with all of the students in the group, and to check with them every day of the following week to see which ones are working. As with achievement difficulties, the goal of assessing a student's attitude difficulties is to ensure that he or she does not stay in a negative situation for a significant length of time.

	Table 11.8
	Group Evaluation
1.	We check to make sure we understand directions.
	Always Never
2.	We share our materials and remember to take turns.
	Always Never
3.	We help one another.
	Always Never
4.	We praise one another.
	Always Never
5.	We listen without interrupting
	Always Never
	Signatures:

Source: Adapted from the Saskatchewan Department of Cooperation and Cooperative Development (1983).

SUMMATIVE EVALUATION *- read.*

At certain periods, summative evaluation must be done with respect to the needs statements developed for the student, which may be in the achievement area and/or the behavioural area. Standardized tests or class examinations might be used to assess achievement, while student reactions to the implementation of a cooperative learning approach in the classroom might be used to evaluate behaviour. It is helpful to remember the availability of computer software that summarizes detail on a regular basis. The Autoskill program discussed earlier records students' work on a day-to-day basis, and provides summarized printouts to both the student and the teacher.

It is important for teachers to know for whom they are evaluating programs. If a teacher were to evaluate a program as part of a larger group of teachers trying to assess the effect of certain types of programs, a systematic approach—perhaps involving a certain amount of standardized testing—would be in order. However, if the primary reason for the summative evaluation was to determine the success of the child's placement in the current program, the teacher's focus would more likely be on altering the program or the environment.

Table 11.9 Completed Work				
Student _____ Week _____				
Behaviours	Evaluation			
	Good	So so	Poor	Comments
1. Attendance				
2. To class on time				
3. Homework done				
4. Assignments done				
5. Attention to lesson				
6. Peer interactions				
7. Organization of materials				

Table 11.10 Evaluation of Notes				
Specific Aspects	Total Possible	Self	Peer	Teacher
Notes Complete (charts, diagrams)	2			
Accuracy	2			
Overall Neatness	1			
Title Page Introduces Topic Well	1			
Title Underlined	1			
Labels in Capitals	1			
Gluing is Tidy	1			
Corrections Made	1			
Comments				

Summative evaluation is especially important in determining the degree to which regular-class integration is possible for a student. The information revealed might mean that more preparation—either emotional or aca-

Table 11.11 Behavioural Checklist								

Name ———————————————   Date ———————————————

Behaviour of concern	Pete	Doug	Mary	Rose	Frank	Pia	Dave	Vito
Swearing								
Fighting								
Talking to peers								
Calling out								
Mouthing off to teacher								
Walking out of class								
Falling asleep								
Gum chewing								

Table 11.12 Mathematics Problems			

General Hypotheses about why Students have Problems in Mathematics	Degree of Problem		
	Serious	So So	Not Serious
1. Reduced time spent in teaching math.			
2. Acceptance in community that math is not essential for adult survival.			
3. Poor preparation for teaching math at the elementary-school level.			
4. Lack of readiness skills in visual-motor and spatial areas.			
5. Problems in abstract and conceptual thinking.			
6. Poor attitudes and motivation, math anxiety.			
7. The pervasive effects of reading problems.			
8. Inadequate mastery of prerequisite skills.			

Source: From Bachor and Crealock (1986).

No

demic—is required before the student is ready to continue in the integrated setting. It may, however, be possible for the resource-room teacher to come into the regular class and work directly with individual students, giving them the extra skills and confidence they need to stay in the setting.

Summative evaluation is also important in determining how well a student is functioning in a large-scale program. For example, given a choice between integrating a student into a whole language program or into a program that is based on direct instruction, the teacher must know which teaching approach best matches that student's skills and temperament. Students with learning and behavioural problems often respond better to the reasonably structured approaches and one-to-one situations that direct instruction can offer. In contrast, students involved in a whole language program may need to be taught in a team-teaching situation where there are two teachers and forty to fifty students, or in a regular class where a teacher's aide is available to students who need to have their communication skills supplemented. However, rather than assume that a student cannot handle a certain program, the teacher should place the child in what appears to be the most favourable environment, and then observe his or her progress frequently.

Programs for special-needs students should be reviewed at least yearly by the inclusive team, the parents, and the student, and fine-tuned according to the findings of the review. Parents should be given opportunities outside of the review to contribute to the success of their child's educational program—one of the issues addressed in the following section.

◆ RECORDING AND REPORTING PROGRAM PROGRESS

Recording and reporting the progress of educational programs is done to share information with significant people, who depending on the issue, may include the student, parents, the district-level special education committee, and the in-school team. Sharing information helps to determine whether the student is functioning well within the prescribed program.

Reporting occurs at different stages. At the informal stage, the teacher discusses concerns with the family and the inclusive team. This initial discussion usually results in informal changes to the program. If these are not sufficient, the teacher generally makes a formal referral to the inclusive team, which results in a testing period that may require the services of the special education consultant, and/or the psychologist, psychometrist, social worker, and other professionals on the team. Parental consent is needed to conduct tests for intelligence and emotional difficulties, while concerns about academic and classroom behaviour are usually assessed by teachers. During the testing period, parents are often interviewed to determine the strengths and difficulties that their child exhibits at home. All of the above information is used to make an initial committee decision, which is reviewed regularly by the team and the parents.

GRADING No

As was pointed out in Chapter 9, there are many issues involved in grading students with special needs, the chief among them being marks, how grades are reported, teacher comments, and the anecdotal information that is shared with pertinent others. With respect to marks, the approach to grading also reflects the type of program in which the student has been placed. For instance, if the student is in a mastery program, where the criterion for completion of units is 85 percent or better, then marks reflect time to complete academic units as well as knowledge of material. Mastery or direct instruction approaches to grading are best suited to core subjects such as computational mathematics, decoding skills in reading, and spelling; they are much less effective when applied to more open-ended subjects like science, history, reading comprehension, and narrative writing.

Grades may be reported as pass/fail, satisfactory/unsatisfactory, excellent, satisfactory, and needs improvement. Because this type of reporting tells little beyond whether the student can work at grade level, many schools use anecdotal comments instead of marks, especially for students in the primary and junior grades; other schools use a report-card system that is based on criterion-referenced measurement.

THE TEACHER-PARENT CONFERENCE   No

One effective way for parents and educators to share information is to set up an interview for which Dembo (1991) provides the following guidelines:

1. Give advance notice to parents of the need for a conference and provide options on time and date.
2. State the purpose of the conference when contacting parents.
3. Review the student's records and collect all information related to the conference.
4. Have a folder of the student's present work available to discuss with the family.
5. Prepare a tentative list of questions to ask parents.
6. Anticipate parents' questions and, before the conference, assemble as much information as possible to answer these questions.
7. Select a suitable site for the conference. Normally, it is held in the classroom, but in some cases it may be conducted in a consultant's office or even in the parents' home.
8. Create and maintain a positive attitude. The special education team should be aware of how easy it is for parents and teachers to become defensive about a student's lack of progress, and should do their best to prevent that situation from developing by avoiding a negative attitude.
9. Use language that is understandable to parents. Teachers tend to use technical language with which parents are unfamiliar, thereby reducing the chances for a successful interview.

When sharing information with parents, the teacher should begin by describing the student's strong points. This puts the parents in a good frame of mind and enables them later to give a positive answer to their child's question, "What did she/he say about me?" The teacher should be tactful when describing areas that need improvement, especially when asking parents for direct help and support in sharing the responsibility for a behavioural or attitudinal problem. As well, the teacher should be cautious about giving advice and about promising parents that a certain program is going to be successful. Instead, the teacher should simply describe a program that he or she considers to be worthwhile, and invite parents to share their perceptions, observations, and general impressions of how as child is progressing in terms of achievement and attitude toward school.

The teacher can begin the last phase of the conference with a brief summary, followed by a course of action that the parents and the teaching team have agreed upon. The interview and current plan should be reviewed with the parents to ensure mutual agreement on the remedial approach. The conference should end on a good note, with the teacher expressing positive statements about the student and appreciation for the cooperation that the parents have shown. (A full discussion of the teacher-parent partnership is presented in Chapter 7.)

◇ SUMMARY

NO

In this chapter, we have discussed components of program planning as they relate to the scope and sequence of the curriculum, and to the sharing of information between educators and parents. In describing programs and evaluation methods used in social skills, core academic areas, and strategy training, we have recognized that the growing number of students with special needs who are being integrated into the regular classroom has influenced program planning. With fewer students being taught in the one-to-one or small-group format of segregated classrooms, needs and goal statements are increasingly reflecting the importance of effective teaching for all students in environments that encourage cooperative caring, teaching, and learning.

All students should be offered educational programs that are compatible with their individual learning strengths and weaknesses. School administration units should provide a range of educational opportunities that will enable students to develop to their fullest potential, and empower both themselves and their parents in the process (C.E.C., 1990).

QUESTIONS
◆◆◆◆◆◆◆◆◆◆◆◆◆

1. How would a teacher use cognitive approaches in remediating students with special needs?

2. Should extra resources be allocated to students with advanced cognitive abilities?

3. How important is it to shift power and responsibility from educators to students and parents?

4. Is it cost-effective to increase spending on computers for exceptional students?

5. How can a teacher plan for maximum use of time in program planning?

REFERENCES

Armstrong, S., & McPherson, A. (1991). Homework as a critical component in social skills instruction. *Teaching Exceptional Children, 24*, 45-47.

Bachor, D., & Crealock, C. (1986). *Instructional strategies for students with special needs.* Scarborough, ON: Prentice-Hall.

Bransford, J. D., Hasselbring, T., Barron, B., Kulewicz, S., Littlefield, J., & Goin, L. (1988). Use of macro-contexts to facilitate mathematical thinking. In R. Charles and E. A. Silver (Eds.), *The teaching and assessing of mathematical problem solving* (pp. 125-147). Hillsdale, NJ: Lawrence Erlbaum.

C.E.C. 8.201, 8.307 (1990, December). *Keeping in touch.* Quarterly newsletter from the Canadian Council for Exceptional Children office, pp. 3-4.

Centre for Special Education Technology (1989, June). *Tech use guide* (Contract No. 300-87-0115). Reston, VA: U.S. Office of Special Education Programs, Department of Education.

Church, S. (1991). Change: What teaching is all about. *IBC Journal: A Newsletter for Teachers, 2*(1), 1-3.

Clarke, J., & Wideman, R. (1985). *Cooperative learning: The jigsaw strategy.* Scarborough, ON: Student and Community Services, Scarborough Board of Education.

Collis, B. (1988). Research windows. *The Computing Teacher, 16*(1), 6-7.

Crealock, C. (1981). The creative problem solving approach in mathematics. *Ontario Mathematics Gazette, 19*(3), 18-21.

Crealock, C. (1989). The on-task and off-task behaviour of exceptional students in segregated and mainstreamed classrooms. *Canadian Journal of Special Education, 5*, 25-32.

Crealock, C. (1991). Problem-solving training with young offenders. *Education and the Law.*

Crealock, C. (1993). The Grid Model. *Teaching Exceptional Children, 25*(3), 33-37.

Dembo, M. H. (1991). *Applying educational psychology in the classroom* (4th ed.). New York: Longman.

Dunn, R. (1988). Commentary: Teaching students through their perceptual strengths or preferences. *Journal of Reading, 31*(4), 304-309.

Dunn, R., & Dunn, K. (1978). *Teaching students through their individual learning styles.* Reston, VA: Reston Publishing.

Egnatoff, W. J. (1988). The schools, computers, and learning project. *CALM Newsletter, 4*(1), 9-10.

Fiedorowicz, C. (1986). Training of component reading skills. *Annals of Dyslexia, 36*, 318-334.

Fiedorowicz, C., & Trites, R. (1986). *Follow-up study of the effectiveness of the autoskill CRS program.* Unpublished final report, Ministry of Education, Toronto, ON.

Foster, R. (1990). *The effect of telecommunications on the written language development of hearing impaired adolescents.* Unpublished M.A. thesis, University of Western Ontario, London, ON.

Fry, R. (n.d.) *Graph for estimating readability.* New Brunswick, NJ: Rutgers University Reading Center.

Gardner, J., Palmer, T., & Shallhorn, J. (1987). *The reading edge: Sharpening reading and study skills.* Toronto, ON: Ontario Secondary School Teachers' Federation.

Golick, M. (1973). *Deal me in!* Guilford, CT: Jeffrey Norton.

Golick, M. (1986). *Reading, writing and rummy.* Markham, ON: Pembroke.

Golick, M. (1987). *Playing with words.* Markham, ON: Pembroke.

Graves, D. H., & Hanson, J. (1983). The authors' chair. *Language Arts, 60*, 176-183.

Gresham, F., & Elliot, S. (1989). Social skills deficits as a primary learning disability. *Journal of Learning Disabilities, 22*, 120-124.

Grossen, B., & Carnine, D. (1993). Phonic instruction: Comparison research and practice. *Teaching Exceptional Children, 25*, 22-25.

Harris, A., & Sipay, E. (1980). *How to increase reading ability: A guide to developmental and remedial methods* (7th ed.). New York, NY: Longman.

Heller, H., Spooner, F., Anderson, D., & Mims, A. (1988). Homework: A review of special education classroom practices in the southeast. *Teacher Education and Special Education, 11*, 43-51.

King, A., & Peart, M. (1992). *Teachers in Canada: Their work and quality of life.* Queen's University, Kingston, ON: Social Program Evaluation Group.

Kropp, P. (1980). *Series Canada.* Toronto, ON: Macmillan.

Manang, N., Slemon, A., & Martin, J. (1991). *Strategies in judging numerical quantity.* Paper presented at the meeting of the Canadian Society for the Study of Education, Kingston, ON.

McBride, A. (1989). *A computer-assisted writing process.* London, ON: London Board of Education.

McCarthy, B. (1980). *The 4MAT system: Teaching to learning styles with right/left mode techniques.* Barrington, IL: Excel.

McLean, L. (1990). Time to replace the classroom test with authentic measurement. *The Alberta Journal of Educational Research, 36*, 78-84.

McLurg, B. (1990). *The oral-written language relationship.* Unpublished manuscript, University of Western Ontario, London, ON.

Mims, A., Harper, C., Armstrong, S., & Savage, S. (1991). Effective instruction in homework for students with disabilities. *Teaching Exceptional Children, 24*, 42-44.

Nagy, P., & Traub, R. (1986). *Strategies for evaluating the impact of province-wide testing.* Toronto: Ontario Ministry of Education.

Noble, L. (1990, December). *Teacher observation checklist of student social behaviours in the class setting.* Paper presented at the meeting of the Exemplary Practices, Toronto, ON.

Palincsar, A., & Brown, A. (1984). Reciprocal teaching of comprehension-fostering and comprehension-monitoring activities. *Cognition and Instruction, 1*(2), 117-175.

Parry, M. (1990). *Cooperative learning: A handbook for effective integration.* Unpublished M.A. research project, University of Western Ontario, London, ON.

Pearl, R., Donahue, M., & Bryan, T. (1986). Social relationships of learning-disabled children. In Torgeson, J., & Wong, B. (Eds.), *Psychological and educational perspectives on learning disabilities.* Toronto, ON: Academic Press.

Regosta, M. (1982, April). *Computer-assisted instruction and compensatory education: The ETS/LAUSD study-overview of the final report.* Washington, DC: U.S. National Institute of Education.

Rogers, W. T. (1991). Educational assessment in Canada: Evolution or extinction.? *The Alberta Journal of Educational Research, 27*, 179-192.

Saskatchewan Department of Cooperation and Cooperative Development (1983). *Working together, learning together.* Saskatoon, SK: Stewart Resources Centre.

Semmel, D., Semmel, M., Gerber, M., & Karp, J. (April, 1990). *Speed of retrieval of simple multiplication facts and the develop-*

ment of automaticity. Paper presented at the meeting of the American Education Research Association, Boston, MA.

Solnick, J., Rincover, A., & Peterson, C. (1977). Some of the reinforcing and punishing effects of timeout. *Journal of Applied Behaviour Analysis, 10*, 415-424.

Stein, N., & Trabasso, T. (1982). What's in a story: An approach to comprehension and instruction. In R. Glaser (Ed.), *Advances in Instructional Psychology, Volume 2*. Hillsdale, NJ: Lawrence Erlbaum.

Wong, B. Y. L. (1986). Metacognition and special education: A review of a view. *The Journal of Special Education, 20*, 9-29.

CRITICAL INSTRUCTIONAL CONSIDERATIONS

W e believe that one's ability to regulate and control learning and interact with others in mutually satisfying ways are powerful life skills. From our perspective, people who can learn independently and are socially competent have more successful and satisfying life experiences than those individuals who are dependent learners and lack social ability. The purpose of this section is to reinforce the importance of self-empowerment and social development, as well as to provide suggestions for helping students maximize their academic and social learning potential. Chapter 12 focuses on strategies that can help students acquire, retain, retrieve, and apply information. The chapter treats learning strategies from both a theoretical perspective and in terms of practical applications. Some educational researchers and practitioners consider cognitive and metacognitive strategy instruction, with its focus on how to learn, to be one of the most beneficial teaching methodologies available for children with learning difficulties. Although there is theoretical and empirical support for teaching cognitively based learning strategies to students who are underachieving, we need to

A NOTE FROM THE AUTHORS

increase our understanding of how to teach these strategies and how to evaluate their impact with respect to students' approaches to learning.

In Chapter 13, we detail the components of social ability and present a variety of assessment and intervention approaches that have proved to be successful in developing aspects of children's social competence. Because children spend so much of their time in schools, where they are exposed to many social situations, the classroom would appear to be an appropriate place for promoting students' ability to initiate and maintain positive relationships. This chapter attempts to capture the complexity of human social ability while providing systematic direction for teachers and other involved individuals.

The focus of Chapter 14 is on the classroom as a community of learners in which differences among students are recognized, celebrated, and used in positive ways to benefit all students. This chapter emphasizes the social dimensions of learning and proposes a holistic approach to language learning as vital in the transformation of regular classroom into effective learning communities.

THE USE OF LEARNING STRATEGIES IN THE CLASSROOM SETTING

CHAPTER 12

CHAPTER OBJECTIVES

To define the term "learning strategy."

To describe the relationship between cognitive learning strategies and information processing.

To explore the benefits of using learning strategies in the classroom.

To identify a variety of learning strategies appropriate for students with learning difficulties.

To describe the steps needed to ensure the successful implementation of a strategy.

Stan Bernstein was a quiet, serious-looking 15-year-old who had just entered Grade 10. By the time the first reporting period arrived in November, it was obvious to all Stan's teachers that he was not achieving. He was, in fact, receiving failing marks in all of his classes.

Stan was referred to Irene Molinger, a guidance counsellor, to determine what the problem was. Stan told Ms. Molinger that he attended every class, although he admitted he was sometimes late because he would get confused about what day it was and go to the wrong class first. Stan said he had worked on all of his class assignments, but often wouldn't finish them on time; he would not hand in incomplete assignments. He also said that high school was much harder than he had anticipated.

Later Ms. Molinger checked into Stan's school file to see how he did in elementary and junior high school. All his marks were generally "satisfactory," sprinkled

with an occasional "needs improvement." There were common themes throughout the years, such as "Stan could do better if he tried harder" and "Stan is disorganized and often loses his personal belongings." Ms. Molinger spoke to all of Stan's current teachers and found that he rarely turned in assignments or contributed to class discussions, and that he scored low on all the tests given in the academic subjects. His scores on tests in his option subjects were average, but, again, he never turned in assignments.

Ms. Molinger set up an interview with Stan's mother, who entered the meeting visibly upset. She told Ms. Molinger that she was "very tired" of always having to monitor Stan's progress, and to make sure that he had all his assignments done on time—she had done this throughout her son's schooling. Mrs. Bernstein said that during the last three years of junior high, she had hired an expensive tutor to work with Stan for an hour each week, but she felt that it was time Stan stood on his own. Stan was bright, she thought, and would often amaze her with some of his ideas and thoughts, but school had always been difficult for him, and if Stan wanted to go into the other academic stream, it was fine with her.

With permission from Mrs. Bernstein, Ms. Molinger transferred Stan to the less academic stream in January, intending to monitor him closely. Due to her busy schedule, she did not see Stan in class until February when she sat in on one of his science classes and observed him working on a lab experiment and recording data in his logbook. The science teacher, Mrs. Gibbons, later informed her that Stan was the brightest boy in class, always knowing the answers when called upon, but that unfortunately, he never turned in assignments and was therefore falling behind in his marks.

Ms. Molinger next went to Stan's radio broadcasting class, only to find that Stan had not yet arrived. The teacher, Mr. Worman, told her that Stan was often late. He also said that although Stan worked hard in class, he did not turn in assignments. As they were talking, Stan walked in. He apologized to Mr. Worman, explaining he had thought it was Wednesday and had gone to his auto mechanics class. He had also forgotten his notes, and had to go back to his locker to retrieve his binder. Ms. Molinger realized that Stan needed much more than placement in lower-level classes—he desperately needed organizational strategies if he was to survive high school.

The next day, Ms. Molinger invited Stan to her office to set up an intervention plan. He told her that he was bored by the general-stream classes and missed his old classes, especially biology. Ms. Molinger replied that she thought many of his difficulties were due to a lack of organizational strategies. He needed a system to help him keep track of the days, his classes, and assignments. Stan said that he really didn't know how to do this because his mother had always organized things for him in the past.

For the next two weeks, Stan and Ms. Molinger met each day. During this time, Ms. Molinger showed Stan how to use a daybook to mark down his daily classes and record his assignments. They worked at breaking down assignments into parts, planning how and when each part would have to be completed if the assignment were to be done on time. Ms. Molinger helped Stan set up a monitoring system to check whether he was keeping up with assignments and getting to class on time. She also encouraged him to re-examine his thoughts about handing in incomplete or imperfect assignments. Stan began to realize that "something was better than nothing," and that teachers could grade "something" but could not grade "nothing."

During the two-week period, Ms. Molinger also assessed Stan's reading comprehension. She found that although Stan was able to read grade-level passages without errors, he had problems remembering facts and ideas, which made it difficult for him to answer interpretive questions. Stan was a passive reader, who believed that reading the words once was sufficient—there was no need to stop and think about what he had read. Ms. Molinger explained to him the concept of being an active learner, of taking charge of one's own learning. She worked with him on the RAP (Read, Ask Questions, and Paraphrase) strategy, and showed him how to use semantic maps to plan his work before reading, after reading, and before writing. Stan seemed dismayed by the effort needed to learn these new strategies, but said he would try them on his own for the next few weeks.

After the two-week intervention period, Ms. Molinger was not able to see Stan individually for a month. Around that time, Mrs. Bernstein phoned her to thank her for the "miracle" that she had performed on her son. She said she had never seen Stan more eager to go to school every morning, and more willing to go upstairs to do his homework in the evenings. Flattered by this phone call, but a bit skeptical, Ms. Molinger called Stan into her office the next morning. She was surprised at how confident he looked. Before she could say a word, he sat down and told her that he had set three goals for himself. First, he would not score below 70 percent on any of his subjects; second, he would complete and hand in all of his assignments on time; and third, he would get back into the academic stream next year.

Stan said that RAP had really helped him. He was still using semantic mapping to plan his assignments and writing projects, and had begun marking his texts with highlighters to help him remember important passages. As well, he had not been late to class for a month. Stan proudly showed Ms. Molinger his neatly organized binder, where he had developed a new system to help him keep items current and tidy. For the first time in his life, he was actively planning and participating in his learning, and feeling good about himself.

◇ INTRODUCTION

Why do some students appear to learn quickly while others do not? This question has preoccupied generations of teachers, parents, and undoubtedly students themselves. Recently, cognitive psychologists have suggested that the differences observed between strong and weak students may be related in part to what students understand about the learning process. From this perspective, learning is seen as a knowledge domain similar to science or history. The more knowledge the student has regarding the domain of learning, the more efficient his or her learning is likely to be.

Gagne (1985) suggests that the development of successful learning is related to: (1) the use of strategies for selectively attending to the most informative aspects of an instructional stimulus; (2) strategies for effective encoding of new material for easy retrieval; (3) knowing the conditions under which a given strategy is effective; and (4) monitoring the effectiveness of one's strategies. Other studies support Gagne's position that successful students demonstrate greater proficiency than do unsuccessful learners in applying these and other learning strategies. The current mainstreaming emphasis will introduce a wide range of learning needs into the classroom. Teachers who are knowledgeable about learning strategies can help students with a history of learning problems make a more successful transition into the regular classroom.

In this chapter, we examine a number of questions related to strategy use. First, what are learning strategies? Second, what is the rationale for using learning strategies with students? Third, what type of learning strategies are available for developing academic skills? Fourth, what factors should a classroom teacher take into account before providing instruction in strategy use?

As a starting point, it is useful to establish just what we mean by "learning strategies." Gearheart (1985) describes strategies as plans, actions, steps, and processes that are designed to accomplish any learning or problem-solving task. Both teachers and students can employ strategies to achieve their respective learning outcomes. Teachers might use strategies to help them decide what and how to teach. For students, the central role of strategies is to help them "learn how to learn" (DeRuiter, 1983).

◇ LEARNING STRATEGIES FROM DIFFERENT THEORETICAL PERSPECTIVES

From a developmental perspective, children's conception of the world is continually undergoing change and growth. The strategies children use to assist this growth also undergo change both in complexity and efficiency. As the child's understanding of a domain deepens, the type of learning strategy and manner in which it is applied reflects this change in understanding. Teachers wishing to encourage strategy use must have an understanding of the student's current conceptualization of the learning domain, and, moreover, be aware that efficient use of complex strategies occurs over a period on time and is linked to the student's cognitive development.

The sociocultural approach, based on Vygotsky's (1986) theory, proposes that the culture evolves certain tools for dealing with those aspects of the world that it considers central and important. Within this framework, the child is seen as "the inheritor of cultural tools." One tool common to all human cultures is language, which, according to the sociocultural perspective, is the most important tool. Each discipline also has its own "tools of the trade" that should be taught. In practice, this belief led to curricular approaches such as the *inquiry method*, which involved, for example, teaching map reading and library research skills in Social Studies. The sociocultural approach thus moved considerably closer to teaching children strategies by providing children with the tools of a discipline and teaching them how to use them.

Many current advocates of the sociocultural perspective have integrated elements of the information-processing point of view. It is from this perspective that Gagne and Driscoll (1988) suggest that strategies can be used to assist the learner with the attentional, storage, encoding, and monitoring demands placed on any information processor. Obtaining the attention of the learner is central to achieving a learning goal. Learners may use a variety of techniques to sustain engaged time on task. In most children, the ability to sustain attention increases with age and experience in the learning environment.

An attentional strategy used by older students when reading involves underlining key points in their textbooks. Other strategies that help sustain attention and assist with comprehension involve having students generate questions and seek out responses to the material they are reading. Critical to such strategies is the ability to identify what is important in a reading passage. Brown and Smiley (1978) suggest that children below the sixth grade encounter difficulty in determining the key points in a passage, and are unlikely to put strategies such as underlining to effective use.

The ability to sustain and monitor one's attention can have a significant impact on academic productivity. While children identified as having an attentional deficit disorder experience difficulties in maintaining on-task behaviour, all students encounter some difficulty in this area. The ability to attend is not an either-or condition but one that is best viewed as a skill falling along a continuum. For some students, the ability to attend is hampered across virtually all learning situations; the attending difficulties of other children may be related to specific content or types of instructional delivery.

Given the frequency with which attending difficulties are reported by classroom teachers, a strategy designed to increase attentional behaviour through self-monitoring might prove useful for a wide range of learning needs. Hallahan, Lloyd, and Stoller (1982) provide a technique that has had some success in helping student increase their attending skills, and, in some cases, improve their academic productivity. Myers and Hammill (1990) identify the following aspects of Hallahan's self-monitoring strategy.

1. The teacher operationally defines what is meant by on-task behaviour and provides examples.
2. The teacher models the procedures that the student is to follow as well as self-assess and self-record if he or she is on task.
3. The student is auditorilly cued by a tape recorder that emits a signal on a random schedule. At that moment, the students asks "Was I paying attention?" and indicates either a "yes" or "no" response on a tally sheet provided by the teacher.
4. As on-task behaviour becomes established, the self-recording and cuing signals are faded.

While Hallahan's strategy is clearly not a direct academic strategy, it may prove useful in further developing some of the skills needed for efficient learning.

As learners proceed from attending processes to the task of storing information, they are confronted by the storage limitations and rapid information decay characteristic of short-term memory. As was discussed in Chapter 4, learning strategies that help maintain information, and increase the likelihood of its transfer to long-term storage, include verbal *rehearsal* (e.g., repeating a seven-digit phone number) or *chunking* (e.g., recognizing that a ten-digit number is actually made up of an area code, a local exchange, and a four-digit unit). Both strategies are useful for tasks that require simple recall.

Encoding is the process by which the learner brings some form of meaningful organization to incoming information. While the means by which this happens varies across learners, the ultimate goal is to make the material highly memorable. Classroom teachers can increase the likelihood of recall in their students by helping them focus on the more meaningful aspects of the material. For example, teachers can augment vocabulary development in beginning readers by using methods that enhance semantic encoding; rather than simply being taught in isolation, the new words can be presented in sentences, accompanied by pictures, or integrated into a task that requires students to create their own sentences using the words (Gagne and Driscoll, 1988).

Strategies to enhance *retrieval* of encoded information may include analogies, mnemonics, and notetaking. There is a clear relationship between encoding and retrieval in that efficient encoding greatly enhances the prospects for retrieval. For example, if the notetaking efforts of students reflect a high degree of organization, they are far more likely to be helpful in the studying process, and, consequently, more beneficial at the time of the examination.

Thus far, we have examined the means by which strategies can assist learning at each stage of the information-processing model. For the most part, the strategies identified are general in nature and not tied to any particular knowledge domain. Later in this chapter, we examine how specific strategies designed for particular knowledge domains also serve to assist the learner with the processes of attending, storing, encoding, and retrieving

know this rrly

◆ encoding: the process of transforming stimuli so that the information may be stored in long-term memory and retrieved for later use

information. For now, having addressed the potential of learning strategies, we turn our attention to establishing a rationale for their use in the classroom setting.

◆ WHY USE LEARNING STRATEGIES? *yq*

While learning strategies hold value for all students, they can be particularly valuable for students with learning difficulties. Deshler, Schumaker, Alley, Warner, and Clark (1982) argue that students with a history of learning problems frequently reach a learning plateau approximately equivalent to a Grade 4 or 5 achievement level. This level of achievement is thought to reflect the point at which basic skills have been consolidated and the student is now prepared to apply those skills to such areas as expository writing, math applications, reading comprehension, and extracting information from content textbooks (Myers and Hammill, 1990). For the student to successfully use these skills, a greater awareness of *how to learn* is necessary. Strategy training may, therefore, significantly assist students in discovering how to approach a learning task.

Myers and Hammill (1990) identify a number of advantages associated with strategy training, particularly for students who experience learning difficulties. Perhaps the most important of these advantages is that learning strategies focus on instructional procedures rather than on internal processing; specifically, they offer the student a "plan of action" for approaching a task.

Despite the potential value of strategies, many students with learning problems—and specifically those with learning disabilities—fail to employ efficient learning strategies. Torgesen (1980) refers to these students as *inactive learners*—inactive in the sense that they fail to organize, plan, and integrate information, thereby decreasing the likelihood that the information will be retained and generalized. While many students do not produce strategies independently, they can make use of strategies if they are explicitly taught. Deficiency in strategy use among learning-disabled students has been interpreted, using Flavell's (1985) concept of production deficiency, to mean that the student has the capability to carry out a strategy but does not produce the strategy spontaneously. This would seem to imply that children with learning difficulties would benefit from explicit instruction in learning strategies.

◆ TYPES OF LEARNING STRATEGIES

An eight-stage organizational scheme—developed by Weinstein and Mayer (1986)—to help conceptualize both the variety and complexity of cognitive strategies is presented as follows:

yes

518 -19
diff btwn
strategies.

1. *Rehearsal strategies for basic learning* involves strategies that are particularly effective in developing a factual knowledge base. While a heavy concentration on this type of learning has been criticized, it is still the case that a student's ability to engage in deeper forms of information processing is dependent on the acquisition of a strong knowledge base (Schmeck, 1988).

2. *Rehearsal strategies for complex tasks* involve learning tasks that require more than simple recall. Specifically, the student is expected to interact with the material in a more active fashion. For example, the tasks of copying and underlining material presented in a lecture assist the student not only in recalling specific information but also in engaging, at a later time, in more meaningful processes such as elaboration or organization (Weinstein and Mayer, 1986).

3. *Elaboration strategies* are dependent on learner input to make new material more meaningful. Through the use of verbal or imaginal devices, the learner constructs a bridge between information that is known and information that is to be learned. For example, the visually based keyword mnemonic strategy can been very effective in helping students assimilate factual information in a wide range of academic content domains. This type of elaboration strategy is frequently used in second-language learning.

4. *Elaboration strategies for complex learning tasks* involve dealing not with single items, but rather with larger units of material. Such tasks as paraphrasing text or developing visually based conceptual maps are methods students can employ to make material more meaningful to them. An increased demand for student interaction with material to be learned is characteristic of this stage.

5. *Organizational strategies for basic learning* involve techniques for imposing order on information. For example, when having to remember a number of Canadian geographical locations, it is useful if the learner perceives that the locations might be organized by assigning each site to the appropriate province.

6. *Organizational strategies for complex learning* involve the development of interrelationships in a body of material. Perhaps the most common example of this method is developing an outline for the chapter of a textbook. In doing so, the learner is given an opportunity to unite the strands of the chapter, which frequently upon first reading seem disjointed. Moreover, the outline provides a useful set of retrieval cues.

7. *Comprehension monitoring strategies* involve establishing learning goals, assessing the degree to which these goals are being met, and, if necessary, modifying the strategies being used to facilitate goal attainment (Weinstein and Mayer, 1986). To successfully implement this strategy, students need to know their own learning characteristics; the demands of the task; which strategy is most appropriate; how to execute the strategy; and how to assess the degree to which the goal has been met.

8. *Affective strategies* involve deliberate actions that the learner feels will produce a working climate supportive of goal attainment. For example, students who have negative feelings about mathematics may need to practice positive self-talk to reassure themselves of the prospects for success. Alternately, students who are particularly bothered by external noise may restrict their studying to the library.

◇ APPLYING LEARNING STRATEGIES IN THE CLASSROOM

MEMORY LEARNING STRATEGIES

terms

◆ mnemonic: technique for remembering that aims to connect new information with prior knowledge

Examples of elaboration strategies used to enhance the memory processes of encoding and retrieving are mnemonic devices. **Mnemonics** has been used in educational settings dating as far back as the Greeks, but it has only been in the last ten years that the educational potential of mnemonics has been widely demonstrated. Scruggs, Mastropieri, and Levin (1987) suggest that mnemonic strategies for both exceptional and nonexceptional populations have yielded some of the most dramatic educational benefits of any single intervention studied to date.

terms

◆ keyword method: a mnemonic device that links new words or concepts with similar-sounding cue words

A variety of mnemonic systems have been used in schools, including verbal mnemonics using rhymes, songs, sentences, and visual mnemonics based on mnemonic pictures and visual imagery. Perhaps the most successful memory strategy employed to date is the **keyword method**, an associative mnemonic technique that uses what Levin (1983) has called the three Rs: stimulus recoding, semantic relating, and systematic retrieving. If for example, a subject was to remember that the old English word "carline" means "witch," "carline" is first recoded as "car" (an acoustically similar and recognizable word that is easily pictured). Next, the keyword "car" is related to its meaning "witch" by means of a pictorial interaction, such as a picture of a witch driving an expensive sports car. Finally, when the subject is subsequently asked to recall the meaning of "carline," a systematic retrieval path has been established: "carline" leads to the keyword "car," which leads to the image of the witch driving the sports car, which, in turn, enables the response "witch."

MEMORY STRATEGIES AND VOCABULARY DEVELOPMENT

read through 520 - 521

Current research on the keyword method has focused on its application to school-based learning. Marini (1991) investigated the efficacy of the keyword technique in vocabulary instruction with gifted and gifted learning-disabled junior high-school students. Students were seen individually for two twenty-minute sessions. In the first session, students were informed that they would be learning vocabulary words and would be given a short quiz at the end of the session. Moreover, they were free to use any method of study they wanted to learn the fifteen words and their meanings. As Figure 12.1 indicates, stimuli for the free-study condition involved the presentation of a line drawing of

Figure 12.1
Free–Study Condition

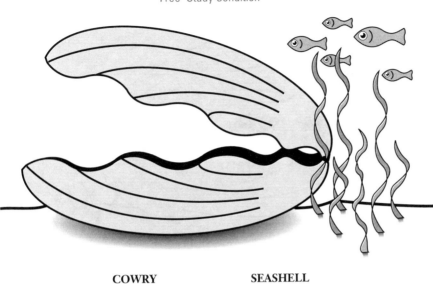

COWRY   **SEASHELL**

the target word with its appropriate verbal label. Each stimulus was presented for twenty seconds. At the conclusion of the first session, students tried to recall the meaning of each of the fifteen words that were presented.

For the second session, students saw a new set of old English words. On this occasion, however, each of the fifteen vocabulary words was represented by a line drawing depicting an interaction between the keyword and the meaning of the old English word (see Figure 12.2). The experimenter then presented each interactive picture for twenty seconds and said: "The word clue (keyword) for 'cowry' is cow, and cowry means 'seashell.' Remember this picture of cows in a seashell? Remember this picture of what? And cowry means what? (Mastropieri, Scruggs, Levin, Gaffney, & McLoone, 1985a). All fifteen words were presented in the fashion described above, followed by a recall test during which the experimenter provided the old English word and the student was to give its meaning.

The findings depicted in Figure 12.3 suggest that both gifted and gifted learning-disabled students recalled vocabulary items better when using the keyword mnemonic than when using a free-study condition. Gifted students increased their recall of the material from 78 percent to 94 percent, while the recall performance of the gifted learning-disabled students increased significantly from 56 percent to 92 percent. The strength of these findings should encourage educators to explore further the benefits of this memory strategy for developing a wide range of vocabulary items.

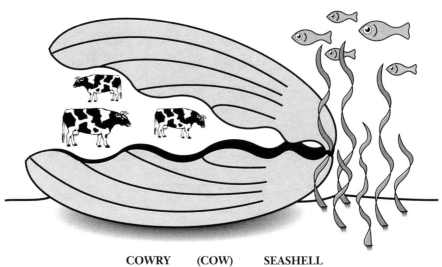

Figure 12.2
Keyword Condition

COWRY   (COW)   SEASHELL

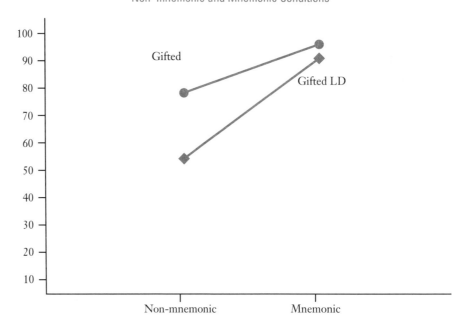

Figure 12.3
Gifted and Gifted LD Subjects' Recall for
Non–mnemonic and Mnemonic Conditions

THE KEYWORD METHOD AND SOCIAL STUDIES — *know what terms are only*

Levin et al. (1983) instructed average and gifted junior high-school students in the use of a keyword-pegword mnemonic strategy to learn the historical order of American presidents. The **pegword system** (one is a bun, two is a shoe, three is a tree, etc.) has been found to be particularly effective when the sequence of material under study is important. To help them recall that Buchanan was the fifteenth president, students were first provided with the keyword for Buchanan, "cannon" (acoustically similar and easily pictured concrete word), a rhyming pegword for number five ("hive"), and a seasonal referent for the appropriate number decade (spring equals 1 to 10, summer equals 11 to 20, etc.), all in an interactive summer beach scene (second decade equals 15). The systematic retrieval route for recalling what position President Buchanan held involved the following: Buchanan to cannon, to hive (5), on a beach scene, to 15. This example of a mnemonic memory strategy is quite complex given that it involves the use of both the pegword and keyword systems. The overall findings of the study indicated that both average and gifted students in the mnemonic condition recalled significantly more presidents than students in a free-study condition. This finding is particularly interesting, given the commonly held belief that high-ability students spontaneously produce effective cognitive strategies, for it suggests that even students identified as cognitively gifted can profit by explicitly taught mnemonic strategies.

◆ pegword system: mnemonic strategy that involves the use of rhyming pegwords, as in one is a bun, two is a shoe, and so forth

The successful application of visual mnemonics has not been limited to only average and gifted students. A number of researchers (Pressley, Johnson, & Symons, 1987; Pressley, Levin, & Delaney, 1982) have demonstrated the value of mnemonic instruction for students with learning disabilities. A series of studies (Mastropieri et al., 1985a; Mastropieri, Scruggs, McLoone, & Levin 1985b; Mastropieri and Scruggs, 1987) involving these subjects examined the use of direct instruction, free study-methods, and mnemonic learning strategies across a variety of content areas, including vocabulary development, scientific factual knowledge, and U.S. history text material. In virtually all cases, the use of mnemonic learning strategies produced significantly higher recall levels than either the free-study or direct instruction conditions.

In a rather unique application of mnemonic learning strategies, Nakane (cited in Higbee and Kunihira, 1985) developed a program of mnemonics for Japanese students named **Yodai**, which covers arithmetic, algebra, geometry, trigonometry, calculus, inorganic and organic chemistry, physics, biology, spelling, grammar, and the English language. The system makes use of commonly understood materials to teach new skills. Fractions, for example, are learned as bugs with heads (numerators) and wings (denominators). The multiplication of fractions involves putting heads together and putting wings together. What is unique about Yodai mnemonics is its emphasis on teaching the *processes* of problem-solving (rules, principles, procedures), rather than simply the facts.

◆ Yodai: program of mnemonics— developed for Japanese students—that focuses on the process of problem-solving across a broad range of curriculum domains

In an attempt to Americanize the Yodai method of mnemonic strategies, Kunihira (Higbee and Kunihira, 1985) used swimming pools and jogging as familiar American activities to teach students to add, subtract, multiply, and divide fractions. In Higbee's and Kunihira's adaptation, a fraction is represented by a jogger with a number on his shirt (numerator) and patches on his shorts (denominator), and operations with fractions are represented as poolside activities.

Stevenson (cited in Higbee, 1988) developed a mnemonic system to teach language skills to learning- and language-disabled, retarded, emotionally disturbed, and ESL children. The program focuses on the skills of listening, speaking, reading, spelling, vocabulary building, penmanship, and grammar for students in kindergarten through twelfth grade. As part of the system, Stevenson developed the *peanut-butter-and-jelly sandwich mnemonic*, which is used to learn spelling and pronunciation of one-syllable words with vowel combinations like "oa," such as "coat." The consonants are slices of bread, and the vowels are the crunchy peanut ("o") and the smooth jelly ("a.") When a child eats a peanut-butter-and-jelly sandwich, he or she hears the crunchy peanut butter but not the smooth jelly.

EDUCATIONAL BENEFITS OF MNEMONICS STRATEGIES

Levin (1981) identifies a number of factors that should encourage classroom teachers to employ mnemonic strategies. First, mnemonics has been found to be effective, as evidenced from the review above. Second, the effort and time needed to introduce mnemonics is modest considering their benefits; in most cases, mnemonic instruction is accomplished in less than thirty minutes, with the occasional review session required to maintain the strategy. Third, mnemonics is versatile in that it can be used across a wide range of academic content and with students of varying ability. (It should be noted that more complex imagery-based mnemonics, such as the keyword method, are more appropriate for students at or above the Grade 4 level, whereas more elementary mnemonics, such as the pegword system, can be used with very young students.) Fourth, most children enjoy using mnemonics and tend to see the activity in terms of a game. Fifth, and perhaps most important, is the fact that both students and teachers quickly recognize the value of mnemonic strategies in consolidating factual information.

Despite the demonstrated value of mnemonic strategies, there is continued hesitancy to make widespread use of them in schools. Critics of these strategies frequently raise the point that they keep students focused on factual information and thus prevent them from developing true understanding. However, Higbee (1978) argues that the development of factual knowledge is frequently a prerequisite to engaging in more complex cognitive activities such as creative thinking or critical analysis. Whereas most students have mastered basic information at an almost automatic level, students with learning problems must expend valuable cognitive resources on the recall of basic information, leaving relatively few resources for more complex processing. For example, students who have not mastered the multiplication tables may not be able to solve a mathematical word problem because they lack the required factual knowledge on which the problem is based.

A second criticism of mnemonic strategies is that students may come to use them as a crutch. Higbee (1978) points out that such dependency is rare. Students usually find that they no longer need to recall the original mnemonic association because the new material has become automatic to them. It should be noted that automaticity of basic skills is central to further development in a number of academic areas.

Finally, and perhaps most central to the reservations many psychologists and educators have about mnemonic strategies, is the perception that they are mere "tricks." This perception has been nurtured by the depiction of memory strategies, largely by entertainers and entrepreneurs, as somewhat mystical in nature. However, as the research above indicates, mnemonics are being increasingly seen as a legitimate area of investigation and application.

◇ SELF-INSTRUCTION STRATEGIES IN MATHEMATICS LEARNING

While memory learning strategies currently attract a great deal of interest, they are by no means the only method of strategy use. For example, cognitive strategies such as self-instruction have been found to be helpful in assisting a wide range of students with various aspects of mathematical learning. Genshaft (1982) found covert self-instruction to be effective in reducing math anxiety in a population of adolescent girls. Leon and Pepe (1983) found that self-instruction helped upper-elementary students who had learning disabilities, as well as educable mentally handicapped students, with basic math computation skills, and they proposed the following procedure:

1. *Model.* The teacher models overt self-instruction as he or she computes the math problem.
2. *Reproduce the model.* The teacher and the student compute a problem together, with the student using self-instruction.
3. *Self-instruct overtly.* The student uses self-instruction as a guide as he or she computes problems, while the teacher assumes a monitoring role.
4. *Fade self-instruction.* The student whispers self-instruction statements as he or she computes problems, while the teacher monitors the process.
5. *Self-instruct covertly.* The student uses covert (nonverbal) self-instruction as he or she computes problems (Sheinker, Sheinker, & Stevens, 1984).

COGNITIVE BEHAVIOURAL STRATEGY FOR REGROUPING

A particularly difficult concept for students is regrouping. Gearheart, DeRuiter, and Sileo (1986) suggest that the cognitive behavioural strategy offered by Meichenbaum and Goodman (1971) may be of assistance in guiding students through this concept. The strategy involves a five-step procedure and is presented below.

1. "What am I going to do? The sign is subtraction" or "The problem asks how many are left" or "The problem asks how much of the———— is ————, so I will subtract.

2. I start with 26, so my answer will be less than that. I'm going to take away 8, which is close to 10, so my answer will be closer to 16.

3. Will I need to trade? I have 6 ones and I want to take away 8 ones.

4. Yes, I will need to trade one of the tens for 10 ones. This will leave 1 ten and make 16 ones. Sixteen ones take away 8 ones leaves 8 ones (or 8 and what number makes a group of 16). Eight and 8 are 16, so I'll have 8 left.

5. Now I'll do the tens column. I have 1 left there and I'm not going to take away any tens, so I'll have 1 ten in my answer. OK, I have 1 ten and 8 ones. My answer is 18. I figured it would be close to 16. Is it close to 16? Yes, I must be right."

No.

In a study conducted by van Luit and van Der Aalsvoort (1985), students were taught to provide a running dialogue as they worked toward a solution. During the dialogue, the students were expected to both ask and respond to a series of questions that had been taught to them using a modelling procedure. This regrouping strategy, together with the one proposed by Leon and Pepe (1983) is useful in identifying skills the student has mastered, along with areas characterized by faulty or partial knowledge.

◇ SPECIFIC LEARNING STRATEGIES FOR DEVELOPING READING SKILLS

Know what terms before leave section

Recently, the field of reading remediation has focused on reading comprehension skills. Strategies in this area can be effective in dealing with a variety of comprehension difficulties, including the ability of students to summarize text, to monitor their comprehension, and to enlist background information in their reading (Swicegood & Parsons, 1989). Tama and Martinez (1986) suggest that reading comprehension skills can be significantly improved if students are provided with strategy instruction in this domain.

◆ SQ3R method: a reading comprehension strategy that involves survey, question, recite, and review steps

One of the best known reading comprehension strategies is the **SQ3R method** developed by Robinson (1961). SQ3R has been used with a variety of learning needs (Lupart & Lupart, 1989), and consists of the following five steps:

1. **S**—Survey a chapter quickly.

2. **Q**—Convert subtitles to questions.

3. **R**—Read to locate the answer to one of the questions.

4. **R**—Recite and make notes of the answer.

5. **R**—Review the material.

The *survey* step of SQ3R involves skimming the material to get a general view of what the text is about. The student should make note of headings, accompanying illustrations, and summary sections. At the conclusion of the survey step, the student should have both a general organizational framework to help integrate new information and enough information to assist him or her with the *question step* of SQ3R, which involves generating questions of interest that might be prompted, for example, by headings, subheadings, or the content of a chapter summary; this step nicely illustrates the engaged component of effective strategies. In the *read step*, the student seeks out answers to the questions raised. During the *recite step*, the students look away from their notes and attempt to answer each question in their own words. In the *review step*, the student tries to recall as much information from the text as possible, rereading portions if necessary. The primary purpose of the review section is to reinforce the retention of the learning.

It should be emphasized that the success of SQ3R appears to be dependent on the degree of training students receive. Adams, Carnine, & Gersten (1982) indicate that Grade 5 students who received explicit training over a four-day period in each of the above five steps produced comprehension scores significantly higher than those of their untrained counterparts.

In an adaption of the SQ3R strategy, Schumaker, Deshler, Alley, Warner, and Denton (1982) developed **Multipass**, which involves the substrategies of *survey*, *size-up*, and *sort-out*. In Multipass, each of these three main components is taught individually by trained teachers in a six-step instructional procedure as follows: (1) initial assessment; (2) description of the substrategy; (3) modelling by the teacher; (4) learning the steps in the strategy; (5) practice with the strategy; and (6) feedback (positive and corrective) to the student (Gearheart et al., 1986).

◆ Multipass: highly structured reading comprehension strategy in which survey, size-up, and sort-out substrategies are taught in a six-step instructional procedure

As part of the survey strategy, the student is expected to read (in sequence) the chapter title, introductory paragraph, table of contents, major chapter subheadings, subtitles, captions of illustrations, and summary paragraph. The size-up substrategy involves a more in-depth analysis of what is being read. At this stage, students are instructed to search for textual cues such as boldface print. A question relating to the highlighted text is asked and the surrounding text is searched for an answer. Finally, in the sort-out phase, students are directed to answer questions at the end of the chapter. For those questions where no answer is forthcoming, students are to return to the text until a correct response can be located.

Tierney and Cunningham (1984) developed a model of comprehension strategies that helps students activate their background knowledge and attention, guides them while they are reading, and helps them review, question, and synthesize material that is read. Sorrell (1990) organized a group of strategies, based on the Tierney and Cunningham (1984) model, that include an organizational technique called *TELLS Fact or Fiction story mapping*, a schema-based technique that is used while reading (see Chapter 10), and *question-answer relationships* that are implemented at the conclusion of the reading session. The TELLS Fact or Fiction strategy, a guided comprehension probe that serves to orient students to the reading material, consists of the following five steps (Sorrell, 1990):

1. **T**—Study the title.
2. **E**—Examine the pages to find out what the story is about.
3. **L**—Look for important words.
4. **L**—Look for hard words.
5. **S**—Identify setting.

Facts or Fiction involves determining whether the story is a factual or fictional work. This reading strategy, like those discussed above, places great importance on engaging the student with the reading material, thereby replacing passive reading with active reading.

◆ LEARNING STRATEGIES FOR ENHANCING WRITTEN LANGUAGE SKILLS

Harris and Graham (cited in Sheinker, Sheinker, and Stevens, 1984) developed a very effective strategy approach for helping mildly handicapped students develop a greater understanding of the writing process. The application of this procedure resulted in student compositions that were judged to be of a significantly higher quality than those produced before training. Sheinker et al. (1984) summarize the Harris and Graham strategy as follows:

1. Teacher models and student practices a task-specific strategy. The teacher provides a definition and example of a specific language skill (e.g., use of action words). The student practices applying the skill.
2. Current performance level and training goals are reviewed. Use of the targeted skill (e.g., use of action words) is charted, and the training goals and rationale for skill improvement are discussed.
3. Strategy steps and self-statements are introduced. A five-step strategy includes looking at a stimulus picture and recording action words, generating a story idea to incorporate these action words, and improving the story (e.g., adding more action words). The teacher models and the student practices generating appropriate self-statements.
4. The teacher models the learning strategy and self-instruction. Using a new stimulus picture, the teacher models four types of self-instruction: problem definition, planning, self-evaluation, and self-reinforcement. The student identifies the four types and records examples of each.
5. The student memorizes strategy steps and examples of the four self-instruction types.
6. Strategy steps and self-instruction are practiced. The student sets a goal for the number of action words he or she will use, practices the learning strategy and self-instruction with new stimulus pictures (initially using

thinking aloud and fading to covert self-instruction), and charts the number of action words used.

The impact of this training was still evident in a followup several months later, although Harris and Graham recommend "booster sessions" to ensure the long-term maintenance of strategy use.

Schumaker and Sheldon (1985) developed a more task-specific sentence-writing strategy that can be used to teach principles of sentence construction and expression. In this strategy, the student learns a set of steps and formulas that facilitate the identification and production of different types of sentences. Students can make use of the acronym PENS to recall the basic components of the strategy in the following manner:

1. **P**—Pick a formula.
2. **E**—Explore words to fit the formula.
3. **N**—Note the words.
4. **S**—Subject and verb identification comes next.

For many students who have difficulties with written language, the teacher's first goal may simply be to get the student to write. When this initial obstacle is overcome, the student needs to become aware of the importance of evaluating his or her own writing. The first level of evaluation need only be concerned with the more technical aspects of the writing process. Schumaker, Nolan, & Deshler (1985) developed a strategy that can help students determine if their writing has made proper use of such elements as capitalization, punctuation, margins, paragraph indention, and spelling. The strategy, referred to as COPS, enables students to examine their own writing in light of the following four questions:

1. **C**—Have I **capitalized** the first word and proper names?
2. **O**—How is the **overall** appearance? Have I made any handwriting, margin, messy, or spacing errors?
3. **P**—Have I used end **punctuation**, commas, and semicolons correctly?
4. **S**—Do the words look like they are **spelled** right? Can I sound them out, or should I use a dictionary?

A more advanced writing strategy that deals with theme writing, known by the acronym TOWER, involves the following:

1. **T**—Think
2. **O**—Order ideas
3. **W**—Write
4. **E**—Edit
5. **R**—Rewrite

While students can use the COPS and TOWER strategies as a starting point to evaluate their writing, they can also obtain helpful information by sharing their writing with their peers. For more mature students, classroom newspapers can be developed, with student editorial boards, to give students an opportunity to share their writing with others.

Spelling has been identified as one of the factors that can seriously hamper students' writing progress. According to Graves (1988), poor spelling skills is the major source of writing block in elementary students. Wong (1983) developed the following *self-questioning strategy* for Grade 6 students in need of spelling remediation.

1. Do I know this word?
2. How many syllables do I hear in this word?
3. I'll spell out the word.
4. Do I have the right number of syllables down?
5. If yes, is there any part of the word I'm not sure of spelling? I'll underline that part and try spelling the word again.
6. Now, does it look right to me? If it does, I'll leave it alone. If it still doesn't look right, I'll underline the part I'm not sure of spelling and try again. If the word I spelled does not have the right number of syllables, let me hear the word in my head again, and find the missing syllable. Then I'll go back to Steps 5 and 6.
7. When I finish spelling, I tell myself I'm a good worker. I've tried hard at spelling.

No.

The above strategy can be especially effective if combined with one of the more promising educational devices to date—the computer—as we discuss in the next section.

COMPUTER-ASSISTED INSTRUCTION (CAI)

To appreciate how the microcomputer can assist the student with written language problems, it is useful to examine Graves's (1983) proposed sequence of writing development, which is as follows:

1. Spelling
2. Motor aesthetic
3. Convention (punctuation, etc.)
4. Topic information
5. Revision

During the early stages of writing, students are preoccupied with the first three skill areas. As written language develops, these areas become relatively automatic, allowing cognitive resources to be directed toward the communication aspect of the writing. However, for students with written language difficulties, the first three stages of writing develop very slowly and significantly delay further writing. Seemingly simple tasks like handwriting can continue to be a problem for some students well into their adolescence (see Figure 12.4). Poplin (1983) suggests that students with learning disabilities are comparable to their nonlearning-disabled peers in areas of thematic maturity, but lag behind their peers in the mechanical and stylistic aspects of written language; the difference between what some students produce orally versus what they produce with paper and pencil can be quite dramatic.

While computers cannot teach the student to write, they are useful in creating an environment in which the teaching/learning process as it relates to written language can flourish. Several factors account for the success of the computer as a tool in the writing process. First, as previously indicated, many students with written language difficulties possess extremely poor handwriting and spelling skills, which serve to reinforce the inferior image these students have of themselves as potential writers. Some of them simply stop participating in writing classes, forgoing all chances for remediation in this area (Lindsay and Marini, 1988).

Word-processing software can greatly assist students who are overwhelmed by the mechanical aspects of writing. First, it organizes the spatial aspects of the task by automatically beginning at the top left-hand corner of the screen and moving down the screen in an orderly left-to-right sequence; second, it eliminates the mechanical aspects of producing legible handwriting; third, it allows students to obtain a clean, attractive printout of their writing effort at any time; and fourth, it facilitates considerably the revision process, which can be an onerous task when the pen-and-pencil approach is used.

In a computer demonstration project involving adolescents with learning disabilities, Lindsay and Marini (1988) found significant changes in the written language skills of these students when computers were used. The on-task time for the writing activity, which ranged from five to twenty minutes in its traditional pen-and-pencil mode, increased in many cases to forty minutes under the computer approach. At the same time, there was improvement in the quality of students' compositions in terms of organization and content, and students who had shown little enthusiasm for the traditional writing system began composing with computers on a daily basis.

During the early stages of the project, the computers were used almost exclusively in the Language Arts classroom, but as the students became more comfortable with them, their use was extended into other curriculum areas for the purposes of notetaking and project submissions. Computers were also used for writing letters home, for producing a school newspaper, and, in the case of one student, for creating a personal micro-diary. While the task of writing remained a challenging one, the positive attitude many of these students now brought to the task made them more open to systematic instruction in this area. It is at this point—when students are motivated—that learning strategies can most effectively assist students in developing their writing skills.

Figure 12.4
Writing Sample of a 15-year-old Student with Learning Disabilities

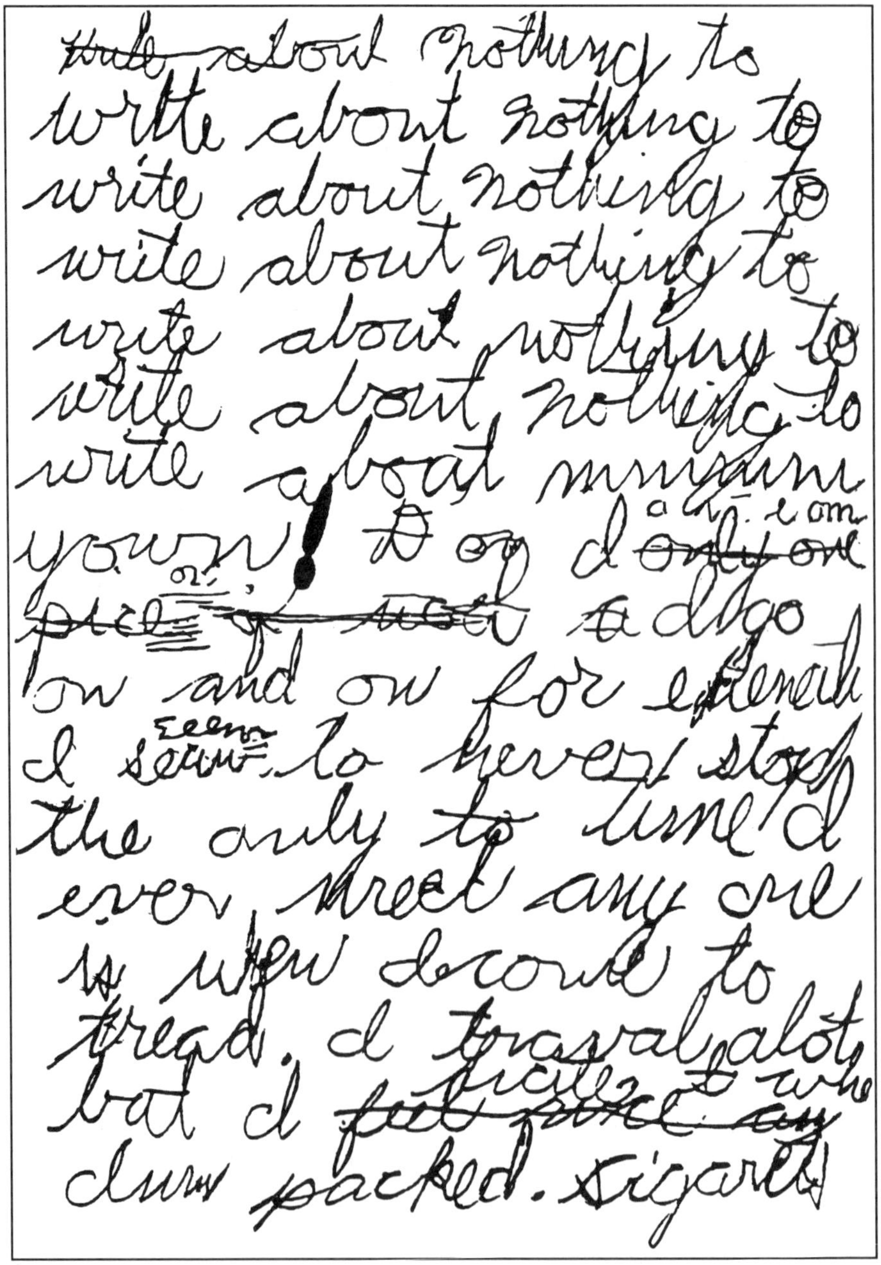

◆ TEST-TAKING STRATEGIES FOR VARIOUS TESTING FORMATS

The importance of test-taking skills has attracted significant attention in the past few years. National education organizations and the media have together become a vehicle for promoting numerous programs claiming to enhance memory, to turn students into human calculators, and to improve grades. The common thread in all these programs is the notion that students can and should take greater responsibility for their learning. Classroom teachers are becoming increasingly aware of the importance of providing their students with test-taking strategies. In most testing situations, teachers are seeking information about their students' comprehension of the material presented in class. When a student's performance is negatively influenced by poor test-taking skills, the information communicated by his or her test score may be misleading, thus leaving the teacher with a lack of accurate information with which to inform his or her teaching. The strategies that follow should prove helpful in creating a more valid testing experience for both students and teachers.

MULTIPLE-CHOICE TEST ITEMS —read throug— *[handwritten]*

Increasingly, students at the elementary and secondary level are encountering the multiple-choice (MC) testing format. Many students, particularly those experiencing learning problems, do not perform well on MC tests. Observations of unsuccessful test-takers have revealed at least two sources of difficulty. First, poor test-takers do not generally spend sufficient time reading the question component or stem of the MC item; the stem of an item frequently contains information the test-taker can use to eliminate incorrect options. Second, racing through the stem in order to choose an option frequently establishes a frenzied pace, which only adds to the student's anxiety.

To help students gain control over the testing situation, we have developed the following affective strategy:

1. **S**—Stop reading at the end of the stem and cover the options with an index card.
2. **R**—Reflect on what information the stem provides and what you know about the specific content area the question addresses.
3. **R**—Respond silently to the question with what you believe might be the correct answer. After completing the task, remove the index card to reveal the possible options.
4. **C**—Confirm your possible response with one of the options the question offers.

Many students, particularly those who experience anxiety during MC exams have reported that the SRRC strategy has helped them to feel more in control during examinations, and has helped to maximize their performance.

Devine and Meagher (1989) suggest additional strategies for approaching a MC test item, which can be used by students in both elementary and secondary grades.

pay attn to PB.

1. *Turn the stem into a question.* For some students, a stem such as "The field of psychology is concerned with" is more difficult to respond to than the question "What is psychology?" While the reasons for this are unclear, there is evidence that converting open stems into complete questions tends to increase test scores (Violato & Marini, 1989).
2. *Try elimination.* While students frequently perceive the chances of selecting the correct answer in a four-option item as one in four, it is more likely that through the process of elimination they will only have to choose between two options. Even with questions they find very difficult, students usually possess enough knowledge related to the item to make the elimination of one or more options possible.
3. *Watch for qualifiers.* Options that contain absolutes such as *never, only, always* or *all* are frequently incorrect responses. All too often, test constructors use these options to avoid the effort needed to develop valid and plausible distracters. Rarely intended to serve as correct responses, such options usually point to poor test construction.
4. *More words tend to be right.* In any well-designed MC item, there is only one correct option. To accomplish this, test writers ensure that the correct option is complete and accounts for all the possible information. Sometimes the need to construct a valid correct option results in inadequate attention to the construction of the distracters. As a result, the distracters may be considerably shorter than the correct option; therefore, from the test-taker's perspective, long and complete options frequently represent the correct option.

ESSAY-TYPE EXAMS

read

In responding to essay questions, students must know the relevant content and organize their time efficiently. All too frequently, students provide complete responses to the first one or two questions on the exam, but, due to poor time allocation, submit only partial answers to the remaining questions. Many factors contribute to this problem, but perhaps one of the most important relates to comprehension of the question. A question that is poorly understood usually results in time-consuming false starts. While the required content for essay questions will naturally vary, the student should find it helpful to have an understanding of the terms that define the task (e.g., compare, contrast, define, evaluate, and summarize).

SENTENCE COMPLETION TEST FORMAT

One of the most frequently used test formats at the elementary level is the sentence completion or fill-in-the-blank format. A student's success with this type of format is strongly related to how well the item has been constructed. For example, selecting the correct response for the completion item "Columbus discovered America in ———" is considerably more difficult than responding to "Columbus discovered America in the year ———." Students can employ a number of strategies to help ensure the correct response. First, they can examine the item for grammatical clues, subject-verb agreement, and consistent language; second, they can use the number—or length—of blanks as clues; and third, as a last resort, they can guess.

NO

A STRATEGY APPROACH FOR SECONDARY STUDENTS

While the above strategies can be used with both elementary and secondary students, some researchers have focused their efforts on the secondary-school population. In an attempt to address the learning needs of learning-disabled adolescents, Alley and Deschler (1979) developed a strategy intervention model to help students acquire skills that can assist them across academic domains. This approach is thought to be more appropriate for the secondary-school level given that students are faced with a variety of content domains and a critical need to develop skills that will contribute to their functioning as self-learners. Under the strategy intervention model, students are taught test-taking skills that are applicable to a variety of testing situations. The focus is on developing strategies that the student can generalize to numerous learning conditions. Among the skills the program teaches are self-questioning, visual imagery, and paraphrasing. The role of the teacher in delivering this intervention program is to help students learn how to learn.

NO

❖ RECOMMENDATIONS FOR TEACHING AND IMPLEMENTING LEARNING STRATEGIES

Gagne and Driscoll (1988) offer the following five recommendations for teaching learning strategies.

1. *Match strategies to the processing requirements of the learning task.* If, for example, the learning goal involves the retention of the main ideas in a selection of expository prose, the student might be directed to use a chunking strategy to increase the amount of information held in short-term memory. In directing students to use a particular strategy, the complexity of the strategy must be taken into account. In other words, the strategy must be developmentally appropriate for the student. Visual mnemonic learning devices provide a good example of how a teacher might move from simple to complex learning strategies. Classroom applications of visual mnemonics have revealed that younger students

Read - 36

have difficulty applying the keyword method. Therefore, in introducing visual mnemonic strategies to elementary students, teachers might begin with the pegword system, followed by the keyword system, and, finally, a combination of these two strategies.

2. *Provide learning strategies instruction consistent with the student's current knowledge and skill level.* While learning strategies designed for specific content areas can be effective, initially more general learning strategies should be taught. Domain-specific strategies are more likely to succeed when the student has obtained a sufficient knowledge base in the content area.

3. *Arrange for extensive practice in strategy use.* Practice helps the student spontaneously produce the strategy when appropriate. In addition, it enables the student to generalize the strategy across a wide range of content areas and learning conditions. The Marini (1991) study discussed earlier in this chapter exemplifies the importance of strategy practice. As was pointed out, the findings indicated that both gifted and gifted learning-disabled students effectively used the keyword method. However, ten days after conducting the study, the experimenter discovered that the strategy had scarcely been used in the classroom setting; in fact, on the followup test, a number of students needed to be reminded how to use the strategy. The lesson from this single experiment underlines the need for continued practice of any strategy in the classroom setting.

4. *Prompt students to use strategies at appropriate times.* While practice helps the student maintain the strategy, understanding *when* the application of a particular strategy is appropriate poses a more difficult task. A simple reminder may suffice for some students; but others—particularly those with learning disabilities—may require very explicit prompting, which ideally should contribute to the student's ability to transfer the strategy to different yet related tasks.

CAUTIONS IN IMPLEMENTING LEARNING STRATEGIES

Despite their great promise (particularly as teachers face a greater range of abilities in their classes), some cautions about learning strategies should be noted. Sheinker et al. (1988), for example, have expressed the following caveats: (1) Learning strategies are not a panacea and should not be substituted for learning techniques that have already proven themselves effective; (2) Strategies should not be an add-on to the curriculum, but should be presented to students as an integral part of the instructional sequence; and (3) Before attempting to implement cognitive strategy training in a classroom, teachers should be thoroughly familiar with the specific aspects of the strategy that researchers have found to be effective.

◇ CONCLUSION

In this chapter, we reviewed the ways in which learning strategies can contribute to successful school performance. Strategies may be general in nature, applicable across various content areas, or specific to a particular academic domain. Research suggests that students of virtually all ages and ability levels can be taught to be effective in applying strategies to their academic tasks. Students with a history of learning problems—particularly those about to be reintegrated into the regular classroom—may especially benefit from learning strategies, which can offer them a means of improving their academic performance while enlarging their understanding of—and control over—their own learning processes.

QUESTIONS
◆◆◆◆◆◆◆◆◆◆◆◆◆◆

1. How does the introduction of learning strategies change the teacher-student relationship?

2. What methods can be employed to determine the effectiveness of a learning strategy?

3. How would you respond to critics who argue that time spent on implementing learning strategies would be better spent on teaching specific academic content?

4. What techniques could you employ to help students develop their own learning strategies?

5. How early in a child's school experience do you think learning strategies should be introduced?

REFERENCES

Adams, A., Carnine, D., & Gersten, R. (1982). Instructional strategies for studying context area texts in the intermediate grades. *Reading Research Quarterly, 18*(1), 27-55.

Alley, G., & Deschler, D. (1979). Teaching the learning disabled adolescent. *Strategies and methods*. Denver: Love Publishing.

Brown, A. L., & Smiley, S. S. (1978). The development of strategies for studying. *Child Development, 49*, 1076-1088.

DeRuiter, J. A. (1983, February 4). Presentation to Denver Academy, Symposium on Learning Disabilities.

Deschler, D. D., Schumaker, J. B., Alley, G. R., Warner, M. M., & Clark, F. L. (1982). Learning disabilities in adolescent and young adult populations: Research implications. *Focus on Exceptional Children, 15*, 1-12.

Devine, T., & Meagher, L. D. (1989). *Mastering study skills: A student guide*. Englewood Cliffs, NJ: Prentice-Hall.

Flavell, J. H. (1985). *Cognitive development* (2nd ed.). Englewood Cliffs, NJ: Prentice-Hall.

Gagne, R. M. (1985). *The conditions of learning* (4th ed.). New York: Holt, Rinehart and Winston.

Gagne, R. M., & Driscoll, M. P. (1988). *Essentials of learning for instruction* (2nd ed.). Englewood Cliffs, NJ: Prentice Hall.

Gearheart, B. R. (1985). *Learning disabilities: Educational strategies* (4th ed.). St. Louis: Times Mirror/Mosby College.

Gearheart B., DeRuiter, J., & Sileo, T. (1986). *Teaching mildly and moderately handicapped students*. Englewood Cliffs, NJ: Prentice-Hall.

Genshaft, J. L. (1982). The use of cognitive behaviour therapy for reducing math anxiety. *School Psychology Review, 11*, 32-34.

Graves, D. H. (1983). A researcher learns to write. Toronto: Heinemann.

Hallahan, D. P., Lloyd, J. W., & Stoller, L. (1982). *Improving attention and self-monitoring: A manual for teachers*. Charlottesville, VA: University of Virginia Learning Disabilities Research Institute.

Higbee, K. L. (1978). Some pseudo-limitations of mnemonics. In M. M. Gruneberg, P. E. Morris, & R. N. Sykes, *Practical aspects of memory: Current research and issues* (p. 146-147). London: Academic Press.

Higbee, K. L. (1988). Practical aspects of mnemonics. In M. M. Gruneberg, P. E. Morris, & R. N. Sykes, *Practical aspects of memory: Current research and issues* (p. 403-408). Chichester: John Wiley & Sons.

Higbee, K. L., & Kunihira, S. (1985). Cross-cultural applications of Yodai mnemonics. *Educational Psychologist, 20*, 57-64.

Leon, J. A., & Pepe, H. J. (1983). Self-instructional training: Cognitive behaviour modification for remediating arithmetic deficits. *Exceptional Children, 50*(1), 54-60.

Levin, J.R. (1981). The mnemonic '80s: Keywords in the classroom. *Educational Psychologist, 16*, 65-82.

Levin, J. R., Dretzke, B. J., McCormick, C. B., Scruggs, T. E., McGivern, J. E., and Mastropieri, M. A. (1983). Learning via mnemonic pictures: Analysis of presidential process. *Educational Communication and Technology Journal, 3*, 161-173.

Lindsay, P., & Marini, A. E. (1988). Microcomputers and children with learning difficulties: Releasing the potential. In J. Beishulzen, J. Tobin, & P. R. Weston (Eds.), *The use of the microcomputer in teaching and learning* (pp. 131-144). Amsterdam: Swets and Zeitlinger.

Lupart, J., & Lupart, M. (1989). Reading-disabled adolescents: Evidence for a top-down attention deficit. In J. Dumont & H. Nakken (Eds.), *Learning disabilities: Cognitive, social and remedial aspects* (pp. 55-62). Amsterdam: Swets and Zeitlinger.

Marini, A. (1991). The keyword technique in vocabulary instruction with gifted and gifted learning-disabled junior-high school students (Submitted for publication).

Mastropieri, M. A., & Scruggs, T. E. (1987). *Effective instruction for special education*. Boston: Little, Brown/College Hill.

Mastropieri, M. A., Scruggs, T. E., Levin, J. R., Gaffney, J., & McLoone, B. (1985a). Mnemonic vocabulary instruction for learning disabled students. *Learning Disability Quarterly, 8*, 299-309.

Mastropieri, M. A., Scruggs, T. E., McLoone, B. B. and Levin, J. R. (1985b). Facilitating the acquisition of science classifications in LD students. *Learning Disability Quarterly, 8*, 57-63.

Meichenbaum, D., & Goodman, J. (1971). Training impulsive children to talk to themselves: A means of developing self-control. *Journal of Abnormal Psychology, 77*, 115-126.

Myers, P. I., & Hammill, D. D. (1990). Learning disabilities: Basic concepts, assessment practices, and instructional strategies (4th ed.). Austin, TX: Pro-Ed.

Poplin, M. (1983). Assessing developmental writing abilities. *Topics in Learning and Learning Disabilities, 3*, 63-75.

Pressley, M., Johnson, C. J., & Symons, S. (1987). Elaborating to learn and learning to elaborate. *Journal of Learning Disabilities, 20*, 76-91.

Pressley, M., Levin, J. R., & Delaney H. D. (1982). The mnemonic keyword method. *Review of Educational Research, 52*, 61-91.

Robinson, F. P. (1961). *Effective study*. New York: Harper & Row.

Schmeck, R. R. (1988). Individual differences and learning strategies. In C. E. Weinstein, E. T. Goetz, and P. A. Alexander (Eds.), *Learning and study strategies: Issues in assessment, instruction, and evaluation* (pp. 177-189). New York: Academic Press.

Schumaker, J. B., Deschler, D. D., Alley, G. R., Warner, M. M., & Denton, P. H. (1982). Multipass: A learning strategy for improving reading comprehension. *Learning Disability Quarterly, 5*(3), 295-304.

Schumaker, J. B. Nolan, S. M., & Deschler, D. D. (1985). *Learning strategies curriculum: The error monitoring strategy*. Lawrence, KS: University of Kansas.

Schumaker, J. B., & Sheldon, J. (1985). *Learning strategies curriculum: The sentence writing strategy*. Lawrence, KS: University of Kansas.

Scruggs, T. E., Mastropieri, M., & Levin J. R. (1987). Implications of mnemonic-strategy for theories of learning disabilities. In H. Lee Swanson (Ed.), *Advances in learning and behavioral disabilities: Memory and learning disabilities*. Greenwich, CT: Jai Press.

Sheinker, A., Sheinker, J. & Stevens, L. J. (1984). Cognitive strategies for teaching the mildly handicapped. *Focus on Exceptional Children, 17*, 1, 1-5

Sheinker, A., Sheinker, J., & Stevens, L. J. (1988). Cognitive strategies for teaching the mildly handicapped. In E. L. Meyen, G. A. Vergason, & R. J. Whelan (Eds.), *Effective instructional strategies for exceptional children* (pp. 194-215). Denver: Love Publishing.

Sorrell, A. L. (1990). Three reading comprehension strategies: TELLS, story mapping, and QAR's. *Academic Therapy, 25*(3).

Swicegood, P., & Parsons, J. (1989). Better questions and answers equal success. *Teaching Exceptional Children, 21*, 4-8.

Tama, M., & Martinez, D. H. (1986). *Reading comprehension and the learner disabled reader: Generalizations from five years of research (1980-1985)*. Paper presented at the annual meeting of the National Reading Conference, Austin, TX.

Tierney, R., & Cunningham, J. (1984). Research on teaching reading comprehension. In P. Pearson (Ed.), *Handbook of reading research* (pp. 609-655). New York: Longman.

Torgesen, J. K. (1980). Conceptual and educational implications of the use of efficient task strategies by learning disabled children. *Journal of Learning Disabilities, 13*, 364-371.

van Luit, J. E. H., & van der Aalsvoort, G. M. (1985). Learning subtraction in a special school: A self-instructional strategy for educable mentally retarded children with arithmetic deficits. *Instructional Science, 14*, 179-189.

Violato, C., and Marini, A. E. (1989). Effects of stem orientation and completeness of multiple-choice items on item difficulty and discrimination. *Educational and Psychological Measurement, 49*, 287-295.

Vygotsky, L. S. (1986). *Thought and language*. Cambridge, MA: MIT Press.

Weinstein, C. E., & Mayer, R. E. (1986). The teaching of learning strategies. In M. C. Wittrock (ed.), *Handbook of research on teaching* (3rd ed.). New York: Macmillan.

Wong, Bernice Y. L. (1986). A cognitive approach to teaching. *Exceptional Children, 53*(2), 169-173.

DEVELOPING SOCIAL ABILITY IN THE CLASSROOM

CHAPTER 13

CHAPTER OBJECTIVES

To provide a conceptual framework for understanding the nature of social ability.

To review the general components of social ability.

To provide examples of measuring devices to assist the teacher in social assessment.

To discuss intervention techniques for enhancing social development.

To provide ways to increase social integration.

The first year of junior high school is a difficult time for most students, requiring them to make many new adjustments. Some schools even hold unofficial extremely embarrassing initiation ceremonies for the newest members of the school early in the year. The transition to junior high was not too difficult for students attending St. James School, because the elementary school and junior high were part of the same school and were in the same building. Initiation rites were not allowed, and the students were familiar with many of the teachers who taught in the junior high wing. Yet there still were adjustments to be made: to new peers, to junior high dances, and to having more teachers and more responsibilities. Most of the students just entering junior high at St. James adjusted to these changes.

Jonathan, a small 13-year-old who had recently moved to the Calgary area from British Columbia, was very unhappy when he first entered Grade 7 at St. James School. He had no friends and didn't know how to go about making them. Jonathan's difficulties were not immediately apparent to most of his teachers, who saw him as a quiet boy who sat in his seat during class and did his work as expected. Students seemed to stay away from Jonathan, and some overtly showed their disdain by making fun of him. The teachers could see no obvious reasons for these peer reactions. Jonathan continued to come to school riding city transit by himself. He would leave school immediately after the bell rang and go home, unaccompanied by friends.

In early October, Jonathan approached the guidance counsellor, Mr. Earle, and told him that some older students were beating him up at the bus stop and in the halls. Mr. Earle followed up on this and found the culprits. He called them into his office where he asked them why they picked on Jonathan. They told Mr. Earle that Jonathan bugged them. He would seek them out in the hallway and say to them, "Want to fight? I can beat you up," and he would follow them, sometimes touching their heads. The next day, Mr. Earle followed Jonathan between classes. He saw Jonathan walking the halls by himself, trying to make contact with others by saying "Hi!" and reaching out to tousle their hair. Most students responded by moving away. Mr. Earle asked Jonathan to his office where he told him that it would be more appropriate for him not to touch the other kids on the head, and that he should stay away from the older kids. Jonathan agreed and left the office.

Three weeks later, the junior high school at St. James celebrated Hallowe'en by holding a dance after school on Friday afternoon. It was the first school dance for most Grade 7 students. They crowded into the gym, stood by the walls, and talked to their friends. Teachers came to the dance to relax with the students and to watch them have fun. Mr. Earle, who was chatting with a group of students, witnessed a sad sight. The lights had not yet been turned off—to indicate that the dance had actually begun—although the music had just started. There was Jonathan, on the floor, performing an ill-advised and poorly coordinated breakdance. Students gathered in a circle around him, laughing and making fun of him, while he continued his dancing with a big smile on his face. When Jonathan had finished dancing, the other students retreated from him. The lights went off and some of the students found partners and started dancing in the darkness. Shortly afterwards, a large group of students formed a line dance, which a person could join without having a partner. Jonathan tried to join in the line dance by roughly breaking in between two people—then he tried to get a girl to dance with him by taking her arm and pulling her to the dance floor: on both occasions, he was told in no uncertain terms to back off. Jonathan left the dance early and went home.

Mr. Earle realized that Jonathan badly needed help with interacting appropriately with his peers. Jonathan was unaware of the unspoken rules of conduct in different situations, such as never start dancing at a school dance before the lights go off. He had difficulty reading social cues, mistaking the children's laughter during his breakdancing for approval and enjoyment when it was actually ridicule. Also, Jonathan had no idea how to make contact with other kids, resorting to roughness when trying to include himself in the dancing.

On Monday morning, Mr. Earle phoned Jonathan's mother and voiced his concerns about her son's lack of social skills. She replied that although Jonathan was very unhappy at school, she was very pleased by the fact that this was the first school Jonathan had attended where she hadn't been phoned all the time and told stories about the trouble he had gotten himself into. Throughout his school life, she explained, Jonathan had been friendless, picking fights with his peers and being teased in return.

Although he was very kind to his younger sister, who was severely mentally handicapped, other children never came to the house to play—nor did he go to theirs. Naturally, Jonathan's mother was very willing to have Mr. Earle work with her son on his social skills.

Mr. Earle thought long and hard as to the type of program that would be appropriate for Jonathan. He spoke with Jonathan's teachers. For the most part, they agreed that Jonathan had no social problems in class, but at St. James School most of the class work was done individually and socializing did not occur. The drama teacher mentioned that Jonathan did have difficulty working on some group projects, partly because most of the students did not want to work with him.

Mr. Earle decided to sit in on one of Jonathan's drama classes. He arrived just as the drama teacher was dividing the children into groups. Their task was to work together to create, using only their body parts, a machine with moving parts. Jonathan had a lot of ideas and directions for his peers. At first they listened, but when he wouldn't let anyone else interject a comment, they started to ignore him. Finally, they developed a plan themselves and told Jonathan what to do; he looked unhappy, but did what he was told.

Mr. Earle decided to recruit several boys in Jonathan's homeroom class to be part of a social skills group with Jonathan, giving the boy a chance to practice new skills with his peers, as well as facilitating the transfer of these skills to other social situations that occur in school. Mr. Earle spoke to Jonathan's homeroom teacher and asked her to suggest four boys who would benefit from learning how to work cooperatively, and who would be good role models. He then phoned the parents of the boys whom the teacher had enlisted to ask their permission for him to work with their sons for two hours once a week.

At the first meeting, Mr. Earle informed the boys that they would be meeting each week to learn more about how to get along better with others, and to work together on a project: the boys were to plan, create, and direct, and act in a video by themselves; they were also to decide who would see the video following its completion. For the first hour of the session, Mr. Earle taught communication skills (listening, speaking, body language), as well as learning to be assertive without being aggressive. He engaged the boys in role-plays and discussions of real-life situations that they had experienced, or known about. During the second hour, the boys were free to work on their project, with Mr. Earle available to coach them on their social skills or to assist them with their production. The boys decided to make a video for their homeroom class on communication skills. Much planning and prop-making went into the video, as the boys took turns filming, directing, and acting. Jonathan appeared to really enjoy these sessions. He learned to direct in a more appropriate manner by taking into account the feelings of the other students in the group. Interestingly, he preferred to act the parts that portrayed how *not* to communicate.

The boys met for six two-hour sessions. At the end of the sessions, they showed their film to their classmates, who applauded and cheered. Jonathan later told Mr. Earle that he was very proud of the production, and that he felt his other classmates seemed to have more

respect for him. Mr. Earle followed up the social-skills group with individual weekly half-hour counselling sessions with Jonathan that focused on problem-solving strategies for making friends, and for avoiding being victimized. During these sessions, Jonathan was encouraged to analyze situations from various points of view (other people's perspectives), to generate alternate responses or action plans, to choose a response set, and to evaluate his plan.

Three months after the social-skills program had ended, Jonathan had yet to make friends that he would see after school. However, his behaviour in the halls was more appropriate, and the four boys from the social-skills group were very nice to him and would often help him if he were in a difficult situation. Jonathan's mother phoned Mr. Earle to tell him that her son seemed much happier in the morning, and more eager to go to school.

◆ INTRODUCTION

Effective education requires attention to both the academic and social development of students. This is particularly true within the context of inclusive education. As noted in an earlier chapter, one major underlying assumption and potential benefit of social integration is that it will foster interaction and acceptance of all children in the classroom. However, the evidence indicates that many children with learning and behavioural problems interact less frequently and more negatively with their classmates, are poorly accepted by their peers, and do not model the behaviours of their peers as a result of increased exposure to them (Gresham, 1982); this reflects a need for teachers to develop the social ability of many of their students. In this chapter, we discuss the nature and importance of social ability, with emphasis on the methods used for social assessment and intervention. Specific procedures for promoting social integration are also described, along with programs for enhancing students' social skills.

◆ THE NATURE AND IMPORTANCE OF SOCIAL ABILITY

Social ability is important because it is required for successful and pleasurable participation with others in society. Many teachers rate social ability as more likely to lead to life success than variables such as IQ and aptitude (Getzels & Jackson, 1961). Despite its perceived importance, there is no comprehensive and universally agreed-upon definition of social ability. Definitions given by a variety of researchers and social theorists differ in emphasis and vary with respect to their conceptual underpinnings. For example, some emphasize overt behaviours and social skills (Argyle, 1981; Cartledge & Milburn, 1978), and others focus on the importance of cognitive structure and processes (Meichenbaum, 1980). Some emphasize individual characteristics such as motivation, empathy, and emotion (Ford, 1982; Ford & Tisack, 1983; Wrubel, Benner, & Lazarus, 1981; Zigler & Trickett, 1978), while others emphasize social contexts, tasks, and situations with respect to social behaviours (Dodge et al., 1982, 1985, 1986). Further complicating the matter is the fact that the literature also represents different theoretical, assessment, and intervention focuses with target populations that range from well-adjusted children and adolescents to maladapted children and clinically disordered individuals.

◇ SOCIAL ABILITY FROM A THEORETICAL PERSPECTIVE

From our perspective: (1) social ability represents an integration of the socio-cultural, cognitive, developmental, and behavioural theories of social development; (2) acceptable behaviour is different across cultures, specific situations, sex, and age groups; (3) individuals sometimes behave in particular ways because to do so is reinforcing (Bandura, 1969, 1977a, 1986); and (4) social ability is largely influenced by how we process social information, what stage of development we are in, and how the ideas regarding our behaviour have been transmitted to us (see Chapter 3).

Social ability is a function of age and culturally appropriate cognitive, affective, and behavioural facets that permit an individual to engage successfully in interpersonal relationships. These facets range from being able to take care of oneself with respect to personal maintenance to being able to evaluate critically one's own capabilities and resources in problematic situations (Anderson & Messick, 1974). Socially able individuals set goals for themselves, think about their actions, evaluate their actions with respect to their goals, and regulate their thoughts and emotions (Bandura, 1986). Additionally, socially competent individuals perform behaviours they believe will effect rewarding outcomes, and avoid acting in ways that might cause negative outcomes (Schunk, 1987). People are motivated to behave in terms of their expectations for success or failure (Bandura, 1986; Rotter, 1954; Weiner, 1972, 1979), and by their drive to satisfy basic needs (Maslow, 1970).

◇ THE INTERACTIVE COMPONENTS OF SOCIAL ABILITY

We view social ability as a global construct that is made up of many interactive components. These major components provide the framework from which we will discuss assessment and intervention methods, and are outlined below:

1. *The absence of social-skill deficits.* This component focuses on the absence of specific behavioural deficits, which interferes with appropriate social functioning.
2. *Positive cognitive-affective characteristics.* This component includes a range of affective characteristics that can influence one's interactions with others, including self-concept, locus of control, and learned helplessness.
3. *Effective communication and role-taking.* This component refers to how individuals express their thoughts and feelings and how well they understand the ideas and feelings of others.
4. *Particular social contexts.* This component refers to the specific and general situations in which social behaviours take place.
5. *Accurate social cognition.* This component refers to how individuals think about themselves and others and how well they make social decisions and solve social problems.
6. *Appropriate social goals.* This component includes the range of desired outcomes resulting from the social behaviour. These goals include making friends, playing with others, joining a group, and avoiding conflict.

Many children in inclusive classrooms lack social ability due to difficulties in one or more of the areas noted above. Failure to deal with social disabilities may have unfortunate consequences for some children. For example, a student's rejection by peers is related to school dropout (Ulman, 1957); while social status problems early in a child's school experience are associated with later juvenile delinquency (Roth, Sells, & Golden, 1972), academic underachievement, and adjustment problems (McCandless, 1967). We now discuss in more depth the above components of social ability—components that we believe are the most important areas for teachers to consider with respect to social assessment and intervention.

THE ABSENCE OF SOCIAL-SKILL DEFICITS

Social skills are specific behaviours that people perform when interacting with others. Research indicates that many students with learning and behavioural problems have deficient and/or inefficient social skills (Gottlieb, 1981; Gresham, 1982, 1985; Madden & Slavin, 1983) in, for example, introducing oneself, controlling anger, apologizing for one's actions, saying thank you, asking to join a group, and ending a conversation.

According to Gresham (1988), social-skill problems can be divided into four types: social-skill deficits, performance deficits, self-control skill deficits, and self-control performance deficits. Children with *social-skill deficits* either do not possess the necessary social skills needed to interact appropriately with their peers or do not know one or more steps involved in the performance of the skill. Children with *performance deficits* may have the social skills required for effective interaction with their peers, but do not perform them adequately, either because they lack the motivation to perform the behaviour or because they have had little opportunity to perform the behaviour. Thus, a child who has demonstrated in the past that he or she can perform the behaviour probably has a performance deficit rather than a social-skill deficit.

Children with *self-control skill deficits* have typically not learned a particular social skill because some emotional response or condition (such as anxiety) has prevented them from acquiring the skill. These children tend to be unable to control impulsive or disruptive behaviour, and often act without considering the consequences of their behaviour. Children with *self-control performance deficits* know how to perform the skill, but do so inconsistently or infrequently due to their inability to control their emotions. Thus, the major difference between these two deficits is that children with social self-control skill deficits have never learned the social skill, whereas children with self-control performance deficits perform the skill inconsistently.

POSITIVE COGNITIVE-AFFECTIVE CHARACTERISTICS

At any developmental level, the success or failure of a social interaction is influenced by self-perception. People who view themselves as liked, wanted, able, and worthy tend to face their day-to-day encounters with confidence, while those with low opinions of themselves tend to avoid others and withdraw from social interactions. A child's past experiences shapes his or her self-image. From our perspective, social ability is largely influenced by children's view of themselves and by the degree of control they think they have over their environment. Hence, we believe that the three most important affective characteristics of social ability/disability are self-concept, locus of control, and learned helplessness, which are discussed below.

Self-Concept

It is a widely held belief that *self-concept* is centrally involved in the learning process of children (Scheirer & Kraut, 1979; Wylie, 1979). Children must be able to see themselves in positive ways, to look at their own flaws and limitations, to trust their capabilities, and to try new approaches in order to have continuing successful interpersonal relationships. How others respond to your behaviour and performance influences your self-perceptions and how you respond to others. Studies comparing the self-concepts of learning-disabled children with those of their nondisabled peers indicate that children with learning disabilities have more negative self-concepts (Pearl & Bryan, 1979). Bryan and Bryan (1978) discovered that children with learning disabilities were more likely to be ignored by their teachers and peers when they initiated action, and that they have unsatisfactory social relationships due to their low self-concepts and peer unpopularity.

However, many children with learning and behavioural problems who rate themselves low with respect to academic self-concept (Boersma & Chapman, 1979) are like other children in terms of general self-esteem (Bryan, 1986). It is important, therefore, for teachers to keep in mind that children's self-perceptions of ability may change across different situations, and that this can affect their performance in various ways.

Teachers can promote positive self-concept by developing learning strategies for areas in which students feel they need to be more successful (see Chapter 12), and by establishing comfortable learning environments in which children have opportunities to talk, work, and share together (see Chapters 9 and 14).

Locus of Control and Learned Helplessness *– yes   pay atten to term!*

Locus of control focuses on the degree to which individuals believe themselves to be in control of their actions. Children with an *internal locus of control* believe that events in their lives are largely determined by their own efforts, whereas children with an *external locus of control* view the outcomes of events to be controlled largely by chance or other circumstances outside their influence. Many children with learning and behaviour problems have a high external locus of control, while children without these problems typically have a high internal locus of control.

Pearl and Bryan (1979) explored the locus of control in children, with and without learning disabilities, in Grades 3 to 8. They found that children without learning disabilities were more likely to attribute their failures to not trying hard enough, while children with learning disabilities were more likely to attribute their failures to the difficulty of the task. In a study of Grade 3 and 5 children, Andrews, Mulcahy, and Darko-Yeboah (1990) found that, although children with and without learning disabilities did not differ from one another with respect to accepting responsibility for their failures, only those children with average to above-average achievement accepted responsibility for their successes. The above research suggests that children with learning disabilities, in tending not to attribute their success to their own effort, will therefore be less likely to sustain any effort that contributed to the positive outcome. This research also suggests that in social situations, children with learning disabilities might fail to perceive successful interactions with others as being in their control and the result of their own efforts; conversely, they may attribute rejection by their peers to themselves and not to external factors outside their control.

The concept of **learned helplessness** is closely related to locus of control. Seligman (1975), who developed the theory, describes learned helplessness as occurring when individuals learn that there is no relationship between their behaviour and their ability to make changes in their environment. Over the course of repeated failures, a person comes to believe that he or she is unable to influence a situation and gives up trying. According to Seligman (1975), people with feelings of learned helplessness fail to initiate responses, fail to learn, and suffer from degrees of emotional disturbance. Seligman's original model of learned helplessness was reformulated to incorporate an *attributional perspective* (Abramson, Seligman, & Teasdale, 1978). According

◆ learned helplessness: occurs when individuals learn that there is no relationship between their behaviour and their ability to make changes in their environment

to this model, people's attributions for outcomes influence future expectancies of outcomes and reactions to them. A person who attributes negative outcomes to stable causes will likely expect negative outcomes in the future, which may result in helplessness. Causes can affect both global and specific areas of one's life. For example, students may believe that they lack ability in all school subjects or just in one specific subject. Global attributions will more likely result in helplessness. Negative events may be attributed to internal reasons (e.g., poor memory) or to external reasons (e.g., poor teaching), with internal attributions being more likely to result in helplessness.

The implication of the above information is that teachers need to assist students in developing an internal locus of control, as well as external, specific, and unstable attributions for negative events. In other words, teachers need to show students that there are ways in which they can control their social interactions, and to discuss with them particular situations that are beyond their control. Borkowski and his colleagues (Borkowski, Johnson, & Reid, 1987; Borkowski, Weyhing, & Carr, 1988) have paired attributional training with strategy training to influence students' expectancies and behaviours. Attributional training with cognitive strategy instruction helps students realize that they can control their learning and behaviour, and that there is a relationship between strategy use and success. Providing credible attributional feedback to students for their successes positively affects achievement expectancies and behaviours (Schunk, 1982; Schunk & Cox, 1986; Schunk & Rice, 1986). Moreover, teaching students to attribute failures to low effort enhances effort attributions, expectancies for success, and achievement behaviours (Andrews & Debus, 1978; Chapin & Dyck, 1976).

EFFECTIVE COMMUNICATION AND ROLE-TAKING

Communication and role-taking are two interrelated concepts that are essential for successful social interaction. Being able to express one's thoughts, feelings and views, as well as being able to understand the ideas and feelings of others, is an integral part of developing and maintaining interpersonal relationships. The ability to effectively communicate with others and to take on the role of others (*role-taking*) greatly determines one's social ability.

In order to communicate effectively, a person needs to be able to initiate, maintain, repair, and terminate conversations (Speckman & Roth, 1982), take the perspective of his or her communicative partner, and convey a message gesturally (through body movements), linguistically (through words), and paralinguistically (through pitch and intonation) (Speckman, 1981). Research suggests that children with learning problems may be sending out messages to others that they do not wish to convey. Bryan, Sherman, and Fisher (1980) report that learning-disabled children spend less time looking at a communication partner (giving the impression of disinterest), engage in shorter and more furtive looks, use a greater number of hand illustrations, and smile less often than nonlearning-disabled children. Bryan, Wheeler,

Felcan, and Henek (1976) found that children with learning disabilities are more likely than their nonexceptional peers to make competitive statements in conversation, and less likely to make considerate statements.

Noel (1980) found that elementary students with learning disabilities are less effective in providing descriptive information about objects than are nonlearning-disabled children, due to a limited use of labelling in their verbal descriptions.

Bryan, Donahue, and Hurm (1981) investigated the communicative competence and peer relationships of children as they engaged in a small-group problem-solving task. The results indicated that children with learning disabilities were less persuasive with their conversational partners than are their nonexceptional peers; furthermore, they were more negative toward others after receiving praise for their communication ability. Dickstein and Warren (1980) found evidence of role-taking deficits in 5 to 10-year-old children with learning disabilities. In a similar vein, Horowitz (1981), in investigating the ability of children to take another person's point-of-view, found that children with learning disabilities perform less well on interpersonal tasks that require taking an alternative viewpoint.

Children with learning disabilities perform less successfully than those without in a variety of aspects related to speaker and listener roles. Pearl and Cosden (1982) investigated children's understanding of social interactions and found that children with learning disabilities generally make more social comprehension errors than do nonlearning-disabled children. Bryan et al. (1981) examined the conversational competence of children with learning disabilities when placed in a dominant social position. Although they were cooperative conversational partners, their strategies for initiating and sustaining the interaction differed from those of their nonexceptional counterparts. They asked fewer questions and were less likely to produce open-ended questions; in turn, their conversational partners were less likely to provide elaborate responses to their questions. Donahue, Pearl, and Bryan (1980), who examined children's understanding of conversational rules for repairing communication breakdown, found that children with learning disabilities are less likely to request clarification of inadequate messages and consequently make fewer correct referent choices than do nonlearning-disabled children.

The above research suggests that children with learning disabilities are: (1) less proficient than nonlearning-disabled children in taking another person's point of view during interpersonal situations; (2) more egocentric (unable to understand the feelings and positions of others, and to adjust to the different needs of their listeners); and (3) unable to function efficiently in both speaker and listener roles, particularly in their inability to provide sufficient information for communication to be adequately shared and understood. The emerging view from social status research is that rejection of children with learning and behavioural problems is related to their inefficient and deficient uses of language in social contexts. This implies that teachers should provide supportive verbal communication climates in the classroom (see Chapters 9 and 14), and encourage open dialogue and discussion with students in both large-group and small-group formats.

PARTICULAR SOCIAL CONTEXTS

In order to adequately evaluate and develop a child's social ability, teachers must take into account the *social context*, which includes the general social context (home, classroom, school playground), as well as the specific social context (friendship-making, peer-group entry, conflict resolution). Other variables such as age, gender, peer status, and interpersonal familiarity should also be considered.

It is important for teachers to keep in mind that an individual may not perform the same way across all situations (McFall, 1982). Situational parameters (e.g., time and place), as well as the behavioural responses of other individuals during and prior to a particular occurrence of behaviour, need to be considered. For example, as noted by Foster and Ritchey (1979) "grabbing a toy … may be an adaptive response if a child's possessions have been taken by another without permission. The same response will be socially inappropriate if the toy belongs to another child. Rating both responses as they were equivalent would mask salient aspects of the social context, thus limiting the social validity of the data" (p. 627). Thus, compiling a behavioural repertoire based on what others consider to be indicative of successful adjustment and social ability is not in itself an adequate prescription for remediation. Rather, as Scandura (1977) suggests, one needs to consider the content domain, the situation in which the behaviour occurs, the underlying competencies of the child, and the way he or she processes information; for any given social situation, there may be several possible solutions due to the interaction between the nature of the situation and the personal characteristics of the child.

The interaction of social skills, affective characteristics, communication, role-taking, and social context is represented by the following example. John wants to make friends with another boy in his Grade 4 class named Peter. In order to accomplish this, he must first determine the best time to approach Peter. John will then go to Peter and introduce himself with appropriate remarks and behaviours. During the initial stages of introduction and throughout the dialogue, John will need to display appropriate nonverbal behaviours (e.g., contingent smiling behaviours and comfortable distance), as well as be able to maintain conversation, repair communication breakdown, demonstrate empathic understanding of Peter's position and viewpoints, and provide suggestions and direction for further interaction. Social skills are important because, for example, John may have social-control deficits and may reduce his chances for getting to know Peter better by failing to ask followup questions. Social context is also important to consider because John's success may additionally be contingent on such things as where and when he decides to initiate his interaction with Peter; approaching Peter in class, for example, may be disrupted by classroom events such as teacher assignments and directions to students.

While research on social ability has generally failed to identify the social contexts that present problems for exceptional children, Dodge, Coie, and Brakke (1982) found deficiencies in aggressive and socially rejected children to be most evident in particular situations (e.g., being provoked by a peer or pressured by social expectations). The implication from this and the above discussion is that teachers need to consider social contexts when remediating social difficulties. At the same time, they should take into account the role of social cognition in the development of social ability, as discussed below.

No

ACCURATE SOCIAL COGNITION

Social cognition refers to the knowledge and cognitive activities employed by people in dealing with the social world (Pearl, 1987), and is considered to be an important mediator in the socialization process. According to some theorists, cognition is intrinsically social (Chandler, 1977) because human knowledge is a social product (Kuhn, 1962), which is flavoured by the norms, values, and motivations of people in society (Forgas, 1981). The way children view themselves, the way they conceptualize social situations, and the way they process information from social interactions has important implications for how they relate to parents, teachers, and peers. A major underlying assumption of social cognition theory is that we are best able to predict and control what goes on around us if we can identify lawful relationships and invariants that explain our own and other people's behaviour across a variety of situations (Weiner, Graham, Taylor, & Meyer, 1983). Social cognition and social ability are related in the sense that how we reason about ourselves, about other people, and about social situations is a major determinant of our overall social ability.

Not specific

Although research on the relationship of social cognition to social ability is somewhat limited, there is evidence to suggest that the ability to process information efficiently and to employ efficient strategies is related to effective social behaviour. Some researchers have found that socially competent adolescents are more cognitively resourceful than are socially incompetent adolescents (Pellegrini, 1980; Spivack, Platt, & Shure, 1976; Spivack & Shure, 1974). Other researchers have found that children with learning and behavioural problems respond to problem situations randomly and impulsively rather than by employing efficient problem-solving strategies (Hallahan & Reeves, 1980; Torgesen, 1977). There is also evidence that deficiencies in cognitive problem-solving skills are associated with the social adjustment of emotionally disturbed children (Shure & Spivack, 1972) and impulsive teenagers (Spivack & Levine, 1963).

Jahoda (1958) suggests that psychological health is influenced by one's ability to recognize and admit a problem, to reflect on possible solutions, to make decisions, and to take action. In terms of a social problem-solving framework, Goldfried and d'Zurrella (1969) outline a series of steps that an individual must take in order to behave in a competent manner. According to this model, an individual must be able to: (1) identify and understand the problem situation that is confronting him or her; (2) search for possible alternative solutions as ways of dealing with the situation; (3) make a decision based on the possible consequences of particular actions, and; (4) act out a response choice.

Research suggests that children with learning and behaviour problems display maladaptive behaviour not because they prefer conflict, but because they do not have effective strategies for producing more satisfactory resolutions (Harris, 1984; Torgesen, 1977). A growing body of literature indicates that these children fail to use systematic or organized strategies for solving problems (Finch & Spirito, 1980; Hallahan, Lloyd, Kasiewicz, Kauffman, & Graves, 1979; McKinney & Haskins, 1980); have difficulty producing problem-solving plans (Hall, 1980), and seldom generalize previously learned problem-solving strategies to new problems (Lloyd, 1980).

In addition to knowing *how* to think, an individual must also know *what* to think when facing a social problem. For example, he or she should have an awareness of the person variables (e.g., self-concept, locus of control, and motivation) that can affect the successful completion of a social task, as well as an awareness of task variables (e.g., knowledge of the task parameters and strategies that can be used to perform the task). According to Larson and Gerber (1987), these awareness skills are significantly related to positive social outcomes.

While researchers have noted that many children with learning and behaviour problems tend to misperceive social situations (Freemont, Seifert, & Wilson, 1977; Freemont, Wallbrown, & Nelson, 1978; Wiig & Semel, 1976), the exact role of social perception in these children's social ability remains unclear (Gerber & Zinkgraf, 1982; Maheady & Maitland, 1982). Nevertheless, there is no disputing that many children with learning and behavioural problems tend to be poor at judging the moods and positions of others; have difficulty maintaining independent activity and interpreting social situations, and often appear to do or say inappropriate things—all of which can cause them to be rejected by their peers. It follows from this, and from the earlier discussion, that teachers should help children develop their social decision-making and problem-solving capabilities, as well as help them interpret the motives, intentions, and feelings of others.

APPROPRIATE SOCIAL GOALS

It is important to take a child's *goals* into consideration in order to better appreciate his or her cognitive processing and social behaviour. According to Ford (1982), social ability is the "attainment of relevant social goals in specified contexts, using appropriate means and resulting in positive developmental outcomes" (p. 324). The research program of Baumrind (1975) has provided evidence that socially competent children are goal-oriented—that is, they actively choose their own goals rather than passively adapt those imposed on them by others in their environment.

White's (1959) concept of *competence motivation* proposes that competent children have goals related to influencing and mastering their environment. As previously discussed, many children with learning and behavioural problems exhibit low self-concept, external locus of control, and learned helplessness. It can be postulated that many of these children lack goals related to influencing and mastering their environment, and instead are more likely to adopt goals imposed by the environment. Moreover, some children choose inappropriate goals (see Chapter 9) that lead to inappropriate behaviour.

Ford (1982) found that adolescents who are judged to be competent in challenging social situations assign high priorities to interpersonal goals such as helping and getting along with others. Other research has found that socially competent individuals are better able to deal with interpersonal problem situations and to provide strategies or plans for resolving them (Pellegrini, 1980; Spivack et al., 1976).

Research has also shown that children with learning disabilities differ from their peers not only in their selection of social strategies but also in their goals for social interaction (Renshaw & Asher, 1983). Carlson (1987) found in her study of second- through fifth-grade students that children with learning disabilities differ from their nondisabled peers in terms of the goals they adopt in a peer-conflict situation. Unlike the majority of their peers, children with learning disabilities tend to approach peer conflict as a win-lose situation. The goals they choose in peer-conflict situations indicate a nonassertive or powerless orientation toward interpersonal negotiation. Carlson attributes the less efficient strategies and goals of these children to their lower self-concept, lower expectation for success, and external locus of control.

As the above discussion suggests, some children in inclusive classrooms need help in setting appropriate social goals. In addition to helping students with their academic goals, teachers should try to guide students toward making reasonable social goals and encourage them to commit themselves to attaining these goals. Having discussed the interactive components of social ability, we now focus on ways to assess these components.

◆ ASSESSING THE COMPONENTS OF SOCIAL ABILITY

Previous discussion suggests that teachers need to be cognizant of the influence that cognitive, affective, behavioural, and environmental aspects have on a child's social ability. Before introducing ways in which teachers can assess the various components of social ability so that intervention programs can be developed and implemented, we should point out underlying principles that are related to the assessment of children's social ability. First, a child's social disability may be due to an interaction of many factors, and thus assessment can be enhanced by using several measures rather than only one. Second, social behaviours vary considerably as a function of age, sex, peer group, time of day, and social context. Third, observations of behaviour are more valid if done by more than one person, and in more than one setting, before judgments are made. Finally, every behaviour should be viewed on a continuum, for example, from "mild" to "severe" or from "always present" to "never present."

Assessment practice should be thought of as an interactive process. In other words, the relationship among affective (self-concept), behavioural (social performance skills), cognitive (social problem-solving), and environmental (specific social context) variables should be analyzed. This process is less overwhelming than it might appear. For example, a teacher might suspect that one of her students has difficulty joining groups of children. She might begin by observing the student in a variety of social contexts (e.g., playing at recess, eating lunch in the cafeteria), and with various groups of children, and then try to determine whether the child has a social-skill deficit or a performance defect. Moreover, the teacher should note if there is any variance in the student's performance with respect to the particular social context and group of children, as well as determine whether the child has peer entry as a personal goal. Finally, the teacher should evaluate the child's communication style during social interaction, and find out how the child feels about his or her ability to join groups of children. Once this information is collected and analyzed, the teacher is in a much better position to determine the child's particular social needs and to design an intervention program. We believe that the process of defining the specific behaviours; observing and recording their occurrence in the social environment; assessing the child's perceptions of the particular social interaction; and analyzing the information in order to design social program plans provides an ecologically valid way of determining a child's social ability.

ASSESSMENT OF SELF-CONCEPT AND LOCUS OF CONTROL

The primary method of evaluating children's self-concept and locus of control is to use norm-referenced tests. These tests measure students' performance in relation to their (norm) group, and provide such information as **percentile rank**, **standard score**, and age/grade equivalent. For example, The Piers-Harris Children's Self-Concept Scale (1984) is a self-report measure designed to aid in the assessment of self-concept in children and adolescents. It can be used to identify areas of relative strength and vulnerability in children across six dimensions: the child's perception of his or her problematic behaviours; the child's self-assessment with respect to intellectual and academic tasks; the child's attitudes concerning his or her physical characteristics; the child's emotional state; the child's evaluation of his or her popularity; and the child's degree of satisfaction and happiness about his or her life. An example of a test for locus of control is Crandall's Intellectual Achieve-

◆ percentile rank: an individual score below which a given percentage of individuals scored; e.g., a percentile rank of 75 means that 75 percent of test-takers scored below the individual's rank

◆ standard score: a score that has a mean and a standard deviation

ment Responsibility Questionnaire (Crandall, Katkovsky, & Crandall, 1965), which examines children's beliefs about their responsibility for outcomes in academic-achievement situations in order to determine their degree of internal or external locus of control.

Figure 13.1

A Teacher-Made Self-Concept and Perception of Ability Scale for Young Children

Name ————————————

Date ————————————

1. I like school.

2. I am a good student.

3. I have many friends.

4. I work well with other children.

5. I like reading.

6. My spelling is always right.

7. Math is easy for me.

8. I do well in school work.

9. I am proud of the work I do.

10. I am good at solving problems.

Teachers can create checklists to assist them in determining the cognitive-affective adjustment of their students. For example, teachers could observe and record behaviours, such as "gets easily frustrated" or "reacts negatively to being corrected," in order to become more aware of their student's behaviour (see Table 13.1). They can also design rating scales (see Figure 13.1) to investigate their students' thoughts and feelings about themselves and their perception of ability across a variety of areas. Moreover, teachers can interview students (see Table 13.2) to gain more information about how they view themselves. When interviewing, the teacher should: (1) refrain from threatening questions; (2) gain information through unstructured lead questions; (3) use probes to obtain specific information; (4) clarify unclear responses through further questioning; (5) follow up areas in which the student shows emotional involvement; (6) be alert to sensitive subjects and handle them diplomatically; (7) answer any direct questions the student poses; and (8) complete the interview before the student becomes tired or bored.

ASSESSMENT OF COMMUNICATION SKILLS

Social communication skills are the foundation of social ability. In fact, communication disabilities play a central role in the social-skill deficits of many

---

Table 13.1
Cognitive-Affective Checklist

Name _____

Observer _____

Directions: Place a check in "Yes" column if the behaviour was observed. Place a check in the "No" column if the behaviour was not observed.

	Yes	No
1. Child pays attention.	_____	_____
2. Child gets angry easily.	_____	_____
3. Child is difficult to manage.	_____	_____
4. Child lacks simple social graces.	_____	_____
5. Child is slow in answering questions.	_____	_____
6. Child has difficulty organizing thoughts and actions.	_____	_____
7. Child has difficulty expressing meaning through words.	_____	_____
8. Child has difficulty understanding other people's feelings.	_____	_____
9. Child acts impulsively.	_____	_____
10. Child solves problems independently.	_____	_____

---

children with learning and behaviour problems (Bryan, 1986). The best way for teachers to determine which social communication skills to teach is by conducting informal natural observations (Cartledge & Kleefeld, 1989). This method requires teachers to target communication skills (e.g., listening to others, complimenting others, speaking clearly, asking for clarification, initiating a conversation); to monitor their students' use of these skills across a variety of social situations; and to rate their students according to their ability to use the targeted skills on a checklist sheet (see Table 13.3).

Another way of determining the social communication abilities of students is through the teacher-student interview. The teacher should tape-record the interview and ask questions that require more than one-word responses. In order to tap the morphological, syntactical, and semantic abilities of their students, teachers could use a number of standardized tests, such as Test of Language Development (Hammill & Newcomer, 1988), or The Clinical Evaluation of Language Functions (Wiig & Semel, 1987). (For further information on oral-language assessments, see Chapter 10.)

Table 13.2
Student Interview

Name: _____   Date: _____

Relevant Background:

_____

_____

_____

_____

Questions:

1. What are your favourite subjects in school?
2. What things do you like about school?
3. What is your least favourite subject in school?
4. Do you like reading?
5. Who do you like to play with at school?
6. Is making friends easy for you?
7. What is the most difficult thing to do in school?
8. Do you feel good about how much you are learning?
9. Do you experience a lot of success in school?
10. What gives you difficulty in class?

Summary Information from Interview:

_____

_____

_____

_____

ASSESSMENT OF SITUATIONAL CHARACTERISTICS

In order to design and implement an effective intervention program for children with social disabilities, teachers need to identify the particular social contexts in which the child displays maladaptive behaviour. One of the few formal assessment measures in this area is The Behavior Rating Profile (Hammill, Bartel, & Bunch, 1984), which examines the home, school, and interpersonal environments of the student from the perspective of a particular student and his or her parents, teachers, and peers.

Informal assessments can be constructed by generating a taxonomy of problematic social situations for students at school. One example of a taxonomy comes from Dodge et al. (1985), who, with the help of elementary school teachers, developed a Taxonomy of Problematic Social Situations for Children in order to better isolate those situations that might lead to peer conflict (e.g., peer-group entry, response to provocation, and response to failure). Teachers can develop their own taxonomies by recording situations that represent common social situations (e.g., small-group work projects, riding the bus, lining up for recess, introducing oneself, apologizing for misbehaviour),

Table 13.3
Communication Skills Checklist

Directions: Record the rating of the students' communication skills using the following scale: (1) very good, (2) good, (3) satisfactory, (4) poor, (5) very poor.

Names	Listens to others	Looks at the speaker	Asks questions	Clarifies messages	Repairs breakdowns	Understands ideas	Initiates conversations	Terminates conversations	Conveys messages gesturally	Smiles at others	Provides descriptive information	Provides alternative views	Sustains conversations	Adjusts to needs of others	Acts interested in others	Comments
Cheryl	3	3	3	2	2	5	1	1	4	3	2	2	1	1	3	A little egocentric
Thomas	1	1	1	4	4	3	1	4	4	4	2	3	1	3	4	Has difficulty making transitions
Jenna	1	2	2	2	2	3	3	3	3	3	3	2	1	1	1	Enjoys talking to others

and by rating students with respect to their social ability in these specific areas (see Table 13.4).

Table 13.4 Behaviour Rating in General Social Contexts			

Name: ————————————————

Date: ————————————————

Directions: If the child generally demonstrates appropriate social behaviour in the particular social context, circle 1; if the child occasionally shows appropriate social behaviour in the particular social context, circle 2; and if the child seldom demonstrates appropriate social behaviour in the particular social context, circle 3.

	Behaviour Rating		
Social Context	Often (1)	Sometimes (2)	Seldom (3)
1. Small-group activities.	1	2	3
2. Large-group discussion.	1	2	3
3. Walking in the hallways.	1	2	3
4. Eating lunch in the cafeteria.	1	2	3
5. Playing in the gym.	1	2	3
6. Outside activities during recess.	1	2	3
7. Inside activities during recess.	1	2	3
8. Travelling in the bus.	1	2	3
9. Playing on the school grounds.	1	2	3
10. Educational field trips.	1	2	3

ASSESSMENT OF SOCIAL COGNITION AND SOCIAL GOALS

Recent advances in cognitive psychology have led to major shifts in the focus of student assessment in both the academic and social domains. Cognitive assessment and intervention focus on the investigation and development of students' approaches to academic and social tasks. Cognitive assessment is based on at least three premises: (1) we can systematically analyze and translate cognitive performance into specific component processes (strategies); (2) we can systematically enhance cognitive performance by training students to employ efficient strategies in their day-to-day performance; and (3) the student plays an active role in his or her cognitive performance.

Assessing students' social strategies, as well as their knowledge of cognitive processes (metacognition), can give a teacher greater insight into their awareness and employment of strategies, and thereby lead to more appropriate remediation and instruction. In cognitive assessment, both the teacher

*＊ 60-d
questions asked*

and student examine the strategies a student uses to perform a certain skill. The intent is to discover how students process information and approach a task, as well as how they perceive their efforts. In this approach, both teacher and student are active participants in the learning and assessment process, as they work together to develop strategies that are relevant to the student's profile of abilities and individual needs, as well as to the teacher's desired outcomes.

The two most common methods used to assess cognitive processes are *verbal self-report measures* obtained before and after a child's performance (Meyers, Pfeffer, & Erlbaum, 1985), and *think-aloud procedures* (Bereiter & Bird, 1985). Two problems teachers might have with verbal reports are (1) obtaining a complete and accurate account of the child's reporting; and (2) having to depend on his or her verbal ability. The focus should be on making the report as complete as possible, rather than on trying to establish unequivocal accuracy. When using self-report measures, the teacher should minimize the amount of probing, make the inquiry as soon as possible after a child does something that is not understood or explained, and use "how" questions rather than "why" questions. One danger of the think-aloud procedure is that, by directing the student to verbalize all thoughts while performing a task, it may interfere with his or her ability to carry out the task. Meichenbaum and Goodman (1971) suggest that the teacher use several types of protocols in order to uncover similar response patterns across the different methods.

Two of the most common standardized measures used to assess children's social problem-solving skills are the Means-End Problem Solving (MEPS) instrument (Shure & Spivack, 1972) and the Matching Familiar Figures Test (MMFT) (Kagan, Rosman, Day, Albert, & Philips, 1964). The MEPS test is composed of six brief stories, each of which portrays a different problematic social situation. In each story, the sex of the protagonist varies to match the sex of the subject. Only the beginning of a story and its outcome are presented. The child's task is to "fill in the middle part" or "tell how the ending got to be that way." The child's responses are scored for three variables, which are then summed to provide a total MEPS score: (1) relevant means—the number of discrete steps the protagonist takes in a coherent plan to achieve the specific goal; (2) obstacles—the number of potential obstacles to goal attainment recognized by the protagonist; and (3) time references—the number of times the subject recognizes the passage of time as a component of the problem-solving process.

Although the MEPS test has adequate reliability and can discriminate between socially maladjusted and adjusted children (Kendall, Pellegrini, & Urbain, 1981), this measure has some methodological flaws (Maag, 1989). In an attempt to address these flaws, Lochman and Lampron (1986) developed the Problem Solving Measure for Conflict (PSM-C), which scores both quantity and quality of responses, contains more realistic story content, and scores for different interpersonal contexts (e.g., peers, teachers, and parents), as well as for the nature of others' intent in conflict (e.g., ambiguous or hostile provocation).

In addition to the skills that are assessed in the MEPS test, Spivack and Shure (1982) propose five other skills they believe to be significant for effective interpersonal problem-solving, namely (1) the ability to generate a variety of solutions to problems; (2) the ability to consider consequences of social acts; (3) the ability to recognize that one's actions and feelings are reciprocally related to the actions and feelings of others; (4) the ability to be sensitive to social problems both generally and specifically; and (5) the ability to recognize that behaviour may reflect motives or antecedents that are not readily discerned. As with the MEPS test, the assessment of these five skills involves presenting hypothetical stories to children and asking questions that require them to think of solutions, consequences, or explanations with respect to a particular social interaction.

In assessing goals, teachers can construct protocols by which they can interview children about their goals. They can also present social situations to children without an explicit goal in order to assess what their goals would be for a particular situation; alternatively, goals could be designed and offered to the children to rank order for the purpose of assessing their goal preferences. As described in Ford (1982), teachers might develop questionnaires to assess such things as children's goal-directedness. For example, children might be asked to endorse one of a pair of opposing statements, such as "I like to set goals for myself" and "I don't like to set goals for myself," or to rank order a list of social and nonsocial goals. Examples of social goals would include "having lots of friends" and "helping other people with their problems," while examples of nonsocial goals would include "earning lots of money" and "having or getting a steady job."

ASSESSMENT OF SOCIAL SKILLS AND DEFICITS

The most common forms of social-skill assessment are sociometric measures, ratings, behavioural role-plays, and naturalistic observations (Gresham & Elliott, 1984; Maag, 1989), to which we now turn our attention.

Sociometric Measures

The two most frequently used procedures are **peer nominations** and **peer ratings**. These two measures identify different aspects of children's status. Peer-nomination techniques require children to nominate their peers in relation to socially relevant criteria such as play partners and best friends (Gresham & Elliott, 1984). This type of measure can help identify which children are accepted or rejected by their peer group, and assist teachers in selecting children who appear to be in most need of social-skills training. The peer-rating approach gives children a list of their peers to rate on the basis of specific criteria (Asher & Hymel, 1981). For example, on a scale of

◆ **peer nomination:** a sociometric measure whereby students nominate their peers in relation to socially relevant criteria such as play partners and best friends

◆ **peer rating:** a sociometric measure whereby students rate their peers on the basis of specific criteria; e.g., group work or play abilities

one to five ("not at all" to "very much"), children might rate each of their classmates on how much they like to do group work or play with them. The rating scale allows the teacher to be aware of each child's attitude toward each peer (Maag, 1989).

Teacher Ratings

Children can be rated by their peers and by their teachers. There are various measures that can be used to help identify specific deficit areas and behavioural tendencies, such as response to peer provocations, disruptiveness, assertiveness, impulsiveness, and so forth. Some of the more popular rating scales are: The Social Behaviour Assessment (SBA) (Stephens, 1978, 1979, 1980); The Guess Who Scale (Gottlieb, Semmel, & Veldman, 1978); The Walker Social Skills Curriculum Scale (Walker et al., 1983); The Progress Assessment Chart of Social Development (Gunzberg, 1980); The Pupil Behaviour Rating Scale (Lambert, Hartsbough, & Bower, 1979); The Kohn Social Competence Scale (Kohn, Parnes, & Rosman, 1979); The Behaviour Problem Checklist (Quay & Peterson, 1975); The Child Behaviour Checklist (Achenbauch, 1978); The Teacher Rating Scale (Conners, 1969); The Matson Evaluation of Social Skills with Youngsters (MESSY) (Matson, Rotatori, & Helsel, 1983); The Taxonomy of Problematic Social Situations (TOPS) scale (Dodge, McClaskey, & Feldman, 1985); and The Teacher Rating of Social Skills (TROSS) scale (Clark, Gresham, & Elliott, 1985).

Behavioural Role-Plays

Behavioural role-plays require students to respond to various fabricated social-interaction scenarios. This procedure is advantageous because it provides ways for students to perform social skills that are not easily observed in naturalistic settings. It also allows for observation of particular strengths and weaknesses, and helps discriminate social-skill from social performance deficits (Gresham & Elliott, 1984).

Naturalistic Observation

Assessment of behaviour that occurs in natural settings is the most ecologically valid method of assessing children's social skills (Asher & Hymel, 1981). This type of assessment allows the teacher to analyze environmental antecedents and consequences that may either be maintaining or preventing socially appropriate behaviour (Maag, 1989). Naturalistic observation also enables a teacher to systematically observe and record students' specific behaviours while they are engaged in social interactions.

Conclusion

The above examples of assessment approaches reflect the important dimensions to consider with respect to our proposed components of social ability. Teachers can use the preceding assessments, observations, interviews, and ratings to form a diagnostic profile of the student, and to initiate program decision-making and planning. It is important to understand (1) that the assessment of students' social ability should reflect the multifaceted nature of human social functioning; (2) that assessing social performance is no less an arduous and time-consuming assessment process than assessing students' academic performance; and (3) that the assessment task is the responsibility of not just the teacher but also the other team members (e.g., parents, teacher's aides, principals, other teachers, social workers, psychologists, nurses, occupational therapists, etc., who can and should assist with information gathering, information sharing, and eventual decision-making.

◆ ASSESSMENT TO INTERVENTION

The assessment to intervention process can begin with a focus on just one of the factors that contribute to social ability (disability), and then expand to include other areas as time and circumstances permit. For example, the assessment team might decide to concentrate its efforts on fostering a particular child's self-concept. It could begin by assessing how the child differentially perceives him or herself within and across different social contexts, which might lead to refinements in the social-intervention approaches. As teachers continue to interact with the student, they can obtain more information about how the student plans, approaches, and evaluates various social tasks, which may indicate a need to develop further his or her information-processing abilities. Essentially, through this process, team members are able to isolate the student's specific social skills and deficits, which will assist the teacher and others in making more specific program modifications.

As described above, assessment and intervention are interactive components, with assessment leading to intervention and intervention leading to further assessment. The continual interaction between assessment and intervention results in better teaching and learning, as do continual teaching, monitoring, and evaluation. Having discussed ways of assessing social ability, we turn our attention to specific ways of developing the social ability of our students.

◆ INTERVENTION APPROACHES AND ACTIVITIES

As we have noted, the first step in program planning and intervention is the identification and verification of the student's social needs. Second, long-term objectives should be established, followed by specified short-term objectives. Third, materials, instructional techniques, and personnel requirements should be considered, along with decisions about whether the environment, instructional process, or materials need to be modified. Lastly, procedures need to be designed to provide continuous feedback on the effectiveness of the program decisions vis-à-vis the student's social needs (see Chapter 9 for further discussion of teaching and lesson planning). We now present some intervention approaches that correspond with the interactive components of social ability.

INTERVENTION RELATING TO COGNITIVE-AFFECTIVE CHARACTERISTICS AND SOCIAL CONTEXT

Teachers should be aware of the social needs of their students and continually strive to create a caring and mutually rewarding and beneficial environment (see Chapter 9). It has already been pointed out that many children with learning and behaviour problems have relatively low self-perceptions with respect to self-concept and locus of control, which have negative impacts on their social ability. Teachers can positively affect children's self-perceptions by giving students opportunities to become aware of their strengths and limitations, and to make adjustments in their learning and behaviour.

Students need to be guided toward trying new ways of doing things. Teachers should not be afraid of students making mistakes because making mistakes in the process of learning is a normal experience. It is only when children come to see themselves as failures that they continue to have failing experiences and avoid trying new approaches and taking risks. Thus, teachers need to develop students' self-responsibility by showing them how to organize and monitor their own actions. This is done by creating classrooms in which students can express their viewpoints, and feel free to question, explore, and expose both knowledge and behavioural limitations without fear of ridicule. An open and trusting classroom atmosphere comes about when a teacher is proactive, nurturing, helpful, positive, democratic, fair, and consistent.

In terms of contextual variables, the teacher may need to modify the environment and social tasks in order to meet the needs of particular students. For example, he or she might provide distractible and inattentive students with fewer activities and perhaps reduce the stimuli associated with a given task. For children who have a difficult time dealing with multiple demands, and who therefore behave inappropriately, a teacher might select and reinforce particular demands. Some students may require careful structuring of activities, with specific rules and guidelines to follow, whereas other students may need more assistance in generalizing their performance in one activity to other activities.

Developing children's social ability in relation to specific situational contexts requires the teacher to observe and analyze a student's social behaviour (successes and difficulties) with respect to different types of tasks, different groups of children, and different social situations. It also requires the teacher to scrutinize the characteristics of the tasks and settings. Two methods of teaching that reflect this approach in developing children's social ability are discussed below.

Diagnostic-Prescriptive Teaching ✓know this

Diagnostic-prescriptive teaching uses diagnostic information to modify educational programs for children. It typically involves a multidisciplinary team approach toward assessment and intervention. The information gathered by the teacher, other professionals, and parents is used to plan an appropriate program. This approach requires members of the collaborative team to observe and assess the child and to make instructional modifications where necessary. The diagnostic findings of the team members are then translated into a prescription for teaching. Next, the recommendations are implemented and modified where appropriate. Lastly, the student's behaviour is closely monitored in order to record progress and determine the success of the prescribed program.

◆ diagnostic-prescriptive teaching: a collaborative approach to developing children's skills in which diagnostic information is used to modify the student's educational program

Diagnostic-prescriptive teaching emphasizes the role of the teacher in all of its phases, especially in providing an educational program that considers the total dynamics of the student's learning and development. Smith (1983) provides the following eight steps as a guide to developing children's social ability:

1. Objectively observe and evaluate the student's classroom social abilities.
2. Objectively observe and evaluate the nature of the student's successes and difficulties during different types of social interactions.
3. Scrutinize the characteristics of alternative social tasks and social settings.
4. Compare and contrast how information gained from Step 3 might interact with the observations from Steps 1 and 2, so as to result in more favourable social development.
5. Consult with the student, present program modifications, and decide together about directions to take.
6. Set short-term goals.
7. Make appropriate modifications and teach.
8. Evaluate progress after a reasonable period. If successful, continue teaching similar but higher-level objectives; if unsuccessful, retrace Steps 1 to 7.

Precision Teaching – know

Precision teaching requires teachers to record on charts the daily behaviour of their students (see Figure 13.2). This method gives teachers an ongoing reporting system and enables them to monitor and discuss with others the student's behaviour and the results of intervention procedures. Precision teaching involves three major activities. First, the teacher pinpoints the behaviour to be changed or improved. Second, the objectives and

◆ precision teaching: an approach to developing children's skills that involves pinpointing the behaviour(s) concerned, establishing objectives for performance, and charting daily progress

Figure 13.2

Daily Record of Students' Social Behaviour

Student Names	Gives Help When Needed	Compliments Others	Speaks Clearly	Uses Appropriate Body Language
James	✓	✓	✓	
Sylvia	✓		✓	
Joan		✓	✓	✓
Bob	✓	✓	✓	✓
Terry			✓	✓
Samantha	✓	✓	✓	✓
Frank	✓	✓		✓
Kelly	✓	✓	✓	
Curtis			✓	

expectations for performance are established (e.g., the student will compliment others, when appropriate, at least three times a day). Finally, the teacher implements the instructional plan and charts the daily progress of the students.

As White (1986) notes, precision teaching allows teachers to become students of "pupil's behavior, carefully analyzing how the behavior changes from day to day and adjusting the instructional plan as necessary to facilitate continued learning" (p. 522). Lindsley (1972) proposes the following seven principles of precision teaching: (1) teachers learn best by studying the behaviours of their students; (2) rate of response is the universal measure of behaviours; (3) student performances need to be charted; (4) direct and continuous monitoring should be undertaken; (5) behaviours need to be functionally defined; (6) building behaviours should be emphasized over eliminating behaviours; and (7) the impact of environmental influences on students' behaviour needs to be analyzed.

SOCIAL COGNITIVE PROBLEM-SOLVING AND GOAL ATTAINMENT

There has been a growing tendency to use social cognitive problem-solving interventions with children who are having difficulty with their interpersonal relationships. In the Think Aloud Program by Camp and Bash (1981), which focuses on developing students' approach to problem-solving, children are initially trained to organize their actions in accordance with four questions: What is my problem? What is my plan? Am I using my plan? and How did I do? The Interpersonal Cognitive Problem Solving Program by Spivack and Shure (1976) targets specific problem-solving skills such as identifying a problem, choosing alternative plans of action, and appreciating the consequences of actions. The goal of these and other interpersonal problem-solving programs is to foster the use of a sequence of cognitive operations or skills required for an individual to develop and maintain positive relationships, to identify and resolve social problems, as well as to facilitate social competence.

Programs that focus on developing children's strategic thinking try to help children to organize their ideas and conceptualize their social interactions in a systematic fashion. These programs advance the idea that improving children's social information processing can aid them in making decisions, describing their ideas and feelings, explaining their point of view, and supporting what they have done. We now review the teaching methodology used in the Strategies Program for Effective Learning and Thinking (SPELT) (Mulcahy, Marfo, Peat, & Andrews, 1986), which is aimed at improving children's problem-solving and decision-making in both the academic and social domains (see Figure 13.3). In broad terms, the overall goals of SPELT are: (1) to have students become active learners, thinkers, and problem-solvers; (2) to have students become more independent, plan-oriented, and strategically efficient in their approach to learning and development; and (3) to have students become more aware of—and in better control of—their own thinking processes.

The teaching methodology in SPELT involves three phases. In *Phase 1*, students are introduced to a number of cognitive strategies and shown how these can increase their ability to acquire, think about, remember, retrieve, express, and apply information and ideas. As students practice the strategies in specific situations, they begin the process of consciously building a personal repertoire of useful tools for dealing with new situations and problems.

At the start of Phase 1, students are presented with a problem or task that would be difficult to solve or complete without using a strategy. For example, a real or hypothetical situation such as the following might be presented: *You walk into the gym to play basketball. Five of your friends are there, and they are arguing. A fight breaks out, during which time some gym equipment is damaged. After the fight, your friends approach you. You are all standing together when the gym teacher walks in. He sees the broken equipment and turns to look at you—your friends do the same.*

Figure 13.3

SPELT Instructional Model

Continuum

Phase 1
Goals:
Metacognitive Empowerment:
a) Raise students' awareness that strategies exist.
b) Illustrate that the systematic use of strategies improves learning.
c) Increase of active involvement and interaction in the learning process.

Direct teaching of strategies in content areas, for example:

Phase 2
Goals:
Students will:
a) maintain strategy use (as developed in Phase 1).
b) be able to evaluate present strategy use.
c) modify/extend strategies taught in different settings, situations.
d) be actively involved in the learning process.

1) Teach for transfer by facilitating the use of stategies previously taught in different subject areas and/or with different applications, allowing for modification and extension.

Phase 3
Goals:
Students will:
a) monitor, evaluate, and generate effective and efficient strategies to improve learning.
b) be actively involved in the learning process.

Content–based assignments are presented, from which the students generate strategies to complete. The use of Socratic dialogue acts as a catalyst for student evaluation of present strategic use, leading to their modification, extension, and/or the generation of new strategies.

Language arts → Social studies
→ Social competence
Math → Science
→ Language arts
Science → Math
→ Social competence
Study skills (one subject) → Test–taking (All Subjects)
Test-taking (Language arts) → Test–taking (Math)
Social competence → Language arts
→ Social Studies

2) Strategies presented in Phase 2 are used to facilitate transfer and to develop critical thinking skills.

All subject areas should be involved with strategies used in skill areas such as those illustrated:

Math → Problem-solving
→ Calculation
Language arts → Comprehension
→ Memory
→ Test–taking
Social studies → Compehension
→ Memory
Making friends
Social competence → Group interaction
→ Lunchroom behaviour

The teacher has students discuss this situation to determine the extent to which they are currently equipped with effective problem-solving strategies. Then the teacher counters ineffective strategies proposed by students to handle the situation by providing them with a step-by-step description of an effective strategy (see Figure 13.4).

Figure 13.4

Social Problem–Solving

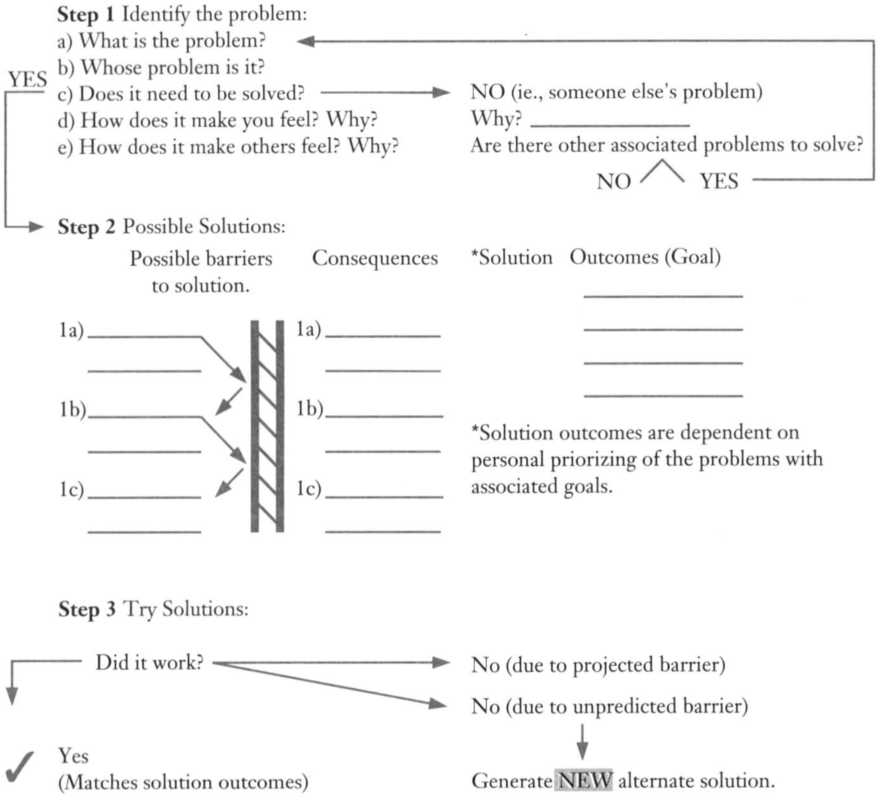

Step 1 Identify the problem:
a) What is the problem?
YES b) Whose problem is it?
c) Does it need to be solved? ——————→ NO (ie., someone else's problem)
d) How does it make you feel? Why?   Why? _____
e) How does it make others feel? Why?   Are there other associated problems to solve?

NO ⋀ YES

Step 2 Possible Solutions:

Possible barriers   Consequences   *Solution   Outcomes (Goal)
to solution.

1a) _____   1a) _____   _____

1b) _____   1b) _____   _____

*Solution outcomes are dependent on
personal priorizing of the problems with
1c) _____   1c) _____   associated goals.

Step 3 Try Solutions:

Did it work? ←——————→ No (due to projected barrier)

No (due to unpredicted barrier)

✓ Yes
(Matches solution outcomes)   Generate NEW alternate solution.

The next step is for the teacher to model the strategy using the same activity or problem-solving situation presented to the students. The entire strategy is modelled using a think-aloud procedure. For example, in terms of our example, the teacher would say something like: "Now, let's see, the first thing I need to be clear about is, what is the problem? As I see it, the problem is fighting in the gym. Next, whose problem is it? I believe the problem belongs to the other boys who were fighting. Let's see, does it need to be solved? No, not by me—it's someone else's problem because I was not fighting. Are there other problems to solve? Yes, it looks that I am being blamed for equipment breakage." Following this modelling exercise, students memorize the parts of the strategy through verbal rehearsal drills. These drills should at first include visual aids, and be rehearsed until the strategy parts can be verbalized quickly and accurately, without visual cues.

The next step is to have students practice applying the strategy to similar social problem-solving situations. This can be done through paper-and-pencil activities, discussion episodes, and role-plays. During the practice sessions, the teacher should give students positive and/or corrective feedback, and return to verbal rehearsal if the strategy parts are forgotten. Lastly, an activity or problem similar to the preceding ones should be assigned to the students as a post-test. Comparing their performance on the pre- and post-tests should give students some idea as to the efficiency and/or effectiveness of their strategy use; the teacher should review this information with the students to ensure that they understand the implications of the comparison.

Students are encouraged in Phase 1 to express their impressions and experiences as they learn and apply new strategies. Control of their own learning becomes more apparent, however, as students enter *Phase 2* teaching, which has as its major emphasis the systematic transfer of the strategic repertoire established in Phase 1 to a wide variety of situations, settings, and applications. In this phase, teachers discuss strategy adaptations, modifications, and/or extensions, emphasizing how these changes can improve strategy use. Students begin to realize that once a strategy is learned, it is not carved in stone but can be modified. Specific strategies are also taught in order to enhance students' ability to systematically analyze the effectiveness and efficiency of their present repertoire of strategies. During Phase 2 teaching, the control of students' learning is gradually shifted from the teacher to the pupil, as students acquire the skills of critically analyzing and discussing their own strategy use, and then using this information to modify or extend the strategies taught in Phase 1.

By the time students begin *Phase 3*, they will have acquired a large repertoire of strategies that they have found to be effective and useful. These strategies, supported by the metacognitive empowerment developed during the first two phases of instruction, serve as a knowledge and experience base for further generation of strategies during Phase 3 instruction. In this phase, situations and problem-solving tasks are presented to students with a minimal amount of teacher guidance. Discussion centres on the analysis of how the task was approached by various students. As in Phase 2, the strategies generated in Phase 3 are evaluated, leading to further refinements and applications.

For both Phases 2 and 3, teachers engage in Socratic dialogue and reciprocal teaching (teacher- and peer-led discussions) whereby they gradually transfer responsibility for questioning and discussion to the students. Unlike Phase 1 and parts of Phase 2, Phase 3 is more student-controlled than it is teacher-controlled. A problem-solving approach to learning and teaching is ultimately established in which students are assigned the responsibility of solving problems. SPELT involves not only teaching strategies but also helping students to deal more effectively with their emotions and desires in academic and social situations. Students are also guided toward an awareness of their needs and goals that enables them to appreciate more fully what they want to gain from their interactions with others, as well as to become more efficient at planning and obtaining their desired goals.

REMEDIATION OF SOCIAL-SKILL AND PERFORMANCE DEFICITS

Earlier in the chapter, we pointed out that social-skill problems could be divided into social-skill deficits, performance deficits, self-control skill deficits, and self-control performance deficits. Gresham (1981, 1984) proposes remedial approaches to these four types of social-skill deficits, which are presented below.

Intervention for Social-Skill Deficits

According to Gresham (1981, 1984), children with social-skill deficits either do not have the social skills required for appropriately interacting with others or they do not know one or more critical steps involved in the performance of the skill. He suggests that social-skill deficits can be remediated primarily through modelling, behavioural rehearsal, or coaching procedures. *Modelling* requires children to attend to specific demonstrated behaviours, to retain the information presented to them, to execute the modelled behaviour, and to be motivated to perform the behaviour (Bandura, 1969, 1977b). Modelled behaviour can be presented to children by teachers or peers, and through role-playing scenarios, films, videos, or television. Although effective modelling behaviour is considered to be an important and influential teaching skill, and although some research suggests modelling to be effective in facilitating social interaction, behavioural change resulting from it has not been sufficiently validated (Gresham, 1981).

Behavioural rehearsal involves reinforcing children's performance with respect to predetermined criteria and providing opportunities for children to practice certain social skills. Although this approach is often successful when used in conjunction with certain tasks and situations, it is limited in terms of its effectiveness in generalizing the behaviour across different situations and contexts.

The *coaching approach* involves verbally instructing children in social skills, giving them opportunities to practice these skills with teachers and peers, and providing feedback to children with respect to their performance and progress. Research indicates that coaching augments sociometric acceptance and status of children (Gottman, Gonso, & Schuler, 1976; Oden & Asher, 1977), and helps to reduce aggressive behaviour (Zahvi & Asher, 1978) while increasing conversational behaviours (Bondy & Erickson, 1976).

Intervention for Performance Deficits

According to Gresham and Elliott (1984), children with performance deficits have appropriate social skills but do not perform them adequately. Strategies for remediating social performance deficits include peer initiations (Strain, Shores, & Timm, 1977), sociodramatic activities (Strain, 1975), social reinforcement approaches (Allen, Hart, Buell, Harris, & Wolf, 1964), token reinforcement programs (Iwata & Bailey, 1974) and group contingencies (Gamble & Strain, 1979). Generally, the focus of these approaches is to modify the environment in order to facilitate positive social interaction, rather than to teach particular social skills. *Peer initiation* activities are directed at getting students' peers to initiate social interaction with children who are not socially interactive. In sociodramatic activities, students practice various social skills by taking on the roles of characters in children's stories. *Reinforcement programs* are generally aimed at rewarding individuals or groups of children, contingent on their performing satisfactory behaviours. According to Gresham (1981), while all of these approaches show promise for training social skills, more research is needed to demonstrate their efficacy in promoting peer acceptance and positive social interaction of children in inclusive classrooms.

Intervention for Self-Control Skill Deficits

Gresham and Elliott (1984) note that self-control skill deficits are indicated when children fail to acquire social skills due to anxiety or impulsiveness. Self-control performance deficits are indicated when a child demonstrates specific social skills in his or her behaviour but performs them inconsistently due to emotional problems. Interventions for children with self-control performance deficits focus on providing them with strategies that inhibit inappropriate behaviours and reinforce appropriate ones (Bolstad & Johnson, 1972; Rosenbaum & Drabman, 1979). Remediation for children with self-control skill deficits usually involves anxiety-reduction techniques combined with modelling and self-control strategies (Meichenbaum, 1977, 1985).

Meichenbaum (1980) and Meichenbaum and Goodman (1971) developed a cognitive-behavioural training program that focuses on teaching children to generate spontaneously, and to employ cognitive strategies and self-instruction. In self-instruction, the individual verbalizes the statements or procedures and develops mental images that facilitate controlling, prompting, directing, and maintaining behaviours under a variety of circumstances. The teacher models the self-statements and the students rehearse these statements (initially aloud and then covertly). The focal point of the training is not to teach the individual *to* think but *how* to think. This is accomplished by encouraging the individual to be a collaborator in the generation of cognitive strategies. In the training program, the individual learns when and where to use particular strategies as well as how to employ them prudently.

Meichenbaum suggests the following guidelines for using cognitive behavioural self-instructional training with children: (1) use the child's personal medium of play to initiate and model self-talk; (2) use tasks that strongly facilitate the use of sequential cognitive strategies; (3) have children cognitively model while performing for another child; (4) progress at the child's own rate; and (5) build a package of self-statements that include coping and self-reinforcing elements.

NO

In the next two sections, we discuss two social-skill programs that are designed to foster positive social skills in elementary students and adolescents.

A SKILLSTREAMING PROGRAM FOR ELEMENTARY STUDENTS

Skillstreaming the Elementary School Child (McGinnis & Goldstein, 1984) is a program that focuses on the maintenance and generalization of learned social skills. In this program, students' social needs are identified through a social-skills checklist and recorded on a chart. Social skills such as asking for help are task-analyzed into specific steps and also charted by the teacher so students can refer to them during the teaching-learning process. The skillstreaming approach has four basic components: modelling, role-playing, feedback, and transfer of training. In the first step, the teacher *models* the social-skill steps, which the students then identify. Next, the students, under the guidance of the teacher, identify situations in which they could use the skill and practice (*role-play*) the behaviours that have been demonstrated (modelled) by the teacher; this second step helps students learn how to perform the social skill. The third step, *feedback*, occurs after each role-play. The teacher and students discuss things that could be done differently, and provide encouragement of the participants. The participants in the role-play also evaluate their own performance. The final step, *transfer of training*, focuses on generalizing the learned social skills through a structured sequence of homework assignments. This step provides opportunities for students to practice the skills in real-life situations, and involves the following four stages:

NO

1. *Homework.* The students and teacher choose situations at home and at school in which the child is going to practice the skill.
2. *Red Flag.* The student is told that, at some point during the day, the teacher will create a situation in which the child will be expected to perform the social skill. For example, if the skill is dealing with teasing, the student is told that the teacher will tease him or her during the day. When the teacher has teased the student and the student has reacted by practicing the social skill for dealing with teasing, the teacher calls "Red Flag." Then together they evaluate and discuss the student's social behaviour.
3. *Self-recording.* The students who know the steps well and show success with the first two stages, write the steps down on a self-recording sheet. During the day, the students record when the steps of the skill were practiced and evaluate their performance.

4. *Keeping a tally.* The students list the social skills and tally each time they practice the skill.

This structured social-skill program consists of sixty social skills arranged in five groups: classroom survival skills (asking for help, following instructions, setting a goal); friendship-making skills (introducing oneself, offering help to a classmate, suggesting an activity); skills for dealing with feelings (expressing feelings, dealing with anger, recognizing another's feelings); skill alternatives to aggression (responding to teasing, avoiding trouble, negotiating); and skills for dealing with stress (coping with boredom, reacting to failure, and handling group pressure).

A SOCIAL SKILLS PROGRAM FOR ADOLESCENTS (ASSET)

The ASSET social skills program (Hazel, Schumaker, Sherman, & Sheldon-Wildgen, 1981) provides a set of training procedures to help adolescents gain important social-interaction skills. The program includes resources and methods to be used in teaching the following eight social skills:

1. *Giving positive feedback.* This skill teaches students how to thank and compliment someone.
2. *Giving negative feedback.* This skill teaches students to give feedback in a calm and nonthreatening manner, to offer their own perception of the situation, to ask for the other person's perception, and to suggest changes.
3. *Accepting negative feedback.* This skill teaches students how to listen to criticism without getting angry, walking away, or taking other inappropriate actions.
4. *Resisting peer pressure.* This skill teaches students how to say no to peers who try to get them to perform some inappropriate behaviour, as well as how to give reasons for not engaging in the activity and how to suggest alternative activities.
5. *Problem-solving.* This skill teaches students how to deal with their interpersonal difficulties, how to evaluate their solutions, and how to choose the most desirable solution.
6. *Negotiation.* This skill teaches students how to solve interpersonal conflicts in mutually acceptable ways.
7. *Following instructions.* This skill teaches students how to acknowledge and carry out instructions in ways that avoid conflict.
8. *Conversation.* This skill teaches students how to initiate and maintain conversation.

The lessons for the social skills include explanations from the teacher about the nature of the skill and its specific steps, and about why the skill is important for the students, as well as homework assignments that provide opportunities for students to practice the skills. Moreover, each lesson reviews the homework and social skills from previous lessons, and contains activities that illustrate the realistic use of each skill. Teachers are expected to model each skill and allow students to practice and demonstrate the use of the particular social skills in class time before they are given homework assignments.

SOCIAL-INTEGRATION INTERVENTION

Many children with learning and behavioural problems have difficulties interacting with others (Kauffman, 1985). The fact that these children will be part of the inclusive classroom makes it necessary for teachers to help them establish positive social relationships. One of the major reasons for advocating the social integration of all children is that the process will provide an opportunity for everyone to develop an acceptance and respect for the individuality of others (Schulz, Carpenter, & Turnbull, 1991). For the social integration of children to occur, teachers must plan and approach the development of social integration in a consistent and systematic fashion. We now review two intervention approaches that can facilitate this process.

Cooperative Learning

Cooperative learning refers to the structuring of learning groups so that students can work together to achieve common goals. This approach fosters the development of interaction skills, instils in students an appreciation of individual differences (Hoben, 1980), and enables individuals to cooperate rather than compete with each other (Madden & Slavin, 1983).

Slavin, Madden, and Leavy (1984) combined cooperative learning and individualized programming in an intervention called Team Assisted Individualization (TAI). Students work in heterogeneous groups and help each other understand and complete assigned academic tasks. Although the cooperative element of this program is appealing, there is limited evidence of its effectiveness in promoting peer acceptance. Johnson and Johnson (1980, 1986), after investigating the effects of cooperative learning on the social integration of children with learning and behavioural problems, concluded that students can benefit from cooperative learning groups as long as teachers follow these guidelines:

- Specify the instructional goals of the lesson.
- Reward group efforts and not individual achievement.
- Teach students the skills they need to work cooperatively with others.
- Help students solve their problems without taking over their problems.
- Monitor and evaluate each group's progress and provide assistance where it is needed.
- Ensure that students can adequately see and use classroom materials.
- Provide clear information regarding objectives and criteria for success, as well as expectations for working together.
- Provide closure to the lesson by reviewing the progress of each group.

Teaching Cooperation Skills: The ASSIST Program

The ASSIST (Affective Skills Sequentially Introduced and Systematically Taught) program developed by Huggins (1986) provides a variety of activities, for both primary and intermediate grades, designed to increase students' growth in three critical areas (self-concept, dealing with feelings, and interpersonal relationships), and to allow students to practice the social skills that are related to the lesson concepts. The cognition-oriented lessons and experiential activities in the ASSIST curriculum are grouped into manuals: Building Self-Esteem in the Classroom, Teaching Cooperation Skills, Teaching Friendship Skills, Helping Kids Handle Anger, and Creating a Caring Classroom. The Teaching Cooperation Skills manual contains the following eleven lessons:

1. *Learning to work together.* Students learn what cooperation means, and how to work with a partner on a learning task.
2. *Working in a group.* Students learn how to assume the roles of a group while engaging in small-group activities, and how to evaluate their own behaviour.
3. *Learning how to listen to others.* Students learn good listening skills.
4. *Encouraging others to share their ideas.* Students learn how to promote cooperation in small groups.
5. *Responding to others in group discussion.* Students learn how to link, restate, and summarize other students' contributions when engaged in small groups.
6. *Cooperative problem-solving through brainstorming.* Students learn how to work together and generate many ideas for solving given problem situations.
7. *Cooperative decision-making through consensus.* Students learn to cooperate by striving for consensus with respect to given problem situations.
8. *Dealing with conflict in cooperation groups.* Students learn adaptive coping skills for dealing with conflict in groups.
9. *Learning to negotiate and compromise.* Students learn skills that can effectively resolve conflict situations that arise in cooperative learning situations.
10. *Working cooperatively on a long-term situation project.* Students learn how to negotiate and reach consensus while implementing a simulated adventure.
11. *Using cooperation skills in classroom meetings and discussions.* Students learn how to express themselves during classroom meetings and discussions.

PEER TUTORING

Peer tutoring is an arrangement in which one student is paired with another for the purpose of accomplishing a defined goal. A child who is competent in one particular academic area is usually paired with a student who is having

difficulty in that area. The peer tutor needs to be trained by the teacher with respect to instructional procedures, reinforcement methods, and ways to provide feedback. Peer tutoring can lead to a greater appreciation of students' strengths and weaknesses (Schulz, Carpenter, & Turnbull, 1991), and foster positive relationships between students (Delquadri, Greenwood, Whorton, Carta, & Hall, 1986). In implementing peer tutoring, teachers can provide an overview of the learning concepts to the entire class, and then organize groups in which selected tutors can review, modify, and perhaps extend the concepts with their peers.

Teachers need to carefully select tutors and base their selection decisions on such things as the student's ability to exhibit age-appropriate social behaviours, and to be a good listener and helper. Designated tutors should, of course, be willing participants in the process. Teachers should closely monitor the peer-tutoring arrangements, evaluate their progress, and provide feedback to the students on their participation. Although many students can be trained to be excellent tutors, they can never be expected to replace the teacher in program planning and instruction.

The positive results of peer-tutoring in many classrooms has led to the establishment of school-wide peer-support programs. These programs provide learning situations in which students listen to and help facilitate the growth and development of other students (see Appendix 13.1 for a sample newsletter compiled by a peer-support team).

Table 13.5
Developing Social Ability in the Classroom

Interactive Components of Social Ability	*Aspects of Social Components*	*Assessment Methods*	*Intervention Methods*
Absence of Social-Skill Deficits	Social-skill deficits Performance deficits Self-control skill deficits Self-control performance deficits	Sociometrics Behavioural role-plays Norm-referenced tests Checklists Rating scales	Modify environment and social tasks Improve Children's self-perceptions Develop specific social program plans
Positive Cognitive-Affective Characteristics	Self-concept Locus of control Learned helplessness	Interviews Natural Observations	Promote social problem-solving and goal attainment
Effective communication and role-taking	Taking another person's point of view Being a good speaker and listener	Taxonomies Questionnaires Think-aloud procedures	Model appropriate social behaviour Coach students in social skills
Particular social contexts	Social settings Social situations	Self-report measures	Use role-taking activities
Accurate social cognition	Problem-solving Strategic thinking Decision-making		Reinforce satisfactory social development
Appropriate social goals	Goal-directedness		Initiate peer support and peer tutoring programs Promote self-control Use cooperative learning arrangements

◆ CONCLUSION

In this chapter, we reviewed the principle components of social ability, methods of assessing students' social ability, and several intervention approaches (see Table 13.5). The underlying themes of this chapter were (1) that the inclusive classroom offers important opportunities for children to develop interpersonal competence; (2) that the development of social ability is every bit as important as instruction in basic academic skills and content areas (Cullinan, Sabournie, & Crossland, 1992); and (3) that the promotion of students' social ability should be a team effort involving students, teachers, and parents.

QUESTIONS
◆◆◆◆◆◆◆◆◆◆◆◆◆◆

1. List the major components of social ability.

2. Describe some ways in which teachers can assess the social ability of their students.

3. Describe some specific ways in which teachers can develop social ability.

4. Name the four general classifications of social skills problems and suggest how teachers might remediate these problems.

5. Discuss some of the social skill programs that are available to teachers to implement with their students.

NO

◇ APPENDIX 13.1
_____

THE PEER SUPPORT TEAM NEWSLETTER

Hi, we're the peer support team. We presently have nine students on the team: Autumn, Stacy, Elizabeth, Carrie, Chris, Kerri, Leah, Eric, and Alicia make up the team.

The group was founded in September. We did role-playing, problem-solving discussions, and studied our conflict-management procedures. Soon we composed a theme song, we advertised ourselves, and we put together our peer support booklet. In the booklet, we gave a little history, who we are, the kind of problems peer support handles, the benefits, our referral, our counselling-notetaking form, and articles to help us do our jobs better.

Using our advertising, we went about our jobs—outside helper, inside counsellor, and tutors.

We have also started viewing films to improve our skills.

What Peer Support Means to Me

Peer Support means helping kids.
It also means prevention.

If kids learn to talk to you,
then they'll talk before doing something tragic.
I think that Peer Support is very important.
I am very proud and honoured to be on the
Peer Support Team.

Who We Are

A peer support member is someone who cares about others and who talks to them about their thoughts and feelings. Rather than being an "Advice-giver" or a "problem-solver," a peer support member is a sensitive listener who uses communication skills to facilitate self-exploration and decision-making.

The peer support team is composed of supervised students who have been trained to help other students think through and reflect on problems they might be experiencing.

What Kinds of Problems Do Peer Support Members Handle?

Peer support students are good listeners. They have learned about the process of decision-making. They can handle any problem that needs a friendly ear. These could be worries about school, family, loneliness, shyness, relations with peers, and just plain needing someone to talk to. *Peer support members are trained to recognize when a student has a serious problem that should be dealt with by a supervisor. Confidentiality is an important aspect of training.*

What Services Can the Peer Support Team Provide?

Some of the services that a peer support team can offer:
1. General information about the school.
2. Orientation for new students (to be included in next year's program).
3. Tutoring: reading, math, other.
4. Spontaneous Discussion—talking to a peer about a concern.
5. Help with personal communication, anger management, conflict resolution.

Benefits

What are the benefits of being a member of the peer support team?
1. Increased self-awareness.
2. Improved communication and listening skills.
3. Improved self-esteem.
4. Knowing you are helping others in the school.
5. Being part of a team.

Referral to P.E.E.R. Counsellor:

Student's Name: ————————————   Grade: ————————————

Teacher: ————————————   Date: ————————————

Check the service you want:
———————— General information about the school
———————— Orientation
———————— Tutoring—math, reading
———————— Talking about a personal problem
———————— Problem-solving

Comments:

——

——

——

——

——

——

Peer Counselling Record

Name: _____   Date: _____

What I did that caused me to be here now.

_____

_____

_____

_____

_____

What I can and will do tomorrow to improve.

_____

_____

_____

_____

_____

_____

_____

_____

_____

(Student's signature)

_____

(P.E.E.R. counsellor's signature)

Followup checks: _____ (Dates)

Note: This newsletter was developed with the assistance of Deborah Hamilton.

REFERENCES

Abramson, L. Y., Seligman, M. E. P., & Teasdale, J. D. (1978). Learned helplessness in humans: Critique and reformulation. *Journal of Abnormal Psychology, 87,* 49-74.

Achenbauch, T. M. (1978). The child behaviour profile: 1—Boys aged 6-11. *Journal of Consulting and Clinical Psychology, 46,* 478-488.

Allen, K. E., Hart, B. M., Buell, J. S., Harris, F. R., & Wolf, M. M. (1964). Effects of social reinforcement of isolate behaviour of a nursery school child. *Child Development, 35,* 511-518.

Anderson, S., & Messick, S. (1974). Social competency in young children. *Developmental Psychology, 10*(2), 282-293.

Andrews, G. R., & Debus, R. L. (1978). Persistence and the causal perception of failure: Modifying cognitive attributions. *Journal of Educational Psychology, 70,* 154-166.

Andrews, J., Mulcahy, R., & Darko-Yeboah, J. (1990). *Perception of behaviour and achievement at different ability levels.* Paper presented at the Canadian Psychological Association annual conference, Ottawa, Ontario.

Argyle, M. (1981). The experimental study of the basic features of situations. In D. Magnusson (Ed.), *Toward a psychology of situations: An interactional perspective.* Hillsdale, NJ: Lawrence Erlbaum.

Asher, S. R., & Hymel, S. (1981). Children's social competence in peer relations: Sociometric and behavioural assessment. In J. D. Wine & M. D. Smye (Eds.), *Social competence* (pp. 125-157). New York: Guilford.

Bandura, A. (1969). *Principles of behaviour modification.* New York: Holt, Rinehart, & Winston.

Bandura, A. (1977a). Self-efficacy: Toward a unifying theory of behaviour change. *Psychological Review, 84,* 191-215.

Bandura, A. (1977b). *Social learning theory.* Englewood Cliffs, NJ: Prentice-Hall.

Bandura, A. (1986). Social foundations of thought and action: A social cognitive theory. Englewood Cliffs, NJ: Prentice-Hall.

Baumrind, D. (1975). The contributions of the family to the development of competence in children. *Schizophrenia Bulletin, 14,* 12-37.

Bereiter, C., & Bird, M. (1985). Use of thinking aloud in identification and teaching of reading comprehension strategies. *Cognition and Instruction,* 131-156.

Boersma, F. J., & Chapman, J. W. (1979). Academic self-concept in elementary learning disabled children. *Psychology in the Schools, 16,* 201-206.

Bolstad, O. D., & Johnson, S. M. (1972). Self-regulation in the modification of disruptive classroom behaviour. *Journal of Applied Behaviour Analysis, 5,* 443-454.

Bondy, A. S., & Erickson, M. T. (1976). Comparison of modelling and reinforcement procedures in increasing question-asking of mentally retarded children. *Journal of Applied Behaviour Analysis, 9*(1), 108.

Borkowski, J. G., Johnson, M. B., & Reid, M. K. (1987). Metacognition, motivation, and controlled performance. In S. J. Ceci (Ed.), *Handbook of cognitive, social, and neurological aspects of learning disabilities, Volume 2.* Hillsdale, NJ: Lawrence Erlbaum.

Borkowski, J. G., Weyhing, R. S., & Carr, M. (1988). Effects of attributional retraining on strategy based reading comprehension in learning disabled students. *Journal of Educational Psychology, 80*(1),46-53.

Bryan, J., Sherman, R., & Fisher, R. (1980). Learning disabled boys' nonverbal behaviours within a dyadic interview. *Learning Disability Quarterly, 3,* 65-72.

Bryan, T. & Bryan, J. (1978). Social interactions of learning disabled children. *Learning Disability Quarterly, 1,* 33-38.

Bryan, T. (1986). Self-concept and attributions of the learning disabled. *Learning Disabilities Focus, 1*(2), 82-89.

Bryan, T., Donahue, M., & Hurm, C. (1981). Learning disabled children's conversational skills: The TV talk show. *Learning Disability Quarterly, 4,* 250-259.

Bryan, T., Wheeler, R., Felcan, J., & Henek, T. (1976). "Come on dummy": An observational study of children's communications. *Journal of Learning Disabilities, 9,* 53-61.

Camp, B. W., & Bash, M. A. S. (1981). *The think aloud series: Increasing social and cognitive skills.* Champaign, IL: Research Press.

Carlson, C. (1987). Social interaction goals and strategies of children with learning disabilities. *Journal of Learning Disabilities, 5,* 306-311.

Cartledge, G., & Kleefeld, J. (1989). Teaching social communication skills to elementary school students with handicaps. *Teaching Exceptional Children, 22,* 100-105.

Cartledge, G., & Milburn, J. F. (1978). The case for teaching social skills in the classroom: A review. *Review of Educational Research, 1,* 133-156.

Chandler, M. J. (1977). Social cognition: A selective revision of current research. In W. F. Overton & J. M. Gallagher (Eds.), *Knowledge and Development, Volume 1.* New York: Plenum.

Chapin, M., & Dyck, D. G. (1976). Persistence in children's reading behaviour as a function of N length and attribution retraining. *Journal of Abnormal Psychology, 85,* 511-515.

Clark, L., Gresham, F. M., & Elliott, S. N. (1985). Development and validation of a social skills assessment measures: The TROSS-C. *Journal of Psychoeducational Assessment, 4,* 347-356.

Conners, C. K. (1969). A teacher rating scale for use in drug studies with children. *American Journal of Psychiatry, 126,* 885-888.

Crandall, V. C., Katkovsky, W., & Crandall, V. J. (1965). Children's beliefs in their control of reinforcements in intellectual academic achievement behaviours. *Child Development, 36,* 91-109.

Delquadri, J., Greenwood, C. R., Whorton, D., Carta, J. J., & Hall, R. V. (1986). Classwide peer tutoring. *Exceptional Children, 52*(6), 535-542.

Dickstein, E., & Warren, D. (1980). Role taking deficits in learning disabled children. *Journal of Learning Disabilities, 13,* 33-37.

Dodge, K. A., Coie, J. D., & Brakke, N. P. (1982). Behaviour patterns of socially rejected and neglected preadolescents: The roles of social approach and aggression. *Journal of Abnormal Child Psychology, 10,* 389-410.

Dodge, K. A., McClaskey, C. L., & Feldman, E. (1985). Situational approach to the assessment of social competence in children. *Journal of Consulting and Clinical Psychology, 53,* 344-353.

Donahue, M., Pearl, R., & Bryan, T. (1980). Learning disabled children's conversational competence: Responses to inadequate messages. *Applied Psycholinguistics, 1,* 387-403.

Finch, A. J., & Spirito, A. (1980). Use of cognitive training to change cognitive processes. *Exceptional Education Quarterly, 1,* 31-39.

Ford, M. E. (1982). Social cognition and social competence in adolescence. *Developmental Psychology, 18*(3), 323-340.

Ford, M. E., & Tisak, M. S. (1983). A further search for social intelligence. *Journal of Educational Psychology, 75*(2), 196-206.

Forgas, J. P. (1981). *Social cognition: Perspectives on everyday understanding.* New York: Academic Press.

Foster, S. L., & Ritchey, W. L. (1979). Issues in the assessment of social competence in children. *Journal of Applied Behavioural Analysis, 12*, 625-638.

Freemont, T., Seifert, D., & Wilson, J. (1977). *Informal diagnostic assessment of children.* Springfield, IL: Charles C. Thomas.

Freemont, T., Wallbrown, F., & Nelson, E. (1978). Social misperception and its implications for counselling. *Personnel and Guidance Journal, 57*, 149-153.

Gamble, R., & Strain, R. S. (1979). The effects of dependent and interdependent group contingencies on socially appropriate responses in classes for emotionally handicapped children. *Psychology in the Schools, 16*, 253-260.

Gerber, P., & Zinkgraf, S. (1982). A comparative study of social perceptual ability in learning disabled and non-handicapped students. *Learning Disability Quarterly, 5*, 374-378.

Getzels, J. W., & Jackson, P. W. (1961). *Creativity and intelligence.* New York: Wiley

Goldfried, M. R., & d'Zurella, T. J. (1969). A behavioural analytic model for assessing competence. In C. D. Spielberger (Ed.), *Current topics in clinical and community psychology, Volume 1* (pp. 151-196). New York: Academic Press.

Gottlieb, J. (1981). Mainstreaming: Fulfilling the promise. *American Journal of Mental Deficiency, 86*, 115-126.

Gottlieb, J., Semmel, M. I., & Veldman, D. J. (1978). Correlates of social status among mainstreamed mentally retarded children. *Journal of Educational Psychology, 70*, 396-405.

Gottman, J., Gonso, J., & Schuler, P. (1976). Teaching social skills to isolated children. *Journal of Abnormal Child Psychology, 4*, 179-197.

Gresham, F. M. (1981). Social skills training with handicapped children: A review. *Review of Educational Research, 51*, 139-176.

Gresham, F. M. (1982). Misguided mainstreaming: The case for social skills training with handicapped children. *Exceptional Children, 48*, 420-433.

Gresham, F. M. (1984). Social skills and self-efficacy for exceptional children. *Exceptional Children, 51*, 253-261.

Gresham, F. M. (1985). Utility of cognitive-behavioural procedures for social skills training with children: A critical review. *Journal of Abnormal Child Psychology, 13*, 411-423.

Gresham, F. M. (1988). Social competence and motivational characteristics of learning disabled students. In M. C. Wang, M. C. Reynolds, & H. J. Walberg (Eds.), *Handbook of special education—Research and practice, Volume 2: Mildly handicapped conditions.* New York: Pergamon.

Gresham, F. M., & Elliott, S. N. (1984). Assessment and classification of children's social skills: A review of methods and issues. *School Psychology Review, 13*, 292-301.

Gunzberg, H. C. (1980). *Progress assessment chart of social competence.* London: SEFA.

Hall, P. (1980). Information processing and cognitive training in learning disabled children: An executive level meeting. *Exceptional Children Quarterly, 1*, 9-15.

Hallahan, D. P., & Reeves, R. E. (1980). Selective attention and distractibility. In D. K. Keogh (Ed.), *Advances in special education, Volume 1* (pp. 141-181). Greenwich, CT: JAI Press.

Hallahan, D. P., Lloyd, J., Kasiewicz, M. M., Kauffman, J. M., & Graves, P. W. (1979). Self-monitoring of attention as treatment for a learning disabled boy's off-task behaviour. *Learning Disability Quarterly, 2*, 24-32.

Hammill, D. , Bartel, N. P., & Bunch, C. O. (1984). *Teaching children with learning disabilities and/or behaviour problems.* Boston: Allyn & Bacon.

Hammill, D., & Newcomer, P. (1988). *The Test of Language Development-2: Intermediate.* Austin, TX: Pro-Ed.

Harris, W. (1984). *Making better choices: A curriculum for teaching cognitive planning and social skills to improve social and academic behavior.* University of Maine.

Hazel, J. S., Schumaker, J. B., Sherman, J. A., & Sheldon-Wildgen, J. (1981). *ASSET: A social skills program for adolescents.* Champaign, IL: Research Press.

Hoben, M. (1980). Toward integration in the mainstream. *Exceptional Children,* (October), 100-105.

Horowitz, E. (1981). Popularity, decentering ability and role taking skills in learning disabled and normal children. *Learning Disability Quarterly, 4*, 23-30.

Huggins, P. (1986). *The ASSIST Program: A Validated Washington State Innovative Education Program.* 7024 North Mercer Way, Mercer Island, WA 98040.

Iwata, B. A., & Bailey, J. S. (1974). Reward versus cost token systems: An analysis of the effects on students and teacher. *Journal of Applied Behaviour Analysis, 7*, 567-576.

Jahoda, M. (1958). *Current concepts of positive mental health.* New York: Basic Books.

Johnson, D. W., & Johnson, R. T. (1980). Integrating handicapped students into the mainstream. *Exceptional Children, 46*, 89-98.

Johnson, D. W., & Johnson, R. T. (1986). Mainstreaming and cooperative learning strategies. *Exceptional Children, 52*(6), 553-561.

Kagan, J., Rosman, B. L., Day, D., Albert, J., & Philips, W. (1964). *Information processing in the child: Significance of analytic and reflective attitudes. Psychological Monographs* (Whole No. 578).

Kauffman, J. M. (1985). *Characteristics of children's behaviour disorders* (3rd ed.). Columbus, OH: Merrill.

Kendall, P. C., Pellegrini, D. S., & Urbain, E. S. (1981). Approaches to assessment for cognitive-behavioural interventions with children. In P. C. Kendall & S. D. Hollon (Eds.), *Assessment strategies for cognitive-behavioural interventions* (pp. 227-286). New York: Academic Press.

Kohn, M., Parnes, B., & Rosman, B. L. (1979). *Kohn Social Competence Scale.* New York: Martin Kohn.

Kuhn, J. S. (1962). *The structure of scientific revolutions.* Chicago: University of Chicago Press.

Lambert, N. M., & Hartsbough, C. S., &, Bower, E. L. (1979). *Pupil Behaviour Rating Scale.* Monterey, CA: CTB/McGraw-Hill.

Larson, K. A., & Gerber, M. M. (1987). Effects of social metacognitive training for enhancing overt behaviour in learning disabled and low achieving delinquents. *Exceptional Children, 54*(3), 201-211.

Lindsley, O. R. (1972). From Skinner to precision teaching. In J. B. Jordan & L. S. Robbins (Eds.), *Let's try doing something else kind of thing: Behaviour principles and the exceptional child* (pp. 1-11). Arlington, VA: The Council for Exceptional Children.

Lloyd, J. (1980). Academic instruction and cognitive techniques: The need for attack strategy training. *Exceptional Education Quarterly, 1*, 53-63.

Lochman, J. M., & Lampron, L. B. (1986). Situational social problem solving skills and self-esteem of aggressive and non-aggressive boys. *Journal of Abnormal Child Psychology, 13*, 527-538.

Maag, J. W. (1989). Assessment in social skills training: Methodological and conceptual issues for research and practice. *Remedial and Special Education, 10*(4), 6-17.

Madden, N. A., & Slavin, R. (1983). Mainstreaming students with mild handicaps: Academic and social outcomes. *Review of Educational Research, 53*(4), 519-569.

Maheady, L., & Maitland, G. (1982). Assessing social perception abilities in learning disabled children. *Learning Disability Quarterly, 5*, 363-369.

Maslow, A. H. (1970). *Motivation and personality.* New York: Harper & Row.

Matson, J. L., Rotatori, A. F., & Helsel, W. J. (1983). Development of a rating scale to measure social skills in children: The Matson Evaluation of Social Skills with Youngsters (MESSY). *Behaviour Research and Therapy, 21*, 335-340.

McCandless, B. R. (1967). *Children, behaviour and development.* New York: Holt, Rinehart, & Winston.

McFall, R. M. (1982). A review and reformulation of the concepts of social skills. *Behavioral Assessment, 4*, 1-33.

McGinnis, E., & Goldstein, A. P. (1984). *Skillstreaming the elementary school child.* Champaign, IL: Research Press.

McKinney, J. D., & Haskins, R. (1980). Cognitive training and the development of problem solving strategies. *Exceptional Education Quarterly, 1*, 41-51.

Meichenbaum, D. (1977). *Cognitive behaviour modification.* New York: Plenum.

Meichenbaum, D. (1980). Cognitive behaviour modification with exceptional children: A promise yet unfulfilled. *Exceptional Education Quarterly, 1*(1), 83-88.

Meichenbaum, D. (1985). *Stress inoculation training.* New York: Pergamon.

Meichenbaum, D., & Goodman, J. (1971). Training impulsive children to talk to themselves: A means of developing self-control. *Journal of Abnormal Psychology, 77*, 115-126.

Meyers, J., Pfleffer, J., & Erlbaum, V. (1985). Process assessment: A model for broadening assessment. *Journal of Special Education, 19*, 73-89.

Mulcahy, R. R., Marfo, K., Peat, D., & Andrews, J. (1986). *A strategies program for effective learning and thinking (SPELT): Teachers' manual.* Edmonton: Cognitive Education Project, University of Alberta.

Oden, S., & Asher, F. R. (1977). Coaching children in social skills for friendship making. *Child Development, 48*, 495-506.

Pearl, R. (1987). Social cognitive factors in learning disabled children's social problems. In S. J. Ceci (Ed.), *Handbook of cognitive, social, and neurological aspects of learning disabilities, Volume 2.* Hillsdale, NJ: Lawrence Erlbaum.

Pearl, R. A., & Bryan, J. H. (1979). Self-concept and locus of control of learning disabled children. *Journal of Clinical Child Psychology, 8*, 223-226.

Pearl, R., & Cosden, M. (1982). Sizing up a situation: LD children's understanding of social interactions. *Learning Disability Quarterly, 5*, 371-373.

Pellegrini, D. (1980). *The social cognitive qualities of stress resistant children.* Unpublished doctoral dissertation, University of Minnesota.

Piers-Harris Children's Self-Concept Scale. (1984). Western Psychological Services, Los Angeles, CA.

Quay, H. C., & Peterson, D. R. (1975). *Manual for behaviour problem checklist.* Unpublished manuscript.

Renshaw, P. D., & Asher, S. R. (1983). Children's goals and strategies for social interaction. *Merrill-Palmer Quarterly, 29*(3), 353-373.

Rosenbaum, M. S., & Drabman, R. S. (1979). Self-control training in the classroom: A review and critique. *Journal of Applied Behaviour Analysis, 12*, 467-485.

Roth, M., Sells, S. B., & Golden, M. M. (1972). *Social adjustment and personality development in children.* Minneapolis: University of Minnesota Press.

Rotter, J. B. (1954). *Social learning and clinical psychology.* Englewood Cliffs, NJ: Prentice-Hall.

Scandura, J. M. (1977). Structural approach to instructional problems. *American Psychologist, 32*, 33-53.

Scheirer, M. R., & Kraut, R. E. (1979). Increasing educational achievement via self-concept change. *Review of Educational Research, 49*, 131-150.

Schulz, J. B., Carpenter, C. D., & Turnbull, A. P. (1991). *Mainstreaming exceptional students* (3rd ed.). Toronto: Allyn & Bacon.

Schunk, D. H. (1982). Effects of effort attributional feedback in children's perceived self-efficacy and achievement. *Journal of Educational Psychology, 74*, 548-556.

Schunk, D. H. (1987). Peer models and children's behavioral change. *Review of Educational Research, 57*, 149-174.

Schunk, D. H., & Cox, P. D. (1986). Strategy training and attributional feedback with learning disabled children. *Journal of Educational Psychology, 78*, 201-209.

Schunk, D. H. , & Rice, J. M. (1986). Extended attributional feedback: Sequence effects during remedial reading instruction. *Journal of Early Adolescence, 6*, 55-66.

Seligman, M. E. P. (1975). *Helplessness: On depression, development and death.* San Francisco: W. H. Freeman.

Shure, M., & Spivack, G. (1972). Means-ends thinking, adjustment and social class among elementary school-aged children. *Journal of Consulting and Clinical Psychology, 38*, 348-353.

Slavin, R. E., Madden, N. A., & Leavy, M. (1984). Effects of cooperative learning and individualized instruction on mainstreamed students. *Exceptional Children, 50*(5), 434-443.

Smith, C. R. (1983). *Learning disabilities: The interaction of learner, task and setting.* Toronto: Little, Brown.

Speckman, N. (1981). Dyadic verbal communication abilities of learning disabled and normally achieving fourth and fifth grade boys. *Learning Disability Quarterly, 4*, 139-151.

Speckman, N., & Roth, F. (1982). An intervention framework for learning disabled students with communication disorders. *Learning Disability Quarterly, 5*, 429-437.

Spivack, G., & Levine, M. (1963). *Self-regulation in acting out and normal adolescents* (Report M-4531) Washington, DC: National Institute of Health.

Spivack, G., Platt, J. J., & Shure, M. (1976). *The problem solving approach to adjustment.* San Francisco: Jossey-Bass.

Spivack, G., & Shure, M. (1974). *Social adjustment of young children: A cognitive approach to solving real life problems.* San Francisco: Jossey-Bass.

Spivack, G., & Shure, M. B. (1982). The cognition of social adjustment: Interpersonal cognitive problem solving thinking. In B. B. Lahey & A. E. Kazdin (Eds.), *Advance in child clinical psychology, Volume 5* (pp. 323-372). New York: Plenum.

Stephens, T. M. (1978). *Social skills in the classroom.* Columbus, OH: Cedars Press.

Stephens, T. M. (1979). *Social behavior assessment.* Columbus, OH: Cedars Press.

Stephens, T. M. (1980). *Technical information: Social behavior assessment.* Columbus, OH: Cedars Press.

Strain, P. S. (1975). Increasing social play of severely retarded preschoolers with socio-dramatic activities. *Mental Retardation, 13,* 7-9.

Strain, P .S., Shores, R. E., & Timm, M. A. (1977). Effects of peer social initiations on the behavior of withdrawn preschool children: Some training and generalization effects. *Journal of Applied Behavior Analysis, 10,* 289-298.

Torgesen, J. K. (1977). The role of non-specific factors in the task performance of learning disabled children: A theoretical assessment. *Journal of Learning Disabilities, 10,* 33-41.

Ulman, C. (1957). Teachers, peers and tests as predictors of adjustment. *Journal of Educational Psychology, 48,* 257-267.

Walker, H. M., McConnell, S. R., Walker, J., Holmes, D., Todis, B., & Golden, N. (1983). *ACCEPTS: A curriculum for effective peer and teacher skills.* Austin, TX: Pro-Ed.

Weiner, B. (1972). *Theories of motivation: From mechanism to cognition.* Chicago: Markham.

Weiner, B. (1979). A theory of motivation for some classroom experiences. *Journal of Educational Psychology, 71,* 3-25.

Weiner, B., Graham, T., Taylor, S. E., & Meyer, W. (1983). Social cognition in the classroom. *Educational Psychologist, 18,* 109-124.

White, O. R. (1986). Precision teaching-precision learning. *Exceptional Children, 52,* 522-534.

White, R. W. (1959). Motivation reconsidered: The concept of competence. *Psychological Review, 66,* 297-333.

Wiig, E., & Semel, E. (1976). *Language disabilities in children and adolescents.* Columbus, OH: Merrill.

Wiig, E., & Semel, E. (1987). *Clinical Evaluation of Language Function: Revised.* San Antonio, TX: The Psychological Corporation.

Wrubel, J., Benner, P., & Lazarus, R. (1981). Social competence from the perspective of stress and coping. In J. D. Wine & M. D. Smye (Eds.), *Social competence.* New York: Guilford Press.

Wylie, R. C. (1979). *The self-concept, Volume 2.* Lincoln, NB: University of Nebraska Press.

Zahvi, S., & Asher, S. (1978) The effect of verbal instructions on preschool children's aggressive behavior. *Journal of School Psychology, 16,* 146-153.

Zigler, E., & Trickett, P. K. (1978). I.Q., social competence and evaluation of early childhood intervention programs. *American Psychologist, 33,* 789-796.

LIVING AND LEARNING IN A CLASSROOM COMMUNITY:

A HOLISTIC PERSPECTIVE

CHAPTER 14

CHAPTER OBJECTIVES

To discuss the role of a learning community as a means of *including* all students.

To present a holistic view of oral and written language learning.

To discuss the role of a classroom community in language learning.

To provide guidelines for creating language-rich learning environments in the classroom.

To discuss the role of language in learning curricular subjects.

It is reading time in Mr. Dudley-Marling's Grade 3 classroom. Catherine, Fatima, John, Crystal, and Peter are sitting in a circle on the carpet. Without any teacher direction, they begin to share and discuss the books they are reading. Their reading selections are entirely a matter of personal choice.

John: I'm glad Peter found these books down in the library for me. They're called *Dr. Jekyll and Mr. Hyde*, *The Phantom of the Opera*, and *The Vampire*.

(*Catherine is looking through one of John's books.*)

John: (*to Catherine*) Look at the second picture of that.

Crystal: (*to anyone who is listening*) This book isn't that exciting.

John: (*still talking to Catherine*) That doesn't kill him. That kind of does. Look at the pic-

tures of him. You might want to read that over.

Fatima: Here, Catherine, give it to me. We're reading those.

Peter: Mr. Hyde is crazy. Look at him. Look at Mr. Hyde. That looks like this guy, dude.

Crystal: Maybe it is …

Fatima: A vampire.

John: It could be. No, that's probably the driver of the coach. They're going to show his face here. Catherine! Catherine! They're going to show his face. (*Catherine flips through the book.*) Find the one where the girl takes off his mask. There. It shows his real face.

Catherine: He has no wounds.

Peter: "And yet he walked on—"

Crystal: And it shows a picture of all the (*unintelligible*).

Fatima: (*to the teacher*) We're all reading these kind of books.

Peter: And we're looking at the pictures.

Crystal: Yeah. I'm going to look at the pictures and then try to read it.

John: I'm reading that after this. I like these books. I'm glad Peter got them out.

Peter: (*after a pause*) A big scorpion.

John: I know.

Fatima: I hope he doesn't eat those things.

John: Huh? Oh!

Crystal: "Kiss to my forehead." Huh?

John: Where is it? "Because you have (*unintelligible*)." Yuck.

Crystal: Sickatating.

Fatima: (*to Crystal*) You're up to that page so quickly?

Crystal: No. I'm just looking at the pictures.

Peter: Look at this book. They're two pictures of him.

John: Yeah. I know.

Fatima: (*Unintelligible*) pictures in it are not even scary.

Crystal: I want to see it.

Fatima: Wait!

John: Look at Dracula. Look at the pictures in that one.

Crystal: Oh, *nice* pictures (*sarcastically*).

John: (*after a pause*) This doesn't make sense.

Peter: What?

John: Look. First Mr. Hyde, the bad guy, was kept in a mansion—

Crystal: Yeah.

John: —and now after this guy, the butler, gave Mr. Hyde some food he turned back. He's (*unintelligible*) it.

Catherine: That doesn't make sense.

Peter: I know. He doesn't remember anything.

Fatima: He probably didn't eat after he took the medicine.

John: So the drug—

Peter: Probably—

John: Isn't permanent yet.

Peter: Or the drug probably makes you normal once you eat.

John: Yeah, probably. And then after you have something to drink or something like that—

Fatima: Then you turn back like the potion you drank.

John: Yeah, something like that. Like a hairy animal. Hey, why don't we make a little group that reads all this?

Crystal: I can bring one of my Dad's scrapbooks in. It has really old vampire pictures in it.

Peter: Real ones?

John: You three could check out more. We could sign out *King Kong*.

Fatima: We're starting a little group.

John: Yeah, we're starting a little vampire group.

Catherine: He's evil, he's powerful, he's thirsty for blood.

John: We're going to get out two (*unintelligible*) and then we'll have a five group.

Crystal: I'm going to get a piece of paper and write a little bit about it.

John: I'm not. I'm reading more. Where's my bookmark?

Teacher: Can I ask you a question? Are you going to read together every day like this?

Crystal: Yeah.

John: Yeah. We're all reading. And we started this group. We all read books. We tell each other about it and then if you done the book you give it someone else.

Crystal: If we put all our ideas together we can make a chapter book. (*They've decided to make notes on the books they are reading.*)

Fatima: And publish it. But no pictures. I'm not very good at pictures.

Peter: We'll have to get *King Kong* out.

John: Then we'll have five books. This is good. He coulda died if this potion didn't work. He coulda died.

Fatima: Instead of me and Crystal's caterpillar book, we can make like a, like um—

John: —a scary book.

Crystal: Yeah.

(*There is some discussion about who is going to get which books for the group to read.*)

John: We've got to name the club. The Scary Book Club.

Catherine: No! The Vampire Club.

John: I know. The Scary Creatures Club.

Fatima: Yeah.

Peter: The Scary Reading Club.

Crystal: Who knows how to spell scary?

Peter: S-c-a-r-y.

John: The Scary Reading Books Club?

Catherine:	No, the evil. Evil.	
John:	The Evil Reading Books Club?	
Catherine:	Yeah. It sounds better.	
John:	No, the Scary, Evil Books Club.	
Crystal:	Yeah.	
Catherine:	You know what I can do? I can bring a whole envelope full of pictures and stuff from when me and my mom went to this place and it said Dracula's House or something like that.	
John:	Dracula's Castle.	

Catherine: I could put it in a big envelope and we could make a big picture.

John: I went there too. A carnival or something. I went into this scary house.

Peter: So did I.

John: The last time there were ghostbusters—

Fatima: Yeah.

John: —and I got a prize and there's this snake pit (*gets lost in loud conversation*).

Crystal: I'll try to bring all my vampire books.

(*The teacher ends the session.*)

◇ INTRODUCTION

A developing interest brought together five students, depicted in the vignette, who wanted to read, write, and talk about "scary books." Over the next few weeks, several other students joined this group while another group of students formed to read and discuss comic books. As members of these spontaneous literature-sharing groups, students were challenged to extend their reading and writing skills as they used literacy to fulfil their intentions (Peterson & Eeds, 1990; Short & Pierce, 1990). The students in the Scary, Evil Book Club, for example, turned their interest in horror stories into account by using language to share, support, react, challenge, question, negotiate, discuss, and respond.

One of the students who later joined the Scary, Evil Book Club was Nader, whose family had only recently emigrated from Afghanistan. Nader's participation in the club enabled him to become a part of the classroom community from which he had been formerly excluded. The relationships Nader developed as a club member soon extended beyond reading and outside of the classroom. For Nader, reading was a way of entering the community, both within and outside the classroom.

yes

The successful inclusion of exceptional students in regular classrooms depends on more than their mere physical presence. Unless exceptional students are integrated into a working community of learners in which they can learn with and from their peers, they risk being segregated *within* the regular classroom. Within an active community of learners, student diversity nurtures the community and differences are celebrated as resources upon which all members of the community can draw. Here all students are valued for the unique background knowledge and experience they bring to the community.

In Ms. Jackson's Grade 2 classroom, for example, Anthony, a student who struggles in reading, is a recognized expert on dinosaurs. Similarly, Daniel, a Grade 8 student who spends part of his day in a resource room for students with learning disabilities, is well known—and frequently sought out by students and teachers alike—for his expertise with computers. In these class-rooms, exceptional students are valued for their contributions to the learning community. They are not viewed as a drain on classroom and teacher resources. Nor does the community ignore the unique needs of exceptional students. The student who has difficulty with spelling, for example, can draw on the support of each member of the community; in effect, each student has twenty-five teachers instead of just one.

yes

Within a classroom community, social interaction is the means by which students and teachers come to learn, live, and work together. Perhaps the most obvious way groups of people come together is through the use of language. This chapter focuses on how teachers can create a community of learners in which students learn oral and written language and use language to learn. While the majority of examples provided in the chapter are taken from an elementary setting, we believe that the principles underlying these examples generalize to all learners. In the section that follows, we discuss the theoretical perspective on language learning that informs this chapter.

◆ A HOLISTIC PERSPECTIVE ON LANGUAGE LEARNING

> Three-year-old Ian is eating dinner with his family. When he has emptied his glass, he hands it to his mother and asks, "May you please give me some more juice?"

Ian's request demonstrates his considerable understanding of language and the world in which he lives. Ian has learned that language is a powerful tool for getting things done. He can use language to acquire goods and services, to obtain information, to entertain, to assert, to report, to describe, to label, and so on. He knows thousands of words and how to use various word-ordering rules for encoding his increasingly complex understanding of the world.

yes

Ian also knows something about how the physical and social setting interact to affect both what he says and how he says it. His request for juice, for example, is made to someone who is able to respond (his mother and not a guest), and in a place where he is likely to get it (in the house and not at the zoo). And his request form ("May you please?") is a recognition of his social position relative to his mother. (If his sister had been pouring juice instead, he would probably have said something like, "Anne, give me some juice, too.") What's remarkable is that Ian, like other children, learned all this in less than four years.

How do children learn so much about language in such a short time? The most important discovery children make that sets them on the path of language learning is this: *language works*. Toddlers learn, for example, that it is much more efficient to ask their parents for something to drink than to cry while their parents run through a list of possibilities for the tears. But efficiency is not the only motivation for language learning. Language opens up new possibilities. Language makes it possible to talk about objects that are no longer present ('ball gone"), to assert ownership ("mine!"), to describe ("ball big"), to question ("where doggie?"), and so on.

But to tap the power of language, children must also learn language forms—vocabulary and syntax—and, as we noted earlier, the choice of appropriate forms is a function of the physical and social setting. Children learn language forms and how the physical and social setting affect language use by being immersed in a "veritable language bath" (Lindfors, 1980) in which they are exposed to frequent demonstrations of language use in a range of social and physical settings. They also have regular opportunities to try out language for themselves in these settings.

The point here is this: children learn language and can *only* learn language by hearing and using language in a range of authentic language settings. In authentic settings all language systems—syntax (i.e., word-ordering rules), semantics (i.e., meanings or, more accurately, the linguistic representation of our world knowledge), and pragmatics (i.e., rules that govern the use of language in context) are naturally present (Bloom & Lahey, 1978; Lindfors, 1987). Figure 14.1 illustrates how semantics, syntax, and pragmatics come together in any genuine instance of language use. Also present in any instance of language use are the various physical, social, and cultural factors that affect these systems. In authentic language settings, there are speakers who have real purposes for speaking and audiences who are genuinely interested in what speakers have to say. In authentic language contexts, children learn, for example, how topic, content, choice of words, and word-ordering rules are affected by audience and purpose.

yes

These intricate and complex relationships can be learned only in real language situations because those are the only places they can be found. For example, in clinical language settings where contexts are created for the purpose of explicitly teaching language, children learn only how language functions in clinical settings. It is uncertain whether what is learned in these settings will generalize to other environments (Spradlin & Siegel, 1982). To learn language, it is crucial that language learners be exposed to a wide range of communicative contexts.

Classrooms are potentially rich language-learning environments where communication skills can be embedded in purposeful activity (Abkarian, 1981). Snow, Midkiff-Borunda, Small, and Proctor (1984) state: "The child will engage in meaningful communication throughout his or her daily activities, and the active use of facilitative features in the language exchanges will increase the child's communicative competence" (p. 83). Here talk helps nurture and sustain the community which, in turn, nurtures and sustains talk. However, in many classrooms, students' opportunities to participate in meaningful language experiences are restricted. In these classrooms, teachers do most of the talking and much of this talk follows the pattern of teacher elicitation-student response-teacher evaluation (Gonzales & Hansen-Krening, 1981; Edwards & Furlong, 1978; Dillon & Searle, 1981). This pattern gives students few opportunities to use and learn language in their

Figure 14.1

A Representation of Genuine Language Use

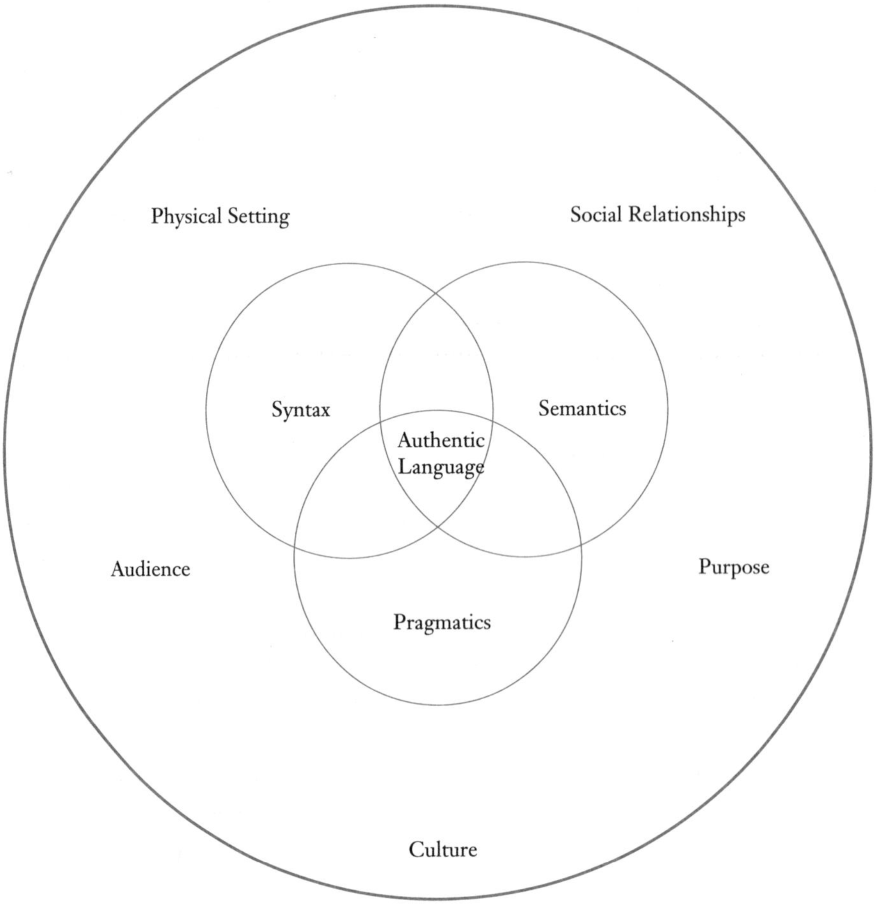

Physical Setting

Social Relationships

Syntax

Semantics

Authentic Language

Audience

Purpose

Pragmatics

Culture

Adapted from Bloom & Lahey (1978).

yes

classrooms (Dudley-Marling & Searle, 1991). It also tends to discourage students from using language to reflect upon their own knowledge and personal experiences, which would help them make sense of instruction (Barnes, 1976; Dyson & Genishi, 1983; Edwards & Furlong, 1978; Searle, 1975).

The situation may be worse for underachievers, a group likely to include many students identified as exceptional. Teachers have been found to ignore more often the comments of low achievers (Cherry, 1980); to provide them with fewer opportunities to respond to questions (Rist, 1970); and to wait less time for low achievers to answer questions (Good, 1980); and to criticize their public responses more often than those of higher-achieving students (Good, 1980).

Where the above patterns exist, students will learn only the language of schooling, which may prepare them only for more schooling (Dillon &

Searle, 1981). However, within an active, vital community of learners, students have opportunities to learn and use language for a variety of purposes and within a range of social settings. Such opportunities challenge students to increase the language skills by which means they become members of a community (Dudley-Marling & Searle, 1991).

yes

◆ A HOLISTIC PERSPECTIVE ON READING AND WRITING

In this section, we review some of the assumptions behind the socio-psycholinguistic model of reading and writing that inform this chapter. This model has been strongly influenced by both psycho- and sociolinguistics (hence the term "socio-psycholinguistic") and is based upon a substantial body of research on written language (reading and writing) and written language development (Cochrane-Smith, 1984; Durkin, 1966; Goodman & Goodman, 1979; Hall, 1987; Kantor, Miller, & Fernie, 1992; Stephens, 1991; Taylor, 1983; Teale & Sulzby, 1987; Wells, 1986).

No

READING AND WRITING AS LANGUAGE PROCESSES

From a socio-psycholinguistic perspective, readers and writers, like speakers and listeners, construct meaning from and with texts by simultaneously drawing upon their knowledge of language (e.g., vocabulary and syntax, etc.); their background knowledge and experience (e.g., if they are reading a story about wild animals, they will construct meaning by drawing upon their knowledge of wild animals from books, TV, visits to the zoo, etc.); their knowledge of texts and text structure (e.g., "Once upon a time …" signals a fictional story, probably a fairy tale); and their knowledge of the conventions of print (e.g., sound-symbol relationships).

Yes

Importantly, as with oral language, these various language systems are not independent of one another. When readers and writers set out to construct meaning from texts, they use the various systems in concert, each one affecting and being affected by the other. Edelsky (1984) states that language systems "not only operate in context; they also are interdependent, each one having consequences for the other. In any instance of genuine … language use, a choice in one system has ramifications for what choices or interpretations are possible in another" (p. 9). If, for example, readers do not possess requisite background knowledge, they may be forced to rely more heavily on their knowledge of sound-symbol relationships. It is important to recognize, however, that relying too heavily on one cuing system—phonics, for example—will interfere with readers' ability to construct meaning from texts (Goodman, Watson, & Burke, 1987).

Reading is most effective when readers can draw upon all of their linguistic and nonlinguistic knowledge to make sense of texts. Readers do more than sound out words. In fact, phonics rules used in isolation are notoriously unreliable (Smith, 1978; Weaver, 1988). Readers use their knowledge of sound-symbol relationships in concert with their knowledge about language and about the world. So what readers must learn how to do is not to just sound out words, but to use their knowledge of letter-sound correspondences in contexts in which they simultaneously draw upon their knowledge of language, their knowledge of the world, *and* their knowledge of phonics.

Reading (and writing) processes are not monolithic, however. The degree to which readers rely on phonics, for example, is a function of their purpose (in many instances of school literacy, for example, reading *is* sounding out words), their background knowledge, their skill as readers (poor readers may be more likely to depend on sound-symbol relationships (Goodman, Watson, & Burke, 1987), and the social context. Therefore, school literacy, with its emphasis on discrete skill instruction, involves processes that bear only a faint resemblance to the range of skills and literate behaviours readers and writers use outside of school (Myers, 1992), or even to unofficial literacy practices within school (Gilmore, 1983, 1986). Encouraging students to engage in many different literate practices helps them discover the range of processes associated with various literate behaviours.

HOW READERS AND WRITERS CONSTRUCT MEANING

According to traditional views of reading (and writing) instruction, texts have meanings that have been encoded by their authors. The reader's task is to decode the author's meaning. The assumption here is that meaning resides in the text. In contrast, from a socio-psycholinguistic point of view, readers do not *extract* meaning from text. Rather, they *construct* meanings, which are influenced by the text but are also influenced by the reader's background knowledge, values, beliefs, and his or her reading of the social context. Two readers from different religious traditions, for example, will have markedly different understandings of a biblical reading. It would make no sense to conclude that one has "gotten" the meaning and the other has not. As Goodman (1984) notes:

> Meaning is not a characteristic of texts. Rather, texts are constructed by authors to be comprehended by readers. The meaning is in the author and the reader. The text has a potential to evoke meaning but has no meaning itself (p. 81).

What is important is to see how authors and texts interact with reader beliefs (e.g., culture) to produce meaning. What the reader "knows" affects his or her reading of the text while, at the same time, the text affects what the reader knows. Both the knower and the known are changed in the course of knowing (Rosenblatt, 1978). A similar argument can be made for writing. Goodman (1984) states:

> In a transactional view, the writer constructs a text through transactions with the developing text and the meaning being expressed. The text is transformed in the process and so are the writer's schemata (ways of organizing

knowledge). The reader also constructs a text during reading through trans-actions with the published text and the reader's schemata are also trans-formed in the process through the assimilation and accommodation Piaget has described (p. 80).

READING AND WRITING AS SOCIAL ACTS

"Being literate is *not* primarily a mental ability, but a social one" (Gee, 1992, p. 122). The uses to which literacy is put, how meaning is made, what mean-ings are available, and even what counts as literacy vary across cultures (Bloome, 1986; Gee, 1992; Heath, 1983; Kantor, Miller, and Fernie, 1992; Taylor & Dorsey-Gaines, 1988). As a social act, literacy is a way of getting along in communities and can thus be an important influence in shaping communities.

NO

Traditional approaches to literacy instruction see reading and writing as processes that are primarily in the reader's (or writer's) head. By ignoring the social influences of literacy learning, these approaches may leave many stu-dents poorly prepared to use literacy outside the culture of schooling. According to Myers (1992),

> [d]efining literacy skill as a collection of socially constructed practices sug-gests that the traditional skill-based school instruction cannot transfer to lit-eracy use in other contexts. The skills of exercises are not the same as the skills of literacy in other social contexts (p. 302).

Traditional approaches to literacy instruction prepare students to function in school (Myers, 1992). Expanding our definitions of literacy can help our stu-dents realize the potential of literacy to affect their lives in the community *outside* of school.

◆ LEARNING LANGUAGE IN A COMMUNITY OF LEARNERS

Frank Smith (1981) observes that learning always occurs in the presence of demonstrations and that what is learned is whatever happens to be demon-strated at the time. Language learners discover the power of language, for example, by observing other people demonstrate how language is used to get things done. In addition to demonstrations, learners also need frequent opportunities to engage in whatever it is we want them to learn (Smith, 1981). Learning to read, write, speak, and listen all depend on regular oppor-tunities to try out language in a range of physical and social settings.

yes

The diverse community of learners in the inclusive classroom has the potential to provide exceptional students with powerful demonstrations of how language works, as well as opportunities to try out language for various purposes within a range of language contexts. In this section, we discuss some of the ways teachers can foster these opportunities for the benefit of all stu-dents, including those students for whom language learning may be a struggle.

LANGUAGE DEMONSTRATIONS IN A COMMUNITY OF LEARNERS

NO

> Jane teaches in an inner-city, primary level class for students with learning disabilities in Denver, Colorado. When students enter Jane's classroom the first thing they see is the daily lunch menu posted in front of the doorway. Separate schedules for the day and the month are posted in the same area. Several commercial book posters are displayed throughout the room. Each student's name and a brief biographical sketch are written on a chart and posted on a wall. Six Shel Silverstein poems have been copied and illustrated by the teacher on large pieces of tagboard and then displayed around the room. Students' written work is displayed under the blackboard in the front of the room. A bookcase in the middle of the room contains nearly 100 books for the students to read. Each day Jane selects one or more of these books to read to her class (Dudley-Marling, 1990, p. 39).

Language-rich classrooms immerse children in language, demonstrating to students different language functions and giving students the data they need to continue to develop as language-users. Jane surrounds her students with print, demonstrating what print is for (e.g., to inform or entertain) and how print works. A print-filled environment also demonstrates the teacher's enthusiasm for literacy. Conversely, a dearth of environmental print risks demonstrating to students that print has little value in their lives. Moreover, classroom literacy instruction that focuses on meaningless fragments of reading and writing may also demonstrate that reading and writing are meaningless (Smith, 1981).

Classrooms that give students opportunities to read and write throughout the day, and share what they are reading or writing, enable students to provide powerful demonstrations for each other. Students who frequently talk about their reading and writing demonstrate to their classmates the various purposes for which people read and write; different topics for writing; new authors to read; the struggles all readers and writers experience as they try to make sense with and from print; the problem-solving processes of readers and writers; and so on. Literate classrooms also demonstrate that reading and writing are important qualifications for becoming members of the classroom community (Smith, 1988).

Similarly, teachers who promote student talk throughout the day and across the curriculum provide students with meaningful demonstrations of both the forms and functions of language. Students who are encouraged to work in cross-age or cross-ability groupings, for example, are exposed to demonstrations of effective conversational behaviour and, perhaps, models of more mature language use. Teachers who choose activities that stimulate the use of language for functions like thinking and problem-solving provide students with illustrations of how language is used for these purposes.

But regular demonstrations of written and oral language use depend on teachers giving students frequent opportunities to use language throughout the school day. In quiet classrooms students learn only to be quiet; in classrooms where teachers do most of the talking, students mainly learn to listen to the teacher. Providing students with regular opportunities to use language is the subject of the next section.

ENGAGING IN LANGUAGE USE IN A COMMUNITY OF LEARNERS

The principal goal for language teaching is to encourage students to use language to fulfil a greater number of language functions (thinking, problem-solving, etc.) in a greater number of physical and social settings (e.g., Dudley-Marling & Searle, 1991). In order to construct meaning in an increasing range of language settings, students must expand their understanding of the world, their ability to use appropriate vocabulary and word-ordering rules, and their ability to adapt their use of language according to the context (e.g., certain topics are appropriate with friends but not with teachers).

Teachers promote language development by furnishing students with data about how language can be used and how it works (i.e., demonstrations). But teachers also need to provide students with frequent opportunities to try out their language in various contexts, as well as settings that challenge students to use their latent linguistic resources in order to get their needs met in those settings (Rosen & Rosen, 1973). In other words, we want to expose students to authentic situations that call language forth (Jones, 1988), as well as motivate them to stretch their language abilities and to construct meaning as they use language for different purposes and audiences, and in various settings.

As a first step in helping students grow as language-users, teachers need to construct a physical environment that is congenial to language learning. Traditional arrangements of desks and chairs in rows are usually part of a deliberate effort to discourage student talk. The practice of physically separating "distractible" students from the rest of the class may prevent talk altogether. Alternative arrangements facilitate—even initiate—social interaction and talk by enabling students to face each other. In some elementary classrooms, for example, desks have been replaced with round or rectangular tables. Other classrooms cluster desks facing each other or allow students to rearrange their desks for talk as needed. Still other classes retain the traditional arrangement of desks and chairs, but set aside places within the classroom for talk as students require.

Teachers also invite talk with the presence of interesting things to discuss. A demonstration of something as simple as a slinky going down steps in a science class, for example, may stimulate many interesting exchanges as students attempt to discover the physical principles that explain the slinky's behaviour. The physical environment can also call forth particular kinds of language. The presence of novel objects in the classroom, for example, may invite students to use language for functions like questioning and speculation (Dudley-Marling & Searle, 1991). Construction activities can encourage the use of language for forward planning (Tough, 1976). A science experiment may invite the use of language for logical reasoning and predicting. The classroom environment, by responding to students' interests, may also affect the complexity of students' language (Cazden, 1970).

Similarly, a print-filled environment demonstrates the uses of written language and invites students to engage in reading and writing. A prominently displayed collection of reading materials—including books, magazines, comics, catalogues, labels, brochures, telephone directories—and the posting of schedules, directions, announcements, and students' written work motivate students to read, even for as basic a reason as getting along in the classroom community. Loughlin and Martin (1986) conclude that students are more likely to be drawn to material that is placed at their eye level and is visible from their desks. It is also important that print in the classroom be refreshed regularly if it is to remain inviting to the students. But perhaps the most important factor in the potential of print to invite reading is its genuineness. Something written to communicate an authentic intention (e.g., a teacher posting a response to a note from a student about a book the student had read) is likely to be read more than something written to teach reading (e.g., a collection of phonics rules on a chart).

Placing materials strategically can also encourage writing. Positioning notepads and pencils by reference materials invites students to take notes (Loughlin & Martin, 1987). Sign-up sheets for centres, activities, or conferences with teachers give students practice in writing their names. Memo pads labelled "To" and "From" give students the incentive to send (and read) notes, an activity that teachers can further encourage by assigning mailboxes to children and writing notes to them.

Teachers can also stimulate language use and language learning by permitting students to work together in small groups. Small-group work enables both elementary and secondary students to engage in extended conversational interactions in which they learn, among other things, about the give-and-take of conversation and about how to address the needs of listeners who differ from each other in terms of background knowledge and experience. Within a small group of peers, students learn about the importance of staying on topic, of turn-taking, of repairing misunderstandings, and so on. In the small-group context, children also have authentic reasons for attending to language forms. The following example from Strickland, Dillon, Funkhouser, Glick, and Rogers (1989) is illustrative.

Neeta: This is my favourite part, but not the funniest. He puts it on the bed.
Katrinah: What is "it"?
Neeta: Put it on …
Katrinah: What is "it"? I don't understand what "it" is.
Bahar: What you're talking about … What's that red thing? You say it.
Katrinah: Yeh.
Neeta: She (*referring to an earlier discussion*) just said it. A cat ring.

Katrinah: Then why don't you say that instead of just saying "it," "it," "it"? (p. 198).

Here Neeta learns about the consequences of failing to satisfy listeners' needs for explicitness.

Teachers who routinely change the composition of small groups, and who use audiences from outside the classroom, also help students learn how to adjust the form and content of their spoken language to accommodate the needs of different audiences. In some schools, for example, teachers provide opportunities for students in the junior and intermediate grades to collaborate with primary students. Other teachers expand the range of audiences for students' talk by regularly inviting parents and other members of the community into their classrooms. Still others give assignments that require students to interview members of the community.

NO

A similar argument can be made vis-à-vis students' writing. Church (1985) notes the potential effect of group interaction on student writing:

> The group can celebrate with the writer over a good piece and commiserate over one that is going badly; they can also share the writer's relief over a problem solved ... the group interaction helps ... by extending the author's own understanding of his or her own text. A reader's comment, interpretation, or question may cause the writer to take a different perspective and see new possibilities to explore (p. 178).

Teachers can expand the range of audiences for students' writing by encouraging students to write letters to penpals, to exchange notes with classmates, to write thank-you notes to adults who visit their classrooms, to write to companies or organizations for products or information, and to share their writing with classmates. In sharing their writing with others, students learn about how editing and revision can support their writing intentions (Graves, 1983). Expanding one's audience is especially important in secondary settings where students tend to write exclusively for their teachers, who respond more as evaluators than as interested readers.

Teachers can themselves become audiences for students' language by engaging them in authentic talk. In a study of teacher-student language in three classes for students with learning disabilities, Dudley-Marling and Searle (1991) discovered one teacher who regularly engaged students in what they call "talk-around-the-edges." The following conversation (which occurred when students were hanging up their coats upon entering the classroom) is illustrative.

Melissa: I like those socks (*referring to a friend's socks*).
Teacher: Aren't they pretty socks? You've pretty socks, too.
Melissa: Yes, I like them.
Teacher: All sorts of fanciness on the socks.
Melissa: They're at the BiWay [a local discount store]. But not on this street or Thornhill. But they're on this, my old street, where we used to live.

Teacher: I see.
Melissa: At the BiWay. There's very cheap.
Teacher: Is it in Willowdale?
Melissa: On (*unclear*) street.
Teacher: Oh.
Melissa: There's elastic on so I can roll them.
Teacher: Yes, they look good that way.
Melissa: Like this? Or that?
Teacher: I like them rolled over. What do you like?
Melissa: I like it down (Dudley-Marling & Searle, 1991).

In the above example, the teacher gives Melissa an opportunity to engage in the give-and-take of conversation, models effective conversational behaviour, and in so doing gets to know this student better. When Melissa says, "There's very cheap," the teacher responds by asking where she bought her socks ("Is it in Willowdale?"), not by correcting her grammar. By confirming her interest in what Melissa has to say, the teacher invites her to continue the conversation.

Teachers can also become (nonevaluative) audiences for students' writing. As we mentioned earlier, some teachers routinely exchange notes with their students. Elementary and secondary teachers may correspond with students via dialogue journals (Roderick & Berman, 1984; Staton, 1988) or reading response journals. Still other teachers engage in written conversations with their students. *Peer collaboration* is another means of stimulating language development. Collaboration encourages language development by providing frequent opportunities for talk and by placing different demands on students in their alternate roles as speakers and listeners. Discussing the potential of collaborative writing, Daiute (1989) observes that "when young children collaborate on writing tasks, they use talk to elaborate their writing and to become more familiar with words, ideas, and composing processes" (p. 657).

It is essential that language teachers create an atmosphere of trust in which students feel free to make mistakes and try out language. Piaget has taught us that children learn by taking chances, and, from a Piagetian perspective, it's fair to say that *children learn by making errors*. Young children, for example, test the meaning of words and language forms by trying them out, only gradually gaining control over them. If students are reluctant to try out their language—because they are afraid of making mistakes—they will be severely disadvantaged when it comes to written and oral language learning.

Similarly, teachers who focus on the correctness of forms (e.g, grammar and spelling) may discourage students from stretching their written language ability by experimenting with the forms and functions of language. Learning-disabled children frequently take an overly cautious approach to writing—writing very little, relying on words they already know how to spell—because to take chances would be to risk failure. But until students engage in extended acts of writing (and reading), they cannot learn how to use written language to construct meaning within their social and cultural communities.

Teachers can stretch the linguistic resources of their students by giving them frequent opportunities to use oral and written language in their classrooms. Of course, teachers can't just set out the books, put pencils and paper around the room, rearrange the furniture, and then sit back and watch students' language grow. Creating language-rich classrooms is important, but teachers also need to respond strategically to the language needs of individual students. Teachers who observe, for example, that a student is not using language for problem-solving need to create settings that are particularly likely to encourage the use of language for problem-solving. Teachers may get students who consistently miss the point of stories to participate in story-sharing groups so as to gain a sense of how other students go about constructing meaning from texts (see Dudley-Marling & Searle, 1991 for an extended discussion of a strategic approach to language teaching).

No

◆ USING LANGUAGE FOR LEARNING

The benefits of a vital community of learners extend beyond the language arts. Language-rich classrooms also enable students to use language as a means of drawing upon their own experiences to support learning in other areas, including curricular subjects.

From a Piagetian perspective, children become active initiators of their own learning when they construct knowledge by modifying their own ideas (Long & Bulgarella, 1985). More than the accumulation of knowledge, learning is the integration of old knowledge and new knowledge in a process Piaget calls *accommodation*. The social context provided by the learning community permits social interactions in which students use language to draw upon their background knowledge, experience, and culture in order to support and sustain learning and make knowledge their own.

As an illustration of how students use language to make learning their own consider the following example in which a group of high-school girls discuss prejudice and the problem of arranged marriages for Greek girls.

> Cause my mother's got a cousin in America right? He comes over here to get married. He comes over, we went down to my aunt's to meet him, right? He comes up with this fiancé. Going home I asked my mum, "When did your cousin meet his fiancée? I didn't know he was engaged." She goes, "He met her this morning." I goes, "You mean he met her this morning, she's now engaged to him to be married, and they're going to live together in the States." And she goes, "Yeh." I goes, "That's crazy, your cousin's bloody mad." I really do think he is because, I mean, she met him in the morning and she's engaged to him the same day. I mean, how much could you say in one morning, with everyone else about, when you're meeting all our, you know, all your friends and that, you know, they have quite a bit of a get-together. So how could you really get engaged? You know, she's going to the States and live with him." (Searle, 1988, p. 27).

Connecting to the lesson
What you know.

The girl in the above example draws on an experience with her mother's cousin in order to arrive at an understanding of the problems associated with arranged marriages. Similarly, a teacher who begins a geography lesson by encouraging students to talk about their travels enables them to draw upon their own experience to make sense of the lesson.

Writing can be used to similar advantage as a medium for learning. For example, a teacher might begin a lesson on aquatic animals by helping students write down some of the things they already knew about life in the sea. This gives students the opportunity to activate their background knowledge and use it to make sense of the lesson (Bayer, 1990). Without opportunities for students to make learning their own, all learning is reduced to rote learning, which is likely to be soon forgotten simply because it was never truly learned in the first place (Holt, 1982).

Another means by which students learn is by engaging in collaborations with other people. From a Vygotskian perspective, learning is facilitated through collaborations in which students, as members of a community of learners, use language to share, discuss, debate, collaborate, and question. Students "construct knowledge by modifying their previous ideas, rather than by accumulating new bits transmitted from the outside, and the exchange of ideas among peers stimulates such modification" (Kamii & Randazzo, 1985, p. 124). In the following example from Barnes (1992), secondary students working in small groups are asked to do an experiment about air and then discuss among themselves what happened and why it happened.

S: What about, what about this glass of milk, though, Glyn?
G: Well, that's 'cause you make a vacuum in your mouth …
S: When you drink the milk, you see … you …
G: Right! … You, you make a vacuum there, right?
S: You, you make a vacuum in the … er … transparent straw …
G: Yes.
S: Carry on.
G: And the, er, air pressure outside forces it down, there's no pressure inside to force it back up again so …
S: OK. (Barnes, 1992, p. 40)

When students are confronted with questions or conflicting points of view, they are forced to clarify, analyze, synthesize, speculate, and evaluate their thinking (Bayer, 1990). In the above example, a group member helps clarify another's thinking "by questioning, by insisting upon explicit answers, and by setting up an explanatory framework" (p. 40). In general, if students do not have opportunities to engage in social interaction with others who offer a range of alternative points of view, there will be no new viewpoints to incorporate into their thinking and hence no intellectual development (Bayer, 1990). The opportunities for language use that emerge from a vital community of learners not only encourage language development but also are fundamental to students' learning.

Talk is more than a medium for thinking and learning—it is also an important means by which we learn how to think. From a Vygotskian perspective, thinking is an internalization of dialogues we've had with others. We learn to think by participating in dialogues, and our ability to think depends upon the many previous dialogues in which we have taken part. As a writer learns to anticipate the response of potential audiences, a thinker learns to anticipate the reactions of potential listeners. Barnes (1992) states: "In dialogue speakers take up statements that have gone before and develop them: one adds a qualifying condition, another suggests a cause or a result, another negates the whole statement, another reformulates it, and another qualifies one of the objects which it refers to" (p. 90). Thus, the chance to participate in dialogues with peers and teachers will influence the quality of students' thinking. We may not be able to literally teach students how to think, but we can offer dialogue as a model of effective thinking and, at the same time, invite students into the process of dialogue so they can assimilate effective thinking strategies.

The influence of the learning community on students' learning and thinking is a function of the quantity and quality of learning experiences the teacher provides. As we pointed out earlier in this chapter, one way teachers can enable students to use their language and experience to make sense of classroom learning is through the use of small-group discussions. This arrangement allows students to use talk as a means of drawing upon their background knowledge and experience, which they can use to construct meaning and extend their comprehension as they are exposed to the views of their peers.

How effectively small-group discussions stimulate language and learning depends, in part, on the nature of the task. Open-ended tasks, in which a number of responses are possible, are generally most effective (Jones, 1988). Asking students to describe, for example, instances of pollution they come across in their neighbourhoods, and to use their descriptions to make some general points about the major causes of pollution in these areas, is likely to be more effective than a closed task in which students are asked to list seven major causes of pollution (Jones, 1988). In the former case, students are free to speculate and test ideas, since there are no right answers; in the latter case, however, there is an implication that there are right answers, and students may be reluctant to speak for fear of giving a wrong answer and attracting ridicule.

The product of small-group discussion can also influence the quality of student talk. Students who are asked to use small-group discussion to answer a set of questions will likely not take as many risks as students who are asked to sort a list of statements into those with which they agree and those with which they disagree (Jones, 1988). In general, narrowly defined outcomes will almost certainly limit the breadth and depth of discussion.

The development of the learning community and students' willingness to use learning talk is also related to the degree to which students are able to take control of their own learning. Based on his observations of both primary and secondary classrooms, Jones (1988) concluded that

> [g]iving the learners the feel that they were in control of the learning and were in a position of greater expertise meant that they were much more ready to explore ideas and express themselves through talk than they would be if they were in a position of relative ignorance (p. 121).

The respect teachers model for students' ideas will also influence students' willingness to engage in exploratory learning talk. Teachers who display their respect for a range of ideas and opinions, and who consider their own opinion as just one of many points of view, encourage students to use talk as an important tool for exploring ideas. Conversely, if teachers use talk to impose their own ideas on students, then students will be reluctant to engage in learning talk. As Barnes (1976) states, "A classroom dialogue in which sharing predominates over presenting, in which the teacher replies rather than assesses, encourages pupils when they talk and write to bring out existing knowledge to be reshaped by new points of view being presented to them" (p. 111).

Genuine learning occurs against a background of previous knowledge and experience against which students construct knowledge for themselves. Written and oral language are the principal tools by which learners activate their knowledge and experience. Teachers, in turn, support student learning by building on students' knowledge and experience, and by making the necessary connections between what students know and what teachers hope they will learn (Bayer, 1990).

◇ ACTIVATING A COMMUNITY OF LEARNERS: A PERSONAL ACCOUNT[1]

Before the school year began I wrote in my notes, "To fill our classroom with our voices and our lives will be a major goal for me next year." Community was important to me because I believed that the development of a vital community of learners would provide a rich social context for our literacy program. Early in the year, I planned many activities that I hoped would help build community in our classroom. During the first week of school, for example, each child interviewed and wrote a brief biography about one of his or her classmates. I also hoped that singing, field trips, and small- and large-group discussions would nurture the community. I can find no evidence, however, that my explicit attempts to foster community made any difference.

[1] During the 1991-92 academic year, Curt Dudley-Marling endeavoured to create a community of learners in a Grade 3 class. He documented his experience using reflective and descriptive field notes, audiotapes, photographs, and photocopies of students' written work. The discussion that follows is based upon preliminary analyses of his data.

But the community did come together as my students brought their lives into our classroom.

I began with the assumption that a community was a vital prerequisite to an effective reading and writing program, but what I found was that literacy becomes an important means by which students built and maintained relationships. Catherine, [2] Jenifer, and Barbara, for example, often took turns reading poems to each other. Fatima, Roya, Denise, and Lila sometimes acted out stories together. Crystal sometimes read stories to groups of several students. Other students read stories chorally or took turns reading books. The Scary, Evil Book Club described in the opening vignette became the means by which Nader entered the classroom community. Writing also brought students together. Students used a message board to exchange notes. Many students wrote collaborative stories or wrote stories about one another to initiate or nurture friendships. Including the names of classmates in stories served a similar function. These are just a few examples of the ways students used literacy to come together.

My hypothesis is that students used literacy in this way because they had complete control over both the topics and audiences for their reading and writing. This enabled them to use reading and writing to come together, but it also enabled them to activate the community that already existed between them. Most of my students had known each other since kindergarten and many lived in the same neighbourhood. *I didn't build community as much as I welcomed the existing community into our classroom.* This is an important observation, I think, because many of the instructional arrangements we find in classrooms have the effect of keeping students' lives out of the classroom. Teacher-controlled curricula, for example, make it difficult for students to relate what goes on in their lives to what goes on in the classroom. And teachers spend an inordinate amount of time discouraging social interaction among students.

IMPLICATIONS

As the above account illustrates, a vital community of learners enables students to learn from and with each other, and to make meaningful connections between their lives and learning at school. But the transformation of classrooms into learning communities requires more than creative activities for building community. Creating communities may have more to do with what we don't do than what we do. From a sociocultural perspective, classrooms that limit social interaction, collaboration, and cooperation also limit students' opportunities to extend learning beyond the walls of the school.

Transforming classrooms into learning communities is a formidable task. Teachers require training as well as administrative and community support. It is especially important for teachers to see models of learning communities

---

[2] As they were in the opening vignette, students' names have been changed to protect their privacy.

in action. Having this approach modelled in their university classes would be a good start.

In bringing their lives into the classroom, students also bring conflict, pain, racism, and sexism—a phenomenon Britzman (1991) calls "Pandora's pedagogy." This can be frightening for teachers, but it also presents an opportunity. Within a community of learners, teachers can help students learn to deal with interpersonal conflict (see Fine, 1990 for a discussion of conflict-resolution strategies), offer support and comfort when students need it, and confront hateful attitudes (e.g., racism) that threaten the community and society in general.

◆ CONCLUSION

Special education is rooted historically in the limited ability of regular classrooms to accommodate the broad range of intellectual, physical, and socio-emotional differences that exist naturally among people. Recently the convergence of various social, political, economic, and pedagogical factors has resulted in exceptional students spending an increasing part of their educational day in the regular classroom. But without significant changes there is little reason to believe that including exceptional students in the regular classroom will be automatically successful. Traditional classrooms, driven by rigid, lockstep curricula and an emphasis on the transmission of knowledge from teachers to students, will never be congenial to the needs of students with special needs.

In the inclusive classroom, the tremendous diversity of backgrounds and experiences that students bring to the classroom will be not only recognized but also seen as a valuable resource for learners. If the benefits of this diversity are to be tapped, classrooms must be transformed from places where the teacher occupies the centre stage to places where students and teachers, as members of a community of learners, share the stage together. Teachers who work to create a vital community of learners in their classrooms provide a context within which differences can be celebrated and used to everyone's advantage. In these classrooms, students use language to learn and learn to use language through a mutually beneficial relationship in which the community provides the necessary conditions for language learning while the language of students and teacher nurtures and sustains the community.

QUESTIONS
◆◆◆◆◆◆◆◆◆◆◆◆◆

1. Based on your experience what are some of the ways that students with exceptional needs are segregated within the regular classroom?

2. How does the holistic view of language learning differ from your own experiences as an elementary or secondary student?

3. How might a secondary teacher go about fostering a community of learners in his or her classroom?

4. Think of some of the elementary and secondary classrooms you have observed. How have you observed teachers inviting students to engage in oral and written language?

REFERENCES

Abkarian, G. G. (1981). A non-verbal child in a regular classroom. *Journal of Learning Disabilities, 14*, 138-139.

Barnes, D. (1992). *From communication to curriculum.* 2nd ed. Portsmouth, NH: Boynton/Cook Publishers, Inc.

Bayer, A. S. (1990). *Collaborative-apprenticeship learning: Language and thinking across the curriculum, K-12.* Katonah, NY: Richard C. Owen.

Bloom, L., & Lahey, M. (1978). *Language development and language disorders.* New York: John Wiley & Sons.

Bloome, D. (1986). Reading as a social process in a middle school classroom. In. D. Bloome (Ed.), *Literacy and schooling.* Norwood, NJ: Ablex.

Britzman, D. (1991). Decentering discourses in teacher education: Or, the unleashing of unpopular things. *Journal of Education, 173*, 60-80.

Cazden, C. (1970). The neglected situation in child language research and education. In F. Williams (Ed.), *Language and Poverty* (pp. 81-101). Chicago: Markham.

Cherry, L. (1980). A sociolinguistic approach to the study of teacher expectations. *Discourse Processes, 1*, 374-393.

Church, S. M. (1985). Blossoming in the writing community. *Language Arts, 62*, 175-179.

Cochrane-Smith, M. (1984). *The making of a reader.* Norwood, NJ: Ablex.

Daiute, C. (1989). Research Currents: Play and learning to write. *Language Arts, 66*, 656-664.

Dillon, D., & Searle, D. (1981). The role of language in one first grade classroom. *Research in the Teaching of English, 15*, 311-328.

Dudley-Marling, C. (1990). When School is a Struggle. Richmond Hill, ON: Scholastic-TAB.

Dudley-Marling, C., & Searle, D. (1991). *When students have time to talk: Creating contexts for learning language.* Portsmouth, NH: Heinemann.

Durkin, D. (1966). *Children who read early.* New York: Teachers College Press.

Dyson, A. H. & Genishi, C. (1983). Research currents: Children's language for learning. *Language Arts, 60*, 751-757.

Edelsky, C. (1984). The content of language arts software: A criticism. *Computers, Reading, and Language Arts 1*, 8-11.

Edwards, A. D., & Furlong, V. J. (1978). *The language of teaching: Meaning in classroom interaction.* London: Heinemann.

Fine, E. S. (1990). *Interrogating silences: Collaborative production of dramatic text in a special education classroom.* Unpublished doctoral dissertation, University of Toronto.

Gee, J. P. (1992). *The social mind: Language, ideology, and practice.* New York: Bergin & Garvey.

Gilmore, P. (1983). Spelling Mississippi: Recontextualizing a literacy-related speech event. *Anthropology and Education Quarterly, 14* 235-255.

Gilmore, P. (1986). Sub-rosa literacy: Peers, play and ownership in literacy acquisition. In B. B. Schieffelin & P. Gilmore (Eds.), *The acquisition of literacy: Ethnographic perspectives.* Norwood, NJ: Ablex.

Good, T. C. (1980). Classroom expectations: Teacher-pupil interactions. In J. H. McMillan (Ed.), *The social psychology of school learning* (pp. 79-122). New York: Academic Press.

Goodman, K. S. (1984). Unity in reading. In A. C. Purves & O. Niles (Eds.), *Becoming readers in a complex society: Eighty-third yearbook of the National Society for the Study of Education.* Chicago: University of Chicago Press.

Goodman, K. S., & Goodman, Y. M. (1979). The development of initial literacy. In L. B. Resnick & P. A. Weaver (Eds.), *Theory and practice of early reading.* Hillsdale, NJ: Lawrence Erlbaum.

Goodman, Y. M., Watson, D. J., & Burke, C. L. (1987). *Reading miscue inventory: Alternative procedures.* Katonah, NY: Richard C. Owen.

Gonzales, P. C., & Hansen-Krening, N. (1981). Assessing the language learning environment in classrooms. *Educational Leadership, 38*, 450-452

Graves, D. (1983). *Writing: Teachers and children at work.* Portsmouth, NH: Heinemann.

Hall, N. (1987). *The emergence of literacy.* Portsmouth, NH: Heinemann.

Heath, S. B. (1983). *Ways with words: Language, life, and work in communities and classrooms.* Cambridge: Cambridge University Press.

Holt, J. (1982). *How children fail* (2nd ed.). New York: Delacorte Press/Seymour Lawrence.

Jones, P. (1988). *Lipservice: The story of talk in schools.* Philadelphia, PA: Open University Press.

Kamii, C., & Randazzo, M. (1985). Social Interaction and Invented Spelling. *Language Arts, 62*, 124-133.

Kantor, R., Miller, S. M., & Fernie, D. E. (1992). Diverse paths to literacy in a preschool classroom: A sociocultural perspective. *Reading Research Quarterly, 27*, 201.

Lindfors, J. W. (1980). *Children's language and learning.* Englewood Cliffs, NJ: Prentice-Hall.

Lindfors, J. W. (1987). *Children's language and learning* (2nd ed.). Englewood Cliffs, NJ: Prentice-Hall.

Long, R., & Bulgarella, L. (1985). Social interaction and the writing process. *Language Arts, 62*, 166-172.

Loughlin, C. E., & Martin, M. D. (1987). *Supporting literacy: Developing effective learning environments.* New York: Teachers College Press.

Myers, J. (1992). The social contexts of school and personal literacy. *Reading Research Quarterly, 27*, 297-333.

Peterson, R., & Eeds, M. (1990). *Grand conversations: Literature groups in action.* Richmond Hill, ON: Scholastic-TAB.

Rist, R. (1970). Student social class and teacher expectations: The self-fulfilling prophecy in ghetto education. *Harvard Educational Review, 40*, 411-451.

Roderick, J. A. & Berman, L. M. (1984). Dialoguing about dialogue journals. *Language Arts, 61*, 686-692.

Rosen, C., & Rosen, H. (1973). *The language of primary school children.* Baltimore, MD: Penguin.

Rosenblatt, L. (1978). *The reader, the text, the poem: The transactional theory of literary work.* Carbondale, IL: Southern Illinois University Press.

Searle, D. (1975). A study of the classroom language activity of five selected high school students. *Research in the Teaching of English, 9*, 267-288.

Searle, D. (1988). Language: A tool for learning. In M. Chorny (Ed.), *Teacher as Researcher* (pp. 5-32). Calgary, AB: Language in the Classroom Project, University of Calgary.

Short, K. G., & Pierce, K. M. (1990). *Talking about books: Creating literate communities.* Portsmouth, NH: Heinemann.

Smith, F. (1978). *Reading without nonsense*. New York: Teachers College Press.

Smith, F. (1981). Demonstrations, engagement and sensitivity: A revised approach to language learning. *Language Arts, 58,* 103-112.

Smith, F. (1988). *Joining the literacy club: Further essays into education*. Portsmouth, NH: Heinemann.

Spradlin, J. E., & Siegel, G. M. (1982). Language training in natural and clinical environments. *Journal of Speech and Hearing Disorders, 47,* 2-6.

Staton, J. (1988). ERIC/RCS Report: Dialogue journals. *Language Arts, 65,* 198-201.

Stephens, D. (1991). *Research on whole language: Support for a new curriculum*. Katonah, NY: Richard C. Owen.

Taylor, D. (1983). *Family literacy: Young children learning to read and write*. Portsmouth, NH: Heinemann.

Taylor, D., & Dorsey-Gaines, C. (1988). *Growing up literate*. Portsmouth, NH: Heinemann.

Teale, W. H., & Sulzby, E. (1987). *Emergent literacy*. Norwood, NJ: Ablex.

Tough, J. (1976). *Listening to children talking: A guide to the appraisal of children's use of language*. London: Ward Lock Educational.

Weaver, C. (1988). *Reading process and practice: From socio-linguistics to whole language*. Portsmouth, NH: Heinemann.

Wells, G. (1986). *The meaning makers*. Portsmouth, NH: Heinemann.

*I*n this final section of the book, we offer some views about the Canadian educational scene as we approach the 21st century. As an introduction, we posit a list of ten trends, which is presented below. Our vision has been shaped by our personal involvement in education over the last twenty years and by our observations of significant developments in the field of education, particularly with respect to conceptualizations of teaching, learning, and the children we serve in our schools.

1. *Patterns of practice are emerging that indicate a greater willingness among educators to consider alternatives to categorical-based educational systems. From our perspective, this reflects a trend toward tolerance for student differences.*

2. *The current transitions in schools suggest that there is a movement toward preventative as opposed to*

reactive education. A central aspect of this movement is its focus on student responsibility and involvement in the learning process. The philosophy and practice associated with this movement will enable schools to more clearly demonstrate their commitment to educational quality and equity.

3. *The world is becoming an increasingly complex place in which to live and work and is therefore creating a need for its citizens to develop, maintain, and build helping networks. One such network in the educational context is the partnership between the school and home. Over the past few years, we have seen a closer and more respectful relationship develop between teachers, parents, and other educational participants. We believe that the educational field will take more of a lead in formulating*

EMERGING ISSUES AND FUTURE DIRECTIONS

methods that will fulfil the lifelong learning needs of people and thereby enable them to better deal with the challenges created by advances in the social, technological, political, and economical arenas.

4. Recent advances in education and psychology suggest a greater interface of theory and research with practice, which will result in a more solid foundation for changes in school programming and service delivery for all students.

5. The last few years have seen increasing evidence of educational policy development and implementation being driven by bottom-up as opposed to top-down decision-making practices. This process is being reflected in the increasing number of schools where collaborative consultation practices are consistently employed, as well as in school districts where individual school-based decision-making practices are being promoted. We anticipate that collaborative consultation and professional information-sharing will be adopted by more schools and school districts in the future.

6. The growing respect in our society for people who are capable of solving our complex problems and producing successful transitions suggests to us that in the field of education, innovations related to improving student learning as well as professional expertise and practice will be sought and supported. We think that one example of this future innovation (which is already happening in some parts of the country), is the restructuring of school curriculum to better prepare students for the types of information and problems they will face in the 21st century.

7. The significant increase of advertising on television related to education is a sign that those in corporate and political arenas (particularly in North America) are becoming increasingly concerned about our future ability to compete on a global basis. This suggests to us that excellence in teaching will be at a premium in the future.

8. The last two decades have seen school districts, schools, and teachers make many changes in their policy and practice to accommodate exceptional children in the mainstream. From our perspective, future adaptations to policy and practice will have to include the hiring of trained educators who are more holistic and flexible in their approach to planning and instruction. We expect that more universities and colleges across our country will develop new integrated teacher training programs that will provide further support for the merger of regular and special education.

9. We predict further changes in the organizational structures and procedures of the educational system that will allow teachers to teach and manage student diversity efficiently and effectively.

10. We have noted in this book a trend toward shared responsibility among all teachers in meeting the needs of all students in inclusive educational settings. We now predict that professional education associations will become more supportive of teacher empowerment. In other words, we think that in the future teachers will increasingly take the initiative in improving their own schools, facilitating the education of all children through teamwork, and accepting greater responsibility for their own professional growth.

We look forward to being a part of these trends and wish you good luck in your journey into the field of education.

ON TO THE FUTURE

The following is an example of a reflective writing activity in which each student's talk is transcribed and his or her actions are described.

Meet Brian, a Grade 1 student, as he explores ideas and constructs meaning with his peers, and adds yet another variation to the theme about Bears. Brian spends a good deal of his time listening intently to the stories of other students. He then follows up with excellent questions and comments as he synthesizes what appear to be unrelated ideas. The class looks forward to Brian's input as he adds a unique twist to what appeared to be a finished story.

Although he possesses strong intrapersonal talents with excellent verbal skills, Brian was reluctant to write and publish any of his stories. However, his bear story, entitled "Me and My Bear," was published, with extra copies printed for his peers. Brian's story was eagerly read and many students illustrated their copies to clarify meaning for themselves. Children begin at an early age to actively process and link information by using the strategy of "imaging."

Brian stood on his chair to read the story aloud. Janet, a child who often demonstrates linear thinking, was the first to raise her hand when Brian invited questions and comments from the community.

Brian: Yes, Janet.

Janet: Why did you buy the bear?

Brian: Well, I had ten dollars on me and instead of looking I saw a bear and bought him.

Rose: Brian, is that true? *(Rose reads and writes about nonfictional stories of bears in their natural habitat.)*

Brian: No, it's not true.

Reflection: *They are naturally distinguishing between fiction and nonfiction, a skill required at this age by the curriculum of studies.*

Figure 15.1

Brian's Original Story

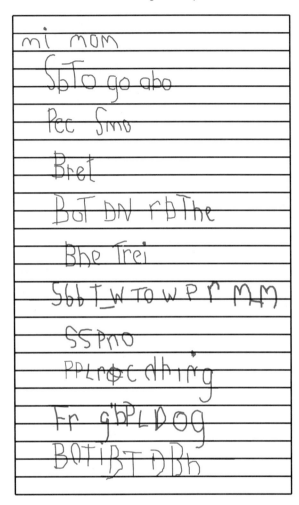

Kris: Brian, I put a circle around the word saying store in the story and made it into a sign.

Reflection: *Note example of Kris's illustration of Brian's story. He uses his spatial talent to build meaning for himself. The attention of the whole class zeroed in on the word "store" as they found it in the text. There was some pondering dialogue about it being Hooperman's Store.*

Jack: Is there only one store, Brian?

Brian: Yes, because the typewriter put it there.

Teacher: *(facilitating) Could everyone focus for a minute please? Has anyone heard of a little mark called an apostrophe that authors put before an 's'—like at the end of Hooperman's?*

Figure 15.2

Brian's Published Story

Me and My Bears

by: Brian

My mom said, " Go and pick some berries."......

but I ignored the berry tree.

Instead I went to Hooperman's store.

People were buying guard dogs and stuff......

but...... I bought a bear!!

People didn't like him...... but I bought him.

We played and

played

and

slept together.

(There is more discussion about the fact that there was only one store that belonged to Mr. Hooperman.) *That little mark called an apostrophe is put there to show that this is Mr. Hooperman's store. Authors do that (demonstrating on the blackboard).*

Brian: Yes, it was Hooperman's Store.

Reflection: *I noted that something seemed to be bothering Brian. There was a pause in the community. I waited.*

Janet: *(still not satisfied)* Brian, did you pick the berries for your mother?

Inviting Janet to watch, Brian asked a few children to gather in the centre of the community of learners *(the desks are arranged in a circle, leaving a wonderful central space)* to help him mime his story. They quickly established the imagined location of Hooperman's Store and the berry tree. Brian began the mime as he walked, deliberately ignoring the berry tree. A few shoppers *(peers)* entered the store to buy guard dogs *(peers)*. The guard dogs were led away. Then Brian walked in, bought the bear, and walked out as the

Figure 15.3
Kris's Copy of Brian's Story

KRIS

Me and My Bears

by: Brian

My mom said, " Go and pick some berries."...

but I ignored the berry tree.

Instead I went to Hooperman's store.

People were buying guard dogs and stuff......

but.... I bought a bear!!

People didn't like him...... but I bought him.

We played and

played

and

slept together.

remaining shoppers made a big deal of pretending to not like the bear. Brian and his bear *(a peer who is unable at this point to read, tell, or write stories and yet was fully involved in the learning process)* continued on a fairly long journey ending up, to the surprise of everyone, at the berry tree. This turn of events generated a lot of discussion. For example, "Did the bear eat all of the berries?" "Did you pick any berries for your mom?" "I thought you said you played and played and then slept together?" This question was prompted

because the action of playing and sleeping were omitted during the mime.

More discussion was generated about the "neat" way the story ended back at the berry tree, where it had begun. This provided an excellent example of a circular story. The children were encouraged to use simple sketches to review the sequence of the story using the following storyboarding diagram at the blackboard.

Figure 15.4
Kris's Copy of Brian's Story

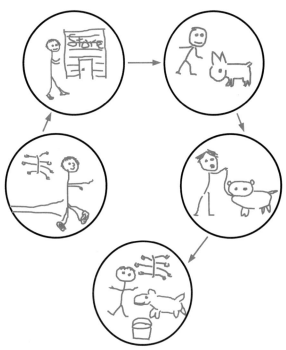

While some of the children watched, others added to the drawing. There was a lot of talk guided by Brian, who talked at length about his plans to write Chapter 2 of his story, which would involve a surprise when he and his bear returned home with a pail of berries for his mother.

The learning time was further enriched when the whole class was invited to enjoy a circular story about a family encountering bears while picking blueberries.

Reflection: *Within the community of learners, Brian was able to explore his ideas as well as develop interpersonal relationships. Brian experienced mind-stretching support from his peers as they helped him to shape his story through the use of questioning and mime. These strategies also helped him to organize and clarify his thinking. It was during the mime that Brian's body language revealed his growing confidence as he led his bear to the berry tree. Until that point, Brian's oral responses had been unsure. Now he was talking excitedly about writing Chapter 2 of his story. What appears to have been about twenty-five minutes of unstructured time actually was controlled by the community's hidden structure, which encouraged imagination to soar and skills to be internalized in a meaningful context.*

Brian's mother had joined the community that day and was pleased to see how what seemed to an adult to be a very short and disjointed story could bring about learning with so many dimensions. Although her son

was reading at a Grade 4 level, his writing and learning style was celebrated by children with different learning styles and varied degrees of uniqueness. She was surprised to see how he used mime to transfer his oral storying to print. This inspired her to plan a trip with her son to the zoo, where Brian could observe the antics of bears as they interacted with each other. After enthusiastically sharing the learning opportunities of the trip with the principal, permission was granted for the trip to be part of Brian's regular school day as he extended his learning beyond the walls of the school building.

Note: This vignette was written by Mrs. Anne Green, a teacher at Mossleigh Demonstration School.

◇ INTRODUCTION

Young people attending schools of the future will come to know learning differently. The opening vignette reveals a snapshot of what we envision inclusive classrooms of the future will be like. The students experience and celebrate new learning in the community of learners, and each child's journey, though different from that of his or her peers, is acknowledged and supported. In the Grade 1 class depicted here, students discover the major role that personal experiences, interests, and passions play in their learning.

The teacher orchestrates the interaction within the classroom using teaching moments as they fit the classroom discourse. Sensitive to the various learning styles and learning strengths of each student, the teacher creates opportunities for dialogue, sharing, and involvement. The teacher in our example uses reflective writing as a tool to understand the delicate balance between structure and the independence that enables students to employ skills as they construct their learning. The teacher is an active participant involved in the learning community, and her role is clearly one of facilitator. Her reflections are constructed as she observes the students actually individualizing their own program. Reflections are linked with professional reading, inclusive teaming, and collaboration with other teachers and support professionals to understand how children make sense of learning. Parents are invited to join the community of learners, and their involvement can lead to other new experiences that will assist the child. Within the inclusive community of learners, children blend creative thinking and logic as they build upon their own ideas and those of others. At all times, the focus is on helping children retain responsibility and control throughout their learning experience as they embark on their journey of lifelong learning.

The learning community as described above is no doubt already coming into being in many schools and classrooms across Canada. Unfortunately, school organization and practice, which are based on a special education approach, deny many students with exceptional learning needs access to such classrooms. Inclusive schools of the future must be driven by the belief that learning is maximized when students are provided with experiences that build on their existing competencies and that are responsive to their learning needs. This is achieved by creating instructional systems that incorporate a wide variety of strategies and supports to deliver inclusive and supportive services. Alternative learning options and varying amounts of learning time must be provided for students with exceptional needs, and teachers, parents, and students should expect variation in the learning progress of each individual. According to Wang (1992), "No special labeling is needed to provide different instruction for different students, and momentary problems in learning are not viewed as failures, but as occasions for further teaching" (p. 2). This quote captures the essence of the vignette about Brian. Whether a student has been identified as having exceptional needs is no longer a relevant issue—in a community of learners the needs of *all* students must be served.

A growing number of school districts across Canada are engaged in a review of their current systems and practices, and are considering productive ways of eliminating segregationist practices (Porter & Richler, 1991; Porter & Collicott, 1992; Flynn & Innes, 1992). Stainback, Stainback, and Bunch (1989) point out that one of the greatest barriers has been the continued operation of the dual system of service delivery for regular and special education. Blythman (1988) describes the current school context by stating that "[t]he emphasis has moved from specialist provisions, compensatory strategies and "Band Aid" (Elastoplast) solutions to what in effect has been a more fundamental appraisal of mainstream schools, their organization and curriculum" (p. 53). In a similar vein, Sailor (1991) notes that the two most notable reforms to emerge in special education in the past decade are (1) the move to integrate students with low-incidence and severe disabilities into general education schools and classrooms, and (2) the move to retain students with mild and moderate disabilities in the general education classroom. At the same time, there has been a parallel reform movement in the general education system, which began with specific changes in curriculum and instructional techniques, and more recently has shifted toward the systematic reorganization of school governance structures, policy, and resource allocation at the school site.

Sailor (1991) argues for an amalgamation of the above two movements to better serve the needs of all students, and suggests that the time is at hand for a *shared educational agenda*. It has been emphasized throughout this text that current systems of special and regular education are in a state of transition as they move toward a unified and holistic system of appropriate education for all students. More so than any previous decade, the 1990s hold promise for a revolution and revitalization of educational practice. Before we can speculate on the most productive means of breaking down existing barriers, and, correspondingly, what our schools might look like in the next century, it is essential to have a clear picture of the present context. This will be briefly reviewed in the following section as we consider where we are in recognizing and dealing with the barriers to inclusive education.

◆ PRESENT CONTEXT

SCHOOLS IN TRANSITION

Current literature is flooded with a rash of new terms and phrases associated with a growing concern over the quality and delivery of education in today's schools (Treffinger, 1991). Issues associated with terms such as the pursuit of educational excellence, educational reform, effective schools, regular education initiative, the collaborative school, program continuity, back to the basics, and at-risk students have been widely described and debated in the literature, and we are beginning to hear these terms being used in educational meetings and everyday discussions in schools throughout North America.

In Chapter 2, our analysis of the historical progression of inclusive education in Canada concluded with the suggestion that the 1990s would be the decade for the unification of the currently separate systems of regular and special education. It must be re-emphasized that we are not recommending that one system merely be appended to or incorporated by the other. Clearly, successful unification will involve the creation of an entirely new system that will encompass the best of what both systems now offer.

There is no question that, over the past three decades, significant advances have been made with respect to the provision of education for children with exceptional needs. In virtually every province, there are more services, personnel, and resources allocated to serving the needs of these children. Many advancements, such as the development of innovative curriculum, curriculum-based assessment procedures, improved evaluation and record-keeping, and student-centred approaches to teaching and learning, have been of particular benefit to students with exceptional needs (Will, 1986). Nevertheless, these advances have also incurred substantial costs to the system.

One problem that has emerged over the past thirty years is the isolation and fragmentation of students, personnel, and resources due to the categorical and dual development of the general and special education systems. A related problem has been the creation of a dual system of decision-making, which left general education teachers and systems increasingly disenfranchised by specialized service provisions. This has resulted in a growing discomfort on the part of general education teachers with respect to serving a diversity of student needs in the general education classroom. Many of these educators would prefer to maintain the status quo by preserving a system that delineates between regular and special education roles and responsibilities for both teachers and students. Moreover, the hierarchical structure currently in place in most school systems has increasingly removed teachers from any significant participation in decision-making. Matters such as class placement, curriculum selection, and in-class interventions are currently being made by other specially trained educators or by consultants representing other disciplines such as medicine or psychology.

As a potential solution to the problem of isolation and disenfranchisement of teachers, many educational reform leaders are proposing a new organization of education that is based on strategies and practices designed to support commitment as opposed to control (Rowan, 1990). Tied to the broader vision of effective inclusive schools are critical features such as teacher involvement in decision-making, redefinition of teacher roles, increased instructional time and innovative instructional approaches, support systems for teachers, collaborative networking and teaming, communal rather than hierarchical patterns of school organization, and principal empowerment to implement school-based solutions (Idol, Paolucci-Whitcomb, & Nevin, 1987; Rowan, 1990; Smith & Scott, 1990; Will, 1986; Porter & Richler, 1991; Porter & Collicott, 1992; Flynn & Innes, 1992; Villa & Thousand, 1992). Some educational reformers are also calling for a renewed emphasis on efficacy and excellence (Creemers, Peters, & Reynolds, 1989; Goodlad, 1990), while others are demanding greater equity and personalization of learning for all students in a unified educational system (Lipsky & Gartner, 1989; Stainback & Stainback, 1990; Stainback, Stainback & Forest, 1989; Villa, Thousand, Stainback, & Stainback, 1992).

Clearly, education is in a state of transition. Educational reformers are simultaneously trying to grapple with two seemingly paradoxical educational problems: (1) creating a renewal of interest in quality and excellence in education; and (2) eliminating inequitable systems of education that isolate both students and teachers. In confronting these problems, educators have advanced in the literature numerous concepts and innovations. Some have focused their plans on the regular education system and have addressed only the excellence issues (Gallagher, 1991), whereas others have emphasized the complex challenges associated with meeting the special education needs of students in a fair and equitable manner (Block & Haring, 1992).

Not surprisingly, there have also been instances of discord, especially when one interest group is threatened by the changes proposed by another, or when philosophical directions or organizational structures are seen to be incompatible. As with any movement for change, it must be anticipated that there will be critics who argue convincingly for the preservation of educational options for students with exceptional learning needs, and who see full inclusion of students with exceptional needs as a risky undertaking, cautioning that such systems offer no choice of educational options to students who may be better served in settings other than the inclusive classroom (Lieberman, 1992; Vergason & Anderegg, 1992). It is our belief that it is possible to achieve the goals of efficacy and equity in Canadian educational systems, and that the power to create this reality is encompassed in several emerging themes, which are described next.

◇ EMERGING THEMES

PREVENTATIVE EMPHASIS

It has often been noted that segregation practices as they have evolved over the century in the school and community have created a society that is uncomfortable with, and consequently rejecting of, individuals with handicaps or notable differences (Stainback & Stainback, 1989). Teachers are all too familiar with the teasing and cruelty that children bestow on one another, not only on those with handicaps but also on those who exhibit any difference at all, be it in size, culture, or name, to suggest a few. The systematic implementation of inclusive education could ultimately lead to a significant turnaround in this trend of intolerance toward difference. Regular teachers will have a significant role to play in providing instruction and opportunities that will help students understand and respect individual differences, as well as in modelling accepting and supportive behaviour toward all students. A unified educational system will bring all students and teachers together, and the artificial barriers created by segregation and categorization practices will diminish and hopefully disappear. Once the necessary attitudes, skills, and values become inculcated in the schools, we will no doubt see the positive outcomes of this preventative approach in the larger community as well.

Support for a preventative approach is also found on other educational fronts. Reschly (1987), following an in-depth discussion of learning characteristics of mildly handicapped students, recommends placing "greater emphasis upon the prevention of low achievement and mildly handicapping conditions" (p. 53). This is in response to the growing number of students in the United States who are at risk for school failure. A recent Government of Canada (1991a) document states that Canada has the largest percentage of high-school dropouts (30 percent) of any of the industrialized countries. The existence of a major subpopulation of undereducated students has far-reaching implications not only for schools but for society in general. A continuation of this trend will clearly diminish prospects for Canada's participation in the global community, especially on the economic front (Wiederholt, 1989). Moreover, as McCann (1991) observes, "any child who fails to graduate and become a productive member of society will become a significant cost to society" (p. 16). These concerns are echoed in the Government of Canada (1991b) document *Prosperity through Competitiveness*.

There have been recent attempts to define the population of at-risk students. Presseisen (1991) targets a number of student subgroups, including school dropouts, students with reading, mathematical, and functional deficiencies incurred by specific learning problems, and language-deficient students. Reynolds and Birch (1988) identify as subgroups of concern "minorities within minorities" (who are currently dealt with under migrant education and bilingual education), victims of child neglect and abuse, drug-handicapped learners, and school-age parents. To this list one could add children with AIDS, children from dysfunctional families, and children who live in rural or remote regions of the country.

As a viable alternative approach to our current categorical-based systems, McCann (1991) recommends a personalized system of service that stresses the need to delineate those personal characteristics that might put an individual at risk, as well as the environmental conditions that contribute to the problem. In a similar vein, Slavin (1990) recommends early education and preventative instruction.

The work of Slavin et al. (1991), who have pursued a preventative approach, shows particular promise. These researchers have systematically implemented programs that combine prevention and early, intensive, and continuing intervention to create a *neverstreaming* solution for at-risk students. Slavin et al. (1991) note that "once a student becomes academically handicapped ... neither mainstreaming nor special education or remedial education is likely to bring the child up to age-appropriate age-achievement norms" (p. 373). Consequently, efforts are best directed at early detection of students who are potentially at risk for school failure, and at the provision of intensive supportive services to ensure that these students experience success and, most importantly, stay in the mainstream. Slavin et al. (1991) describe a number of programs—including Success for All, Reading Recovery, and Prevention of Learning Disabilities—that are based on a preventative approach, and the collective results are exceedingly promising. As the authors suggest, neverstreaming approaches offer powerful solutions to two of our most difficult problems for schools in transition: teachers are supported in their efforts to meet a greater diversity of student learning needs in the general classroom, and preventing or reducing severe learning problems at the outset makes appropriate accommodation in the inclusive classroom more probable.

One of the greatest fears classroom teachers have about inclusive classrooms is the threat of increased behaviour problems (Stainback, Stainback, Moravec, & Jackson, 1992). Indeed, many resource teachers can attest to the close association between behaviour problems and students who have a long history of learning problems. It is generally believed that school failure and low self-concept combine to create an eventual pattern of behaviour problems in the classroom. Cullen (1985) has carried out a number of studies that show a direct link between these factors. As a viable solution to the problem, recent advances in adaptive education strategies (Wang, 1992) have demonstrated not only that such procedures can have a positive effect on school achievement for exceptional learners, but that such programs can also be readily implemented in a regular classroom program. It is critical, therefore, that successful preventative practices be seriously examined as potentially powerful means for educational reform. In addition to the suggestions offered in Chapter 9, educators can benefit from new approaches in an inclusive education context, which are beginning to appear in the literature, as well as from approaches to behaviour management that have proven successful in the past (McGee & Menolascino, 1992; Haring & Kennedy, 1992).

EFFECTIVE SCHOOLS

It is widely recognized that educators know considerably more about education and what makes for effective practice than what the schools actually enable them to do. For example, although teachers have, on average, four years of professional preparation, once they become practicing teachers the bureaucratic demands of schools prevent them from tapping much of this professional expertise (Skrtic, 1991). One of the current areas of promise for promoting successful inclusive schools is effective school research. Lezotte (1989) defines an effective school as "one that can, in outcome terms reflective of its teaching and learning mission, demonstrate the joint presence of quality (acceptably high levels of achievement) and equity (no differences in the distribution of that achievement among the major subsets of the student population)" (p. 28).

Effective school research has been carried out over a twenty-year period, with much of the work based on the comparative examination of effective and less effective schools. By the 1980s, although the primary characteristics of effective schools had been identified, there was little information with respect to how these schools might be brought about (Lezotte, 1989). Three primary issues emerged: (1) school boards mandated their local schools to become effective, and teachers and school administrators viewed the process as yet another top-down model of school development; (2) school principals, believing that they were solely responsible for school effectiveness, resisted the process, citing lack of expertise to instigate change and their own doubts about improving school achievement for students from deprived families; and (3) teachers erroneously interpreted the drive for effective schools as suggestive of the fact that they were not doing their best, and saw the process as one in which they would be compelled to work harder.

Despite the above barriers, effective school research continued, first on a school-by-school basis, and later on the basis of district-wide programs. Stimulating change was the notion that the primary unit of planned change should be the individual school, with all members of the school staff involved and the principal providing leadership. Successful initiatives were implemented as a long-term change process, with a general goal of continuous school improvement, the use of research as a basis, and the delineation of facilitating school and district policies, practices, and procedures. Finally, it was recognized that effective schools require the commitment of all school staff, and that this depends primarily on teachers choosing to become involved and believing that they have control over the change process.

For those who are primarily involved in working with children with exceptional needs, the current conceptualization of effective schools holds great promise. For several decades, special educators have been grappling with the problem of how to produce maximal learning for students who experience difficulties in the regular education system. Within the limiting structures of a categorical system of special education, it has become increasingly apparent that despite the growth of special programs and resources, many of our students do not meet the criteria of eligibility to receive such help and are consequently left to continue to fail in the regular education system. It is encouraging to note the reporting of a number of successful innovations in inclusive schooling in Canadian (Porter & Collicott, 1992; Flynn & Innes, 1992; Porter & Richler, 1991) and U.S. (Schattman, 1992; Jackson, 1992; Kaskinen-Chapman, 1992; Cross & Villa, 1992) educational systems. A school or district-wide commitment to effective schooling for all students is a positive and, more importantly, proven means of ensuring quality and equity for all students.

LIFELONG EDUCATION

At one time it was widely upheld that the knowledge of a culture could be carefully sequenced and parcelled into curricula by grade levels. Education and thus teaching involved the transmission of this knowledge base to students. It is now commonly recognized that such thinking is flawed, and that given the technological and ideological advances of recent times, effective education must go well beyond building an adequate knowledge base by showing students how to learn (Cornish, 1986) and how to critically question and evaluate new information (Wiggins, 1989). In other words, students must learn to engage in effective problem-solving and to transfer their learning to other thinking domains and, more importantly, to real-life situations. The traditional image of the student as a passive recipient of knowledge is being replaced with the image of students and teachers interacting dynamically in a community of learners, with the teacher providing the necessary student-centred support to enable learners to become socially and academically competent and self-instructive, and able to engage in self-directed learning (Wang, 1992).

Noting the related need to provide intelligent curricula to encourage students to become lifelong learners, Cornish (1986) observes that "[y]oungsters must acquire during their school years the skills and attitudes that will enable them to gain all kinds of new skills and understandings many years later. The ability to learn in later life is crucial if they are to succeed as workers, citizens and people" (p. 13). These skills and attitudes will be crucial in helping individuals to upgrade the professional and work-related expertise that they need to survive in the rapidly changing workforce of the future.

Coombs (1982) recommends that our efforts be directed toward "building a progressively broader and more diversified 'learning network'—combining formal, nonformal, and informal modes of education—to serve the evolving lifelong learning needs of all members of the population" (p. 146).

Wiederholt (1989) raises a further challenge by arguing that the large-scale efforts associated with the general education initiative (GEI) or the regular education initiative (REI) are too narrow in perspective, and that educators should instead be more broadly concerned with advocating a policy of improving students' quality of life. Such thinking lends support to an emphasis on lifelong education.

Contemporary educators and prospective teachers have a tremendous challenge awaiting them, in that they *can* and *must* become the models of lifelong learning. As the reality of inclusive education enters our schools and our communities, its success will depend on the teacher's ability to be an autonomous learner. Recognizing that an adequate knowledge base is essential for meeting the needs of all students in the classroom, effective regular teachers will seek out and demand professional development opportunities. Moreover, effective schools will reflect the fact that maximum growth and development in the classroom can accrue only from collaborative consultation practices and the promotion of ongoing school-based problem-solving. Lifelong learning for teachers is thus a necessary companion to inclusive schooling.

CHILDREN-CENTRED EDUCATION

Wang & Peverly (1987) note that "[a] prominent and recurring theme in the history of school reform efforts has been the recognition that one fundamental task of effective schooling is to enable individual students to become active learners who assume responsibility for acquiring knowledge and skills and sustain a pattern of self-directed, lifelong learning" (p. 59). This represents a significant change in the traditional delivery of education in the regular classroom.

In his discussion of future trends in education, Lewis (1981) suggests that "one major shift would be in the relationship of the teacher and the learner. The old paradigm made the teacher responsible for the student's learning, with the student obliged to learn. The new paradigm of a learning society shifts the responsibility for learning to the learner" (pp. 66-67). In this context, the responsibility of the teacher is not so much to teach knowledge, but rather to use professional expertise and available resources to stimulate the learner to construct his or her own knowledge and skill base, understanding, insights and values.

According to Wang and Peverly (1987), the two critical categories of learner competence are "students' ability to be responsible for their own learning and behavior, and students' ability to be self-instructive in the learning process" (p. 59). Perhaps the most serious barrier to special education endeavours in the past was the failure to recognize the potential benefits of encouraging students to self-regulate their own learning. Although individualized learning has long been a hallmark of special education practice, it has only recently been understood that the critical element for effective learning is the promotion of self-direction and self-instructive skills in learning

(Wang, 1992). Research on self-regulation, involving both exceptional and nonexceptional students, has led to a variety of interventions that have been effectively used to improve learning efficacy and efficiency of students (Wang, 1992; Tarver, 1992).

Further support for student-centred learning comes from educators who are particularly concerned about the consequences of school reform for gifted students. For example, Schatz (1990) sees the removal of artificial barriers created by our traditional categorical systems of special education as a positive change, but he expresses grave concern that restructuring will result in a lowering of the ceiling of achievement expectations, which some consider to be already dangerously low for gifted students. This entirely legitimate concern lends support to the adoption of a student-centred approach. Many leading experts assert that by carefully attending to the goal of ensuring that able students are sufficiently challenged and encouraged to become self-instructive in the classrooms of the future, the wealth of expertise that has been generated in the field of gifted education over the past few decades can contribute significantly to improving the quality of education in the mainstream. While some leaders in gifted education continue to advocate a range of program options (Clark, 1992), others have been quick to point out the logical fallacies and pedagogical flaws that underlie segregated gifted programs, asserting that all students, including those identified as gifted and talented, can have their needs met in the regular classroom (Sapon-Shevin, 1992).

The concept of student-centred learning is a daunting one for the regular classroom teacher who has anywhere from twenty-five to thirty-five students. Indeed, the simple computation of total teaching time divided by the number of classroom students gives the average student about twelve minutes of individualized time per day, deployed over five or six different subject areas. Carnine (1991) offers a useful alternative to the student-centred versus teacher-centred dilemma. The concept of **child-centred instruction** helps to defray the notion that student-centred learning means individual attention, and correctly places the emphasis on using a variety of strategies in the classroom to promote independent learning and the engagement of all students. Whether this occurs through individual, small-group, or whole-class based activities is of minor consequence—what matters is that students become active participants in a community of learners.

child-centred instruction: instructional process that focuses on developing active, self-directed individuals who ultimately become independent, lifelong learners

FROM ISOLATION TO COLLABORATION

The isolation problem is readily observed in the practice of teaching in general. Although the majority of teachers spend the greater part of their professional day encouraging and orchestrating student learning, they have very limited opportunities to share and discuss their teaching challenges and successes with colleagues or other adults. Most schools do not attempt to systematically identify teaching excellence. Unfortunately, it is usually the least

competent teachers who become the focus of public discussion and scrutiny, and thus teachers—particularly the exceptional ones—strive to avoid the limelight. Lacking opportunities to celebrate and assist one another, teachers look for direction in the teaching models they experienced in school. Schools without collaborative networks and professional supports in place leave teachers to rely on their own experiences and problem-solving abilities and thereby force them into a trial-and-error pattern of learning (Rosenholz, 1985).

All too often, teachers who do manage to attain excellence in teaching become overwhelmed by the demands imposed by an unsupportive and iso-lated system, and consequently fall victim to burnout, or, worse yet, opt to leave the teaching profession. Indeed, Smith and Scott (1990) suggest that teacher isolation, which has become the norm in schools, may be the primary factor in teachers' resistance to change in general and, more specifically to accepting and accommodating exceptional needs students in the regular classroom: "Under the best of circumstances, change imposed from (or even suggested by) the outside can be viewed as threatening. And apprehensions about change are reinforced when one must face that change alone" (p. 10). For schools to become successfully merged into a unified system of educa-tional delivery, it will be critical to develop effective communication and col-laboration between teachers (Graden & Bauer, 1992) and support personnel (York, Giangreco, Vandercook, & Macdonald, 1992).

One of the more predominant trends over the past decade has been the development of educational collaboration. Among its major features are: a commitment to shared responsibility for meeting the needs of all students through the use of a wide variety of practices and structures; a commitment to work together, and to share and develop expertise as equal partners (not in a hierarchy); the belief that quality education is largely determined by what happens at the school site; and the belief that teachers should be involved in the decisions made about school goals and the means for achieving them. As Smith and Scott (1990) describe it, "[c]ollaboration depends inherently on the voluntary effort of professional educators to improve their schools and their own skills through teamwork" (p. 2).

Inasmuch as it is recognized that collaborative schools are site-based, it is logical to expect that a variety of configurations are possible. Whereas some proponents have specifically developed collaborative consultation approaches as a basis for shared interaction between regular and special education teachers (Idol, Paolucci-Whitcomb, & Nevin, 1987), other recent publications see collaborative consultation as a necessary precursor to effective inclusive schools and classrooms (Graden & Bauer, 1992; Nevin, Thousand, Paolucci-Whitcomb, & Villa, 1990). Whether the impetus comes from regular education or special education is not as important as the fact that advocates of collaboration are overwhelmingly positive about the potential of inclusive teaming for making schools more effective and collegial environments in which to practice the profession of teaching. Smith and Scott (1990) point out that "[a]n inherent characteristic of collaborative norms and practices is that they cannot be imposed on a school's personnel by outside authorities" (p. 72). Consequently, the decision to become a collaborative school, or for teachers to engage in inclusive teaming, rests with the school and the professionals within it. In contrast to the traditional hierarchical structure of the school, principals must be prepared to share the responsibilities of instructional leadership, and they must have the competence to define the team's common purpose and to provide the supportive structures to help teachers accomplish the work. Teachers must be prepared to work together as a team and to accept responsibility for school improvement and professional growth.

From the perspective of those who support a merging of special and regular education, collaboration has the potential to become a powerful tool in such a transition. In the following section, we examine trends at all levels of education that hold considerable promise with respect to the merging of regular and special education and subsequent creation of effective inclusive schools and classrooms.

◆ BUILDING THE FUTURE

For Wang (1990), the challenge facing educators of future schools is "to apply all forms of extant knowledge (as derived from research on teaching and school effectiveness, and from experience in the implementation of innovative educational practices) to the structuring of a coordinated, well-managed, and inclusive universal educational system that effectively meets the instructional and related service needs of individual students" (p. 4). In order to effect a successful transition of Canadian schools toward inclusive schooling, necessary changes at four distinct levels can be delineated. Whereas it is recognized that a multitude of factors could be suggested for any given level, for the purposes of the present discussion, only the major areas will be cited. The four levels include federal and provincial, school district, school, and classroom.

FEDERAL AND PROVINCIAL LEVEL

Research Support

Probably the most pressing need in Canada for future development in education is for research studies to be carried out, in Canadian educational contexts and with Canadian students. Funding for educational studies is limited in comparison with that for other disciplines such as medicine or the sciences. The Canadian practice has been simply to adopt and generalize the findings from research conducted in other countries, particularly the United States.

In the redeployment of resources that will need to accompany the transition of schools into a unified system of education, research and the role it can and should play must be considered. Although many educational administrators declare their belief in the necessity of research to support school practice, in many school systems such research programs are nonexistent. As Reynolds and Birch (1988) have convincingly argued, the continuing trend of diminishing resources demands that educational practice become cost-effective, and this can only be achieved through the systematic examination of what is being practiced (i.e., program evaluation) and the effectiveness of these efforts in meeting the learning needs of all students (i.e., research). According to Stainback and Stainback (1989), "Research can provide the basis of development and refinement of programs, procedures, and techniques that can allow for quality education to occur within groups of students with diverse needs in integrated regular education classes" (p. 264-265).

Consolidation Initiatives

There is a critical need for Canadian educators to become more proficient at identifying what works in Canadian educational contexts for Canadian students. Across Canada, there are few resources available to promote the sharing, dissemination, and critical reflection of successful educational models and practices. Two recent Government of Canada (1991a, 1991b) documents may well set the stage for a national education debate. The $20 million program described in these documents is meant to raise concern about Canada's prospects for competing in the global economy of the next century, as well as to stress the critical importance of improving Canada's education system, in that the future well-being of the nation will depend on the competencies and education of its people.

McConaghy (1992) notes that the above federal documents provide few recommendations for actual change in Canada's schools. Moreover, he warns that Canadian companies and businesses will be required to take on more responsibility for employee training and education. At the present time, private industry in Canada spends a mere 0.3 percent of its gross domestic product on training, whereas the U.S. spends twice that amount and Germany eight times as much. The two Government of Canada documents, although they help to highlight economic and educational issues, will have little impact if matters are simply left at the discussion level. The next few years will be a critical time for Ottawa to show leadership in these areas.

One of the few existing structures for national education concerns is the Council of Ministers of Education, which meets periodically and carries out projects such as the *Special Education Information Sharing Project* (Council of Ministers of Education, 1989). Other national perspectives on the educational needs of exceptional children come from advocacy groups and their publications (e.g., the *Learning Disabilities Association of Canada Newsletter*), occasional book publications such as Csapo and Goguen (1989) and Winzer (1989, 1990), and a recently launched journal called *Exceptionality Education Canada*. However, the successful transition of schools will depend on the creation of new forms of information consolidation, in order that all provinces and school jurisdictions might benefit from knowing about successful practices across the country.

general.

Defining the Vision

At the provincial level, there is a critical need to review existing policies, and to revise these in developing a clear delineation of the vision of inclusive education, along with specific actions to support this vision (Villa & Thousand, 1992). David and his colleagues (David, 1990; David, Cohen, Honetschlager, & Traiman, 1990) have provided a set of recommendations directed at positive restructuring and at stimulating action at the district level. Others suggest that provincial departments make a gradual shift from the role of compliance policeman to facilitator and assistance provider (Wang, 1992; Mills & Hull, 1992). This shift could be brought about in a variety of ways, including initiating provincial or regional conferences, networking organizations, providing time for staff development and meetings, offering technical assistance and training, using provincial and brokered services, identifying and promoting best educational practices, creating fiscal incentives, and, finally, securing progressive legislation.

David et al. (1990) further propose that initial work begin on a small scale, with pilot demonstration projects, and that systems be allowed certain freedoms or waivers from existing provincial rules to facilitate restructuring efforts. Accordingly, school systems should be held accountable for maintaining a clear focus on the goals and objectives of restructuring, and ultimately for demonstrating general school improvement and increased student performance.

Alignment

Given that educational matters are predominantly a provincial concern, there is a need to ensure that the major provincial participants in education are in alignment. Flynn and his colleagues (Flynn & Kowalczyk-McPhee, 1989; Flynn & Innes, 1992) argue that these participants must be sufficiently aware of the philosophy and direction of transition, and must be collectively willing to channel their efforts in the same direction. Thus, it is essential that provincial departments of education, faculties or departments of education in universities, school districts, teachers' unions, parent groups, and students pull together to create effective schools that can meet the needs of all students. A perusal of current documents describing provisions for exceptional students in each province clearly reveals that provinces that have encouraged and developed this kind of alignment are much more advanced in the transition process than are the less aligned provinces.

general

One example of cooperative effort, described by Miller (1991) and called the Integrated Special Education-English Project (ISEP), was specifically designed to support the merging of special and regular education through a combined special education and English teacher-preparation program. The integration of these two previously separate programs resulted in the effective preparation of English teachers in carrying out English instruction with handicapped and nonhandicapped students. The experience gained through such projects can be used to guide other university faculties of education in developing and implementing new teacher preparation programs that ultimately support the broader educational goal of initiating inclusive education in nonthreatening, productive ways.

University teacher preparation can be another effective means of supporting the merger of special education and regular education. Stainback and Stainback (1989) outline four critical steps in the facilitation of merger in higher education: (1) strengthen collaborative and cooperative efforts between special education and regular education programs and faculty; (2) restructure organizational units so that they emphasize consulting and support services as opposed to special education; (3) reorganize program offerings and content by consolidating the knowledge base and best practices of regular and special education, eliminating categorical-based preparation programs; and (4) coordinate with state (provincial) and local agencies to promote certification by instructional area as opposed to a category of student.

SCHOOL-DISTRICT LEVEL

Facilitating Organization

Flynn and Kowalczyk-McPhee (1989) caution that the change process is sure to fail without "well-designed structures, policies, and procedures [to] allow the individual energies developed by alignment and personal power to translate effectively into collective results" (p. 37). School divisions or districts have a critical role to play in the transition process, first in articulating the vision and then in ensuring that their policies and regulations are sufficiently supportive yet flexible enough for schools to define and accommodate the needs of the local community. Many of the strategies outlined by David et al. (1990) in a previous section would be equally applicable at the school-district level. In the past decade, a number of Canadian school districts have made the commitment to full integration for all students. Porter & Richler (1991) provide a detailed account of how a school system might facilitate organization, and brief accounts have been reported in southern Ontario (Little, 1985), Quebec (Frigon, 1988), and several public districts in Manitoba, Saskatchewan, and British Columbia (Porter, 1990).

general.

Service Coordination

Within every community, there are existing resources and services that augment and overlap with the provisions of schools. As school divisions move into new and collaborative forms of service provision, maximal benefit will be derived from efforts to facilitate and encourage community coordination of schools with a variety of agencies, including health and welfare, family services, and employment assistance. Wang, Reynolds, and Walberg (1987) stress that the "new morbidities" of current society (e.g., child abuse, drug addiction, and broken family structures), and their recognized association with special education referrals, make it imperative that schools collaborate with other community service agencies not only to improve the coordination of services but also to ensure that schools delimit some of the ever-increasing special functions they have recently undertaken with respect to serving exceptional children's needs. This kind of service coordination should be initiated and coordinated at the school-division administration level. Falvey, Coots, and Bishop (1990) provide a current account of the processes involved in developing a caring community to support volunteer programs.

SCHOOL LEVEL

Organization of the Environment

Many leading advocates of education reform emphasize that future efforts in serving students with special needs will require the redeployment of available personnel and material resources (Reynolds & Birch, 1988; Wang, 1990). Current roles and systems of educational program delivery will need to evolve in such a way that all participants (i.e., general education teachers, special education teachers, administrators, school psychologists, parents, and students) are brought into closer partnership so that their potential contributions are recognized and facilitated. More specifically, Reynolds and Birch (1988) suggest that, "for the future, education of marginal students requires radical changes in the training, deployment, and certification of school personnel" (p. 352). The particular framework that is used may vary substantially from school to school and from community to community, as each locale tries to capitalize on its existing strengths and resources. Nevertheless, as we have noted elsewhere in the text, a number of excellent approaches have been implemented effectively at the school level. Some of the most promising are described below.

Moving from Professional Bureaucracy to Adhocracy

yes!
yes!

Dr. Tom Skrtic has become a leading spokesperson in the move toward educational reorganization. In a recent interview (Thousand, 1990), he discusses some of the major obstacles that we are facing. One lies in the organization of the profession and the way that schools are structured. Essentially, the professional bureaucracy of schools runs counter to the two primary goals with which schools are currently grappling: (1) the personalization or individualization of services; and (2) the pursuit of excellence. The current organizational structures of the educational system (i.e., legislation, provincial, district, and school policies) are based upon standardized solutions for specified groups of students. This has resulted in a "means-ends inversion," or what Skrtic describes as "a situation in which professionals begin to favor their general principles (or standard ways of doing things) over the particular needs of their clients" (Thousand, 1990, p. 31). Within regular education, we see the parallel of the standard curriculum (i.e., means) as the driving force in most regular education classrooms, as opposed to the appropriate education of all students (i.e., goals).

As a viable solution to the present educational dilemma, Skrtic proposes an adhocracy-based school system that "deploys its professionals in multidisciplinary teams and coordinates their work through mutual adjustment" (p. 31). **Adhocracy** demands that educators use and share their professional expertise to invent novel and successful ways of meeting the needs of all students in their jurisdiction.

◆ **adhocracy**: a school system in which educators are encouraged to share professional expertise in creative and innovative ways to meet student needs

School-Based Inclusive Teaming

A number of recent studies and reports have suggested that school-based inclusive teaming is a powerful means of promoting the atmosphere, motivation, and commitment needed to create a successful merger of special and regular education. Essentially, teaming offers a professional means of sharing both expertise and experience in productive problem-solving with respect to students who are experiencing difficulties in the school. Jenkins and Pious (1991) propose that teaming be nonhierarchical in design, and that problem-solving for individual students be shared among all individuals who are directly involved in educating the student. Accordingly, classroom teachers or specialists can contribute to the problem-solving associated with analyzing a child's learning difficulties, with examining the child's instructional environment, and, finally, with offering solutions. (For a full discussion of inclusive teaming, see Chapter 6.)

Cooperative Professional Development

Most educators would agree that professional development is the key to the ongoing growth and effectiveness of the discipline. Whereas in the past there was a tendency for educators to bring in outside experts, the more recent focus has been on using inside expertise to foster the professional growth of all teachers. Smith and Scott (1990) suggest a variety of ways to capitalize on in-school resources, including peer observation, peer coaching, teaching clinics with expert teachers, teacher institutes, mentor programs, and teacher support teams.

Schools are increasingly being encouraged to promote what Treffinger (1991) calls **entrapreneurship**. This refers to systematic and deliberate efforts to create innovative teaching and effective schools within the supportive framework of administrative encouragement. In contrast to the practice of entrapreneurship in which only the individual benefits, the entire school stands to gain from this form of entrapreneurship. To give a brief illustration, Treffinger (1991) points out that since much of the training emphasis for specialists for gifted students has centred on areas such as productive thinking, problem-solving, and decision-making, these individuals could provide leadership by sharing their expertise with regular classroom teachers and by assisting them to empower the thinking of their students through such strategies and methods.

◆ **entrapreneurship:** systematic efforts to promote innovative instruction in effective schools within a supportive administrative framework.

An example of entrapreneurship is provided in a recent study by Johnson and Pugach (1991). In this study, the needs of students with mild learning and behaviour problems were met using a peer collaboration approach in which teachers were encouraged to develop and implement instructional and behavioural interventions themselves, rather than relying on the direct service of the special education teacher. The authors describe peer collaboration and inclusive teaming as "a structured, four-step, collegial dialogue in which the initiating teacher focuses on the classroom problem, while the peer partner, or 'facilitator,' guides the first teacher and assures that the steps in the process are followed appropriately" (p. 456). Working with a sample of forty-eight elementary and junior high-school teachers in the intervention group and forty-three elementary school teachers in a control group, Johnson and Pugach found that teachers involved in the peer collaboration training group showed a significant increase in their tolerance and understanding of the range of cognitive abilities in the classroom. Other recent studies of full inclusion (Stainback, Stainback, Moravec, & Jackson, 1992) and adaptive education strategies (Wang, 1992) have similarly highlighted the importance of professional development in creating successful inclusive education environments.

Recognize and Reward Excellence

Earlier in this chapter, we noted that teaching is generally regarded as a highly isolated profession. As a possible means of reversing this situation, Treffinger (1991) recommends that schools take deliberate steps to identify excellence in teaching and then recognize and reward it. Clearly, at the school level at least, it is important to search out teachers who experience success in meeting the needs of heterogeneous students, and to create numerous opportunities for other staff members to observe, reflect, and collaborate with such peers. A visible model of excellent teaching can be highly effective in motivating others to strive for excellence in their own classrooms. Rewarding such efforts not only helps generate new levels of productivity in a school but also provides tangible confirmation that one's teaching efforts are valued and supported.

CLASSROOM LEVEL

Attitude Change

Current school reform leaders (Bilken, 1989; Lipsky & Gartner, 1989) make the resounding claim that the essential ingredient for the successful merging of schools into a unified educational system is a total reconceptualization of the notion of disability. Disability is something that is defined by the culture, and schools have developed numerous administrative policies and structural arrangements to foster the attitude that it is the disability that must be dealt with and not the individual. Accordingly, Biklen (1989) states that "disability has a series of meanings that extend far beyond its observable or objective reality" (p. 236). For some, this translates into dangerous stereotypical views about "special" ways to interact with disabled students, such as the belief that a blind student is incapable of negotiating his way around the school and community, or that a student with a mental handicap is incapable of learning how to read. Such thinking is wedded to the notion that the label defines who the student is, and that it is the social meaning of the label that dictates the student's placement, program, and potential. Numerous educational practices, such as the designation and training of regular and special teachers, testing, and special curriculum, are driven by these attitudes.

What is needed to change this kind of thinking in the schools? In proposing an alternate vision for persons with disabilities, Lipsky and Gartner (1989) stress the need to focus on individual rights of autonomy and decision-making authority. Such an emphasis encompasses the following beliefs:

(1) A statement as to the *right* to control one's life; (2) An expression of belief in the individual's *capacity* to do so; and (3) A recognition of the *benefits* to the individual to do so (p. 260).

Biklen (1989) offers a number of suggestions to support the general goal of achieving effective schools, and quality and equity in serving the individual student. Specific recommendations are:

1. The elimination of labelling students, programs, and teaching staff by category.
2. A change in the social organization and authority, focusing on the empowerment of those who have been most systematically divested (i.e., exceptional students, teachers, and parents).
3. The elimination of testing as a gatekeeping mechanism defining who's in and who's out with respect to special programming.
4. A need to consider the social and emotional as well as the academic growth of the student.
5. A need to redirect integration efforts beyond simple curriculum revision (p. 247).

The above changes must necessarily begin in the regular classroom. It is hoped that their widespread adoption will eventually make difference ordinary.

New Century Curricula

Carnine (1991) raises two important concerns with respect to current thinking about curricula. First, he notes the subtle yet prevalent influence of psychology or, more specifically, what he refers to as the **motivational-developmental perspective**. This perspective is based on the widely accepted belief that exposing students to developmentally appropriate experiences and using interesting materials will result in learning. The second concern involves the use of comprehensive textbooks that offer little more than surface coverage of a wide variety of topics. Carnine (1991) notes that, although such "teaching for exposure" is a well-established practice in American classrooms, it does little to foster the kind of self-instructive thinking that students will require to deal with an increasingly complex world.

Thousand and Villa (1991) convincingly argue that the traditional developmental curricula of the current century will simply be inappropriate for the 21st century. The knowledge explosion of the 20th century necessitates curricular restructuring that will truly prepare students for the kinds of thinking that will be needed in the next century. Treffinger (1991) astutely points out that many of the ideas that have been generated in the gifted education field may have particular relevance here. This perspective is supported by Keating (1991), who describes such components as critical and creative thinking as "the preparation needed for acting effectively in terms of some particular discourse and practice (e.g., a scientific discipline, a field in the humanities, an art form)" (p. 73).

◆ motivational-developmental perspective: the belief that effective learning is based on a student's exposure to developmentally appropiate experiences, materials, and tasks

habits of mind: a mind set or thinking pattern that is the outgrowth of knowledge acquisition, socialization practices, and experiential learning

Both Keating (1991) and Wiggins (1989) stress the importance of developing **habits of mind**, which refers to the socialization of essential knowledge-acquisition and problem-solving abilities, including suspending belief, questioning to clarify an idea's meaning or value, and being able to express one's thoughts with clarity in both written and oral communication. Keating (1991) asserts that we must go well beyond the mere teaching of basic skills of cognition in order to instil in our students a commitment to act upon expertise, to move toward rational inquiry, and to participate in public discourse.

Thousand and Villa (1991) elaborate further on what a new century curriculum might look like by emphasizing the need to focus on a community service ethic that will prepare students to participate effectively in a global community. In essence, the futuristic view of curriculum is both dynamic and community relevant, with the ultimate goal of helping students develop the thinking abilities needed to cope with the ever-increasing complexities of adult life and to instil a desire for lifelong learning.

Teaching Strategies

It has been emphasized throughout this text that numerous teaching strategies have been generated over the past few decades that can vastly enhance teaching effectiveness for exceptional and nonexceptional learners alike. According to Walberg and Wang (1987), adaptive learning approaches that are geared to individual student learning needs and abilities are far superior to traditional methods such as teacher-directed and group-paced instruction, which are unfortunately predominant in today's schools. While it may be too soon to delineate those strategies that may have the greatest value for inclusive classrooms, the challenge for teachers of the future is to reflect on their teaching experiences and to seek out innovative ways to implement a variety of approaches. In doing so, Treffinger (1991) notes, teachers become more autonomous, and supporting teacher autonomy leads to "increased ownership and investment in program development and improvement" (p. 7).

Teacher and Student Commitment

Recent explorations of schools and school effectiveness have revealed a pervasive lack of commitment on the part of both students and teachers, particularly in the urban school divisions. Familiar indicators of this are seen in various student behaviours such as lateness, poor attendance, low academic achievement, dropout, and disorderly behaviour. Teacher behaviours such as careless lesson planning, absenteeism, late arrivals and early leaving, and a general lack of enthusiasm for teaching are similarly indicative of lack of commitment.

Firestone, Rosenblum, and Webb (1991) discuss three types of commitment that are germane to effective teaching and learning in general, although specifically directed at high-school contexts. First, *commitment to place* refers to a general loyalty to the school; second, *commitment to students* is the key element in developing strong emotional bonds with students; and third, *commitment to teaching as an activity* is tied to one's developing perceptions of the craft of teaching and a concomitant desire to foster high achievement in students. All three components must be in place to ensure maximal effect. For example, even if a teacher demonstrates a high degree of involvement and loyalty vis-à-vis the school, and is widely recognized as warm, caring, and responsive toward students, he or she may lack the competence or the will to help students reach their full potential.

In a similar vein, commitment to place and commitment to learning on the part of the student is essential and requires that students not only attend classes regularly and on time, but that they take the business of learning seriously by making the most of the challenges that are offered by the school. When teachers and students are prepared to commit fully to the school, a cyclical pattern of healthy and mutually reinforcing relationships develops, which contributes positively to the quality of education. The factors needed to ensure this kind of commitment are defined by Firestone, Rosenblum, and Webb (1991) as follows:

- *Relevance* refers to the process of bringing meaning to school activities, especially for students.
- *Respect* grows out of consistent interactions in which individuals feel and believe that they are being treated with decency and fairness, particularly when they are involved with a more senior peer or one who has higher authority.
- *Support* refers to having a pleasant, well-maintained working environment and adequate instructional materials, as well as administrative clarity and consistency in designing and applying the rules and procedures. The provision of personal assistance to help an individual achieve a worthwhile goal is another type of support considered relevant here.
- *Appropriate expectations* refers to the procedures and incentives within the school to ensure that quality instruction and achievement remain a top priority for teachers and students respectively.
- *Influence* refers to the fact that most teachers are vastly uncomfortable if they are not allowed to participate in school-based decisions, particularly those that have an impact on their day-to-day teaching.

Collectively, the above recommendations can serve as an effective framework for students and teachers as they take positive steps to ensure a joint commitment to fostering school improvement and promoting standards of excellence in their classrooms and schools.

Inviting Partnerships with Parents and Community

Teachers inviting partnerships with parents and families is a longstanding practice in special education and, as detailed in Chapter 7, one with numerous benefits. Buswell and Schaffner (1990) see parents as having a significant role in supporting inclusive schooling. First, they can provide teachers with their vision of future possibilities for their child. Second, parents can instil in teachers positive attitudes by being effective models of unconditional acceptance and support of their child, and by encouraging teachers to recognize his or her strengths and capabilities. Third, parent advocacy can be an essential bridge in promoting successful inclusive schooling, especially at times when new challenges or obstacles are faced. Finally, given their long-term experience in making adjustments and coping with difficulties associated with their child, parents can offer constructive strategies to teachers who are working with that child. As Buswell and Schaffner (1990) conclude, such partnerships "can bring a focus to inclusive schooling that can help guide educational programming for each student that is positive, supportive, caring, and purposeful" (p. 222).

Other sources advocate an even broader community-referenced learning perspective (Peterson, LeRoy, Field, & Wood, 1992), as well as extracurricular activities (Falvey, Coots, & Terry-Gage, 1992), to support inclusive schooling efforts. We have only scratched the surface of community support, and initial efforts suggest that there is a rich foundation to be tapped. Educators of the future are the best resource we have to mine this potential wealth.

◆ SUMMARY

In our concluding chapter, we have attempted to pull together many of the current and optimistic ideas that we believe will eventually shape future education practice. The fundamental question that arises is: how best to proceed with the process of change in regular and special education that has been outlined in this chapter? If we accept the analysis of leading experts (Skrtic, 1991; Thousand, 1990; Thousand & Villa, 1991), who advocate a new adhocracy approach to the organization of schools, then we must attend to the professional preparation and development of the teachers who will play a pivotal role in the future success of all our schools. Thousand and Villa (1991) describe the teacher of the future as a personalizer of curriculum and instruction, who uses eclectic, inventive approaches to select, combine, and reorganize as required to meet the diverse student needs that arise in day-to-day practice.

Capturing much of the current futurist thinking, Thousand and Villa (1990) predict that the role of the teacher in the 21st century will be to "actively engage students in their own and others' acquisition of (a) humanistic, public service ethics; (b) communication, information-seeking, and problem-solving skills; and (c) core curricula deemed essential by the community" (p. 557). Similar in his vision of the future, Skrtic (1991) succinctly outlines what the larger educational picture might look like:

> The successful school of the 21st century will be one that produces liberally educated young people who can work responsibly and interdependently under conditions of uncertainty. It will do this by promoting in its students a sense of social responsibility, an awareness of interdependency, and an appreciation of uncertainty. It will achieve these things by developing students' capacity for experiential learning through collaborative problem solving and reflective discourse within a community of interests. The successful school in the post-industrial era will be one that achieves excellence and equity simultaneously—indeed, one that recognizes equity as the way to excellence. The successful school in the post-industrial era will be one that produces cultivated citizens by providing all of its students with a progressive education in an adhocratic setting" (p. 233).

Proposals for how a unified education system that accomplishes the dual goals of excellence and equity might be established have been made throughout this text. Whether our education systems can bring this ambitious undertaking to fruition is an open question. Regardless of the outcome, we firmly believe that classroom teachers are the most important participants in the transition and restructuring of our schools, and we hope that readers of this text will become involved in the quest for excellence and equity in the teaching of all students.

no

QUESTIONS
◆◆◆◆◆◆◆◆◆◆◆◆◆

1. Delineate the importance for successful inclusive education of the excellence and consolidation initiatives shared among professionals.

2. What role can parents play in helping to build a unified educational system?

3. Discuss the responsibility of the federal and provincial governments with respect to the development of inclusive education.

4. What concerns should be addressed at the school-division level to accommodate needs of the local community and its special population?

5. List the similarities between lifelong education and child-centred education.

REFERENCES

Biklen, D. (1989). Making difference ordinary. In S. Stainback, W. Stainback, & M. Forest (Eds.), *Educating all students in the mainstream of regular education* (pp. 235-248). Baltimore, MD: Paul H. Brookes.

Block, J. H., & Haring, T. G. (1992). On swamps, bogs, alligators, and special educational reform. In R. Villa, J. S. Thousand, W. Stainback, & S. Stainback (Eds.), *Restructuring for caring and effective education: An administrative guide to creating heterogeneous schools* (pp. 1-24). Baltimore, MD: Paul H. Brookes.

Blythman, M. (1988). From the other side of the wall. In. L. Barton (Ed.), *The politics of special educational needs* (pp. 32-57). Philadelphia: Falmer.

Buswell, B. E, & Schaffner, C. B. (1990). Families supporting inclusive schooling. In W. Stainback & S. Stainback (Eds.), *Support networks for inclusive schooling: Interdependent integrated education* (pp. 219-229). Baltimore, MD: Paul H. Brookes.

Carnine, D. (1991). Curricular interventions for teaching higher order thinking to all students: Introduction to the special series. *Journal of Learning Disabilities, 24,* 261-269.

Clark, B. (1992). The need for a range of program options for gifted and talented students. In W. Stainback & S. Stainback (Eds.), *Controversial issues confronting special education: Divergent perspectives* (pp. 57-67). Boston: Allyn & Bacon.

Coombs, P. (1982). Critical world educational issues of the next two decades. *International Review of Education, 28*(2), 143-157.

Cornish, E. (1986). Educating children for the 21st century. *Curriculum Review, March/April,* 13-17.

Council of Ministers of Education, Canada (1989). *Special education information sharing project: Summary of responses.* Vol. 2, no. 7.

Creemers, B., Peters, T., & Reynolds, D. (Eds.). (1989). *School effectiveness and school improvement.* Amsterdam: Swets & Zeitlinger.

Cross, G. C., & Villa, R. A. (1992). The Winooski School System: An evolutionary perspective of a school restructuring for diversity. In R. Villa, J. S. Thousand, W. Stainback, & S. Stainback (Eds.), *Restructuring for caring and effective education: An administrative guide to creating heterogeneous schools* (pp. 219-237). Baltimore, MD: Paul H. Brookes.

Csapo, M., & Goguen, L. (Eds.). (1989). *Special education across Canada: Issues and concerns for the '90s.* Vancouver, BC: Centre for Human Development and Research.

Cullen, J. L. (1985). Metacognitive approaches to classroom failure. In D. L. Forrest-Pressley, G. E. MacKinnon, & T. G. Waller (Eds.), *Metacognition, cognition and human performance* (pp. 267-300). New York: Academic Press.

David, J. (1990). What is restructuring? *Work-America, 7*(2), 1.

David, J., Cohen, M., Honetschlager, D., & Traiman, S. (1990). *State actions to restructure schools: First steps.* Washington, DC: National Governor's Association, Centre for Policy Research.

Falvey, M. A., Coots, J. J., & Bishop, K. D. (1990). Developing a caring community to support volunteer programs. In W. Stainback & S. Stainback (Eds.), *Support networks for inclusive schooling: Interdependent integrated education* (pp. 231-239). Baltimore, MD: Paul H. Brookes.

Falvey, M., Coots, J., & Terry-Gage, S. (1992). Extracurricular activities. In S. Stainback & W. Stainback (Eds.), *Curriculum considerations in inclusive classrooms: Facilitating learning for all students* (pp. 229-237). Baltimore, MD: Paul H. Brookes.

Firestone, W. A., Rosenblum, S., & Webb, A. (1991). Restructuring schools: Building commitment among students and teachers. In K. M. Kershner & J. A. Connolly (Eds.), *At-risk students and school restructuring* (pp. 101-107). Philadelphia, PA: Research for Better Schools.

Flynn, G. J., & Innes, M. (1992). The Waterloo Region Catholic School System. In R. Villa, J. S. Thousand, W. Stainback, & S. Stainback (Eds.), *Restructuring for caring and effective education: An administrative guide to creating heterogeneous schools* (pp. 201-217). Baltimore, MD: Paul H. Brookes.

Flynn, G., & Kowalczyk-McPhee, B. (1989). A school system in transition. In S. Stainback, W. Stainback, & M. Forest, (Eds.), *Educating all students in the mainstream of regular education* (pp. 29-41). Baltimore, MD: Paul H. Brookes

Frigon, O. (1988). Stopping segregation. *Entourage, 3*(1), 35-39.

Gallagher, J. J. (1991). Educational reform, values, and gifted students. *Gifted Child Quarterly, 35,* 12-19.

Goodlad, J. I. (1990). *Teachers for our nation's schools.* San Francisco, CA: Jossey-Bass.

Government of Canada (1991a) *Learning well ... Living well.* Ottawa, ON: Minister of Supply and Services.

Government of Canada (1991b). *Prosperity through competitiveness.* Ottawa, ON: Minister of Supply and Services.

Graden, J. L., & Bauer, A. M. (1992). Using a collaborative approach to support students and teachers in inclusive classrooms. In S. Stainback & W. Stainback (Eds.), *Curriculum considerations in inclusive classrooms: Facilitating learning for all students* (pp. 85-100). Baltimore, MD: Paul H. Brookes.

Haring, T. D., & Kennedy, C. H. (1992). Behavior analytic foundations of classroom management. In W. Stainback & S. Stainback (Eds.), *Controversial issues confronting special education: Divergent perspectives* (pp. 201-212). Boston: Allyn & Bacon.

Idol, L., Paolucci-Whitcomb, P., & Nevin, A. (1987). *Collaborative consultation.* Austin, TX: Pro-Ed.

Jackson, H. J. (1992). Full inclusion at Helen Hansen Elementary School: It happened because we value all children. In R. Villa, J. S. Thousand, W. Stainback, & S. Stainback (Eds.), *Restructuring for caring and effective education: An administrative guide to creating heterogeneous schools* (pp. 161-168). Baltimore, MD: Paul H. Brookes.

Jenkins, J. R., & Pious, C. G. (1991). Full inclusion and the REI: A reply to Thousand and Villa. *Exceptional Children, 57,* 562-564.

Johnson, L. J., & Pugach, M. C. (1991). Peer collaboration: Accommodating students with mild learning and behavior problems. *Exceptional Children, 57,* 454-461.

Kaskinen-Chapman, A. (1992). Saline area schools and inclusive community CONCEPTS (Collaborative Organization of Networks: Community, Educators, Parents, The Workplace, and Students). In R. Villa, J. S. Thousand, W. Stainback, & S. Stainback (Eds.), *Restructuring for caring and effective education: An administrative guide to creating heterogeneous schools* (pp. 169-185). Baltimore, MD: Paul H. Brookes.

Keating, D. P. (1991). Curriculum options for the developmentally advanced: A developmental alternative to gifted education. *Exceptionality Education Canada, 1,* 53-83.

Lewis, A. (1981). Education: Bridging past, present, and future. *Journal of Thought, 16*(3), 61-71.

Lezotte, L. W. (1989). School improvement based on the effective schools research. In D. K. Lipsky & A. Gartner (Eds.), *Beyond separate education: Quality education for all* (pp. 25-37). Baltimore, MD: Paul H. Brookes.

Lieberman, L. M. (1992). Preserving special education .... For those who need it. In W. Stainback & S. Stainback (Eds.), *Controversial issues confronting special education: Divergent perspectives* (pp. 13-25). Boston: Allyn & Bacon.

Lipsky, D. K., & Gartner, A. G. (1989). Building the future. In D. K. Lipsky & A. G. Gartner (Eds.), *Beyond separate education: Quality education for all* (pp. 255-290). Baltimore, MD: Paul H. Brookes.

Little, D. M. (1985). A crime against childhood—uniform curriculum at a uniform rate: Mainstreaming re-examined and redefined. *Canadian Journal of Special Education, 2*(1), 91-107.

McCann, R. A. (1991). At-risk students: Defining the problem. In Kershner & J. A. Connely (Eds). *At-risk students and school restructuring* (pp. 13-16). Philadelphia, PA: Research for Better Schools.

McConaghy, T. (1992). Ottawa sets the stage for a national education debate. *Phi Delta Kappan,* 498-500.

McGee, J. J., & Menolascino, F. J. (1992). Gentle teaching: Its assumptions, methodology, and application. In W. Stainback & S. Stainback (Eds.), *Controversial issues confronting special education: Divergent perspectives* (pp. 183-200). Boston: Allyn & Bacon.

Miller, D. E. (1991). Merging regular and special education teacher preparation programs: The integrated special education-English project (ISEP). *Teaching and Teacher Education, 7,* 19-23.

Mills, R. P., & Hull, M. E. (1992). State Departments of Education: Instruments of policy, instruments of change. In R. Villa, J. S. Thousand, W. Stainback, & S. Stainback (Eds.), *Restructuring for caring and effective education: An administrative guide to creating heterogeneous schools* (pp. 245-266). Baltimore, MD: Paul H. Brookes.

Nevin, A., Thousand, J., Paolucci-Whitcomb, P., & Villa, R. (1990). Collaborative consultation: Empowering public school personnel to provide heterogeneous schooling for all—or, who rang that bell? *Journal of Educational and Psychological Consultation, 1*(1), 41-67.

Peterson, M., LeRoy, B., Field, S., & Wood, P. (1992). Community-referenced learning in inclusive schools: Effective curriculum for all students. In S. Stainback & W. Stainback (Eds.), *Curriculum considerations in inclusive classrooms: Facilitating learning for all students* (pp. 207-227). Baltimore, MD: Paul H. Brookes.

Porter, G. L. (1990). *Integrated education as a paradigm question: Policy perspectives of Canadian school superintendents.* Unpublished doctoral research, Syracuse University, Syracuse, NY.

Porter, G. L., & Collicott, J. (1992). New Brunswick School Districts 28 and 29: Mandates and strategies that promote inclusive schooling. In R. Villa, J. S. Thousand, W. Stainback, & S. Stainback (Eds.), *Restructuring for caring and effective education: An administrative guide to creating heterogeneous schools* (pp. 187-200). Baltimore, MD: Paul H. Brookes.

Porter, G. L., & Richler, D. (Eds.). (1991). *Changing Canadian schools: Perspectives on disability and inclusion.* North York, ON: The Roeher Institute.

Presseisen, B. Z. (1991). At-risk students: Defining a population. In K. M. Kershner & J. A. Connolly (Eds.), *At-risk students and school restructuring* (pp. 5-11). Philadelphia, PA: Research for Better Schools.

Reschly, D.J. (1987). Learning characteristics of mildly handicapped students: Implications for classification, placement, and programming. In M.C. Wang, M.C. Reynolds, & H. J. Walberg (Eds.), *Handbook of special education: Research and practice, Volume 1, Learner characteristics and adaptive education* (pp. 35-58). Toronto: Pergamon.

Reynolds, M. C., & Birch, J. W. (1988). Facing the future. In M. C. Reynolds & J. W. Birch (Eds.), *Adaptive mainstreaming* (pp. 311-382). New York: Longman.

Rosenholtz, S. J. (1985). Political myths about educational reform: Lessons from research on teaching. *Phi Delta Kappan,* January.

Rowan, B. (1990) Commitment and control: Alternative strategies for the organizational design of schools. In C. B. Cazden (Ed.), *Review of research in education, 16* (pp. 353-389). Washington, DC: American Educational Research Association.

Sailor, W. (1991). Special education in the restructured school. *Remedial and Special Education, 12,* 8-22.

Sapon-Shevin, M. (1992). Including all children and their gifts within regular classrooms. In W. Stainback & S. Stainback (Eds.), *Controversial issues confronting special education: Divergent perspectives* (pp. 69-81). Boston: Allyn & Bacon.

Schattman, R. (1992). The Franklin Northwest Supervisory Union: A case study of an inclusive school system. In R. Villa, J. S. Thousand, W. Stainback, & S. Stainback (Eds.), *Restructuring for caring and effective education: An administrative guide to creating heterogeneous schools* (pp. 143-159). Baltimore, MD: Paul H. Brookes.

Schatz, E. (1990). *Ability grouping for gifted learners as it relates to school reform and restructuring.* Wisconsin. (ERIC Document Reproduction Service No. ED 327 047).

Skrtic, T. M. (1991). *Behind special education: A critical analysis of professional culture and school organization.* Denver, CO: Love Publishing.

Slavin, R. E. (1990). General education under the regular education initiative: How must it change? *Remedial and Special Education, 11*(3), 40-50.

Slavin, R. E., Madden, N. A., Karweit, N. L., Dolan, L., Wasik, B. A., Shaw, A., Mainzer, K. L., & Haxby, B. (1991). Neverstreaming: Prevention and early intervention as an alternative to special education. *Journal of Learning Disabilities, 24,* 373-378.

Smith, S. C., & Scott, J. J. (1990). *The collaborative school.* Oregon: ERIC/NASSP.

Stainback, W., & Stainback, S. (1989). Common concerns regarding merger. In S. Stainback, W. Stainback & M. Forest (Eds.), *Educating all students in the mainstream of regular education* (pp. 255-274). Baltimore, MD: Paul H. Brookes.

Stainback, W., & Stainback, S. (Eds.) (1990). *Support networks for inclusive schooling: Interdependent integrated education.* Baltimore, MD: Paul H. Brookes.

Stainback, S., & Stainback, W. (1992). Schools as inclusive communities. In W. Stainback & S. Stainback (Eds.), *Controversial issues confronting special education: Divergent perspectives* (pp. 29-43). Boston: Allyn & Bacon.

Stainback, W., Stainback, S., & Bunch, G. (1989). Introduction and historical background. In S. Stainback, W. Stainback, & M. Forest (Eds.), *Educating all students in the mainstream of regular education* (pp. 3-26). Baltimore, MD: Paul H. Brookes.

Stainback, S., Stainback, W., & Forest, M. (Eds.). (1989). *Educating all students in the mainstream of regular education.* Baltimore, MD: Paul H. Brookes.

Stainback, W., Stainback, S., Moravec, J., & Jackson, H. J. (1992). Concerns about full inclusion: An ethnographic investigation. In R. Villa, J. S. Thousand, W. Stainback & S. Stainback (Eds.), *Restructuring for caring and effective education: An administrative guide to creating heterogeneous schools* (pp. 305-324). Baltimore, MD: Paul H. Brookes.

Tarver, S. G. (1992). Direct instruction. In W. Stainback & S. Stainback (Eds.), *Controversial issues confronting special education: Divergent perspectives* (pp. 141-179). Boston: Allyn & Bacon.

Thousand, J. S. (1990). Organizational perspectives on teacher education and renewal: A conversation with Tom Skrtic. *Teacher Education and Special Education, 13*(1), 30-35.

Thousand, J. S., & Villa, R. A. (1991). A futuristic view of the REI: A response to Jenkins, Pious, and Jewell. *Exceptional Children, 57,* 556-562.

Treffinger, D. J. (1991). School reform and gifted education—Opportunities and issues. *Gifted Child Quarterly, 35,* 6-25.

Vergason, G. A., & Anderegg, M. L. (1992). Preserving the least restrictive environment. In W. Stainback & S. Stainback (Eds.), *Controversial issues confronting special education: Divergent perspectives* (pp. 45-54). Boston: Allyn & Bacon.

Villa, R. A., & Thousand, J. S. (1990). Administrative supports to promote inclusive schooling. In W. Stainback & S. Stainback (Eds.), *Support networks for inclusive schooling: Interdependent integrated education* (pp. 201-218). Baltimore, MD: Paul H. Brookes.

Villa, R. A., & Thousand, J. S. (1992). Restructuring public school systems: Strategies for organizational change and progress. In R. Villa, J. S. Thousand, W. Stainback, & S. Stainback (Eds.), *Restructuring for caring and effective education: An administrative guide to creating heterogeneous schools* (pp. 109-137). Baltimore, MD: Paul H. Brookes.

Villa, R. A., Thousand, J. S., Stainback, W., & Stainback, S. (Eds.). (1992). *Restructuring for caring and effective education: An administrative guide to creating heterogeneous schools.* Baltimore, MD: Paul H. Brookes.

Walberg, H. J., & Wang, M. C. (1987). Effective educational practices and provisions for individual differences. In M. C. Wang, M. C. Reynolds, & H. J. Walberg (Eds.), *Handbook of special education: Research and practice, Volume 1, Learner characteristics and adaptive education* (pp. 59-92). Toronto: Pergamon.

Wang, M. C. (1990). Learning characteristics of students with special needs and the provision of effective schooling. In M. C. Wang, M. C. Reynolds, & H. J. Walberg, (Eds.), *Special education: Research and practice: Synthesis of findings* (pp. 1-34). Oxford: Pergamon.

Wang, M. C. (1992). *Adaptive education strategies: Building on diversity.* Baltimore, MD: Paul H. Brookes.

Wang, M. C., & Peverly, S. T. (1987). The role of the learner: An individual difference variable in school learning and functioning. In M. C. Wang, M. C. Reynolds, & H. J. Walberg (Eds.), *Handbook of special education: Research and practice, Volume 1, Learner characteristics and adaptive education* (pp. 59-92). Toronto: Pergamon.

Wang, M. C., Reynolds, M. C., & Walberg, H. J. (Eds.). (1987). *Handbook of special education: Research and practice, Volume 1, Learner characteristics and adaptive education.* Toronto: Pergamon.

Weiderholt, J. L. (1989). Restructuring special education services: The past, the present, the future. *Learning Disability Quarterly, 12,* 181-191.

Wiggins, G. (1989). The futility of trying to teach everything of importance. *Educational Leadership, 47*(3), 44-59.

Will, M. (1986). *Educating students with learning problems—A shared responsibility: A report to the secretary.* Washington, DC: Clearinghouse on the Handicapped, Education Department. (ERIC Document Reproduction Service No. ED 279 149).

Winzer, M. (1989). *Closing the gap: Special learners in regular classrooms.* Toronto: Copp Clark Pitman.

Winzer, M. (1990). *Children with exceptionalities: A Canadian perspective. (*2nd ed.). Scarborough, ON: Prentice-Hall.

York, J., Giangreco, M. F., Vandercook, T., & Macdonald, C. (1992). Integrating support personnel in the inclusive classroom. In S. Stainback & W. Stainback (Eds.), *Curriculum considerations in inclusive classrooms: Facilitating learning for all students* (pp. 101-116). Baltimore, MD: Paul H. Brookes.

COPYRIGHT ACKNOWLEDGEMENTS

p. 10 Excerpt from Marfo and Nesbit, 1989: From M. Csapo and L. Goguen, *Special Education Across Canada: Issues and Concerns for the 90s*, Centre for Human Development and Research, 1989. Used by permission.

p. 11 Excerpt from Jones, 1986: From B.F. Jones, "Quality and Equality Through Cognitive Instruction," in *Educational Leadership*, April 6–11, Association for Supervision and Curriculum Development, 1986. Used with permission.

p. 12 Excerpt from Snow, 1989: Judith A. Snow, *Educating All Students in the Mainstream of Regular Education*, Paul H. Brookes Publishing Co. (Baltimore, MD), 1979, p. 223. Used by permission of the author and publisher.

p. 15 Excerpt from Stainback and Stainback, 1984: From "A Rationale for the Merger of Special and Regular Education," by W. Stainback and S. Stainback, *Exceptional Children*, *51*, 1984, pp. 102–111. Copyright 1984 by The Council for Exceptional Children. Reprinted with permission.

p. 17 Excerpt from Jenkins, Pious, and Jewell, 1990: From "Special Education and the Regular Education Initiative: Basic Assumptions," by J.R. Jenkins, C.G. Pious, and M. Jewell, *Exceptional Children*, *56*, 1990, pp. 479–491. Copyright 1990 by The Council for Exceptional Children. Reprinted with permission.

p. 29–30 Chapter 2 vignette: From Rick McConnell, *The Edmonton Journal*, 14 September, 1991. Reprinted by permission.

pp. 35–36 Excerpt from Hallahan and Kaufman, 1991: From D.P. Hallahan and J.M. Kaufman, *Exceptional Children: Introduction to Special Education*, 5th ed. Boston: Allyn & Bacon.

p. 64 Excerpt from Roberts, 1987: From David Roberts, "New Brunswick Special Education: A New Beginning," *Education New Brunswick—Journal Edition*, 1987, pp. 17–18. Reprinted by permission.

pp. 91–92 Table 3.1, Metacognitive Interview Guide by Dr. Judy Lupart, University of Calgary, and Dr. Margaret O'Brien, Mount Saint Vincent University. Used with permission.

p. 93 Excerpt from Sternberg, 1984: Adapted from Robert J. Sternberg, *Mechanisms of Cognitive Development*, pp. 165–166 (Copyright © 1984), reissued by Waveland Press, Inc., Prospect Heights, Illinois. Reprinted with permission from the publisher.

pp. 119–120 Excerpt from Stainback and Stainback, 1984: From "A Rationale for the Merger of Special and Regular Education," by W. Stainback and S. Stainback, *Exceptional Children*, *51*, 1984, pp. 102–111. Copyright 1984 by The Council for Exceptional Children. Reprinted by permission.

pp. 120–21 Excerpt from National Joint Committee on Learning Disabilities (NJLCD), 1987: From National Joint Committee on Learning Disabilities, 1987, "Learning Disabilities: Issues as Definition," *Journal of Learning Disabilities*, 10 (2), pp. 107–108. Reprinted by permission.

p. 121 Excerpt from the Association for Children and Adults with Learning Disabilities, 1985: From Association for Children and Adults with Learning Disabilities (ACLD) Board of Directors (1985), "Definitions of Specific Learning Disabilities," *ACLD News Briefs*, 158, pp. 1–3. Reprinted by permission of LDA of America.

p. 121 Excerpt from Ysseldyke, Algozzine, and Epps, 1983: From "A Logical and Empirical Analysis of Current Practice in Classifying Students as Handicapped," by J. Ysseldyke, B. Algozzine, and S. Epps, *Exceptional Children*, *50*, 1983, pp. 160–166. Copyright 1983 by The Council for Exceptional Children. Reprinted with permission.

p. 127 Excerpt from Marland, 1972: From S. Marland (1972), *Education for the Gifted and Talented*. Report to the Congress of the United States by the U.S. Commissioner of Education.

p. 127 Excerpt from Renzulli, 1978: From J.S. Renzulli, "What Makes Giftedness? Re-examining a Definition," *Phi Delta Kappan*, 60 (3), 1978, pp. 180–184. Reprinted by permission of the author.

p. 173 Excerpt from Ashworth, 1988: From M. Ashworth, *Blessed with Bilingual Brains: Education of Immigrant Children With English as a Second Language*, Pacific Educational Press, 1988, p. 5. Reprinted by permission.

p. 179 Table 5.1, Characteristics Used to Measure Cultural Distance: J.H. Schumann, "Social and Psychological Factors in Second Language Education," in J.C. Richards, ed., *Understanding Second and Foreign Language Learning: Issues and Approaches*. Newbury House/Heinle & Heinle Publishers, 1978. Reprinted by permission of the publisher.

p. 182 Excerpt from Bock, 1970: Philip K. Bock, *Culture Shock: A Reader in Modern Cultural Anthropology*. New York: Alfred A. Knopf, 1970, p. ix. Reprinted by permission of the author.

p. 196 Excerpt from Gosch et al., 1974 and Mohan, 1982: Reprinted by permission of Little, Brown and Company.

pp. 222–23 Excerpt from Charles and Malian, 1980: From C.M. Charles and I.M. Malian, *The Special Student: Practical Help for the Classroom Teacher*, C.V. Mosby Co., 1980, p. 31. Reprinted by permission.

p. 225 Table 6.1, The Changing Role of the Student, and Table 6.2, The Changing Role of the Teacher: From *Teaching Thinking: Enhancing Learning—A Resource Book for Schools ECS to Grade 12*, 1990, p. 11. Reprinted with the permission of Alberta Education.

pp. 225–26 Excerpt from New Brunswick Department of Education, 1988: From *Working Guidelines on Integration*, Department of Education, Province of New Brunswick, 1988, p. 12. Reprinted by permission.

p. 237 "Teachers learning lessons of violence." From *Calgary Herald*, 23 June 1990. Reprinted by permission of the Calgary Herald.

p. 252 Excerpt from Gorham, 1975: From "A Lost Generation of Parents," by K.A.A. Gorham, *Exceptional Children*, *41*, 1975, pp. 521–525. Copyright 1975 by The Council for Exceptional Children. Reprinted by permission.

p. 252 Excerpt from Larson, 1987: From "An Inside Look at the 1986 Clarissa H. Hug Teacher of the Year: An Interview with Judy Larson," *Teaching Exceptional Children*, *19*, 1987, pp. 37–39. Copyright 1987 by The Council for Exceptional Children. Reprinted by permission.

p. 260 Excerpt from Kroth, 1985: From R.L. Kroth, *Communicating with Parents of Exceptional Children: Improving Parent-Teacher Relationships*, 2nd ed., Love Publishing, 1985, p. 10. Reprinted by permission.

p. 265 Excerpt from Davis, 1980: From W.E. Davis, *Educator's Resource Guide to Education*, Boston: Allyn & Bacon.

p. 267 Excerpt from Jowett and Baginsky, 1988: From S. Jowett and M. Baginsky, "Parents and Education: A Survey of Their Involvement and a Discussion of Some Issues," *Educational Research*, 30, 1988, pp. 36–45. Reprinted by permission of Routledge Publishing.

p. 278 Excerpt from Bos and Vaughn, 1988: C.S. Bos and S. Vaughn (1988). *Strategies for Teaching Students with Learning and Behavior Problems*, 2nd ed. 1991, adapted from pp. 341–343. © 1991 by Allyn & Bacon. Reprinted by permission.

Second Edition (Boynton/Cook Publishers, Inc., Portsmouth, NH, 1992).

pp. 622–23, 634 Excerpts from Reynolds and Birch (1988): From *Adaptive Mainstreaming: A Primer for Teachers and Principals*, 3/e by Maynard C. Reynolds and Jack W. Birch. Copyright © 1988 by Longman Publishing Group.

pp. 636–37 Excerpt from Lipsky and Gartner, 1989: From D.K. Lipsky and A.G. Gartner, *Beyond Separation Education: Quality Education for All*, Paul H. Brookes Publishing Co., 1989, p. 260. Reprinted by permission.

p. 637 Excerpt from Biklen, 1989: From D. Biklen, *Educating All Students in the Mainstream of Regular Education*, Paul H. Brookes Publishing Co., 1989, p. 247. Reprinted by permission.

p. 641 Excerpt from Skrtic, 1991: From T.M. Skrtic, *Behind Special Education: A Critical Analysis of Professional Culture and School Organization*, Love Publishing Co., 1991, p. 233. Reprinted by permission.

the idea that different language forms may be processed by the brain in parallel, and therefore in competition with each other. 184

Componential subtheory A subtheory of Sternberg's triarchic theory of intelligence which refers to the use of information-processing components for strategy construction and complex problem-solving. 93

Computer-assisted instruction (CAI), 7
effectiveness of, 498–99. *See also* Autoskill; Computers

Computers
purchasing guidelines, 496–97
software choices, 496–98
as used in writing, 497, 530–31

Conductive disorder, 140

Congenital deafness, 140

Constitution Act (1982), 46

Consultation
competency areas in, 228
as component of inclusive teaming, 219–21

Consultative-collaborative model A system of service delivery based on the collaboration of educational professionals in meeting the needs of all students in the general classroom. 243
assessment procedures in, 242
levels of service delivery within, 242

Context (social)
assessment of, 557, 559
as component of social ability, 500–501
intervention relating to, 564–66

Contextual subtheory A subtheory of Sternberg's triarchic theory of intelligence which refers to the ability to bring control to one's life by making adaptations in one's environment. 94, 95

Contingency contracting, as behaviour management strategy, 268–69

Continuous chronologue, as information-collection technique, 312–13

Controlled processing, 93–94

Cooperative learning
initiating, 493
as social intervention method, 575

Council for Exceptional Children, 39

Creativity, as aspect of giftedness, 128

Criterion-referenced test A form of testing in which students are evaluated on the basis of their ability to meet a particular standard. 297, 505

Cultural distance model, 178–80
psychological/social variables in, 180–82

Cultural relativity The notion that all ideas and perceptions are particular to the cultures in which they are developed and experienced. 202

Culture, as a multivariate phenomenon, 175–76

Culture shock The complex of feelings and reactions that typically occur when a person moves from one culture to another. 182
degrees of, 182
psychological effects of, 183

Curriculum
competency requirements, 475–76
new century vs. traditional, 637–38

Curriculum-based assessment (CBA), 301
applied to trial lessons, 321
approaches to, 323

Custodial provision Depersonalized care facility for exceptional children that provides minimal basic physical care. 36

Cystic fibrosis A hereditary respiratory disease characterized by chronic pulmonary dysfunction and pancreatic deficiency. 158

Decontextualized assessment Assessment in which the measurements taken do not parallel what is occurring in the classroom. 297

Deinstitutionalization The movement to remove disabled individuals from residential institutional care and place them in home community settings that support and foster their independence and quality of life. 40

Delayed cognitive skills, 122
characteristics and needs of students with, 342
definitions of, 121–24
influence of box model on field of, 85

Developmental theory. *See* Cognitive developmental theory

Dewey, John, 77

Diabetes A hereditary metabolic disorder characterized by excessive amounts of glucose in the blood and urine. 159

Diagnostic-prescriptive teaching A collaborative approach to developing children's skills in which diagnostic information is used to modify the student's educational program. 565

principles and practices, 565

Direct Instruction System for Teaching Achievement and Remediation (DISTAR), 81
for mathematics, 456
for reading, 427–28

Discourse competence, in language learning, 188

Discrimination learning A behavioural principle in which a person learns to respond to different environmental conditions and/or to similar stimuli. 427

Disequilibrium State of imbalance that results from an inability to use existing schemes to interpret a new situation. 99

Distal placement Placing exceptional students in the location farthest from the mainstream. 32

Divisional support services team, 242

Dossier A teacher-directed, cumulative, and representative record of student attainment and learning. 306
establishing, 306–7
guidelines, 308–11

Due process Provision of U.S. Public Law 94–142 to ensure professionals and parents adequate and fair practice in the screening, identification, and placement of exceptional students. 51
as component of PL 94–142, 49, 51

Duration recording, as technique for counting behaviour, 315–16

Duschenne's muscular dystrophy, 157

Educational counselling Counselling approach that centres on the provision of information to parents. 277

Educational history, Canada vs. U.S., 33–34

Educational psychology Scientific study of factors important in creating educational environments that promote and nurture a child's intellectual and personal growth. 78

Educational psychology theory, 76
applications to inclusive education, 78–80
behaviourist, 78
cognitive, 78
functionalist vs. scientific, 77–78
information-processing, 83–96

Educators. *See* Regular classroom teachers; Teachers

Efficient learners
characteristics of, 133
response mechanisms of, 135
strategies for memory storage, 147–48

EFL English as a Foreign Language. 190

Egocentric speech A child's second level of language development—evident from ages 3 to 7— which is directly connected to thinking. 105, 106, 108

Ego-permeability The extent to which a person is open to challenge and change. 181, 201

Elwood case, 50

Encoding The process of transforming stimuli so that the information may be stored in long-term memory and retrieved for later use. 517

Entrapreneurship Systematic efforts to promote innovative instruction in effective schools within a supportive administrative framework. 635

Epilepsy An impairment of the nervous system characterized by recurrent and sudden disturbances of movement, sensation, and behaviour. 158
types of seizures, 158

Equilibrium State of balance in which a person uses accommodation and assimilation to increase development both quantitatively and qualitatively. 99

Equity, as goal of inclusive education, 9–10

ESD English as a Second Dialect. 190

ESL English as a Second Language. 189

ESL education
characteristics and needs of students, 342–43
future of, 205–7
instructional guidelines on, 199–205
types of programs, 191–97

ESL programming
immersion vs. submersion, 195–97
mainstreaming, 194
self-contained, 191–92
transitional, 192
withdrawal, 192

Eugenics movement Early 20th-century movement that advocated legislation to prevent procreation by mentally retarded individuals. 37

Evaluation. *See* Assessment

Event recording, as technique for counting behaviour, 315

Exclusion, as period of progressive inclusion, 35

Executive functioning. *See* Metacognition

Experiential subtheory A subtheory of Sternberg's triarchic theory of intelligence which refers to a person's ability to learn from past situations and to use

tural limitation or immaturity evidenced by a child's inability, despite adequate instruction, to use a strategy. 87

Memory
    box model of, 84–85
    levels of analysis model of, 85–86
    long-term (LTM), 88, 134–35, 136, 149–50
    metamemory, 88
    performance, children vs. adults, 87, 88
    procedural, 135
    semantic, 135
    short-term (STM), 88, 134, 135, 136, 147–49
    strategies for enhancing, 520–25

Meningitis, 141

Mentally handicapped A level of intellectual functioning and adaptive skills low enough to prevent a child from obtaining benefits from ordinary school education. 41

Mental retardation. *See* Delayed cognitive skills

Mentor Person with special skills or knowledge who tutors less-experienced learners in the domain(s) of interest. 244

Mentoring, 234

Metacognition Awareness and self-regulation of basic learning strategies and executive processes that deal with planning, monitoring, and evaluation of one's learning. 89, 135, 136, 150
    aspects of, 90
    regulation and control as dimensions of, 136

Metacognitive empowerment The ability of individuals to reflect on and control their learning and behaviour. 336

Metacognitive knowledge Self-knowledge about cognitive abilities and resources. 89
    dimensions of, 89
    enhancing, 150–51
    in reading, 89

Metacomponent An executive process that deals with planning, monitoring, and evaluation aspects of information processing. 93

Metamemory Self-knowledge about memory capabilities. 88

Metamemory performance The selection and assessment of strategies that are most appropriate for carrying out a task. 88

Methods and resource teacher, 243

Minimal pairs A pair of words that differ in meaning while differing in only one individual sound. 205

Mnemonic Technique for remembering that aims to connect new information with prior knowledge. 520

Mnemonic learning strategies
    benefits of, 524–25
    keyword method, 520, 523
    pegword system, 523, 524
    Yodai, 523–24

Modal model. *See* Box model

Modelling, as social intervention method, 571, 573

Monoplegia, 156

Montreal Children's Memorial Hospital, 37

Morpheme The smallest meaningful unit of a language, whether a word or a specific element such as a prefix or suffix. 449

Motivational-developmental perspective The belief that effective learning is based on a student's exposure to developmentally appropriate experiences, materials, and tasks. 637

Multiculturalism, as philosophy, 170

Multi-level instruction The use of various task presentation and response formats to accommodate students' differing learning styles and abilities. 224

Multipass Highly structured reading comprehension strategy in which survey, size-up, and sort-out substrategies are taught in a six-step instructional procedure. 527
    substrategies, 527

Muscular dystrophy A disease in children that is characterized by a deterioration of the muscles. 157

Mutual regulation, as conceived by Case, 101–2

Myopia Nearsightedness. 138

National Institute of Mental Retardation, 40

Native peoples
    language needs of, 198–99
    treatment of in colonial period, 172

Neverstreaming System of service delivery that combines the practices of prevention and early, intensive, and continuing intervention for at-risk students. 221, 623

New Brunswick, 35, 499
    education legislation in, 63–64
    school district initiatives, 242–44

Parent volunteer programs, 263–64
  establishing, 275–77

Pavlov, Ivan, 80

Peer collaboration, 227, 635
  as language learning strategy, 602

Peer nomination A sociometric measure whereby students nominate their peers in relation to socially relevant criteria such as play partners and best friends. 561

Peer observation, 220, 234

Peer rating A sociometric measure whereby students rate their peers on the basis of specific criteria; e.g., group work or play abilities. 561

Peer support, 224, 227

Peer teaching Instruction of one student by another in a structured situation in which materials are well planned and organized. 344
  as social intervention method, 576–77

Pegword system Mnemonic strategy that involves the use of rhyming pegwords, as in one is a bun, two is a shoe, and so forth. 523

Percentile rank An individual score below which a given percentage of individuals scored; e.g., a percentile rank of 75 means that 75 percent of test-takers scored below the individual's rank. 554

Perception, 134, 135, 136, 150
  defined, 146

Perceptual deficits
  indicators of, 146–47
  teaching children with, 146–47

Performance deficits, intervention for, 571–72

Permissive legislation Legislation that permits but does not legally require school boards to provide educational services for students with special needs. 49

Phonics teaching, as strategy for mastering decoding, 479

Physical impairments
  defined, 156
  teaching children with, 157–58
  types of, 156–57

Physical/occupational therapist, role in inclusive education, 239–40

Piaget, Jean, 96, 100, 602, 603
  implications of theory, 99–100
  intelligence viewed as adaptation process by, 98

stages of cognitive development as conceived by, 96, 151

Piers-Harris Children's Self-Concept Scale, 554

Placement The determination of where a student with special needs is to receive special education services. 297, 300

Portfolio Material chosen by students that reflects their ongoing academic achievement. 306
  establishing, 306
  guidelines, 308–11

Positive parenting principles Procedures followed by parents to create mutual learning and sharing experiences between themselves and their children. 262

Precision teaching An approach to developing children's skills that involves pinpointing the behaviour(s) concerned, establishing objectives for performance, and charting daily progress. 565
  principles and practices, 565–66

Prejudice A feeling or expression of judgment about others based on unfair and faulty overgeneralization. 178

Prereferral intervention Steps that are taken prior to referring a student to formal intervention. 301

Preservation The process by which members of an immigrant cultural group protect their own interests and identity. 180

PRESL Preschool English as a Second Language. 191

Prince Edward Island, 50, 51, 499
  education legislation in, 66

Principal, 624
  as administrator, 232

Prior knowledge Knowledge that is already part of a person's cognition. 133

Proactive classroom management
  classroom environment as element in, 343–48
  meeting students' needs as element in, 339–43
  teaching approaches and, 334–39

Problem Solving Measure for Conflict (PSM-C), 560–61

Procedural memory, 135

Process questioning A form of questioning in which students' attention is focused on their own learning and thinking processes. 337

Production deficiency The inability to use a learning strategy spontaneously even when it is part of one's repertoire of strategies. 87, 518

NOTES

NOTES

NOTES

NOTES

NOTES

To the owner of this book

We hope that you have enjoyed *The Inclusive Classroom: Educating Exceptional Children*, and we would like to know as much about your experiences as you would care to offer. Only through your comments and those of others can we learn how to make this a better text for future readers.

School _____ Your instructor's name _____

Course _____ Was the text required? _____ Recommended? _____

1. What did you like the most about *The Inclusive Classroom?*

_____

_____

_____

2. How useful was this text for your course?

_____

_____

3. Do you have any recommendations for ways to improve the next edition of this text?

_____

_____

4. In the space below or in a separate letter, please write any other comments you have about the book. (For example, please feel free to comment on reading level, writing style, terminology, design features, and learning aids.)

_____

_____

_____

_____

Optional

Your name _____ Date _____

May Nelson Canada quote you, either in promotion for *The Inclusive Classroom* or in future publishing ventures?

Yes _____ No _____

Thanks!

FOLD HERE

MAIL ⇒ POSTE

Canada Post Corporation / Société canadienne des postes

Postage paid
if mailed in Canada

Port payé
si posté au Canada

**Business
Reply**

**Réponse
d'affaires**

0107077099   01

Nelson

TAPE SHUT

TAPE SHUT

0107077099-M1K5G4-BR01

Nelson Canada
College Editorial Department
1120 Birchmount Rd.
Scarborough, ON M1K 9Z9

PLEASE TAPE SHUT. DO NOT STAPLE.